ONE ON ONE

MY JOURNEY WITH HALL OF FAMERS FAN FAVORITES AND RISING STARS

JANE MITCHELL

FOREWORD BY
DICK ENBERG AND TONY GWYNN

For John —
Enjoy the Good Sports Story
and your own journey.
Thanks for your support of STARPALs
and me.
            Jane Mitchell
            6/9/18
Perpetuate the
Positive

One on One: My Journey with Hall of Famers, Fan Favorites and Rising Stars by Jane Mitchell

Jacket/Cover/Color Insert Design: *Mark Mrowka*

Author Jacket Photos: *Melissa Jacobs*

Interior Design and Layout: *Sweet Dreams Publishing of MA*

Editorial Services: *Shayla Perry, Jayne Pupek, Jan Coker Proofreading & Editorial Services, Neysa Jensen*

Contributing Editors: *Ann Mitchell, Kelly Morris Buh, Candace Edwards, Robyn Mitchell-Stong, Tammy Payne, Todd Tobias*

Published by Sweet Dreams Publishing of Massachusetts
36 Captains Way, East Bridgewater, MA 02333
www.publishatsweetdreams.com

For more information about this book go to www.janemitchelloneonone.com

Library of Congress Control Number: 2010931772
ISBN-13: 978-0-9824461-7-1
Printed in the United States of America
Copyright © 2010, by JCM Communications, Inc.
Second Printing 2011

This book is dedicated to:
my parents for their love and encouragement …
the players who trusted me with their stories …
and the fans who welcomed us into their homes.

"Baseball and Home: Where the Sky is Blue
and the Heart Knows No Limits."

—Jane Mitchell, 1997

Table of Contents

Foreword

For more than fifty years, I've been privileged to fill the best seat in the house, witnessing some of sports' most mesmerizing and inspiring moments, sharing them with television viewers and fans. When I'm not behind a microphone, I'm an avid fan, enjoying how others present the action. So in 1997, when I learned of a new Padres television partnership in my hometown, San Diego, I was curious how the cable channel's programming would look, sound, and feel. Game broadcasts aside; I had an early answer when I saw a young woman reporter, introducing players in pre-game segments and on a show, *One on One*.

Her voice, writing, and presence were of high quality. She wasn't simply reciting statistics, or the mundane, but was offering insightful player stories. Men viewed as strong, tough heroes to fans were openly candid in her interviews, sharing not only their victories, but also their vulnerabilities. They seemed at ease in sharing childhood dreams, teenage trauma, professional and personal flaws throughout their major league journey. In 1999 while featuring San Diego Chargers, there was no surprise she transitioned from baseball to football, seamlessly.

Her research, command of the language, and choice of interview segments meshed with her soothing, yet confident delivery, creating an ideal host. It's been Jane's attention to detail, her writing, her ability to make players comfortable, and her obvious passion for her work that have made her universally popular in our city. She understands not only how to produce a good television show, but recognizes how we, as viewers, can best appreciate a story when it flows from one point to the next, chronicling defining moments. Jane makes us feel as if she's not only asking the questions we want to ask, but also the questions many might not even think about asking. And she listens. I believe she's been successful and popular because she is genuine, caring, and relentless in capturing the qualities and essence of her subjects.

At the end of a show, I felt I thoroughly knew her subject. I was not alone. *One on One* touched fans across the spectrum: men, women, and children. When a program doesn't lose its freshness, you can watch it over and over, even the same episode, and find something new each time. Like a rich symphony, that's a credit to the depth of her study. Indeed, her work is timeless; a good reason why she has survived so long in a world that often sees programs quickly come and go.

In 2002, I had an idea for a feature story about my personal physician, who plays in a "60 and over" adult baseball league. If anyone in San Diego could do it the right way, it was Jane. So I called her and was pleased with her receptive enthusiasm. She proceeded to produce a two-part story for the Padres pre-game show in her signature professional and entertaining style.

In 2004, I became her subject. She interviewed me for a Channel 4 program, *Forefront.* I was impressed by Jane's preparation, approach, listening skills, questions, and professionalism. I could tell she had taken hours to read the advance copy of my autobiography, cover to cover, therefore, never asking the obvious, but allowing an interview to become a warm conversation. I'm accustomed to being the interviewer, so when the tables were turned, I not only enjoyed the process, but it confirmed my high expectations of her talent. When I became the Padres television announcer in 2010, she then featured me on *One on One*. I was equally delighted by the experience.

She may not have a national job, or national name recognition, but her work is consistently of network caliber. Maybe that's a good thing, because she has full control over the content and quality, allowing a more personal touch. Jane has a way of exploring one's challenges without exploiting them. She isn't afraid to ask questions on tough or sensitive topics, but artfully does it without embarrassing or criticizing. She finds the good and positive in her subjects, and helps us understand and care who they are as people, not just athletes.

Many of you have not seen her in action, so now you have the opportunity to read the stories from her many fascinating interviews, as well as the insights into her behind the scenes stories. For those who have watched *One on One* and feel you know Jane, reading her personal reflections will warmly inspire you even further. There's no doubt that her upbringing and journey have influenced her approach and compassion. She has not only found her niche, but created one. Over the years it has been a delight to watch her progression and consistency, and now her account in these pages pulls it all together for which, enthusiastically, I'm delighted to say, *OH MY!*

—Dick Enberg

As a rookie, I remember Steve Garvey telling me about what it takes to be a major leaguer: that you're going to have to deal with the media, whether you went 4-for-4 or 0-for-4, because the media needs somebody they can depend on to be honest with them. He was right. I've been around the game a long time and have met many reporters. Some are willing to go in-depth, while others just want the quick, sensational quote. Some get it, some don't. That's why some players are guarded; they aren't sure who they can trust and who might put words in their mouths.

Jane is unique. Even early on I noticed she had this way of disarming guys, and a special ability to get them to talk. Sometimes she had to weave around some touchy subjects, but she always got there. She's been successful because she did it in a way that everybody respected. She didn't come in knowing the answers. She just knew how to ask the questions.

Put yourself in our shoes. We are putting trust in someone to portray our image, our reputation, and even our personality. Jane has proven to be trustworthy. It isn't that she is "creating" our image, but through her style helps reveal who we are.

In February 1997, I didn't know anything about Jane when she was coming to my house. I learned she was thorough, not only with her questions, but also by including my wife and family. By that June, I had already seen her first two shows and was curious how mine would turn out. I remember being really surprised and telling my wife, Alicia, "She got it. She understands. This is going to be a good thing."

Jane was part of the new Padres TV deal, but someone with less awareness and less professionalism might not have made it from the players' standpoint. She respected our space around the game and at the field, and that made me respect her role and her work all the more.

The fact that she and her show have been around for fourteen seasons? Nobody plays for fourteen seasons for one team anymore, and I should know. Players come and go. Reporters come and go. Jane has been a mainstay for a reason. I remember telling her when she started, that if she did this really well, people will know. And that's exactly what happened. You could ask anybody in town and say *One on One,* and her name's going to come up, and that's a testament to how well she's done her job.

Alicia and I appreciate how Jane has been a very positive addition to the sports world. She not only tells our story, but also sees beyond the obvious into why we love and play the game. She helps fans understand that the game is more than baseball for many of us. It's about dreams, work, achievement, faith, connecting with people, and contributing to our community.

I think the thing that I learned in doing these *One on One* pieces, is that fans realized how honest I was. I didn't know that. I was playing and didn't know how people really perceived me. I learned that fans really thought I was pretty honest; pretty straightforward, and I like that. I think that's great, because that's what I tried to be every day: as honest as I could be.

And so as much as she's learned about baseball over the years, I think she's taught us something, too. She's taught us that it's good to think beyond just the game, to the bigger picture, and that sometimes to express that, you need to take the time to sit and talk.

For me, it was really amazing to see it come full circle in 2009 when Jane featured my son Anthony. The night of the debut I was scrambling to get to the TV to watch his story. It was awesome. The thing that I remember about that, and I told my wife this, is that here's a guy who has been in his father's shadow forever, and now all of a sudden, he's got his own *One on One*. In this town, that's a big deal when you can be one of those people on Jane's show. So I was very proud that I got to play the sidekick this time instead of the lead guy.

Like my father said, "Work hard, and good things will happen." Jane works hard, with good intentions. And with her television show and now this book, good things have happened.

—Tony Gwynn
Hall of Fame, 2007

Introduction

After a lifetime of being around storytellers and twenty-four years as a professional journalist in television, I am thrilled to be writing this book about my life and the lives of others I've had the privilege of interviewing. If you are from the San Diego region and a Padres or Chargers fan, you have likely watched Channel 4 San Diego and possibly my program, *One on One with Jane Mitchell*. If so, thank you for watching and for taking an interest both in me, and more importantly, the more than one hundred athletes appearing on the show, many of whom have donned Padres or Chargers uniforms and are featured in this book.

I believe this book and these athletes' stories transcend a uniform. Even if you're not from San Diego and have not seen the show, you will still undoubtedly find interest in the journeys of Ted Williams, Tony Gwynn, Junior Seau, Drew Brees, and many other athletes you've heard about, watched, and admired over the years. I hope you'll enjoy hearing about my experience, bringing their stories to you—the fans. You might have read different things about them, heard them speak, or watched them play, but in many cases *One on One* was the first and arguably the most comprehensive account of their personalities, their lives, and their stories. So, you might be from Paducah, Kentucky, where Steve Finley grew up, and are interested in knowing how he got his start; or you are a Chicago White Sox fan, will forever consider Geoff Blum your hero, and want to hear his perspective on that time in his life. Perhaps David Wells, Dave Winfield, Luis Castillo, and Doug Flutie are among the inspiring athletes who have piqued your interest. For whatever reason you've picked up this book, I thank you and hope you find my version of their biographies fulfilling, informative, and inspiring.

These stories, along with the love and support of my parents, served as inspiration in my writing this book. In fact, my father's knack for storytelling is one of the reasons I'm a journalist. Another reason is my mother's tenacity to have me start writing about our family travels around the world as a child. Their loving energy and gypsy spirits embraced my talents. They believed in me. That is why I was able, excited, and motivated to pursue my dream of being a journalist, a news reporter and eventually, a documentary-style storyteller. Never would I have anticipated that my storytelling would be in the realm of sports.

One irony of my writing this book involving sports, or even being involved in the world of sports myself, is that my father thought baseball was boring; especially baseball on television. When he occasionally watched sports on TV, it was football—the San Diego Chargers and sometimes college games during the bowl season—and only while he was doing something else at the same time, such as ironing. He was one of the original multi-taskers, probably because my mother thought just watching TV was a waste of time.

Another inspiration for this book: my father served in and survived three wars—World War II, Korea, and Vietnam—but he couldn't beat ALS (Amyotrophic Lateral Sclerosis), the disease that claimed the life of baseball great, the "Iron Horse," Lou Gehrig. Call it fate or serendipity, but my position of being in television with a community-minded station, covering mostly baseball, and having gone through my father's illness have all intersected with a positive synergy that allows me to use my profession and my passion to help others with this dreadful, degenerative, and fatal disease. That's why part of the proceeds from this book will go toward the Greater San Diego Chapter of the ALS Association, which also helps to fund the research efforts of the National ALS Association. I consider my volunteer work with the chapter as part of my father's legacy. Anything I can do to help families and patients with ALS is an honor, a privilege, and a calling.

While my job is to do the interviews, I'm often asked how I came to be the one to sit with San Diego Padres, Chargers, Hall of Famers, sports legends, fan favorites, and rising stars. People want to know how I ended up in the enviable position of being in their living rooms talking about life, their family, their passion for sports, and other dimensions that make them who they are both on and off the playing field. My answer: I've had to pay my dues and work intense hours, but nothing just happens; there's always a back-story.

One vivid example of this is when I remind people that the All-Time Saves Leader Trevor Hoffman didn't just become a great closer, he once was a little boy too, and, no less, a child with only one kidney. The home movies showing him playing in the backyard with his two big brothers illustrate to anyone watching—children, adults, athletes, and fans alike—that he had challenges and choices along the way that got him where he is today, and where he is headed: likely—although he would never assume such an honor—to the National Baseball Hall of Fame.

So indulge me in a few pages as I share my own back-story, the evolution of Channel 4 San Diego and the *One on One* program, and the behind-the-scenes anecdotes of some of the most interesting, fun, and endearing people I have ever had the pleasure of learning about and sharing with fans and viewers.

Some of the athletes I interview stay in San Diego, others move on to different teams—a few have died—but their stories are timeless. It was hard to narrow the selections from nearly one hundred shows, so I hope those not discussed in depth know that I appreciate them and their stories as well. I am honored, humbled, and thankful that so many of my featured guests have agreed to share their thoughts on their interview experience, their take on the final product, and what *One on One* has meant to players and to the community.

When I started with Channel 4 San Diego and produced the first *One on One* show, I said I wanted this to be "family TV." Meaning, while serious subjects might be broached, it would be presented in such a way that children, their parents, and grandparents could watch with no concern for inappropriate subject matter, no revealing of surprise skeletons in the closet, no dirty laundry. I'm staying true to that and to who I am in this book. There may be some stories that didn't make air, a few that are a little too serious for a child but in general, this book is for family reading as much as the shows are for family viewing.

In this memoir—for my story and the back-stories—I've double-checked a number of things with those involved with various parts of my journey, but most of the stories and quotes included are based on my memories, records, opinions, experiences, and how something was relayed to me. I've indicated if it is a direct quote.

In my interviews, I ask people to open up and be vulnerable as I explore their journey, ask about defining moments, triumphs and tragedy, successes and failures, lessons in love, loss, fame, and humility. Here, I turn the tables and ask the same questions of myself, with honest and sincere answers.

I believe in giving credit where credit is due, and I am so grateful to those who have helped me. At the same time, whether on matters of love, career, or office politics, if I bring up a negative or sensitive situation, I do not point fingers or place blame. I share some challenging moments in my life and career from my perspective, my perception, and possibly my take on someone else's perspective—but it is all based on my experience. If someone was involved in a challenging time, they likely know who they are; no one else needs to.

While I appreciate all the good things, good people, and opportunities in my path, I know that those positive influences and the obstacles I faced have made me who I am, and therefore able to persevere. I have learned so much from others and thank you for your curiosity and support in opening these pages. Enjoy!

CHAPTER 1

My Story From the Beginning

From Tolerating Sports to
Having One of the Best Gigs in the Game

The Family Tree

In my interviews with guests, I ask about their family tree, to know who's who and to understand at least the facts, if not the family dynamics. In that spirit, I share with you my family tree. I was born the youngest of four on March 22, 1963, in Coronado, California. My mother, Ann (Lydieann) Juanita Glick Mitchell, a teacher, was two months shy of turning forty when she delivered me, a big baby at nine pounds, twelve ounces, and twenty-one inches, long and thin. My father, "J" Wallace "Wally" Mitchell, a Lt. Commander in the Navy, was forty-four. My brother, Jerald, or "Jerry," was fourteen, Scott was eight, and my sister Robyn was five.

Jerry, who now goes by "Mitch," is the only one who called me by my middle name. My mother let him choose the name, and he chose Candace, or "Candy," after the homecoming queen he had a crush on in high school. Being a lot older, he helped take care of me and often babysat. He graduated from college and built a career as an entrepreneur and an expert in franchising and real estate. My brother Scott had a sense of humor and did not like school. After being around my sister's influence, he connected with the world of medicine in high school and has been an operating room technician for thirty years. My sister, Robyn, was the quiet hard worker who wanted to get out of high school early to become a doctor. She graduated at sixteen. Even though she struggled with standardized tests, her willingness to learn Spanish and her determination, discipline, and dedication allowed her to achieve her dream, and my mother's dream for her. She became an MD through the Universidad de Autonoma in Guadalajara, Mexico, the University of Maryland, and the University of California in Los Angeles, where she now is an associate professor in the Department of Family Medicine and oversees a clinic where she uses her Spanish fluently when seeing patients.

Have You Always Been a Sports Fan? Oh, Nooooo!

Since I entered the world of sports in 1996, I'm often asked, "Have you always loved sports?" Most people assume I have, considering I'm in this line of work. My answer however, is "Oh, no." As a little girl, I went to a few Padres baseball games, mostly for a school or Girl Scout outing. I can still hear the announcer reading the line up and saying with a big, booming voice, "Daaavvve WIIIINNNN-FEeeee-LD," but I could not have told you anything about Dave Winfield until twenty-five years later. I played girls' Bobby Sox softball for two years in fourth and fifth grades. My teams were the Red Barons and the Little Green Apples, named after Coach Appleton. Organized sports were not a required, nor expected, extracurricular activity for girls in the mid-'70s, but I liked the camaraderie and fun of being a part of a team. I was a girly-girl, making sure the ribbons in my long ponytails on either side of my hat matched my team uniform, be it red or green. I was often a pitcher. Being the confident girl in the center of attention suited my outgoing personality, but I did not want that pitcher's role. I was afraid of a batter's comebacker ball or line drive would hit me in my face. I don't recall that ever happening, but the possibility was nerve-wracking enough. I preferred centerfield because it took the longest time for a ball to get to me, reducing the chances of my getting hurt.

I was somewhat athletic and, with my lanky body, could run fairly fast. It wouldn't be until later, at fourteen that I would be forced to limit some of my physical activities following back surgery. Even so, in college at UCSD, I played on intramural sports teams merely for the social aspect and to be with friends. When I did participate, I preferred playing defense in our basketball games; offering enthusiastic growls to intimidate the opponent was more effective than my offense would ever be.

I liked the experience of sporting activities, but I was not a sports fan. I was happy moving on to the next activity of the day, whether it be shopping, lunching, painting, or studying. At times it seemed as if I lived in the library. With any of my boyfriends, from college until my role with Channel 4 San Diego, I simply "tolerated" sports. I would watch football on TV with them knowing the time trade off would mean going to a museum or eating out later. I would go to a baseball or football game as an outing, not as an addiction. In college, I watched the 1984 World Series on the little television in my family's kitchen, but only because the Padres were playing. Even then, I only caught the end of the games after returning home from studying.

In graduate school at Northwestern University in Chicago, I attended one football game. The Wildcats weren't very good then, but even if they had been, my only interest in going was to be able to say I showed my school spirit at least once. On the opposite end of the spectrum, on January 26, 1986, my friends and I were up all night, roaming the streets, caught up in the euphoria of the Bears winning the Super Bowl. We moved from one packed bar to the next as part of a wave of celebration, even though I couldn't relate to the happy and boisterous Bears fans. It snowed earlier that week, but it was a deceptively clear night. I wore Keds® tennis shoes expecting that my down jacket I had enough cover to keep me warm. What I didn't realize until it was too late was that the melting snow made for wet streets and wet feet, so going into a new bar, for me, was more for defrosting my feet than drinking. Sports were never really a part of what I cared about in life, until they became a door to a new world.

Don't Take My Picture

An eight-millimeter home movie filmed by my father shows me sitting with my mother and talking into a tape recorder at two years old. There wasn't any sound on the film. It was just a captured moment of a baby discovering a new toy; not what my parents imagined their little girl would do professionally someday, but evidence of an early affinity for it, and somewhat prophetic. To get there, I would first have to get through my bashful stage. My mother says I was shy until I was four. I hid behind her skirt. I cried when she and my father left me with a babysitter, my siblings, or at preschool. No one knows why, but I did not like having my picture taken most of the time either. While there are many childhood photos of me smiling, even posing, there are plenty showing my pouting lower lip, cringing as I'm being pulled into the picture with tears in my eyes. Mitchell family game night changed that.

I was only four, but I vaguely remember the evening we were playing Charades in our living room. My mother whispered in my ear what I should act out: a seed that turns into a flower. I stepped into the center of the room, curled up into a little ball on the floor, and slowly stretched my skinny little body high toward the ceiling, imitating a sprouting flower. They guessed correctly. I smiled. It was a real life metaphor for how I emerged from my shyness. My camera-happy father and family nurtured my confidence as I gradually became more joyful and relaxed about being in the center of pictures and later orchestrating them. I won an instant camera at a Bingo game in fourth grade, which went with me everywhere for a while. I became a shutterbug and loved documenting every moment on both sides of the camera. The cameras have changed, but the shutterbug remains.

Gypsy Parents: A Navy Kid's Education

I have traveled to more than sixty countries, mostly on trips with my parents and family from childhood through college: Western and Eastern Europe, parts of the Middle East, Asia, and South America. Those trips were not vacations at four- or five-star hotels with taxis, nice suitcases, and dining out at restaurants. We stayed at youth hostels, one- or two-star hotels, and sometimes in our car. We had backpacks or military duffle bags and usually ate at the local markets and bakeries. My parents had a gypsy spirit. They wanted to see the world and give their children an education through travel. That was ambitious on modest salaries. With their depression-era background to draw from, they were resourceful and knew how to do a lot with a little. They showed us the world on a shoestring budget. The book *Europe on $10 a day* was intended to be ten dollars a day per person, but some days we stretched it to being ten dollars a day for the whole family.

Some of my adult choices and preferences (especially for traveling and clothes) are very different now, but I believe much of who I am and how I got here is rooted in my upbringing and what I learned about my parents' backgrounds as well. My parents were raised during the Great Depression of the 1930s. Both their parents were divorced, which was not common back then. My father was an only child, born in Utah and raised in Seattle. He was named after his father, but his parents didn't want him to be a junior, so they just gave him the initial "J." His mother, Lula Mae, and her relatives lost a lettuce farm due to weather, causing them great hardship. Grandma Lula told us she never ate lettuce again. We visited her in Seattle. When she moved close to us, my father was devoted to her care until she died when I was in high school. My grandfather, James Wallace Mitchell, died before I was born. Back in the 1930s, he owned a plumbing store where my father worked until he enlisted in the Navy in 1939, when he was twenty.

My mother had her own challenges growing up. Her oldest sister, Emagene, died at ten from polio. Her parents, Ralph and Mary Ruth, divorced when she was eight. My grandmother was a beauty school teacher in Los Angeles and attended the Amy McPherson Bible School to become a missionary. She sang and played guitar to jail inmates. In July 1936, my mother, her younger brother Bobby, and my grandmother embarked on a nineteen-day voyage to the Philippines on the British freighter MS Rexinore. My mother's other older sister Mina, then nineteen and a Los Angeles telephone operator, did not go and planned to send them part of her $18 weekly salary. My grandmother intended to start a beauty school and become a missionary on Negros Island. That didn't work out, and they were stranded for several months. When they returned home that December, at just forty years old, grandmother Mary Ruth became sick and was later diagnosed with a brain tumor. Because of her religion, Foursquare Gospel, my grandmother did not believe in dancing, alcohol, card playing, or doctors. Even so, she was taken to the hospital; however, it was too late. Although the surgery was successful, it left her paralyzed on her left side. She later died of pneumonia. It was 1938, and my mother, who was fourteen at the

time, went to live with her father and her grandparents. She didn't like how much her grandparents argued, so she chose to be on her own, working as a nanny, living with families, and cleaning houses while she went to high school and college during World War II.

As a young woman, my mother did not want to marry because she never wanted to love someone so much she would be sad if they were gone; losing her mother was painful enough. Her attitude toward marriage changed when she met my father.

After the war, my mother was working her way through school at the University of Washington as a dancing teacher in Seattle with the stage name "Miss Star." Even though dancing was against her mother's religion, my mother loved to ballroom dance: jitterbug, the waltz, and the rumba. My father's mother told him the way to meet girls and to eventually find a wife was to know how to dance, so he ended up taking lessons from my mother. They have different versions as to how they connected: She says she inadvertently taught him incorrectly, then he had to come back so she could re-teach him the steps. He told me he *pretended* not to learn very fast so he would *have* to keep coming back.

While they loved each other, my mother was afraid of getting too close and left for seven weeks, selling stationery at colleges on the Pacific Coast. She asked everyone for advice as to whether she should marry my father. She says there were many young men willing to advise her, suggesting she might date them instead. But she finally returned, realizing he was the one for her. My father welcomed her back and then one day they went to buy a ring, with no formal proposal. They married at a small church near the University of Washington campus. I've always loved looking at their black and white wedding pictures, with their small wedding party, chrysanthemums, and a reception that cost twenty-five dollars, all paid for by my father's mother. My favorite photo is of them dancing. They looked so happy and such a perfect fit.

After they married, my mother finished college—10 years after she started—and became a teacher (elementary, special education, reading specialist).

At thirty-one, my father took a test to become an LDO (Limited Duty Officer) and failed. A year later, he took it again and passed. They started their family while he was stationed in San Diego. All four children eventually learned the basics of ballroom dancing. When we traveled or went to a military officer's club, or the Hotel Del Coronado, my father would take turns dancing with his girls; first my mother, then my sister, then me. We were never embarrassed. He was such a good dancer with his smooth moves and gentle control, and always wanted us each to feel special on the dance floor. I can follow almost anyone's lead, but his will always be the best.

My parents loved the San Diego climate and especially Coronado, where my father was frequently stationed at Naval Air Station, North Island, for aviation maintenance. They knew this was the place for them. My mother worked for the City of San Diego Child Care program, so they could live in government housing for twenty-one dollars a month. Following their thrifty ways, they saved and borrowed enough to buy property in Coronado in the '50s. Eventually, after moving to Washington state, Washington, D.C. and the Pentagon, and then Guam, all four Mitchell kids graduated from the same high school, which is unusual for a Navy family.

Other than Coronado, I spent my childhood years from 1967 to 1969 in Guam, my father's last overseas assignment. Even though I was very young when we were stationed there, certain Guam memories are still brilliant in my mind: the vast blue ocean, the swaying palm trees, and the high humidity. We lived on Agana Air Force Base. Our house at 416 West Sunset was typical cinderblock Navy housing with rattan furniture and no air conditioning, just fans. Screens kept most of the island critters out, but geckos and huge cockroaches still found their way inside. We had a few familiar things from home, including my father's childhood player piano and a big white rocking chair where I had to be rocked by my mother every day. There were island rules to follow: no walking in the grass after dark to keep the rabid shrews from biting our feet, and no climbing over the fence to the tangan-tangan grove because the fence was on a cliff, and it was a long way down to the bottom.

The Guamanian people were friendly and hospitable. With my mother meeting families of her students at Dededo Junior High School and my father being outgoing and friendly as well, we were often invited to the fiestas and treated to great food, including giant pigs cooked in the ground. At home, my brothers, Jerry and Scott, played football in the street using breadfruit. Breadfruit is a football sized squishy fruit that carries in the air, but makes a mess on impact. I sometimes got the messy end of the deal when I would put my hands up to try to catch it, and instead, they threw the breadfruit *at* me. They thought it was funny. I did not.

I don't remember ever realizing the United States was involved in a war in nearby Vietnam. My father's role with aviation maintenance was critical for the planes in that region. When I think of that time, I just picture helping my father pin his stars and bars to his khaki uniform in the morning before he would go to work. I'm sure he didn't need my assistance, but he was so patient in letting me help. The scariest thing was typhoon season. We would fill the bathtub with clean water to have in case the plumbing was ripped out or the water supply was contaminated after a storm. The candles were always ready should we lose power. We had some threatening storms, but only one big one during our two years there. Usually, Guam was sunny, hot, and humid, with the bluest skies, whitest clouds, and greenest trees. My mother, an oil painter, captured the atmosphere in several paintings. They hang in her home, and I have a few in mine. Some paintings even have a little bit of the sand stuck to them from dropping them upside down while painting at the beach.

Being stationed in Guam was the impetus for our family traveling a lot. We made a trip to Japan—a pristine, organized country—where we stayed in equally lovely youth hostels that were inexpensive, clean, and convenient. The fairly refined, albeit cheap, style of travel was not exactly what was in store for us on the six-week trip home to San Diego the summer of '69. That was the start of something crazy, contagious, and character-building.

That summer could be another book for the Mitchell annals. For the purpose of explaining my formative years, here are some highlights: First, imagine a family of six with big Navy duffle bags as our suitcases. We flew MAC (Military Air Command) flights. The flights were free, but on a standby basis. If after all the active duty and higher-ranked military personnel boarded and there was room, then we were on. If not, we waited for another flight and found something to do in the meantime. We usually had good luck and good timing. Once on the plane, there were rarely real airline seats, just netting, and no meal service. They did provide box lunches. Uncle Sam would get us there, but it wasn't going to be fancy. In two months we made a number of stops from Japan to Thailand, and then west to Europe.

There were several significant stops, beginning with India. The Taj Mahal was stunning, but the contrast with the poverty in the streets was shocking. At the time, the government was trying to control the population and I remember seeing the billboards encouraging just two children in a family with a sign for a boy and a sign for a girl. I remember feeling very sad about that, telling my mother that if we had been from India, I might not have been born. We had a taxi driver, Polly, as our tour guide for several days. We don't know what happened to him. For the longest time, even after I outgrew them, I kept some orange leather sandals we bought at a market he had taken us to. We had collected peacock feathers we found on the ground, and for years, we kept those feathers in a vase in our home to remind us of our time there.

Europe was next. My parents decided we would travel Europe in a Volkswagen van. Not a camper, just a van. It was a tight fit for sleeping when we couldn't find a cheap hotel. My parents were in the front seats. Robyn and Jerry were in the middle, longer seats. Scott was in the back curled up over the engine, and I was on the floor, on newspapers, wearing my mother's coat as my blanket. Scrunched, but safe and dry, we managed. It was not so terrible; we were, after all, seeing the world.

My father served thirty years in the Navy during three wars: World War II, Korea, and Vietnam. His final assignment was as Commanding Officer of the Aircraft Maintenance Department, NAS North Island, back in Coronado. I remember his office by an airplane hangar and the fried eggs and hash browns we'd some-

11

times have for lunch at the Gedunk, or snack shop. He retired after I finished first grade in 1970. I remember the ceremony outside the hangar. He was wearing his white uniform and during his speech, he worked through a lump in his throat, then fought back a few tears as he walked between two rows of Navy men saluting him. He loved the Navy, but I was glad he would be home.

Our Island in the Sun

Coronado is actually a peninsula with a long, skinny tail-like strand and a road that goes south to Imperial Beach, but we call it an island. Construction on the big blue bridge across the San Diego Bay began a few months before we left in 1967, and was finished a few weeks before we returned in 1969. It connects San Diego to the main island, also home to the Navy base. I had an active imagination and a craving for adventure. My little partner in that was my new best friend, Pam Johnson. We met in first grade and she lived across the street from our Crown Elementary School, so it made for an easy commute to go to her house at lunchtime. I usu-

ally packed my own lunch at home: Monterey Jack cheese on healthy wheat bread with Miracle Whip®. On special days, Pam's mother would make us toasted peanut butter and marshmallow sandwiches on white bread. The Johnsons were my second family, and Mrs. J still calls me "Janie-face" to this day.

Pam and I had bikes with baskets, a good place for our dolls and stuffed monkeys. We often took them down the street to a dirt alley between the school and the military base, imagining the weeds were part of the wilds of Africa and pretending we were Jane Goodall, studying the chimpanzees. Pam's backyard had a wonderful little playhouse where we made mud pies topped with inedible pink berries from a shrub-like tree. At my house, along with our playmate Leslie Taylor, we played school. We put my big green chalkboard up on my closet door handles as if it were the front of the classroom. One of us would be the teacher, the others the students, along with our stuffed animals. Then there were the times we would plan great, extravagant carnivals or fairs for my backyard. We would make tickets and planned to charge an entry fee for the different booths. We imagined popcorn and beanbag games. We had great big ideas, but didn't follow through with many of them. Still, the planning process was fun and exercised our creativity.

With my mother working as a teacher at Oneonta Elementary School in nearby Imperial Beach, Pam and I would go to school with her when our school district had a day off and hers didn't. Pam went with me until fourth grade, when she and her Navy family were stationed in Virginia for four years, returning for eighth grade. In my mother's classroom, we were teacher's helpers with reading, math, and art. I enjoyed it when I was at the same level as her second graders, but I realized I didn't enjoy it as much as I advanced. I wondered about her second-graders, *If I can do this reading or math now, why can't you?* My patience was tested, a sign that perhaps teaching would not be my forte, at least not for a while. Pam, on the other hand, became a teacher. She always loved books and credits the exposure to the classroom with my mother as an early influence on her choice to be a teacher.

It's interesting to see how our different personalities would be an indicator of where we would end up. For example, sometimes I would come by Pam's to meet her to go to school, which started at 8:15 a.m. When I arrived at her house at eight, she sometimes still had her pink spongy curlers in her hair, or her mother would be combing her curls into pigtails. I would be thinking, *Let's go, we're going to be late!* We were opposites. They calmly and slowly moved through their routine, while I had a sense of urgency to meet a deadline. Maybe it was from my family's mix of my father's orderly military routine and my mother's last minute way of getting ready for work. We always moved fast, it seemed, so that was my "norm."

Contrary to that, I could also be a terrible procrastinator, such as when it came to cleaning my room in elementary school. Before my mother's inspection, I would cram everything under the bed. I seemed to "put off things today that I could do tomorrow" as the saying goes, even though I could not do it tomorrow because that's when it was due. Once in fourth grade, I had to read a book. I had known about it for a week, but had avoided it. The night before the reading was due, my sister Robyn rescued me. Knowing I was too tired to read, she read the book out loud to me, nudging me every now and then so I would stay awake. I passed the assignment the next day, but it was not fun.

It was the beginning of some tough lessons about procrastination. One of the books that finally helped me realize the benefits of efficiency was *Cheaper by the Dozen*, first published in 1948. It is about the Gilbreth family of twelve children and their parents, Lillian and Frank Gilbreth. They were industrial engineers and "efficiency experts" starting in 1910. My father had a similar approach to getting things done. For example, if I was in the garage, parking my bicycle, even if I had a book bag in one hand, if I saw a load of laundry to be carried upstairs, I was taught to pick it up, then deliver the contents room by room in the order I passed by them, lastly dropping the books in my room or the kitchen to do my homework. It was not strictness as much as an exercise in being efficient and saving time by saving actions.

I had chores starting in first grade, including drying and putting away the dishes, taking out the trash, dusting, or helping with laundry. Even though we were told we should contribute to the housework, sometimes my mother put quarters in the laundry basket to encourage us to fold the clothes. She said whatever change we found we could keep. My father did most of the cleaning because he didn't take on a full-time job after he retired. He did real estate investments, fixer-uppers, hunted in the fall, and was "Mr. Mom." My mother cooked most of our dinners and Dad helped with breakfast and lunch. Robyn didn't do, or have to do, as much around the house by high school because she had to study, and my parents accepted that reason. I did not, but it was hard to be mad at Robyn, because she was sweet, genuine, and convincing. She made up for it by being a doctor, a fantastic cook, and a generous sister, daughter, wife, and mother.

One of the unexpected dividends of breaking my bad habit of procrastination was what my mom called, "stick-to-itiveness." I thought she created the word, but it means perseverance and persistence. I point to a few factors for the evolution of my stick-to-itiveness. When I was little, if I didn't clean my room or do the dishes completely, my mother used to say that was like having a "half-baked potato," and expected me to finish the job. My father agreed. It set a new standard for my work ethic and quality of work. I had higher expectations for myself. Over time, I applied that expectation to others and in things that mattered, such as a group project or an assignment, expecting "fully cooked potatoes." This is not to say I haven't fallen short on delivering, and I have even accepted that sometimes you can just "do so much just to get it done," but the bar was set to at least make an effort.

The other factor in this work ethic evolution emerged from the times when I was mad about having to do a task or being told to do it again more completely. I was dumbfounded on occasion when I thought it was fine. These tasks included cleaning the bathroom, dusting, sweeping the garage, or organizing my room. In those cases of being corrected, sometimes in a fit of childish fury and with a few deep sighs, I put my head down, focused, and did the task to the extreme, and usually well. It might have taken me longer, or I might have just worked faster, but I was going to see it through. It was my way of saying, "I'll show them!"

Even after I had been obstinate, my parents praised me for the follow-through, and that positive reinforcement taught me that just doing it right the first time, or at least giving more effort to doing it right the first time, was not only more productive, but more rewarding. It didn't happen overnight, but seeing a job done well felt good and motivated me to do better.

As a little girl, I was bothered on Saturdays when I had to do housework before I could play with my friends. But having chores and responsibilities instilled in me a sense of priority and appreciation for the mundane, as well as the advantages, relative luxuries, and true love that my parents and environment afforded me. What also kept me grounded was my time spent at Graham Memorial Presbyterian Church. My father went to services nearly every Sunday when he was home. My mother believed in God but didn't attend church on a regular basis. Church and religion were not forced on us, but encouraged, and I found the spiritual environment fulfilling. My father always sat in the front left pew facing the minister and the very simple cross inside the lovely white-steepled church. He sang on key and with such heart. He always held my hand, or our hands, depending on who joined him that day. I remember the grape juice and cubed white bread for communion at Christmas and Easter. I understood their symbolism and appreciated the unpretentious and practical custom. It felt more comfortable to me, compared to some of the more formal environments I had experienced when we traveled and visited many Catholic churches in South America and Europe.

My sister became a Christian in high school. I believed in God and Jesus Christ, went through the church program, and was baptized in the eighth grade. I didn't understand everything, but at the core, I knew that God had given me gifts, and it was up to me to use them for good. I believed He loved me and that my faith would give me strength and get me through challenges in life, whatever they might be. I enjoyed the youth group meetings and outings, the positive influence of the church family, singing in the choir, and playing in the bell choir. My parents belonged to an adult couples' group, The Mariners, that would often have a Sunday potluck dinner at our house, and the church members were friendly and supportive of anything my sister and I did in school or beyond. There were a lot of churches in Coronado, and many friends attended when the youth groups met together. I was never good at quoting scripture, but felt peace in my heart and a

responsibility to do right and good, partly because of this spiritual connection.

I was also very grateful. Our house was beautiful with oak hardwood floors, oak paneling, white walls, and a view of the ocean. My father and brother, Jerry, designed it, and the family moved in three weeks before I was born in 1963. We have a picture of me as a baby in the house. My mother didn't want me to get hurt or sick, so she did not take chances with visitors at our new home for about three months. Any of my siblings' friends who wanted to see me as a baby had to stand on the patio and look through the window. I was the fourth child, and my mother was especially cautious with me. It might have been because she felt so fortunate. Seven months earlier, she had gone to the doctor for an X-ray as a requirement to teach in South Bay and Imperial Beach. Before they took it, she asked to have the lead shield put on her. She didn't know she was pregnant, but she followed a feeling that she might be, and put that big lead cover on before the X-ray. Not long after, she learned she was expecting me. There's no telling if her intuition to wear that lead vest really made a difference, but she has often said that had she not followed that feeling, I could have been very different, possibly being born with any number of mental or physical disabilities.

The mid-century clean lines of the house were inspired by the famous architect, Frank Lloyd Wright, and adapted by Don Manning, my parents' contractor.

The dining room table, china hutch, end tables, and other items added later were designed by my parents, made in Taiwan, and shipped back after we left Guam. The large crystal chandelier they bought in Italy still hangs in the house. My father's childhood player piano was a magnet for singing and playing for Mitchell family gatherings. Matching dressers and night-stands in the master bedroom had been made by my father in the early years of their marriage. The room colors were pure seventies—gold, green, orange, and brown. We didn't have a lot of knick-knacks or fancy decorations, just several of my mother's paintings from Guam, plus landscapes, still lifes, and portraits.

The dining room table and the cushions from the couch made for great forts, and my parents always welcomed sleepovers for my girlfriends and me. They loved it when we wanted to do projects, whether baking, tea parties, or high school floats. My parents rolled up their sleeves and were right there with us, or when we wanted just kid time, they stepped away and allowed us to be creative and have fun.

While our towels, linens, and clothes were from the Navy Exchange, garage sales, or second hand stores, we never felt deprived. My mother taught Robyn and me to sew, producing a number of wraparound skirts and hot pants that were the popular style in the seventies. Once or twice a year, before school started and maybe at Christmas, we had a shopping spree at the exchange. While my parents provided what we needed, what we wanted was a different story. My parents' fiscal values and spending habits reflected growing up in the Depression.

I had to do a lot of justifying before I would get anything they deemed frivolous. One time, I had to rationalize the need for a plastic gumball machine. I explained that I would be saving them money by buying gumballs in bulk. That year, the gumball machine was wrapped and under the Christmas tree. Then there were those three pair of the popular and trendy Dittos® jeans. I went to great lengths detailing why they were practical and durable for school and play before my mother would buy them. The posturing and pontificating helped in my point-counterpoint and negotiating abilities. I must have taken after my father in this respect, because he liked to weigh the pros and cons of a situation. My mother often interpreted it as arguing, giving her reason to think I would be a good lawyer. I saw it as debating and showing all sides of an argument. A journalist wouldn't be too far off the mark.

While they were thrifty during the year, my parents did not skimp on our summer education through travel. With my father retired, my mother, the teacher, also had her summers free. Jerry was in college and starting his business career. Scott joined us a few more summers, and then it was just down to Robyn and me. Each summer we left behind our home at the beach and alternated going to the Pacific Northwest in our Airstream trailer to enjoy trout fishing and berry picking, to traveling overseas—Central and South America (another wild ride), Europe (this time, there were only four in a van, after my parents, Robyn, and I ditched the backpacking idea). Later, when it was just my parents and me during my sophomore year in college, we took a ten-week trip to New Zealand, Australia, and Asia.

During those many years of travel I was exposed to the contrasts of beautiful churches and shrines with poor people outside them. I had seen the beauty of the Andes Mountains and the contrast of a Marxist leader in Chile with armed soldiers in the street. I had seen the pristine, calm, and organized countries of Switzerland and Liechtenstein. We may not have been princes or paupers, but we saw the spectrum of cultures. This made an indelible mark in my heart and memory, as I realized the privileged life we lived.

There is one day I point to as a defining moment in my developing view of the world. One hot summer day in Istanbul, Turkey in 1976, my parents, sister, and I walked the long road up to the citadel, the old fortress in the middle of the city. My father was always in the lead. Robyn was usually beside him. My mother and I were in the back. Two significant things happened that day. First, a girl about my age, thirteen, joined me in our walk. We didn't speak the same language, but she took my hand as we walked that dusty path, as if we were friends. People lived in the parts of the citadel once manned by soldiers. It was quiet and peaceful. Children were running around us, curious about the visitors. My father saw a little old, wrinkled woman making tortilla-like flat bread over a small fire. He went up to her to take her picture. She took the bread and tore it, giving half to him and keeping half for herself. It was a gesture of peace and friendship, and it showed me how different we can be, yet we all share the same desires for love, peace, and friendship.

From Vowels to Earl the Pearl

My mother taught me to read in Guam when I was four. I enjoyed how she used a phonovisual chart and sang a song to teach me my long and short vowels: "Baby wants a cake, aa, aa, aa, Baby wants a tree, ee, ee, ee ... but the mama says 'No, oh, oh.'" The principal at the elementary school wrote my parents a letter informing them that the school had given me the option of staying in kindergarten or going on to first grade. My mother says I said, "no," to advancing early because I liked being in one corner reading to the students while the teacher was reading to another group. My parents let me stay. By second grade, I tested as a "gifted" student and was assigned to classes for the gifted program. I was eager to participate and truly loved school and learning.

For someone who had once been so shy, I was just the opposite early on in elementary school. It seemed there was always something I just had to share with someone else in class. I don't think I was chatty as much as felt I had important information to relay to my classmates. Sometimes, however, that was when the students were supposed to be quiet. One time, an educator put tape over my mouth, the consequence for being one of the talkative kids. It might have made me more disciplined, or taught me to practice self-control, but it was embarrassing and hurtful. Nevertheless, it didn't keep me from expressing myself.

Thankfully, expressing myself also had its roots in my mother's creativity. My mother had my sister and me write about our experiences while traveling, starting when I was in the second grade. Whether it was our three months in Central and South America, or driving to Alaska seeing bears and magnificent glaciers, the writer in me was being nurtured whether I wanted it to be or not. Sometimes, I just wanted to be on vacation, but I now appreciate Mom requiring that of us. She had a philosophy echoing the teachings of educator Dr. Van Allen which she used with her students: If you can tell your story, you can write your story. If you can write your story, you can read your story, and read what other people have written.

For eight of her thirty-one-and-a-half years of teaching, she compiled her students' stories as they progressed. School assistants or parents typed them, added in their drawings, and then printed the pages at the school print shop. With the help of parents, volunteers, and students, "Mrs. Mitchell's Room 5" made books using fabric and cardboard for the covers, and heavy duty thread, hand binding them together. The homemade book-publishing project meant each child could see, touch, and experience his or her own development that school year.

My mother's classroom projects were often a family affair. Our dining room table was covered with the papers for the book project, the kitchen filled with ingredients to take to the classroom for a baking project, and huge containers of ice cream for the students at our house, before taking her class to the beach for a field trip every year. Her students were from middle- to low-income families and she wanted to make them excited about school and learning and expose them to the possibilities education can bring. My mother had the ideas. My father helped her get them done. As she wrote in the front of the 1985 edition of her class's book: "To my husband Wally who warns me not to, but helps me when I do." We helped her as well. She didn't mind if things were messy, or paint or flour flew everywhere, as long as it was cleaned up afterward. There were rules, but she was a fun and loving teacher, and we could see how much joy and reward she had every school year. She taught eleven years before we returned from Guam, and then second grade for twenty more years before retiring in 1989.

Her enthusiasm for encouraging creativity was a constant in my life, as she taught me about writing journals and poetry, painting, and playing the piano, and listening to me practice the clarinet for four years.

She helped me with three school projects in particular—writing three books. Each was an assignment for three of my favorite teachers. In seventh grade English class with Noel Brewer, the book was *Herman the Hermit Crab Hunts for his Home*. I received an A+, and Mrs. Brewer said in her notes: "Good story. Technically perfect, you had a good editor."

For my eighth grade English class with Kathy Clark, the book was *A Very Rare Breed*, based on life lessons from our puppy, Danny. My sister also helped edit this one. My grade was A++. Mrs. Clark said the illustrations were "very professional," the mechanics were "great," and the neatness "stupendous." She commented, "This was worth waiting for. I love it. An outstanding job." I'm wondering if I asked for an extension.

The third project was in ninth grade art with Tom Luedk. *How the Oyster Got Its Pearl* featured Olly the Oyster and Earl the Pearl illustrated with colored pencil drawings. I don't have the notes or grade, but I think it was an A.

My mother had learned the concept of the homemade book project from her music education professor, Mr. Frye, at San Diego State College. She showed me her story called "Jerry Had a Birthday, He Spent it at the Zoo." It had water-color illustrations and a poem in the form of a song. She passed on what she learned by helping her students and me.

While we didn't use a song as the foundation, we collaborated on the stories, developing each little character and their struggle, journey, and resolution. She asked me to imagine what they would think by relating to experiences in my own life about change, fear, adventure, security, and love. For example, she asked, "How would you feel if you were a crab and had a seagull swooping down on you, or your clothes were getting too tight and you needed a new shell?" We worked together on the editing and the production of the book, with fabric covers and hand-stitched binding, thanks to my father's strong hands. These were pre-computer days, so each was handwritten. I painted or sketched all the pictures with a little assistance from my mother on the details, because I could never quite get proportions right. My people did not look very realistic, but the crab and sea critters were easier for me. The collaboration didn't come without some arguments or exasperation. Sometimes I would be tired and say, "It's good enough," but she said it needed to be clearer or corrected. She was usually right. Most of the time, though, we had fun in the process, and were excited to see the final project.

I have seen how sometimes parents take over a project for their child, to either get it done faster or better, or to help them get a higher grade. That was not so in my case. I had to do the work. I had to execute the plan. I also embraced the help and guidance I needed. If I had done it alone, I would have completed the projects. However, I wouldn't have learned as much along the way. I dutifully gave my mother credit as editor on all three books. It has been more than thirty years since those projects, and my mother has been a valuable editor on this book, as well. We have still had some arguments about grammar and style, but she is proud, and I am thankful for her guidance and help. Now that I know the process and we are in the digital world, we will publish those three children's stories, and perhaps her story, too.

While I was outgoing and interactive with friends and in school, some situations nearly paralyzed me, and I have my mom to thank for freeing me from this confining fear. For example, at social or cultural events, I would comment how I liked what someone did, such as a museum tour guide, a musician playing the piano, or an actor from a play. Mom would encourage me—almost demand of me—to go up to meet them. I froze. My feet felt as if they were in cement. I had no nerve. I could not imagine walking up to someone famous, or older, and saying anything—a compliment, asking a question, or requesting an autograph or a picture. I was petrified, embarrassed. I would stare at my mother and shake my head no as she was saying, "Just go up there. You can do it." Somehow, nine times out of ten, I did it. Sometimes she went with me, other times she just gave me a little push and waited to see if I would do it. Nike® might have used the phrase "Just Do It" for advertising in the late '80s, but my parents were saying that—about work, travel, and setting goals—their whole lives, and certainly as they raised their children. A real turning point came the summer of 1976 in Greece when I emerged from that final state of a petrified feeling.

My parents, sister, and I were traveling and stopped by a military base celebrating America's Bi-Centennial. Miss America 1976, Tawny Godin, was starring in a USO show entertaining the troops. I wanted to meet her, and with encouragement from my family, I approached her to say hello and have my picture taken with her. That experience—and just finally accepting that it did not hurt to ask, that they would either talk with me or not, that they would be cordial to me or not, that they would take a picture with me or not—helped me to understand that either way, it was worth the risk. Even though I was still a little apprehensive at times, had to plot my move, or had butterflies, being encouraged to step out of my box as a young girl was liberating, and possibly the final piece of the puzzle that led to my epiphany the next year.

My 8th Grade Epiphany

As a family of storytellers, how we captured the story progressed with technology, too. My parents seemed to have the "document-the-moment" gene. They had eight-millimeter film reels from before they were married, reel-to-reel audiotapes, audiocassette tapes, then every new format of video that developed in the 1970s and '80s. The Mitchell family archives are plentiful, with many moments (including eating Thanksgiving meals) captured on tape, on paper, and in our minds' eye.

After the summer in Turkey in 1976, my father tried to send the pictures to that little girl. We never knew if she received them. I wrote about my day on the citadel that fall in school. I also had the personal victory of talking with Miss America and a picture to prove it. My confidence level matched my interests, and it all came together one night.

I had always wanted to go to Egypt. Maybe it was the pyramids and the idea of seeing where civilization began. One evening in eighth grade, I sat in our living room, curled up in a big, soft green and gold velvet floral rocking chair. My father was on the couch. We were watching a news report from the peace talks in Cairo. I don't remember what was being said. I do remember distinctly seeing a man holding a microphone standing in front of the pyramids reporting on the story of the day. In that moment, that very moment, I said to my father, "Wow, that man travels the world, tell stories, is on TV, and gets paid for it. That's what I'm going to do."

I had found my future, what I was meant to do. I was going to be a reporter, and I was determined to find out everything I had to do to achieve that goal. I just didn't know that something else would either delay that or keep me more focused, depending on how I handled it. That something happened later that year.

My First Real "Curve" Ball: Scoliosis

There was nothing unusual about the day I went to the nurse's office in seventh grade. She said to bend over and hang my arms to the ground while she ran her hand down my spine. She noticed it was curved a little and told my parents and me we should keep an eye on it and check it in the next six months or so. Those six months came and went. Soon, it was nine months later, the following summer between eighth grade and my freshman year in high school. My father's words and concern seemed more annoying than telling. "Get your little wing back," he would say, urging me to stand up straight and make my shoulder blade flat. I just sighed and tried, and none of us really thought much about it. I didn't feel any pain. I was somewhat tall at 5'2" and a bit gangly, but healthy. Finally, after a summer of traveling to Seattle with my parents and a few weeks of camping in Hawaii with my mother, my parents were concerned about my posture. So, we went to an orthopedic surgeon, a specialist at Balboa Naval Hospital, Dr. Richard Browning. He was wonderful. The news was not. That curvature of the spine had progressed rapidly to a sixty-degree curve. The X-rays showed how my spine looked like a question mark. The diagnosis: A severe case of idiopathic scoliosis. Idiopathic meaning they didn't really know what caused it. Perhaps it was from a growth spurt where the bones grew faster than the muscles could stretch, or from not using both sides of my body equally, or maybe my not being too athletic. It's not a disease, but a condition. Pulmonary tests indicated I was breathing with essentially only one lung. The curve of the spine was crushing the other lung and my organs.

The good news was that the twisting was above my waistline and therefore considered a "C" curve, as opposed to curving at the two ends, creating an "S" curve. The bad news was that if I didn't have surgery right away, it would continue to progress and crush my internal organs. Doctors predicted that without surgery, I could be severely crippled and perhaps die by the time I was thirty years old. That's a lot to hear when you're fourteen. Surgery was set for three weeks.

The odyssey began. I saw the anesthesiologist, who had me undergo hypnosis sessions. The reason for hypnosis was so that in the middle of surgery, they could take me off anesthetic, wake me up, and ask me to move my hands and feet to make sure I wasn't paralyzed. The hypnosis would allow me to not feel or know the pain I might have felt while being awakened with my entire back cut open.

It was terrifying to imagine what was going to happen, but I had tremendous love and support from my family, especially my parents and my sister, Robyn, who was going to be a doctor.

I checked into the hospital on Sunday, November 13, 1977, and underwent many tests. They had a hard time finding my veins for drawing blood and for inserting the IVs, and I still have the tiny pinpoint scars in my elbow crease from all the times

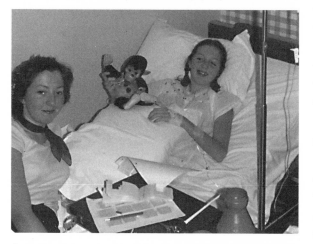

they poked me. The worst was the one on the top of my hand. Robyn tried to make me feel better by using a little straw and tape and attaching it to Mr. Buttons, my favorite stuffed monkey. It didn't hurt less, but I laughed and felt better.

My parents didn't seem to care about the hospital rules and visiting hours. My mother, especially, was feisty and determined to be there for me the night before surgery. Early the next morning, the hospital staff wheeled me down the hall. The last thing I remember about that morning was seeing my mother's face as she said she loved me and rode the elevator to the basement holding my hand. She said, "You have braces on your teeth and you will have a brace on your back, and when they're all off you can compete to be Miss Coronado like Robyn did." It was high-risk surgery and I was so scared.

The six-hour surgery was intense. They opened my back from about four inches below my neck down to my waist. While they often use cadaver bone now, at the time, they went inside and around to my hipbone to the body's "bone bank." They took bone, then after stretching my spine two inches, used it to fuse five

vertebrae. They attached a stainless steel Harrington rod at the top and bottom of my spine to hold it in place while the fusion set. After the hypnosis strategy and determining I could move my feet and hands, they sewed me up.

The surgery was a success, but the next three weeks were horrible. I was in terrible pain and discomfort as that huge incision, along with everything else, healed. My parents were amazing, making sure I had the care, pain medicine, and silence I needed. I didn't want any noise. No talking. No TV for at least two weeks. I cried. I hurt. One nurse said I should toughen up. My mother chewed her out saying, "This is no time for her to toughen up. She's allowed to cry. Just get her medication and be gentle." I was grateful for Mom's strength when I was so weak. The worst was when they had to flip me every few hours to prevent bedsores and to keep my circulation going. I was on a Streicher Frame bed, the two sides like two pieces of bread, and I was the middle of the sandwich.

I had a round open-faced pillow for my head when I was face down. The nurses would say, "One, two, three, flip," and turn me fast. If they went too slowly, my body would slide on the boards and it felt as if the wound was wide open. It was very painful.

At some point, they removed the stitches. These were not the kind that dissolved or were little threads that just pulled out. These were big, heavy threads that didn't seem to want to come out, but they did, with a lot more tears and screaming.

By the two and a half week point, it was time for the body cast. They wheeled me into the cast room, lifted my little ninety-pound body with that giant incision on my back, and balanced me on a two-inch wide fabric band—the pivot for wrapping a cast around my body. I screamed loud curdling screams, enduring the most excruciating agony. An hour or so later, I was covered neck to hip and around my torso in forty pounds of wet plaster. A few days later, the cast was dry—ten pounds of water had evaporated. They cut a hole out of the cast in my stomach area so I could breathe and function better. The pain had subsided. Now, it was just getting used to my new outlook on the world. Literally.

For the first time in nineteen days I was sitting up as I moved into the wheelchair to leave the hospital and go home early in December. It was an odd sensation, but my new perspective didn't really hit me until we arrived at the house. With this thirty-pound plaster shell around my body, I moved slowly. I gingerly walked up the stairs and through the front door, feeling like I was Alice in Wonderland. Everything had shrunk. The piano was two inches shorter. The chandelier was two inches lower. I realized I had grown two inches overnight from the surgery. That is a lot when it is all of a sudden and not over time. A bizarre sensation, but it was so good to be home. I was grateful to be alive and not paralyzed.

I wore that body cast for six months. I went to school and could have easily been the oddball made fun of because of how I looked in the big, bulky cast. I wore T-shirts, smock dresses my mother custom made, and drawstring pants—the only things that would fit. I knew I could count on my best friends to be kind and helpful, but I wasn't sure about others at school. Kids can be cruel. That's why I will always appreciate Molly Barnum. Molly was one of the most popular girls. She also had a big heart. She set the tone at school by cheering me on, helping me around campus, and in her own way, made sure no one made fun of me, and they didn't. Molly made those six months much easier.

My parents also made the best of the situation. They drove me place to place or I walked. When I felt daring, I hopped on a bike, even though that wasn't advised because my mobility was fairly limited, especially my head's turning radius. Thankfully, I didn't crash or fall. I wasn't allowed to get the cast wet, so no showers, just sponge baths. To wash my hair, I stepped up to lean back on our kitchen roll-around-island, and my sister or my girlfriends, Pam Johnson and Anne Watson, tilted me down to the kitchen sink, always with grace and a giving attitude.

I felt I could finally resume my goals on May 16, 1978. That's the day the cast was removed. The medical technicians split it on the two sides with a saw and pulled it off. I felt so light, as if I could fly. I cried out of sheer relief and joy. It was over. Pam wrote me a "Cast Off" poem that day. The page is yellowed now. The writing is black except for the words "cast" and "back," which are in red. Two lines read: "It's nice to see [you're] back in the swing of things, which joy and happiness it brings. You may have felt like a castaway, now [you're] here to stay. You've gathered much nerve, all due to your spinal curve."

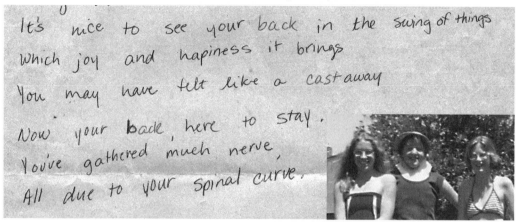

That cast, with my friends' autographs and messages, is wrapped in plastic and stored in a cupboard. I look at it every five years or so as a tangible reminder of what I went through and how fortunate I am to have had the help and support when I needed it. It might not have had the same impact because I didn't want to be an athlete, but when I see people, especially athletes, who have gone through some sort of life-changing surgery, I can relate. My scar is probably among the longest, too. While it has faded with time, what someone might see is just a reminder of my lifesaving experience.

A Mexican Adventure

My best friend, Pam, had returned to Coronado in eighth grade, and a new friendship with Anne Watson made the three of us inseparable through high school. Anne and Pam met in English class. An invitation to join them one afternoon making ice cream at Anne's house sealed the deal on this trio.

We have remained close, even through different career paths, and even when miles separate us. Both of them are married with children, but we can still pick up right where we left off, even if it has been months. For years, we have always made the point of having lunch or dinner, just the three of us, when we are in Coronado during the summer or the holidays. We often reminisce about one adventure in particular.

After our freshman year in high school, we persuaded our parents to allow us to go to Mexico for a month with about ten other students and one Spanish teacher. It was a language immersion program where we would live with a family and speak only Spanish for four weeks. This was not to a major metropolitan city, but San Cristobel de las Casas, in the mountains of Chiapas, Mexico.

After a stop in Mexico City, we traveled to the town. It was rustic with stone walls and a lovely square in the city center. There was one charming hotel, lush with tropical flowers and birds. Pam, Anne, and I were assigned to live with a family. The gate opened into a house designed around a garden. At first it felt elegant and inviting, but we would soon learn their definition of modern did not coincide with ours. The shower was a pipe that came out of the wall and drained down the hallway and into the garden. The walls had a few more cracks than we felt comfortable with. In the kitchen it was their tradition to keep one pan of beans on the stove around the clock. We were there one month and we are quite sure that pan never was emptied of beans. They just kept adding new ones to the mix.

It wasn't a bad situation, but it required some adjustment. I think it was less shocking to me because I had traveled more than my friends had. Still, it was a long way from home and we just had each other when we were scared, sick, or bored. I won't go in to details about our trip to the ruins of Palenque and how we fought the old amebas. When you're sick in a foreign country, that's when you know who your real friends are.

One night, when the three of us were walking home to our villa, we sensed someone following us and wondered if they meant us harm. Our hearts started pounding and our adrenaline was pumping. We discussed how we didn't want them to know where we were staying or that we were three American girls. I said, "Walk like a man. Walk from the knees down." So we waddled down the street fast, thinking if we walked that way they wouldn't see us as girls, swinging our hips. I don't know if that in any way deflected their attention or made them lose interest, but that moment of feeling "we were in this together" strengthened our bond. We didn't go out much after dark because of that. We amused ourselves by pretending our beds were surfboards and by watching the ducks walk around inside the house. We did learn Spanish, and after those four weeks, I said goodbye to Pam and Anne as they went home and I went to see my sister and mother in Guadalajara where Robyn was starting medical school. It was a much calmer time, and my Spanish came in handy. All these experiences offered perspective for my blossoming profession.

Journalism 101: TV and Print

My surgery and newly fused spine meant no contact sports, nothing that would jar or put undue pressure on my back for the next five years. That would not be a problem for me. I played a little tennis, swam, and was active but had no interest in being the next gymnast or basketball star. I was happy on the sidelines. I did play an occasional flag football game until I broke my radius bone on my left arm when a sophomore boy playing defense plowed into me. I had learned how to ski in Portillo, Chile when I was nine, and I joined my family for spring skiing when I was younger. After my surgery, I would go on ski trips, but unless it was sunny and all powder, I was too frightened to ski. Falling or hitting ice and losing control terrified me, thinking I would twist my back and dislodge my rod. The biggest things I lifted were my pen and a typewriter in my quest to be a reporter.

Student government was part of that. I was elected to the Sophmore Class Cabinet, then Junior Class President. Going into my senior year, I lost the Associated Student Body president election, but I was re-elected class president. I wasn't popular in the traditional high school sense. I wasn't a cheerleader, an athlete, and certainly not the cutest girl. I have been told both in comments in my yearbook and throughout life that people felt I could be friends with, or at least was friendly with, students across the spectrum, and that I didn't alienate people, but rather, made them feel included. That seemed normal to me, perhaps because I had traveled and was accustomed to diversity and adaptability. Also, I didn't want to leave someone out, just as I didn't want to be left out.

This might have stemmed from an experience in elementary school. A few boys (and they know who they are) teased me a lot; what we now call bullying. They called me "Goober Eyes," because, I suppose, they thought my eyes were big and presumably ugly. My parents told me my eyes were big and beautiful. The boys also stole my shoe once and threw it in the boys' toilet. Then when they were told to take it out to dry, they put it on the workbench in the classroom with a vice grip, making it difficult for me to remove. I never understood why they went to such lengths to frustrate me. I didn't do anything to them. I thought they were my friends. My feelings were hurt. I was a little bit of a teacher's pet, so I wondered if maybe that was why they chose to bother me. Finally in fourth grade, my teacher, Sammy Denhoff, helped me see the light in this complicated world of boys and girls.

Mrs. Denhoff had a long black and gray ponytail, wore glasses on the top of her head, long skirts, sandals, no makeup, and was tough and loud. She loved being a teacher, and I loved her direct way of communicating with us. One time when I was upset, she pulled me aside quietly and told me the only reason the boys continued to tease me was because they either liked me, or were getting a reaction from me. *Well, of course they were getting a reaction,* I thought, *they were being mean to me.* She advised that if I just stopped reacting to their childish pranks, they would stop doing them. It was all I could do to bite my tongue and not react during their attempts to tease. It went against my nature of speaking up and defending myself. Somehow, I stopped reacting, the pranks stopped, and those classmates who didn't move on to other places returned to being my friends. I don't know what they learned from all that, but I learned to pick my battles, take the high road, and to relax a little when people teased me. I believe this contributed to my desire to be inclusive once I hit high school, because I knew what it felt like to be left out. Plus, I liked organizing people and events, was willing to do the work, and seemed to have success at it. I also learned even more about time management, and coordinating different personalities and responsibilities.

I held myself accountable, too, as a leader and because I wanted to do the right thing. I did not drink or smoke ever in high school, and have never done drugs. If I found myself in a situation where there was drinking or smoking (cigarettes or marijuana), I left. I believed that more could be gained by doing the right thing than the wrong thing. I let my parents know where I was and what time I would be home, and thankfully, my closest friends had a similar take on things.

As a child, I also learned from watching my brothers. They were relatively good as teenagers, but it was the late sixties and early seventies after all, and there were times they made my parents unhappy. I would sometimes see my parents talking in the kitchen about a situation with my brothers, and my mother would cry. I knew I didn't want to be the one to cause that. I was not perfect. I could be a little sassy at times, usually because I wanted my way, but I always felt bad afterward and apologized.

I barely dated in high school. Maybe I was too straightlaced or more mature than the boys who might have thought about asking me out. I'm not sure. I was certain about right from wrong and thought about consequences two and three steps down the road; and that included not having sex in high school. I was not only scared of the whole concept, but I didn't want to disappoint my parents. I wanted to live by what I had learned in church, and I was driven by achieving goals that would get me to college and into my career. I had fun, was involved in all school activities, and had friends in all categories (popular kids, athletes, surfers, and in the band and drama group). But I did not want to get in trouble. It was just that simple to me.

While being a broadcast journalist was my goal, I wanted experience writing at a newspaper, too. I convinced the local newspaper, *The Coronado Journal,* to let me be an intern and work for free. I began by writing obituaries. While not the most pleasant topic, it served as a lesson about how the details of someone's life are important; not only to strangers reading about the person who died, but to that person's family and friends. I didn't get a byline, but I cared about doing the story well. The byline finally came when I wrote a feature about gold coins found in the ocean on display at a local jeweler. It wasn't riveting or breaking news, but it was satisfying to see my name in print at seventeen.

I was also on the yearbook staff as a section editor and the business manager with the guidance of my dynamic and influential journalism teacher, Mrs. Margaret Wright. Mrs. Wright had confidence in me and urged me to pursue my goals, including applying to a competitive journalism camp sponsored by the California Scholastic Press Association. I was accepted and received a one hundred dollar scholarship to buy a new Smith-Corona® manual typewriter. I joined thirty other students with aspirations to work in print or broadcasting from across California,

Oregon, and Washington for three weeks at Cal Poly, San Luis Obispo the summer between my junior and senior years.

One moment stands out the most from that camp—July 30, 1980. Playing the role of a print reporter, I had to write news stories from around campus or adapt one from the newspaper. We wrote under a mock deadline. On my typewriter, I pounded out a story about a regional high school controversy. The subject is not important, but what was significant about that assignment was the note from the teacher who graded it. When I saw it, I nearly jumped out of my chair. The comment at the top of the page read: "This reads like a TV news bulletin. Needs more detail." The score was a 67 out of 100. Not good. Had I wanted to be a print

reporter, I might have been disappointed or discouraged by the seemingly critical and condescending comment, but I was thrilled. I even wrote, "All right!" on the top of the page. I kept that paper with that big blue-inked comment. I plan to frame it.

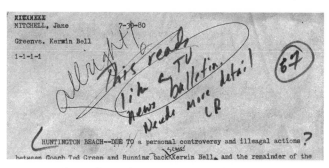

In spring of 1980, my junior year, I took a chance on something that took a lot of encouragement from my parents. I tried out for the Miss Coronado pageant. Singing or dancing were not required. I didn't think of myself as particularly attractive, but I knew performing and public speaking were important to my development if I wanted to be on TV, eventually. My sister, then a pre-med student, had tried twice and placed third when she was sixteen, then second when she was seventeen. This was a stretch for her, being a very quiet, focused person. I had cheered her on. This time, she was there for me. I was contestant number "8" of eight, among girls far better looking than I. I didn't think I had a chance, but I suppose the interview and the live question and answer session impressed the judges. I was honest and articulate, telling them of my recent medical challenges and my goals to be a reporter. When asked if I believed I could "have it all," I told how my mother set a great example by being a wife, mother, and professional. Of course, my father videotaped it, but it's the one tape in our archives we cannot find.

As the last contestant, I was in the middle of the stage. They announced the second runner up, then the first runner up. I thought I didn't place at all. Then, they announced the new Miss Coronado 1980: "Janie Mitchell." I was shocked and happy. At just seventeen years old, I was the youngest, at the time, to have the title. I wasn't into the whole "beauty queen" thing, but it was a great experience for public speaking and it allowed me to be a representative of my community. It also helped keep me on track. I was excited to have a second chance after that surgery to seize life, an education, and a career.

In 1980, cable television was still fairly new. Cable companies were creating programming and were required to provide public access. This was a great venue for me. In my junior year, my mother received a telephone call from Stan Antrim, who oversaw Televents, Coronado's local cable company at the time. Stan had seen my writing in the *Journal* and figured I had an interest in media. He asked my mother if she thought I would like to work behind the scenes and run camera for a new production. The host was going to be a classmate, a girl who was a smart, popular, athletic star of the school. Again, my mother stepped in, suggesting to him that I should be the host *in front* of the camera, not behind the scenes, because I wanted to be a news reporter. I said, "Oh, Mother," and agreed to work on the production. Soon after, the girl didn't want to do the show anymore; she was going to be a doctor, not a journalist. Scott Stagliano, another classmate, was the producer/director. He asked if I would step in. Of course, I did. The show was called *Coronado Corner* and was designed to bridge the gap between the high school and the community. Perfect fit. It was a weekly thirty-minute program without commercial breaks.

I prepared for my first show—an interview with the high school's student body president, Jon Herron. As we began rolling tape that day in the studio, I asked him about his background, what it was like to have his mother in city government, playing on the water polo team, his vision for the community, and his goals for college and beyond. After about twenty minutes, I had exhausted all my questions and curiosity. I could not think of one more question to ask, could not squeeze one more answer out of my subject, or think of one more thing of relevance to say. There were no commercials to go to, so I wrapped things up and they rolled credits for about ten minutes as we sat there. I laugh about it now. Thank goodness it was public access. I couldn't get fired. I wasn't even getting paid. By the next show, I learned to always have other questions or pieces of information to go to and to stretch when necessary. Running out of questions has not happened since, either as a student or as a professional—even when I'm doing live television and having to tap dance or stretch alone or with a subject.

I recently found the research for twenty-eight of the thirty *Coronado Corner* shows I hosted. They looked oddly familiar, and not all that different from how I have been preparing for in-depth interviews for fourteen years at Channel 4 San Diego. I researched the pertinent facts about the guests and their activities. I wrote questions or words that would trigger questions I was curious about. Even then, I felt that if someone was going to give me their time, I owed it to them and to the viewers to at least have done my homework, and then be ready to listen and go with the flow.

At my high school graduation, I gave the Senior Class President's speech. It was similar to the one I gave after eighth grade at my middle school graduation, when eight of us each took a letter in the word "progress." Mine was "E." I said in both speeches that we should all approach each day and live with "effort, energy, and enthusiasm." I love alliteration. Those words reflect my outlook still. Several years later, in 1998, I used those three "E" words when summarizing Trevor Hoffman's approach to life for my show, *One on One*.

Meeting my "American Idol"

I was never one to have an obsession over a teen pop star or movie star. I had no desire to be famous, but I did have role models beyond my parents. When I decided I wanted to be a reporter, I began watching the news even more. My father often clipped articles about two women I admired in the business: Jane Pauley, new to NBC's *Today Show* then, and Judy Woodruff, a White House correspondent. I also admired the "On the Road with Charles Kuralt" features on CBS's *Sunday Morning*. I was drawn to their presentations, their individual styles, and their intelligence. I imagined I could be in their position someday. The articles about Jane Pauley, specifically, talked about how she was a Political Science major in college and felt it was important to have an education that included history, politics, economics, and literature. She shared that someone can learn the skills needed to be in TV, but a broad-based education prepared one for thinking, listening, and knowing how and what questions to ask. I agreed and proceeded to map out my course.

Having traveled all my life, I didn't have the urge to leave home for college as some of my friends did. I would be gone soon enough. Plus, if I lived at home, my parents promised me a new car, a Volkswagen Rabbit. It wasn't really because of the car, but being at home seemed easier and more comfortable for me. I applied to three schools in San Diego: The University of San Diego, San Diego State University, and the University of California, San Diego. I was accepted into all three, but wanted UCSD the most, probably because my sister graduated from there and my dad had taken Poli Sci classes there as he worked toward (but eventually didn't complete) his bachelor's degree. I had good grades and average SAT scores. To make it into a fiercely competitive state school felt like a huge achievement, and I was going for it.

The summer after high school graduation in 1981, my parents, sister, and I went to England, Ireland, Wales, and Scotland. This would be the last big trip we would take as a foursome. Robyn had to leave a little early to get back to complete her fourth year of medical school. By the end of July, my parents and I were in London for Prince Charles' and Princess Diana's wedding. Along with a half million others, we decided to camp out on the streets to watch the procession. We found a spot in front of Buckingham Palace and stayed all afternoon, into the night, and the next day with all the Brits who were madly in love with their royal family. I could not believe what I was seeing and hearing. With the nicest of manners, the crowd applauded when the police came by and asked people to step back behind the cones. They applauded again when the street sweepers came through, and again when the geese flew over. Everyone was so happy.

Not even seeing the royal couple later that day, just ten feet in front of me in their carriage, could mean more to me than what happened early that morning. I looked behind me to see how the U.S. television crews were setting up stages. NBC's *Today Show* was right there. The anchors' backs were facing Buckingham Palace. Seeing them gave me a rush of adrenaline. I got up the nerve to try to meet the crew. I introduced myself to the security guard at the "do not cross" tape several yards from the stage. I told him it would mean so much if I could go over and introduce myself to the anchors. I said they were very well known in America and I wanted to be just like them. He let me cross. In my jeans, raincoat, and tennis shoes, I walked up behind the stage where the anchors were sitting in their seats. No one stopped me. In what I thought seemed like a commercial break, I said, "Excuse me, Ms. Pauley." She turned and said hello. "My name is Jane, too. Jane Mitchell. I'm going to college to be a Political Science major and I want to be a reporter just like you." In the most sincere, genuine manner, she said, "Good for you. You're doing the right thing. Tom, this is Jane. She wants to be a reporter, too." Tom Brokaw said to me, "Good for you, kid. Good luck." With the commercial break almost over, they quickly said goodbye. I was elated and encouraged as I walked back to my parents and the events of the day.

Some twenty years later, I told Bob Costas that story when I met him covering Dave Winfield's Hall of Fame induction. Bob, a broadcaster with NBC sports, encouraged me to write to Jane Pauley at NBC and tell her of my experience. I did. I received a lovely note back from her. I don't know if she or someone in her office read my thank you letter, but I appreciated the response. I'm still grateful for that two-minute commercial break on July 29, 1981. I carried that moment with me all the way through college, graduate school, and into my first job. Years later, when I finally had a paycheck for doing what I loved, I knew I had made it; maybe not anchoring the *Today Show,* but I had made it.

Not Waiting for Opportunity to Knock

Television is a competitive field. There are 210 markets with about three stations per market, and only so many on-air positions. That competition didn't scare me. I just decided to give myself better odds by being prepared. In college, I continued implementing my father's slogan, "Don't wait. Anticipate." UCSD had a lot to offer, but hands-on journalism experience was not one of them. I had to create opportunities to gain practical experience. I originally double-majored in Political Science and Communications, but I quickly determined that the Communications classes there often criticized the very business I wanted to be a part of. So, I majored in Poli–Sci, added Literature/Writing and Visual Arts as minors, and pieced together a plan to fit my goal. I focused strictly on academics the first two years— academics and a trip down under.

During my sophomore year, my mother needed a respite to de-stress from work and severe migraines that had taken their toll on her. She took a year's sabbatical from teaching, and she and my father decided to take a big trip to fulfill one of my father's dreams: fishing in New Zealand. They planned to do a circle route with Pan American Airlines, meaning the trip would begin in Fiji, and as long as they kept moving forward, they could make several stops: New Zealand, Australia,

Singapore, Thailand, Hong Kong, and Japan. They asked if I would like to take a quarter off from school (ten weeks) to go with them. My first reaction was, "No, I am in love with my first real boyfriend and could not be away from him that long." My mother thought maybe there was some truth to the term "love sick," and said I needed to snap out of it. If he really loved me, he would be there when I came back. I finally decided the adventure would be fun. After some tears and a send-off, once my parents and I got in the plane, I switched gears, pulled out the maps, and began to plan our trip.

As far as my dad's fishing dream, 1983 happened to be the year of drought. The fish were hard to find because they sought the cold water deep in the lakes and streams, and they weren't biting. What he did catch tasted musty from the warm surface water. The sheep to person ratio at the time was twenty million to three million, and I think we saw a good portion of them dotting the green hillsides and pastures as we drove a rented Winnebago® for a month. We also soaked in the amazing scenery, saw kangaroos in Australia, stayed at Green Island, and snorkeled on the Great Barrier Reef. We met warm and friendly people. We explored parts of Asia, and this time, I was old enough to appreciate more of the culture and food than when I was a child. I processed the contrasts more as a student and a critical thinker. When we returned from that ten-week trip, I was happy to learn my mother was right. My boyfriend was waiting.

Back at the academic adventure, my grades improved quarter by quarter as I figured out that procrastinating really could hinder me in college, and I learned how to juggle the full-time class workload better. No more having my sister help me with my book reports at ten o'clock at night, as she did when I was in fourth grade. Waiting until the last minute to cram for Spanish or Logic would not cut it. Certainly, there was no margin for error in turning in anything late, especially for Professor Sam Popkin. One time, I pulled an all-nighter, drove ridiculously fast in my VW® Rabbit that morning, and parked illegally just to get in my seat as the buzzer rang at nine o'clock. Some fifteen years later, I would occasionally see Prof. Popkin at ball games in San Diego. He boasted I was one of his best and favorite students. I told him I had used something I learned in his class about the "What have you done for me lately" theory of voting for a political story I covered in Oklahoma. I wonder if he knows how much I feared him, and how the idea of getting marked down for being late terrified me? That discipline was good for me. It helped underscore the importance of deadlines and not missing them.

In my junior year at UCSD, I also found my voice in my academic writing. Instead of trying to impress my professors with academic verbiage and a regurgitation of their lectures, I discovered writing in a more conversational style resulted in better papers with clarity, conciseness, and better grades. The pressure of test-taking was another matter. I panicked after a mid-term in Steve Erie's class on Urban Politics, thinking I had mixed up the theories and made a mess of my test's blue book. I'm grateful to him for looking at me and saying, "Jane, it's just a test. It's not the end of the world. You can make it up. It's just a test." I took everything so seriously. I set such high standards for myself, but when I trusted my writing and my thought process, I did better. I had to go through some stress, but I eventually gained confidence to forge ahead and stop second-guessing myself.

Part of that maturity and confidence came by taking a class my junior year that tapped into my interest in international relations. The Cold War was raging in 1984, and the idea of going to Europe as a reporter and covering NATO (The North Atlantic Treaty Organization) appealed to me. I signed up for a class in a new program called IGCC: The Institute on Global Conflict and Cooperation. Professor Allen Greb was in charge of the coursework. Herb York, part of the Manhattan Project that designed the atomic bomb back in the 1940s, was the Director of IGCC. His focus had shifted to helping in the control and non-proliferation of nuclear weapons. I took the class with my college boyfriend. We were among about twenty-five students involved in the role-playing structured class. Half the students were on the U.S. negotiating team, the other half on the "Soviet" team. It was intense, and at the end of the course we faced people from the real world of arms control negotiations in Washington, D.C., who quizzed us on the "agreement" we had made with "the Soviets." Professor Greb had great energy and respect for his students. I stayed in this program through my senior year.

I loved acting as a "policy maker," but I wanted to be a reporter. At the end of my junior year, 1984, I applied for internship positions on Capitol Hill in Washington, D.C., but they fell through. When the UCSD internship office said the U.S. Office of Personnel Management wanted someone to help with their training program and they had a video production facility, I pursued and was given the internship. My friend, Kathleen Rexrode, and I were roommates at Georgetown University that summer. While we enjoyed being interns in the big city, I moved in like a political appointee on a mission and produced three videos for OPM's internal use. They were designed to help the political appointees, elected officials, and civil servants understand each other's roles and responsibilities. This was not the most compelling topic, but as part of that, I interviewed then Congressman Dick Cheney, the Representative from Wyoming. I still have that VHS tape. In my graduate school folder, I found a letter of recommendation from a senior faculty member, the woman to whom I reported. She wrote in part, "(Jane) was given assignments and responsibilities never given to an intern.... She is assertive and a self-starter with all the self-assurance necessary to be successful in graduate school or any profession she chooses."

I share this only to make the point, to anyone with a goal, that opportunities don't always come knocking with a sign that says "Pick me." Sometimes, you have to go with what you get behind "door number one or door number two," and dive in. You have to be resourceful to make things happen, gain experience or build a track record and a résumé.

My senior year seemed to roll everything into one. I anchored and produced a weekly newscast at UCSD's radio station. My friend, Kathleen, an Economics major, was my go-to economics reporter, just for fun. I'm not sure more than a

handful of people heard us, but it provided me with some "live" experience and recordings I would need later that year.

I also enrolled in the Political Science Honors program. Enthralled with the topic of national security and arms control, I continued to work under Allen Greb at the IGCC. My thesis explored the US-NATO decision-making process on the neutron bomb during President Carter's administration. I lived that topic for six months, practically camping out at various school libraries to write an eighty-page thesis. Personal computers were a new concept, and I wanted one I had seen another student carrying around, even though it was the size of a small suitcase. Not ready for the new high-tech world yet, my parents instead paid five hundred dollars to a woman with a word processor to type my paper. Her computer crashed two days before my thesis was due and lost everything. I had to beg for an extension, and they granted me, and others, an extra day. The woman had to re-type it all from my rough drafts. It was not perfect, but good enough to warrant department honors. I learned that I preferred having control of my own work. My parents eventually bought me a Tandy® word processor from Radio Shack®, and I have typed my own work ever since.

At the same time, I wanted some real TV experience. While I could have taken my chances with the internship office, a little bit of fate stepped in. My mother was at home one day when the doorbell rang. She opened it to find two women, one of whom she had met through another friend. They stopped by to say hello before taking a walk on the beach. My mother thought the woman she didn't know should have some beach attire, so she let her borrow my sister's tennis shoes and her own shorts and a T-shirt. That woman was Jean Morgigno. These two chatted about many things, including their children. "My daughter wants to be a TV reporter," my mother said. "My son is Dennis Morgigno, the anchor at KCST," Jean replied. Networking comes in all forms. I, with no fear at this point, called Dennis, who told me it was all right to drop his name when talking with the News Director, Tom Mitchell (no relation), who was in charge of picking the interns. Tom and I met and he selected me for an internship. I don't know if I would have landed that position without Dennis and our mothers, but I am glad that things fell into place.

I began my internship in January 1985. Willing to do the usual intern duties, including fetching coffee, I was more determined to do something constructive as well, such as make hourly beat calls to the police stations, do research for stories, and log tapes. I would do anything and everything to learn. When I asked to extend my internship a second quarter, two producers asked me to help with their special projects: Sue Strom, for the consumer reports; and Jan Hudson, for a series about San Diego during the World War II era, hosted by the popular weatherman, Bob Dale.

I soaked it all in from them, the staff, and from what I called my "makeup room talks" with co-anchor Laura Buxton. She never seemed full of herself or threatened by the up-and-comers. She encouraged me to persevere. Reporter Jack Gates explained local news reporting to me this way: "Tell them what you're going to tell them. Tell them. Then tell them what you told them." He didn't mean that literally, but it was a formula to get me to think about how to take a big subject and put it into a format quickly, in time to make the evening news. Jack and I have worked together since then—at KNSD and at Channel 4 San Diego—and we still laugh about those words of wisdom he shared back then.

I didn't interact with Dennis much during those six months, partly because of my schedule—sometimes days, sometimes nights. I also sensed an unwritten rule about separating any sort of "connection," so it wouldn't seem as though I was getting special treatment because he, the main anchor, recommended me. I did ask him to read my scripts, even practice scripts. To this day, I know that when speaking about numbers, there are "more than" one hundred people in the room, not "over" one hundred people. "More than" is for quantities; "over and under" refers to items actually over or under something. I don't think I have made that particular mistake, again—at least not in print.

As an intern, I did not chalk up any on-camera experience, by either practicing stand-ups in the field while tagging along with a reporter or in studio when no one was around. I might not have wanted to delay their work day, or perhaps I was still a little scared that I might not be very good at it. Regardless, by that spring, I realized I was not ready for the real world. I didn't have a résumé tape to send out for job applications, so I opted for the next logical step: graduate school.

While in Washington, D.C. during the summer of '84, I had heard that Northwestern University's Medill School of Journalism was among the best in the country. The most appealing part was the final quarter of the one-year master's program. Students went to Washington, D.C. to be correspondents for small stations around the country that subscribed to the Medill News Service. A win-win-win for the school, students, and stations.

With my father's help with the forms, I applied to Northwestern in Chicago, my first choice. Along with a number of questions on a typical application, it required, "In 75 words or less, tell what type of career you hope to pursue." I did it in forty-three words.

In 75 words or less, tell what type of career you hope to pursue:

I plan to pursue a career in broadcast journalism, and hope to report on national and international issues e.g. national and international security, nuclear arms talks, and U.S.-European relations. Eventually, I would like to produce/commentate news-features and non-fiction documentaries.

At the time, I thought the content of those documentaries would be some-thing of the "save the world" kind—uncovering wrongs in society, revealing pow-erful stories that would make a difference to a third world country or America's inner cities—all topics of the idealistic, political, social, and cultural variety.

In addition to Northwestern, I applied to Columbia University in New York, UC Berkeley, and Stanford University for journalism masters programs. I covered my bases and applied to UCLA and Georgetown University for their International Relations programs, thinking I could become an expert, and then apply that to being a re-porter. By the time I was in the middle of my senior honors thesis and my newsroom internship, I received the letters from the schools. Columbia's reply: No (I'm sure my GPA of 3.5 and very average GRE scores were not up to their standards). Stanford: Yes, but it was a one-year program with only one documentary at the end of the year, which did not seem to be enough hands-on experience for me. UC Berkeley, UCLA, and Georgetown all said no. Northwest-ern said yes. I presume they liked all the things I had done to that point. I'm sure my parents' willingness to write a twenty-six thousand dollar check for tuition helped, too. I was just glad to be going to one of the best programs. It delivered on all fronts, combining academics, ethics, history, and practical experience in print and television, and being located in both Chicago and Washington, D.C..

My Last Undergraduate Frontier

With the pomp and circumstance of graduating done and in the photo album, I had one more direct experience with UCSD. I had been selected as one of about fifteen students from the UC system to be part of another arms control simula-tion program. It was three weeks in Bonn, Germany with another fifteen students from Europe, and foreign affairs experts from both Europe and the United States. This time, I would be a Russian. For three weeks, the thirty students and faculty stayed at a small Bonn hotel. We met within our negotiating teams, faced off with each other, and were challenged by our superiors. It again challenged me to see a different perspective politically and socially. Vodka is the beverage of choice for Russians, but we were in beer country, which made for some interesting celebra-tions. Partying had never been high on my priority list, but after those intense weeks and a mock arms-control agreement, we did commemorate the moment. The next day, a miserable hangover reminded me that mixing beverages and any excess was not a good idea—period.

After three wonderful weeks of traveling through France, Portugal, and Spain with my sister, mother, and my mother's childhood friend Audrey, I was ready for my next academic adventure.

First, though, I had to deal with my first heartbreak. I had a great boyfriend in college, but after four years and his being away for law school my senior year, he broke up with me. It was partly because I planned to go to Chicago, wanted a nomadic career, and would not be around. I was crushed and cried for two days. I debated if I should change my mind and go to Stanford to be closer to him and maybe win him back. I was sad and confused. I will never forget what my mother said. As I looked at her through my blurry eyes, she asked, "What does your heart tell you to do? Go to Stanford, and maybe things will work out? Or go to Chicago?" I sat there quietly, calming down from the sobbing, and asked my heart that question. It answered me. In a matter of moments, I knew I needed to go to Chicago, and I did.

The Grad School Reality Check

In my interviews now, knowing we don't have endless time or tape, I often ask the interviewee to sum up the significant aspects of their life. The highlights, the lowlights, and the defining moments. Turning the tables on myself and summing up my graduate school tenure, I would say it was intense. It was exciting being in Chicago and stimulating to be in a class of sixty people from all different backgrounds and educational levels who all wanted to be journalists. In the first quarter, we were required to take an Introduction to Graduate Studies Program designed for students who did not have a journalism undergraduate degree or significant journalism experience. It essentially leveled the playing field, ensuring we all had the basics.

Second quarter, the focus shifted to print reporting in downtown Chicago. I moved to an apartment at Chestnut and State with two roommates and not much more than our clothes, a couple of futons, and paper plates. It wasn't fancy, but it was in the heart of the city and near our downtown classrooms. We were in a prime location in the dead of winter to celebrate when "Da Bears" won the Super Bowl. At the time I was just happy to be part of the elated city. Now, I think about that Super Bowl Sunday and the all-night revelry with a different appreciation.

For the winter quarter, I chose to cover the courts. We were acting as if we were newspaper reporters, working under daily deadlines most days and developing long-form pieces as well. I thought I was a pretty good writer, a good detail person, and good at following directions. Yet, a class with Jack Doppelt presented another reality check.

Professor Doppelt's résumé included reporting at WBBM-Newsradio in Chicago. He was a no-nonsense newsman and a stickler for accuracy and proofreading. I have the red ink to prove it. As for my writing, in general, here are some of his comments from my graded assignments:

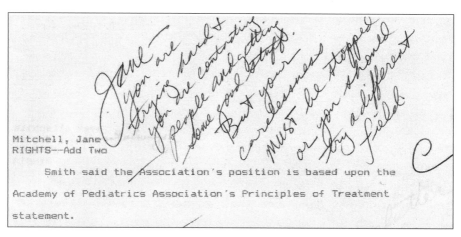

```
Mitchell, Jane
RIGHTS--Add Two
    Smith said the Association's position is based upon the
Academy of Pediatrics Association's Principles of Treatment
statement.
```

"Too much clutter in the lede. Maybe you should pretend like you're on TV."

"Jane—you are trying hard & you are contacting people and getting some good stuff. But your carelessness MUST be stopped or you should try a different field. C"

"Excellent way to get into the story… The best thing of yours I've seen yet. A"

"This lede needs more punch—it's somewhat torturous."

Ouch. *Torturous?*

I did struggle with proofreading, careless spelling errors, and AP (Associated Press) style. In print, especially, there is no acceptable margin of error, as I would sorely learn. More comments:

"A. However, you repeated a misspelling of a lot (2 words). That makes grade a B."

"Jane, your story is told fairly well and should be a B, but the assorted errors in fact take it to an F."

"Jane, very good job. A."

The other teacher who graded papers was an attorney. He used black ink, and his writing was not as large. Some of his comments included:

"Awkwardly written in parts. Some more forceful interviewing might have yielded more too. You chanced a good story, but you didn't execute it as well as you're capable of."

"Quite a competent job, especially making the regulations both understandable and interesting. Your best effort yet. A."

They meant business. I was crushed to think I wasn't seeing some of my mistakes. Professor Doppelt gave me some excellent advice: "Read everything backwards and out of context, so you're not 'hearing' it, but rather reading it." A few more times, with different words and phrases, a few more splashes of red ink, and I finally got it. I didn't want my hastiness to deter me from being considered a serious journalist. I learned to give myself more time to proofread and correct the mistakes, as well as limiting them along the way.

I don't like red ink, and their attention to detail made a big impact on my development and growth. Had they let my errors slide, I would not have benefited. I raised my own expectations, along with what I expect from others writing scripts, letters, or emails. Sometimes it doesn't matter as much, but most of the time, especially in professional circles, it is a clue to me that someone might not care, is being lazy, or is careless. I don't think I was lazy or didn't care, but I was careless. My professors' comments were not like those of that teacher back at journalism camp, but I still have them as a reminder that details make the difference and that I had to work hard at my writing to make it through class.

By spring quarter, the class of sixty was broken into areas of our specialty, and about fourteen of us were in the broadcast group. Rick Brown was our professor. Rick, understated and low-key, was taking a break from producing network news to teach at Medill. His calm demeanor—not what I expected from someone from the chaotic world of broadcasting—certainly helped us as students. We prided ourselves when we could get him to laugh. He was so serious and thankfully, had high expectations, wanting us to learn the right things the right way. He didn't want us to develop bad habits, so he encouraged us to fix our mistakes right away.

We rotated the roles of photographer, soundman, and reporter. On the days I was the reporter, I had about two and a half hours to shoot a story, then two and a half hours in the classroom to log the tapes, write, and edit the story. The segments started out being short: thirty seconds, one minute, and then longer, to what would be typically required on a daily basis in a real newsroom. The

first story I did with sound was about how chick and rabbit sales often went up around Easter time, and how people needed to be aware of the care needed for such holiday-related pets. Rabbits are quiet, so I had only the chick peeping sound in that story. We also learned about photography and framing: for example, being aware of what was behind our heads when we were shooting an on-camera stand-up. One time, a beautiful double-lantern light post on Chicago's Navy Pier seemed far away, but when I later saw the shot in the monitor, I looked like a Martian with the light post—or antenna—coming out of my head. Whether simple or gradually more complex, each was a step in the fun and adventurous learning process, which became easier with practice.

At our designated deadline, Rick Brown opened the door of the editing room and said, "Time's up." I was not allowed to do one more thing to the package. The story would have to "be ready to air," as if we were in the real world. He would sit and watch the piece all the way through once. I hoped he would laugh at the right spots, sigh at the right spots, and seem interested at the right spots, too. Sometimes he did. Sometimes, there was no reaction. My stomach was always in knots. Then he would rewind the tape, play it again, and every time he saw something that was really good, he stopped and commented on what made it good. Every time there was something bad, or needed improvement, he stopped to tell me why. Then he gave me the opportunity to fix the parts per his suggestions. I always did. It didn't necessarily mean I would get a better grade, but I wanted to break any bad habit, do it right, and show him how much I respected his time and input. I got my (parents') money's worth with him.

I have since told Rick how important he was to me and to our class. Several of us, I'm certain, became much better reporters and people because of his attention to detail and because he cared so much about each of us, our potential, and our unique qualities. He made such an impact on how I learned that I have often shared his approach with interns, young reporters, or associate producers who have come under my direction. I don't know if I have done it as well as he did, but I have at least tried to pass it on.

At the end of the quarter, we had a final project. My group was Jay DeDapper, Robin Cantor, Jeff LeShay, and Roger Kissin. Recently, I watched our mock newscast on VHS tape. We sat at a desk in the classroom with one camera, holding scripts (no teleprompters back then). Robin and I anchored, Jay was the director, and all of us produced stories. Mine was about drug testing for jockeys.

Our broadcast group's final quarter was spent in Washington, D.C., where we would each be a correspondent for a particular station that had signed up with the school. I was assigned to 23-Action News in Rockford, Illinois, about ninety miles from Chicago. Before I moved to our nation's capital, I wanted to see the station, so I rented a car and drove west. The fairly flat landscape had a few hills. Just as I was approaching Rockford, looking down into a valley, the 1986 hit by Whitney Houston, "Greatest Love of All," came on the radio.

The lyrics hit me, my eyes welled up, and I started crying as I was driving. Even with my successes, I thought about the challenges I had faced and overcome: my scary back surgery, struggling at times in college, getting a very average score on my GRE and wondering if I would make it into a graduate school; getting lots of red ink on my papers, including an F. I realized I had come through it all with a lot of help and hard work, and I was one step closer to living my dream. So the lyrics struck a chord. A few tissues later, I visited the station. No one there seemed very interested in me or what I was about to do, so I just moved on to Washington, D.C.

Capitalizing on Being in the Nation's Capital

Medill's Washington, D.C. bureau was as exciting and productive as the brochure and its reputation promised. We worked under Lou Prato, a salty broadcast journalist who told it like it was, good and bad. As tough as he was, I appreciated how he critiqued and guided with passion because he wanted us all to succeed. Twenty-four years later, I reminded him how he had made a lasting impact on me, for one.

It was invigorating to know a story I produced and reported would end up in someone's living room in Rockford, Illinois. From covering topics the city's congressional delegates were working on, to how a proposed law might impact the community, the Washington beat was usually serious with an occasional feature. Sports were not on my radar, and I didn't have an interest in them, but I did a story on a Washington Redskins football player, Joe Jacoby, for a Lexington, Kentucky station. He was a big man. I was a flat-footed 5'6", and I craned my neck, holding the microphone to interview him. It was a feature about the things he had done both on and off the field. I remember feeling good about going beyond the gridiron and talking with him about his charity and community work. I had no idea it would be a precursor to my career path ten years down the road.

My mother's mother Mary Ruth Nelson

Knowing Pam since first grade, I consider the Johnsons and Grandma Harmon my second family.

My High School group: Maria, Kerry, Anne, Christina, Julia and Pam

Practicing being a reporter in Chicago during graduate school, 1986.

CHAPTER 2

From Dreaming the Dream to Living It

Thanks for "Paying"; Now Good Luck Getting a Job

To get a job in television as a reporter, usually, you must have a résumé tape—video, digital, or, nowadays, on a website. Whatever the format, it's a sampling of stories showcasing your writing, style, and on-air presence. Between stories in Chicago and Washington, I was confident in my tape, but it came at a steep price. My parents gladly paid the tuition to Northwestern as an investment in my dream and future. However, as much as I valued my education and its reputation, Northwestern's program, at the time, offered little or no networking once we finished our one-year Master of Science in Journalism degree. Thankfully, we had great advice, and a few connections through Rick Brown and Lou Prato. Most people said it could take six months to get a job. I didn't have to work to pay rent yet, but I did have to work full-time to get a job. So I implemented Rick's number one strategy: road trip.

My mother paid for a new interview suit I bought at the Ann Taylor® store on Oak Street in downtown Chicago. Neither she nor I spent a lot of money on clothes back then, so this two hundred dollar purchase was a special occasion. The suit was classic glen plaid wool. Realizing the weather was ninety degrees in the South in the fall, I bought a less expensive thirty-dollar black and white houndstooth short-sleeved dress as a back-up at a department store. Because of the heat, I wore that dress to almost every interview on that trip. I rented a Chrysler® K car, packed the trunk with thirty résumé tapes, a box of printed résumés, a list of TV stations and their news directors' names, and a road atlas. There was no GPS and there were no cell phones in 1986. I just started driving, marking off my route, the cities, and the TV stations I had targeted. I drove three thousand miles in three weeks through the Virginias, Carolinas, and Tennessee. I cruised the back roads and highways, calling my parents from pay phones and small hotels. I interviewed with some twenty-eight news directors, getting in to see almost all whom I called. I usually said something like, "I just finished at Northwestern and I'm going to be in your neighborhood. Could I stop by, meet with you, and convince you why you need to hire me?" I didn't use those words exactly, but they knew the routine. I think my willingness to actually do a road trip showed my determination and made it hard to say no to me.

Of all those stops, I was close to landing a job twice. First, I was offered a position in a small market station in Wilmington, North Carolina. It was a two-year contract, which seemed like an eternity back then. On the up side, the station had the military connection with the Marine's Camp Lejeune nearby, so I would be able to utilize my military family and college coursework background. The offer had a restriction though: I could not move into a bigger market in the region for two years. The possibility of networking to move up was out. The reporter position paid about ten thousand dollars a year, and I would have had to work for a manager with whom I did not feel comfortable. He talked to me as if he were a lot smarter than me (which he might have been) and with inappropriate flirtatiousness. That didn't seem right based on what I had learned from my father. Even though my dad was fairly conservative, he was also progressive, open-minded, not a sexist, and certainly had demonstrated how women should be viewed and treated with respect in the workplace. To make my final decision, I sat down at a German café in Wilmington, and on a white paper placemat listed the pros and cons of accepting the job. The cons, and my intuition, said to pass it up.

After making a stop in Roanoke, Virginia, I was in the running for a reporter position with a salary of eighty-five hundred dollars a year—below poverty level. I could have done it, but by the time I was given a solid offer, another job would come through.

I spent the next month working the phones and mailing letters and tapes to another eighty-plus stations, pitching myself, my degree, and my enthusiasm as part of why I would be a good fit. I explained how I was ready to embark on my career, and that all I needed was a chance. I took my spiel to small markets in California for a few days, piggybacking a job search with my parents' fortieth anniversary celebration: a family picnic at one of their favorite spots, Presidio Park, overlooking San Diego Bay. On my way back to Washington, I stopped in Texas to see someone I was dating at the time. I used Dallas as my hub to interview for a few days in the great state of Texas. I drove north a few hours on a Monday morning to the Sherman-Dennison area for an interview at the small station there.

After the meeting, I walked outside to rain—blinding rain—with storm clouds so dense and dark it felt like the middle of the night in the middle of the day. I had Wichita Falls on my itinerary and had called the week before to say I was coming. It was about two hours west. *Would it be safe in the rain? Would it be worth it?* I called two stations. When I reached the news director, Peggy Quinn, at KAUZ-TV, the CBS affiliate, I explained my situation. She said it would be well worth the drive because she just had a reporter quit that previous Friday. To find a station with an actual position to fill was rare.

Terrified because of the severe weather, I talked to myself driving through that scary downpour and arrived at the station by mid-afternoon. In a world of hurry up and wait, I waited and waited to be able to meet with Peggy Quinn. She had immediate newsroom crisis type things to deal with, so I waited some more. Out of professional courtesy, I called the news director at the NBC station to let him know I would be either very late or would have to pass on meeting with him this time. I didn't tell him this, but I had to take my shot at making an impression where there was a job opening.

Finally, nearly two hours later, at 6:05 p.m., once the news was on the air, Peggy called me into her office. I gave her a second tape, because the one I had sent a few weeks prior was buried in the pile of other reporter wannabes. She popped it in, liked it, and asked an anchor what he thought. They commented to each other as I was standing there, "She has IT: the polish, the look, and great credentials." They then told me it seemed as if I had been reporting for six months (WOW! What I'd been waiting for) and they would let me know about the position.

That night I drove back to Dallas, and the next few days I tried my luck in Austin, with only one meeting, then returned to my little studio apartment in Washington, D.C. With my bags barely unpacked, Rick Brown from Chicago called to say, "Get a thank you letter to that Wichita Falls news director right away." She had called him and said she liked me.

Before the letter was in the mail, on Friday night, November 14, the phone rang. "Jane? This is Peggy Quinn. We'd like to offer you the job. Oh, can you hold?"

Hold? Are you kidding me? I was jumping up and down while I was on hold. About five or ten minutes later, which seemed like forever, she apologized for keeping me waiting while she handled a crisis. Then she made me an offer: "We'll start you at fifteen then after six months, go up to fifteen-five. Is that okay?" Okay? Fifteen thousand dollars? That was almost twice what I would have made in Roanoke. "When can you get here? Two weeks? By December 1?" I was on my way.

While I was doing mass mailings and interviewing, others in my class were, too. Most significant to me was Jay DeDapper, who would become one of my best friends. We had first met in the elevator of the Evanston graduate housing the week our program began at Northwestern. He was wearing a long sleeve white sweatshirt with a black and red anti-apartheid graphic. I agreed with that sentiment, but I was more conservative and had never had a political statement as part of my wardrobe. Despite our differences, I was open-minded and had seen a lot of the world, and he seemed to appreciate that. I also think we connected because we had a shared vision of what we wanted out of the program. I liked to challenge him, and I could listen to him speak on almost any subject. He reminded me a little of my father, who was articulate and had an easy way with words.

Jay had all the makings of a savvy, pithy, smart reporter, as well as having the look and confidence needed in this business. We were each other's cheerleaders both during the program and in our no-holds-barred, pull-out-the-stops, leave-no-small-market-unturned job search effort. In just two months, just a few weeks before I received that call from Peggy Quinn, he landed a weathercaster position in Davenport, Iowa. He quickly proved to be a serious news and political reporter; his forte—we could tell, even in school. He moved up to Phoenix, then New York City as a top-notch political reporter. I criss-crossed the country in the other direction. Anyone who has been in this business, or in the minor leagues of any sport or profession, knows the feeling of finally getting a shot to prove themselves. Wichita Falls was my shot, and it only took two and a half months to get there.

Foreign Correspondent? Welcome to Texas!

I had already sent some of my belongings ahead in boxes on a Greyhound bus. My college friend, Kathleen Rexrode, had been working in Washington, and I had been living in a small studio apartment just down the street from her at Dupont Circle since moving there from Chicago. Two weeks after I accepted the job in Texas, with my bags packed, we cooked Thanksgiving dinner at her place. It was my last meal in Washington before my next frontier. At five the next morning, I hopped in a taxi with my suitcases, watched the sunrise through the back window, and was Texas-bound. I caught the connecting flight from Dallas to Wichita Falls. The plane must have been a crop duster at one point. Yikes. What was I getting myself into? In a vibrating plane that felt like it was going to shake, rattle, and not get us there, we flew low along the flat, brown winter landscape that was soon to be "home." *Really,* I asked myself again. *What am I getting myself into?*

I had the weekend to find a place to live. The rent of my little apartment was $265 a month. I would gradually decorate it with second-hand furniture and a few key buys at Target®, including a folding table and chairs for my dining room. Shipping a lot of my things by bus from Washington seemed like an economical idea, but I lost one suitcase, and, sadly, it was the one carrying the kilts my parents had bought me on our 1981 trip to Scotland.

With a place to lay my head, I started that Monday, December 1, 1986. I had wanted to be a correspondent in a foreign country, but as I have joked whenever recanting my experience there, I felt like I was in one, once I was in Texas. That is not a slam. I like Texas. It's just unique—polite, down home, with its own view of the world. While I enjoyed the change and the twang, this California girl felt like a foreigner for a while.

I also felt very far away from home. Every December my father would write our family's holiday greetings letter to friends. It covered the whole page top to bottom, front and back, in his very legible cursive writing, and he even drew a little holly in the corner. He summarized the year overall, and for the part about what I was doing, he explained I had graduated and embarked on my job search:

> "It was hard for new grads to crack the barrier and get a job, but she did, in Texas. So now we have a television reporter at KAUZ-TV in Wichita Falls, TX, and she is happy, and we are proud."

It was hard to be away from my family at Christmas for the first time, but living the dream was a great gift. A week later, my parents drove my new Honda® Accord out from San Diego and I paid for it—$221.23 a month—even on my small salary. We used their military privileges and went to Sheppard Air Force Base's exchange to stock my bachelorette apartment with food and a fifteen-inch television. By the way, the guy I had been dating in Dallas married someone else. Sometimes, it's not about being in the same time zone, but in the same place in life.

From Dead Cows to Tornadoes: Early Adventures in Local TV News

Foreign correspondent, transplant, whatever I was, I had the time of my life covering "Rattlesnake Roundups" and "Dead Cow Disasters" for farmers. I learned that if cows eat too much winter wheat, they get gas that won't escape, so farmers have to "poke" them or give them baking soda so they don't die. I sold that story to CNN. At the time, the fairly new 24-hour news channel was looking for content from around the country, and I was thrilled to have some stories with national appeal during my time in Texas. The exposure was a welcomed validation early in my career, and the little extra money—$125 a story split with the photographer—sure did help.

The small photography staff helped me as a rookie reporter: Blaise Labbe, with his Cajun style, kept me calm in new news situations; and just back from a war zone in the Middle East, Jim Allen taught me how to manage the terrain of breaking news. Then there was Harold Ferguson. Harold was a former Navy enlisted man in his mid-forties who had spent time in San Diego and returned home to Texas to raise his family. He was an experienced photographer with a wonderful eye and had so much enthusiasm that I fed off his zest for telling a good story. He also encouraged me to try a few things when I wasn't quite sure. For example, when we did an economic story about the growth of the pork production business, I had written a stand-up that was a math equation about the price of pork.

Instead of just pointing to a pig, he urged me to get in the middle of a pigpen, squat in the mud, and say my stand-up. I did, and it was challenging because the stand up had several words that started with a "P." If that tongue twister wasn't hard enough to memorize, the first time I said, "So when this two-hundred pound pig goes to market," I touched the hog and it squealed so loudly, I almost fell into the

mud. We laughed so hard, it took me about twenty takes to finally get one good take for the final story.

Harold was my creative partner in a series I developed to explore the Texas and Oklahoma region called "Texoma Travel Log." We visited places in the area to show what viewers could do for a getaway. We captured a chuckwagon ride in Amarillo, a wild animal park with ostriches, and the botanical gardens in Dallas. I was able to tap into my love for travel and get paid for it. The eighth grade epiphany was being realized.

Eventually, I also applied my Political Science background to covering small-town politics. In trying to be thorough, I ended up getting under the skin of a mayor who had the audacity to call my news director to say, "That little *@!#% (yes, he used a bad word), Jane Mitchell, is asking too many questions." To which my new news director replied, "It's her job to ask questions. It's the answers you need to worry about." I appreciated the professional support.

It was hot. It was cold. Humidity was ninety-five percent in the summer. Hail pounded down with a forty-below wind chill factor in the winter. Chicago had nothing on this, other than snow. Anyone who has worked in a small TV market will have plenty of stories to tell about the stories they covered, the people they met, and the sometimes less than basic facilities they used to get the job done. They're the situations that test us, shape us, and ultimately determine if we have the patience and determination to stay and grow in the business.

I knew I was on the right track when I learned within a few weeks of being there that no one had ever done an extensive television report on the Europeans who trained at Sheppard Air Force Base. The program called ENJJPT, or the Euro-NATO Joint Jet Pilot Training Program, was unique in that pilots from NATO coun-

tries trained with the Americans. Their motto at the time: "If we train together, we can fight together." My two years of studying US-NATO relations, my background growing up in a Navy family, and traveling all came together. Before I knew it, I was interviewing generals and pilots with foreign accents and a range of stars and credentials. It could have been overwhelming to a twenty-three-year-old rookie, but I seized that opportunity.

Part of telling the story was seeing what it was like to train in the planes. The colonel in charge considered which plane would be best for me to ride in. He told me the T-38 could break the sound barrier and required just one step for the ejection seat. The T-37, or "Tweet," wasn't supersonic, and required two steps for the ejection seat. He thought the T-37 was preferable because it wasn't so intense and it was less likely I would accidentally eject myself. Captain Brian Bishop (who, I learned recently, went on to be a general in charge of troops in Afghanistan) was the instructor pilot who sat next to me in the cockpit. He even handed over the controls part of the time as we flew up to twelve thousand feet over the flat Texas land in wide-open air space.

It was awesome, and I managed to not get sick or black out as we pulled 2.5 Gs. That's a lot of g-force for someone who was not an athlete or accustomed to any kind of intense physical activity or exertion. I boast about that part of my life résumé any time I am around pilots. Upon landing, I was treated to the real-deal first ride initiation ritual: a dunk tank that looked more like a shallow baby pool on the tarmac. It wouldn't have been so bad had it not been January in North Texas. The water was cold. The dunking was on videotape, thanks to Harold, and of course I included it in the story. There I was, surprised and shivering in a water-drenched flight suit. More than anything, the flight that day and being around the pilot training for a few weeks gave me a greater appreciation of what the pilots must do to earn their wings.

That four-part series, which I wrote and edited, aired on Armed Forces TV in Europe, on CNN, and in some major cities with a military contingent. It was the perfect combination of my background, my interests, a little bit of expertise, and my passion for storytelling. The series is still among my mother's favorites. Even though the '80s hair and makeup make me cringe just a little, it was a defining moment. I proved to myself I could do more than the quick news story.

Even so, I wanted to improve and was proactive about two things. First, I sent copies of my stories to Dennis Morgigno back in San Diego. He watched them and replied with support, "You're looking good, kiddo." He also offered detailed constructive criticism about content and performance. For example, in a February 1987 letter he wrote:

```
Prisons 1:     Opening SOT was too long, we lost focus on the
story during it.

Prisons 2:     You sounded as though you were reading the voice
over from the studio and doing it in a monotone.

Eagle:   Would have been nice if we didn't need a magnifying
glass to see the vulture!

You're making lots of progress!  Keep pushing.
```

I also applied the Rick Brown way of critique to myself. After a story aired, whether I had been rushed to get it done or had ample time, I watched the air-check (the recording from the aired newscast) and broke it down. Was I talking too fast or too slow? Did the story flow? If I noticed something, I would make note, then the next time I went in to the audio booth, I would think about what I wanted to change and whatever suggestions Dennis or others I respected had offered. That also

included my on-air look, makeup, or expressions. This is a visual business, and if others were watching me, I had better watch myself to see what they're seeing, for better or worse.

Just getting the job done every day was not always fun and not always easy, and that's where Tammy Payne enters my story. Tammy was the co-anchor at KAUZ-TV when I arrived. She was beautiful, confident, smart, and welcoming. One moment, specifically, revealed what a nurturing person she was and how she was not threatened by "the new girl." I was working the afternoon-evening shift and returned to the station at about nine o'clock for a ten o'clock newscast. I had ten minutes to write something before I had to edit it and be on set as the lead story. It was a complicated issue at a small town's city council meeting with so many facets, my head was spinning. *Where do I start?* Tammy calmly said to me, "Just boil it down, Jane. Boil it down." She asked, "What was their purpose tonight? What did they do? What's next?" I felt if I left information out, it would cheat the story and the audience. I always had a difficult time writing "short." She helped me immensely. "Just boil it down, Jane. Boil it down." We became fast friends, and even when she moved on for her career, she was only a phone call away for advice and guidance. Her spirit, faith, ethics, and support mean the world to my family and me. In a business where there can be cutthroat politics, I was fortunate to have met someone who just wanted to help me be the best reporter and person I could be.

Another coworker, Bret Johnson, offered assistance in a more matter of fact way, with his Texas twang and wry humor. One day I struggled to get my story written and edited. It made the newscast, but missed its slot in the show by a few minutes. Another new news director (I had four while at KAUZ) looked at me with such disappointment, I was crushed. It was particularly important everything flowed that day because a company bigwig was in town, and the news director wanted to make a good impression. Just my luck. I was so upset and stressed that I had failed I went to the parking lot crying. Bret sought me out and said, "Mitchell, if you can't take that, then you have to get out of this business, 'cuz it's all about being able to take the pressure. It's not the end of the world. Just get over it. It will be okay." He was right. I shook it off and I don't recall missing another deadline there. Sadly, Bret, who moved on to be a successful and well-loved reporter in Dallas, died unexpectedly of a stomach condition in 2009. That story was the first I thought of to share with our mutual friends and former KAUZ colleagues, Chris and Dana Hanks.

Dana was a great sounding board and friend too. She was a very good reporter and anchor, who downplayed the drama and intensity of the business. When I was perplexed by someone's duplicity or stressed by the uncertainty of the workplace, she reminded me, "It's okay. Whatever's going to happen, will happen, and you'll be fine. That's their problem, not yours." I don't remember what exactly, but something difficult happened early in my experience in 1987 that led my father to write this in a letter:

"So glad you are busy and doing well. Continue to play your cards right and protect yourself. It can be a double cross, survival situation if you are not well informed and too trusting. Remember my favorite 'Don't Wait. Anticipate,' followed by, 'Have plans and alternatives ...' Love, Dad."

When I imagined my career, I envisioned the positive. I didn't know how much I would develop, or need to develop, beyond just improving my journalistic skills. As a little girl, I remember a class assignment to write a Haiku, a Japanese poem, describing how we viewed ourselves. One of mine had to do with my being a rubber band, able to stretch and be flexible. The other I vividly recall was: "I am like a china plate, handle me with care, or else I will break." This is pertinent because, especially early in my career, I was not only on my own and growing up, I was seeing a variety of coworkers, too, some more competitive and less compassionate than others. My first job offered at least two eye-opening experiences that not only helped me evolve as a person, but also develop another layer of Teflon®.

First, I was confident in my reporting skills, but sometimes became very nervous when I was on the anchor set. I wanted to overcome this and be better. I was a fill-in anchor on the weekends with co-anchor, Bret Johnson, who made me relax because he was at ease and funny. But it was harder when I anchored alone. Management was trying out reporters to take over the noon newscast. While I did fairly well, sometimes it took me a while to shake the nerves and not have them affect my voice. I just forgot to breathe and ran out of air in the middle of a sentence, having to swallow to take a breath. It happens. I expected that was forgivable, but I learned someone had pointed out that flaw to the news director—not necessarily to help me or out of concern that I appeared too inexperienced, but perhaps to sabotage my chances of learning and growing. The specifics don't matter, but I realized some people, whether out of their own jealousy or insecurities, would go behind someone's back for their gain, or someone else's loss. When I discovered this, I confronted the situation, but my power of persuasion did not prevail. I didn't get that particular position and had limited anchoring opportunities there, but I took the high road, and kept looking at the big picture.

The second specific experience painting another coat of Teflon® on my otherwise sensitive self was a mild case of sexism. No one at the time was talking about what was or wasn't appropriate in the workplace. The Clarence Thomas-Anita Hill story that brought the sexual harassment dialogue to the country was still a few years away. I had already rejected a job where I sensed some sexism, but this example was different—it could be interpreted as a compliment, depending on one's perspective. At the time, I was a news reporter not a sports reporter, but the office was small, so we overlapped in space and conversations. One day, I was standing nearby when a news manager and a sports reporter were talking about their challenge in getting an interview with a coach who had either been resisting an interview or was reluctant to schedule a time with the sports reporter.

I was wearing a conservative top, a skirt that was just above the knee, pantyhose (yes, we *had* to wear them back then), and two-inch heels—normal, professional attire. In front of the sports reporter and a few others, the news manager said a sentence seared into my memory: "Well, let's send Jane. With those legs, he'll stop whatever he's doing and give her the interview." In one sentence, really two words—those legs—I went from feeling respected for my professionalism to being an object. I was stunned. I almost didn't know what to say, especially to a supervisor. In a constrained, yet deliberate and diplomatic voice, I looked right at him and said, "I certainly hope you would think that I could get the interview because I'm a good reporter, and not because of my legs." I don't know if he realized how inappropriate his comment was, and he probably thought he *was* being complimentary, but I realized there was yet another battle to fight, when all I wanted to do is my job and be judged on my integrity and performance. I think my semi-bold statement stuck. I don't recall another such comment for the duration of his or my time there. My father was right. I had to beware. I also had to have plans and alternatives.

I knew that while I was a contributing reporter to the Wichita Falls community telling stories that affected the community's politics, schools, and cultural landscape, that first job was also where I could make some mistakes and not get fired. It's generally accepted that smaller market television stations have turnover, especially if the reporter is not from the area and wants to move on. So, as much as I enjoyed it, I was on a mission to move on and move up.

I had been dating an Air Force pilot whom I had met in Wichita Falls. He moved to Arizona, so in my effort to look for a new job, I visited him and interviewed at several stations in Phoenix and Tucson. It was a Tucson news director who helped me more than he may ever know. I have tried to figure out who it was exactly, but I am sure of this: In his office, he popped in my résumé tape and watched with me. Afterward, he went back and pointed out something I had never noticed, but bothered him. He said in my live shots when I started a new thought or answered an anchor's question, I began my sentences with either "well" or "now." The words were almost my launching pad for each sentence or thought, the equivalent of a more refined "umm" or "ahh," stalling or buying time between content. In general, one might not notice, but a concentrated sampling of my work showed I had a habit to break, and I made an effort to do that. That's not to say I never say either of those words (my mother reminds me, "A well is for water"), but I have always appreciated how he took time to offer constructive criticism when he had nothing to gain.

The Richest Man in America Helps Me Land the Job

By October 1988, I had already been sending out tapes trying to get that elusive second job. If not to a network job (a little ambitious), certainly to a bigger market. I was home on my day off one September afternoon when I answered the phone to this: "Jane. This is Dave Cassidy in Tulsa." I had responded to an advertisement in *Broadcasting Magazine* seeking a reporter. Dave Cassidy read my résumé, saw

I was a fellow Northwestern University graduate, and liked my tape. He said he might have an opening and asked me not to do anything until I heard from him in the next few weeks. Of course, I kept sending out tapes, but hoped I would hear from him. On Thursday, October 13, the newscast producer asked if I could do an extra story and cover the opening of the new Walmart® in town. It was big news. The angle was the big store moving into a town that's only had mom and pop shops. What did Walmart® have to say about that? What would the store's impact be on those smaller stores and the economy? Oh, and by the way, Walmart® owner Sam Walton would be there. Just that week, *Forbes* magazine had named him the Richest Man in America for the fourth year in a row.

Okay. I would do it. Turn a quick story for the ten o'clock news. My photographer and I were at Walmart® and I, of course, wanted to interview Sam Walton. Why wouldn't I? I asked his public relations person, who kindly said, "Ah, that's probably not going to happen. Mr. Walton doesn't do interviews." *Oh. Hmmm. Really?* I thought. I needed to hear it from him, so I decided I would just ask him myself. In a sea of trademark red, white, and blue baseball caps the various employees, managers, and ownership folks were wearing, I saw Sam Walton coming down an aisle. "Mr. Walton, I'm Jane Mitchell with KAUZ-TV. I was hoping I could do a quick interview with you about your new store." He looked right at me and said he was busy, but maybe in a few minutes. All I needed was a maybe. So I waited and waited, and to my, and his PR person's surprise, Sam Walton walked over to me. We started rolling, and I started asking questions: What's it mean to be opening such a store here? How do you see this impacting the community and the job market? What's your philosophy of life and business? His answers were short, pithy, and passionate. My last question: "Mr. Walton, today *Forbes* magazine named you the Richest Man in America—what's your secret to success?" I can't find that story, with the answer, but I can hear his final comment as if it were yesterday. He said, "and now I've got to go," and turned around and walked away. Wow.

I knew how I would end the story even before I wrote the bulk of it. After I included his soundbite, "now I've got to go," I said, "Places to go. People to meet. Billions to make. Jane Mitchell, Channel 6 News."

What I didn't know was that fantastic energy and that little coup were only part of what would make this one of the best overtime days ever. When I returned to the station, I went to my desk and plopped my notebook and bag down. Just like the feather in the movie *Forrest Gump* that comes slowly floating down, down, down, a little piece of paper torn from a yellow legal pad flew up in the air then slowly floated down in front of me. It was a scribbled phone message a colleague had taken and tossed on my desk. The message: Call Dave Cassidy.

I called him that night, and he was still at his office. He told me he had an opening and wanted me to come up to Tulsa to interview. He also wanted me to bring another tape and include the story I did that night so they could see my work on "just a regular news day." The story was the interview with Sam Walton. A few weeks later, I interviewed with Dave and the executive producer, Jim Loy, and showed them the Walmart® story. They loved it. I liked them a lot and was thrilled to be hired on the spot. They asked if I would call my station right then and give my two weeks' notice, which I did. My goal was to be in my first job for two years. I was there one year and eleven months. Beating the goal, I moved to Tulsa, Oklahoma before the holidays. I too had places to go, people to meet, and maybe not billions, but a career to make.

Ding Dong! Hong Kong Calling!

Part of my job search in Texas led me to apply for a reporter position in Hong Kong. It would be reporting in English, but I could learn Cantonese and would finally be working overseas. I had just accepted and started the job in Tulsa when I found out that of the more than 110 people who applied from across the country and Canada, I made the top ten for two positions. The news director was Hong Kong-born and U.S.-educated. He encouraged me to fly to Los Angeles for the interview because I had a lot going for me—my background, my travel, my education, and my drive. I met with him in L.A. on my day off, but a few weeks later he told me I just didn't have enough TV experience. I didn't get the job, but trying out Tulsa-time was fine by me.

The Hong Kong position also seemed appealing to me because I was still dating the Air Force pilot I had met in Wichita Falls. At this point, he was either Europe- or Asia-bound for assignment. The idea we would both be in the same part of the world sounded exciting, but I didn't get the job and I wasn't prepared to quit my career for his. We remained friends, but this time, I realized being in the same time zone *was* important to me for a long-term relationship.

Tales from Tulsa: What? I'm Going to Florida?

I hadn't been at my new desk in the KOTV Channel 6 newsroom more than a few weeks when the assignment editor stood from his perch announcing there was a fire in Miami and they needed to send somebody: "Jane, you're going!" *Miami,* I thought, *Wow, I can't believe they're sending me to Florida. This must be big, and they must have a lot of confidence in me.* I started gathering my things and turned to Brett Shipp, the reporter who sat just across the aisle from me. He was from Texas and had a little bit of an accent. In a half-whisper I said, "Oh my gosh, they're sending me to Miami." "That's great, Jane," he said so supportively. "Be careful. See you when you get back." I met up with the photographer and we went to the airport—a private airport—and walked out to the runway to a small plane and a pilot. Something didn't add up. How were we going to fly from Tulsa, Oklahoma to Miami, Florida in a small prop plane? "Oh no, we're not going to Miami, Florida," they said. "We're going to Miam-ah, Oklahoma."

"Miamah, Oklahoma?" I had assumed that everyone was saying Miami with a Texas and Oklahoma accent. They were, but it's because the town of Miami,

Oklahoma is pronounced with an "ah" at the end, not an "ee." I could not believe it and was a little embarrassed. We flew to the town ninety miles away where a small strip mall had a minor fire, and I called back to say there really was no story. I could get an interview, but it was inconsequential: little damage, no injuries. I was glad they said never mind and to just come home. That underscored KOTV was a good news operation that would go the distance for a story, but not make it into something it was not just because we had literally gone the distance. On the other hand, when I saw Brett next, I sarcastically thanked him for not clarifying the state where this "Miamah" town was. We both laughed. That was a good little indoctrination into life in TV in Tulsa.

My three years there were a lot more serious than my experiences in Texas had been, starting with the subject matter. I covered crime, city hall, and the education beat. Brett Shipp and I covered a controversial education bill, broke the story of a statewide teachers strike, and then stood in the rain at the state capitol when it was over. I received my first Emmy nomination with Brett for that coverage. We lost to a Denver station's coverage of the San Francisco earthquake, which was understandable. While in my Tulsa apartment in 1989, I watched the World Series on television between the San Francisco Giants and the Oakland A's. I recall hearing broadcaster Al Michaels describe the earthquake during the Battle of the Bay and seeing my home state in dire straits.

Severe weather was part of the daily reporting equation—from being scared to death that the live-truck photographer and I would be caught in the trail of a tornado around midnight, to then seeing the dramatic devastation at dawn, and being puzzled by how debris could be strewn for two miles, but a bucket by a gas station never moved an inch. In the winter, there was the time I was standing on the street at five-thirty in the morning at forty-below, warning people to avoid going outside because of the frigid cold temperature and black ice on the roads, and wondering why we had to be outside to communicate this, never quite understanding the logic of some live television. Still, I did it, gloved hands frozen to the microphone. I did investigative stories from plane crashes and drug deals, to topics of freedom of speech and the right to congregate. Some of the people in those factual and sometimes emotionally charged stories didn't always like what I said, even calling me at work or at my unlisted home number on occasion with carefully worded threats. That serious subject matter put my journalistic fiber to the test. It was challenging, but I again grew as a person and as a reporter.

In 1990 when President George H.W. Bush drew that line in the sand and the first Gulf War was underway, the whole newsroom, like every other newsroom across the country, watched in amazement and kicked into high-speed-work-mode. We told the local stories from the people working all night to the families sending their loved ones off to the Gulf, and then later, the reaction, fear, and strength of the families from Oklahoma whose sons were prisoners of war. Often, in between the serious matters of the day, it was good to have a matter of the heart.

Do We Have to Watch *SportsCenter* Again?

A hot summer night in June of 1989 would open my eyes not only to new love, but also to sports. In Tulsa, on a Thursday night of ninety-degree heat with equally high humidity, the place to go after the newscast was a sports bar with a patio on South Peoria. Many of the young, single TV-types went, and this was one of the first times I decided to go along. At a table next to me, I kept hearing this one person cracking jokes—the sarcastic kind. The kind that come from someone very smart and witty. I asked what he did. He said he was a sports photographer and occasional reporter at another station. "You've missed your calling," I said. "You should have been a comedian."

A few weeks passed, and because I was doing the grueling, yet somewhat enviable assignment of the five o'clock local news cut-ins during the network morning show, I could no longer make those Thursday night gatherings. But one weekend, the sports anchor at my station said to me, "I know someone who wants to go out with you. Would you go out with him?" I said, "It depends who it is." He said, "John Anderson," the witty guy from the bar. I said, "Heck yeah!" A half hour later, John called and asked if we could meet at the same sports bar that night. I already had plans to see a movie, but told him my friend and I would stop by. We did, and that was it. John and I dated for two and half years.

During that time, Bob Stevens, our main sports anchor, had taken a job in Cleveland. John Walls from Channel 8 (KTUL) was hired to fill that spot at my station. Soon after, John Anderson was hired as a sports reporter and weekend anchor. We were now working together, sitting about three desks apart. I was thrilled for him, recognizing he had so much potential that he could go far in this business because he was such a good writer, storyteller, and had a good grasp of the human condition. His journalism degree from the University of Missouri served him well. Plus, he was funny.

John, from Green Bay, Wisconsin, was unconventional. He loved the Packers fourteen games out of the year, but two games a season, he "sided with the NFL team in Chicago due to an unwavering love for Walter Payton." As a Missouri alum, he was a fervent fan. He taught me that if I was going to spend time with him, I could not like the University of Kansas Jayhawks. "Why?" I asked. He adamantly relayed, "Because that is just how it is when you're a Mizzou fan." Fan loyalty 101.

When the news hit in 1989 about the Padres selling sushi at Jack Murphy Stadium, John sparred, "It just isn't right," and that hot dogs are the appropriate fare for baseball. *SportsCenter* on ESPN was still fairly new, but I wasn't interested in the daily sports details, just the big stories, such as the World Series or Super Bowl. Regardless, while I sometimes complained, "Do we have to watch *SportsCenter* again?" I did watch as part of our time together.

His passion for the Packers, the Bears, the Cubs, and Joe Paterno gave me a foundation of what it meant to be a true fan before I even knew I would care about it. I also learned he was a true journalist. When the Gulf War hit, he was turning in stories with heart, soul, and substance. As it turns out, I was right about his potential, and he moved up from Tulsa, to Phoenix, to ESPN, to anchoring *Sports-Center,* which didn't surprise me. John was a talented man and an exceptional and supportive friend when I faced a life decision I could have never imagined.

The Scary Summer of '91

I was packing the last of my things into my suitcase in my Tulsa apartment one June evening when the phone rang. It was my sister, Robyn. I was flying home the next day for a week's vacation to see my family in Coronado. The last time I had been home was for the holidays six months earlier, and Robyn said she was looking forward to seeing me. But I could hear something in her voice as she told me, "I just want you to be prepared. Dad has lost a lot of weight since you've seen him, and he just looks a little different. We're not sure why, but I just want you to be prepared."

What could I do with that except get on a plane, get home, and see for myself. At the airport, Dad greeted me with his big smile, hug, and kiss as he embraced me saying, "Janie Doll!" He always got a little choked up when it had been a long time since we'd seen each other. He was so sweet and loving. He was also, most definitely, thinner—forty pounds thinner. Something just wasn't right.

He could still ride his bike and was driving, but his mobility was more limited. His strength was not the same. He was too skinny. I left that week concerned. I knew I would be back in a few weeks for my friend Pam's wedding. Maybe he would be better by then. He was not. When I saw him in July, he would sit in the chair, worn out, falling asleep in the middle of the day, almost as if he were having a stroke. He wasn't sleeping at night. He didn't have the same kind of energy he usually had, but why?

Robyn was watching closely and noticed that if he started to fall asleep at night he couldn't consciously breathe deeply, so when he breathed shallowly, he wouldn't get enough oxygen, and therefore, he never got to REM, or restorative, deep sleep. He would wake up to get more oxygen, and the cycle continued. Robyn figured this out by borrowing the pulse oximeter from the emergency room where she worked for two years. She put it on him while he slept and watched his oxygen level drop from the normal 98% to the low 70s. No wonder he would wake up: he was suffocating. We needed answers as to the culprit.

Four Things Before I Die

While I was back in Tulsa, my parents and sister were going to local doctors to evaluate Dad's situation. Thank goodness we had a doctor in the family who could help direct the questions and relay the information in a calm, compassionate way. Robyn's medical credentials, determination, and bedside manner helped us all. Even now in writing this, I rely on her and my mother for the details about my father's timeline while I was away.

My sister and her husband, Steve, were going on a bike riding trip for ten days for their anniversary over Labor Day weekend and wanted to leave their son, Ryan, just one year old at the time, with my parents. Knowing my father wasn't up to par, I offered to come home and help. The night before I was getting on the plane from Tulsa back to San Diego, my father called me. I thought it was just one of those calls to make sure everything was set for my travel plans. Never would I have imagined hearing what he was about to say. "There are four things I want to do before I die." *Die? Who's talking about dying?* "I want to look at all the slides from our travels," he told me. "I want to transfer all the film to video. I want to put those colored thumbtacks on a big map showing all the places we've traveled, and I want to tell my life story." *What was he talking about? What could be happening?*

When I was home that Labor Day weekend—seeing him weakening and knowing there was so much uncertainty—I knew I had to be home for more than a few days. It was a feeling, a voice, a calling almost, I couldn't ignore. It was so hard to get on that plane to go back to Tulsa, but I did. When I returned to work, all I could do is think about being back in Coronado, helping to figure out what was going on with my father, helping my mother, and doing those four things Dad wanted to do. It was hard to focus.

God, Please Give Me a Break

It didn't help that I was dealing with some other challenges at the same time, namely, a new person in management who was not my biggest fan. I don't have any bad feelings now or harbor any grudges, but this was a time of tribulation. It is a tough business. You cannot expect everyone to like you all the time. I was a good reporter, but that new person inherited me, along with most of the staff. As productive and solid as I was at my job (subjectively speaking), I seemed to be held to some kind of higher standard, as if the new person wanted to see me fail or quit, because I didn't "fit" the look or style that manager preferred in TV news reporters. Management by intimidation did not sit well with me and did not feel good. For example, when I was filling in for the morning cut-ins, thirty seconds before I went on the air for an update, the manager came storming into the studio and said, "See me as soon as you get off the air," naturally making me stressed, so I didn't perform as well as I should or could have. Another time, on a slow news day, the manager hovered over my cubicle saying, "So, Mitchell, how are you going to earn your paycheck today?" If that were said in jest, I could have laughed it off, but it was not.

In conversations about my career development, the manager told me, "You probably will never make it in a market bigger than Tulsa. You just don't have it." When I said I had people in the business telling me otherwise, saying I had good qualities and potential, the manager's nearly exact words were, "Your friends are just telling you what you want to hear." I said thank you for the opinion and asked what I could do to get to the next level. With no answer, the conversation was topped off with this, "Prove me wrong, Jane. Prove me wrong."

September of '91, at twenty-eight years old, I was feeling tremendous pressure to succeed, to change that manager's mind so I would have a more pleasant work experience, or to find another job. I had already sent out dozens of tapes and inquiries to stations in the west, and had spent some vacation time and long weekends interviewing in Phoenix and Tucson and trying to build my connections in San Diego. Plus, by then, I knew something was wrong with my father. I had heard that saying, "God doesn't give you any more than you can handle," but this was ridiculous. I worked hard. I was honest. I tried to be a good person and go to church when I could. I used to say, "I have plenty of character, God, thank you. What more do you want from me?" It felt as if everything was just collapsing on me, but all I could think about was my dad.

After I returned from that Labor Day weekend, I was on a shoot and shared my frustration with news photographer and friend, Cathy Curtin. How could I be in Oklahoma, I asked, when my family needed me? She said, in the most supportive, compassionate voice, "Then go, Jane. Go. The company has to let you go. This is an emergency. Find out what your options are." The human resources department gave me the option of an emergency leave of absence. I could take up to six weeks and would still have my job if, and when, I returned.

Dad tried all forms of film and video to capture the Mitchell moments.

Mom and Dad hiking in New Zealand on the last big trip I took with them in 1983.

My parents with Robyn, her husband Steve, and baby Ryan.

Dad with his friend Andy Adams, on one of their last hunting trips before Dad got sick.

CHAPTER 3

I Can Get Another Job, I Can't Get Another Father

The Diagnosis: Part One

My sister Robyn had been doing a lot on the medical front, so she was able to interpret the doctor-speak for us and make a plan. She and my parents went to the Mayo Clinic in Scottsdale in late September of 1991, just after I returned to Tulsa, for a more complete evaluation. From what they tell me, it was a very thorough, all hands on deck approach from all angles: neurology, pulmonary, cardiology, and more. The doctors called Brazil and ruled out the chances of Dad having a tropical disease they thought he might have contracted from a trip my mother and he had taken in 1989. My father had cut his elbow on some glass and it was still swollen and odd looking a year later, but that was not the problem. They also said it was not Lyme disease, something that could have been possible because he had gone hunting the fall of 1990. That's also when my brother Mitch, hunting with him, recalls our father having a hard time sitting in the saddle and having shortness of breath, things he just chalked up at the time to a little old age.

Then the Mayo doctors ruled out heart problems. They did confirm what Robyn had suspected—the reason Dad was falling asleep in the day was because he had Sleep Apnea, causing him to wake up hundreds of times a night. It was determined he could breathe in oxygen, but could not breathe out to dispel the carbon dioxide. The diaphragm seemed weak, which would account for the breathing difficulties, and his other muscles were being hindered, too. They knew he had been in the Pacific in World War II, lived in Guam, and he had been in a recent minor car accident that certainly jarred him and caused him stress. Such conditions had been associated with neuromuscular problems.

Doctors thought it could be some kind of muscular dystrophy, or possibly a variant of ALS, Amyotrophic Lateral Sclerosis. Robyn had read about it in a small paragraph in a medical book, and my mother had heard it called Lou Gehrig's Disease. This was bad news, but it was not confirmed.

In layman's terms, what happens with ALS is the light switch that controls the brain's communication with the muscles turns off. The muscles gradually shut down, resulting in atrophy. A medical explanation is that the neurotransmitter that sends the message from nerve to nerve and finally to the muscle is made, but not able to be received. Hence, the muscles never receive the message or the stimulation, resulting in atrophy and weakness. There was nothing that could be done to stop or reverse the condition.

When they called to tell me this potential diagnosis, I was shocked and didn't believe it. I barely even remember the phone call now. I was in denial, likely because it was not certain. I mentioned it at work to learn that a colleague's friend had ALS. She said it was a disease known to affect men in their late thirties, so I thought it couldn't possibly be the same thing because my father was older. Even so, the concept didn't make sense, as so little was known about ALS. Still, that potential diagnosis solidified my plans.

My sister remembers the day she, Mom, and Dad went to a neurologist who specialized in ALS. The specialist confirmed that Dad had an ALS-like condition. He said a biopsy and labs showed the classic findings with some variations which accounted for his slowness of progression, although it didn't seem slow to my family. The expert said his breathing was much too affected to be in a current study about the disease. Robyn and my mother recall how Dad felt disappointed by this. If he was going to have an illness, he wanted to put up a fight, not give in to the disease until he just couldn't do it anymore. He also wanted his illness to be used for the good of others and for his suffering to count. He would do anything to be in a research study, but they said it was too late.

After that appointment Robyn was at my parents' home. She remembers: "Sitting on the porch, overlooking the Pacific Ocean with Pt. Loma and Fort Rosecrans on the horizon, discussing with Mom that Dad had symptoms of ALS. His eyes welled up and with a soft voice he sighed and said, 'I always wondered how I would die. I never imagined this.'"

I admire Robyn and am in awe of her strength to be there with our parents during that time and to share the news with me. She was seeing this through the eyes of a daughter and a doctor, and we relied on her so much to help us through that frightening time.

Like father, like daughter. I wanted to fight for him, too. Having the emergency leave approved, I kept my apartment in Tulsa and flew home by early October. I could ask questions. I just didn't always understand the answers, even when Robyn tried to explain them to me once I was home. I was in denial, feeling as if we could beat this thing.

Being the more emotional child of the family and equally determined to get things done, I had to grab on to what I could control—coordinating doctor appointments, helping my parents with their rental property, organizing bills and paperwork—all the things that were just more difficult for them to get a handle on in between everything else. More than anything for me, those four things my father wanted to accomplish were on my mind and on my to-do list.

I sorted the slides. I ordered a giant world map from National Geographic. I pulled out all the film canisters from actual movie film my father had taken even before he met my mother, as well as all the different formats my home-movie-happy-father had shot over the years. I labeled them, logged them, and had them transferred to VHS, equating to about forty hours of tape. Then I made a plan to videotape my father telling his life story.

It was all he could do, some days, to hold his head up by leaning on his very thin hand and arm. Breathing was becoming more difficult and deliberate. We used the living room as our studio. My father sat in a wood and rattan rocking chair. The rocker allowed him to move and adjust a little as he was going along. The big windows provided natural light. I put our home video camera on a tripod, pulled up a chair, and began asking questions. We started at the beginning: his childhood, his parents, his military service, meeting my mother, and having children. We branched out to traveling the world, his biggest accomplishments and challenges. I asked him to share his faith, what he wanted to tell his children and grandchildren, and what he wanted his legacy to be. I learned things I never knew, details I might never have asked about. I heard emotions and perspectives that may have always been there, but came out differently as we both focused and listened, and I'm sure, because he knew life was never going to be the way it had been.

We could only do the interview sessions a half hour at a time. It was too taxing and uncomfortable for him much after that. In the six weeks I was home, we managed to tape five and a half hours of his telling his life story. I recorded another hour as he shared my mother's favorite stories about their fishing and travel adventures.

I didn't know if I would ever watch those tapes. I thought maybe I would want the man I married someday to see them so he would know my father. That hasn't happened yet. I gave copies of the tapes to my mother and siblings, but to date, I haven't viewed them. Still, it's comforting to know I can, and that I was able to help my father tell his story, just as he wanted.

Homeward Bound

What those six weeks showed me was that I needed to be in California. I could not do what I needed to do for my family in Oklahoma. My options were to quit my job altogether or take a leave of absence for up to one year with no paycheck. My parents would cover my health insurance. At the end of one year of leave, I would be eligible for "some kind of a job" within the group of stations, including a station in Sacramento. There was no promise of a reporting position, but something.

Trying to make an informed decision about the impact on my career, I asked a talent agent I had heard about through colleagues. She advised me not to get off the air, "because people will wonder why you aren't reporting.... That something was wrong with you … and once you're off the air, it's almost impossible to get back on the air." With that information, I thought, *That just doesn't seem right to me,* and *it just doesn't matter.* After hanging up the phone, sitting at my dining room table, I concluded: *I can always get another job. I can't get another father.* It was the most difficult, yet easiest, decision of my life. My mind and my heart were made up. I was going home.

My sister flew to Tulsa right after Thanksgiving. We shipped things home and packed my Honda® with the last of my belongings, including my hamster, Sammy. He had been a Valentine's present from John nearly two years before. John knew how important my family was to me and supported my decision. Not knowing what would ever come of us (life is never easy), I kissed him goodbye, and with tears in my eyes and my heart in my throat, got in the car, and Robyn, Sammy, and I headed west to California for the next chapter of my life.

Overqualified. Ever Grateful.

While I wanted to be with my family as we figured out what was going on, I still wanted to work, so I applied to the different stations in San Diego for reporting, producing, or any position they had open. My parents and I needed some time away from the stress of the challenging time, so my father was a good sport and let us plan a trip to Hawaii. We stayed on Oahu for about a month in military housing on the beach. They were simple but comfortable cabins, reminiscent of those many trips we'd taken around the world. This time, I did all the driving, and we had a wheelchair for my dad. He had never really liked being at the beach or in the heat much, but it was January and fairly mild, so he knew it wouldn't be too bad. Plus, he wanted my mother and me to do something we liked. He was always willing to oblige our wants and needs, and he could find joy and happiness just being together. Robyn and her little boy Ryan came out for a week. My father was given another blessing to look forward to when Robyn announced on Valentine's Day that she was

expecting another child, and her baby was due in October, the month of my father's birthday.

Perhaps it was my "forward thinking" gene, but I changed the message on my answering machine to say I was traveling, but would check messages. Sure enough, toward the end of the trip, there was a message from Keith Esparros, the executive producer at KNSD-TV, the NBC affiliate where I had done my internship.

I met with Keith when I returned. He had a writer/field producer position open, but his concern in hiring me? "You're overqualified, Jane. I'm afraid you'll get here and be so frustrated because you're just so overqualified." I assured him I needed to be in San Diego for family reasons. I just wanted to get my foot in the door and have a job in news, and I would give one hundred percent to whatever task I was assigned. With a great big smile, he said okay. I will forever be grateful to Keith for believing in me and for hiring me. I feel good that I held up my end of the bargain. To put the financial part of this move in perspective, I went from making nearly $35,000 a year in Tulsa, Oklahoma (decent pay for the cost of living there) to about $20,000 a year in San Diego with a considerably higher cost of living.

Four months into the job at KNSD, Keith asked me to start reporting on the weekends and to field-produce and write three days a week. I wasn't expect-

ing this, but they needed me, and I was raring to go. I worked that schedule for two and a half years. I think Keith was glad I had a chance to apply my talents and skills a little more, too. I eventually received a pay increase to about $24,000. Still not much for my level of experience, but working in San Diego was an investment in my family that paid both personal and big-picture dividends.

It was so much fun being a weekend reporter, often being the lead story for the Saturday and Sunday newscasts. I covered hard news and features, and became pretty good at "making a silk purse out of a sow's ear," as my long time weekend photographer partner, Tom Tokar, called it. Slow news days can test your creativity and stretch your capabilities, especially when you have to fill a minute-thirty or two-minute time slot. That might not seem like a lot of time if you're not in television, but it takes a good half day or more sometimes to gather the elements, write it, and have visuals and an editing strategy to make it interesting for viewers. Even so, I still had a hard time keeping things short and to time. I was glad the weekend producer, Jeanne Phillips, cut me some slack when I needed more time, because she knew I would deliver on busy as well as slow news days.

I would come home after those weekend reporting days and tell my parents all about my experiences. They usually had watched the news, so they had seen my stories. They commented on the story itself, what I was wearing, my makeup, or how I sounded. Usually, they were just proud of me. One Sunday, I sat in the living room debriefing with my father as we had many times before over the years. I was wearing a cream white wool suit. My hair was in a ponytail and I was dolled-up with TV makeup. He was sitting there in that rocker, propping up his head with his thinning arms, and wearing one of his blue or yellow T-shirts and a big smile. I don't remember too many other details, just the feeling I had when he looked right at me and said how proud he was of me, how thankful he was, how much fun it was for him to watch me on TV, and how happy he was that I was not far away in Tulsa or Texas anymore. Then he said something I will never forget: "It was worth getting sick to bring you home."

I don't know if he really believed that, in terms of getting sick, but the sentiment behind it was sincere. That's a kind of love I can't begin to define or measure. I always knew how much he and my mother wanted the best for me. I hadn't realized how much he missed me while I was off "doing my thing." He never made me feel bad that I was away. He encouraged me to pursue my dreams. With tears in my eyes and a lump in my throat, I told him I loved him. To know how he felt to have me closer to home, I can only say it made me feel all the more loved.

The Diagnosis: Part Two

Getting sick was an understatement. After starting at KNSD in March of 1992, the real reason I came home would rear its ugly head. While we had been told my father had symptoms of ALS, by that spring of 1992, it was confirmed. I was in the office with the neurologist and my parents when he said to us, and I remember this almost verbatim: "Get your things in order. Take your last trips. Go home, and prepare to die. You have six months to two years to live."

I was more angry than sad in that moment. I could not believe he would be so cold, that there wouldn't be a plan to try to beat this disease. This didn't seem possible, not for my father, a healthy and vibrant man at seventy, now frail at seventy-one. He had taken care of his body his whole life. He didn't smoke or drink, and served his country for thirty years in three wars. He was fit and an outdoorsman. He had gone hunting every year, hiking in the cold, and exploring fields and mountains. He had hauled boats into lakes and rivers to fish. He had built and renovated houses for fun, pushing wheelbarrows and hammering nails—the epitome of the handy man. He was not big, but he was energetic and strong, with great stamina and endurance in any physical activity he ventured into. He was still so young to us. He still had so much to do in life.

My mother and I especially didn't want to accept, and certainly did not grasp, the reality of the diagnosis. Our attitude was that we were just going to be his cheerleaders and his caregivers. My brother Jerry concurred. We were going to try anything and everything to keep him going and comfortable. We were in denial as we tried to conquer this beast that was gradually taking Dad's strength and his ability to function. On a daily basis, we wanted him comfortable, to keep fighting, and to try to enjoy life and family. We established Sunday dinners to get everyone who was in town over to the house to eat Mom's cooking and just be together.

Robyn came down from Orange County about every two weeks for two days. Jerry, who lived a few blocks away, helped with some of my parents' business paperwork, house logistics, and handyman tasks my father could no longer do. He was very good about seeing him often, even if it was just to stop by and say hello.

My brother Scott, who lived in San Diego at the time, was in the medical field and saw so many different kinds of sick people. He had a difficult time facing the reality of the illness, but with his sense of humor, Scott provided my father with some healthy levity during his visits.

For the most part though, my mother and I were his caregivers every day. We did our best to physically manage his needs. Dad was losing weight and had little strength to even walk to the bathroom, or from the bed to a chair, so we had to adjust. We tried to accommodate him as just a matter of logistics, so he didn't feel useless or inept. It's not what you expect to do, ever, for a parent, so I tried to maintain respect and treat him with dignity, especially in the most awkward and personal of moments. He, in general, had a great sense of humor about it. We kept coming up with new contraptions to make things easier. For example, adding pads and pillows to the wheelchair to try to support his shrinking and boney body, introducing a shower stool for bathing, and installing handrails by the toilet. When he had an itch he couldn't lift his hand to scratch, I would use a tissue or cotton swab to alleviate that annoyance for him. Every day, I learned a little something more about my father's patience. Every day, I realized how much he needed us.

Gradually, he required more than just our ingenuity and care. A BiPAP machine helped his diaphragm breathe out so he wouldn't accumulate carbon dioxide. He went from using it at night to all the time, even plugging it in the battery charger of the car when we went somewhere. He could still talk, but in half-sentences, breathing in between. Eventually, his shrinking body was too heavy for my mother or me to move on and off the wheelchair or shower chair. The family decided we needed help. Dad was not critical, but he had the option of hospice care because he had a terminal illness, so we accepted that care. Between that and other health workers, he had dignified assistance for his baths and personal needs. He also received physical therapy to keep his circulation going. There was not much help or information at the time. We talked with the hospice workers, but their approach was more for someone who was critical, terminal, and ready to die any day. My father had some time, we just didn't know how much or how little. Still, the hospice workers were kind, understanding, and provided us a break, while giving Dad their full attention.

I was living in and managing my parents' small apartment building just ten blocks away. In the mornings, I would go to the house, help with what I could, then get ready for the night shift at KNSD from 2:30 - 11:30, and start all over again the next morning. On my days off or when my schedule changed, I went to the house in the evenings. Getting my dad ready for bed was part of the routine, but also a special time. I wanted him to have a good night's sleep. Part of that for him was reading the Bible.

He couldn't read anymore because it was too hard to focus, and he couldn't hold the heavy book. He asked me to read it to him. I usually did, gladly. I admit, and regret, there were times it just seemed like another thing to do that day. I was so exhausted and emotionally drained sometimes, I just did not give that time, that gift of reading to him, as selflessly as I should have. I don't know if he picked up on it, but I felt bad I wasn't as patient as I could have been. I always kissed him goodnight, though. He always said thank you and I love you. After I had gone home, I know he and my mother had some long and scary nights. It was hard on her to see her strong husband of more than forty-five years fighting a losing battle, but she was devoted, supportive, and a fighter, too.

Even when I was snippy, impatient, or very definite in my decisions or declarations at times, I don't remember my father ever raising his voice to me my whole life—never—until early December 1993. By then, I was living in an alley apartment just a few blocks away. It was the back part of the house my parents first bought in the late fifties and had kept as a rental. I had so much going on at the time between work, family, and a trip to New York City for my girlfriend Kathleen's surprise thirtieth birthday party. Then I received a phone call from my father who had something he wanted me to do.

A long time friend was in town. It was Andy Adams, my dad's old hunting partner of twenty-some years, whom I had known since childhood. My father wanted me to come over and say hello. I was frustrated because I felt so busy. I said, "Dad, you enjoy Andy. He's your good friend. I just can't come over right now." He replied, with all the strength he had, "Please, do this for me." "But why," I whined. "Why is this so important? He's *your* friend!" "Because," he told me, as forcefully as he could with pauses between his words as he struggled with his breathing— "you're my daughter and I'm proud of you, and I want Andy to see how you've grown up." Wow. I had no idea that's what this was about. My heart sank, thinking I had been so selfish. Right away, I went over to the house to say hello and visit with my father and Andy. I know Dad was pleased I did. This taught me to listen a little better, between the words.

You Just Don't Have "It"

Throughout the first two years at KNSD, a few full-time reporter positions opened up. As much as I was willing to do the split-assignment routine, I kept throwing my hat in the ring for the full-time reporter position. Decision-making management at the time didn't see me as the right fit. I took them up on their open door policy, and got up my gumption to share my goals and ask advice. Those conversations included the suggestion that I would be better suited as a producer, that I should "just hang around and become part of the furniture to see what might happen," and "Oh, by the way, you just don't have 'it' … that 'breakthrough' quality we're looking for." *Part of the furniture? What, like a footstool?* I wanted to be a chandelier. I wanted to make my mark. I didn't just want a job, I wanted a career doing what I loved and what I thought I was good at doing. I said thank you for that perspective and asked that I be kept in mind, and I went about my work with a smile on my face.

I told my parents about these types of conversations. My father, who raised two daughters to be strong and independent, kept saying, "Just don't ever let them keep you down." My mother would say, "What's wrong with them?" and then encourage me to visualize myself reporting full-time, while offering her reassuring mantra, "Where there's a will, there's a way."

My parents also suggested that if I didn't like doing the news thing, I should start my own business of interviewing people for their families, as I had done with my father. We could call it "Living Legacy" or "This is My Story"—something meaningful for posterity. That idea was prophetic, as I would find out.

The Final Friday Night Conversation

On Tuesday January 4, 1994, I was sick with a cold. I didn't want to go to my parents' house, afraid I might pass something on to my father. His frail state would not do well with a cold or the flu. I was at my apartment when the phone rang, and it was my news director informing me I had won a Golden Mike. This was a big deal. The competition was between television stations from all of Southern California, including Los Angeles. The awards ceremony was in a few weeks in Los Angeles. He congratulated me, and I called my parents.

The story I won for was called "Major Dad's Triplets." The photographer/editor I worked with for the story was John Avey. It was about a major in the Marines who was staying home with his triplets while his wife, also in the service, was overseas in Somalia. To watch him change diapers and feed three babies was entertaining and impressive. I presume the judges liked the way I told the story, juxtaposing the description of his usual military duties with seeing him tending

to his fatherhood duties. I was thrilled, especially because I was only reporting on weekends, and it was rare to have the time to do a feature story with any depth.

I told my father that if I had an acceptance speech at the ceremony, I was going to dedicate it to him, because he

served his country and his family and was such a great example for us all. It was a bright moment in an increasingly difficult time.

My parents and sister were looking into the procedure of a tracheotomy, which would involve inserting a tube into a hole made in Dad's throat to help him breathe better. There were many pros and cons. The doctor said very few patients elect this because of the potential for infections and pneumonia, and it would require full-time nursing care. My father didn't want to die, but he knew he was going to die. He was not afraid of death, but he was afraid of the dying process. He certainly didn't want to die stressfully or in pain. That's why this decision was so big.

My memory about those few days is blurred. I was feeling better Thursday and went to the house to see my parents, and also for something I vaguely remember. I was part of the family conference in which all four of us kids and Mom and Dad had a meeting with a doctor on the phone, discussing the options should Dad need intubation and a tracheotomy. Having a tracheotomy meant he would have to re-learn to speak and that would involve holding his breath. With his diaphragm weakening, this was not a good scenario.

Friday, my parents had another meeting with the doctor and Robyn by phone, and my father had made his decision. He did not want the tracheotomy. He was at peace with his decision, and had come to terms with his situation. Even with his resolve, he had expectations of living as long as he could. I went to work that Friday night, and in between writing a script, I called them and asked what they were doing. My mother said they were having some clam chowder and "Daddy's telling me about a hunting trip and a big elk." I said, "Sounds like you're having a nice evening. I'm going to get back to work. I'm reporting tomorrow morning, so I'll come by after that. I love you! Good night."

Saturday morning, January 8, 1994, my assignment was a story about an animal clinic helping catch and treat feral cats. I had just finished the interviews and we were getting in the car shortly after noon when someone at the station called my photographer, who handed the phone to me. "Jane, you need to get home right away. It's your father."

For anyone who has ever heard words like that, you know the feeling of complete shock, helplessness, and fear. I couldn't breathe. I couldn't focus. My photographer couldn't drive me home fast enough. I remember running up the stairs, almost like I was flying, or being propelled into the back bedroom, and seeing my father in bed asleep. But he wasn't asleep. He was gone. Gone. No more words. No more conversations. No more smiles. I hugged my mother so tightly. I fell to my knees. I fell apart. It was too soon. There was still so much more to do, to say, and to share.

My mother told me my father had planned that coming Monday to give me a message on videotape about his idea of the man I would marry. He had also shared with my mother his idea of using the alphabet so he could communicate when he lost his voice, which was the next step in the disease's progression. Both my mother and I just thought he was invincible and would be handicapped forever, but forever came too soon.

It had been a rough night for my parents. My dad was having difficulty breathing. His body, perhaps, just couldn't take it all anymore. He was awake all night, and so was my mother, trying to make him comfortable. The BiPAP machine had settings, and he preferred the air to be cool. My mother had called the company about the machine and how to adjust it to suit his preferences better, but they couldn't come out until the next day. The hospice person was there. Somehow the setting was turned down very low. My mother remembers how he seemed to be asleep, then she looked away for a moment, and when she turned around and looked at him again, he was gone. My sister believes, and my mother concurs, that once he fell into a deeper sleep, he went peacefully and without pain or suffering.

Still, losing him then was not how it was supposed to be. My mother and I thought he would just keep living for years; that he would be able to implement his plan of blinking once for no and twice for yes, once he couldn't talk anymore; that we would be able to tap into his brilliant mind and have conversations with him, even if he could mostly just sit and listen. My sister was calm and I couldn't understand that. I was so angry she was not crying. She told me it was because she had already cried her tears, she had accepted his decline more than we had, having seen him every two weeks, compared to our seeing his decline gradually every day. She knew his soul was at peace and his body was worn out. She needed to be strong for her two children. I wasn't strong. I was a mess.

The Eulogy: Setting His Record Straight

That next week, we had a memorial service at our church, Graham Memorial Presbyterian. The night my father died, I read his own eulogy, his thoughts about his life. He had dictated it to a caregiver who was helping us with him and some other projects. I didn't know he had done this. It was three pages long.

Nearly eighty people came to the service. I wore a navy blue suit with a gold ribbon on the collar. It was the closest thing to a tribute to the Navy I had in my closet. Dad liked that suit. I had looked in the mirror that morning before I walked out the door and swore I saw my father's face looking back at me. I could feel him, as if he were comforting me, but I already missed him so much. At the church, a friend from work, Denise Yamada, brought me a teddy bear. I called him Wally Bear. Even at thirty years old, I needed an extra hand to hold.

It was a sad service. Even though we wanted to celebrate his life, it was still sad. I had been adamant about inviting people to say something about him. I knew I wouldn't have the strength, but other friends and family might. They made comments such as, "Wally related to people through their stories ... he was a good listener ... and even when he was sick, he had a keen interest in what others were doing." My station was kind enough to let Tom Tokar videotape the service. It was something my father would have wanted, and I wanted to have it for some day.

The minister read some of my father's words from that three-page message he had left for us:

"In those pre-Navy years, I hiked, fished and hunted and no matter where I was, I had a reverence for my surroundings. It was God's country created by Him for our enjoyment.... Only a half block from where I'd been raised as a boy I met my best friend, Ann....We were blessed with a wonderful son, Jerald on 1 February 1949.... My return to Whidbey, Ann's teaching there and the birth of our second son Scott all took four years.... Our travels took us to Washington, DC for three years, where one of God's loveliest creatures was born to us, our daughter Robyn.... In 1963, a second wonderful daughter, Jane, came to live with us ... all this time my faithful ..."

When the pastor reached the end of that page, he ad-libbed: "Sort of abruptly, he never finished it, although he did finish it where he wanted to... in a way, Wally is telling us that life goes on when each of us goes Home."

What? No! There were three pages! My mother looked at me, and our whispered, but powerful conversation in the front pew went like this:

MOTHER: He did finish his thoughts. You have to stand up and say what he said on page three!

JANE: Are you kidding me? I'm a mess.

MOTHER: You have to, Janie. You're your father's daughter, and you're a journalist! You have to set the record straight!

I don't know if it was the look in my mother's eyes, the strength by which she squeezed my hand, or my father's spirit just overpowering me, but somehow, I stood up and talked with a quiver in my voice, but, I see now, with an unexpected calm. Watching the tape of the service for this book, I'm reminded exactly of what I said and what was on that third page. "As a journalist, I have to set the record straight. He did finish it... he said this would be the last place the letter would be read. So he did want to say goodbye to everyone.... And in these last few days, talking to people about where he is now, it's what my big brother (Jer) said, 'He's right in here. He's right in our hearts." I then explained how I had felt his presence in the mirror, and finished by saying, "So I salute you, Dad. You were the best, and you'll live through us."

Later, we had a small service at Fort Rosecrans National Cemetery at Pt. Loma, which overlooks San Diego Bay and Coronado. We can see it from our house. There the traditional military honor with a 21-gun salute was somber and final. The military personnel handed the warm bullets to my mother, who then put one in each of our hands. I said, "Like his warm heart." Robyn said, "He survived three wars, but couldn't beat this disease." It's surreal to say goodbye to someone forever, but as my big brother said, he's right here in our hearts.

While we all grieve in our own way and in our own time, I look back on those two and a half years home with my father with little regret. I feel I did just about everything I could have done. Maybe I could have been a little more patient at times, but I think he understood. We checked off three of the four things on his list: we transferred all the film to video, watched and categorized a lot of the slides, and told his life story on videotape. As for the fourth item, I still have the map in the shipping tube. We didn't get those pins in them, but maybe someday.

I learned a lot about not only planning ahead, but living in the moment, too. While I have always been sentimental, this heightened my awareness about telling someone special that I love them and why, apologizing if I hurt someone's feelings, acting on ideas, not letting go of dreams, and always keeping my priorities straight. Looking back, I wish I had been more sympathetic and let him know he didn't always have to be so strong. I wish I had let him—always the student and analyzer—be more descriptive in what this disease and dying were like, rather than trying to just fight with a good attitude. I wish I had let him know it was okay to be sad. Not that he would ever wallow, but I wish I had encouraged him to share more what he was feeling: the good, the bad, and the scary.

Sometimes, we all need a good cry when we're dealing with such difficulties. We had a few, but I wonder if we had enough. I do believe we said all we had to say in terms of what we meant to each other and how we appreciated our family trips and adventures. We reminisced a lot, and that was good. Maybe there is never a good time to say goodbye. There is never enough time left. That's from my perspective, how a child feels for her father. It was even more difficult for my mother, losing her life partner and best friend of forty-seven years.

Two Years Later... The Phone Call

I took that next week off, returning to work as California was dealing with the Northridge earthquake that hit January 17. You might think the newshound in me would be ready to be back for such a big story, but I was not. I could hardly talk, sometimes, just thinking about losing my father. The only thing good about returning was it got my mind off of things for a little while, but I felt as if I was in a fog, or just faking, getting through the day. My work didn't suffer, but it was physically and emotionally hard to not only deal with my feelings, but to know how much my mother was hurting, too.

A few weeks later on a Friday afternoon, a producer, Greg Dawson, tapped me on the shoulder and said he had my story set for Sunday. I was the station's representative to go to Los Angeles to interview President Bill Clinton with two other reporters. The president had just taken office and would be in L.A. for a town hall meeting. I wondered, *Why me? Why wouldn't they send one of the main anchors?* Nonetheless, I accepted they had already decided I could do it, and of course, I knew I could.

The plan was that the crews would rendezvous with President Clinton at an auxiliary airport terminal and ask questions relevant to San Diego concerns— military base closures, the border, and the economy. His advance team had set up three folding chairs in a half-circle in front of a fourth folding chair for him. Someone found a fake ficus tree to put in the background. When he arrived, he was escorted up the long ramp to our set-up. He went through the line, greeting each of us individually. When he came to me, he shook my hand, looked right into my eyes as I introduced myself, and he said, "Hello Jane, it's good to meet you." In those five or ten seconds, for each of us, President Clinton seemed locked in and focused. I understood better what had been described as his charisma and ability to connect with people.

The other stations' anchors on this assignment were Hal Clement and Adri-enne Alpert. The three of us had discussed in advance what we wanted to touch on and began our very civilized questioning. Our allotted fifteen minutes with him stretched to thirty, and he didn't seem bothered or in a rush. His answers were on point, and predictably, when a question was not perhaps what he wanted to talk about, he gave a great answer to a question that was not asked. I knew I was Jane Mitchell from a local station in San Diego, not White House Correspondent Andrea Mitchell, so I posed basic questions and didn't try to do a point-counterpoint ses-sion. The adrenaline was pumping. I was happy to be on this assignment and excited to get back to San Diego in time to get the story for the eleven o'clock news. The station showed confidence in sending me, so that seemed to be a good sign.

That confidence was short-lived. By the end of the summer, for reasons not really explained to me, management decided to take me off the air and have me produce behind the scenes. I thought, *Stay inside all day and move pieces of a show around like a puzzle? This is going to drive me crazy.* But I did it. As much as I appreci-ated their support, my friend and fellow field producer, Jill Underwood, and others were frustrated for me. They said they could not believe my positive attitude when I told them, "I know there's a reason for this. I know this will lead to something."

Part of that attitude stemmed from my need to be in San Diego. I needed to be home now, for my mother. I looked around at other stations. I sent tapes to markets that would be an easy flight away. Keith Esparros, who had hired me at KNSD, had moved to a station in Los Angeles and twice offered me a writing job there. Moving to LA for that didn't feel right at the time. I would be asked to not search for an on-air position for six months, and the pay wouldn't have been much more than what I was making in San Diego. I wanted to report. The combination of factors just didn't add up or feel right.

Although I wasn't moving, I was ready for a change. This became clear to me when I covered a story about a boy named Tyler who had been hit and killed by a drunk driver. I interviewed the boy's grandmother about her loss, and in her grief, she seemed to want to explain her anger toward the drunk driver. I fought back tears as I talked with her, and cried once I sat inside our news car. I was not only sad for her, but because I thought of another Tyler, my nephew, who was about that boy's age. I thought I was tough enough to cover the daily tragedies, but realized it was becoming too hard on my heart. It was becoming more difficult to leave those stories at the office.

After I was taken off the air, I learned to show-produce the four o'clock one-hour newscast. It was complex and frustrating. On my first day, they said I was going to be in the booth alone during the live show. I said, "No, I do not know what I'm doing, you cannot set me up for failure." I practically demanded an experienced live show producer be in there with me. They agreed. By day two, or so, when I was on my own, I had some eye-opening and frustrating moments, too. For example, when I asked the anchors to wrap up, and they kept talking. It was unnerving because there was so much pressure on the producers to go to a commercial in certain time blocks and start the second half hour on time. This had to do with television ratings. I barely could get the show timed correctly, so it was doubly disconcerting when some of the anchors didn't always pay attention. I remember thinking and then saying to them that as an on-air person, I always—*always*—listened to the producer in my ear, because the producer is primarily responsible for managing and running the show. I couldn't understand why they would not listen to me. I stood up for myself, gained more confidence, and actually became good at producing because I had determination, a sense of survival, and help from the much more experienced directors. Producing live television is another animal. Give me a microphone to tap-dance any day instead of that. Again, I knew this producing assignment had to be for a reason, and it was.

It had been little more than two years since my father died, and I had started taking little trips or an annual vacation with my mom. By March of 1996, the weekend of my birthday, Mom and I went to San Francisco for a fun and much needed change of scenery. Before I left, I received a message on my work voicemail from my friend and former news anchor, Dennis Morgigno. The tone of his voice sounded as if it were about something personal, not urgent or business related, so I waited to call him when I returned from the trip. It was personal, but with a twist.

Dennis had been off the air for a while and was doing some consulting with Cox Communications in San Diego. We met for dinner and he told me his good friend, Dan Novak, at Cox was planning to do a special channel that summer while the Republican National Convention (RNC) was in the city. Dennis knew I felt I was stagnating professionally and wanted a challenge. I wanted to make sure it would be a bi-partisan or non-partisan channel, and he said it would be. The goal was to tell the San Diego story to the forty-thousand-plus visitors, and to tell the RNC story to the greater San Diego region. My part would be a four-month contract, and I would be the assignment editor, producer, and reporter, working with a small staff and freelancers. He told me he thought I was the only person in town who, 1) would be up for such a challenge and 2) could do it. That meant a lot coming from Dennis. That he would recommend me to Dan meant a lot, too.

It was a risk. I would need to quit my full-time job with benefits, for a four-month freelance contract with a good salary, but without benefits, and no promise it would lead to anything after those four months. Regardless, I sensed it would be a great professional experience, and I could be on the air. It felt right.

I made an appointment to meet with Dan Novak. I was producing the four o'clock newscast that week at KNSD and drove out to his office one evening after the show. The old building in El Cajon was far from glamorous. The administrative assistant, Barbara Cheek, greeted me at the reception area. The ceilings were low and the carpet and furniture run down, but I was excited when I saw Dan and his welcoming smile. I vaguely recognized him from a telethon where Dennis said we had met a few years before. I liked that Dan was outgoing and friendly. He asked about my views on work and I assured him I was a hard worker, a self-starter, and a go-getter all rolled into one. We talked for a few minutes and he gave me a piece of paper with a list of about twenty things on it. "These are the things you'd be responsible for as the producer of this project," he said. The list included interfacing with network cable providers, creating a marketing plan, and interacting with government and other entities. I wasn't sure what those things were. Then I saw, "Create programming and produce stories and shows about San Diego." I looked right at him and said, "I know how to do about five of the things on this list." Thinking I was sunk, he said, "That's okay. We can work with you on the other fifteen!"

After twenty minutes of talking, he asked me, "Do you want to think about it? Can you let me know maybe by tomorrow?" I said, "Oh, I've thought about it. I

 have an answer." He asked again "So, do you want to let me know maybe tomorrow?" I said, "Are you offering me the job?" He said, "Yes, I guess I am." "Then I guess I accept." "How soon can you start?" "I'll give my notice tomorrow."

Two weeks and a day later, I was raring to go but had no idea, really, what was in store. I would soon discover it would lead to what Dan would call "the next frontier."

CHAPTER 4

The Making of *One on One*

A Baseball Rookie Ventures into New Territory

Quitting IS What It's Cracked Up to Be: The Biggest Professional Risk of My Life

My scoliosis caused me to adopt a fairly cautious approach to life on the physical front. I chose certain activities for fun and fitness and avoided anything that might result in injury, such as sky diving or skiing. People might not see the scar from my surgery, but I know it's there, so I do not take physical risks knowing I have five fused vertebrae and a rod in my back.

But when it comes to other kinds of risks, count me in. Quitting my job in Tulsa to move home to San Diego for my father and family was a big risk. Quitting my job at KNSD for a four-month contract to go to Cox was even bigger. What would happen after four months? I could always get a writing job, maybe the one Keith Esparros offered me up in Los Angeles, or I could do freelance work. Despite all the unknowns, I decided it would still be worth it.

An Investment of a Lifetime

This non-partisan channel would be a big project. The goal was to tell the San Diego and Republican National Convention stories. No live coverage. Nothing daily—it would just be informative, creative, and substantive. The *Cox Convention Connexion* effort resulted in fourteen one-hour shows. Dennis Morgigno, well known as a former television anchor in San Diego, would be our host. I would be an on-air reporter as well as the show and channel's producer. Dan Novak would dip back into his on-air days and be the second reporter.

The show included features about San Diego, the history of political conventions, and behind the scenes preparations for a significant event for a city and region. The features weren't just the quick minute-and-thirty or two-minute stories the news organizations would do. We wanted to be different. Stories were three to seven minutes long in categories such as "Beyond the Beach" to showcase San Diego's high-tech industry and "Road to San Diego" to tell the history of how the city was chosen to host the convention. We had colorful graphics, "man on the street" interviews with San Diego trivia to add some fun and information to the shows, and the San Diego skyline as our backdrop for our on-camera introductions.

We rounded out a four-hour block of daily programming with political movies and other relevant programming from our cable partners. The main content was a new daily one-hour magazine show that repeated several times in a twenty-four hour period. Whatever time people were back in their hotel rooms or tuning in at home, the channel was on. I enjoyed the menu of topics, considering I was a Political Science major, journalist, and a native San Diegan.

There was a small staff made up of full-time employees and several freelance producers, editors, and photographers. Some came from journalism and communications backgrounds and had worked in the local cable world, but few had daily broadcast news experience. Dan Novak gave me the green light to not only organize and coordinate the content of the channel, but to bring the production values up to a standard that would be expected in a major market. This was my first attempt at using what I learned from Rick Brown in graduate school to constructively critique the current production elements. I watched something all the way through, then watched again, offering suggestions based on my criteria. Some of my suggestions and requirements were welcomed by people including Nick Davis. Nick was married with two daughters, had played football at Purdue, had a big booming personality, and an equally big heart. I appreciated his can-do attitude and the fact that he understood and respected my plan of attack.

Some of my strategy, however, faced resistance or maybe even resentment, because I was the outsider coming in with authority, energy, and ideas. Change was good for me, but early on, not everyone seemed to like change. It was my first big lesson in managing—other than student government and fill-in producing a newscast. Coming from a broadcast news background with deadlines around every hour and having worked through my childhood procrastination challenges, I was surprised by the various perspectives about how to get things done. I had one speed—full speed ahead. We had a big job to do in less than four months. When I

shared some of my concerns with Dan Novak, he understood and supported me, setting the tone and encouraging those who were involved to either get on board or step aside. Almost everyone got on board, and that made for a smoother and more exhilarating ride.

The field producers produced about one hundred feature packages (stories) that Dennis, Dan, or I would voice (narrate). I produced and voiced more than fifty. My stories were easily two or three times the length and far more complex than a typical two-minute daily news story. Producing fifty of those was the equivalent of doing six months' regular work in less than three months, which was much more than I had produced in a while. The content was exciting, though. For example, through Dan Novak's contacts, we coordinated having the legendary broadcaster Walter Cronkite tape a comment about the history of political conventions on television and about a pioneer in the business, his friend Sig Mickelson. I didn't interview Mr. Cronkite, but I talked with his assistant in New York and sent the questions for him to answer. Dan and I spent many hours around a table with color-coded index cards and a computer, finalizing my rough drafts of how the fourteen shows should be organized. I also wrote the anchor on-camera scripts and produced the fourteen programs. It was the largest television jigsaw puzzle I had ever faced.

I was grateful, in particular, for my associate producer, Jen Hardin Marchesini, whom I had known from KNSD, and for my intern, Erin Krueger. Both were roll-up-your-sleeves young women who embraced the details and the big picture possibilities of the project. We had several freelance photographers and editors, including Dan Roper. Dan and I clicked as we began editing projects. He had been Dan Novak's teaching assistant at San Diego State University, had his Master of Education degree (with a technology emphasis), and had produced and hosted a local cable surfing show, *Wavelength*. He was smart, creative, and hard working. Having not been in the broadcast news world, he took my suggestions and guidance well to adapt from a fast-editing MTV style to a more classic look and feel for our broader audience and my sense of what would be a better fit. He had a myriad of ideas and was willing to shoot and edit at any hour.

Along with Dan Novak and Dennis Morgigno, I was part of a bigger Cox team for this project. That team focused on the technical aspect of the channel, such as getting fiber optic cable into the hotel rooms downtown so hotel guests could see the channel, marketing the channel, and managing the government and community relationships with those willing to carry the channel.

It was a fast-paced four months. I had ten, twelve, and even eighteen-hour days filled with shooting, writing, overseeing editing, and meetings. Having barely enough time to do anything other than work, my mother and I were curious about what my freelance salary would equate to for those four months. We did the math and it was about five dollars an hour, an investment of a lifetime. When the *Cox Convention Connexion* aired in August for fourteen days, it was a success from both a company and community standpoint. It turned out to be the launching pad to what Dan Novak called our "next frontier."

Station Break: *A Salute to Teachers*

Toward the end of the project in August, Dan Novak asked if I would extend my time for one month to take over producing *Cox Presents: A Salute to Teachers.* 1996 marked the sixth year Cox had produced a live two-hour Academy Awards-style, black-tie event honoring teachers and announcing the County Teachers of the Year. *Salute* was the brainchild of Dan Novak and Sandy Murphy from Cox, and Jim Esterbrooks from the San Diego County Office of Education. Dan had been both the executive producer and show producer. I accepted his offer to be lead producer and it turned into another intense and all-consuming four weeks doing something I had never done before: producing a live two-hour scripted event with video elements, student performances, and an emcee—all on the stage of the two-thousand-seat Civic Theatre in downtown San Diego. Aside from the television content, there were many moving parts: professional lighting, props, scenery changes, sponsorship components, graphics, a printed program, and coordinating with the emcee—all of which seemed monumental to me.

Thankfully, I was able to rely on many people who had been part of the previous shows. Still, when there were issues or conflicts surrounding the production that flowed to or from me in some way, as the lead producer I had to either find a solution, rely on Dan Novak for advice, or make a decision on a matter I was not so certain about. By September, there was a basic format and elements in place, but I re-vamped many components, including creating a new template for the script and show elements and establishing a flow and a style that became a solid foundation for years to come, taking it to what Dan and others called "the next level."

My background in news, story, and show producing came together in a way I could never have anticipated. Not only was I behind the scenes, but beginning in 1997, during the live production, I would take off my headset, leave the production truck, and go on stage in my evening attire to make a presentation as an on-air representative of Channel 4 San Diego. For thirty seconds, I shared how I was inspired by my teacher-mother and my story-teller-father, and gave kudos to teachers, including my high school journalism teacher for encouraging me to work toward my dream. Other times, I was part of the Channel 4 on-air team's banter as we announced the next teacher finalist.

Dan Novak, Deborah Davis-Gillespie, Carla Hockley, Jim Esterbrooks, and Richard Taylor were other co-producers for the show. We were part of a bigger committee, dividing the work and tasks from show themes and content to administration. We interfaced with sponsors, performance groups, and the community. The hosts ranged from comedians to our own Padres broadcaster Matt Vasgersian and anchor Dennis Morgigno. With our Padres connection, Tim Flannery, Steve Finley, and Trevor Hoffman showed their support by being guest presenters. In

1998, we began using Director Tom Ceterski and various camera crew and producers, including Nick Davis, from the live Padres games to take that aspect of the production to yet another level.

I must have lived on adrenalin, pure drive, and the desire to succeed and please, because I produced *Salute* for nine years, while still being fully engaged in my baseball and *One on One* related responsibilities. After the 2004 show, my managers decided it was time to lighten my workload and focus on *One on One,* hosting our non-sports interview show *Forefront,* and other projects. Carla Hockley moved up to lead producer, carrying the torch while adding her own ideas. I'm proud of those nine years of celebrating teachers and elevating that production. The show celebrated 20 years in 2010. During my tenure as producer, our producing team received five Emmys for Special Events Coverage, and I won an Emmy for writing the segments the year we paid tribute to Ted Geisel and the story of *Dr. Seuss.*

Back to Baseball: How'd You Like to Help Create This Thing?

Somewhere between 1995 and 1996, Dennis Morgigno, as a consultant to Cox Communications, had wanted to create a local channel with local programming. He brought that idea and a plan to Dan Novak and Bill Geppert, the new vice president and general manager of Cox Communications in San Diego. The Republican National Convention (RNC) presented an opportunity to create such a channel, and it worked, but it was limited to that subject.

In the summer of 1996, amid the RNC programming, Dan Novak hinted there might be something else for me in the fall, but all he would say was that it was sports-related and it might give us a chance to do new programming we had talked about. For one, I wanted to take the public affairs show up a few notches for a program we could call *Living Legends,* featuring the stories of important and compelling San Diegans. We had so many ideas, but how to fund them? Who would watch? What channel would they be on? The logical place would be number 4 on the dial, where Cox carried its local programming. Dennis and Dan had mapped out ideas on paper and I offered a brainstorm of ideas, excited about the possibility of something developing.

This is not intended to be a comprehensive history of the channel's development; however, for this book, I talked with some of the key people involved in the creation of the channel to help round out the perspective. In the 1980s and early 1990s, televised Padres games were limited. At most, about fifty road games were aired on different stations, with Pay-Per-View being the only other option for fans to catch the games on TV. In 1996, KFMB-TV was the rights holder for the San Diego Padres games, broadcasting about eighty road games a season. While KFMB's contract was up after 1997, Dennis Morgigno recalls learning KFMB would be open to getting out of its contract early, if possible. He shared that information with Cox's Bill Geppert. Good timing, as Bill was also seeking a way for Cox to connect with the community in a new and different way. So Bill met with Padres President Larry Lucchino.

Larry recalled: "I thought it was important that the new Padres, as we were calling them, would go out and get as many games on television as possible. And the best way, of course, to do that was with a cable rights bid to regional sports delivery. And then that's kind of where it came from. Bill and Cox were the dominant players in San Diego, and so their aggressiveness in coming to us was reciprocated by our desire to have as many televised as possible."

Bill remembered the meeting this way: "When we got into the programming topic, it was really all about branding. It was really not about sports, it was about how do we create a vehicle by which we can help brand and tell our story about our community involvement, engagement, our products and services, as we were just about to launch telephone service, Internet service.… All of that was brand new. And we were transforming ourselves from being the cable company to the communications company. We had a sense about what he [Larry] wanted to do and what we wanted to do, and it was just converging. And, frankly, no one was doing it. We were putting games on a fiber optic backbone; that had never been done before. We were doing home games and away games. We had a traveling production group. We were putting a whole channel together with the centerpiece being the Padres. That had never been done before."

Negotiations took place and a deal was in the works. I was at the news conference at Jack Murphy Stadium in September 1996 when Larry explained the new venture with Cox, and how he and Padres owner John Moores believed that "the more games you put on television, the more people will come to the ballpark." Doubters might have questioned if this would work. Larry often relayed how back in the late thirties, when the idea of putting games on the radio was presented, doubters thought people wouldn't go to the ballpark if they could hear the game for free on the radio. That fear was not realized, of course, and fans continued to flock to ballparks.

So by the late '90s, with the proposal of one hundred games on TV, skeptics might have wondered whether fans in San Diego would still turn out at the ballpark. The business partners involved in the venture—modern day visionaries—were willing to take a chance. Beyond that, they wanted to build a relationship between the players and the fans, and that meant more than just televising the games. It meant creating a whole channel. The visionaries, and those of us hearing about it, called it an experiment, with confidence that with the right formula it had a good chance of succeeding.

Fortunately for me, Cox and the Padres needed someone with a television background to help create both the channel and the programming surrounding the games. Coming off the summer project and *Salute*, I had proven myself on enough levels that I was a prime—and maybe the only ready, willing, and able—candidate who was also immediately available. It didn't seem to matter that I didn't have a sports background; I could tell stories and produce television. Dan Novak asked if I would be interested and, of course, I was. Since graduate school, I had dreamed I would someday own my own production company and work with people I liked to work with—those with creativity, talent, great ideas, and a good work ethic. This was a chance for me to have the excitement of an entrepreneurial experience without any of the financial risk or need for capital investment. I was energized by the prospect.

Sunday, September 29, 1996 I sat on the sofa in my mother's front sunroom by her kitchen and watched television: the San Diego Padres playing the Los Angeles Dodgers. In the ninth inning, with Trevor Hoffman on the mound, the Padres won, clinching the National League West Division. It was one of the few games I had paid attention to all season, having been engulfed by the RNC channel, then *Salute.* I didn't normally watch baseball on TV and had not been following the Padres. However, at this point, I was intrigued.

Knowing the new Padres-Cox deal was done, by that October, Dan Novak recalls his mission:

> "I was looking for people who would do whatever it takes to help create something brand new that had never been done before. Everyone else who had launched a regional network had a meaningful infrastructure behind them. We were just us. I knew that with limited ability to hire full-time employees, I had to hire the right folks and had to have folks who could do it all, or at least were willing to roll up their sleeves and make it up as they went along. I knew Jane was really motivated to be a part of the 'next great frontier' as Bill and I were calling it. And with Dennis' history and recommendation, I thought it was a good fit."

Dan was encouraging his direct boss, Bill Geppert, to create a position to hire me as a full-time producer/reporter. I still didn't know whether it would happen, so I put out feelers for freelance work. Dan was very encouraging and hopeful, but made no promises for weeks. Just before a planned vacation with my mother, he offered me the position. The salary was adequate. We were all taking a chance with the experiment, so I was willing to start low, knowing it was a good company with benefits and, more importantly, a unique opportunity. I reiterated I would do anything and everything, as long as I could be on the air. Dan assured me that was fine by them. Wow. What a contrast to what I had experienced the four years before at my previous station. There, other than two years of part-time weekend reporting, I was not factored into their on-air staff because I was told I didn't have "it"—the qualities they wanted for an on-air reporter. Cox was now giving me the opportunity to just go for it and to be me. I took that vacation to Hawaii and officially started at Cox on November 11, 1996.

What's Our Name? What's Our Number? Mission Identity

We had only four months before our first spring training game was scheduled to be televised live on March 13, 1997. With much to do, everything seemed to happen all at the same time. Our long to-do list included figuring out our identity, hiring the right people to round out our game and non-game production crew, developing non-game programming, deciding what the channel would look like, how it would operate, and how it would be carried out to the community with other cable companies. I was not in the technical/operations part of the equation because that was not my forte.

I was in the middle of the process of deciding our look and what we would be called. I didn't know anything about graphics or marketing per se, but I did know TV—the good, the bad, and the "What were they thinking?" I had good intuition, too, I suppose, so Dan Novak asked me to drive to Los Angeles to meet with two highly recommended prospects for our graphic design and promotions needs. I met them in a hotel lobby. Ismael (Ish) Obregon was cool, hip, creative, and confident. Ed Roth was quirky, funny, and seemed to get the feel-good, hometown image we wanted to project. I liked them. The same day, Dan had a game producer in from Phoenix he wanted me to meet before the prospect had to catch a flight. So I drove fast to get back to San Diego to meet Scott Hecht. He was another good fit and had my vote.

Within a matter of weeks, Ish spent the day with Dan, Dennis, Brenda Lovitt of the Cox marketing staff, and me to show us his options of what our 4 would look like. What was our name? 4 Padres? 4 San Diego? While we expected in the long run it would be "4 San Diego," we settled on "4 Padres" to start, because the Padres would be our base programming, and we wanted people to know where to find the games. We would refer to it in narrative writing and verbally as Channel 4 Padres, but the logo would not have the word "channel" in it.

Ish showed us what the four could look like: four dots, a square four, a round four, and a skinny four were among the myriad of options. My argument was that people say the word "channel" even though they might not see it in the logo. So the logo needed to be simple, but strong, and not too confusing or fancy when someone was trying to figure it out.

We narrowed it to a few, and with others' feedback, made a decision on the angular four, essentially the same four the station has had all these years with some technical improvements and color tweaks.

Dan narrowed the candidate list for the game producer down to Scott Hecht. Dennis suggested Tom Ceterski as a candidate for the live game director position, because they had worked together at KCST, and Tom had a solid track record of news and live sports production. Tom and Scott got the jobs and took the lead in hiring the crew for the games so we could focus on the other content.

Early in this process, Dennis and I were in a meeting with Bill Geppert. Bill recalls our asking several tactical questions about the plan, and what Bill said then has stayed with me all these years:

> "'Jane, I'm giving you the canvas; you're the painter. I'm giving you an idea what kind of painting I want, now go paint. You know, that's what you do. That's your genius to this. And this is where your talents and skills are.' And I said, 'Far be it from me to tell you how to paint, because I don't paint. We're creating art together.' And I remember the look on your face was like, ooh, one, 'I've never heard that before.' Two, 'Wow, this is going to be fun and interesting.' And, three, kind of a scared, 'Uh-oh.' And from that it was, 'You go out and figure out what kind of programming we need to do around it.'"

Info-what? My First "Pitch"

That November, the Padres needed an infomercial to promote the 1997 season, ticket prices, and season ticket holder packages. Swamped with work at this point, I still knew very little about the team. Regardless, Dan Novak asked me to take a crack at writing a fifteen-minute show that would be looped on the channel. Dan recalls:

> "Jane joined the small team and hit the ground running. She worked long hours and wanted to be a part of everything. This helped her round out some of her skills that she hadn't had to use before."

Beyond that, I had not seen much of the season, so I asked the Padres to provide talking points they wanted included—the stars, the story lines, the prices, and the fan benefits. This was coming off the 1996 National League West Division year, and even though the St. Louis Cardinals had swept the Padres in the Division Series, I could see there was much to celebrate and to be excited about.

With this task at hand, one day in early December, I sat at my work computer to write. Other than an hour for lunch at Rubio's for fish tacos with my brother Scott, I focused on writing that script for nine hours. I wrote and wove the points of interest, strictly going by what they provided and a sense of what a fan or I would be drawn to. I didn't think about it as a hard sell, but as a story. I left some holes for interview comments that could be added later if needed, but otherwise, it felt fairly complete.

Because the Padres didn't know my television voice delivery, or know *me* very well at that, I read the script into a tape recorder so they could get a feel for my voice, the pacing, and the poetry. Part of it went like this:

> "Last year we asked you to keep the faith, and you did and it showed. In the stands, on the field, in our hearts and in the record books. For the first time, in a long time, we had a winning season... as National League Western Division Champs... That was '96. Wow. Now it's '97 and we want you on our

team. Be part of the energy, be part of the emotion, be part of the action, be our 10th player.... We'll do our part, but we need you there. We want you there and we're glad you care. Thanks for keeping the faith and we hope you'll keep on believing."

Within a matter of days, I heard from the Padres front office. Don Johnson with the marketing department, for one, told me I captured the year, the team, and the mission, and "got them" like no one else had. If nothing else, if things didn't work out at Cox, I figured I could get work as an infomercial scriptwriter. Soon after, I sat in an editing room with Bob Shroder at his HVS Productions studio. This is where we had spent the summer editing the RNC related stories and shows. On the Padres project, Bob edited as I scrambled to find bits and pieces of video from boxes of tapes from the team, and we put that fifteen-minute piece together in a few weeks. It was on Channel 4 before there was a Channel 4. It wasn't my best *journalism*, but it served the purpose, and never again would a fifteen-minute piece be that *easy*.

Faces and Places: Whom Do We Want to Know?

Until late December of '96, Dan Novak and I, along with about five other employees participating in the new channel, were based in an old building in El Cajon. It had low ceilings, old furniture, little ventilation, and was musty. I had taken Christmas Eve and Christmas Day off to be with my family at my sister's home in Orange County. The next day, I returned to our building and a flooded mess. Our area was uninhabitable, so we temporarily relocated to the main company building, sharing cubicles and office space, while Dan and Dennis searched for a new home for our small group. By early 1997 we relocated to half a floor of a small office building in Little Italy near downtown San Diego. It wasn't glamorous, but it was a start. I had an office with big windows and bookshelves that would fill with notebooks and scripts pounded out on my computer as that office became my home-away-from-home for many long days and nights the next several years.

Dennis Morgigno recalls how, at that time, he, Charles Steinberg, the Padres' vice president of public affairs, and I, all agreed on a singular strategy.

> "If this venture was going to be successful, we needed to get the viewer more involved in Padres baseball, which meant helping them know the players, coaches, and front office personnel in ways they couldn't by just watching the games. So we devised the pre-game show, *Prime Time Padres* (Scott Hecht came up with the name and Charles loved it), to provide a vehicle for you (Jane) to tell the personal stories."

Prime Time Padres would include highlights, interviews on the field, and my features about players, the game, fans, and anything baseball related.

I met Larry Lucchino at the first news conference in September, but the first time I recall talking with him since I had been hired for this venture was at a planning meeting that winter. Dan, Dennis, and I met with Larry, Charles, and Larry's consultant friend, Jay Emmett, who had been at the forefront of the sports and entertainment industry. We discussed what we all wanted to achieve with the channel and programming. Dan told them I would be doing the features. I felt as if they looked at me asking, "Who are you?" I told them of my news background, and while I didn't know a lot about baseball, I knew about storytelling, and I was just like many of the people they were trying to reach. Dan backed me up. They nodded their heads and we moved on to figuring out what stories to tell and which players to feature.

This is where one of my favorite "If we knew then what we know now" stories comes in. There were several players on the list for me to profile. I needed background information and newspaper clippings for my research, so the media relations team, led by Charles Steinberg and Glen Geffner, invited me to come to their offices at the stadium where their media relations assistant would be happy to help me sort through the files.

On that day, I introduced myself to the assistant and explained what I needed. The tall, twenty-three-year-old with a mild northeastern accent seemed uncertain about me. He had been described to me as a baseball purist with a great love and respect for the game. I sensed he wondered how I could do my job without a sports background, and he might have actually asked me that question. His skepticism didn't concern me; after all, I had butted heads with that mayor in Texas years before, among others, so this was just another challenge. I thanked him for assisting me with the files and told him I would do my homework and get my facts straight as I began interviewing players. I might not have let on that I wasn't sure how all this would go, that I too was a little nervous about the sports part of the equation but had no doubt I would figure it out.

Eventually, after watching the first shows that spring, my work seemed to answer his question. He complimented me on my grasp of the game and how I wove that into the stories. Half-teasing with an "I told you so" tone, I said I appreciated that he recognized how I tried to do the players, and the game, justice. That media relations assistant was Theo Epstein.

Theo eventually was promoted to work under the Padres' general manager, Kevin Towers, went to law school, and became Larry Lucchino's protégé. When Larry left the Padres for the Boston Red Sox for the 2002 season, Theo followed, and at the end of the 2002 season was named general manager at just twenty-eight years old. Then the youngest GM in baseball, Theo is credited with being a key architect of two World Championship teams. That's a long way from organizing file folders with newspaper clippings and assisting a veteran reporter who was a rookie in the sports world. It's also a reminder that great things are possible with focus and perseverance.

Back at that brainstorming meeting about whom we wanted fans to get to know, we concluded we needed to introduce current stars, fan favorites, and others in the Padres organization key to the team. Considering it was winter, the person we featured depended upon whom we could shoot before spring training, and before everyone had gone to Arizona for camp. The first short list included Tony Gwynn, a perennial All-Star and batting champion and long time Padre; Tim Flannery, a fan favorite as a player who had returned as the third base coach; John and Becky Moores, then new owners who had injected money, charity, hope, and a winning attitude into the community; and Ken Caminiti, the 1996 National League MVP who had shoulder surgery in the off-season and whose readiness for Opening Day was still questionable. The plan was to shoot the interviews with the idea of doing feature stories, several minutes in length, at the most.

John and Becky Moores, Tim Flannery, and Tony Gwynn were set for the end of January and beginning of February. They were all local and therefore easier to schedule once they agreed. The request came from the Padres, I just had to do the research and coordination. One person on that short list who lived out of state was Ken Caminiti. With unanimous agreement to spend the money on travel for his story, Padres Director of Media Relations, Tim Young, Padres videographer, Mike Howder, and I went to Texas for two shoots in February. Stop one: pitcher Trevor Hoffman's home near Dallas to show him and his wife Tracy in their off-season home and talk about 1996. Stop two: Houston to interview Ken Caminiti.

Could You Throw a Little Something Together for a Show?

Ken Caminiti's full back-story is before his script later in this book, but here is the crux of what happened once I returned from that fast three-day trip to Texas. Exhausted but enthused, I attended a planning meeting about programming for the new channel. When the small group asked what I had to offer, I told them I had a surprisingly great interview with Ken Caminiti that was emotional and powerful. My boss, Dan Novak, asked if I could throw that together into a half-hour uncut show. "Oh, sure," I said confidently. "It will need a name," he said. Something like *Up Close,* but that was already taken by Roy Firestone. Then he said, or I suggested, "How about one-on-one?" We discussed how it was both a sports term and an interview term that sounded good.

At Dan's suggestion, I called a recommended graphic design company to assist in developing the show's look. Knowing I had also done a few other in-depth interviews with Flannery and the Moores, and that Tony Gwynn's was in the works, it was likely we would have a series of these "uncut" shows. The graphic designer, Tonya, suggested *One on One with Jane Mitchell,* because I would be the regular host, the common denominator from show to show. Having my name in the title seemed pretentious, even a bit egocentric. I had never been the focus of anything television-wise, and few in the viewing world knew me. She assured me it was the right way to go to establish a host for the viewer. I called Dan to explain her rationale, and in about ten seconds, he said okay. That would have required meetings upon meetings and focus groups at most stations, but not here. I couldn't believe it. In a matter of moments, *One on One with Jane Mitchell* was born. Well, almost.

Give Me a Canvas; I'll Get the Paint

Given the opportunity to do something new and different, I was going to do it the best I could. I don't know if it was a storytelling instinct, my imagination, or my desire to emulate the best of television I had seen over the years, but I felt I needed more than just that interview in Houston. I felt strongly it was important to hear from Ken Caminiti's parents, to see where he grew up, and where he went to high school and college. Even though Dan Novak had a vision of an uncut conversation style program, I convinced him that a photographer and I needed to fly to San Jose to capture all these other elements. More of the details are in the Caminiti chapter, but as I would soon realize, the concept of gathering and showing these details was not only inspiring, but also time consuming.

I knew I would need more help for *One on One* and for all the features planned. Because we were still in the experimental phase, we couldn't hire people for full-time positions at the start, so we found part-time freelancers. Two people were important additions for our early success. First was Megan Mallgrave. A recent graduate from Point Loma Nazarene College, Megan heard about our efforts and contacted me. She was ambitious, a Communications major, a big baseball fan, knowledgeable about the game and willing to help with research, story development, and anything else. She was my associate producer for a few years, and later produced several stories and baseball related series for us.

Second was Jason Bott. Jason and I worked at KNSD-TV at the same time. I didn't know him well, but he produced news and sports. He had heard about the new channel and asked to meet with me in January of '97. I described all the programming we planned to produce and said I was scheduled to go to spring training, too. I reiterated he should not quit his full-time job or have any expectations this could be full-time, and I couldn't promise how much work there would be. But Jason knew there would be plenty of work. He quit his job and took a leap of faith. We joked later about how cautious and naïve I was about the workload ahead. Not only was Jason key those first few years producing stories and shows, but he was, in fact, hired full-time and became an integral part of the station's sports-related programming for more than a decade.

Now I Get It

As I was preparing to go to spring training in Peoria, Arizona for the first time that February, people told me how special it was—the beautiful weather, a new beginning, seeing all the players in their uniforms after the winter break. I had no doubt it would be an interesting experience, but didn't understand why it was such a big deal. Camp opened with pitchers and catchers reporting around Valentine's Day, but that couldn't be the reason for the romance of spring training, could it?

Photographer Dan Roper drove the camera and lighting gear from San Diego, and I flew to Phoenix. We stayed at a two-bedroom apartment designated as our Channel 4 Padres spring training headquarters. We rendezvoused about seven the next morning for our first day of camp and drove to the Padres complex shared with the Seattle Mariners. The sky was blue. The air was crisp. The complex was quiet. We unloaded the camera and went to the top of the little hill overlooking the big, green practice fields. So far, it just seemed like a sports complex to me. Being the Padres' new television partner, we had special access and an invitation to make ourselves at home, so we had breakfast in the team cafeteria. Just before nine, we went back to the spot where we had set up the camera to wait for the team's workday to begin. At that point, I had no expectations and still didn't understand what all the build-up was about.

Then, it happened. The door from the weight room opened, and the pitchers, catchers, and coaches emerged, walking down the slope of steps and on to the red clay track surrounding the field. I could hear the click-clack of their cleats on the cement, the chitchatting of their voices, and the pop of the ball smacking into the gloves as they started warming up. That was it. I got it. The sounds of the game. The smell of fresh cut grass and clean air. The feeling of a new beginning. It was tangible. I got goose bumps. My heart pounded a little faster. In those few moments, I had fallen in love with baseball.

I wrote a feature story for our first pre-game show when the channel launched, March 13, 1997. It's one of my mother's favorites. Seventy-three years old at the time, she didn't care about baseball then but was excited to watch me on TV, and she knew my father would have been proud of me. We both felt melancholy that he wasn't here to experience this new phase of my career, but happily, with her full attention on her daughter's new job, this story was the first taste of why my mother would care about baseball, and perhaps others would too.

Here is the script that captured my love at first sight and the excitement of spring:

• • •

The peaceful quiet of sunrise, it could be any day. But this day, the quiet is the prelude to a symphony of spring, a melody of memories, baseball starting all over again.

TIM FLANNERY: The first day of spring training is all about hope.

The blackbirds sing on the sidelines, a signal that the fields of dreams are awakening, are manicured, plush, and ready for play. In baseball, "Pitchers and Catchers report" rings poetic; a reassurance to the boys of summer that their winter's hibernation is over.

> **TREVOR HOFFMAN:** I'm a baseball fan, so I'm happy as heck to get out on the field and throw that little white ball around and catch it.

The crack of the bat, the pop of the glove, first softly, then harder; a crescendo that makes your heart skip a beat.

> **ROB PICCIOLO:** This is my twenty-third spring. You still get excited to put on the uniform and meet the guys.

> **TREVOR HOFFMAN:** It's a long off-season, and you can't wait to get out.

> The high-fives and hellos of a roster of old friends and new prospects are the lyrics, the language of baseball that returns in February.

> **TIM FLANNERY:** I don't look at my guitar players and say, "Hum, baby!"

With the vibration of the first workout runs, and the staccato of sprints, that melody of memories of the last season begins to play.

> **KEVIN TOWERS:** Not just Cammy. All of them. Finley. Gwynn.

> **TIM FLANNERY:** It just seems we were here last week. You remember what it was like winning the division, and what it was like to have someone beat you in the playoffs.

> **ROB PICCIOLO:** Everyone's good, but there's a lot of competition as we get into it.

Gradually, the sound of cleats and catcher's gear, hats and hardballs, is muted as the fans flock and the players and team talk about the business at hand. Numbers start counting, and box scores start mounting. The pressures and focus shift the intensity to playing, and winning, and sometimes losing. And throughout the year, no matter what comes, think back to this moment, when the crack of bats and the pop of the glove are crisp and clear. Think back to when the blackbird sings as a prelude to a symphony of spring, and know that baseball will start all over again.

• • •

Spring training was an adventure on so many levels, but being new to baseball and the Padres, I had trepidation going to camp, wondering how the players would accept me. I felt all had gone well with Ken Caminiti and Tim Flannery. I was told that the ownership and Manager Bruce Bochy would tell players about their new relationship with Channel 4 Padres, but the real test was what kind of impression I made on the leader of the clubhouse, Tony Gwynn. I believed the interview the day before he drove to Arizona went fine, but seeing him a few days later at camp, I hoped he would acknowledge me. He did. While I didn't know if he put out a positive word or just said nothing, at least I had a feeling I was still safe, with no strikes against me.

I met dozens of players and personnel during the two weeks in Peoria. I learned that some sixty players came to camp either as roster or non-roster invitees. That year, many minor leaguers also came early for instructional league. Their uniforms and schedules were similar, so I was confused as to who was who. Everything was new, but I wasn't shy about asking for guidance to navigate the baseball waters. With my list of names and their connections to stories, I interviewed some twenty players either about the season ahead, life at spring training, or about players and people I was featuring for this new *One on One* program.

We were there every morning by seven-thirty and shot through the end of their workouts at about one o'clock. Dan and I often had to wait to interview players until they completed their treatments and workouts inside. I learned it was often a "hurry up and wait" situation, because most players operated on their own or their trainers' schedule. Only a few were no-shows, despite the fact we had made an appointment. For some, it might have been because they just forgot. For a few others (and only a few) I sensed they lacked professional courtesy or respect for my job, or me, or the media in general, especially when they acted as if their not showing up was no big deal. Some people liked to set their own boundaries. It was the not so nice part of this new venture that didn't feel good to me, but I chalked it up to lesson learned and decided at that point not to take it personally. While always trying to be accommodating to their schedule and space, there would be times to push and times to just not worry about it. I had a job to do, and this was a new concept, a new relationship, and the beginning of building trust and respect. We were not under a major deadline, and, nine times out of ten, plans worked out. After two weeks there, we returned to San Diego with plenty on tape and much work to be done.

Never Pretend to Know Something You Don't: What's a Change-Up?

The romance of spring training aside, I had to learn more than the basics I had absorbed from watching a little baseball over the years, or from all the baseball movies I rented and watched that winter. There was one term I heard frequently when people referred to Trevor Hoffman's pitching. In Texas, we had talked about his being on the mound in 1996 for that final game against the Dodgers when he entered in the ninth with the game on the line. He described the butterflies in his stomach as more like "pterodactyls," a term I could visualize from seeing Hollywood's version of the pre-historic creatures in the movie *Jurassic Park*. What I didn't understand—and what I didn't let on that I didn't understand—was that certain pitch in Trevor's arsenal referred to as the "change-up." I avoided using the term and planned to ask someone else about it later.

Later was at camp. I was just getting to know the game announcers, Mel Proctor and Mark Grant. Mel's background was broadcasting. Mark had been a major league pitcher, including a stint with the Padres. At spring training, I reminded Mark I was a baseball novice and asked him to explain the feared "change-up" to me. With no hesitation, and certainly without making me feel ignorant, he patiently and enthusiastically described the pitch. This is how Mark says he would have described it to me back then:

> "The pitcher uses the same 'arm speed' as a fastball, but because of the change-up grip, the ball does not come out of his hand with the same velocity as a fastball grip. The hitter recognizes fastball, because of the 'arm speed' of the pitcher, and then commits before it's too late. The ball gets to the hitter a little later, and hopefully, the result is a swing and a miss, because his timing was off."

This is how I remember his description:

> "When a pitcher holds the ball a certain way, the batter thinks it's going to be a fastball coming at him at some ninety-plus miles per hour. Actually, the way he releases it, the ball is coming at a slower speed, and the batter swings before the ball gets there and gets a strike."

Not nearly as scientific, but I understood the gist of the pitch and it stuck with me. One new thing down, countless more to go. The change-up definition is a prime example of why I decided early on not to pretend to know something I didn't. I would do my homework, listen, and absorb a lot of the baseball talk and lingo, but if I didn't understand and needed to, I would just ask. I found experts, and even non-experts, happy to help me.

No Chewing, Spitting, Scratching, Swearing, or Jockstraps

There were some things I was quite confident about, and that included making sure our content was not only correct and creative, but also classy. When we started editing *One on One* and other features, I made an editorial decision and an unwritten production rule for what would end up in any final story a producer or I worked on: No chewing tobacco, no spitting, no scratching. Those elements might be part of the game, but I didn't want to focus on them. So, if there was a shot where the player was doing any of these things on video, we should pick up the shot before or after that action or leave it out altogether. When the action was part of a moment that just had to be there, we would take it on a case-by-case basis. I bounced my philosophy off my higher-ups who agreed and endorsed my approach.

Especially with a lot of youngsters watching, we didn't want to condone chewing tobacco or spitting by showing those images if we didn't have to. Chewing sunflower seeds or a mouthful of gum was fine. That, at least, illustrated better alternatives. Scratching and re-adjusting were naturally necessary for a player's comfort on the field, I suppose, but were unattractive actions that I thought better to politely ignore for what would be replayed in stories. The first time we shot my show stand-ups in the Padres clubhouse, we encountered another "attention to detail" challenge—jockstraps. While I appreciated being inside the real environment of the players' world, I made the call that we didn't need to get *that* personal, and added one more thing to the shoot check off list. The crew didn't particularly enjoy it, but seized the task by using hangers to move them out of the shot and replace them when we were done. Whether inside as part of their locker décor or on the field, we didn't have control over what players did, but we did have discretion as to what was used, so I used that discretion.

There are government rules for television about swearing and cursing. While this was cable, it was not a case of anything goes. Channel 4 was establishing itself as a venue presenting and celebrating family and sports programming. From the beginning, I was mindful of not using portions of interviews with players or fans that might be more rough or rude, even if they were just part of their natural conversation. That did not happen very often. Most people were aware of what was appropriate when a camera was rolling, and I often prefaced an interview (live or taped) with something like, "Remember, this is family television, so don't say anything I can't use or that might get me fired!"

On occasion, a slang word made a show, even though it might have seemed a little rough, or might make a mother of a child or a more refined fan cringe. Usually, it was included because it was pertinent to the emotion or to the story. Still, it was a matter of judgment, and if it was going to have my signature on it— which included setting the tone for much of the programming we produced in the beginning— it was going to be real, but tasteful. It wasn't about being a prude, but about not being rude. Whether it was from a one-minute or one-hour interview, making thoughtful choices of what we used and what we weeded out was part of the foundation from the beginning, and I'm proud of that.

Their Territory. My Style.
So, Not in Their Underwear, Thank You

My Padres and Major League Baseball media credentials gave me access to the clubhouse like any other reporter, man or woman. Call me crazy, but I had no desire to mill around the half-dressed players before or after a game, and I didn't need to. I wasn't trying to be the beat reporter, nor was I trying to prove anything. The players had their territory and I had my style, a style that was a matter of what I saw as my role, my comfort zone, and my purpose. I considered where I would be interviewing them, the kind of rapport and trust I would need to develop, and who would be watching. The interviews would be in their homes. I did not want to sit in their living rooms and possibly have their wives wonder if I had seen their husbands in their underwear—or less. I would rarely need to do interviews in the clubhouse or locker room; I could do what I had to do out on the field or at their homes. So I chose not to be in their territory, just because I could.

A year into Channel 4, a woman close to the team told me she sensed and heard from players that they appreciated how I wasn't in the clubhouse with a microphone or hanging out by the lockers, and that they respected me for respecting their space. Granted, being in the clubhouse or locker room is often the best way reporters get post-game interviews for their upcoming newscast, and it is a standard part of the general media coverage process for broadcast and print. But I rarely had that kind of deadline situation with *One on One*. Her comments made me feel good: first, that anyone would notice; and second, that I was building a good, professional reputation with the players as well as the front office.

The 1998 post season was a different story. I was on the road with the team, and due to time constraints, going in the locker room on the road, or the clubhouse at home, was the best and sometimes the only way to get our post-game interviews fast for our post-game show being televised live in San Diego. My first and most vivid memory of being uncomfortable in the situation was after game two of the Division Series in Houston. Twenty minutes after the game ended, reporters and cameras were allowed into the locker room. Men. Women. All equal. The players knew this, and most had showered and dressed by then.

Tony Gwynn was appropriately dressed and prepared for reporters and cameras. I approached him to do a short three-minute interview. As we began, I realized that behind him—the direction I was looking—was the shower area. We had already started rolling tape when someone from the showers walked toward us, around the photographer, and to the locker next to Tony's. I was a little distracted wondering if the naked person was in the shot, and because I could see, in my peripheral vision, the player drying off and dressing while I was interviewing Tony. When we finished the taping and I said, "Back to you in San Diego," I thanked Tony and deliberately kept my eyes at standing eye level. I checked with the photographer to make sure we didn't see anything that couldn't be on TV, and we were safe. The neighboring naked player was amused by my challenging moment, and I made the point, quietly, that this was new territory for me, that I would let him get dressed, and we would be out of his way. It was amusing, but I was embarrassed, and just kept looking up.

Of course, I had to return to locker rooms many times during the playoffs, but that first time in Houston was an eye-opener as to what to expect from what I already predicted would be an uncomfortable situation. From my experience, the clubhouse/locker room for baseball is more calm and modest compared to that of a football team. I've only been to the Chargers' locker room a few times after a game or practice, but modesty, for many, is not part of the equation, even knowing cameras and reporters will be around. Athlete or not, I would not want a camera or people I don't know intimately coming into my dressing room, but that's just part of the professional sports workplace in many cases so everyone can get their job done. I'm glad I've been able to do most of my work elsewhere.

I did take the more conservative approach from the start in how I dressed, too, in line with my norm; specifically, no cleavage on the air or at the ballpark for sure. I kept things very professional as far as gathering a player's phone number or email, and intentionally kept their wives or serious girlfriends in the loop. I tried to be friendly, but not a flirt. I loved my job and this opportunity, and I was not going to do anything on that front to sully my name or that of my employer. If I traveled with the team and saw players in the hotel bar or was invited out (a rarity), I made sure a Padres media person or a Channel 4 colleague was part of the mix.

With time and experience, confident and established in my game, I relaxed a little on the dress code, even traded in tennis shoes, khakis, and logo'd polo shirts for more stylish clothes on the field and on shoots. Some players and their families have become friends socially, but I have stuck to my core values and approach to covering the players when they were with the Padres or Chargers. Maintaining a professional and appropriate decorum is something I have also required of my associate producers and interns, and have offered my perspective to younger female reporters or hopefuls, on occasion. You can't control what others think, but you can, for the most part, control your effort and actions. Having others' respect and self-respect aren't things you list on a résumé, but if you did, they would be at the top of the list of things I strive for and value, along with integrity, trust, a solid work ethic, and compassion.

The Experiment is Working

Opening Day 1997, Dennis Morgigno put on his tuxedo and hosted our first *Prime Time Padres* program. Live, to our new viewers, he introduced what Channel 4 Padres was and the players on our team, including game announcers, Mel Proctor, Mark Grant, and Rick Sutcliffe, the regular pre-game host and long-time San Diego sports broadcaster, Bob Chandler, and me, the feature reporter with a new program, *One on One with Jane Mitchell*. The adrenaline was pumping. Opening Day had new meaning, and it didn't take long for the fans and the players to catch on that we would be a regular part of nearly every home game and some road pre-games, too.

As for my role, Larry Lucchino doesn't recall now that I was new to sports in the beginning:

> "Had I known [you weren't a sports fan], it would've concerned me, but once I saw the first few episodes of *One on One*, I felt a degree of comfort, that you had a certain versatility that gave me some comfort. You added the depth of personality and the history and family to a dimension of players, and that was a concerted philosophy of our team, and so it meshed perfectly with what your vision and goals were at that account."

Our pre-game set was not fancy. It wasn't even a set. For five seasons (1997-2001) Bob Chandler stood in front of the dugout holding a microphone, without a teleprompter, and with just a light and a camera on him. I joined him nearly every home pre-game show for one or more segments, depending on the day. In 1997 and 1998, we knew we were getting the okay from some of the players to be there. Many would walk by and poke their head in the shot, make funny faces, or just hame it up while we were on live. I was about the same height as Bob, so on days I was wearing a higher heel, I took off my shoes for the live shot so Bob and I would be at the same eye level. Needing to focus on the live segment, I didn't have control when utility player Archi Cianfrocco, for example, snagged my shoes or held them up with a sign that read "Jane's Shoes" for all to see. Sometimes we could acknowledge it, other times, we just kept talking about the subject at hand. Bob, the crew, and I also enjoyed when a rookie was being interviewed, and the players were not shy about doing the traditional pie in the face routine as a rite of passage, all captured on television.

In 2002, Matt Vasgersian replaced Mel Proctor as our new play-by-play announcer. Matt and Mark "Mudcat" Grant hosted the pre-game show. Even as the main show hosts changed and we began adding additional reporters in 2002 (first John Weisbarth and Argy Stathopolus, and later, Steve Quis and Jenny Cavnar), I continued my feature segments and live-shots for the show. With more people, however, I wasn't required to be there for every show as I had been for the first five years.

Teaching and Learning on the Job

While many people helped me learn about baseball, none was more willing than Bob Chandler. He reminded me of my father with his gentle way of talking and engaging someone in a conversation. He was flawless and fluid in how he anchored the show, introduced my segments and me, and had a way of making everyone feel confident he had things under control, which he did. In his short sleeve Channel 4 Padres shirts and khaki pants, his homegrown aura was lovable. I was in awe of his knowledge of baseball, San Diego players' stories, and historic events in particular. He was like a walking encyclopedia and could dip into his memory bank with a story or an example and tell it as if it happened yesterday.

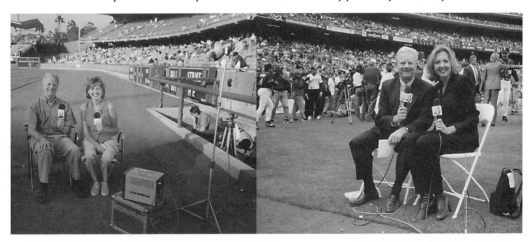

He never made me feel silly or stupid when I didn't know something. He would just teach me on the air, and in teaching me, he taught our viewers. He taught us things such as why they call a pitcher-catcher combo a battery. (One origin stems from the Civil War because artillery pieces delivered missiles to a target, just as the ball was delivered to the catcher and the batter.) That expression "You learn something new every day" was true for those five years with Bob. The bonus? When I did a story about a person or nugget of baseball history, he appreciated my research and storytelling, and there were even times when I happened to gather some information he actually did *not* know.

Tips from Tony Gwynn

There are pages and pages of official rules in Major League Baseball. I've learned the basics and some of the odd ones by osmosis or by inquiring about them. As for a few of the most significant rules that affected me? I didn't learn them by reading the manual, but rather, Tony Gwynn was my guide. Once the season began in 1997, I divided my time between the office and the field at Qualcomm Stadium. I often went to batting practice early to talk with players off-camera to set up stories, or on-camera before they were busy with their batting practice responsibilities. I did my segment on the pre-game show almost every night, which ended about the time of the National Anthem. After the anthem, I would stand next to the dugout to watch the first pitch before heading out.

The location for the television game cameras and the still photographers near the dugout is called the camera well, and at that stadium, it also housed VIP dugout seats very close to the action. The ground in the camera well was dirt. A blue pad covered the ground in the players' dugout area. One day, as the game was starting and I was standing in the camera well to watch the first pitch, I stepped from the dirt onto the blue pad. I didn't think I was in anyone's way until Tony Gwynn, nicely, but firmly, said to me, "Jane, once the anthem's done, this side is our side. That side is your side. You stay on your side, and we'll be okay." No problem. I figured there was some kind of Major League Baseball rule, but with no signs, I appreciated Tony pointing that out to me. He wouldn't have to tell me twice.

There were also unwritten rules of protocol; another area Tony helped me with. The first year of Channel 4, I flew on the team's chartered plane. I asked what I needed to know: dress nicely, be prepared to go up steps rather than a ramp on the outside of a charter plane (so no skirts), be quiet, and go where the traveling secretary put me. Coaches and front office executives sat in the front, media partners and staff were in the middle, and players were in the back. But how far back did the middle go, and when was the back "the back"? I was detectably lost looking for a seat. Tony set me straight saying, "That's far enough. Anywhere in here is fine. Players are in the back. Don't go back there and you'll be fine."

When we returned from that road trip, I saw Tony at batting practice. He inquired if I made it through the rest of the trip okay. I said yes, thanked him for the guidance, and assured him he wouldn't have to tell me twice. "I know," he said. And he didn't.

Beyond the Ballpark: *Channel 4 Super Bowl*

The 1997 season holds great significance for me and for the beginning of the partnership between Cox and the Padres. Baseball-wise, the Padres were last in the division, a disappointment coming off the 1996 season as the Western Division Champions. Being the newbie, I was still optimistic, realizing this game had not been around for more than one hundred years because people just gave up if their team didn't win it all. So I looked forward to the next season.

Before that, we had to launch the next part of our Channel 4 Padres experiment beyond the ballpark to *Channel 4 Super Bowl,* working with the NFL. Similar to what we did for the Republican National Convention in 1996, this would be ten days of around the clock programming leading up to Super Bowl Sunday in San Diego. "Everything But the Game" was both our slogan and our mission. I took the lead on producing and anchoring ten half-
hour magazine shows chock full of features. We hired two former KNSD colleagues and solid on-air reporters, Jack Gates and Corrie Vaus, to round out our feature reporting for that show. We covered the history of Super Bowls in San Diego, the economic impact, the stories of people with connections to many facets of the game and event. Those were all taped and prepared before the ten days leading up to the game. That's when we were working on all cylinders. Jason Bott, Scott Hecht, Nick Davis, and Richard Taylor took the technical lead in the truck for producing and directing the live two-hour programs from the NFL Experience. Dennis Morgigno anchored and I was the live roving reporter and fan getting a feel for all the fun at the NFL Experience. Jack and Corrie were mostly at Super Bowl related events in San Diego, producing those stories for the live show.

It was an immense amount of work with absurd, but necessary, long hours. I was sore most of those ten days from running around at the Punt, Pass, and Kick section and other interactive games. I didn't work out on a regular basis then, so I used muscles I hadn't used in a semi-athletic way in a while. Perhaps the most memorable moments (and one of Jason's favorites) was a segment in the Kid Zone. A twelve-year-old boy and I put on football pads for a playful demonstration, and the kid (in good fun) tackled me. If there were a winner, he was clearly it. Other than being a little embarrassed at my lack of strength and fight against a kid, it made for some fun live TV.

I realized people were watching, really watching, when one Sunday night that winter, I took a break from writing at the office to have dinner in Little Italy with Padres colleague and friend, Charles Steinberg. I was wearing overalls, an orange T-shirt, and no makeup, just feeling like a nondescript customer. As we sat at the table, someone came up to us and said, "Hey, you're the Padres girl!" I was taken aback. Charles looked at me and said, "See, they're watching!" Of course you want people to watch, why else would we be on television or produce shows? But it was surreal to think I was being recognized, and moreover, out of context. The scenario began repeating in unexpected places, such as at Home Depot on a Saturday afternoon or a Thursday evening when I was squeezing in shopping for home repair or gardening projects. It happened with or without makeup, with or without sunglasses. Once, when I was walking the beach on a Sunday morning, someone yelled, "Hi Janie!" I expected it to be someone I knew, because that has been my nickname since childhood. "No," the couple said, "You don't know us, we just enjoy watching you on *One on One* and the Padres channel." When I was perplexed as to why they called me "Janie," they explained how Dennis Morgigno had called me that on the air, so it stuck with them.

Whether it was "Hi Jane," or calling out to me "Channel 4 Padres," or "*One on One*," being recognized was a new reality for me. I enjoyed it, of course, not just for the recognition or taste of celebrity, but because I knew people liked what I was doing and what *we* were doing. They were always such happy, satisfied, and grateful greetings that I felt, and continue to feel, good about that. It's better to be known for something good than something bad, so I have embraced and enjoyed the good vibe. I've always appreciated fans who feel comfortable coming up to me to talk or ask a question, who holler something nice from afar or take the time to send a note or an email, and I thank them for that.

While I was fully engaged in turning out shows and content, Dan Novak looks back at my role like this:

> "Jane and *One on One* were the centerpiece of our non-game programming during the first few years of Channel 4 San Diego. It was our biggest non-game investment of dollars and staff resources because we knew it was different than what anyone else was doing locally and, with few exceptions, nationally. The quality of the shows and interviews was excellent, and it drove talk amongst the sports community and the Padres fan base in our region."

Padres Chairman John Moores reflects on watching *One on One* unfold since the beginning:

> "In all candor, I think I was surprised people opened up as much as they have. It's very hard when you only see people from a distance, especially on television, in their role as a ballplayer, to understand these are people

like all of us and have strengths and weaknesses and foibles. I think you did a very good job. Perhaps it's because you have a non-confrontational personality. You appear to me to be non-judgmental, personally. Most of us are. So I think people found it easy because you are a non-threatening person, and I mean that as a compliment."

Because of *Channel 4 Super Bowl* in 1998, the Padres Channel was being seen as more than just baseball. San Diego fans and viewers weren't the only ones who heard about us. Orange County's Cox 3 station could not carry our Padres baseball games in Angels territory, due to MLB rules, but they could carry our other Padres related programming, including *One on One, Padres Magazine*—the show hosted by Jerry Coleman that replayed pre-game features with homestand highlights and interviews—and our Super Bowl coverage. The *Super Bowl San Diego* magazine show in particular was the launching pad for a news magazine program, *San Diego Insider,* debuting the summer of 1998. Dennis Morgigno anchored with several talented journalists, making a solid team and an award winning show more than a decade in the running.

Now I Get It—Again.
T-shirts, Champagne, and a Lesson in Waterproof Mascara

The last Padres series of the 1997 season was against the Giants in San Francisco, and I was on the road with the team. The Padres lost both Friday and Saturday nights, and their season came to an end. Dan Novak and a few of us went to the hotel bar to talk and toast the end of our first season of Channel 4 Padres. Despite the team's record, we were proud and happy with what we had achieved. Some players were there, including pitcher Andy Ashby. I didn't know Andy well. At spring training, he had given Dan Roper and me a hard time for getting close-up shots while they were doing their stretching. I was never quite sure if he was serious or joking, because other times, he was friendly and said hello, so we just rolled with it as part of our learning process. On this night, seeming a little down about the season, he told me he liked the new channel and what we were doing, and that after the games he would watch the replays of the pre-game show. He liked seeing my features or watching *One on One* and getting to know his fellow teammates. *Wow,* I thought, *players are actually paying attention?* That gave me an extra boost of confidence and energy going in to the next year.

Everyone had a good feeling about the '98 season. The Padres had hired Dave Stewart to be the pitching coach, signed ace pitcher Kevin Brown coming off a World Championship season with the Florida Marlins, and had retained most of the veterans and core of the team from '96 and '97. I had interviewed Kevin Brown and his family at their home in Georgia for two pre-game show profiles to be aired early in the season. There was promise in the air—and rain.

An unusually wet mid-February in Arizona during spring training didn't quell the intensity of the team's general manager, Kevin Towers, and the front office had designed. I spent about ten days at camp that second year, gathering elements for pre-game stories for *One on One* and developing relationships and a rapport with players. At the end of spring training, I rejoined the team in Mobile, Alabama for an exhibition game with their Double-A affiliate, the Mobile Bay Bears. It was rainy there, too. When it came time to board the buses for the airport, a big storm hit. The charter plane couldn't take off in such weather, so we stayed at the ballpark. The players relocated from the chartered bus to inside locker rooms. There, Manager Bruce Bochy gave what players called his "inspiring and motivating" speech. As it was relayed later, the speech solidified how he thought they were winners, and that now the players had to believe it. On Opening Day in Cincinnati, I watched how Kevin Brown was as good as advertised and the Padres won the first of ninety-eight games in 1998. But no game was as significant or as special to me as September 12.

The Padres were in position to clinch the Western Division by the middle of September at the team's last homestand. It was important to us on the Channel 4 team to have that clinch happen when we were carrying the game, preferably that Saturday night rather than on Sunday. Sunday games that year were produced by us with the same announcers, but carried on KUSI with no pre- or post-game show. Saturday, we would all be on hand, with a big crowd, and it would be ideal if the baseball gods were in our favor. I had my earpiece and credential ready and planned to head to the field if it looked as if we were going to clinch. In the meantime, my mother and I were guests of the Padres in seats about ten rows behind home plate. By the bottom of the fifth inning, the Padres were behind the Dodgers 7-0, but even with sighs of frustration from fans around us (and my mother) that clinching the West might not happen that night, I kept thinking and saying, "Don't give up; you just never know." Sure enough, the Padres launched a huge comeback—three runs in the fifth, and five more runs in the sixth to take the lead 8-7.

Earlier that week we had had a production meeting about who would be where for the post-game celebration should the Padres clinch. Mark Grant would be in the clubhouse. Mel Proctor and Rick Sutcliffe would come down from the booth after calling the game. Even though I probably knew the players as well as anyone, I was assigned to be on the field to interview fans. I was disappointed I wasn't considered for the clubhouse location, but I bit my tongue and figured it would be fine.

With things looking pretty good by the sixth inning, I went to the camera well to be ready to go live. They had white T-shirts with "NL West Champions" printed on them if and when the Padres won. I grabbed one and went inside the grounds crew's closet under the stands by the dugout to do a quick change, keeping my jacket on over the T-shirt so as not to jinx anything. I waited in the camera well watching the last few innings with great anticipation. The Padres held the Dodgers, and in the bottom of the ninth the bells tolled and Trevor Hoffman entered the game. It was another nail-biter, and the Dodgers, whose manager was Glenn Hoffman (Trevor's older brother), weren't giving in. In the end—after a single, a wild pitch, a fly ball, and a walk—Trevor struck out two and the celebration began. The whole dugout of players ran out to the mound. The stadium erupted in applause as sixty thousand fans were on their feet cheering.

Mark Grant was in the clubhouse waiting for the players there. I took off the jacket, grabbed a microphone, plugged in my earpiece and was standing on the field near the stands. The players ran inside, popped the champagne, and I was prepared to get fan reaction. Within a few minutes, before I could interview a single person, I saw the players coming back through the tunnel onto the field to celebrate with their fans. The game plan changed. I told the producer I could interview players, he said go for it, and I did as they came by me, or as the photographer and I made our way onto the field—as far as our cables would allow us to go. I talked live with Ken Caminiti, Trevor Hoffman, Carlos Hernandez, and Mark Sweeney, among others. I was in the middle of the action, and it was pure euphoria.

Players were pouring champagne and beer on my head and I could feel it in my eyes and on my shirt. I knew I probably looked like a mess, but I didn't care. I learned three important things that night: First, wear waterproof mascara the night of a potential champagne or beer dousing so you don't have black running down your face. Second, wear an extra layer in case the victory T-shirt is white and you happen to get drenched, because white shirts are see-through when wet. And third, during the heart pounding, swirling, wet, loud, blinding moments of the post-game celebration, take it all in, because it is clear this is what it's all about. Winning. I got it. Again. Every pitch. Every inning. Every game. Everything. The work. The fun. The focus. It was about getting to the playoffs and a chance to go all the way. It all came together for me; it all made sense.

I had bitten my tongue when given my assigned post, but thanks to the players who wanted to celebrate on the field, I was right in the center of the action. For post- season, I wasn't going to bite my tongue again. I nicely, but firmly said I wanted to do post-season post-game coverage and thought I deserved to do it. Dennis and Dan agreed. Mel Proctor and I traveled with the team for the post-game field and locker room interviews (win or lose) for both home and away games to feed into the show. Dennis and Mark anchored from Qualcomm Stadium and downtown locations. Dan Novak traveled with us along with two photographers, Dan Roper for the Division Series, and Nick Davis for the NLCS in Atlanta and the World Series in New York. It was thrilling, even the part where we had to sit on the ground by the garbage trucks at the old Astrodome in order to send our interview tapes from a small deck we jerryrigged and hooked up to a fiber feed. It didn't smell good, and was far from glamorous but we didn't care. We were there.

Eventually, the Padres would put up a good fight and Tony Gwynn would have one of his favorite moments of his career: a home run at Yankee Stadium. But those darned Yankees were one of the best teams ever, and they swept the Padres—two games in New York, then two at home. It was sad. After the fourth and final game, the Padres headed into the clubhouse. The Yankees celebrated briefly on the field, then shuffled inside. All the while, some sixty-five thousand fans stayed and waited, and soon their heroes returned to the field. No champagne this time, but lots of love and tears. I had a lump in my throat as I interviewed Sterling Hitchcock who said, "It's awesome. We wouldn't have gotten where we are without these people. We just want to say thank you. They've been strong for us all year long. These are the best fans in baseball, right here." It was a magical time. Two days later, about one hundred thousand people lined the streets of downtown San Diego for a parade. As a former Yankee and the Padres own "Mr. October," Jim Leyritz said about the Padres' parade compared to the Yankees': "There may have been more people at their parade, but we have more heart right here." The journey was worth celebrating. Yes, only in San Diego.

Charles Steinberg, Tom Catlin (whom I had hired as a freelance producer, and later was hired by the Padres), and I co-wrote a sixty-minute documentary called *A Season of Heroes*. It was truly a creative collaboration: Charles composed the music, I narrated it, and Tom, Chase Peckham, and Sandy Gonzalez from the Padres' production staff edited most of the show. This was a long, non-stop six weeks, as we wove every moment and nuance of the season together with words, video, pictures, emotion, and music. With most of it done, the refining and tweaking were in the capable and creative hands of Dan Roper the final two weeks. Since my father died, I took a trip once a year with my mother, and in '98, we had scheduled a two-week trip to Europe long before any talk of producing a documentary. I felt confident being away and returned two weeks later, just hours before the show's premiere. I had been part of the brainstorming session suggesting it be a community event with the Padres, Cox, and other sponsors. That December night, several hundred from Cox, the Padres, players, and guests from the community dressed up to celebrate and watch the documentary on a big screen at the Civic Theatre in downtown San Diego.

I had not seen the final rendition, but had no doubt it would be great, and it was. Amid powerful music and images, my narration told of an emotional season:

> "What a ride. The most splendid season ever for the San Diego Padres, who captured our hearts, enraptured our souls, and taught us more about being winners than we could have ever imagined."

The surprise for me was that after the words "captured our hearts," a three-second image of a woman blowing a kiss to the camera appeared, a symbolic kiss to the season. Not many know this, but that's my mother. Tom had taped the shot the last night of the World Series when I pointed her out and she waved and blew me a kiss. He saved it. As much as I loved co-producing that documentary, Tom's little, but kind and thoughtful addition of my beautiful mother makes watching it all these years later extra special for us both. *A Season of Heroes* was awarded an Emmy for Best Documentary, and in November of '98, voters approved a proposition

for a new ballpark. Channel 4 had helped tell the Padres' story about the need and potential for a downtown ballpark. I had done several pre-game stories on the road in 1997 and 1998 about how other cities were benefiting from new or re-vamped parks, or building new ones. With the exciting and victorious year for the Padres, 1998 will long be summed up with those three words, "What a ride…"

"It was the most visible piece of our effort to connect the players and front office with the fans. From the outset, it was a different kind of local sports television—much more personal. Jane allowed fans to get to know the people they were rooting for—which only deepened that connection. From our first year—her player profiles and *One on One* clearly set us apart from the way other local rights holders were connecting fans with their teams….

"I think one of the things that makes us [Channel 4 San Diego] different is that most other rights holders use sports people exclusively in the production of their telecasts. We took someone who was not a sports person—but who was a good storyteller—and turned her loose on sports subjects. I think that helped create a different perspective for our fans….

"The one possible downside in all of this is that Jane deepened the connection between player and fan to the point that, no matter how good a player was or wasn't, fans always felt a real sense of loss when they left. Thus, trades and free agent departures were felt harder by Padres fans who didn't want to see people they'd invested so much in emotionally—leave."

—Dennis Morgigno,
Channel 4 San Diego, 2010

CHAPTER 5

Preparation:
It's All in the Details

Doing My Homework

I'm often asked how long it takes to produce a show from start to finish. It's difficult to answer, because it's hard to quantify, or even to count, the hours and days devoted to one show, especially when balancing several projects at a time. With that qualification, here is the basic process I developed that has evolved from just doing it over time, discovering what worked and what did not.

First, I ask a subject, or work with a team to ask the subject, to do the interview for the show. Some answer quickly, others take time. Regardless, once they have agreed, the next step is coordinating the date and location of the interview. If it is the off-season and they live away from San Diego, sometimes we travel there with just one camera and a photographer (usually Dan Roper) to capture them and their families in their hometown environment, interview their parents or high school coaches, and get a look at their life away from San Diego. If it is in season, we coordinate doing the interview in San Diego, and depending if his family (wife and/or children) is here or lives elsewhere, I might have two sessions—one with the subject and one when his family arrives. I work with each set of circumstances to make it happen. The planning alone, getting the shooting schedule on the calendar and finalizing the logistics, equates to several hours.

Next, the research and collection of visuals involves calling wives, parents, and teachers to track down scrapbooks, home movies, and yearbooks to visualize their story. This takes time, coordination, and a lot of cooperation. Some contacts are quick to act on the task of digging up those elements. Others are busy, and it gets down to the wire before we receive the items. Nine times out of ten, we get it all. Sometimes we have to work with less, just because they can't find pictures, don't have pictures, or didn't have time to find them. It is interesting to see the differences in families and how the era and environment of when they were raised impacts what pictures or videos they may or may not have. Some are such shutterbugs (like my family was) and others—due to a lack of interest, resources, or because of family breakups—don't have as many pictures. I have had tremendous cooperation and help from family, friends, and schools who have provided us with the archival elements to paint the portrait. All those elements have to be processed—scanned, dubbed, or transferred—and made ready for editing. Interns are often a great help with this time-consuming, tedious, but important, aspect of the production.

From the beginning, I have had a limited budget, so to be visually thorough I have to be resourceful and creative. I reach out to local television stations where a player is from, or where he played at some level, and ask for assistance. Sometimes it is just to obtain whatever video they might already have on their shelves. If we're lucky, the sports department covered that player or his team. If not, we might have to settle for generic video or none at all. Many times, I ask the station to spend a few hours to shoot video of the town, the school, the street, and house where a player grew up. They're scene setters as we go back in time for when someone's describing their childhood. When video is not an option, digital pictures suffice.

Sometimes I coordinate to have a subject's parents or coaches interviewed at his home or school. I provide the questions and the photographer/producer asks them. We have even had parents come down to the field when the Padres were on the road and do the interview there, thanks to the road game production crew at Channel 4 San Diego. Location or background isn't as important, I believe, as the content. What matters most to the story is to see and hear someone's parent describe their son as a little boy, or hear a coach relay the special qualities or challenges someone had in high school. So as long as the visual is acceptable and we have good audio, we are able to use interviews, no matter how we gather them. Content and perspective make for a more thorough, informative, and sometimes emotional, portrait.

Next is preparing for the interview. I have an intern or my associate producer help do an Internet search or review the media guide to gather the basic information known on the person. Sometimes there is a lot. Other times, very little. Often, my *One on One* is the first comprehensive piece on someone. Either way, I weave the facts—where they grew up, schools attended, teams, etc.— into my list of questions document. I tweak and tailor the notes and questions to the person, weaving in information and stories I've gathered by talking with family, friends, and coaches. Sometimes I'll write out the questions as part of my thought process and preparation. I may or may not ever ask a particular question, but it helps me solidify the information and record my curiosity, regardless if it's part of the interview.

Lights, Camera, Action!

On the day of a shoot, the crew and I rendezvous at the station with ample time to gather the equipment and travel to the subject's home. As the producer, it is my responsibility to factor in travel time, print directions, order sandwiches to take with us for the crew and guests, and keep things on track, including communicating the amount of time we have to set up, shoot, and any other relevant concerns or heads up points. For example, if it's a shoot on a game day with the Padres, we generally have to arrive by ten in the morning to set up, do the interview, shoot any of the activities at the house (a tour of his sports collection, a hobby, or playing with his family), and break down the equipment by one-thirty or two o'clock so the player can leave to get to the ballpark. That is a tight window, but we make it work. In all of this, it is the photographers' responsibility to have the right equipment, lighting, batteries, and tapes. On location, they and the crew move the furniture and set up the two or three cameras and lights for the most flattering and artistically aesthetic atmosphere. Sometimes our crew is a photographer with an intern or a production assistant; other times, we have two photographers and a few assistants, depending on what's available.

During the set-up time, I talk with the player and his wife, if he's married and she's there. I double check some facts of their background, maybe look through some pictures or get a quick tour of their home, building a rapport and making sure they feel comfortable as we sit down for a conversation. We put on microphones, ask everyone to shut off their mobile phones, see that any noisy animals, children, or house-guests are out of sight and quiet, and then I begin the interview. About every thirty minutes (the length of a tape) we stop, switch tapes, and continue until we're finished.

In the midst of a long interview that can sometimes go in different directions, my notes are like a mini-road map should I need to reference them. That way, if the subject doesn't bring something up I think may be important or revealing, it's in my head and on paper as a reminder. Because I don't know how an interview will go, I'm prepared. When other unexpected topics or moments arise that I assess to be even better than what I had anticipated touching on, then I can pass on talking about some of the planned topics on camera. The information may still be woven into the show if I deem it important. Plus, we usually only interview the main subject for an hour or hour and a half. While that might seem like a long time, there's a lot of ground to cover, and we can't always cover everything.

For those who like to talk a lot, or who veer off on tangents talking about other people or general topics, I have to bring them back around to the things I feel are relevant to the show at hand, which is *their* story. For example, if I ask about their struggles climbing the ranks through the minor leagues, and they spend several minutes expressing their frustration about the state of the game, I have to bring them back around to their specific situation. I rarely use their general opinions on such matters. Starting in about 2005, and before drug testing was regular and required, I felt compelled to ask a player about steroid or illegal substance use while in baseball or football. The question was really about their accountability and their position on the matter, not about the details of the policy and controversial topic.

I understand the players and their stories better when I start at the beginning of their timelines. This helps me see how one life event leads to the next, or how a decision triggers something on their journey. Aside from just getting the facts, listening gives me so much more insight than just checking off events on their chronology. While we have a lot to cover, not being in a rush allows the guests to share things they might be excited to talk about that I may or may not know anything about. Some questions might not lead to compelling or substantive answers or information. Others result in an emotional or funny moment that takes me by surprise, and takes things in a different direction.

Some examples will be described in my back-stories throughout the book, but here's one unexpected discovery: As I was interviewing Eric Owens in 2000, he talked about how he was frustrated he was traded from the Reds, to Florida, to Milwaukee after 1997, where he had spent the '98 season bouncing again between the majors and Triple A. He said, "I really didn't understand, and probably didn't cope as well as I should have with the way that things were going for me."

I wasn't sure what that meant as I sat there and listened, but I could feel there was something more. He shared that in 1997, his first marriage was not going well, his father's health was weakening due to heart problems, and that his dad died when Eric was playing winter ball in Venezuela.

ERIC: "It was really devastating on me. When he died, my life was not in order... I was not the same person I am today."

JANE: "How did it change you?"

ERIC: "It changed me by looking at life and knowing that baseball and things are not quite as important. That maybe going out after a game is not the best idea every night. Maybe [what was better was] going back to your room, watching a movie, and living your life for God."

By listening and perhaps because he felt safe, the interview, which was not harsh or accusatory, allowed the crux of the problem to be revealed: That he couldn't really blame the teams for not playing him the way he thought he should be played, because he was acknowledging there was more going on. He was going out after games, partying, which no doubt affected his performance, energy, and attitude. I asked if he had lost focus.

ERIC: "I think maybe I did. I took a step away. I think that God put me to the bottom of the barrel before he was going to bring me back up... And I started to realize that my family, and my mother, and the people surrounding me—they were giving me leeway, but they really wanted to see me become the guy that I was, not the guy who I was turning into."

To set up what happened next, I summarized for the viewers what I had learned had impeded his progress:

Impatience, immaturity, partying too much...

ERIC: "Eventually it catches up to you... your performance level starts going

110

down… I think that is what Barry Larkin and people were trying to teach me, and I just didn't get it."

BARRY LARKIN: "I hear guys talk around the league about him, and what they talk about now is what he does on the field, as opposed to what he did last night."

ERIC: "I have turned over a new leaf, and I have changed my life."

No matter the course of the interview, at the end it is my responsibility to make sure I've heard them talk about the things I feel are important to hear them address in their own words, their own voice. Maybe it's only a few sentences. Maybe we go through my list quickly just to get it on tape, but sometimes I just skip it if I don't think it's that critical. I always ask if there's anything I have not brought up that they would want to make sure I, or the fans, know about—a defining moment, an experience, a cause they're involved in, a person who means something to them, or an award or honor they're proud of. I tell them I don't want to find out later there was something significant I didn't know about. I assure them I won't think they're bragging or being egotistical, but I just want them to share the story or the information. It might not be a big topic, but often they remember something such as giving credit to someone who has helped them, or mentioning a new business venture or charity they're involved in. They know themselves, their projects, and their history better than I do, so I'm giving them a chance to fill in more gaps. In the end, I decide what makes the show and how I paint the portrait, but the day we spend together gives me not only information, but also a real feel for their different dimensions.

Writing and Editing: The Jigsaw Puzzle

When the show is aired, my goal is for the viewers to feel they have heard a seamless story with the answers to questions they might expect, learn facts they didn't know, and get the essence of the person they thought they knew, or someone they didn't know anything about. In the end, it should be smooth, easy to understand, and feel complete. I have heard some in television say the sign of a good program is that you leave them wanting more. While that might be good for mysteries or fiction, and there is always more to know, I believe it is more satisfying and fair to the viewer and the subject not to leave people guessing or hanging. I prefer to tie it up with a bow, put their story in perspective, punctuate a facet of their journey, or offer a launching pad for what might come next.

To get there is like facing a massive jigsaw puzzle—pulling all the facts, the best parts of the interview, and the visuals together. I usually create a list or an outline of the points I want to make. Not just the obvious, but also perhaps a study in contrasts or a quirky aspect of their personality that needs mentioning. Sometimes it's important to spend more time on one area, and just hint or address another topic with a turn of a phrase, a sweeping sentence, or a reference that at least paints a stroke of color on their portrait, even if there isn't time to go into great detail.

After the research and interviews, I review all the elements, then I sit down to write. I have calculated it takes about one hour to write what ends up being one minute on the air. That includes writing, thinking, re-arranging, adding, and subtracting. I tend to write best with no distractions, at home, when I have big blocks of time. I often sit and write for five to eight hours in a day, and sometimes more if there is a looming deadline to begin our editing. Generally, I complete the first segment first, then as that is underway in editing, I move on to the next. I have to anticipate what areas might need more time and focus as I divvy up the time for each segment. It is easier said than done.

After I have put the puzzle together on paper, it's usually too long. I try to go back through the script to shorten it, but this show is very much a "feel thing," and that massaging happens in the edit room. The sound of my voice (or track), the interview, and other SOTs (sounds on tape) are put on the digital line with our nonlinear edit system. Dan Roper and I then sit in the room and listen to it and reduce it down to time, which is twenty-four minutes and thirty seconds for a half-hour show with room for commercial breaks. For example, if it took a person thirty seconds to elaborate on a point, we have to cut that description in half without losing its essence. This is the hardest part of the process. It's important to let things "breathe" and to give Dan time for music and natural sound. While some extras must go, I am a stickler for not deleting or cutting something if it is important to the subject's story. I'll re-write or tweak so it's included somehow. If

it's just something fun or extra, it often has to be shortened or deleted all together, ending up on the digital cutting room floor.

Once we're about at time for the segment or the whole show, Dan begins editing. While we took longer the first few years, our production schedule allows about eighty hours (eight ten-hour days) to edit a half-hour program. Sometimes it is two work weeks in a row, or it's spread out due to scheduling. Dan has pulled some incredibly long days and nights because technical challenges or unexpected issues have interfered with the allotted editing time. Somehow, either routinely or not so routinely, we get it done. He can work alone or with the help of the associate producer while I'm writing another part or busy with other responsibilities. I'm always there at the end to find those final pieces of video, to trim the final extra content for time, to listen to the audio mix, and to make sure we have everything right.

There have been times when, after looking through a show, something jumped out at me. A date or a reference doesn't make sense. *Did I get it wrong? Did I miss something?* Sometimes my mind works overtime and I awake in the middle of the night with an odd feeling. The only way to explain why something might be wrong is that I'm processing so much information, sometimes from different sources or from my notes, and I'm human. Even after double-checking, I have misread or misinterpreted notes resulting in an error. I'm being honest because it's a reminder for young journalists or anyone in the field to be sure to double check. I would rather be vague than wrong. I have seen firsthand how some people don't know the facts or timeline of their own life. They get mixed up and sometimes it takes, for example, seeing a picture with a date to bring to light that something was off. I have awakened in the middle of the night triggered by watching a segment that may have been completed a few weeks after I first wrote it. If I, indeed, had something wrong, it gets fixed. That can be stressful and frustrating, but it's better to be right. Rarely has something hit the air that was incorrect. If it does and we catch it right away, we fix it and replay the corrected version. We aren't perfect, but in fourteen years we've only had to make a few tweaks due to inaccuracy.

Nick Hundley cooking with me as photographers Justin Renoud and Dan Roper roll tape.

Spring Training dinner with John, Lya, Matt, Mark and Argy.

Make-up Artist James Overstreet works his magic on Jenny Cavnar and me for a photo shoot.

In the booth with Broadcasters Mark Grant, Tony Gwynn and Steve Quis.

Could never get One on One done without the help of the Chargers and Padres media relations staff including the Padres' Warren Miller here with Dick Enberg.

Sharing a spring training moment with young Padres fans Desiree and Theresa— also among my all-time favorite Starbucks® baristas!

CHAPTER 6

Lessons from the First Ten Years

The 1998 Reunion

Having been around the Padres since 1997, I have benefited from longevity and the perspective of being part of incredible moments in the team and city's history. The ten-year anniversary of the Padres' second National League Championship title was in 2008. The Padres organization chose to recognize the anniversary by bringing the '98 team to PETCO Park in July when the Padres played Atlanta. Even though the 2008 Padres were not having a very good season, it was a worthy sentimental journey to revel in the moments that created a special bond between players, fans, and all those a part of that Season of Heroes.

Former players Kevin Brown, Carlos Hernandez, Donne Wall, Brian Boehringer, Greg Vaughn, Wally Joyner, Steve Finley, and pitching coach Dave Stewart were among the more than a dozen who returned for the commemoration. Trevor Hoffman, still with the Padres, and Tony Gwynn, a Channel 4 broadcaster by now, joined their former teammates for a ceremonial first pitch and tossing balls and

shirts back into the stands to the fans as they had done a decade before. The evening was a freeze-frame in time, long enough to remember how good it can be. Some of the '98 squad looked as if they could have pitched or played that day, but stories of aches, pains, surgeries, and age were reminders that one's body can only hold up so long to compete at the major league level. Missing, of course, was Ken Caminiti, who died in 2004.

After the pre-game interviews with several players, I appreciated being invited to the president's box to reminisce and catch up with the '98 team. Even though I was among the "next to the inner circle" group close to the team, I was still young in the sports reporting part of my career back then. So, it was a little surreal to think I was now talking to these former teammates on more equal footing. Not in terms of athleticism, but in terms of age, and all being able to relate to a common experience. I felt respected and appreciated for my role in covering the team, telling their stories, and being there with the champagne, tears, and parade in a magical time. That night I pulled out my National League Championship Series ring that's tucked away in a special drawer. I was one of the fortunate few on the Channel 4 team in '98 who had received a personalized official ring— just like the players'—as a gift from the Padres.

A Haberdashery of Responsibility

Being in on the ground floor as a founder of Channel 4 San Diego with our tiny staff, my focus from the beginning through 2004 was manyfold. I continued to be the lead producer of *Cox Presents: A Salute to Teachers* that our committee and staff worked on for eight months of the year. The core of my work was sports-related as producer/host of *One on One,* reporter and co-producer with Scott Hecht then Nick Davis for *Prime Time Padres,* as well as overseeing the content produced by the contributing field producers. I was the Executive Producer of *Padres Magazine,* and produced or hosted several related specials. I practically lived in my office and tried to take one day off a week, sometimes two, but rarely did during those first several years. I did escape to Maui for a week every February before spring training and a week in the fall and for the holidays. Otherwise, my schedule was fairly nonstop. We were a start-up with a lot to do and to manage.

By 2001, Dennis and I shared the anchor/interview role of a non-sports in-depth interview program called *Forefront,* produced by Carla Hockley. It had a regular pace of production for about eight years. My nearly forty editions included Ralph Rubio of Rubio's Fish Tacos; Irwin Jacobs, the UCSD professor who pioneered the cellular phone industry and co-founded Qualcomm; Wyland, a kid from Detroit who fell in love with the ocean and made it his mission to paint whales and sea animals all over the world to raise awareness; and Zhondra Rhodes, the brilliantly colorful clothes designer and artiste from England, who nurtured her creative niche in Del Mar. Two other favorites were from the music world: the eclectic singer-songwriter, and my friend, Steve Poltz, and Marvin Hamlisch, the brilliant composer of my first musical, *A Chorus Line.* The variety of people was vast.

On occasion, we featured sports figures for *Forefront,* but it was for their bigger roles beyond the game. I interviewed former Chargers quarterback Stan Humphries, whose golf event had supported charities; Rolf Benirshke, the former Chargers kicker who came back from a devastating illness to play seven more years and has been key in raising awareness for the disease and the Crohn's & Colitis Foundation of America; and Dick Enberg, the legendary sports broadcaster who called San Diego home and was chronicling his story in an autobiography.

It was a new challenge, because the three-camera shoot was largely interview driven, and I didn't do any writing to fill in the blanks or summarize parts of their story. So the preparation was more intense and thorough than for most of my *One on One* interviews. It was similar to cramming for a big exam, so I would be familiar with more of the content, having less time for exploration. I still had to listen, and the interview experience was stimulating and enriching.

Once the interview was complete and I memorized and shot the on-camera standup on location, I was mostly cleared of show responsibilities. Carla and the editors completed the shows masterfully. It was good to stretch myself cerebrally with so many topics in between my athletes' biographies. It was rewarding to give exposure to fascinating people and be recognized for taking my interviewing skills to a different dimension. It's another of our signature, Emmy award-winning shows, but just very different from *One on One*.

Classics: A Good Story Never Grows Old

For the first several years of *One on One,* we would play the newest edition over and over within the month it debuted. Then, after football season, we would replay a mix of the previous year's Padres-related shows until the next season, and the cycle would begin again. As long as a player was still on the team, his show could replay. However, once he was gone, we took it out of circulation and it stayed on the shelf. Part of the thinking was that if the player wasn't a Padre anymore, why remind fans that he's gone, for better or worse. That was fair and made sense. On the other hand, at the end of 2006, I suggested *One on One* was part of the Padres' and Chargers' history, and some of that history was going to waste on the shelves, so why not play them as classics? Our new vice president and general manager, Craig Nichols, liked the idea, and in a brainstorming session we decided I should update the older programs with answers to "Where did they go?" or "Where are they now?"

After researching, calling former players, and writing the new stand-ups to put the story in historical context, *One on One with Jane Mitchell Classic* was launched the spring of 2007. That allowed viewers to re-connect with old favorites who were part of the team's history. For those new to San Diego, or who were just children or not even born when Channel 4 began in 1997, the *Classics* introduced them to these names and faces they had only heard about over time. Thirty shows are in the *One on One Classics* rotation as of 2010. I even catch myself stopping and watching one once in a while. Other than a few different hairstyles, and the length of my skirts from higher to lower now, the show takes us to a time and place for the team and that player's life. The reaction from fans about *Classics* is a testament to how much San Diegans treasure the program's rich history, and to the people featured as part of San Diego sports history.

Turn and Face the Change: A Few "Ah-Ha" Moments

I ask guests to share some of the difficult moments of their journeys that might have brought them down or built them up, that caused doubts or confusion, that hurt their feelings, or increased their confidence. The answers, and how someone gets through those peaks and valleys are, I believe, what make us human, fallible, and offer clarity about who we are or who we want to be, no matter the profession. I am no different.

It was rewarding to know my company trusted me with so many projects, and I relished that fact and the dedication it required. For seven years, 1997 through the end of 2003, the station and all my responsibilities consumed most of my life, six to seven days a week, not only with baseball and *One on One,* but *Salute,* too. There were many weeks from August through October that *Salute* associate producer Carla Hockley and I were the only two at the office at ten and eleven o'clock at night, part of a ten- to fourteen-hour day, working on the seemingly endless list of pre-production details of the teacher event. We knew it was late when Nick Davis would come back to the office after producing a live Padres game to do post-game office work. Many times, Dan Roper was in an edit room working on *One on One,* and I would bounce in and out to also help with that project. For me, it was an intense combination of work, fun, reward, and growth.

We had evolved in what we were doing beyond baseball and other local sports (women's soccer, high school, and college coverage), and so had our staff. Our "little engine that could" was a powerful train moving along a big and fast track. Our team was growing and changing, and naturally the dynamics evolved, too. My colleagues were talented, smart, and motivated. Some had significant experience and it showed with remarkable work and results. Others were newer, still learning, but with great potential, and part of my position was to help oversee, nurture, and guide them.

Since I began at Cox, I embraced something I wasn't sure I ever would do—teach—namely, with interns or entry-level production assistants, associate producers, and some reporters. It might not have always felt like teaching because we were moving so fast at times, and I had to quickly map out the assignments and hope they were enthused and interested enough to grasp the details and execute the plan. That was a lot to expect of some, I realized, and the learning curve couldn't always keep up with the fast track. That was okay; if they tried and improved, progress was good. Some interns didn't care for the less than glamorous work, but at least had the exposure to know what they didn't want to do. Others reminded me of myself and friends of mine who were so eager to learn and help that they blossomed right before our eyes.

I hired several interns to be associate producers, especially in the first eight years. Some stayed a while as they worked with me specifically, then were offered more responsibility. Several launched their careers from Channel 4, as it was a great place to start right out of college. I tried to guide them based on what I saw and what they wanted to learn. I wanted their internship or work to be fun and beneficial, so I offered opportunities to watch and participate. It has been rewarding to see so many take advantage of that, and fun to be part of their new experiences and growth.

I remembered what it was like to have a tough and less than compassionate boss at various stages of my career, and I didn't want to be that boss. It wasn't easy, however. No question, I had the "half-baked potato" and "efficiency expert" factors from my background that I'm sure I relayed at times in one way or another to those I supervised or to my peers. My own shortcomings and patience were occasionally tested. I appreciated some coaching from peers as I tried to teach, meet my own deadlines, and meet my bosses' expectations. I underscored striving for the best—my best, their best—and wanting the best for our final product and the viewers. No one watching would likely care or need to know about how challenging a project was, although they would likely notice if something was done well or not done according to our normal standards. The viewers deserved to see a high quality product in the end. I was not alone in expecting excellence, but speaking only for what I could direct and control, I set the bar high and expected to reach it. My mantra when I or someone else thought something was going to be hard was to ask, "But is it possible? If it is, let's do it. If it's not, then let's find another way. There's always a way, always a solution. Always."

While not perfect, I have tried to give constructive and useful guidance, pass on some of what I have learned, and offer a reality check of what it takes, while encouraging their dreams and passions, even in a changing industry. I am so appreciative of the words, notes, and phone calls from those many interns and associate producers over the years, expressing their gratitude for what they learned, and their opportunity at Channel 4. Even after playing school and helping my mother as a little girl, I now better understand why teachers love their jobs and watching their students evolve.

As far as our full-time staff, one of my favorite newcomers appeared on the scene in 2002. We were carrying a show called *High School Sports Weekly*. One afternoon, the TV in my office was on and a reporter's voice caught my ear. I walked in to Dennis Morgigno's office and asked, "Who's that guy? He has great energy." It was John Weisbarth. I was glad Dennis hired him as one of our new reporters. I told John I believed he had the potential to be at ESPN in five years because he seemed to have "it," as well as confidence, a command of sports, and a good work ethic. I enjoyed being at John's first spring training. He was excited to meet and interview Padres' third base coach Tim Flannery, one of his childhood heroes. As of this writing, John is not at ESPN, but has excelled establishing himself as a key part of our on-air team. I'm proud of him on another level: coincidentally, we're from the same hometown.

While our Channel 4 team was still adjusting and evolving, it was no longer in that intense start-up mode. That different mode meant some rearranging of assignments and organization. For me, it was an opportunity to focus more on managing and producing my specific program, *One on One*, pre-game segments, and co-hosting *Forefront* and other specials. I would contribute to the other shows, rather than having the managerial and production workload and responsibilities in so many categories. Some of what I did was redirected to other capable producers. It was a change of pace, but welcomed and needed. I could not have, and should not have, kept up the rigors of the first eight years anymore. I was encouraged to take a couple days off each week. This would also allow me to schedule time to do more community events and appearances on behalf of the company and have some balance in my life.

Still, after having my fingers in so many projects for so long, I had to readjust my thinking a little. It was suggested I read the book *Who Moved My Cheese?* by Spencer Johnson, MD. I did, and it helped explain how things happen that you don't always have control of. Sometimes it is good, sometimes you're not so sure.

In December of 2002, my friend Rachel Gershwin gave me the book *The Purpose Driven Life,* by Rick Warren. It could not have been a more perfectly timed Christmas gift. It brought me back to my faith, starting with the first sentence, "It's not about you," and the concept that God has a plan. It also asks, "What drives you?" I had always felt I was able to control my destiny by my choices, my work ethic, and my determination, combined with love and support. I was driven by doing good deeds and using my gifts and talents, and not by money, guilt, pain, or fame. I never entered this business just to be on TV, but rather broadcasting just suited my personality more than print journalism. I believed God gave us free will to make choices and make our path, and that I was on my right path, connecting with people and relaying stories to make a positive difference in the world. In what can sometimes be a highly ego-driven business, that book also helped me recognize how when difficult, unkind, unloving, or frustrating things happen—whether of my own making or someone else's—I can become stronger and better, more loving and more patient, by letting go of needing to have all the answers and so much control, and by having faith and following my heart.

It gave me permission to not have to figure everything out on my own. I accepted and embraced the train's new track, adjusted, and, thankfully, I'm still standing: stronger, happier, more grateful, and more fulfilled than ever. I again experienced that when change happens—whether you choose it or it chooses you—as long as you believe you're operating with integrity and in a good environment, the rewards of resilience can be immense.

This time of transition and ah-ha moments also happened the year I turned forty. I didn't regret implementing the qualities that helped me through my twenties and thirties—striving for excellence, quality control, a relentless work ethic, passion, and compassion—but I still felt a little unsettled. Then I read an article validating what I was feeling. Like the woman in the article, I had worked almost twenty years in the real world trying to prove myself, to get to a place of success and respect, in a dynamic, innovative, competitive, and ego-driven field. Now, I wanted it to be okay to breathe, to stop trying to prove myself every day, and to just do what I loved, have more time to be creative, enjoy the work more, contribute to my community and society, and let go of the need to control everything. I realized, ah-ha, it was okay.

Throughout this transition and our channel's growth, I also understood better that people, even those in the same profession, have different paces, and that's also okay. At this point, for me, there could be a finish line of sorts, or at least a rest stop, where it was also safe to finally exhale. Oddly, it wasn't always easy after eight years of managing so much, but a little less work—with a little more flexibility and personal time—was liberating. It equated to an unexpected gift not only of time, but a sign my company valued, respected, and trusted me. After a trio of ah-ha moments, I felt I could turn a page, and write a few more, too.

You Oughta Write a Book

After interviewing Ted Williams in 2000 and then going to Cooperstown for Dave Winfield's induction in 2001, I recall talking with my mother about how unexpected my career had turned out to be, not the reporting and storytelling part, but the sports part. I had come to take a lot of it in stride, but was quickly reminded how unique my position was when my mother would ask, "What are you doing today?" My answer was, "Just going to the field to grab some interviews." She would comment how I made it sound a bit blasé, so routine, as if it were no big deal. It's not that I didn't appreciate it, but it was my work world. There had been many moments when I pinched myself, realizing how rare and special it was to meet and spend time with elite athletes. So many people had asked me what it was like to interview someone or to be in their home. I would share some of my experiences, and they were always interested to know more. My mother suggested I write a book about it. I thought, *Maybe I will.*

I put the idea aside, thinking that five years of *One on One* might not be quite enough of a track record for a book. A year later, Cox Vice President/General Manager Bill Geppert and I were talking about some of my experiences and my odyssey and adventures of meeting such stellar athletes. He also suggested, "You oughta write a book."

Again, I put it aside while work and life issues kept me busy. Then, in the fall of 2006, I finally had the gumption to broach the subject with the new man at the helm of Channel 4, Craig Nichols. My idea was to tell my story and answer the many questions I had received about my background, my experiences interviewing the athletes, and also include their stories. Craig was enthusiastic about my vision from the beginning, and he and Cox approved of my using the scripts, notes, and images from my years producing *One on One*. I visualized a book similar to Charles Kuralt's *On the Road with Charles Kuralt*. He was a wonderful storyteller with CBS. I had watched and admired his work for years. His book was a compilation of transcripts from his televised stories. Mine would be similar, but I would include my story and the back-stories of this most unusual pairing of a non-sports fan with what I would call *Hall of Famers, Fan Favorites, and Rising Stars*.

Considering I write for a living, it was hard to write on my regular days off, so tackling this independent project has been spread out over time. I kept the project quiet for more than three years as I spent my vacations, a week or ten days at a time, writing at condos, cabins, and friends' getaway homes. I skipped a few of those annual trips with my mother to write. She had hip surgery in 2008 and was not up to traveling anyhow, so it all worked out. I seemed to be single at vacation time, so vacations became writing retreats. I set my Mac laptop aside long enough to treat myself to massages, nice dinners, and some relaxation time too, often in Maui at my favorite sanctuary the Grand Wailea Resort and Spa. The first three years I tallied 300 hours of book time; in 2010, while working full-time, I racked up another 1,700 hours for writing and all the dimensions to get it in print by November 11, Veterans Day, and my book launch fund-raising event.

This book has required my mother's term, "stick-to-itiveness." Now, in my twenty-fourth year in television, my fifteenth baseball season so far, almost four years of filling the pages of documents on my new iMac, and tracking down every person included to have their permission to use their picture, and more, here it is. It was hard to narrow which of the shows to feature, but it came down to a few things: the most significant for the evolution and emotion of the show and my journey, and players with hometown connections and/or broad appeal in the world of professional baseball and football. I wish I could include all the show scripts, but perhaps that will be in the sequel.

Must be fate. This was the street in Kauai near where I started writing my book in 2007.

Set up with my laptop and notes, a tropical view on a writing retreat 2008.

Writing in snow and sun, after four years, the book is done!

CHAPTER 7

The Back-Stories and Their Stories

Everything but the Audio and Video: Interpreting a TV Script for Your Reading Pleasure

You have just read about the in-depth process of researching, interviewing, writing, and editing a half hour or one-hour show. In our TV production, the script is written with various TV lingo and guidelines such as: SOT (sound on tape, a person being interviewed); TRACK or "VO" (my voice reading the script); or NAT SOUND (natural sound of, for example, the crowd roaring, an announcer's call of a highlight, a crashing wave at the beach). *For more explanations, see the Glossary on pages 635-636.*

As the reporter and producer working with an editor, we use those as guidelines for the script to keep things organized. Viewers never see such cues. They just see and hear the result. Think of the scripted show as a highly sophisticated and creative paint by numbers project. In the end, when it is complete and in a frame, the viewers don't know what is underneath or in the behind-the-scenes details, they just see the final piece of art. In the case of *One on One*, it is a video portrait with many layers and textures of information, archival images, and sound.

How does that help as you're reading the stories, the transcripts of the televised show, in black and

	SHOW OPEN Graphic: From Channel 4 San Diego... This is a special one-hour edition of One on One with Jane Mitchell....
Home run Faces... World Series images	**TRACK 01** With big bats **NATS:** 1, 2, 3 hits, action
	TRACK 02 and big smiles... the boys of the Park View Little League All Stars... became the Boys of August.... The Blue Bombers... the 2009 Little League World Series champions.
Childhood pics... PV player shots... Winning Championship Game video images	**NATS** **TRACK 03** Follow their glorious journey... from little boys... to young men... to champions.
	01 SOT: JANE ON CAM STANDUP Lots of little boys dream of being part of a big league clubhouse, and for the Blue Bombers, we just might see their name on a major league uniform some day. But what they have already accomplished is something few can claim and we all can celebrate Park View's story is centered around baseball but is so much more... as the team from Chula Vista not only captured a title... but captured our hearts.
	PART A Music...
ESPN – action Home video – PV uniforms... SB tournament ESPN televised action A loss (Williamsport vs. Texas?) A win ...	**TRACK 04** With every pitch... snag... throw... and hit... the team of tiny... and not so tiny... giants... blazes their victory trail. From hot summer, less than glamorous games... to the spotlight on national television and ESPN Through adversity they find triumph... Through it all... they've grown up.

123

white? I have removed the TV lingo and cues that are both unnecessary to you and could be confusing. What I wrote that a viewer heard on television with my voice is the narrative. I will indicate whenever someone else speaks, including the main subject. If it is someone other than the subject, their name will be indicated. If it is a fan and we didn't use their name, it will just say, "Fan." In the scripts, the quotes are presented as they occurred on television, transcribed from on-camera interviews, and are the words of those being interviewed, with a little editing for clarity.

Use Your Imagination

Here is the reader-participation part. These TV shows included music and natural sound. The scripts are adapted so you can read the stories easily, but also get a sense of how viewers heard and saw the portraits on television. Use your imagination about the "roar of the crowd," "crack of the bat," and "pop of the glove." I will help you along at times, and the pacing will provide the rhythm and emotion of the story. For those of you who have never seen the TV program, it will be like reading the book before you see the movie. For those of you who have seen the show, this will be an opportunity to absorb the stories in a different format, but with some familiarity, like catching up with an old friend.

Coming Up Next ...

Each chapter gives a back-story to that show. In the back-story, I share some of the reasons I featured that particular person. I set the scene and give details about the program or shoot I found interesting, humorous, or otherwise significant, so not every back-story will hit on the same topics. I also weave in answers to some of the most frequently asked questions I am asked as they pertain to particular subjects or shows. (*You can find more questions and answers in the FAQ section on pages 617-619.*)

So whether you are reading start to finish or just flipping to a player or person you are especially interested in, I hope you enjoy learning about their journeys. The show is their story, but as Dennis Morgigno told me long ago, it is also my story to tell with my style. I choose what words I write and say. I choose what parts of the interview to use. I decide what to elaborate on, what to touch on, or what to leave out. In the writing part alone, I humbly, and with great effort and

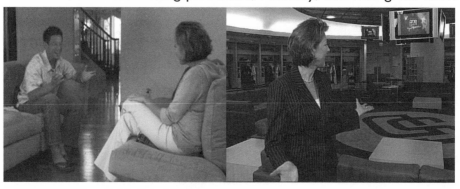

pride, have put together the jigsaw puzzle of words, facts, and elements. I have painted the portraits with much care, attention to accuracy, and emotional detail, weaving in their tangibles and intangibles in an effort to capture their essence.

This continues to be a rewarding undertaking fifteen years into the show's existence, with timeless and sometimes transforming stories. Now it is your turn to live or re-live the stories of your heroes, your idols, your neighbors, or just some good people you might want to know about or introduce your children to through these pages. I hope you feel as if you are in the living room with us, flipping through their scrapbooks, rewinding their videotapes, learning about each of these influential figures. If you are a student or aspiring producer or reporter interested in the process, this will help you appreciate the number of things on the to do list for such a program. It is a lot of work, much fun, and for me, a labor of love.

KEN CAMINITI

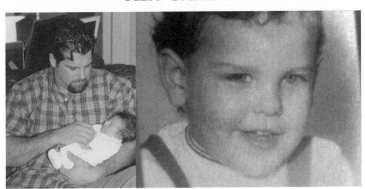

"The part of the show when you talked about his background
was the most interesting for me, especially in retrospect, because Ken
was … more of a warrior than anybody I knew in any sport,
but certainly baseball. You could see Ken as a youngster,
how he was so utterly intense."

— JOHN MOORES, PADRES CHAIRMAN, 2010

In the spring and summer of 1996, I was so caught up in the television project surrounding the Republican National Convention I did not realize the Ken Caminiti sensation was buzzing around the stadium and the city.

I had not witnessed his stellar feats at third base or his powerful at bats. I had not heard about the Snickers® incident in Mexico, nor seen his stoic presence contrasted with his sparkling eyes and smile in the dugout or off the field. These were all part of his mystique that had captivated a community of baseball fans. I was clueless and out of the loop, until early September when it looked as if I would be involved in the new Padres television venture. With the RNC behind me and a few weeks before my first *A Salute to Teachers*, I sat on my mother's couch and watched the Padres beat the LA Dodgers, clinching the Western Division. I picked up on some names, especially Ken Caminiti.

The first time I met Ken was that fall at a Padres' awards banquet. I was among several reporters getting a quick interview about the season I planned to use somewhere as we were developing the channel. While the deal between the Padres and Cox had been made at this point, the channel still didn't have a name, and I didn't have time to explain it or my potential involvement. I'm sure my introduction was brief and meaningless to him, but not for me. I remember the crowd around him, and how quiet he was—almost uncomfortable with all the attention. I wouldn't come to understand that, or him, for a few months.

We were in the high-speed mode of creating Channel 4 San Diego by November 11, 1996 when Cox hired me full-time. My assignments included orchestrating the programming surrounding the live Padres games: the pre-game show, a magazine show—whatever we could come up with. My mission was to help connect the fans with the players by telling their stories, letting the fans get to know the players as people, not just "guys in a uniform." As we were thinking about whom to profile first for the new baseball season, Ken Caminiti was an obvious choice. He had just won the National League MVP award and was rehabbing from shoulder surgery. The big question was: would he be ready for Opening Day?

The plan was to go to his off-season home in Houston. Having no track record with the Padres yet, it seemed smart to go there with people who knew Cammy, as he was called. It would likely make him feel more comfortable, and I would be considered part of the family, which might make things go more smoothly, especially in a fairly tight time frame. The Padres' public relations staff explained the situation to him, and with his approval, the plan was in motion.

Before that trip, a few people who knew Ken well suggested, "He's a quiet guy, so good luck. He doesn't talk much, and don't ask him about his drinking problems of the past. He won't want to talk about that." *Thanks for the advice*, I thought. *I'll take it from here.*

In early February 1997, I traveled to Texas with the Padres' director of entertainment, Tim Young, and the team's lead videographer, Mike Howder. After making a stop in Dallas to interview pitcher Trevor Hoffman, we arrived in Houston. I had done my homework, reading what little had been written about Ken Caminiti, looking at some of the Padres' music videos highlighting him, and asking people about him. I mapped out my questions about his childhood, family, sports, and the various steps in his journey, including his outstanding season of 1996. I created enough of a guideline, based on facts and my own curiosity, to be sure I wouldn't miss anything.

On the morning of our shooting day, February 4, we arrived at the gym where he was doing his rehab following his shoulder surgery. We put a small microphone on him and followed him through his routine. I asked him about his progress and he demonstrated how far he had come by throwing a ball or lifting his shoulder, comparing it to his starting point. It was clear how far he had to go to be ready for the season. His physical therapist helped by describing his progress in layman's terms.

After that two-hour session, we grabbed some sandwiches then headed to his house—a two-story home in a Houston suburb. It was comfortable, with pictures of family and a dining room table filled with baseball memorabilia from people who wanted autographs. His wife, Nancy, and three daughters were there, too. Nancy had just had their third baby a week earlier. We set up in the living room—just one camera and a few lights. He wore a blue and white plaid shirt and jeans and sat on a couch. I wore a conservative jacket over a white T-shirt

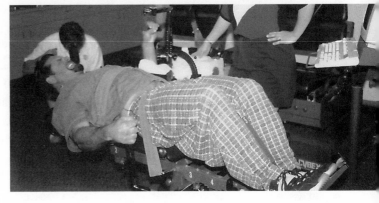

and khaki pants, and sat in a chair. I could not have anticipated this interview would eventually change the course of my career and launch a whole new dimension to San Diego television.

I started from the beginning of his life, and as we went along, I could tell he had so much inside him. It wasn't that he didn't like to talk, it just seemed as if he needed time to think and express himself. The rush of the typical pre- and post-game interviews was not necessarily his comfort zone, and that might have been why people thought he didn't have a lot to say. Given time, and with some patience, I discovered, he would open up. One specific topic arose about the relationship with his parents. That opened the door to talking about his rebellious times as a teenager, challenging times in the early part of his career, and his faith. While referencing his special year of 1996, our dialogue went like this:

JANE: Do you have a sense of why this was your year?
KEN: I don't know. I accepted the MVP award a couple nights ago, and part of my speech was God gifted me this year, and He really looked after me.
JANE: Tell me about your relationship with God.
KEN: Well it's been a rocky one for me cuz in '87-'88 I asked Him into my heart—Jesus Christ—but I didn't do it for all the right reasons ..."

While my questions were simple, his answers revealed so much. I could tell during the interview this was going to be something special. If he had not brought up the subjects I had been warned not to broach, would I have brought them up anyhow? Probably. How could I cheat him, his story, or the viewers of something that was personal, but significant? I'll never know, but I do know I followed not only his lead, but also my intuition, in delving into both obvious and sensitive topics. I had already planned to ask all my interviewees about their philosophy of life, what guides them, or their faith to give them an opportunity to share that side of themselves. In Ken Caminiti's case, just asking about his year opened that door to something that was in his heart.

After three tape changes—about an hour and a half of interview—I turned to Tim and Mike and asked, "Can you think of anything else? Anything I missed?" Surprised by how much we talked and how much he shared, they couldn't think of anything else.

I don't share this to claim I inspired this quiet man to open up. I tell this because in this new venture, I learned it was okay to follow my instincts and to be myself. No matter how much I prepared, just listening and caring showed him respect, hopefully a genuine concern, and made him feel comfortable to express himself. In the bigger picture, it was the unexpected prelude for what was to come. At the time, getting to know players on a personal level was not the norm, certainly not through interviews in their homes. This was fairly new territory, and I was charting the course of the content and my style, not even knowing yet where this would all end up.

We completed the sit-down interview with Nancy beside him and met his girls, including their newborn Nicole, who looked so tiny in his arms. I commented on how he had an All-American family. "All American," he laughed, "with the toys, the blind dog knocking over the lights. Yeah, All-American!"

Cammy took Mike, Tim, and me to dinner that night at Papa Deaux's. I still have the souvenir glass from the restaurant. Mike reminded me recently how when we walked in to the restaurant, ESPN was airing the recorded ESPY awards program where Cammy was accepting the honor for Best Baseball Player. So many people at the restaurant did a double take when they saw Cammy—a former Houston Astro, the NL MVP with the Padres—on TV and right there in person. No question, he exuded an air of distinction, even in his plaid shirt and jeans and accompanied by a posse of three unknowns from San Diego.

When I returned from Texas, I had a meeting to discuss programming with Dan Novak and a few other Cox employees (*see Chapter 2*). With the green light to do a half hour program, I felt it important to supplement Cammy's story with details. So at spring training I interviewed his trainer and saw Cammy in uniform, counting the days until he would be—hopefully—ready for the season. I also believed it was important to hear from his parents, to see where he grew up, went to school, and began his athletic career. My boss agreed. When I returned from ten days in spring training, photographer Cord Cameron and I flew to San Jose for the day to see where it all began for Ken Caminiti.

His childhood home where his parents still lived was modest and in a fairly middle-class neighborhood. They welcomed us and offered more insight about their son. They gave me a bag of home movies and pictures and pointed out the cul-de-sac where young Ken rode his bike. A stop at his high school and San Jose State University provided more content and texture.

I had never written any television script longer than five minutes, other than that Padres ticket info-mercial. It was exciting, but a bit overwhelming, to think how much material I had to work with. The Houston interview, the family interviews, all the highlights and photos from home movies through the pros, plus spring training, and player and coach interviews. I was about to launch into a documentary-length biography and wanted to meld enough of the baseball and sports part of his story to satisfy the knowledgeable sports fan without too many statistics that might alienate a casual fan like me. How would I make it only a half hour? This was a contrast to my background, coming from daily broadcast news, where most stories were about two minutes. It was a huge opportunity and undertaking.

The writing adventure and pure hard work began—hours of sorting through tapes, making an outline, and writing. Finally, with a thirty-page script in hand, I asked Dennis Morgigno to review it. He let me be me in my writing, but he also helped me to finesse and streamline some parts I did not always know how to boil down, so they would make sense and be accurate. In those edits, I was ada-mant that I not leave out anything or the essence of something I felt important to Ken Caminiti's story, including the sensitive aspects of his struggles with alcohol and his faith. I learned from Dennis' guidance how I could present a circumstance that people could relate to without sounding critical, accusatory, or judgmental.

I never could have imagined that my script—the writing, the pacing, and the emotion I wanted to convey—would evolve into something so comprehensive, musical, and meaningful, as I believe it did. I harkened to my earlier years of writing with my mother's guidance, thinking about alliteration and rhythm and to the guidance of Rick Brown, sharing about how a viewer "hears" a story. In concert with my work and vision, the synchronization came together because of my editor, Dan Roper. He absolutely "got me," and got the story from the beginning. He felt it. He lived it. He made it sing. It was the start of a beautiful working relationship, a true partnership in making it all come together.

Thankfully, the program was a hit. People commented about the details, the candid interview, about seeing the pictures and learning who Ken Caminiti was, and how he evolved with the team and in life.

He would go on to be a star and a hero for the 1998 season in which the Padres played the New York Yankees in the World Series. Ken Caminiti was truly loved, and he loved San Diego. After the '98 season, the Padres were embarking on a rebuilding phase. He was a free agent and signed with Houston, closer to home. Fans would see him when he played in San Diego for Houston, then Atlanta. He would always get a round of applause when he returned to San Diego, but things would not be easy for him.

What we didn't know in 1997, and what we would not find out until after he retired, was that part of his "wow" factor while playing with San Diego was not just natural brute strength. Ken Caminiti shocked the sports world in 2002 when he told *Sports Illustrated* he had taken steroids during his MVP 1996 season and beyond, and that he thought others in baseball had too. That revelation—considered the first public admission of anabolic steroid use by a professional baseball player—rocked Major League Baseball and contributed to the eventual exposure of such steroids in the sport, which launched a Congressional investigation and, eventually, a more defined steroid use policy in baseball.

In 1997, however, no one was talking about steroid use, performance enhancing drugs, or human growth hormone, so it did not even occur to me to ask Ken Caminiti what specifically he was taking as part of his fitness or vitamin regimen or to even think he might be doing anything that would cause him problems later on.

By 2004, it was a matter of public record that Ken Caminiti had also struggled with cocaine and substance abuse and that he and Nancy had divorced. The last time I saw and talked with him was February 2004. He was at the Padres spring training camp in Peoria, Arizona. I went up to him without a camera or microphone, just as a friend, gave him a hug, and asked how he was doing. He told me "okay," but that he really hoped he could work a lot more with the Padres, either at camp or throughout the season. To the extent I had come to know him over the years, I felt he was a lost soul trying to find his way back. Again, I could see it in his eyes. It seemed he wanted so much to be okay. He gave me a hug, and I said I hoped things worked out, and that I would see him back in San Diego.

The season went by, and on Sunday evening at about ten o'clock on October 10, 2004, my phone rang. It was a CNN radio reporter in Atlanta, who remembered I had profiled Ken Caminiti. She asked if I had heard the news he had died that day in New York of an apparent drug overdose, a heart attack, or something sudden. I had not. She interviewed me about my memories of him. After I hung up, tears flowed down my face. I was sad that he just couldn't quite overcome his struggles, and that he didn't get a chance for his new beginning.

I never asked him about the steroid use in person or on camera. In the end, his choices and challenges were between him and God. While I didn't like the idea of using such substances, I admired him for being honest and helping bring the serious subject to light. No matter how history or people may judge him, he will forever be part of a magical time in San Diego, part of a special collective memory, and part of my journey. There's much to learn from how he played, how he lived, and how he battled.

In the spring of 2005, Ken Caminiti would have been forty-two. The Padres honored his memory at a pre-game ceremony. They invited his parents, siblings,

Nancy, and their three girls. It was heartbreaking to see how they had lost a man they loved, but heartwarming to see how the fans, players, and organization embraced him and his family. I will always be grateful to the Caminitis, and especially Ken, for allowing me to come into his home and personal life to explore and share his journey.

In 2007, we launched *One on One Classics,* adding new on-camera stand-ups and information to older favorite editions. Ken Caminiti was, of course, our first *Classic,* and I incorporated into the show how the Padres honored him after he died.

He was my first *One on One,* and I pay tribute to him by sharing the script from the show debuting April 8, 1997.

• • •

He did it.

KEN: I'm back!

The National League's Most Valuable Player, Ken Caminiti, defied the odds once again, and made the San Diego Padres' Opening Day line up as the starter at third base. Not a lot of people thought this locker would be full Opening Day, after what Ken Caminiti went through in the off season with shoulder surgery. But underneath that bold exterior is a heart of gold, and this is a remarkable story to be told of the man who by the sheer force of his talent and determination, willed the Padres to a division title last year and is reaching even higher in '97.

His name …

ANNOUNCER: *Ken Caminiti!*

His face, his talent, emerged in 1996 with unbelievable plays, one after the other.

KEN: It was real funny. My wife and I would sit back and we'd reminisce about it now, but back then I would call her on the road and say, "Did you see the game?" And she would say, "What's up with you? You hit another home run." Then I'd call her and say, "Did you see the game?" She said, "No," and I said, "I hit another home run." She says, "You hit another home run?" You know? It was just unbelievable the things I was doing. I couldn't believe it myself.

And through it all, an inspiring yet unimaginable tolerance for pain.

ROB PICCIOLO (Padres Bench Coach): He's the guy that proves to you what mental toughness is.

Around the league, they call Ken Caminiti a throwback—a guy who wants to be in every game, who'll dive for every ball, who'll play through any pain. And in 1996, Caminiti proved just how much he could take. The play: against the Astros April 6,

1996. Derrick May popped up towards left. Caminiti jumped for it and landed on his left shoulder.

> KEN: I remember getting a sharp, sharp pain. I usually don't ask for special attention, but I said I need some time, you know, I need some time, gimme some time 'cuz I was in some good pain. And right after that it got real hot, and then it went kinda numb.

Then, in the next series against Atlanta, a head-first slide into second.

> KEN: And I got the same sensation all over. I dove for Rafael Belliard's ball down the line.

And another dive ...

> KEN: I told the trainers there is something wrong with my arm.

An MRI at the time indicated a slight tear on the left rotator cuff, but nothing cortisone shots and iron-man Caminiti couldn't endure for the whole season.

> KEN: It was considered a dead arm. It was like the pain was done and gone, and it was dead. I had to learn how to play with that just deadness. And I did real well, so I was real happy with that.
>
> JANE: Yeah you did, to say the least.

October 9th, three days after the post season, Caminiti had surgery to repair a severely torn left rotator cuff, two torn tendons, torn cartilage, and bone spurs. Basically, doctors gave him a whole new shoulder.

> KEN: I was miserable, actually not being able to dress myself, not being able to bathe myself.
>
> TRAINER: Here you go, keep it clean ... *[grunt]*

We spent a day with Ken Caminiti in Houston. A day on his road to recovery. It's February 4th, nearly four months after his surgery, and he's come a long way. Catherine Ondrusek is the physical therapist who has become so in tune with what needs to work and when.

> CATHERINE ONDRUSEK: That was the key to keeping him motivated and keeping him fired up—was having success. Every time we started something new, yeah it could be tough, but he had to be able to get through it.

The Cybex machine helps evaluate how much force he can generate while working the muscle. It duplicates the motion he uses to swing a bat or catch a ball and shows the progress of his control and endurance.

> CATHERINE: It's really been remarkable.

In between being a dad and helping with his two daughters and newborn ...

> KEN: I get the girls up in the morning ...

His rehab—physical therapy and conditioning—is four to six days a week.

> KEN: I put them to sleep at night, then I go, I do my lifting.

Eight hours a day. Beginning three weeks after surgery, Ondrusek moved his arm for just twenty minutes, progressing to the point where by the end of December, he raised his arm against a band.

CATHERINE: Merry Christmas. We can get ourselves dressed.

Even break a few habits.

KEN: After I get out of the shower I go to put on my deodorant and I go to the wall and crawl up it.

CATHERINE: You take some things for granted.

KEN: I say, wait a minute, I don't have to do that anymore.

Every exercise, every new phase was complete with the intensity and focus that is pure Caminiti.

[arm work, grunt, heavy breathing, working faster]

KEN: That's one. Tomorrow I'll do two.

Bouncing a four-pound red gel ball from the ground is a vivid reminder of the unbelievable throw Caminiti made in Florida that became his season's signature play. And a reality-check of the extent of the damage, repair, and recovery.

KEN: I feel I'm a little bit away from playing. I'm not a long ways.

Catherine Ondrusek says he's been a good patient, never complaining, never going too far.

KEN: When I'm with my trainer, now that's a different story. I'm a whiny little baby with him. I start thinking back to last year at this time and where I was at. And it gets real frustrating, you know? Everybody says, "Wow, you hit forty home runs last year? Wow. How much do you weigh?" Stuff like that. When you lose fifteen pounds, then you start gaining back all fat, it's just a frustrating time.

That's where his personal trainer of two years, Blake Blackwell, has made a big impact on Cammy. Blackwell, also a new father, has been there every step of the way. From strengthening to developing a strategy for power hitting and creating a diet that will help his body composition and maintain muscle mass.

KEN: He tells me what I'm doing today. "Do twelve. Do twelve. Now do it till you're done."

[Spring training, Cammy swings a bat in the batting cage.]

JANE: You must feel good seeing the progress?

BLAKE BLACKWELL: Yeah, that's mostly what I get out of it is seeing that I can help him out, you know?

And you can't argue with success. Back in a live game at least two months ahead of schedule, Caminiti blasted his first home run of 1997 against the Angels on March 13. From a pennant-winning season to surgery to rehab, to spring training, and into the '97 season, Caminiti's road to physical recovery has given him reason and time to reflect on an indisputably awesome year.

KEN: I always consider myself a player that could help a team and was important to a team, but not MVP status, or have the year that I had. I have always felt that inside. It was there, but I just couldn't put together a year like that.

JANE: Do you have a sense of why this was your year last year?

KEN: I don't know. I accepted the MVP award and part of my speech was God gifted me this year, and He really looked after me, and I really believe that.

Up next, Ken Caminiti opens up about his relationship with God, and guidance, and giving back….

To turn back the pages of Ken Caminiti's life is to see a little boy whose piercing blue eyes, even then, were focused. A dreamer with strong expressions of determination and an attitude of achievement. Ken Caminiti is the youngest of three with a brother, Glenn, and sister, Kerrie. He grew up as Kenny in San Jose, in a house on a quiet street where his parents, Lee and Yvonne, still live.

LEE: Kenny, he was a little "goer." He didn't walk anywhere. He ran from the time he started walking. I don't even know if he crawled, did he?

YVONNE: He did. Well, he tried to fly down the stairs when he was around two and a half. He thought he was Batman and he made it, but, you know, tumbling!

Sports would be Ken Caminiti's passion, his career. He overcame his fear of baseball after a ball hit him for the first time. Caminiti says it didn't hurt as much as he thought it would, so he kept on playing.

LEE: And all the other kids would get out of the way and he'd get the ball. He just had to go where the ball was I guess.

His parents proudly document his career. Pictures, awards, and in a new sound system he bought for them, stacks of videotapes of his games going back to his early days playing his favorite sport at the time—football. That's him on the home movies, number 18.

KEN: For a little guy, I knew how to hit real well. I was considered a defensive back, a monster man. Whatever, wherever the ball was, I read it good.

A serious neck injury ended his dream of professional football, so he started down the long road to Major League Baseball—earning a baseball scholarship to San Jose State. In 1985 he was drafted into Houston's minor league system, and by 1987 Caminiti was in the majors—at twenty-four years old. He married his high school sweetheart, Nancy Smith, in 1987.

YVONNE: Nancy is his perfect mate. She's easy going, laid back.

And although he was very good with a bat and a ball, another relationship wasn't as smooth—the one with his parents.

JANE: Tell me a little bit about that relationship.

KEN: It was a little rocky out of high school and college. I think I rebelled a lot, went down the wrong streets here and there, and just didn't want to listen to the parents and the guidance they are trying to give you. I rebelled hard. To the point where when my minor league career started, they were calling me and wondering why I wasn't doing better here or if I was getting my sleep. So finally, I said, "Just quit it. I'm a grown up, and don't tell me how to live." That kind of attitude. Finally, I just broke it off for a while and did not even talk with them.

YVONNE: I had a suspicion what it was that was just driving him away from us. And he knew, I think, deep down in his heart, we were suspicious.

Suspicious of something Caminiti hasn't talked much about: too much alcohol, and struggling with his game.

KEN: I remember my first year in the big leagues, I was such a scared little boy it seemed like. Managers throw things, and I couldn't deal with that. Instead of saying, you know what, I'm going [to] do the best I can no matter what. I wish I had my attitude now back then; I think I would have been a better player.

To get where he is today took coming face to face with the fact that the tough guy Ken Caminiti wasn't stronger than the pull of the beer bottle. He had a drinking problem.

YVONNE: I think Kenny and Nancy sat down, and I think Craig Biggio and Jeff [Bagwell] made him aware that they were aware that he had a problem, and he didn't think that he did.

But Caminiti's courage shows itself on many levels. And this time, it allowed him to just let go and admit he needed help.

LEE: Something he did on his own, which he did for himself. That was the part. To go through what he did, I'm extremely proud of him for that.

KEN: In '93 when I went in for treatment for myself for alcohol, my parents came down and went through the course with me, and ever since then it's been a real close family. I think a lot closer.

Letting go in '93 reunited Caminiti with his family, arrested his drinking problem, improved his playing, and brought him closer to God. But that relationship didn't come easy, either.

KEN: Well it's been a rocky one for me cuz in '87-'88 I asked Him into my heart—Jesus Christ—but I didn't do it for all the right reasons. I did it for the reasons of trying to make the Christian guys on the team look at me a little different because I was running hard, going out after the games and stuff like that. It wasn't until 1993 when I actually got down on my knees and said the prayers, and watched the little things happen through my prayers, that I really started noticing the difference and seeing how He works. That was my big deal last year, and I tell a lot of people, the way I went about my job was before every anthem or during the anthem I was on my knees and telling Him to look after my family, and I was going to play as hard as I was going to play, and whatever happens happens. And I'm going to hang my hat up and know in my heart that I did my best. And that's all I could have asked of myself.

JANE: It was a blessed year?

KEN: It was.

You can hear it in his voice: this past year and all it encompassed has touched his heart.

KEN: You just have to try and suck in your emotions. It gets kind of tough.

JANE: Why do you have to suck in your emotions?

KEN: I just don't like to appear like a ... it's a guy thing I guess [smiles]!

For Caminiti, looking back is a reminder—not a crutch.

KEN: I can look back at my past and not live in it, and I don't live in my future. I try to plan for my future, but I don't live in it. I just do the best I can.

His surgery and shoulder rehab: a test of his commitment and discipline.

KEN: There is a lot of age involved in my brain nowadays that I don't just do things without thinking about it.

And when asked about his new sense of obligation to be a role model, he says his experiences of success and struggle could make a difference with high school kids.

KEN: The high school level for me would be a challenge, but I think that's where I would hit home the best a lot of times. That's where I started going the wrong ways, going down the wrong roads. I was always a follower, not a leader, and I was happy with that, and I always did what other people did instead of challenging myself and knowing right from wrong and doing it. That's what I do with the kids, is to challenge them to know what's right and wrong, and don't give in to their peers when they know it's wrong, you know? Study and stay in school. To be honest with them, there are drugs out there and they are gonna come your way, and you're gonna be around it sometime unless you shut the door and lock it with a key and don't go outside.

JANE: Now you're a father of three?

KEN: That's scary, but great. I worry about the girls growing up and maybe going the wrong way, and all you do as a father and a parent is try and guide them the best that you can, because they got their own little brain and they are going to do their own things. But you just try and do the right things when they're growing up, and hopefully they do the right thing.

JANE: Do you have a particular saying that you live by?

KEN: "NO!" That's it right there. I believe I am the disciplinarian in the family and they listen to me. I don't think I am real strict on them, but I do want them to respect when I speak to them. That's all I ask.

The Caminiti's house outside Houston is spacious, but even with a multi-million dollar salary, they prefer the "down home" motif rather than pricey interior designers.

KEN: The house is decorated by my girls with their toys and Barbies®; they love to play with them.

An afternoon in the backyard with his girls is not as common as Caminiti would like it to be. That could change as they make plans to move to San Diego year-round. Still, he's a little wistful about how the demanding schedule of a ball player affects fatherhood.

> **KEN:** We have the new addition, and to put her in my arms and for my other ones to come up and give me a hug, it's like, oh my gosh where has the time gone? I spend a lot of time disciplining them, but I need to spend a little bit more time just having fun with them, I think.
>
> **JANE:** Three girls.
>
> **KEN:** Yeah, one more I can have an infield for a girls' softball team.

His wife Nancy is not too hip on that idea, considering she just had a baby, but meet the Caminiti team so far.

> **KEN:** This is Nicole. *[Ken holding the new baby, sitting with Nancy and kisses baby.]* This is our new addition. This is Kendall. Say hello, say hello. And this is Lindsey. Hi. Hi.

Ken Caminiti says Nancy doesn't get enough credit.

> **NANCY:** Well that's nice. I didn't hear you say that.
>
> **KEN:** Yeah, she does the majority of it.
>
> **NANCY:** It's hard because I'm a single parent a lot of the time. You get your routine down and you get used to doing everything yourself, and then when they come back, everything is different again.
>
> **KEN:** I think that's the way it is for a lot of the ballplayers. It's the limelight for us, and you travel a lot, and the guys of course enjoy it. What wouldn't you love about it?

So how is it that a kid who used to fear the speed of a little white ball …

> **KEN:** I was always scared of the baseball until it hit me for the first time.

Grew up to have such a reputation as a tough guy? A man of steel, even "Scary Man"?

> **KEN:** I don't know, but I don't mind it. You know there are a lot of people that say I'm moody, or grumpy, and stuck-up, or whatever, but I just think for the most part, I don't talk a lot … so.

So, who needs to talk, when you can do this?

> *[Highlights]*
>
> **JANE:** Do you ever think you could have had a career like this, but in football?
>
> **KEN:** Yeah, sometimes I think about that for about thirty seconds and I'm glad it happened that way [laughs]! I wouldn't have lasted in football; there are some big, mean, strong boys in that game.

Funny, that's what they say about Caminiti; maybe not the mean part, but strong? Oohh … Just think back to August '96, when he became an instant baseball legend.

So sick and dehydrated from eating bad food, he takes two liters of IV fluids, then asks for a SNICKERS® candy bar. He hits not one, but two home runs.

> KEN: Everyone's asking what's going on? I say, "I don't know." Everyone wants IVs and SNICKERS® in their lockers. It was a dream week, week and a half. That whole month actually was outstanding.

Beyond all the crowds and all the genuine glory for the team, his fame began to really sink in at the end of the season. Story goes: He and his wife Nancy were shopping for a truck in Carlsbad when they stopped to eat at a restaurant.

> KEN: Some friends said, "We heard you ate at Marie Calender's up in Carlsbad today." I said, "How did you know?" "We heard it on the radio." So it's definitely a good feeling to be recognized, and I know that's not going to be forever. I'm diggin' it, and it's a good, good feeling.
>
> JANE: It's got to be overwhelming for so many people to have so much interest in you because of your performance.
>
> KEN: It is. It is definitely overwhelming. That's the worst feeling in the world when you're signing autographs or asked to sign autographs by the parents or kids and you really don't have time, and you get the words, and the looks, and the glares. It's an everyday battle. I try to do my share of signing. It comes to be real hard sometimes for me to go, "Okay it's time for me to get my family, it's late, and get them in bed, too."

But Caminiti says the fans really need to know how important they are to the players.

> KEN: It's a big part of a championship team. You can't win without fan support, I don't think; and how you go onto a field that's excited, and it's exciting, and you feel the energy, and then when you go to a crowd that's got [only] 8,000-9,000, and you can hear yourself thinking.
>
> JANE: Is there something that you don't think the fans know about you that you would want them to know about you?
>
> KEN: No, the least they know about me the better. If they need to know, they can come up and ask me.

Okay, so we asked. Other than baseball, what are your other hobbies? He loves to listen to *Jurassic Park* on his great sound system. And he really digs cars and motorcycles. His garage is closed for shipping to California, but his pride and joy hot pink and black, fully-loaded, customized '55 Chevy got a two page spread in the March edition of *Hot Rod*. Could cars be his focus down the road?

> KEN: I'd like to do some sort of racing. She [Nancy] doesn't want me to, but we've talked about it a little bit. She still won't get into that conversation. I'll start it up a lot, but she'll just kind of like, go back to her book.

Looking into this season, he just wants to play. All the more reason he focused so hard on putting on that uniform Opening Day.

> KEN: I don't mind watching my teammates play, but I'd rather be out there playing if I could.

He's taken a few knocks, had a few shocks, but the adage, "what doesn't kill you makes you stronger" couldn't fit anyone better than Ken Caminiti.

> ANNOUNCER: *The ESPY award goes to … Ken Caminiti.*

And this quiet, intense, and focused man is confident about sharing his milestones and the spotlight with those who count most.

> KEN [ESPY speech]: *What a great honor it is for me to be here tonight …*
>
> JANE: You believe that you were put on this earth to play baseball …
>
> KEN: Yeah, I still believe that because the way He gifted me this year, and I'm able to reach out and do some things for the Lord.
>
> KEN [ESPY speech]: *Number one, I'd like to thank the Lord for the talents He's given me …*
>
> KEN: I'm just trying to do my own thing the best way I know how with some guidance from other friends and people. You know, I'm not a saint by any means, but I try hard.
>
> KEN [ESPY speech]: *I'd like to thank John Moores and his wife Becky, the owners of the Padres. I'd like to thank the Padres for giving me such a great atmosphere.*
>
> KEN: It's just a classy organization to play for.
>
> KEN [ESPY speech]: *I'd like to thank my teammates. My agent, Adam Katz, I'd like to thank him. I'd like to thank my good friend Brian, my personal trainer, Blake Blackwell. Most of all, I'd like to thank my family and my wife Nancy who couldn't be here tonight; we just had a baby girl. And I'd like to say hello to my other two girls, Kendall and Lindsay. Daddy did good. Thank you.*

Sometimes with stardom comes leadership. That's the case with Caminiti, who leads by example and is now sharing and earning the role in the clubhouse with Tony Gwynn.

> TONY: If any young guy was here last year and watched the way Caminiti played with the pain that he was going through, you can't help but be inspired by that.
>
> KEN: Tony is the man, he is Mr. San Diego. So those are some heavy shoes to fill when you have one of the greats saying that you're a good player. And when I came over here the first two months, let's see, I think I had twenty errors, so those shoes are definitely heavy.

Caminiti has earned respect and awards. They are big—like the National League's Most Valuable Player of the year.

> YVONNE: He deserves it. He deserves it. He worked for it. He overcame a lot of things and—God, I'm going to be crying in a minute.

They're significant in the world of baseball and the world of human achievement. But tucked away in his daughter's room is a special honor from the National Italian American Sports Hall of Fame in Houston and some of his best friends from his years with the Houston Astros.

> KEN: They obviously thought I was good enough to receive it, so it's a special award to me.

And there will likely be more, but for Ken Caminiti, just doing what he loves to do—playing hardball hard—is enough.

> **KEN:** I can't go, "Oh, I'm gonna have the year I had last year." I can't do that. I gotta go out there and just do what I did. I'm gonna get on my knees and say, "I'm gonna play the best I can today." I've had people tell me that you are gonna have it hard next year 'cuz you're gonna have to repeat. You know, I look at them and say, "You know what? I'm just gonna go out there, I'm just going to do my best, and if I put that kind of pressure on myself, I guarantee I will fall on my face. Play hard and think, and try not to mess up a whole bunch, 'cuz you might not be here too much longer."

Baseball is part of Ken Caminiti's make-up: his aura, his stamina, his success. But in the end, after some tough innings and some great innings in life, he now knows what's most important to him.

> **KEN:** The Lord and my family.
> **JANE:** Thank you very much.
> **KEN:** You're very welcome.

Whatever the season holds, it has already been an incredible journey for Ken Caminiti. I'm Jane Mitchell. I hope you'll join me next time for *One on One*.

JOHN AND BECKY MOORES

Part of the new channel's mission was to tell the stories of both the players and the key people in the Padres organization. That organization changed dramatically at the end of 1994 when John and Becky Moores bought the San Diego Padres. Larry Lucchino, the Padres' president, was at the helm running and shaping what he called the New Padres. John and Larry were quite public in their new venture, committed to putting a competitive team on the field and to being a part of the community. It was not only the Moores' generous financial commitment, but also their good intentions in following through, that were scoring points and gaining fans. They were accessible, but also exuded a humble profile. They were movers and shakers, transplants from Texas, and a breath of fresh air on the San Diego sports scene.

I didn't know what to expect from them, but I did feel a little pressure, considering these were the new owners, and this was a new business and television venture. The shoot was mid-February, just before my first spring training. The crew and I arrived at the Moores' Rancho Santa Fe house. The ranch-style home had a large yard with exquisite bronze sculptures of children playing and some animals. We chose the living room area for the interview because there was more space for the three cameras and crew. Their home was decorated with beautiful vases, frames, and furniture.

"This business of interviewing is a pretty good skill. I could never do it. Most people couldn't do it. You have a very open way. You don't hide anything. Most people can't do that."

— JOHN MOORES, 2010

John and Becky, with slight southern drawls, were quiet, but very friendly, seeing that we had what we needed. John wanted to wear his green Padres hat—green with a shamrock for St. Patrick's Day. I normally would have preferred no hat inside, but he was proud of the Padres and the new twist of holiday ball caps, and at that stage of the game, I didn't feel comfortable urging him to take it off. Their humility and down-to-earth qualities were particularly appreciated a few minutes into the interview. The lights were too much for the house's electrical system and blew a circuit, over and over. Fortunately, they had an electrician at the house who was able to help, and we just kept resuming the interview. There was

"It was interesting and touching to see how she put together our journey to getting us to this wonderful experience of being part of San Diego and a baseball team. It's one thing to think about it and live it. It's another to see it condensed in a half hour show with all the pictures and her narration. It was lovely."

— BECKY MOORES, 2010

---

nothing we could do, but I felt nervous and wondered if John and Becky would get frustrated by the delays.

In talking with John for this book, in 2010, I reminded him about the electricity issue:

JANE: You were very patient, but we were sweating on the other end.
JOHN: You gotta be kidding me.
JANE: No, just because you were the owners of the Padres.
JOHN: Give me a break.
JANE: No, I remember telling the crew, "don't break anything."
JOHN: Don't break anything? That's funny. That is funny.

As for the interview in general, John remembered something quite specific:

"You asked us, Why did you go off and do this thing [buy the Padres]? And it was curious; nobody had ever really asked us that until you did, and it was nice to be able to talk about it."

Becky's reflections about that day include:

"My very first media interview was with Jane. I have to admit, I was a bit afraid. But Jane made me feel unbelievably comfortable. I didn't feel like I was being interviewed; it was more like I was just having a very enjoyable and re-laxed conversation. I didn't know, at first, that it was going to be so personal, or that I'd get a little emotional talking about 'my guys,' but I appreciated her different approach. It was not at all what I was expecting."

That day in 1997, Becky shared how she had fallen in love with the game, the players, and their families. When she spoke of her boys and the "gladiators," she had tears in her eyes and a slight lump in her throat. While viewers didn't see the electricity issue, they would see what I was touched by: John and Becky Moores, with their millions and good life, had not only come from humble beginnings to make their fortune and later purchase the Padres, but they were emotionally in-vested both in the team and the region.

I came to know them by seeing them around the ballpark and at Padres events. I appreciated how they included me in various Padres front office gather-ings and even invited me to fly in their plane on a road trip to Seattle. The plane ride was an experience in itself, but what showed me another lovely side of Becky was how when she learned I didn't have my car at the airport in North County due to logistics, she arranged to have a driver take me home, to be sure I was taken care of. John has been equally kind in recognizing my work and asking that every show I do be catalogued in his Padres archive for history's sake.

During the 1998 season—the playoffs, the World Series, the parade, the election for the new downtown ballpark—I watched how they managed to stay true to their core values for their Padres family and their San Diego home. With the many challenges that faced them and the Padres after the new ballpark proposition passed, they were not in the public eye as much. By 2004, the ball-park was opening, and I felt strongly we should re-visit their story, because they had forged through the battle and were key to the completion of PETCO Park. They agreed.

A few years later, they began divorce proceedings, and the Padres are being sold to a new ownership group lead by Jeff Moorad. Even so, they are still very much a part of the Padres and the team's legacy. When I shared with John and Becky that I wanted to include the scripts, both graciously replied that was fine, acknowledging you can't change history. The following is the script from the 1997 show and an excerpt from the 2004 edition. They remind us of how their story reflects an important time in San Diego sports and in their lives.

• • •

In this edition of *One on One,* you will meet John and Becky Moores. They come from humble beginnings and are putting their money where their hearts are—in San Diego baseball, in business, and in building a better future for children here and around the world.

> **JOHN** [outside in garden]: This is a piece called "Puddle Jumpers."

Three years ago [1994], John and Becky Moores were quite happy in their Rancho Santa Fe home, surrounded by lush green landscaping and sculptures.

> **JOHN** [outside in garden]: The artist is a gal named Glenna Goodacre that we've gotten real fond of.

It's just what they wanted when they moved from Houston in '89. They were planning to divest from their software company, set financially, for life.

> **JOHN:** We kinda like the notion of havin' a bunch of kids hanging around the place, since ours are gone. I wanted to find the best place in the world to live. I think we were the only people in Houston getting newspapers on a regular basis from North County area.

But they were also planning to move north for part of the year to their other favorite spot, Monterey.

> **BECKY:** I felt like I was over fifty. Your life is over. I was going to garden, and learn photography, and work at the Boys Club up in Carmel, and sort of settle down, live a more settled, quieter life, even though deep in my heart I knew John could never do that.

JANE: At the same time, The San Diego Padres were making national headlines for the fire sale of a number of players by the club's owners. San Diego baseball fans were disenchanted, disillusioned, and really kind of disgusted with what was going on, then enters John Moores. Why did you buy the San Diego Padres?

JOHN: You know, I wish there was a real simple answer for it. The thing obviously doesn't make any kind of economic sense.

JANE: So are you sitting around at breakfast one day, reading the paper, and think, let's do something here? I mean, is it really that simple?

JOHN: No, it wasn't quite that simple. Our son called and said he'd heard the club was for sale. And he said, "Look Dad, if you ever want to do something, do it now, or forget it. It will only come around one time." And when he suggested it, I thought it was a little loopy. But the more I thought about it, I thought, *You know, he's right.*

After someone at the Padres office finally took his call, he began negotiations, and in December 1994 he bought the team for eighty million dollars, with Larry Lucchino as minority owner.

JOHN: So it was a little leap of faith to think that we could be involved in the turnaround. But we still knew it was going to take a lot of talent and a lot of hard work to improve things. And it's still a journey. The journey's not over.

To understand why John and Becky Moores would want to venture on such a journey, it helps to know a little about where they come from. They are both from South Texas and grew up in divorced families. John is the oldest of four children. Becky's two brothers liked sports. She did not. But when John was a little boy, he spent a lot of time on the sidelines with his father, a sports photographer.

JOHN: And football in South Texas is serious stuff, and I looked up at these high school boys like they were Roman gladiators. I was delighted to be there.

He was hooked on sports. But never did he dream he'd one day own a Major League Baseball team. In fact, for a while, he wasn't sure what he would do.

JOHN: I didn't know whether I wanted to be—play third base for the Astros or Secretary of State! It just wasn't clear.

The high school sweethearts married in 1963, and both went to the University of Houston and law school.

JOHN: Part time, full time, sometime, no time! Whenever we could. I think it was harder for Becky than it was for me.

BECKY: Yeah, I was going to say, because I wasn't as smart? Or what are you saying?

JOHN: No, no, no. I think you, well, you did! You worked at it harder than I did, and you had kids to take care of.

He tried the corporate world, working in sales and computer programming at IBM and Shell.

JOHN: I had one year's experience about four or five times, but I'd always been a computer geek. Those things came easily, and they were fun.

The idea on which Moores made his millions was initially offered to IBM. Moores had figured out a way to make IBM's giant mainframe computers run faster. But IBM said no thanks. So Moores took the idea and a thousand dollars and founded his own company, BMC Software.

JOHN: To my utter amazement, it was very easy to develop a product that the market accepted very well. And every time we'd get a little bit of extra revenue, we'd go out and hire somebody to either help us sell it or to develop something new. It worked out very well.

Ready for a change in their early forties, they took BMC public in '91, bringing their worth to some $400 million.

JANE: So suddenly, you have more money than probably most people would know what to do with. How did that change you? Or did it?

JOHN: Well, yeah, it undoubtedly changes what you can do. But the funny thing, the amazing thing from my perspective, is not how much it's changed, but how little it's changed. I don't think we're a bit different.

BECKY: Obviously there are a lot of changes in your life, your lifestyle. Things you can do for your family members. We've given them some opportunities that maybe our kids didn't enjoy.

And a little fun. Their backyard is complete with a tree house that big kids would relish a climb in …

JOHN [home tour]: The world's least frequently used exercise room; I know that.

And even some oversized rocking horses of sorts.

JOHN: I think that's a giraffe. And that one's loosely been called "Puff," or "The Loch Ness Monster," or one or the other.

BECKY: We certainly couldn't own the Padres. We'd have to be able to just afford to go to a game. But I think what I have to watch, what you have to watch, is not taking things for granted.

And that's part of the reason the Moores have been embraced by the San Diego community, the fact that they are down to earth.

JOHN: How could it be any other way than that?

JANE: Well, I think because there are some people in the world of sports and the world of wealth that, they sort of put on a show, and they don't want to be out there, and they don't share their values, and that is why this has been such a refreshing new relationship with you as the owners, and with this community. People say that every day.

JOHN: Well, I hear things like that and I just have to laugh. You know, Becky and I were poor as church mice when we got married, and the number of bonehead decisions that I made in business over the years are enough to fill a bunch of books. So it's kind of hard to be cocky, or I think arrogant. I think, I hate to say, but we're probably more ordinary than not, and I feel very comfortable with that. In fact, I don't think I'd want it to be any other way.

And their way really is a matter of their perspective, their value of family, doing what makes sense, what feels right. The Moores' promises and contributions to baseball fans and business are affecting the region and parts of the world in some surprising ways. That part of their story when *One on One* continues....

Most people who have met John and Becky Moores since they moved to San Diego say they're a breath of fresh air, an unassuming wealthy couple. The Moores don't like to brag about all the things they've done for their adopted hometown. But others are more than happy to do it for them. In fact, John Moores has already found his place in the San Diego Hall of Champions, recognized this year as a Community Champion for his generosity and vision.

[John Moores being applauded at Hall of Champions]

JOHN *[Acceptance speech]: I'm a little embarrassed about all of this, and I've had so much fun with the Padres the last couple of years.*

The list of honors goes on and on, from the American Ireland Fund, to being the first non-African-American to receive the annual Jackie Robinson YMCA's Human Dignity Award for exemplifying the work of Martin Luther King, Jr.

JOHN: There are some things I think people just ought to do for no other reason than it makes them feel good.

John Moores knows what makes him feel good. He knows how to have fun. He knows business. And John Moores knows what he doesn't know.

JOHN: The best thing in the world to do is to hire people that are a lot smarter than you are and have a lot more experience.

When Moores contemplated the Padres purchase, he tracked down a man many felt was the best in the field to operate the club—Larry Lucchino.

JOHN: We called him. We pursued him. There was a real courtship here.

LARRY LUCCHINO: I was able to say quite truthfully, "I'll be happy to help you acquire the Padres, but I'm really in the process of trying to acquire the Pirates, and I'm really intending to go back to Pittsburgh."

JOHN: The challenge was to sell him on San Diego, which you would think would be very easy!

LARRY: I used to describe myself as incurably eastern, but I've found that I have been cured.

JOHN: I had to sell him on the personal chemistry between the two of us.

LARRY: From the first day I met him, when he was in blue jeans and a T-shirt and was not permitted in the hotel restaurant for that reason, I knew I had a different kind of guy here.

JOHN: He's very much a hands-on guy, and he wanted to make sure there weren't gonna be three hands making this cake.

LARRY: You've got to have some harmony and point of view among owner-ship, and John understands that.

JOHN: Baseball is not a passive investment for me.

LARRY: He's got what's most important in life and business, and that is a great sense of judgment about issues, and people, and crises. And we have fun together.

JOHN: I'm extraordinarily happy with what he's done and the way we get along.

What they've done is spearhead three commitments to the San Diego community. First, to field a team worthy of the fans' support ...

JOHN: I've been a sports fan all my life. Generally, I don't care who owns a ball club, whether it's a baseball, football, basketball, or Tiddlywinks! I just don't care. I'm more interested in what happens on the field. It's inconceivable that fans would ever pause to think who owns this ball club or that ball club, unless they're making a lot of mistakes.

Which, rightly or wrongly, is what Padres fans had come to expect from the people who owned the team before.

LARRY: You may have a journalistic first here, because John and I are dis-agreeing on this. I think our fans do know who the owner is, and they're very proud of the way John is owning the team.

The "fire sale" left burn marks throughout the community, but they're healing over nicely now.

LARRY: I saw a fan wearing a uniform, not with a player's number on it. He was wearing a uniform that had a number one on it, and at the top it said Moores.

JANE: The second was to create a warm and friendly environment.

JOHN: You've done your homework! Ballparks ought to be a fun place for families. If they're not, then frankly, we're just missing a business opportunity.

A sound strategy according to the head of the Greater San Diego Chamber of Commerce.

STEVE CUSHMAN: If it isn't fun, you're not gonna do it. Now if people are having fun, that's when they spend money. And that's what it takes, obviously, to employ people. 'Cause what we're really talking about is jobs.

The Moores' daughter, Jennifer, is involved in player and community relations, with the team's third goal for the Padres to play an active part in their community. The team's building or renovating more than sixty baseball fields as Little Padres Parks.

CHILD [at Little Padres Park]: This park was not like this. It had rocks and everything on it. We would slide off the bases. Now it looks like a Padres Stadium field. Thank you, just thank you!

And they also established Padres Scholars to help some high school kids go to college.

BECKY: We had some aspects of our lives that could have been difficult, and nothing like the children we may be dealing with. So we know how important it is to have a good childhood and have some opportunities.

JOHN: It was a struggle for us to go to college, and it just doesn't seem fair, frankly, to see a bunch of nice kids not growing up thinking—not expecting to go to college.

Or for college players to not play baseball in a decent stadium. The Tony Gwynn Stadium at San Diego State University is nothing like it was just a few years ago. Baseball Coach Jim Dietz remembers well.

JIM DIETZ: I mean, the termites were taking over the press box, and I knew I was going to have to tear that down.

But that changed when Dietz met John Moores at a community function.

JIM: And he made some comment, he said, "I understand that your facility is in pretty bad shape." And I said, "That's an understatement John," and that was kind of the end of it.

A month later, Moores asked what it would cost to do the facility right. At first, Dietz gave a lower figure.

JIM: And he said, "I'm not buying that Jim." I gave him a higher figure. He says, "That's more like it."

And a donation of nearly four million dollars transformed the park, but the Moores didn't want the park named after them.

JIM: Oh no. John didn't want any part of that. In fact, they probably would have felt more comfortable had people not even known it was them that donated the money. John asked what I thought about naming it after Tony Gwynn, and I thought that was outstanding because Tony Gwynn, in a lot of ways, is an example of what our program and our university is all about.

The Moores say SDSU reminds them of their alma mater, the University of Houston, to which they've contributed some seventy million dollars. In fact, the more you look at the lives and works of John and Becky Moores, the more it becomes clear that owning the Padres is yet just another dimension from the far-reaching philanthropy that has characterized their lives since they sold BMC Software. Take, for example, the River Blindness Foundation.

JOHN: It had a very simple function, that was to pass pills out to people in the extremely remote locations, principally in Africa, that were in danger of going blind because they'd been bitten by a fly that carries a parasite, and the pills, which were free, merely had to be taken once a year ….

More than one hundred million people are at risk of River Blindness. Drug giant Merck & Company supply the pills; the foundation and former President Jimmy Carter's center in Atlanta distribute them.

PRESIDENT JIMMY CARTER [Carter Center interview]: The program grew more rapidly than anyone had ever anticipated. And about two years ago—John and I were very close friends, we'd go fly fishing together in Alaska and so forth. We had just about reached a limit to what one person could do. So John said, "So Mr. President, why don't you see if the World Bank or someone else can help us with the financing." So I had a meeting at the Carter Center with the World Bank, IMFM, some other major donors.... And the World Bank finally saw the sterling nature of this program that John had created, and said, "We will volunteer to raise $120 million over a ten year period."

JOHN: If this young man will take one pill, once a year for a number of years, he'll never go blind. It's that simple. The challenge is to find them.

PRESIDENT JIMMY CARTER: And last year, eighteen million people were treated free of charge because of Merck's generosity, and because of the innovative spirit of John Moores.

And while another matter doesn't have such dire consequences, John Moores is on another crusade to build a new ball park he says will ensure a bright future for Padres Baseball in San Diego.

JOHN: A new ballpark is going to have to be considered for San Diego, only because the fans and the rest of the United States, where new ball parks have been built, have been wildly enthusiastic.

A recent poll shows that even with the stadium controversy, San Diegans are willing to consider a new baseball-only facility, which probably owes to the Moores' unrelenting courtship of the locals from the Little Leaguers who play on the Little Padres parks, to their parents who cheer on Tony Gwynn and Ken Caminiti. And the Padres are trying to internationalize baseball, reaching into Japan, to Hawaii, and Mexico.

TIM FLANNERY: If you would have done that years ago, people would have griped, people would have complained. When they asked this ball club to go down to Mexico and play, because of what this ownership has done, we will go and do anything for these people.

SCOTT LIVINGSTONE: You know that if you do well, they're going to appreciate it.

Yes they do. And Becky Moores, never much of a sports fan before the purchase, can hardly stay away.

BECKY: I probably saw 150 ... I'm going to say 150 games last year, maybe 152. I mean, it really kills me if I miss a game.

JOHN: I've always been kind of nuts about green things.

John Moores likes the color green, and we don't just don't mean the color of money. From his luck-of-the-Irish green baseball cap to green gardens at his home ...

JOHN: It's a big old bear ...

To a bronzed bear by the artist who designed the bear that sits in front of the Alaskan capitol.

JANE: This must be your other passion?

JOHN: I've been fishing in Alaska a bunch of times, and I've seen these guys just like this. This guy, he's working on a big old salmon.

He also likes the green of a baseball field.

JOHN: Well, I must say, my childhood was in South Texas, and I was never in a place as nice as this. This is the way it should have been.

Maybe that's another reason he and Becky have invested so much in the Padres. But for all that they're doing—for the team, for fans, for business, and others outside the world of sports, the purchase, the partnerships—the passion for America's favorite pastime has affected them, personally. Just listen to the dynamics in this conversation about John's childhood memory of athletes on the field.

JOHN: I looked up to those high school boys like they were gladiators.

BECKY: I really sort of snickered at that a little bit. I mean, I'm being really honest. I just thought it was immature.

JOHN: It is immature!

BECKY: I didn't feel that way even at first with baseball, when I first started really loving it, and loving the guys, and knowing them personally, you know. I still didn't feel like they were gladiators coming out there to play. But at the end of last year, I began to feel that way too! And I was almost embarrassed about it, you know. It was like my heroes coming out there, the gladiators coming out to fight this war. See, it brings tears to my eyes! Because I really think I felt, at one level, I felt bad about being critical of other people over the years, but also felt embarrassed because I felt, gosh, I'm as immature and juvenile as the rest of them.

JOHN: And we've never had this conversation. This is a first ...

BECKY: But there was a feeling—I talked to my sister-in-law about it—is that all of a sudden, when those guys would go out to the field, you did feel they were fighting a battle for you, you know? [Wiping tears] Now I'm going to have a good laugh, and I'm still not quite comfortable with that. I have to allow myself to feel that that's okay.

JOHN: That's okay.

Owning the Padres has changed Becky and John Moores in other ways.

BECKY: I think one thing John left off, and he'd [prefer] that I leave it off ...

JOHN: What's that?

BECKY: Why he bought a baseball team. What I would say is there is probably a little bit of middle-aged crazy there!

JOHN: A lot of middle-aged crazy there!

She says they had never really been social people, preferring to host small dinner parties over gala events.

BECKY: John, I would say, used to be shy. But because of his exposure to the public the last few years, had gotten more comfortable I guess with dealing with public and groups. But I really didn't want to. To tell you the truth, I had no interest. Immediately, with Opening Day last year, I couldn't find him, and they were looking for him to talk to and [I thought] maybe I should go over and introduce myself. And all of a sudden felt this—almost transfixed—into feeling more comfortable meeting people and enjoying meeting people.

In fact, as of the time we visited their home, Becky had done only one other television interview, and that one was very brief.

BECKY: So, I think what baseball did was sort of give me a new lift, a new youthful lift to my life. My sister-in-law [Molly] and Rachel, my twelve-year-old niece, and I spent the summer going on the road trips—that will make me cry! It was a very special summer for us.

JOHN: Well, it was a perfect summer. Perfect. I mean, it would really be hard to equal. I don't know how we could equal that, frankly, this year, unless we did go to the World Series. Even if we are in the Division again, it could never be as meaningful for us, or as exciting.

With financial means most couldn't fathom, their health, and a team re-energizing the record books, the fans, and the city—what more could they want?

JOHN: I'd like the World Series ring, real bad.

The last World Series was won at Yankee Stadium. John Moores discovered, to his surprise, his own competitive nature when he was in New York during the offseason at banquets honoring Bruce Bochy and Ken Caminiti. In both cases, the World Champion New York Yankees were well represented in their own backyard.

JOHN: The juices got flowing pretty good on that one. I really want a World Series ring. I want to be competitive with those guys.

BECKY: I would like my boys to have a World Series ring.

JOHN: I want Tony Gwynn, and I want Caminiti, and I want Finley, and I want Bochy, and I want all those guys to be there—and I think they can do it.

Baseball can have a tough and gritty side. But Moores says life is too short to put up with that.

JOHN: I don't want to be around people that I don't want to be around, it's that simple. And one of the terrific discoveries with the Padres has been I really like these guys. There are just no bad apples, and our goal is to make sure that's a trait of the Padres as long as we're associated with the club. One of the charming things about last season or so has been watching terrific human beings like Ken Caminiti and Steve Finley, who have just blossomed. I mean, we feel a little bit like grandparents, I suppose …

BECKY: Parents! Let's not go to grandparents, please!

JOHN: They've exceeded their expectations and they got there by hard work. There's no doubt about it. They truly, honestly appreciate it.

And, the players appreciate the ownership.

> **KEN CAMINITI:** The owners, Moores, Lucchino, it's just a classy organization to play for.

> **TONY GWYNN:** That's how much respect they have. Not many people who play have been able to say that they love this organization. I do. I do.

Coming off an incredible year and the reality that anything can happen, Moores says he's managing his expectations about the success of the team in 1997.

> **JOHN:** It's dangerous to start predicting where we'll end up. But I'm optimistic. I guess I'm always optimistic.

Whatever John and Becky Moores have learned and earned, they have also taught and shared.

> **JIM DIETZ:** It's so refreshing to see someone who tries to give things back and who are really genuine, good people.

> **JANE** [at the Little Padres Park]: What do you want to say to the people who helped make this happen?

> **CHILD** [at the Little Padres Park]: Thank you!

> **SCOTT LIVINGSTONE:** And they're baseball people, and they love the game, and you love to play for people like that. It's awesome!

> **TIM FLANNERY:** Mr. Moores is doing things for society and for people. He is incredible. The amount of money he gives out. Those are the types of people you want to be wealthy.

> **DONNA FLANNERY:** Our timing couldn't have been better because we left in the Kroc era and missed all that stuff in between, and when we came back, it's just wonderful!

> **LARRY LUCCHINO:** If you want to understand John Moores, you better start with that. You better look at the size of his heart and the generous nature he has.

It is written, "In the beginning, there was no baseball. But ever since, there have been few beginnings as good as the start of a new baseball season. It is the most splendid time in sport." And many would agree. John and Becky Moores, and partner Larry Lucchino have helped make baseball in San Diego a splendid time again.

> **JOHN:** Every day I wake up and can't believe we're fortunate enough to be here.

Think back Padres fans, it's been fortunate for us too. I'm Jane Mitchell. I hope you'll join me next time for *One on One*....

Between 1997 and 2004, much happened in the building of a new downtown ballpark for the Padres. The proposition passed in 1998 and lawsuits, in part, delayed the process. Eventually, the Padres prevailed, and the ballpark was back on track. The following are excerpts from the show debuting April 2004, the week the ballpark opened.

• • •

The new home of the Padres, PETCO Park, reflects San Diego: a showcase not only for a team on the field, but for how this Major League Baseball club is part of the region beyond the box score. The ballpark itself exists thanks largely to John and Becky Moores, who are in their tenth year as the Padres' owners. Now, in a rare in-depth interview, you'll hear their feelings about the emotional and financial toll it's taken to get here, and about their hopes for a new chapter for San Diego.

> JANE: To see it all coming together, that must be a huge sense of relief and satisfaction.
>
> JOHN: Oh, no question. One of the surprises, for me at least, is although I knew the park was beautiful, it looks a lot better with a lot of people in it.
>
> BECKY: The surprising thing is, maybe even though it's all new, it still feels sort of like—I feel at home.
>
> JANE: When I first interviewed you in 1997, you said it was a little leap of faith that you bought the team, and maybe a little "middle age crazy," to use your term, Becky.
>
> BECKY: And I wish at this point we could say it's middle-aged crazy, but, un-fortunately, we're passing—or past—middle age.
>
> JOHN: So you think it's senior crazy?
>
> BECKY: So, yeah, I guess it's senior crazy.

[In terms of the ballpark odyssey:]

> JOHN: Yeah, I didn't anticipate there was going to be quite the public scrutiny. I thought I'd just show up at a ballgame and watch it, and then periodically meet with, you know, a CEO and a GM, and periodically get a signed baseball. I didn't know that it was going to be as intense and demanding as it's been. And I also didn't know, to be quite candid about it, that it was going to be as rewarding as it feels right now.
>
> JANE: Seventeen lawsuits in all. Does it still get you a little irritat-ed when you think about that part of it? How it kind of slowed the process up?
>
> JOHN: Well, it's unfortunate. It cost this ball club a couple of competitive seasons and I think that's not what the voters expected. That's certainly not what I wanted. I must say that nobody should ever feel sorry for anybody that owns a baseball club. I mean, it just doesn't get much better than it does for us, living in San Diego and owning a team like the Padres that operates in this ballpark. I mean, life is absolutely terrific.
>
> JANE: But there were delays and there was a dark cloud ...
>
> JOHN: Yes.
>
> JANE: And that was not a good time or a fun time. And you sort of retreated over the years. You sort of pulled out of the public eye, and we didn't see you, and ...
>
> JOHN: Yeah.
>
> JANE: You clearly seemed ...
>
> JOHN: Well, it was ...

JANE: Down, or out, or mad?

JOHN: Well, it was …

JANE: Or stressed, or all of the above?

JOHN: I don't know that—I don't know that I was mad. The stress was clearly there; there's no question about that. It was an extraordinarily stressful period. But I think it was unavoidable that the project had to go through that sort of process while we were resolving seventeen lawsuits.

BECKY: Certainly it was—I don't know whether to use the word depressing—but it was depressing. It was a down time for us, and I think it was very hard personally. Putting it in perspective: Your health's good, your kid's health's good. You're not starving yet.

JANE: What kept you going then? The positive? The reinforcement? Just the determination to get through this?

JOHN: Well, for better or worse, I just don't quit projects. And there actually was no opportunity to quit. I mean, it's like you …

BECKY: Not like there was a lot of choice.

JOHN: You buy a ticket on the bullet train and you can't get off at midpoint when it's going a 180 miles an hour. And I didn't want to, either.

JANE: But not everyone may have stayed with it and stuck with it. But is it just a matter of—you wanted to win? To finish? To not …

JOHN: No.

JANE: … be defeated?

JOHN: No, it didn't really have anything to do with that; it had to do with the fact that we started—it really wasn't about me winning or losing. It had nothing to do with that. It had to do with the fact that the right thing for the community was to build the ballpark. The right thing for the Padres was to have this ballpark. The right thing for San Diego was to have the Padres here permanently. And, selfishly, the best thing for us was to be able to watch ballgames for a long time in this, the new ballpark. I mean, that's really the big payoff for us ….

March 11, 2004, the first game is played at PETCO Park. It's an exhibition game between San Diego State and the University of Houston. Larry Lucchino, who had moved on to the Boston Red Sox after 2001, was invited by John Moores to throw out the first pitch: a fitting reunion and an opportunity to talk with the two men who had spearheaded this feat. They agreed to do an interview with me in the still unfinished Sony Club restaurant area behind home plate ….

JOHN: You know, we both survived. I mean, that's remarkable. I think we had a terrific collaboration. I think Larry and I are quite different personalities, and I think it probably took the combination of the two, because I think we approached most problems in a different direction. San Diego is a really tough nut to crack, the politics are really hard, Larry is much better at details than I am, and that is why his fingerprints are all over the ballpark.

> "Getting the ballpark built and open was obviously a complete joy, but more than that, it was like the weight of the world was off our shoulders.... There were some truly rough moments in getting it done.... Looking back on it, when we opened the ballpark, there was a wonderful feeling, but I never had a chance to express it until we talked, and Larry [Lucchino] and I sat down ... but we never had a chance just to sit down like old friends and celebrate what we had accomplished together. And it was nice, we said it, it was done, and then it was just time to go on and worry about the next opportunity or problem.... It was sweet. It was a very sweet moment.... Frankly, we wouldn't have been talking about it if we hadn't been there with you."
>
> —John Moores, 2010

LARRY: It's great to be here sitting beside him on this historic night, because there were some really nightmarish moments during the whole process, as you go back to the beginning. It was not an easy thing to do.

And for Lucchino, leaving was a tough time.

LARRY: It was hard to leave, but the opportunity in Boston was so good, it made for a very pleasant alternative, very positive. We love it there. We still feel very deep roots here.

They seem to be a great example of how things can change, wounds can heal, and friendships can continue.

JOHN: I don't know the wounds were ever as deep as some people might have thought. I mean, Larry and I had a great partnership for a long time, and this is the obvious sign of success on this. I feel as good about everything we did as I possibly could. And you know, like all of us say, we're gonna get amnesia about how tough it was over the years. There were some things that were extraordinarily hard, but it kind of seems worth it now.

LARRY: Absolutely, I'd go exactly [with] that. The proof is in the pudding as they say. Look at what the partnership begat, and its something we can all be proud of. It's gonna be a point of civic pride for a long time, and we'll feel a little sense of satisfaction that we helped contribute to that.

JOHN: Absolutely.

"Even the second time, seven years later, after the ballpark was finally opening, and we had all been through a lot, we felt not only obligated to talk about the challenging times, and exciting times, but felt comfortable knowing Jane would treat the sequence of events and our perspective fairly. Not just because she was with the team's TV partner, but because of how we had seen her consistent work and style over the years.

Jane has contributed greatly to Padres fans by connecting them with the players and the organization. Especially in the first decade of being with the team, I have been fortunate to know the players personally—they were my boys—and how they were with their families and what they did for our community. But I still learned so much more about them by watching the shows, and our fans did, too. I was always moved to see them open up with Jane, and allow us all into their lives."

—Becky Moores, 2010

TONY GWYNN

"I think I told you this when you started, that if you do this really well, people will know. And, I mean, that's exactly what happened. You've done that gig so well that you've stamped your name on it in this town and everybody knows it…. And I think, as a working individual, I think that's what we all want, is that we've left our mark, and I think you have."

— TONY GWYNN, 2010

Entering this new world of sports, I was learning relevant names fast. Being a native San Diegan, Tony Gwynn was a familiar name, but I didn't know his importance. When I heard him referred to as "Mr. Padre," I quickly realized his place in the baseball landscape, and he jetted to the top of my list of people to profile. The Padres' public relations staff arranged for us to meet and interview him the day before he was heading to Peoria, Arizona for spring training.

I did my homework. I researched his background. He played basketball at San Diego State, won several Gold Gloves and batting titles, and had a memorable, videotaped conversation with batting great Ted Williams. I felt fine about all of that. The one area I was a little nervous about was making sure the whole "interview at home" experience went well. I had been told Tony was the leader of the Padres' clubhouse. (No pressure.) If everything went well, I would be in. If it didn't, I believed his opinion could squelch our new mission, or at least my part of it. I don't know if he realized he had such influence or if he would have used it had it not been a good experience. I was determined not to find out and to make it a good day.

In February 1997, photographer Dan Roper and I met Tony for the first time at El Cajon Ford at an autograph-signing event. He was cordial and agreeable. I was impressed the moment I shook his hand. We watched and videotaped as people of all ages stood in line to meet him. I liked how he took time with each person, especially the kids, who stopped by the table. Tony was very thorough in explaining to one little boy how to break in a new glove. The boy learned something. I learned something. Eventually, that tidbit made it into the show.

We thought it would be fun to capture Tony doing normal things, including driving home. We kept the microphone on him, and Dan sat in the driver's seat rolling tape as Tony drove and talked. I was driving our Channel 4 car. We could have done a show just on that ride. Tony is personable and truly has the gift of gab.

He and his wife Alicia have a beautiful, spacious home, which is comfortable and unpretentious. We set up around the kitchen table, and I continued to learn all about a man who had a place in San Diego sports like no other. I interviewed Alicia, then his two children, Anthony and Anisha, and talked with Tony outside as we watched Anthony shoot hoops on their basketball court. Who would have known we would revisit that video some thirteen years later for a show on Anthony, who made it back to San Diego as a Padre in 2009?

At the time, it was all just the beginning. Dan Roper and I saw Tony at spring training and throughout the early part of the season. On Tony's thirty-seventh birthday, I interviewed him at the field about his eight home runs already that season—more than he had ever hit in a year—and how he said he was going to decide how much longer he would play rather than retire just because he was an older player. He was matter of fact, as usual. His show debuted in June.

While I hoped for the best, I wasn't sure how Tony would respond to the program. I was certain his reaction would set a tone for others and their openness to my *One on One* mission. I did not dare ask, as that would be too risky, in case he didn't like it. But soon, my curiosity was satisfied. A few days after the show debuted, I went to the stadium early for batting practice. Tony was sitting in the dugout. He called my name, and when I looked over at him, he gave me a thumbs up and said, "Good job. Well done." Tony's validation gave me an added boost of confidence.

For the next four years, I was privileged to watch Tony Gwynn play, see him hit that home run in the World Series at Yankee Stadium in 1998, be part of the effort to capture his "Road to 3,000," then be in St. Louis for hits 2,997, 2,998 and 2,999 and in Montreal for number 3,000. He retired at the end of the 2001 season. The Padres presented a spectacular Tribute to Tony on the field after his final game, and Channel 4 carried it live and replayed the ceremony.

Tony Gwynn's presence, participation, and influence were important in my development as the producer of *One on One* and helped sustain and grow my relationship with the players and the community. He understood the importance of genuinely connecting with fans. He also understood the power of television, good storytelling, and of documenting moments, including his. That doesn't mean I didn't have to work, at times, to convince this humble man that he needed to make time for me and our crew to do our job of telling his story at different stages of his career. My persistence and power of persuasion, in part, prevailed, and he obliged every time, even with his very busy schedule.

In 2003, Tony was coaching at San Diego State University and I wanted to do an update on his life since retiring. We scheduled a shoot in January, before my Maui vacation and annual spring training jaunt. At a cozy coaches' lounge at SDSU's baseball complex, we pushed two overstuffed black leather couches together, set up lights, two cameras, and picked up the story from 1998 to cover his final playing years, his decision to retire, and the transition to coaching.

I was a little excited going in to the interview, because I knew how I wanted to end it. This is a rare scenario for me because, usually, I don't know what might come out of the interview other than the obvious. In this case, I had a little something up my producer's sleeve, and it dated back to the summer of 2001.

When I was in Cooperstown for Dave Winfield's induction into the National Baseball Hall of Fame, I did many interviews about Dave; that's why we were there. I made it known to the Hall of Famers on hand that I was from the Padres' TV station, and several offered comments about another Padre—Tony Gwynn. I saved those taped comments and had them transcribed just for this very occasion. Knowing Tony would never say he deserved to be in the Hall of Fame, I wanted him to hear why others already thought he should and would be there. As we were nearing the end of the session, I read verbatim what Yogi Berra, Don Sutton, George Brett, and others had said about him. It was a priceless moment, to see Tony's expressions of joy and surprise. He was almost speechless. It might not have been a unique interviewing tool, but I felt good knowing I had saved those sound bites for this perfect *One on One* occasion.

Fast forward to December 2006. The Hall of Fame election results would be delivered January 10, 2007, and we wanted to be there to document the presumed phone call informing Tony he had been elected. We weren't alone. After much discussion, it was agreed that a photographer and producer from Channel 4, the Padres' rights holder's station, would be part of the pool video team along with an MLB crew to capture the call and reaction at the Gwynn home. With  the Padres' and Gwynn's desire to keep the number of crew to a minimum, I did not go. I wish I could have been there, but I was glad we had additional video for the show. I was also happy Dan Roper was one of the photographers on location. He deserved to share in the moment and was very good in high-pressure situations. This was a one-time only, nothing-could-go-wrong-technically situation: the lighting, the sound, especially getting "the call" on Tony's mobile phone, and Tony's reaction all had to work—and it did.

That afternoon, after hearing it on the radio then watching the video from the house, I walked from our new building next to PETCO Park to where the Padres had set up a stage and podium for Tony to address the media and fans. I listened to all the questions about the call, his accomplishments, what it meant to go in with Cal Ripken, Jr. All were worthy and appropriate. However, what wasn't asked was something I thought we would all want to hear about, and he would want to comment about, but probably wouldn't bring up himself. So I stood up, and with a little bit of a racing heart, said, "I know you're all about heart and soul, and your family. And I think people would be interested in what you're feeling and what you think your dad would be thinking right now?" He started to answer, but with his voice shaking, stopped to compose himself before he spoke. Some people later commented, "Leave it to you, Jane, to make him cry." I didn't do it with that intention. Rather I was simply seeking an honest, heartfelt answer to a legitimate topic. After all, we in the media and Tony's fans knew how much he loved his father. How could we not honor that relationship by asking about it? Later, I would come to know even more about why that question triggered such emotion.

The 2007 *One on One* season debut would be called "Tony Gwynn's Road to Cooperstown." Two months after the call, the crew and I arrived at the Gwynn home for the interview. It had been ten years since I had been there. Parts of the house had been remodeled, but the large glass case filled with awards and the wall with jerseys and photos marking his career were even more plentiful with another decade's worth of keepsakes. I expected to capture his reflections about his career and life overall, his feelings and thoughts surrounding the Hall of Fame election, and anticipation of what lay ahead. That would indeed be plenty and fertile ground to continue his story, but there would be more.

What I did not expect was how he would reveal to me something very personal about the relationship with his father. Tony had said many times over the years that he and his father argued about whether he should stay in San Diego or go to another city with a team that might have more of a chance to win. Tony had been open about this dialogue as part of his chronology and explanation about why he chose to stay with the Padres, and even why he wanted to prove to his late father that his decision was a good one and the right one for him. So had I just listened, expecting him to recount the same story, I might have missed a revealing link between those arguments and the significance of how Tony's life changed after his father's death. By listening closely, I heard him say that he and his father had argued on a Friday, and the next day, Saturday, his father passed. Having lost my father, I know how significant a final conversation can be. The one with my father was, thankfully, a good one. I could not imagine had it not been. Perhaps that's why I was so in tune when I heard the almost melancholy lilt in Tony's voice as he walked through the timeline. Then, when I commented I had not heard that story before, he said, "Nobody has." This was a special moment, not to be exploited, but to be explored.

After talking with Tony, his wife, Alicia, sat next to him on the couch for an interview. I mentioned to her that I had never heard that story. I remember the exchange vividly, but did not put it in the show because it seemed more like part of the process of the interview, which was not as important as what he shared—at least when there was limited time. That show was about Tony, not about me. Now, sharing about the back-stories of my experiences, here is the conversation between Tony, Alicia, and me recorded as we were settling in for the interview, but was not in the show:

TONY: I didn't let people get close. I did that purposely, and not many people knew that Dad and I argued that Friday and he passed Saturday. I didn't tell that part 'til today, and Jane picked up on it and had to think for a second, *Wait a minute, did he just say they argued Friday and Dad died on Saturday? I did not know that. I need to go back and ask him about that,* and she did, so ...
JANE: My final conversation with my dad was a Friday and he died Saturday.
ALICIA: That was a long interview you guys had.
TONY: I told you, I hit Jane with that bombshell. She had to dig into that one.

ALICIA: Remember, she's a newsperson, a journalist.

TONY: I know, I was surprised. First of all, I couldn't believe that I said it, to be honest. But ...

ALICIA: That'd be the first time that's ever come out.

TONY: I haven't ...

JANE: Well, don't tell anybody else! This show comes out in April!

ALICIA: No. We'll give it to you first. We've been with you for a long time.

Two unexpected things came out of that day: first, a story that helped us understand Tony Gwynn's determination to justify why he wanted to stay in San Diego his whole playing career; and second, my realization that the Gwynns had the confidence to trust me with that information, expecting I would treat it with the care, respect, and the perspective it deserved.

Considering *One on One* and Channel 4 San Diego were the keepers of the largest comprehensive video archive of Tony Gwynn's life, and that he was a broadcaster for Channel 4 games and a San Diego icon, there was no question we should be in Cooperstown to document the pomp and circumstance surrounding his induction into the Hall of Fame. The only question encompassed logistics: Would we have special access behind the scenes to capture some of his special events moments, plus time for a sit-down interview there?

Understanding other San Diego stations would be going to Cooperstown that summer, too, I was protective of our unique relationship with Tony and the Padres, and persistent in what we had to be able to do at the Hall of Fame during the long induction weekend. Because of my two previous trips, I knew what was possible. Other stations should certainly have access, but I believed as part of the Padres family, we needed additional access and assistance. Trying to explain that without sounding arrogant or bossy is challenging when you're in a conference call meeting with Padres and Hall of Fame executives. While they were in agreement, I felt I had to speak up and help give direction because I knew, from experience, what was essential. My station manager, Dennis Morgigno, supported my quest. I was, of course, willing to work within reasonable limits and compromise to accomplish that. Because Tony was going in to the Hall of Fame with Cal Ripken, Jr.—both first-ballot inductees—there would be record-setting media interest. Planning was critical because I didn't want to short-change the final one-hour program, one that would be on television and in the archives for a long time. Thankfully, everyone involved in making the decisions about what we would be able to do agreed on a good plan.

With a notebook including an outline, prewritten anchor stand-up scripts, an itinerary, and game plan, Dan Roper and I traveled to Cooperstown that Tuesday, July 24, 2007—my third time and our second time together. (My first was Dave Winfield's induction in 2001, and our first together was 2005 for Jerry Coleman.) The highway from Albany to Cooperstown was familiar, as were the two-lane roads and tree-lined streets taking us back in time. We coordinated renting a large house outside town with several bedrooms to share with the Padres' production crew: Erik Meyer, Jennifer Hughes, Chris Hardy, and Media Relations Assistant Leah Tobin. We were collaborating on video, interviews, pictures, and coordinating with Tony, so it worked well to share a house.

A few things stand out from that trip. We had access to the Hall of Fame Plaque Gallery, where the beautiful bronze plaques hang in perfect symmetry. Our second night, we set up the equipment in the gallery for my on-camera stand-ups that would connect the various segments of the show. I felt more comfortable this third time, but I also felt more pressure not to miss a single nuance of what this induction meant to Tony and to San Diego fans.

Compared to the other two times in Cooperstown, it was clear the village would swell even more with the induction of Tony Gwynn and Cal Ripken, Jr. No question, there were more Orioles fans than Padres fans, but San Diego was well represented. Beyond that, I was moved by hearing Orioles fans comment on and compliment Tony Gwynn. While they might not have seen him play much in person because he was in the National League, Orioles and Ripken, Jr. fans knew about Tony as a hitter and a quality person in the game. We found ample fan insight and opinions.

The comments were equally abundant from Hall of Famers. Those mostly took place at the beautiful Otesaga Hotel. For this weekend, the Otesaga was locked down except for Hall of Famers, their guests, staff, and anyone with special credentials. We were given such credentials for a few key times. The first was Tony's arrival at the hotel on Thursday, July 26, 2007. We were there when he got off the bus with his family and stepped onto the hotel porch. He greeted me with a hug and hello and we did a brief "How does it feel in this moment?" interview and then followed him inside for check-in and meeting other Hall of Famers. This was a moment that could not be re-created. To hear the natural interaction and comments and to see the genuinely nervous and excited Tony Gwynn in his straw golf hat and special "Number 19" running shoes were priceless moments, and exactly why I lobbied to have the special access back at that spring meeting.

Another such moment came when we were allowed to be on the porch as all the Hall of Famers and their wives or guests were loading up on buses to go to the private party at the home of the Hall of Fame President, Jane Forbes Clark. Even with cameras in tow, we were like flies on the wall, seeing Tony talking with his stellar colleagues, all dressed up and taking in the excitement of this surreal moment.

The sit-down interview in Cooperstown did not come stress-free, however, and I wondered if we would even get it. That Friday, the Hall arranged for a group interview opportunity with writers, television, and radio reporters, and promised we would have him afterward. I had suggested the gathering be set up inside the hotel, just in case the bad weather forecast was correct and to avoid any other potential issues, such as noise from cars or landscape work, which don't mix well with television production. Instead, the interview location was set for outside the golf clubhouse under some trees.

When the rain and thunder were imminent, a spontaneous plan B moved the session inside to the men's locker room at the golf club. Before the rain poured, everyone scurried inside and squeezed into a changing area of the clubhouse. Even with the delay, and knowing Tony's time was tight, I reminded organizers that we were promised a one-on-one interview before Tony had to be elsewhere. All I could do was exhale and wait for the other print and television reporters to finish. When they did, the Hall staff ushered them out, as planned, and we moved in quickly. There was no time to stress at this point, so once we sat down, I focused. Knowing Tony well, and how this part would fit into the show, I felt confident and in control. He was good, too. We did a second taped piece addressing the fans that would play Sunday on the big screen at PETCO Park. Pictures from that session are among favorites, knowing that, even with slightly damp hair, that day had positive results.

After Tony left, I interviewed his brothers and wife for their feelings about Tony's big day. For years, I tried to persuade Tony's mother, Vandella, to do an interview with me. Even knowing I'd be gentle with her, she kindly declined. The

closest I came was August 6, 1999 in Montreal, Canada. We were covering Tony's "Road to 3,000," expecting he would get his 3,000th hit that day facing the Montreal Expos. It was his mother's birthday, and six years to the day that he hit number 2,000. Photographer Tom Catlin and I were in the dimly lit, private restaurant area behind home plate at Olympic Stadium in position to get comments from his

wife, Alicia, and Tony's mother before or after Tony's at-bat. They were ordering dinner, expecting there would be time before the potential big moment. Then, at his first at-bat, Tony hit a single, tallying number 3,000. The small crowd of 13,000 roared, and the Gwynn group was whisked away and escorted out to the field to congratulate Tony. It happened so fast I did not get much of an interview, but we did capture their jubilant moment. By Cooperstown, in 2007, I thought maybe someone would persuade his mother to do an actual interview with me, but to no avail, and that's okay. I have incorporated Mrs. Gwynn's influence on Tony throughout the various shows, because he has always recognized his mother and how much she means to him, and that is part of the heart of his story.

Saturday, July 28, 2007, our two crews strategized to gather several quick sound bites from the Hall of Famers participating in the golf tournament. We could do that at the first and sixth holes, along with dozens of media who all wanted a piece of the big names willing to do interviews, too. Some of our shots weren't so pretty—with radio and print reporters' microphones pushed into the subject's face—but we managed to get what we needed. Most importantly, Tony was gracious in granting me another short one-on-one interview at the course. He made it clear he would take care of those who had stood by him all along, and he did. Padres still-photographer, Chris Hardy, captured several moments of me in action with Tony. I rarely get those, so his, combined with some our interns snapped with my camera, are treasured photos, and I thank Chris for keeping me in the shot as part of documenting Tony's induction weekend experience.

We appreciated being invited to the party for friends and family Saturday afternoon, but for us, it was still work because we were rolling tape. I don't know if we were outside or getting a bite to eat there, but Dan and I were not in position to roll when Tony and Alicia addressed the crowd. It was one of the few times I had heard Tony get choked up, but it was not on tape. Sometimes that's okay too, and I enjoyed taking it in as a guest, even if just for a few minutes.

Beyond the festivities, another mission was on the list. Hall of Fame infielder Rod Carew was one of Tony's idols growing up, especially because of his hitting. Mr. Carew did not golf on Saturday, so there was no opportunity to interview him at the course. The Hall's media relations staff tried to let him know my goal, and they approved my meeting him at the hotel porch quickly, *if* I could find a way to meet with him. Determined to have a comment from the man Tony so admired, I took matters into my own hands. Tony's agent and my friend, John Boggs, agreed to pass along a message, but I still didn't know if Mr. Carew would respond. Then we thought, *Why not just call the hotel and ask for his room?* So I did, and a young man answered—Rod Carew's son. I explained my urgent request, and he suggested I call back in a little while when his father would be there. In the middle of the Gwynn family and friends party, I called again, and to my surprise, Rod Carew answered. He was kind and accommodating, and we met him on the hotel's porch for a five-minute interview. I rarely do this, but afterward, I asked if he would take a picture with me. Persistence paid off. Would the viewers have known the difference if it hadn't worked out? Maybe not, but I had to try because I felt his comments would add poignancy to Tony's story, and I knew he would appreciate hearing from Mr. Carew. I'm not sure if Tony knows this back-story, but if he reads this, he will.

Induction Day, Sunday July 29, 2007 was spectacular. The rain stayed away. The sun was out, and so was a record-breaking number in a sea of fans that filled the field and hill for the outdoor ceremony. We had access inside the fenced area where we placed our camera and were able to say hello to Gwynn family and

friends as they found their seats. We waited for Tony's son, Anthony Junior, to interview him about how his father was handling the big day. Before the ceremony began, I stopped for a few moments and just took it all in, as a reporter and as a fan. I was proud to have come to know Tony Gwynn, to have learned from him, watched him play, and helped share his story. I had goose bumps even in the heat of that sweltering summer day.

As I wrapped up the interview with Tony earlier that year in March, he declared now that he was going into the Hall of Fame, that particular *One on One* would probably be the last one he would need to do, unless he "goes to the moon" or something. With a smile on my face and certainty in my voice, I reserved the right to do one on that, or something else, and he conceded that option. Sure enough, two years later, in 2009, there would be another *One on One* interview with him, but this time, it was about his son. He was happy and proud.

The following script is the one-hour edition of *One on One* debuting August 24, 2007, encompassing Tony Gwynn's life story and his induction into the National Baseball Hall of Fame.

• • •

"Mr. Padre," Tony Gwynn.

> TONY *[HOF speech]: I never really looked at what I did as being anything special. I loved the game. I think that's why you guys are here today, because you love the game.*

Now immortalized in the National Baseball Hall of Fame …

[Jane standing inside the Hall of Fame Gallery]: It's hard to describe the aura of greatness and accomplishment surrounding you here in the beautiful gallery of the National Baseball Hall of Fame in Cooperstown, New York. It is hallowed ground. Not with a sense of arrogance, but rather history, respect, and even confidence that America's pastime will live on for generations to come. Tony Gwynn is now among those enshrined here as one of the best to have ever played the game.

[Symphonic, moving music with images of the historic Hall of Fame]

Elegant, but not ostentatious, a step inside this shrine is a step back in time. Words etched on the wall remind visitors, "In the Hall of Fame Gallery are plaques dedicated to baseball's greatest heroes upon whose shoulders this game has been built." In the grand archway the first inductees, the class of 1936, includes Ty Cobb, Babe Ruth, and Honus Wagner. Along the walls, bronze plaques with images and words are captivating, like reading a good book. But here, there's a new hero, a new character on every page. The words paint pictures of careers on the diamond, decade after decade. Babe Ruth, "greatest drawing card in history of baseball." Hank Aaron, "hit 755 home runs in 23 year career to become majors' all-time homer king." Ted Williams "batted .406 in 1941, named Player of the Decade 1951-1960." And then there's the plaque that gives unexpected goose bumps—the name Willie Keeler. His plaque's description? "Hit em where they ain't. Baseball's greatest place hitter batting champion '97, '98." That's 1897 and 1898, a hundred years before Tony Gwynn would accomplish similar feats. Yet, now, Gwynn joins Keeler and other legends as part of the one percent who make it to the majors and then become brethren in the Hall of Fame.

[Music into list of names at the ceremony]

GEORGE GRANDE (announcer): Say Hey! Willie Mays, Yogi Berra, Brooks Robinson, Reggie Jackson …

To tell Tony Gwynn's journey of becoming a Hall of Famer, we begin at the end, Induction Day, Sunday July 29, 2007.

GEORGE GRANDE: Rollie Fingers, Willie McCovey, Sparky Anderson, Rod Carew, Dave Winfield.

Of the sixty-one living Hall of Fame members, a record fifty-three are on stage for this annual celebration of excellence.

GEORGE GRANDE: Bill Mazeroski, Sandy Koufax, Lou Brock, Johnny Bench, Gaylord Perry, Billy Williams, Ozzie Smith. Please welcome the newest members of Major League's Baseball Hall of Fame, Cal Ripken, Jr. And Tony Gwynn. *[Applause]*

With some 75,000 baseball fans gathered at the outdoor Clark Center site, 25,000 more than the last record crowd in 1999 …

DALE PETROSKY: This is the largest induction ceremony in the history of the baseball Hall of Fame and you're part of it.

JANE FORBES CLARK: The men behind me are the definition of Hall of Famers: character, integrity, sportsmanship, and incredible baseball careers. As the Chairman of the National Baseball Hall of Fame, it's my honor, Tony, to welcome you into our Hall of Fame family.

[Music and applause …]

Baseball Commissioner Bud Selig reads his plaque's inscription.

BUD SELIG: Anthony Keith Gwynn, 'Tony' 'Mr. Padre' San Diego Baseball Club National League. 1982-2001. An artisan with a bat whose daily pursuit of excellence produced a .338-lifetime batting average, 3,141 hits, and a National League record-tying eight batting titles. Consistency was his hallmark, hitting above .300 in nineteen of twenty Major League seasons, including .394 in 1994. Renowned for ability to hit to all fields, frequently collecting opposite-field hits between third base and shortstop. Struck out just once every twenty-one at bats. A 15-time All-Star, a 5-time Gold Glove award winner. Hit .371 in two World Series, 1984 and 1998. Congratulations.

[Music and applause …]

TONY [HOF speech]: For me, this story kind of begins in Long Beach, California. As a kid growing up, my brothers and I watched baseball all the time, played it all the time in our back yard, and for us, I don't think any of us thought that hitting a fig, or hitting a sock ball, or hitting a wad of tape was going to turn into this, just unbelievable.

Tony Gwynn had been to Cooperstown twice before, as a player in 1997 for an exhibition game and tour of the museum, and in May of '07 as an electee, for an orientation. But this time, this sultry summer weekend would be the ultimate visit for him.

TONY [HOF speech]: I played for one team, I played in one town. I told the people of San Diego when I left to come to Cooperstown, they were going to be standing up here with me, so I hope they are just as nervous as I am, because this is a tremendous honor to be here today.

Like those who'd come before and many who'd come this time, travelers know the trek is long but worth the magical destination ahead. With Albany, New York a landmark, one picturesque route is to travel down the interstate exiting onto a two-lane highway: "Cooperstown, 51 miles."

The summer landscape includes clear blue skies, wispy clouds, freshly cut fields with an abundance of lacy white flowers. Lush green trees line rolling hills with old farm houses and horses, and an occasional babbling brook.

The road leads to the doorstep of Lake Otswego, a summertime mecca for locals and visitors with boats and canoes and peaceful days, nestled close to the charming village of Cooperstown. And with ease, the sights and sounds turn to baseball.

[People talking outside of a store …]

167

The store signs reflect a kindred spirit about our "National Pastime." Here, where the flagpole's the center of town, "Rivals" become friends, "Legends are Forever," and "All Baseball Fans" are welcome. And this year, they pay homage to Padre Tony Gwynn.

> **FAN:** Yes, we had to be here. We've been waiting five years to be here. It's giving me goose bumps.

And Oriole great, Cal Ripken, Jr ....

> **FAN:** I was born in Baltimore, but spent a majority of my life in San Diego, since, you know, '71. I get the best of both worlds. I'm just so happy.
> *CAL RIPKEN, JR. [speech]: I was listening to the other Hall of Famers on the bus. They couldn't remember a time seeing this many people, so for us, to come here for the first time on induction weekend and see so many people here, we cannot begin to say thank you enough. So thank you.*

More of Tony Gwynn's induction speech later on *One on One*, but first the career, circumstances, and phone call inviting him here to Cooperstown....

Through 2007, there's never been a unanimous vote for a person on the ballot for the Baseball Hall of Fame. Not even for Babe Ruth, Ted Williams, or Lou Gehrig. But Tony Gwynn, with 98 percent, and Cal Ripken, Jr., with 99 percent, sure got close. They are elite first ballot inductees and received among the highest number of votes ever. Both well above the minimum of 75 percent, and more than Gwynn could ever have imagined. As a kid from Long Beach, a San Diego State basketball and baseball star, and a young outfielder for the San Diego Padres, Tony Gwynn held the Baseball Hall of Fame in high regard. A place for legends. Untouchable. Unreachable.

> **TONY:** I thought it was cool early in my career that I got to play with some guys who I thought were going to be in the Hall of Fame.

What a difference two decades make: a 15-time All Star, with more than 3,000 hits, 8 batting titles, 5 Gold Gloves, and a career .338 batting average; 17th highest, all time.

> **TONY:** I can't lie. When I retired, I watched every Hall of Fame ceremony from the time I retired until January 9th, actually. And, you know, you just don't know.

He retired in 2001 and two years later we sat down with him for a *One on One*, knowing he'd be eligible for election in 2007. He listened to quotes from Hall of Famers gathered during our 2001 visit to Cooperstown for Padre Dave Winfield's induction.

> **JANE:** Ernie Banks said he was going to be there when Tony Gwynn comes into the Hall of Fame. Willie McCovey said, "One of the greatest hitters of all time." Don Sutton said, "If it were possible to waive the five-year rule, they would do it for Tony Gwynn. He'll be here."
> **TONY:** Wow.

JANE: Yogi Berra said, "A shame he's going to retire after this year. But, he feels he's had enough. He'll be in the Hall of Fame."

TONY: Wow. That's nice. It's really nice. And I tell people this all the time because, you know, since I retired I get introduced as "future Hall of Famer," you know, "first ballot Hall of Famer," all that. We have to wait to see, you know. I dread talking about it because I don't want to jinx myself. Believe me, I want to get into the Hall of Fame, but it's not my call. It's not my call.

Fast forward now to early morning January 9, 2007 …

TONY [Reflecting on the day]: Announcement day is a blur, a complete blur.

The Gwynn home in Poway begins to fill with family and close friends. Our cameras and a crew from MLB.com are graciously allowed to document the day.

[Posing for photos, wife kissing Tony on cheek.]

TONY: Everybody in my house, "Ah don't worry about it, that phone's going to ring, that phone's going to ring, that phone's going to ring." And I'm like, "Well, we'll see. We'll see in twenty minutes." And twenty minutes turned to fifteen, to ten, to five, till I sat in my chair and I put my phone right there and I—just sitting there waiting, waiting, waiting. And when it rang and I looked at it and it was 212 area code; I knew that they don't call you to tell you, 'you *didn't* make it,' so …

TONY [January 9 phone conversation]: Hello?

JACK O'CONNELL: Hello. May I speak with Tony please?

TONY: This is Tony.

JACK O'CONNELL: Tony, this is Jack O'Connell with the Baseball Writers Association of NYC. How are you today?

TONY: I am good.

JACK O'CONNELL: I am calling to tell you that the baseball writers have elected you to the Hall of Fame. Congratulations.

TONY: Wow …

JACK O'CONNELL: Tony, are you still with me?

TONY: Yeah, I'm here.

JACK O'CONNELL: I'll give you a minute if you need it.

TONY: Yeah, give me a minute. [Holding back tears.]

JACK O'CONNELL: I understand your feeling, pal.

TONY: Give me a minute …

[Alicia gives Tony a hug and there is applause after he hangs up the phone.]

TONY: I got over my crying and stuff and picked up the phone, called my mom. Said, "Mom, your son's a Hall of Famer." And [clears throat] she didn't—she didn't buckle an eye. She—she said, "I knew it."

Then he calls his brother Chris …

TONY [on phone]: I'm happy, but you know I think about Dad a lot.

TONY, JR. [toasting in kitchen]: I just hope I can put the bat on the ball like you did. You can do it!

[Champagne glasses klink.]

And takes non-stop congratulatory calls …

TONY: All right, thanks Mr. Commissioner.

After a national conference call with writers, Tony changes into a suit, then he and his wife Alicia take off in a limo toward downtown.

TONY [at podium at PETCO Park]: To stand before you today being called a Hall of Famer, is truly more than I could ever imagined. So, and I love you guys, too.

[Applause.]

His late father imagined it. Charles long believed in his son's talent and potential. But by late 1993, while struggling with heart disease, he told Tony he should leave the Padres for bigger opportunities.

TONY: And we argued about it and I just told him, I said, "Dad, this is where I'm supposed to be." You know, he's like, "Man, don't you get tired of losing? Don't you, you know, don't you want a chance to win a world championship?" And I said, "Yeah, but it's not going to mean as much unless I do it here." And so he was upset that day. And I thought about it. It was a Friday, so I thought about it that weekend and was going to call him back and, you know, again try to explain to him the virtues of playing in one city and stuff, and we lost him that Saturday. And so it bothered me for a long time. I wasn't sure if I was going to take his advice or, you know, decide to stay and, you know, after …
JANE: You mean Saturday of that week?
TONY: Yeah, I talked to him on a Friday and I was going to wait over the weekend and talk to him on Monday, but he died that Saturday—Saturday evening.
JANE: I didn't know that, that your …
TONY: Lots of people didn't. I never really talked about that but …
JANE: Was that…. Do you feel guilt? Or regret?
TONY: No, no guilt. Regret in that I, you know, just—you know, I didn't … I … I tried to let him calm down and then call him. Out of this whole twenty years, twenty-five years now of playing baseball and going through some ups and downs and then struggling and having success, that sucks the most; not picking up the phone that day and maybe an hour later, a couple of hours later, just picking up the phone and calling him, but, ah …

Now knowing that dimension of his loss, we better understand his reaction to this question back on announcement day.

JANE: I know you're all about heart and soul and your family. And I think people would be interested in what you're feeling and what you think your dad would be thinking right now?
TONY: Uhh … [pauses for a moment] I think he would be pretty proud today. [Pauses again] *[applause]* I think he'd be pretty darn proud [points to audience].

That special day in San Diego was just the beginning of a six-month emotional odyssey that would eventually make its last stop here (in the Hall of Fame.) The hectic schedule and being honored coast to coast, all coming up on this special edition of *One on One* from Cooperstown....

Tony Gwynn made a career of doing his homework and being prepared. But starting with the day he was elected into the Baseball Hall of Fame, even he wasn't ready for the whirlwind that becoming a Hall of Famer entails. While that beautiful sunny day at PETCO Park is part of the blur of January 9, 2007 for Tony Gwynn, countless fans are clear about what Mr. Padre means to them.

> JANE: Why did you want to come down here today?
>
> FAN: Oh, just to see one of the greatest hitters of all time.
>
> FAN: We love him, we love him because he is faithful to San Diego and he has a place in our hearts.

As Tony Gwynn steps away from the stage, his young and proud San Diego State Baseball team sends him off with the Aztecs' fight song.

> *[San Diego State athletes singing Fight Song]*

While busy with interviews and checking out his new car from the Padres, his wife comments about the call.

> ALICIA: That was the first time I've seen Tony ever break down and need a minute to get his composure.
>
> JANE: What are you thinking about right now?
>
> TONY: I'm thinking about having fun.

Starting with a trip to the Big Apple for a Hall of Fame media blitz with national media, MLB.com, an appearance on the David Letterman Show and the Home Shopping Network ...

> TONY: You know, when it was over, I was like, wow, I just can't believe we just went on national TV to hock our own stuff on national TV!

A day spent autographing memorabilia is topped off with comment by a San Diego fan at the New York airport who told him:

> TONY: "I think most San Diegans are proud of you because you handled things the right way, you played the game, you did your stuff in the community. And I just want to say thank you." And I, you know, in New York, you know, in a commuter airport, that's kind of the last thing you expected somebody to say. You kind of thought he was going to ask if you had a eight-by-ten or something you could sign for him. But when he said that, it just—it kind of dawned on me that a lot of people genuinely are enjoying the fact that you're going to the Hall of Fame.

After sleeping most of the way home ...

> TONY: It was like, did that just happen? Did we just.... Did I just go to New York and sign all that stuff and then ... now here I am back at home. And it's like my cake was still in there from announcement day and people had

brought cookies and cakes and pies and stuff, and I was just like, you know what? I gotta go to work tomorrow.

> TONY [coaching]: Hey pitchers let's go!

Not surprising to his coaches and team.

> TONY [coaching]: Hey Cameron, you gotta touch the bag!
> BRANDON GLOVER (SDSU Center Fielder): This is his heart. He grew up around here and he went to school here and this is his love now. I know that he left his game behind and it's nice that he's in the Hall of Fame and nice to see that he still cares about us and gets back here in a matter of time.

As for being at PETCO Park for announcement day?

> LANCE SEWELL (SDSU Pitcher): It was nice to be able to support him and kind of give back to him for at least a little bit for what he does.
> BRIAN LUCAS (SDSU First Baseman): You try to be as much like Tony as you can because he handled himself so well, so you kind of use him as your ideal person to look at and try to be like, or at least I do.
> MARK MARTINEZ (Assistant Coach): I think he knows what he is on the national stage, but at the same time he loves these kids and he loves coming to work and helping these guys hopefully live a dream.

It's Saturday March 9, 2007. Two months since the call, and the Hall of Fame electee and his Aztecs are playing in the second annual Tony Gwynn Classic at PETCO Park. Between games …

> TONY [on field]: These things make me nervous …

A tribute to him …

> TONY [on field]: I'm thrilled that people remember [clears throat] what I did there on the baseball field. It was a great time in my life.

A precursor to the summer ceremony …

> TONY [on field]: God, that is so hard. How am I going to get through Cooperstown, man. Whoo. It's gonna be real hard.

After the meeting with the umpires and listening to his daughter sing the national anthem, Coach Gwynn has a job to do. Still, the induction speech is a daunting task.

> TONY: We'll get it done, we'll get it done.
> JANE: You'll deliver.
> TONY: I hope so. 'Cause if I don't, I'm going to hear about it for—trust me, I'll be hearing about it forever.

So, he's preparing.

> TONY: Every day I write down something. You know, somebody I need to thank, something I need to—who needs to be remembered.

He keeps his speech under wraps as the spring unfolds and a proud city and team celebrate his journey with a "Countdown to Cooperstown" at the ballpark.

[Music and applause]

In May, his Aztec team is out of contention for the NCAA playoffs. But the silver lining? He's able to travel back to San Diego in time to see his son play. Tony, Jr. had been called up to the bigs with the Milwaukee Brewers.

[Game broadcast] **TONY:** Can't tell you what a rush it is to see him sitting down there man. It's pretty awesome.

By July 19, it's Tribute to Tony Weekend, with the ballpark decorated with brown and yellow bunting—Padres colors his rookie season—and the countdown number down to single digits. On Saturday, there's an on-field ceremony before the historic unveiling of the nine-foot Tony Gwynn statue behind Center Field at the "Park at the Park."

TED LEITNER (Emcee): None having immortalized like this with their image on a statue that will be in this city for this generation and for all the generations to come.

DICK FREEMAN (Padres President): Tony's baseball records are amazing, but he is a lot more than that. To many people, he represents the city of San Diego, and he has represented our city very well. We're lucky, and I mean all of us—San Diegans, Aztecs, Padres—that Tony Gwynn chose to make this city his home for thirty years. Congratulations Tony on your election to the Baseball Hall of Fame. Ladies and gentlemen ... Tony Gwynn.

[Standing ovation]

TONY [on field to crowd]: It's been an unbelievable ride for the last six months, and we are eight days away and counting, and as you can hear my voice is cracking, so you can imagine what is going to happen a week from now. I am honored to be the first guy, the first statue out here at PETCO Park. I'm thrilled to death to be part of it, but more importantly, I'm a San Diegan. Okay? I'm a Padre, and I'm honored that you're honored for me and my family on this trip to Cooperstown next week. I'm honored that you guys came out and supported me and my family when we were out here playing, you know the twenty seasons, the one team. As Mike Cameron just told me "that was the easy part." Going out there and putting the numbers on the board was the easy part. The hard part ... is to let you guys know how much of a part of my career that you were. And so when we make this long trek to New York next week, and I am standing at the podium, I won't be standing there alone. I will be standing there with my family, and this organization, and every one of you. Thank you very much.

[Five second countdown to unveiling begins. 5,4,3,2,1 .... Statue is completely unveiled. Tony looking at it....]

As the game against the Phillies begins, Tony Gwynn takes his spot in the Channel 4 San Diego announcers' booth, sounding relieved and pleased with the statue's likeness and tribute to his father.

> **TONY:** That phrase, "If you work hard, good things will happen," and that was what they put on the back of the statue. And I was at the front looking at it, and when you see that in the back with Charles Gwynn, Sr. underneath, it really meant a lot.

Over the years the Padres have commemorated significant moments in Gwynn's career. Joining the 3,000 Hit Club, retiring from playing, inducting him into the Padres Hall of Fame, retiring his number now perched atop the Batter's Eye in centerfield, and naming a street Tony Gwynn Drive alongside the team's new ballpark which he helped champion. And now, a statue the week before his induction.

> **TONY:** I've been to Cooperstown and I've been a big fan of the game, and even as a kid loved the game. Loved the history, know the players. But to think I'm good enough to be with them. I can't even … it's not going to hit me till I get there.

While he finalized his speech and packed his suitcases, Cooperstown and the Hall of Fame prepared for the big Induction Weekend, including taking Gwynn artifacts from around the museum and placing them here in this special case on Inductee Row. That's next on *One on One*. Plus fans, peers, and Hall of Fame greats talk about number 19, Tony Gwynn….

Long before his induction, Tony Gwynn's twenty-year career was well represented here in the Hall of Fame's Museum, with artifacts from his two World Series years, 1984 and 1998, his 3,000th hit in 1999. Here in the records room, he's on the list of batting champions. He and Honus Wagner—the two players in the National League tied with eight batting titles. Only Ty Cobb has more, with twelve in the American League. While these items are impressive to view year round, Tony Gwynn is showcased all around town as the Hall of Fame lays out the welcome mat for a memorable Induction Weekend.

> *[Music]*

The charming village of Cooperstown swells from 2,000 to more than a 100,000. It's sporting a summer sparkle: flowers blooming, the streets a-buzzing with baseball fans from everywhere. Just down Main Street, the National Baseball Hall of Fame and Museum with banners naming the newest members, Tony Gwynn and Cal Ripken, Jr. Inside, that special display on Inductee Row, featuring photos and artifacts from Mr. Padre and the Iron Man's careers. While mid week visitors have space to meander through the gallery, a record crowd gradually packs the place, a surge the Hall of Fame staff had been expecting.

> **DALE PETROSKY:** When Tony and Cal retired six years ago, the phones started ringing off the hook in Cooperstown. People were asking, "Where can I get a room for 2007?" So we knew it was going to be a huge year.

Store owners and memorabilia dealers stocked up with Ripken and Gwynn items galore.

> **STORE OWNER:** It's basically Cooperstown's Christmas right now!

And while there are more Ripken fans here ...

CLEVELAND FAN: Certainly there's a lot of fan support for baseball in the Eastern part of the U.S., but I think Gwynn gets his due as well.

Indeed each day, more and more of the Padres contingent arrives.

SAN DIEGO FANS: Tony Gwynn, absolutely, we've followed his career from San Diego State all the way through the Padres organization. It's just been a great time.

JOHN MAFFEI (*North County Times* reporter): Good things happen to good people, and this is just great for him.

JANE: Couldn't miss it.

JOHN MAFFEI: Absolutely would not miss it at all.

Nor would the guy who took this rare picture of Tony's first major league hit, former Padre employee, Fred Rodgers.

FRED RODGERS: In the eighth inning I still had two pictures left, so I just put the camera through and just hoped I could catch him hit the ball with the bat. And then after I heard the bat hit the ball, I clicked.

Copies autographed by Tony, on sale in Cooperstown.

FRED RODGERS: I'm proud because, as I told Tony, I was there, I have proof, and I now have proof that I'm here in Cooperstown for the final blessing of his career.

FAN: Well Tony Gwynn has been one of my favorite baseball players of all time. I've grown up, I've lived my whole life in San Diego, so I've always known Tony Gwynn. So him getting inducted into the Hall of Fame is really great.

FAN: When he announced his retirement we started talking about coming back for it whenever it happened. We were pretty sure it was going to happen.

So many reasons to travel here to celebrate ...

FAN: And I'll never forget the time Tony actually stepped forward. I mean, in this day and age, step forward and actually meet the fans? And ah, he looked right at my son and came up to him, gave him a high five, and you know what, that was important. It was important to him.

FAN: I think that everybody, regardless of what team you root for, respects Tony Gwynn—the person he is and the way he plays the game.

Just stop any fan who's *not* wearing Padres gear.

DODGERS FAN: Oh no—loved Tony Gwynn. Ya, ya, I'm a fan of the game.

BRAVES FAN: He was a totally excellent baseball player, he's like the Hank Aaron of San Diego. Total icon, almost like God over there; people loved him.

JANE: You know one of his favorite moments was when he hit that home run in 1998 at the World Series.

YANKEE FAN: We were at that game and the Padres were ahead till the Yankees had that great seventh inning and scored seven runs. And I'm sorry Tony it didn't work out for you, but that's okay, he's still a great player.

FAN: And I think he's good for the game. I mean, I've never heard anyone say anything bad about Tony Gwynn.

Sentiments echoed by two former Padres in Cooperstown for autograph sessions, Graig Nettles and Goose Gossage.

GOOSE GOSSAGE: I mean, if there's anybody that belongs in the Hall of Fame, Tony does. The career he had and to do it with one team like he did is awesome.

GRAIG NETTLES: It was a real thrill to watch him play and to be one of his teammates.

FAN: The fact that he stayed in San Diego, could have made a gazillion dollars going somewhere else, but he was loyal to us, and that means a lot to a fan. It really does.

While the excitement is building in town, it's a travel day for the inductees. That afternoon, the exquisite lakeside Hotel Otesaga is ready for the weekend's Hall of Fame guests. It's locked down for security reasons. But granted special access, we're there first when the Ripkens drive up from Maryland. Then when the Gwynn gang arrives on a bus from the airport, after having flown on the Padres owner's jet, friend and agent John Boggs greets them, including Tony's mother, Vandella, wife, daughter, his brothers, and their families.

JANE: Hey Tony, good—welcome, how was the flight?

TONY: Great.

JANE: Glad to be here?

TONY: Finally yeah, glad to be here.... Let's go on, let's see, let's see what this is all about. It's going to be fun.

Inside, a piano sets the tone for an elegant, well-choreographed, and busy weekend. As the Gwynn's pick up their official name tags and check in, Tony—in jeans, a sport coat, straw hat, and Padres-logo'd shoes—is greeted by familiar faces.

[Hello to Dick Freeman.]

Yet seems a little overwhelmed ...

TONY: Just trying to relax. Have a good time.

The next day, amid a thunderous rain storm, we find a spot inside to sit down one-on-one.

JANE: We saw you come in yesterday, you said, "Let's just go see what it's all about." Once you got inside, what was it all about, who came up to you?

TONY: Tom Seaver was the first guy who came up to me and gave me the standard, how you doing, congratulations, you know, this is going to be great, your family is going to enjoy it. I mean, at least while we're taping this right now, I'm calm. I'm calm. I'm actually looking forward to what's going to happen here this weekend and really trying to enjoy it.

Earlier that day, Ozzie Smith hosted his "Turn-Two" charity event, an opportunity to talk about Gwynn with "The Wizard" and fellow Hall of Famers.

OZZIE SMITH: When I look around I try and figure out what it is that's different about the people that are here as opposed to the other thousands of people that have played the game. It's the degree of consistency of which we do what we do, and nobody's done it more consistently than Tony's done it—his work ethic—he's put everything in.

The Chicago Cubs' Ryne Sandberg ...

RYNE SANDBERG: But Tony was a true professional, and just a student of the game, and probably the purest hitter in the National League that I faced.

Baltimore's Brooks Robinson ...

BROOKS ROBINSON: You could put Tony in ... I mean Ted Williams would put Tony in the same class as he was in when it came to hitting, maybe not the power, but when it comes to outright hitting a baseball.

Kansas City's George Brett ...

GEORGE BRETT: I would always get up in the morning and regardless of what I was sittin' at, I would always look and see how he was doing, and I would use him as a yard stick kinda to figure out how I was doing. He was my benchmark. We were similar type hitters.

TONY: Ahh, so that's nice to hear, then on the other hand, when it comes to practicing your craft, you just do what you do. It's just these guys—a lot of these guys—have no idea how much of an influence they had on my career ... George Brett: I haven't talked to him that much during the course of my playing career, but any time he was on TV, I stopped what I was doing to watch him. Rod Carew has been my idol since *whenever*, and when they were on TV, I stopped what I was doing to watch him hit.

Rod Carew, a line drive, contact hitter, like Gwynn.

ROD CAREW: But you measure a man by what he does for other people, and that's the way I measure Tony Gwynn: as a great person, and a great ball player, and a great friend.

Concurring, the one-time Padre coach and the opposing manager in the '84 World Series, Detroit's Sparky Anderson.

SPARKY ANDERSON: The Tony Gwynns of this sporting world is a hope and a dream that you guide. Not because of what he does on the field; he's going to do that. That's his natural ability. But what he does as a person.

TONY: The writers are the ones who vote you in, but it's the acceptance from the guys who are already in there that allows you to relax and really try to enjoy it. So thus far, it's been pretty good, they all seem to think I was okay.

JANE: We've been here since Tuesday and we've talked to a lot of fans, a lot of San Diego fans, and just baseball fans.

FAN: I talked to Tony this last spring and said, I'm going to the Hall of Fame. Yeah sure you are, so Tony, we're here Tony. [Laughs]

TONY: And I appreciate that because, like I said last week, it's just not about me. I'm the guy being honored, but this story is not just about Tony Gwynn, it's about my team, our team, the San Diego Padres, and our city, the city of San Diego.

JANE: And the fact that people who are fans of the game who may have never seen you, but know you and respect you.

TONY: Yes, yeah, yeah. That's wonderful. Yeah it is because it's a byproduct of lots of things, but probably the most important thing is doing it the right way. When you do it the right way, people let you know. They're not afraid to come up to you tell you, "Hey, I appreciate the way you took care of your business. I appreciate the example you set for our kids." That means more than whatever thirteen hundred or whatever runs or 3,141 hits. To me, having people come up to you means a whole lot more than just the numbers.

With that, he tapes a message to fans who'd be watching Sunday at PETCO Park. Then, he's ready for the parties and the golf to begin. That's next on *One on One*. And later, he takes his place on the grand stage for Induction Day....

Friday evening, the Otesaga Hotel's front porch is the who's who of Hall of Famers in cocktail attire catching shuttles to a private party. Our access allows us to capture the guest list: Wade Boggs, Ozzie Smith, Gaylord Perry, Frank Robinson, Jim Palmer, Al Kaline, Phil Niekro, Lou Brock: living legends. Then there's the newbie, Tony Gwynn, wide-eyed in awe ...

TONY: What doesn't belong?

By the traditional golf tournament Saturday morning, he's more relaxed. The media, a bit more frenzied. There's considerably more this year, and many from the east coast, all vying for angles and interviews during the limited time access to most veteran Hall of Famers. Nevertheless, jump in to ask about Tony Gwynn and the answers come easily.

PAUL MOLITOR: I remember one of my first spring trainings in Yuma, Arizona playing third base, and Tony hit one to my left, so I would move over there, and then he would hit one to my right. He'd hit down the line, and then I would play him in, and he would hit one over the fence. So there were too many things to defend.

WADE BOGGS: When you talk about pure quality hitters, I mean he's as pure as they get.

ROBIN YOUNT: We didn't play against each other much other than spring training. Certainly I saw him on *SportsCenter* highlights enough to know how well he was doing.

DON SUTTON: I admired his unselfish approach to hitting, if it took a ball to the right side to get it done, if it took a double, if it took a swing for a homer, he had that commitment.

CARLTON FISK: I don't think there's been a discouraging word written about that man because he's—I've met him a few times—the nicest fella you'd ever want to meet, and he's a pretty good hitter, too.

ROLLIE FINGERS: Certainly belongs here. Glad I never had to face him.

MIKE SCHMIDT: I used to go out there and watch him feather those little line drives all over the place. And you know, he knew how to play the game.

BILLY WILLIAMS: And this weekend he will receive the glory of being in the Hall of Fame, which he had worked hard to get here.

DAVE WINFIELD: Batting titles, Gold Gloves, leadership. Welcome Tony. You deserve it.

JANE [Jane and Tony at golf course]: A lot of these guys are saying some good stuff about you out here.

TONY: That's cause I, you don't hear them behind closed doors like I do. You know I'm the newbie. I'm the rookie, so it's really weird to be forty-seven years old and to be treated like a freshman again. And all I can do is take it. I just gotta take it, and whatever happens, happens.

As he continues his golf game ...

TONY: I can't tell you how much fun we've had being out here, seeing the fans.

Those fans wait for him along the roadside on the back nine.

FAN: Thank you Mr. Gwynn!

TONY: OK. I gotta go. Thank you. *[Applause]*

After a day on the links, it's Padres party time, a private afternoon affair for friends and family, and with a sentimental thank you to guests. Many are willing to share their thoughts on Tony Gwynn's great achievement.

DICK FREEMAN (Padres President, 2007): Number one, nobody deserves more, and secondly, it couldn't happen to a nicer guy.

SANDY ALDERSON (Padres CEO, 2007): Not only did he have a great career, but he's represented the Padres and the city so well over many years, even since his retirement from the game.

KEVIN TOWERS (Padres GM, 2007): I watched him play in the minor leagues, and then I was fortunate enough as a GM to see a lot of great years and help us win a lot of championships.

JOHN BOGGS (Tony's Agent): To have your first client go in to the Hall of Fame, it just doesn't get any better, and he really hasn't changed. He's the same guy, that's the beauty of it.

JERRY COLEMAN (Broadcaster): The character of Tony Gwynn is the most important thing he owns, and that's what I love most about him.

STEVE GARVEY (Retired player): I mean, once in a great while somebody epitomizes a team, a profession, a city. And Tony's done that.

JOHN MOORES (Padres owner): I don't buy any of the nonsense that he tells people, that he just had to work harder than anybody else. He did work harder than anybody else, but he still is as good as they get.

BECKY MOORES (Padres owner): Well, Tony just means baseball to me, because when I first started watching baseball, Tony was there in right field, and I always thought, *I can't imagine a game without Tony.* So now, I guess he's where he should be. If he's not going to be in right field, he should be in the Hall of Fame.

That night, on their way to a dessert reception, they arrive by trolley to cheering fans and clicking cameras. A red carpet evening before a day Tony Gwynn will never forget.

The plaques here in the Hall of Fame outline a person's career highlights and statistics. What they don't generally detail? Who they are as a person, how they went about their baseball business, and what they had to choose, battle, or resist to get here. Tony Gwynn and Cal Ripken, Jr. are the first to be elected from eligible players from the so-called steroid era. Two men never associated with baseball's blemish. And Gwynn is adamant that years down the road when someone looks at his plaque …

TONY: They're not going to know whether I was clean or not. And so that's one good reason why we do these *One on Ones,* 'cause I can sit here and tell everybody, I'm as clean as it got.

All part of his story, intertwined with the game and the people he loves. And so on Induction Day, the stage is set. Far and wide, fans file in on their blankets and lounge chairs. It's a sea of Oriole orange and Padre gold, brown, orange, and blue, with plenty of signs and sentiments.

SAN DIEGO FAN: I was just envisioning Tony's smile and all he did for the city of San Diego, and every bit of it's been worth it. This is a priceless moment right here.

"MADRES" FAN: We're celebrating a hometown guy. Not just a baseball player, and the country gets to see what we see every day.

"MADRES" FAN: He gave so much to San Diego, we had to come here and give back. Let everyone see what everybody thinks of what he did for us.

San Diegans celebrate Tony Gwynn's favorite spot, his trademark hole between shortstop and third, where he got many of his hits. ESPN's cameras are in position to carry the ceremony live. In San Diego—Padres faithful are hearing his taped message at the Park at the Park.

TONY [HOF speech]: *You know, I went from being a twenty-two year old rookie to a forty-one year old man, and we've all kind of gone through this process together. And it really has been a lot of fun.* [applause]

Induction Day tops off three days in Cooperstown, a mix, his family describes, of anxiety and awe.

> **ALICIA:** Just seeing the old timers come up to Tony and congratulate him, it's like wow, you know, you're in that company, but I'm not sure Tony feels like he is in that company because he says, "Did you hear him say congratulations?" "Yeah, I heard him Tony."
> **CHARLES GWYNN** (brother): We played Little League together; we go way back. Very proud to see him accomplish this, and it's very well deserved.
> **CHRIS GWYNN** (brother): Wow, and my dad, I know he's looking down and it's going to be emotional, but I think we're all going to have a lot of fun with it.

Perhaps it took being here to finally sink in to feel he belongs. And for all the pep talks he gave his son who's following in his footsteps, this time it was Tony Junior's turn.

> **TONY, JR.:** This morning he said he was nervous, very emotional. Last night didn't get very much sleep, but before I walked out the door, I told him everything was going to be all right, you know, that it's no different than playing in front of 75,000, so I think he's going to be good. I think he's going to pull it together.

[Tony's daughter, Anisha, sings the Canadian national anthem … and the U.S. national anthem.]

Just in case a threatening storm were to hit that afternoon—the program order changes. So, to his surprise, Tony Gwynn is batting lead off.

> *TONY [HOF speech]: They've been telling me all day that it's my day. Can I call a time out here, because I need my notes? I'm going to struggle. Hold on …*

And once he settles in, he indeed delivers. No script, just notes and a confident yet down to earth tone that's signature Tony. For a half hour, he chronologically walks through many of his defining moments, giving credit to contributors to his life and career, from Little League to getting a basketball scholarship out of high school to San Diego State.

> *TONY [HOF speech]: Tim Vezie was my first coach there, and he told me that as a point guard, your job is to make sure that everybody on the floor, all your teammates, are better players.*
> **TIM VEZIE:** We thought a lot of Tony because of his leadership, his ability to play. He was a very unselfish player. And at that point in time, I didn't even know he had picked up a bat and baseball. I didn't have any idea. He didn't even care about his baseball ability. All he cared about was his basketball ability.
> *TONY [HOF speech]: At the same time, the reason why I went to San Diego State is so that I could play baseball also, and I played for a guy there by the name of Jim Dietz.*

A mentor and friend throughout his career.

JIM DIETZ: He was very much a team kind of guy. The younger players would go to him. He was very good in the community. The media really liked him. You've been around him, you understand what I'm saying. And he could back it up with great numbers.

Tony Gwynn explains the unusual fact that he'd been drafted by the Padres and Clippers on the same day and then, upon choosing the Padres, worked his way up quickly from the minors in Walla Walla, Washington.

TONY [HOF speech]: There was a cardinal rule when you got to the big leagues, keep your eyes and ears open, keep your mouth shut, and I did that a lot. I kept my mouth shut. I laughed a lot because laughter, I learned later on, would be that thing that would disarm people.

This speech is a long way from one of his first television interviews, the night he logged his first major league hit …

TONY [HOF speech]: … and Pete Rose said to me, "Don't try to catch me all in one night, kid."

Known as the pioneer for using video in baseball, he tells how it all started in June of '83. He was struggling at the plate and on the road …

TONY [HOF speech]: And I called home and I asked my wife, I said, "Honey, do you think you could hit the record button for me?" I would not be standing here today without video, and again, my wife hit the button and all of a sudden, it just opened up a new avenue for me because I learned at this level, it's about knowing what you do when you get in that batter's box. It's about knowing how they are going to pinch hit, how they are going to play you, how they are going to attack you, and you have the game plan to try to attack them.

TONY [HOF speech]: 1984 was really a good year for us, for the Padres. We had some veteran guys in our club, a Steve Garvey, a Goose Gossage, a Graig Nettles, and I was the fortunate one because my locker was right in the middle of all those guys. I really tried to emulate some of the things that Garv told me. He said, "Stay on an even keel." He said, "Never get too high, too low, just go about your business, go about your business the right way."

And willing to listen, too. Especially to Ted Williams at the 1992 All Star game.

TONY [HOF speech]: The first time I had a bat in my hand, he said, "Hey, Tony, how you doing? Give me your bat." I gave him my bat and he started picking his teeth with it. And if you're worth your salt as a hitter, your mind starts to race, it starts to tick, and really what Ted really made me do, he made me think about the art of hitting a baseball. '98, we just had a tremendous team in '98. We were lucky enough to get to the World Series. Won our division, beat the Astros, beat the Braves, and just happen[ed] to play the best team maybe in the history of the game, the 1998 Yankees. I never really looked at what I did as being anything special. I loved the game. I think that's why you guys are here today—because you love the game, you have a passion for it. I have a passion for it. I still have a passion for it. I just don't play anymore.

But when he did, he made an indelible impression on friends and peers.

TREVOR HOFFMAN: Just so extremely proud of the Padre organization to have one of our own go in as deserving as he did.

TIM FLANNERY: There's a little piece of all of us that he took with him, and he made sure we knew that.

BRUCE BOCHY: To watch him on a daily basis, I know I'm lucky. And he's so good for baseball.

CRAIG BIGGIO: Tony is just the best pure hitter that I have ever seen as far as putting the bat on the ball consistently, day in and day out, and hitting the ball hard.

GREG MADDUX: If you needed a guy up there to put the ball in play, he was the guy. It was hard enough to get strike one, let alone three out of him.

KEN GRIFFEY, JR.: He is one of those guys who, if you want to know how to hit, you can watch him, because he will teach you how to hit.

WALLY JOYNER: Wanted to be great and worked hard at it.

TONY [HOF speech]: My father said you work hard, good things will happen. Boy oh, boy, he was absolutely right. I worked hard in the game because I had to. I wasn't talented enough to just get by on ability. There's a responsibility when you put that uniform on that those people, the people who pay to go watch you play, you're responsible, you've got to make good decisions and show people how things are supposed to be done. [Crowd cheers]

TONY [HOF speech]: I'm proud as heck to be a San Diego Padre. I played on one team in one town.

He appreciates the Padres organization and his supportive family, including his mother, who didn't feel well, so stayed at the hotel.

TONY [HOF speech]: Don't feel bad about not being here. We love you, and I'm glad you could make the trip with us. My father passed in 1993, and this would be an event he would love to be at. He would love it. And then my family, my wife, who again, I would not be standing here today without her. Honey, I love you. Thank you. My son is here. He made it yesterday. He and his wife Alyse. Thank you guys for coming. I'm going to be a grandpa in October for the first time, so that child's got no chance, he's got no chance. And my daughter Anisha sang the Canadian anthem and the national anthem. You guys, I'm so proud of you guys, I really am. Your mom did a wonderful job, and I kind of rode in on the back end. You guys make me so proud just watching the way you handle. Being a son of a major league player is sometimes a difficult thing, but you guys have always handled it great. And the rest of my family, and that's you guys, that's the fans, my adopted family, especially my fans from San Diego. It was twenty years, and we had a blast, I had a blast. I truly enjoyed it, but it wouldn't have been nearly as much fun if you hadn't been as supportive as you were, so I say thank you for all of our fans sitting at PETCO Park in the morning. Thank you to the fans who made the trek, thank you to the fans who are here to see everybody. I say thank you because you know what? For the rest of my life, when I come here to the Hall of Fame and I look out and I see as many people as I see here today, I can say in our first time here, our first Hall of Fame weekend, the people were lined up way, way back through the trees. So thank you, everyone. Thank you very much. I really appreciate it. Thank you.

His father raised him with the mantra "Work hard and good things will happen." Tony took it to heart and still lives by it. If you ask him why, he'll just say, "because it's the right thing to do." A simple thought from a man who is anything but: a magician with a baseball bat, a community icon, a proud husband and father, and now, a member of this most exclusive club—the Baseball Hall of Fame.

I'm Jane Mitchell. Thank you for watching *One on One* from Cooperstown, New York.

TIM FLANNERY

"I'm a very private person even though it seems like I'm not, but there are some things that I hold very sacred, and my home is one of them … So the idea of having somebody come in there who I really wasn't familiar with as well, I was a little—I was on guard."

— TIM FLANNERY, 2010

I wasn't sure what to expect from Tim Flannery. I had watched video from the night he retired in 1989 and asked people what he was like as a player. I knew he had been a feature reporter at a local television station, was a musician, and managed in the minor leagues before returning to the majors as the Padres' third base coach. In order to capture his various dimensions, we planned a full day of

shooting the end of January 1997 to coincide with a concert he was playing that night at the Belly Up Tavern in Solana Beach.

A small crew and I arrived at Tim's home in San Diego's North County. He welcomed us with a burst of energy, and I thought *This is going to be fun.* Still, he didn't know me, so I was very mindful of working within our time limit in his home. Their modest two-story house is a harmonious mix of who he and his family are: Southern California surf lovers, baseball fans, and musicians. The evidence? Surf boards in the garage, shelves filled with baseball and family pictures with their three children, and a piano in the living room with boxes of Tim's new CD stacked and ready to go.

This was one of my first long-form interviews, so I was still not sure how long it would take to cover his story—especially someone whom I understood was passionate and talkative. Wow. I was in for a treat, and soon, our viewers would be, too. There were a few special moments the first time I interviewed The Flan Man, as he is affectionately called. One is when we talked about the day he retired. He said he had not looked at the video or really talked about that day for almost ten years. He became a little choked up reflecting on what he had learned he meant to this town and what being part of a team meant to him. I asked out of curiosity; that little key unlocked some emotion he'd held close to his heart for a long time. Another moment was when Donna and Tim had an honest and humble exchange about Tim being "high maintenance," and how their history and love had seen them through a lot.

> "... You make them feel comfortable enough to where they now feel like, you know what, I'm going to open up my heart, and I'm going to open up my soul, and I'm going to let people in."

The Padres released Tim Flannery from his coaching position after the 2002 season, and he reentered the world of broadcasting in 2004—the year the new ballpark opened—as the co-host of the pre-game show on Channel 4 San Diego and one of the Padres' radio announcers. In 2007, Tim returned to the field as third base coach for Bruce Bochy, who relocated to be manager for the San

Francisco Giants. While the Padres and their fans would have preferred to have beaten the Giants on the last day of the 2010 season and made the playoffs, I cheered for Tim and Bruce as they went on to win the World Series. Even as opponents on the field, friendships transcend a uniform.

Tim and I also bonded as friends around the topic of fathers. Mine had died of ALS; his father, Ragon, had Alzheimer's. As anyone who has had a sick parent knows, it's a heart-wrenching experience becoming the caregiver for someone who once was so strong and cared for you. One night when I was with the team in Anaheim in 1997, I saw Tim sitting at the hotel bar, looking contemplative. He was having a hard time with how Alzheimer's was changing his father—the man he knew so well, the man who didn't always know him anymore. While I couldn't relate to that aspect of the disease, I could relate to losing a father. It's moments like this that I've been grateful to not *have* to be an unbiased, disconnected reporter on the outside, and not have to worry about drawing a line at a conversation just because I had a press credential. It felt right to be able to talk and relate to someone as a person with no camera rolling, and to Tim especially, who treated me as an equal.

In 2004, the Padres' young pitcher, Jake Peavy, was a star on the rise. Fans and the Padres organization were excited about him, and he was on deck for a *One on One*. I wasn't sure if I could do a whole half hour on him at first *(see more of his story in the section on Jake Peavy)*, but when I heard he was learning to play guitar from Tim Flannery, I had the perfect solution: If Jake didn't want to play alone, then bring Tim and Jake together for a guitar lesson and singing at Jake's apartment. That visual would not only help tell Jake's story, but show the different generations connecting in both baseball and life. Tim was a good sport to help us create an opportunity to see that side of Jake, and in so doing, showed what a good teacher and mentor he is, too. Their singing and conversation are captured in the show script about Jake.

Wherever his musical talents and baseball life take him, Tim Flannery will always be considered a fan favorite with San Diegans who appreciate his many dimensions. He's also one of my all-time favorite people for his candor, compassion, transparency, and soulful spirit; he's unafraid to carry his guitar and to be a bit of a rebel in the baseball world.

This is the script from the original show debuting July 9, 1997.

• • •

Fasten your seatbelts. Going inside Tim Flannery's secret world is a wild ride with music, a little insight, a lot of love, some inspiration, and satisfaction guaranteed!

DONNA: He is a wonderful dad, husband, and my best friend.

TIM: But I'm high maintenance [laughs].

DONNA: But he's high maintenance!

Baseball's got its stars. Some burn brightly and then are never seen again. Others burn slowly and steadily and become part of the game's fabric. Such is the case of Tim Flannery, who started in the Padres infield and has come back home to his new office next to third base.

If you could bottle up the essence of baseball and sell it as a passionate, color-ful, high-energy extract, you could call it Tim Flannery.

TIM: It's so nice to be able to put this uniform on and do something that I love for a living.

Tim Flannery grew up with baseball in his family. His uncle, Hal Smith, played for the Pittsburgh Pirates.

TIM: But I'd never got to see a game until I was living in Portland, Oregon and my Uncle Hal was on his way out of the game in Triple A, and came through Portland and left us tickets. So I was able to go. It is something that I will never forget. You don't ever forget the smells, the grass, the sounds. I knew what I wanted to do right then and there.

Moving to Anaheim, he became an Angels fan.

TIM: In the seventh inning they would open the stands and let people out. Well, I would sneak in and hope they would tie and play like seventy-four in-nings. As a player, you hated extra innings, so as a player I always knew there was a kid up there wishing that on us.

In high school, Tim met Donna.

TIM: Her brother went to my high school and I saw her come to a football game one night with her brother, and I decided that I'm going to be friends with her brother!

They dated seven years and have been married for sixteen years. He played base-ball at Chapman College in Orange, and was picked up by the Padres in the sixth round of the 1978 draft. A so-called fringe player who worked so hard and played so hard, Tim Flannery became one of the most valued players on the Padres for ten years.

One of his sweetest moments came in 1984 in game five of the National League Championship Series at home against the Cubs.

TIM: There are a lot of things that come through your head when you come to the plate. I mean, you're sitting on the bench watching the game develop and you know your time is going to come, and that time is going to be right in the thick of things with a lot of pressure. I found out a lot about myself at the time. I wanted to be in that situation. So you find out: can you handle the heat or can you not handle the heat; do you want to be in that situation or do you not want to be in that situation; are you a championship player or are you a last place team player? And to be in that situation, there is a huge difference. Destiny had a part in it, but more than anything, I felt really good about the opportunity I had and was prepared and wanted to be in that situation. What I remember most is when I was on first base, the noise of the stadium was so loud that it actually hurt; like I'm on the bottom of a nine-foot swimming pool.

His hit triggered a four-run, seventh inning rally that clinched the title. One of his teammates for five years then, Padres Manager now, was Bruce Bochy.

> TIM: That's who I ran around with on the road. We were both back-up players, so we always played the "B" games in the mornings in spring training. We always played Sunday day games and we always played Cy Young Winners or former winners, 'cause that's when they took their days off. They threw us to the wolves. So we had a lot of good times on the field and off the field as well.

By 1989, it was time to say goodbye to playing.

> TIM: Everyone says, "You should have kept playing." I was finished, no regrets 'cause I gave everything I had.

And San Diego said thank you in a thirty-minute sendoff for him, his wife Donna, and their children.

> TIM: That night, especially the outpouring of fans, it still moves me. [Tearing up.] Phew, it was a great night. I mean, I can't even look at the video, it was a wild night. I haven't really even thought about it much.

But leaving the game brought a tough transition.

> TIM: Your whole life since you were three or four years old, you dream about being a Major League Baseball player. Then all of a sudden at the prime of your life, thirty-two years at the time, the highest time making dollars on the business side of it, everything is snatched from you. It's gone. So after I retired, I went through a four to five month adjustment period where I had to get away.

He escaped for a while to the hills of northern California …

> TIM: And really kind of went through the whole grieving process of leaving the game, healing, and coming back.

Through that time he turned to his faithful friend, his music.

> TIM: I've been playing music all my life and anyone who has played baseball with me, from the first day I walked in the clubhouse through the minor leagues, I've always played my guitar, written songs. It's therapy for me.

It helped. Tim Flannery took his talent for storytelling into the TV studio as a feature reporter for a local TV station for three years with tough assignments, like surfing in Fiji, complete with a down to earth flair that's just classic Flannery. And even less known, but more rewarding than being on the air, was being on stage strummin' a guitar and singing as the opening act for big name performers like Jimmy Buffet, a long-time baseball fan, George Thoroughgood, and Willie Nelson—one treasured moment in time was an impromptu duet, "Son of a Son of a Sailor."

[Tim and Jimmy Buffet singing duet]

But baseball was still in his blood, and when it called again in 1993, Donna encouraged him to seize the opportunity.

> TIM: She saw that I was missing it. She said we'd rather have you homeless and have you home alive than have you home every night the way you're coming home.

Flannery took a pay cut and headed back out on the road as a manager, this time in the Padres farm system.

> TIM: I didn't want to be like anyone else. I said I'm going to manage the way I played, the way that I am.

His Spokane Indians were playing the first place Billingham Mariners. Big game—there'd already been one bench clearing incident.

> TIM: So if anybody hits another batter, the managers are immediately ejected from the game.

Flannery's pitcher made a move.

> TIM: He drilled the next hitter and I knew it was going to happen, I didn't stop it.

Flannery's thrown out.

> TIM: Sometimes you have to do that to motivate your club. So I just expressed myself a little bit, a lot, got thrown out again. Got thrown out twice! When I left the field I'm up in my office pacing, just Irish mad, and I hear on the radio the team's starting to rally. They come back from seven runs to tie the game. Now they go ahead. I got to go on the field, but if you go on the field again it's a seven-day suspension, and when you're making twenty-two thousand dollars as a minor league coach, you can't afford a seven-day suspension.

So he borrowed the mascot's uniform and sat on the bench.

> TIM: And they're coming off the field and I said now's the time. And I started high-fiving and these guys heard my voice and I did a full routine of Louie-Louie that got the whole ballpark going. Everyone said, "You got a lot better timing than the mascot we got!"

He moved up and led Rancho Cucamonga to a California League Championship and then managed the Las Vegas Stars in '95. Archi Cianfrocco played for Flannery.

> ARCHI: He was great. He's a players' manager. He has a passion for the game. He knows the game inside and out.
>
> DONNA: It was really great going back to the minor leagues again. The year after we got married he made it to the big leagues.
>
> TIM: She wouldn't marry me until I got to the big leagues.
>
> DONNA: No, that's not true.
>
> TIM: So I dragged her back through for a few years.

Fate would bring Flannery home again for his second time around in the majors, this time coaching third base. He writes, "After riding buses in the minors, flying airplanes seemed easier than it used to be." And one night in '96, flying 30,000 feet somewhere over Colorado, he wrote a song "Second Time Around" while stargazing out his first class window, flying over a storm cloud.

> TIM: From my point of view, it looked like we were flying over a lighted floor. From the ground, people were looking up at the same storm, but all they could see were clouds, rain, and lightning. Thank God for second chances and a different point of view.

His second time around started with the incredible year of 1996 and some parallels to the last victorious season of '84.

> TIM: To be able to coach and be able to be part of something that was just as good or even better with the chemistry of our ball club, be back in the city I love and work with one of my best friends, Bruce Bochy, then to top it off, sleep in my own bed at night. I mean, what a concept!

But his colorful life hasn't been without some disappointments. When *One on One* continues, Tim Flannery reflects on illusions of the game and inspirations in his life....

With no regrets about ending his playing career when he did ...

> TIM: Oh, have you seen me run to third base? I'm done!

Tim Flannery still gets the natural high from waving runners around third.

> TIM: So when a guy like Steve Finley scores, I feel like I'm running with him. And when [Ken] Caminiti comes around the base, I get off on that energy, that excitement.

Doesn't mind that his decisions don't always work out.

> TIM: What, you want me to hold him up? You don't get anything for a guy on third base, no score!
>
> DONNA: Coaching is wonderful. My husband doesn't have to go out there and hit three home runs and come up in the seventh inning with the bases loaded and pinch-hit.
>
> TIM: I love where I am today, I really do. Where else can you surf great waves and go out and get a carne asada burrito and coach in the big leagues all in the same day? I'm still learning because the one thing you do learn at third base is when you think you've got it figured out, you will see something you've never seen before. You get blamed for things that you had nothing to do with, you get credit for things you had nothing to do with. I really work at it and respect the position. I tell my friends it's like surfing big winter waves. Right when you think you have it wired, right when you think you can take a deep breath, there comes a great set out of the blue, and you end up breaking your board and crawling to shore, and 50,000 people are pointing at you.

It's moments like that which inspire him to pick up his guitar ...

DONNA: We've actually heard some of his songs evolve. He starts banging out a tune, and then before you know it, something else, then the words come. He hears the band behind him whenever he writes.

TIM: I write to the strengths of the band. I have a producer, Andy Machin, he takes these songs and puts a heartbeat to them, and all of a sudden, wow.

Tim Flannery's music isn't about bats and balls. It's about the game of life on the road in Arizona, the Midwest, or the east coast; it's a lonely life sometimes. His music is about the lifestyle, the pressures, the people he meets, and the places he goes.

TIM: When I sing my songs I remember exactly where I wrote them, how I felt when I wrote them.

So, how does he write them? The old-fashioned way—pen and paper. His guitar case is filled with napkins and matchbooks, a trail of his travels and emotions.

[(singing): Inside these walls I am alone, with my feelings and my thoughts ... I'm away from the noise of the world ...]

Spring training 1996, his first day back in the big leagues, this time as a coach, Flannery wrote "Inside These Walls."

TIM: Sometimes it really hurts. This song came to me one night when I really needed it, and it's usually the first song I sing when I get to a new room in a new town. I call it a medicine song.

[(singing): And then I hear your voice echo in the silence ...]

Flannery recognizes what he's learned and shares that with the younger players.

TIM: I grew up a mile from Anaheim Stadium and every night I would look out, and if the Angels won the big "A" would blink on and off. I was drawn to it. It was like Oz. If I could just get there, everything would be perfect. Well, I got there and realized it was a business, and that hurt.

His first realization about the pain of the game came in spring training, 1981.

TIM: I was playing every day, hitting home runs in spring training. Last day of camp, the last hour of camp, Frank Howard said, "Tim, you're the second baseman Opening Day. Congratulations. Go get your stuff and get to San Diego." So we're packing up, we're moving from Yuma to come here to start the season, and they made a trade. And [Frank Howard] said, "Tim, we made a trade." They call me into the office and sent me back to the minor leagues. I cried from Yuma to here, and I'm an emotional guy, and that's something I'm not afraid to—that's me. I remember Donna showing up from school, she was going to UCLA, and she thought I was kidding her. I said I have to pack up and go to Hawaii, I'm getting sent back. Which, you look back and—Hawaii is a great place to be. But when your dream, your passion, and you've worked your whole life to be the starting second baseman in the big leagues, you don't want to go back to Hawaii, or Triple-A, or anything. Coming up that way is one thing, but going down—it's a whole different thing.

[(singing): ... another night ... here inside these walls ...]

Baseball is predictably unpredictable.

> TIM: You've got to respect the game because it will bring you to your knees no matter who you are. You have to respect that and have to understand that; have to know it's just a natural rhythm of the game.

> TIM: What you have to learn in this business is expectations ruin a lot of things. I mean they ruin dinners, they ruin movies, they ruin books, they ruin baseball teams. When you just expect it's going to happen, this game will humble you. It is a cold rotten business at times, but in the middle of all of those types of things, there is some purity that you can find, and some experiences and fun that I wouldn't have traded for anything in the world.

Tim Flannery feels lucky to have achieved a dream, reached some goals in baseball and beyond.

> TIM: But a lot of times you grab those goals and reach those dreams, and you realize that this is good, but this is not what it's all about. It's about the whole journey. I was telling that to the minor leaguers, but I was telling that to myself because there are times when it can get real hard on those ten-hour bus rides, living without furniture, sleeping on the floor. But if you look at it as a celebration of life, if you look at it as a gift, a blessing, it can be the most fun you've ever had, and it sure beats working. I've tried that!

Going backstage for a little Flannery-style rock and roll, and another part of his heart and soul, when *One on One* continues....

Tim Flannery has yet to visit Ireland, but he's found his soul and his song very much connected to Irish folk music.

> TIM: The mandolins, and the guitars, and the penny whistles, and all of the things that I love …

And he feels a kinship with Blue Grass. His Irish relatives settled in the Kentucky hills and he remembers, as a child, listening to his eighty-year-old grandmother play her banjo.

> TIM: This is why I play the music that I play.

Tim Flannery and the Tim Flannery Band spent more than a year working on his second CD, *Secret World*.

It's a culmination of his originals and special songs by some of the artists in his band. Late-night rehearsals and getting in synch before the CD's debut concert mean more than getting it right for Flannery. This was an emotional risk because, for many years, he kept his passion for music low profile.

> TIM: The hardest part is when you let it out, and let people in, and let people know about things that are very important to you, things that are sacred to you.

Including his marriage, his children, his perspective on life.

> TIM: When the season's over with I'm going to continue to play, and when I leave this game—which is going to happen, it's going to happen again—I'm

going to survive again without it. The constant has been my music. So that's why I think that I'm not ashamed anymore to let people in on it, because for a lot of years I didn't want anybody to know about it.

His reasons for writing are simple. It makes him feel good.

TIM: It's the same thing you feel before you walk out the tunnel in front of 50,000 people. It's adrenaline and preparation …

CONCERT ANNOUNCER: *Ladies and Gentlemen, the Tim Flannery Band!!*

Flannery has a way with words and that might be partially due to how his parents raised him. He's the son of a preacher man born in Tulsa, Oklahoma, moved to Oregon and then to Southern California with his father spreading the word.

TIM: I found out that God is very very alive and sometimes you have to make a little bit of sacrifice, sometimes a lot of sacrifice, to find that out. I'm not going to get up and say that this is the way it is supposed to be and if everybody doesn't do it my way, you're wrong. Coaching third base teaches you that. That's my perspective over there. That's not the best perspective, but it's the only one that I have. The guy sitting up there in the top deck—he's probably got a better perspective and can probably make the call better, but I have to make it. And the only thing I can go on is what I know, not what I'm told.

And so he wants his song "Secret World" to be open to interpretation. Your secret world, he says, is any place to gain clarity on who you are and why you're here. His teammates were enthusiastic about being a part of making his music video, the sales of which will benefit charity.

[Flannery Music Video footage]

BRUCE BOCHY: [singing] … and the stars look down on me smiling. [laughing]

He doesn't expect his songs to change the world; they're not meant to.

TIM: If it makes somebody else feel better, which at times I think it does, we keep doing it.

Flannery's *Secret World* helps clarify who he is, why he's here—as a father, a husband, a part of a team—and why he needs to give back. Most of the proceeds are buying Padres tickets for children who otherwise couldn't afford to go to a game.

TIM: Because I know when I saw my first major league game and what it did for me.

Sales of 2,000 albums have already benefitted 600 children who watched in wonder, gratitude, while looking right down the third base line.

[Footage of kids at a Padres game]

BOY 1: Hit a home run!

GIRL: I'm glad he gave us this opportunity.

BOY 2: He gave me and my team some tickets to come to this game.

BOY 3: Thank you a lot for the tickets.

[Kids running bases]

[(music): Secret world … hear the laughter of children … through their eyes I hope we can see … My secret world …]

Tim and Donna Flannery's three children, Danny, Ginny, and Kelly have experienced the extremes of the majors and the minors and their father's music …

KELLY: I like it. He wrote this song about me, and whenever I hear it, it makes me feel good.

TIM: People come up to them and say, "Well what's wrong with the Padres?" And Danny has the great attitude—he says, "It's the third base coach's fault!"

Keeping baseball in perspective is important to Flannery.

TIM: I remember we had just swept Los Angeles in '82, we won four in a row. It was the highlight of my career—when I got home, I found out my brother had cancer. So it was like, I love this game, but it's a game.

[music, singing: I believed you at the altar, the day you said I do, that you would love me forever, whatever we go through. Through the years and through the struggles, through the recklessness of youth, through a world of broken lovers, we're still standing …]

He dedicated the *Secret World* CD to his parents, who taught him Love was Above All Others.

TIM: I wrote a song called "We're Still Standing," which is my song to her, my song to my parents, my song to whoever has been lucky or blessed enough or had enough persistence and guts to stay together.

DONNA: He is a wonderful dad, husband, and my best friend. But he's high maintenance!

TIM: She is probably the only woman who would put up with me. I have things that I have to do, and she allows that and supports that.

Including his music, with another CD sure to evolve in years to come …

TIM: It's great to look back on—and when I'm dead and gone, my kids and their kids can put them on and say, "Dad loves Mom."

[(music and montage of kids, family): Together we will forge on through as we watch our children grow, as they spread their wings and start to fly and learn the things we know. The day to day, you can survive in a world that doesn't show, that love's above all others, 'cuz we're still standing.]

[Music]

Tim Flannery, a Southern California boy from Oklahoma, a baseball man, a husband, father, a musician. While the rules of baseball are black and white, he sees the game and life in full living color. I'm Jane Mitchell, see you next time on *One on One*.

"It was way beyond anything I ever dreamed. It got inside the inner being and this core of who I was as a person, and more than anything, of who my family was, and, you know, what we experienced as players in the organization…. I learned about telling stories. I learned how you can get what you need in a kind way, letting that person say what he needs to say. You make them feel comfortable enough to where they now feel like, you know what, I'm going to open up my heart and I'm going to open up my soul and I'm going to let people in. A lot of times, people will have this idea in their minds of who you are, and then they're going to try and get you to say what they need to be said, and you didn't do that. And that also means you had to work harder because of that, because you didn't have some preconceived idea of how the story was going to go. But it was an honest and it was a true story, and that's something that you can live with forever. I'm still honored to look back at it and chuckle and go, look at us back then. It allows you to kind of go, wow, we're a lot the same people, but there are a lot of changes since."

—Tim Flannery, 2010

LARRY LUCCHINO

"Jane elicited more personal tales from Larry than I had ever seen anyone elicit. And the warmth of the environment that she created—that she creates—somehow got him to be more revealing than he typically might be. He's much more reluctant to have the spotlight be on himself, and somehow, she made that palatable."

— CHARLES STEINBERG, BASEBALL EXECUTIVE, 2010

The first thing I learned about Larry Lucchino in 1996 was how to pronounce his last name. It's *Lew-KEY-no*, not Lew-CHEE-no. I did not want to get that wrong. The second thing I learned was that Larry, the Padres' President/CEO, was a powerful and energetic guy. I could see how he and the more calm but equally visionary Cox Vice President and General Manager, Bill Geppert, could team up to put more than one hundred Padres games on television for this new Cox/Padres partnership the fall of 1996.

Larry had been proactive about being public with John Moores, the new owner of the Padres. The New Padres, as Larry called them, were invigorating, focusing not only on fielding a competitive team, but also on philanthropy and fun for Padres fans and the community. Fans had felt burned since the players' strike and the previous ownership's fire sale—essentially getting rid of all the stars via trades or releases. All except Tony Gwynn, who could and did choose to stay. The Moores-Lucchino team was not only determined to make San Diego a successful business and community partner, but the two were movers and shakers with fight and influence in Major League Baseball as well.

The first time I formally met Larry, in the context of our new partnership, was at a meeting with my boss, Dan Novak, and Padres Vice President of Community Relations, Charles Steinberg. Having only been a weekend reporter in San Diego—and then on our two-week RNC channel—few with the Padres knew who I was. Dan Novak made it clear in that meeting that I would be the one doing the interviews and feature stories. Fourteen years later, for this memoir, I told Larry that I thought he looked at me, back then, as if to say, "Who are you" to which he reflected:

> "I don't remember that kind of reaction. Now, it doesn't mean it didn't happen but I don't remember that kind of reaction. The presence of female sportscasters was still relatively new at that time. Not new, but at least not widespread. So there may have been some reaction to that, but you proved to be exactly the right person for the role that you had, vis-à-vis in-depth analysis of players' personalities on and off the field."

So, back in 1997, while the Padres' contingent might not have been convinced I knew what I was doing baseball-wise, they graciously accepted I was the designated reporter and said they looked forward to working together.

Larry is a type A personality: bold, tells it like he sees it, with a blend of brash and diplomacy. I saw him in action as a tough negotiator at meetings for the development of the channel. I was impressed by how he had a wonderful command of the English language, was quite cerebral, not one for idle chitchat, and was always on the move. He wasn't easy to pin down, and while he didn't wholly intimidate me, he did, a little. The more I talked with him and was around him, though, the more comfortable I felt.

He got to know me as he saw my work the first few months of the season.

When it came time to ask him for a sit down interview, I, with the urging of his inner circle, convinced him it would be a mutually beneficial venture for the fans and the team. This idea of the channel connecting the fans with the team was, after all, partly his idea. Larry reflects on that vision:

"It was to be the easy way to see baseball regularly. It was to capitalize on the game of baseball and that was the principle purpose. The second purpose was to personalize and introduce our players to the town on a regular basis and more intimate basis."

Larry agreed to the interview. I had a challenge ahead.

In preparation, I solicited input from a few who knew him well. I was warned Larry might not sit still for an hour, might not want to talk about personal topics, and would not suffer the fool (that would be me, the reporter) who wasn't prepared. So I prepared by reading about him, asking people in his inner circle about him, and even interviewing his parents while they were at a game during a visit.

That summer of 1997, Padres Manager Bruce Bochy heard I planned to interview Larry. Bruce told me then what he had relayed to Larry, and years later, Larry recalls that friendly warning:

"I do remember Bruce Bochy telling me that 'She'll find out things about you that you don't even know about yourself.' And I said, 'I hope not.' And he said, 'No, trust me, you will. She will.'"

I took Bruce's heads up as a good sign I was digging a little deeper, peeling back a few layers, and still had people willing to sit down with me.

On the day of the shoot that summer, the production crew and I arrived at Larry's beautiful La Jolla home on a hill in a gated community. His living room had big windows that looked out over La Jolla Shores and the Pacific. Unmarried at the time, this was clearly a high-end, exquisitely decorated bachelor pad with everything in its place.

After converting his living room into a set with two cameras and lights, we rolled tape. I had a few butterflies at first, but I don't think he was nervous. This was, after all, a big time Washington lawyer, football and baseball team executive, who had faced far fiercer reporters than me. While he had a motto, "It can be done," he learned I believed that, too.

My preparation seemed to, if not impress him, at least assure him I knew what I was doing. The hour and a half interview flowed smoothly, covering his formative and professional years and his battle and victory over cancer. Then, we broached his personal life, touched on the fact he wasn't yet married, to which the attorney in him interjected, "Is this going to be a cross examination based on my mother's previous testimony?" When lobbing a series of comments from other people describing his strong personality as domineering and impatient, he snapped, "Who said this?" Maybe he had met his match. Not on tough issues, but on matters of the heart, I had no fear. Those are some of my favorite *One on One* moments, and they made it into the show.

His long-time friend and advisor, Jay Emmett, listened in on the interview that day, as did confidante Charles Steinberg, who had followed Larry from the Orioles. What seemed normal to me—to cover all the bases and pull out a few fun surprises—stunned them. To get him to sit for more than an hour and talk about himself? That, they said, was a first.

I asked if he would show me his yard where he had found some peace and quiet in the middle of a busy life. He obliged, and even as the camera rolled on our walk and talk, I could sense a calm about him as he looked out at that spectacular view.

I was learning with every in-depth interview, and this one truly helped me realize it was my responsibility to take control of the situation and make sure I covered everything I felt needed to be covered. If I realized I left something out, or learned about it later, I found ways to do pickup questions at other shoots, or at least ask about it, to weave it into the content of the show as necessary.

To visualize the "busy man" part of the story, we followed Larry around his office to see him in action at meetings, taking phone calls, scurrying from place to place. When the Padres were on a road trip to play the Pittsburgh Pirates, photographer Dan Roper and I went, too. In a fast two days of shooting, we visited where Larry grew up and had sat on his parents' front porch recouping from cancer treatment. We videotaped him around the dinner table with his parents, Rose and Dominic, in that small yellow house on Squirrel Hill he had talked about in his interview. All those elements came together for a comprehensive biography.

Within fifteen minutes from when the show aired September 12, 1997, I received this email from Charles Steinberg:

> "out——STANDING. Beautiful, ambitious, achieving, accurate, very very very impressive. Very Very good. Excellent. I just watched it, by the way. Superb. Big news ... even Larry loved it ... he'll tell you himself, I'm sure. Nice going."

Seeing Larry Lucchino sweat, just a little bit, that day of the interview still makes me smile. I have great respect for him as a person, a humanitarian, a visionary, a tough businessman, and a family man. I appreciate his professionalism, respect, and accomplishments, especially after he moved on from the Padres to the Boston Red Sox, and how he re-connected with the Padres and John Moores in 2004 when their vision of a new ballpark was realized. It does not surprise me how his leadership helped bring two World Championships to Boston in 2004 and 2006.

In 2008, the Larry Lucchino edition became a *One on One Classic*. With new stand-ups, I put his role in Padres history into context, referenced his move to the Red Sox, his marriage to Stacey Ballard, and how they, with her two children, spend time in Boston and La Jolla. Stacey became a friend of mine before she and Larry married, and after our fun but contentious interview about his being single in his fifties, it was good to see he finally met his real match.

This is the original script from the show debuting September 12, 1997.

• • •

Larry Lucchino, a man on a mission for the San Diego Padres.

LARRY: Winning, and winning, and winning.

To understand his vision we look at his past, which was influenced by a legendary sportsman and defense attorney, a battle with cancer, a pioneering baseball success story, and his Pittsburgh roots.

Larry Lucchino's goal is for the Padres to be as much a part of San Diego's pride and culture as the San Diego Zoo. It's not easy to catch up with the energetic minority partner of the Padres, but when you do get him to sit and talk about himself at length, one clear slogan emerges for both his personal and professional goals—the slogan, "It CAN be done."

Larry Lucchino is a lifelong baseball fan who revels in every nuance of the game.

LARRY: The daily-ness of baseball is one of its greatest charms. At the end of the day I know if San Diego has won or lost. I love that sense of competition, I really do.

While the Yale Law School grad no longer paces a courtroom, he still revels in preparing for a case, anticipating the other side's every move. He's thrilled to talk about the team and his vision, but when it comes to personal subjects, he prefers to ask the questions than to be questioned.

LARRY: Is this gonna be a cross examination based on my mother's previous testimony?

But he is also a very public part of the Padres rebuilding process, so we'll let the facts and some impressions state his case. Larry Lucchino is a dynamo. Few would argue with that. It's been obvious since he came on the San Diego scene in January 1995 as the new president and minority owner of the Padres, partnering with Texas transplant, computer software millionaire, and die-hard baseball fan all in one, John Moores.

JOHN MOORES: He's been wonderful. He couldn't have been better.

LARRY: Both John and I are now in the center of mid-life, I guess, and maybe that's a good time to adjust your life's focus.

Larry Lucchino is fifty-two years old, never been married, although he expects to be someday. He has a few regrets, a few failures …

LARRY: Oh yes, you've talked to some of my ex-girlfriends!

And scores of successful ventures from sports, to education, to litigation, to sports, again. While he is inspired by watching the team play or by the view of the Pacific Ocean from his San Diego home, his life and work experiences have a common denominator, how he was raised in Pittsburgh, PA, the city where the Mononga-hela and the Allegheny Rivers form the Ohio; where barges still carry coal; and the house on Suzanna Court, in the hamlet of Greenfield, is home to Dominic and Rose Lucchino. Homemade ravioli is on the menu when their son Larry comes to visit in the house where he grew up.

[In the kitchen]

LARRY: Mom, I'll protect you. I don't want the world to know how you make this sauce.

Larry Lucchino is proud of his Italian heritage and traditions, although he leaves the cooking to Mama Lucchino.

ROSE: He always disappears when I need him.

He was born September 6, 1945 and has one brother, Frank, who's six and a half years older.

LARRY: I was a real Pittsburgh kid. I would say that. I grew up in the city. So we played sports around the clock. I lived in a neighborhood full of kids and relatives, aunts, and uncles. I certainly didn't think that someday when I grew up I was going to be a baseball owner or executive. I didn't think that. Short-stop, maybe, but not the position I'm in.

Education would be a major influence on him, starting at the same school his parents attended, Greenfield Elementary.

LARRY: With great pride, I never missed a day of school. If you talk to my mother, I'm sure she'll tell you about that.

ROSE: We had three feet of snow one year in '52, and he was in kindergarten and he insisted on going to school. I said, "You just can't go today!"

LARRY: And I didn't miss a day of school I don't think for six or seven or eight years!

In the early '60s, kids in Greenfield hit the books, or hit the rougher life just down the road. Lucchino hit the books and sports at Squirrel Hill's Taylor Allderdice High School.

[High school football practice]

LARRY NEIBERG (High school coach): Larry worked hard enough, I would say, to be equal of anyone that was here.

Larry Neiberg remembers Lucchino as an All-City basketball player and the second baseman on the team that won the city championship in '63.

LARRY NEIBERG: He was the type of guy you could count on to lay the bunt down, to hit behind the runner, to get the extra base.

But his forte was basketball.

LARRY: I knew I was good at it and I wanted to be really good at something.

Lucchino says he got his work ethic from his family and friends.

LARRY: It's a Pittsburgh thing. That's an expression people use there all the time: "It's a Pittsburgh thing."

His father had several jobs, owned a bar and a small grocery store. His mother was in charge at home.

ROSE: He was never satisfied at ever having anything half done. It had to be just perfect.

He strived for perfection and had a little friendly competition with his brother.

ROSE: He said, "Anything Frank can do, I can do better."

FRANK: The only thing that he couldn't do better was beat me hitting the tennis ball off the back of my parents' house. We played that time and time again, and he has never beaten me, no matter what he says today. His memory is faulty! Besides being my brother, he's my best friend.

Larry Lucchino showed early signs of presidential power in high school, the senior class president, on the honor roll, focusing his sights on joining his brother as the first generation of Lucchinos to go to college; Ivy League, nonetheless.

ROSE: We can't afford it. [Larry] spoke up and [we] said, "Larry, if you can get admitted to Princeton, you go, because we'll take a second mortgage on the house if we have to."

Lucchino got in and worked at the cafeteria to help pay his way.

LARRY: I ended up in charge of the dining halls with 400-500 employees. I learned a lot of my business ethics and business experiences there.

As a basketball player at Princeton, Lucchino went to the NCAA Final Four in '65 and played with Bill Bradley, now a former U.S. Senator …

BILL BRADLEY: Larry could shoot, dribble, and pass. I particularly liked that he could pass.

DOMINIC: My biggest pride in Larry was when he actually entered Princeton and finished with honors. He just had so much confidence in doing what he could do, that it made me feel very proud.

LARRY: I wasn't sure I wanted to be a lawyer, but I was sure I wanted the rigor and the opportunity of law school.

He graduated from Yale and went to Washington to work on the impeachment proceedings of Richard Nixon for a year. When that ended, a new chapter in his life began. He was hired at a prestigious, high-powered, high-profile Washington law firm, Williams and Connolly, and had a boss who would have a profound influence on him.

LARRY: Everything I have done in sports and the opportunities I've had, have all been directly attributed to him.

Up next on *One on One*, Larry Lucchino's formative years in law, and the business of baseball, and a life-threatening experience that affects how he approaches his family, friends, and the future....

In baseball, there are rookies who learn from veterans who teach. For Larry Lucchino, as a young attorney in Washington, D.C. in the early '70s, his teacher, who grew to be his mentor, was Edward Bennett Williams, another attorney, but also part owner and president of the Washington Redskins.

LARRY: He just decided I would be a good guy to work with him.

Lucchino recalls his first day on the job at the firm Williams and Connolly.

LARRY: The senior partner comes in and you talk sports all afternoon. Hey this is not so hard, but how wrong I was. It was a very rigorous and very demanding place and he was an extraordinary workaholic.

Williams died of cancer in 1988. His funeral reflected the connections and friendships he had ...

[*CNN television report: He was the finest trial lawyer of our time ...*]

His clients ranged from mobsters to movie stars, including Jimmy Hoffa, Frank Sinatra, Joseph McCarthy and the *Washington Post*. Williams said, "Everyone is entitled to a lawyer."

LARRY: We used to ask, what makes Fast Eddie run? He kept running. And running. And running throughout his entire life, and even after he reached this extraordinary level of personal and professional achievement. He loved the competition and the intensity. That was life for him.

And that was life for his protégé, Larry Lucchino.

LARRY: We had a nice, easy connection right away.

Both Catholic, among the first in their working class families to go to college, and hard-charging sports lovers, Williams thrived on contest living in everything; results can be measured, you can succeed.

WILLIAMS: I had to [get] into the free agent market in order to field a competitive team.

Even as he fought cancer, Williams finally achieved a goal to own a Major League Baseball team. In 1979, he bought the Baltimore Orioles.

LARRY: They were going to be a dominant passion for him.

And because the team had had success on the field but couldn't draw the fans, Williams said he'd keep the team in Baltimore if the fans turned out at the gate. And with Lucchino, he began a marketing approach to reach beyond the city limits.

LARRY: He transformed the Orioles into a larger regional team.

Charles Steinberg, now the Padres Senior Vice President of Public Affairs, worked with Lucchino at the Orioles and remembers Lucchino's visions back then.

CHARLES STEINBERG: Vision one: Washingtonians will come to Baltimore for baseball games. Reaction from the native Baltimorian: Yuck. #2 Wrong, #3 Oops, he was right.

Lucchino will not take all the credit.

LARRY: We couldn't have done it without Williams being the person that he was with the presence in both cities.

And in 1983 …

ANNOUNCER: *The Orioles have won the World Series!*

The team slipped a little in '84 and '85, and that September, Lucchino took two weeks off. He and his friend, fellow Orioles board member Jay Emmett, motorcycled across France leaving the world of baseball and business and battles behind— or so they thought. They arrived home just as Lucchino was turning forty and about to be confronted with the biggest battle of his life.

JANE: Take us to that day.

LARRY: We had a large fortieth birthday party, but instead of having that, I was diagnosed with non-Hodgkin's lymphoma. Which is a pretty serious illness.

In a new procedure at the time, Lucchino's own bone marrow was treated and transferred back into his body. With chemotherapy he lost weight, hair, and strength, but found solace on his parents' front porch.

LARRY: I did a lot of sleeping, and I would sleep right here and look out at the world from the porch.

CHARLES STEINBERG: It's 1986, will he be here?

LARRY: Yeah, sometimes I wondered, too …

But like his mentor, he literally worked through it.

CHARLES: In a frail physical state, he'd sit down at the head of the table, "Okay let's go, we've got to beat last year's attendance mark!" We just set an Orioles record and here he is driving us, and nothing is going to stop …

LARRY: I never say it is over, but I feel like it is a distant part of my past.

JANE: It must affect your perspective on life. I can't imagine.

LARRY: For a while I had all these vows and resolutions that I'm gonna be different, and I was gonna take time to stop and smell the roses and all of that, but you find out after a while what you really want to do is get back to a sense of normality; that you're just a regular person again. Maybe part of my loyalty to my friends and family as extreme as it is, it comes in part that I was the beneficiary of so much of their loyalty during that time, so I had the whole second part of my life to say, *Boy, look what my friends and family did for me when I really needed it. If they ever need anything from me, I have half my life to pay them back.*

And half his life to keep on pursuing his visions. In Baltimore, vision number two.

LARRY: I remember the first time I suggested to Ed that we should have a baseball park instead of another combination multi-purpose facility.

Baltimore had lost the Colts and was considering remodeling the stadium for base-ball, but Williams wouldn't sign a long-term lease to keep the Orioles there without an agreement to build a new ballpark. The political powers that were didn't want to lose the team, and the state okayed instant lottery funds to pay for the new ballpark. And on May 2, 1988, Williams, near death, but determined to see his plan through, approved a fifteen-year lease agreement with the state. Then Williams named Lucchino President of the Orioles.

Three months later Williams died. The estate sold the team to a group headed by Eli Jacobs. Lucchino remained a minority owner and in charge of building the ball-park he'd been imagining since 1986.

> LARRY: Something that was traditional and old fashioned, but had lots of modern amenities.

He had the right to approve the details of the park, and he did. For example ...

> CHARLES STEINBERG: The precise shade that the pink brick had to be after baking in the sun to match the red brick of the warehouse ...

While the state had an architectural firm of record, Lucchino brought on board Janet Marie Smith, an architect with experience in urban design, who could help translate his ideas into reality.

> LARRY [Baltimore video clip]: *It's not gonna be a perfect stadium, but it will be a wonderful stadium.*

With the perfect Camden green paint, the best sod grown in Salisbury, Maryland, and a hundred-year-old warehouse preserved behind right field, Opening Day 1992 the vision came to fruition.

> LARRY: We knew we would like that—we at the Orioles would like that kind of ballpark. We didn't know the whole world was going to embrace it as it did.

The team was sold in October '93. Lucchino realized the new majority owner would take an active role in running the club, so he resigned. He worked with the Florida Marlins to help develop plans for a new stadium. But then he began to feel the urge to come home, come back to Pittsburgh. So in 1994, he was part of a group trying to buy his hometown team, the Pittsburgh Pirates. That's when John Moores called.

> JOHN MOORES: I don't think frankly he gave my telephone call a lot of sig-nificance, but he did agree to meet.
> LARRY: What I wanted was a business partner who would be a friend, some-one I could like, and trust, and have fun with.
> JOHN MOORES: We started to talk and it really clicked.

And that was just the beginning.

> LARRY: We came in when the franchise had been victimized by the triple whammy of the '90s.

The California recession, player-management problems in baseball, and an owner-ship perceived as lacking commitment to winning, which stripped the team of all but one veteran player.

> LARRY: We were determined to prime the pump and spend the money to do it the right way and be the best kind of baseball franchise we could be, and then eventually, we thought we could win the folks back. And I think we are well on our way of doing that.

When *One on One* continues, Larry Lucchino in action in his office, in the field, and at home, insight into his unconventional wisdom, and how it may affect where you and future generations watch a ball game in San Diego ....

When Larry Lucchino packed his briefcase and moved from his eastern roots to the west in January 1995, he brought with him his unquestioned intensity, his work ethic, and a reputation.

> BILL BRADLEY: He is loyal and trustworthy, humorous and caring.
> ROSE (Larry's mother): He's a tough boss!
> LARRY NEIBERG: Nothing was given to him. He's earned what he's got.
> JOHN MOORES: He has his soft spots and he has his self-doubts like we all do.
> JANE [quoting others]: A good person, a devoted son, bright, passionate, someone who doesn't get bored or give up. And ...
> LARRY: Uh, oh
> JANE: Domineering.
> LARRY: [laughing]
> JANE: Impatient.
> LARRY: Nonsense!
> JANE: Intolerant of people who aren't prepared.
> LUCCHINO: Who said this?
> JANE: Or don't use common sense.
> LARRY: All those things are probably true; if my friends said them, they're probably true, but I'm not sure that makes me different from a lot of people you've interviewed. I am a little perfectionist about things.

So to say a day in the life of Larry Lucchino can be hectic is an understatement.

> ROSEMARY POHL (Larry's assistant): Larry's phones are non-stop, but he's a make-it-happen kind of person.
> LARRY: It's funny how much smarter you can be, how much more successful you can be if you work just a little bit harder on the problem. We want to be one united, dedicated, determined team and I feel very proud of the quality people we have assembled in the Padres front office.

On this day he's meeting with leaders of business and government, reviewing a survey about fan satisfaction. Charles Steinberg followed Lucchino here from the Orioles. He considers him a coach—a mind coach.

CHARLES STEINBERG: He makes you think, he makes you stretch, he makes you dream, he makes you work.

LARRY: It can be hard on people and it can be hard on yourself. So I try to modulate that a little bit, and San Diego has had a positive influence on me.

San Diego and majority owner, John Moores …

JOHN MOORES: I prefer to think he's getting older!!! I have encouraged him many, many times to stop and smell the roses.

LARRY: You guys ready?

It's pretty clear, a fan runs this organization.

[Larry walking to private game suite and watching game.]

So the experience of going to a game is always a priority.

LARRY: Are the fans enjoying? Are the concessionaires doing their job? I also of course think about winning, and winning, and winning.

His drive is not lost on the fans.

FAN: A very straightforward person; doesn't beat around the bush.

FAN: I think he's trying to bring back baseball for the parents and the kids, and I think that's good.

Fans have been a part of the re-building process with "Tell it to the Padres" meetings and Padres Scholars to help at-risk kids go to college, and the creation of sixty Little Padres parks.

FAN: He's been doing a lot of things in the community, especially what I heard what he wants to do down in Tijuana in that ballpark.

And inspired by both Lucchino's experience with cancer and by a Padres fan Cindy Matters, who died of cancer, the Padres partnered with the UCSD Medical Center for research and to improve the lives of cancer patients …

LARRY: I don't want to be a part of a team that just plays baseball. I want to be part of a baseball team that is part of an entire community.

On the business front, Lucchino is known as a tough as nails negotiator, who often contradicts conventional wisdom for marketing.

LARRY: Conventional wisdom is that you can't go north, can't go east, can't go south, can't go west. So we decided we were going to go north, east, south, and west anyway.

To North County, Mexico, Hawaii, and Japan, and on TV more than ever before by partnering with Cox Communications and becoming the anchor programming on the new Channel 4. Cox General Manager, Bill Geppert.

BILL GEPPERT: He's very progressive in his view, the more exposure to the team, the more involvement you have with the team, the more you're following the team, the more likely you are to come out to the ballpark and watch it on television.

The Padres' next goal? Joining the national trend Lucchino set with Camden Yards, building a new, more intimate, baseball oriented ballpark.

> **CHARLES STEINBERG:** It won't look anything like Camden Yards. That's the point. Make it look like your town and then you celebrate that.

Centerfielder Steve Finley likes the idea.

> **STEVE FINLEY:** Part of the contingency when you sign a lease for a new ballpark is I have to be here to play in that ballpark.
>
> **LARRY:** We want the Padres to be a source of pride. We want them to be a very competitive, solid team, entertaining team, and in order to accomplish this, we can't do it under the current circumstances. We've tried for a couple of years and our losses are enormous. But we're not whining about them.
>
> **JOHN MOORES:** Ultimately we have to financially stabilize the franchise or the franchise will go away. Our goal is to fix the problems that are here and deal with them now and there's no reason we can't do that.
>
> **LARRY:** It's about economic improvement, economic opportunity. If the people of San Diego and the public opinion and political will is that we get a chance to build a ball park for a second time, which is most unusual, we will build the best and most beautiful ballpark in the world. I assure you of that.

Larry Lucchino enjoys the journey, but thrives on results. While 1996 was a Cinderella story, winning the West and the '97 Padres didn't fair as well. Lucchino, the fan, appreciates the game's "anything can happen" nature.

> *[Tony's game winning hit, Larry cheers.]*
>
> **LARRY:** Think about how alive you are. You care. It affects your disposition, your good humor for a while. You care about something other than yourself, a larger group endeavor. It's fun and it does get the juices flowing, both for better or worse.

"I [recall] the first call when you said that you were going to go there [Pittsburgh] and to trust you. And it showed me that this was really going to be a little different than most interviews, that you were going to go all the way back to like its bare roots. My impression was Bochy was right, this is going to be more in-depth than I'd anticipated ... I'm not known for my extended conversations. I do remember the interview at the house and I can still remember it as being kind of playful and fun and maybe that's why it went on so long ... When I saw it at the end, I was relieved. You did a thorough job, and I felt that I was fairly treated, or, not to say there weren't things I wish that I had said differently, but on balance, I thought it was fair and it was a satisfying experience ... [Of Channel 4 and *One on One* ...] It worked. It was perfect. We knew what we wanted to do, and then you came in. We couldn't have conceived a program that captured what we were trying to do in terms of humanizing and personalizing the players."

—Larry Lucchino, 2010

On the "worse" days …

>   **LARRY** [from his backyard looking out at the water]: I come back here and I sit here for a few minutes, and it doesn't seem as important.

His introspective side dedicated palm trees to honor the memory of special people in his life. He values his native Pittsburgh where three rivers meet, and he still cherishes being home on his parents' front porch.

>   **LARRY:** You're always your parents' son when you're at home; you're not anything else.
>   **DOMINIC:** We never dreamed it. He's done fantastic and made us very proud.

From Pittsburgh to the Pacific, Larry Lucchino is still a man on a mission.

>   **LARRY:** I really want to do something for a city I love as much as I've come to love San Diego. So I do feel an obligation to do some things to make baseball work here, and to make some marginal contribution to the quality of life and community that exists in San Diego.
>   **JANE:** What do you want to be known as?
>   **LARRY:** I want to be known as a good friend. I want to be known as a really good friend. That's what I want to be known as, yeah.

Whether the result is another pennant for the Padres, a new ballpark, or working through a personal battle with cancer, there's certainly a lesson to be learned from the way Larry Lucchino lives his life, by his motto: It can be done. I'm Jane Mitchell, hope to see you next time, on *One on One*.

STEVE FINLEY

Steve Finley made playing centerfield look so easy. His low-key personality and on-field productivity combined for an intriguing persona on the Padres. He had come to the team in a blockbuster trade with the Houston Astros in December, 1994. That trade signaled that the new ownership was putting their money where their mouth was. Steve was proving to be a good move, not only for his play on the field, but for helping the team accomplish another goal: being a part of the San Diego community and connecting with fans.

> "Jane's *One on One* program helped the fans see beyond just the player on the field, but see him more as a regular person doing a dream job. All this helped bring the players and fans closer, and really build a community spirit for the team."
>
> — STEVE FINLEY, 2010

Steve set the tone at home for the 1998 season with a walk-off game-winning grand slam the Friday of opening week in San Diego. He was part of the "never say die" Padres who would go on to the World Series that season. Before that, though, I was excited to tell his story and, as quiet and humble as he was, he was open to it.

We arranged to interview him and his wife, Amy, at their Del Mar home. The two-story house was right on the beach, quite the contrast to their Kentucky roots. They were genuine, open, and at ease during the interview, Steve more low key and Amy, very vivacious. To show them with their children, we walked out to the beach with their three boys, playing in the sand and water. They liked photographs and capturing the moment—obvious from the beautiful pictures displayed in their home. This time, images would not be for just friends and family, but for fans. It was one of the first times I had been in public with a crew and a player, where people would walk by and realize who we were videotaping: a Padres star in his own backyard, and one they'd be able to learn about in an upcoming *One on One.*

It was clear to me by now, my second year of the show, that interviews with those who knew someone best from different parts of their life added to the depth of my storytelling. I had talked with Steve's parents on the phone, but my show budget didn't include going to Kentucky to interview them or to tape locations where Steve grew up. So I collaborated with a small TV station, WPSD-TV in Paducah, Kentucky. Eager to help, the reporter agreed to interview his parents for me (with my questions) and tape the town and school. Being resourceful and having such cooperation allowed me to paint a more complete portrait.

This show proved another first: seeing how the program reached beyond San Diego. After I mailed his parents and his college a copy of the program, I learned a coach showed it to young players at the American Legion baseball camp where Steve had once played. The coach saw value in showing them the story of how a kid from Paducah could make it to the majors.

After 1998, Steve Finley signed with the Diamondbacks, won a World Championship ring with them in 2001, and went on to play with several teams through 2007. He and former teammate Carlos Hernandez were on hand for the '98 reunion, both among all-time favorites. Amy became an interior designer and businesswoman. Amy and Steve, since divorced, are raising their five children and

continue their philanthropy in San Diego telling me they were happy to be part of this memoir. While some things change, this profile from their earlier years includes the core of who they were growing up and how they became part of San Diego sports history.

Here's the script from the original show debuting March 31, 1998.

• • •

Steve Finley, the Padres' centerfielder, has a glove like gold, dazzles on the diamond, and has marquee good looks. But if you think he's all business no pleasure—stick around …

STEVE: Anything that has to do with playing, anything, I'll go and do it.

He radiates when he talks about his journey, his family, his California dream. Modesty is Steve Finley's middle name, which makes him a rare commodity in the sometimes ego-fueled world of professional sports. But he's not shy about what he believes in—family, community, and baseball. Some say he's the best kept secret in the game.

ANNOUNCER: Finley has made all kinds of incredible catches, but look at this one!

When a ball is hit toward centerfield, it's almost like a heat seeking missile, seeking and finding Steve Finley's glove. More accurately, it's Steve Finley's radar, his defensive tactics that put him in the right spot to grab and snag, to seek and destroy. His catches never cease to amaze and surprise fans, players, the opposition. But does he ever surprise himself?

STEVE: No. I don't think so. I expect myself to catch everything that's hit up in the air.

He proves the adage "where there's a will, there's a way." Guess that explains why he's a Gold Glover, the only time a Padres centerfielder has earned that title—not once, but twice, in '95 and '96.

STEVE: I'm not flashy, I've never been flashy. When I dive, it doesn't look pretty.

Maybe not pretty, but completely in character.

FRAN (mother): He was a bundle of energy that exploded out of bed every morning, and he did not stop until he was sometimes physically held in bed and read to.

He was born Steven Allen Finley to Fran and Howard Finley, March 12, 1965. He grew up in Paducah, Kentucky, a farm town 175 miles from St. Louis, the nearest big league city.

STEVE: It was slow, but it was country living.

He liked to throw just about anything round, including fruit from his dad's garden.

HOWARD: Who's been throwing my tomatoes? And I'd go back there and they'd just pulled the last green ones off and here it comes. They pulled every tomato off the vine, so that wasn't a very good experience for him; he still doesn't like tomatoes to this day.

His sister Anne, who's three years younger, recalls spending countless summer days at the baseball fields with him.

ANNE: They used to say I'm one of the reasons he's such a good defensive player because I had such a lousy arm as a child. So he was always having to jump and scramble to get the ball.

His parents were teachers at schools he attended.

STEVE: They always made sure I got my homework done and I felt the responsibility because they were teachers. I better do well in school or else.

But another basic took a little more discipline.

STEVE [sitting next to his mom, Fran]: "Steve, get your elbows off the table." When I'm chowing the food down, she's looking around the room … going, "Steve, I don't see anybody here that's going to steal your food …"
FRAN: [laughing]
STEVE: So you know just little things like that happening and I'm going, "Mom, just leave me alone!"

He also values a more intangible lesson …

STEVE: I think a lot of it was just respect. Respect for other people's things, respect for other people, and just in general being a nice person. I don't feel like I could ever be mean to somebody. I go back and look now and that's just kind of the way they brought me up.

Steve Finley, who was skinny as a rail, was all boy.

STEVE: After school, basketball, football, baseball, golf, you name it.

He didn't have a sports idol, didn't even dream, early on, about being a professional athlete.

STEVE: I didn't really know what being a professional player was, I just loved playing sports.

As for Major League Baseball ...

STEVE: My first game that I ever went to was the seventh game of the World Series in St. Louis in 1982; that was the first major league game I saw and it was a good one. I remember the Cardinals won and in a dramatic fashion we ended up even spilling down onto the field. It was exciting and I knew at that point it would be nice to one day be there, but I never really thought about it any more than that.

His mother reveals it might have been a little more than a passing thought. Finley was the sports editor of his high school paper and a classmate told her of a conversation Steve had with some friends then.

FRAN: And he said, "You're going to be reading about me in a newspaper one day." He said, "You're going to hear all about what I have done." And they're going, "Yeah, sure Steve ..." So I think that he knew he was going to do something.

That something?

STEVE: Baseball kind of took over as my main goal sport, and my goal at that point was just to get a college scholarship. I never watched professional baseball, I didn't watch professional baseball until I broke my leg in 1984 and I was forced to sit for a whole summer on a couch in my bedroom, so I watched the Atlanta Braves and the Chicago Cubs.

He was selected to play American Legion baseball in Kentucky, spotted by college scouts, but never picked up in a draft. Still, his skills and good grades especially in math and science landed him a college scholarship at Southern Illinois University, where he began to really develop his talent, and baseball began to take hold of his heart.

ITCHY JONES: The first time I saw him I was not that impressed with him.

But that opinion soon changed. His coach at SIU, Richard "Itchy" Jones, realized Finley was fast and motivated.

ITCHY JONES: He worked very hard, and he accomplished what he wanted, and you could see each year he got a little better—his freshman year, his sophomore year, and on into his junior year.

At the end of his junior year he was drafted by the Atlanta Braves. But he didn't just jump at the opportunity. He valued the goal of finishing college in four years, so the offer had to be enough to make it worth delaying graduation.

STEVE: They made one offer and never came back again, and so that was it.

That summer he played baseball in Alaska, then joined team USA in Europe, then back home against the Cubans. He majored in physiology, prepared to be a chiropractor like one of his mentors. But his decision to turn down that Atlanta offer haunted him for a while.

STEVE: There were a lot of questions in my mind my senior year because I didn't have as good a senior year in college as I really thought I was going to. I was really worried about it at first, but things have a tendency to work out, and it did. It worked out for the best.

Coming up on *One on One*, how doing what comes naturally and a bulldog of a coach help him make it to the majors. And later, Steve and Amy Finley define good times, good fun, and good will....

Call it fate, call it a reward, but Steve Finley, who passed up Atlanta's offer to play professional baseball to instead finish college, got a second chance. And this time, he grabbed hold of what would become his rising star.

STEVE: I was one of the lucky few.

In 1987, Finley was picked up in the free-agent draft by the Baltimore Orioles, who shipped him off to Single-A—the low minors.

STEVE: I was a college senior coming out, so I was maybe a little bit more mature than the high-school kids.

The usual route for a college senior would have been for Finley to spend his second full year in Double-A. Instead, he played only ten games before jumping to Triple-A. All because of the impression he made in spring training on Johnny Oates, then the manager of the Triple-A Rochester Redwings.

JOHNNY: Here's this kid, he did everything right on the field. He ran well, he threw well, he hit.

The big club wanted to bring Finley along slowly ...

JOHNNY: I said, "You've got to be kidding me."

Early in the season, the Orioles were being depleted by injuries and the top prospects in Triple-A were moving up, vacating spots for younger players.

JOHNNY: I said, "I want the Finley kid" and he says, "Okay you can have him for two weeks."

STEVE: And I started hitting a little bit after that, and another few days went by, I started hitting, another few days went by, and I couldn't figure out what was going on. I kept waiting to get sent back.

What was going on? Johnny Oates was fighting to keep him.

STEVE: I was just playing. I was just playing and having a good time!

Oates' hunch paid off. That season, Finley took the Triple-A International League batting title and in '89 earned a spot on the Opening Day starting line-up in Baltimore. It would be a defining moment in his career.

STEVE: I remember that day well.

He's playing right field ...

STEVE: I wasn't nervous, not one single bit ...

And in his typical no-holds-barred effort he races to catch a ball over his shoulder ...

ANNOUNCER: *He reaches up and he makes the catch! And slams into the wall and then hangs onto it!*

STEVE: All I could hear was Brady Anderson telling me I had room, then he stopped saying I had room, and I knew I was going to catch it, so I went ahead and went for it, and it hit my glove, and the next thing I know was slammed into the wall.

ANNOUNCER: *Hello, Steve Finley and welcome to Baltimore.*

STEVE: I caught the ball and threw it back in, then tried to lift my shoulder, and I knew something was wrong,

He had to leave the game.

STEVE: But by the same token, I made that catch and I got a standing ovation. It was the greatest feeling in the world.

While Baltimore valued his speed and potential, Houston needed that, and Finley was traded to the Astros at the end of '91. He tried to look on the bright side.

STEVE: There was going to be no pressure because they didn't expect us to win, so we could really develop.

ANNOUNCER: *Steve Finley has hit it out of the park!*

An every day player, he did develop, posting career highs. Then in December '94, after the Padres' fire sale and just one week after John Moores and Larry Lucchino bought the team, he was traded again.

STEVE: I thought I was going to Boston that year, and that was going to be one of my biggest nightmares if I had to go play in Boston, and I'm like, "Come on, get out of here. Where, where?" They said, "San Diego," and it was like, wooooo, relief, all right.

He was part of a blockbuster deal that included third baseman Ken Caminiti to shore up the defense. But with trade came new pressure.

STEVE: I felt I had to prove what I could do all over again. They told me I didn't, but I kind of always feel that way. I want people to know how I can play, what I can do for them.

Finley credits hitting coach, Merv Rettenmund, for changing his game.

STEVE: After six years in the big leagues I learned how to hit. It's weird, you think somebody should know how to hit, but I learned how to hit my first year over here.

MERV: The hitter has to do it and I say the same things to basically every hitter we bring in here. The words maybe will be a little bit different.

Finley listened and he applied.

MERV [talking to player]: Think of this, if your head's going forward at all, doesn't that make it longer to catch up to your face?

MERV: Once in a while he gets off track, but when he's good, he's just—he's incredible.

STEVE: It has really taken my game to a different level.

To say the least. In 1996, he nearly tripled his career best for home runs from 11 to 30 …

STEVE: Surprised the heck out of me.

Steve Finley says the only person who predicted, early on, that he'd ever be a power hitter was Johnny Oates.

JOHNNY: I said at Triple-A, eventually he would hit some home runs because he has the power.

And with his individual achievements, he loved being part of a team effort to win the West. Early in the '97 season, with a sore elbow, Finley fell into a frustrating slump at the plate, but he never gave up.

STEVE: You just gotta go up to the plate and keep swinging, and keep swinging, and you'll get through it.

He got hot, hot, hot. He became the first Padre in twenty-five years to hit three home runs in a game twice, finishing the season with twenty-eight homers. While challenging, the '97 season said volumes about what makes Steve Finley tick.

STEVE: I want to be up at the plate with the game on the line. Those are situations you have to want. Even when I'm struggling, I want those situations, because I know sooner or later, I'm going to get a hit and somebody's going to pay.

But true Finley fans can't decide which is more fun: watching him swing the bat or taking after a batted ball that mere mortals might let fall.

STEVE: I've gotta find a way to make this look a little more sleek and I just can't do it. I think ever since I separated my shoulder on Opening Day in '89 that I've not been able to dive headfirst. All I do now is kind of a tumble dive just to protect my shoulder.

What he lacks in flash, Finley makes up for with finesse. Experts say he gets one of the best jumps in the game—so he doesn't have to make a flashy dive. But it's not luck. It's homework, and headwork, knowing a batter.

STEVE: How guys hit, who's pitching that day, how they might hit him…. There's a lot of times in batting practice where I won't chase fly balls, but I'll just stand there. The ball will be hit and I'll just look to a spot in the outfield, and that's where its going to land, and that way, whenever a ball is hit in a game, I know exactly where it's going to land.

Nine years in the majors, Finley is proving he's not just getting older, he's getting better.

MERV: He's one of the best players right now, as far as I'm concerned, in all of baseball. He plays a hundred and sixty games a year, he's durable, is mentally strong, and when you put it all together he's got a lot of good years of baseball left.

At thirty-three, Finley's defying conventional wisdom that most players decline as they get older in baseball age, into their mid-thirties, because they fail to make adjustments as they learn the game.

> **STEVE:** The older you get, the more you know. But you have to apply it, too. That's what we're trying to do is apply different things to the swing that you learn or you feel.

From off-season workouts to spring training batting practice, Finley is a constant student of the game, always adjusting to the pitcher who thinks he has Finley all figured out.

> **STEVE:** I still feel like I'm on the upswing of my career; I think I'm finally finding myself as a player.

Others are discovering him too, in different ways. Up next on *One on One*, how Steve Finley handles the limelight, some Finley family fun in the sun, and touching stories of how they help those they care about....

> *[(music): Running down a dream ...]*

Steve Finley is finding fun, love, and satisfaction in work and life. As Tom Petty would say, he's "running down a dream."

> **FRAN:** He gets up every day and he's just joyful that he can do his job.
> **JOHNNY:** He only knows one way to play, and that's as hard as he can.
> **ANNE:** He's just Steve. And he hasn't forgotten about his friends and his family.

It sounds so simple to say Steve Finley is a nice guy.

> **STEVE:** I don't feel I could ever be mean to somebody.

And when you look at how Webster defines *nice*—pleasant, attractive, kind, and good—nice fits Steve Finley. But there's more. He's quiet yet thoughtful, confident without being cocky.

> **STEVE:** Half the battle in being a major leaguer is *believing* you belong there.

And confident that he does belong there, Finley gets great enjoyment from just playing.

> **STEVE:** Anything—play—just play. I like my toys.

Swimming, boogie boarding, fishing, scuba diving ...

> **STEVE:** I'm like a little kid. I think I will always be like a little kid; anything that has to do with playing anything, I'll go and do it.

Even playing baseball underwater, a different sort of centerfield, when Finley was featured on Fox Sports' *In the Zone* ...

> *[Steve on TV show: My lucky baseball ... don't go anywhere without that ...]*

For all his sweet swings and fearless feats in centerfield—Steve Finley hasn't become a household name in the national baseball media.

> **STEVE:** No, I never worry about those things.

Even his breakthrough year of '96 was masked by Ken Caminiti's unbelievable year.

> **STEVE:** No, I didn't feel overshadowed by him. I was glad Cammy was doing what he was doing.

Part of it is probably because he's happy not drawing attention to himself.

> **STEVE:** I go about my business the same this year as last year and the year before that, as I do every year.

But he's gradually receiving more kudos, named the MVP of an international all-star team which played in Japan, and in '97, his first taste of the All-Star team.

> **STEVE:** I had an absolute blast going out there!

He blushes a bit when someone points out his rugged good looks and magnetism ...

> **STEVE:** It's nice that you have fans out there ...
>
> **AMY:** I'm his #1 fan, so I love it. I can't see why they wouldn't be in love with Steve Finley. He is one of the most unaffected people that I know. When we go somewhere, he just doesn't realize the impact he has on people.

The Finleys have three children—Austin, Reed, and baby Blake.

Steve and Amy became friends in college.

> **AMY:** I did not want to be married. I wanted to be an interior designer or an architect. I wasn't going to be married for a long time.

They married in '92.

> **AMY:** Don't think this is what I planned, but my life's wonderful. I have no complaints.

Amy is from Illinois, one of ten children. Her father is one of the original body builders of the '40s, and she's a self-described jock.

> **STEVE:** She's a great mom. I have to call when I'm on the road and I'm getting my sleep, and I'm hearing her just going, "Reed was up at three o'clock in the morning, they were both fighting in the middle of the floor at three o'clock in the morning, Reed and Austin," and I'm laughing, and she goes, "That's not funny."

And for a guy who, as a child, never watched baseball on TV, his son, Austin, is hooked.

> **STEVE:** When I call at night now he goes, "Daddy I saw you on television, you hit a home run tonight."

And he's a mimic, mastering the batting stance of Cammy, Tony [Gwynn] and Daddy. Their hope for their children is simple.

STEVE: Happiness. Just to be happy, support them in whatever they want to do.

Just like their parents did for them. That hasn't gone unnoticed. Finley's mother was named a San Diego March of Dimes Mother of the Year …

STEVE [at event podium]: Mom, thank you for everything you've done. I love you and I'm proud of you.

While family is a priority, the Finleys have to balance the demands of people wanting a piece of his celebrity.

AMY: It's what you accept to be when you do what you do.

But what's optional is how they spend their own time and money, how they use their celebrity to influence others.

STEVE: You do have a responsibility to the public, people that look up to you, and if they see you act a certain way, they might try to act the same way, so you should be acting in a responsible manner.

In his last year, before he becomes a free agent, Steve Finley is earning just under three and a half million dollars …

STEVE: We don't let money control our lives. We try to share our money as much as we can. We'll give to charities.

AMY: You can buy somebody's education or buy a home for somebody that otherwise wouldn't have it, and that's the best feeling I find that we have with our money.

Finley is very much a part of the Padres' community outreach and supports a new ballpark for San Diego in hopes he'll be able to stay and play in it someday. And he was one of the first players to put up ten thousand dollars to establish Padres Scholars in 1995, now one hundred students strong.

STEVE: It's an incentive plan to keep kids straight and off of drugs.

It's made a difference for Bernice Alcantara, a straight A student at Mount Miguel.

BERNICE (Padres Scholars): He pushes us up, giving us self esteem and to try to achieve our goals after high school to go college, to study a career, become someone.

Finley is in a comfort zone around kids …

[Reading *Green Eggs and Ham* with Tony Gwynn]

From a T-shirt and jeans to a tuxedo, Finley represents his commitment to education well. And in perhaps his most visible off-field public appearance yet, he was a presenter for *Cox Presents: A Salute to Teachers* after toe surgery and before a live television audience in October, 1997.

STEVE [on stage]: Both my parents are teachers back in Kentucky, and I think I always respected that, but I don't think I really appreciated it until I became a substitute teacher between my minor league seasons. And believe me, that was an experience!

What they started in Houston is now in San Diego—The Steve Finley Family Foundation, to raise funds and raise awareness for needs, including the YWCA's Domestic Violence Program ...

AMY: The statistics are staggering of abused women and children, and since I'm a woman, and I'm not in that situation, I feel a desperate need to help somebody in that situation.

The YWCA's program provides victims with a hotline for help, a safe place to stay, and counseling for people like Patty, a survivor who's now moved on with her life.

PATTY: Every time they maybe think it isn't worth it, they need to just think of me and remember that there are a lot of people just like me, a lot, who need that help, and who have benefited from it.

The Finleys contribute time and money to Children's Hospital for neonatal care and cancer patients, like Erin Kilian, who's on the road to recovery.

ERIN: The hospital treats your illness, it treats the cancer that you have and stuff, but it's Steve Finley and organizations like that that really treat your heart. They've helped more than they will ever know. I hope they see it in our faces and in our eyes how much they help because we really appreciate it.

The Padres honored him with the Leadership in the Community Award, which he shared with his wife ...

STEVE [accepting award]: She does all the work behind the scenes ...

And gave credit to team owners, John and Becky Moores.

STEVE: They've opened more doors than thought possible for the community.

Steve Finley never imagined living in California ...

STEVE: Now that we've been here, it feels like it should be home.

He loves the Padres.

STEVE: There's one thing about the players on our team, and that is we don't give up.

And he's driven to achieve a professional goal ...

STEVE: World Series Championship—period.

In the end, it's not just how you look or how you play, but how you love that matters. Steve Finley knows that, as he's running down his dream....

You've seen some different sides of Steve Finley, but perhaps one final story sums him up best. It's told by Johnny Oates. When Finley was called to Triple-A in '88 wearing jeans and a T-shirt, he didn't meet the dress code, so Oates lent him a sports jacket. Oates later took it to the cleaners to discover the jacket was ruined because Finley had left a candy bar in the pocket.

JOHNNY: Just to show you what Steve's all about, last summer we had interleague play and it was the first time I'd seen Steve since my days in Baltimore. It was a Sunday day game, and I walk in and there's about a $500 sports jacket hanging in my locker with a Snickers bar in it. He just wanted to thank me for everything I'd done.

Steve Finley—an example of how nice guys really can finish first. I'm Jane Mitchell. I hope you'll join me next time for *One on One*.

DAVE STEWART

"I spoke about a lot of things that day I don't speak about publicly: my kids, personal feelings, about my house, game issues. Those are all things that have always been reserved for personal friends.... My agent Tony Attanasio sent me an email saying he was brought to tears. I don't know if it was that good, but I was happy with it ..."

— DAVE STEWART, 2010

It was big news when Dave Stewart signed with the San Diego Padres to be the club's pitching coach in 1998. A five-time World Series pitcher with two Championship rings, he would not only bring experience, but a unique presence to the pitching staff, showing the team, fans, and opponents that the Padres meant business. He was hired to guide the pitchers, and ultimately the team, to the World Series.

I didn't know anything about Dave early on, but when I first saw him at spring training in '98, I recall a distinctive aura and confidence about him. With his hat pulled down tightly, demonstrating focus, he was big, strong, and serious. His soft-spoken voice did not fit his powerful demeanor. That contrast, in part, made him intriguing, and a perfect candidate for season two of *One on One*. He agreed to my request via the Padres to do the interview.

It was raining the day we met him at his home that January. Rain never makes things easy, but when we drove up to his bachelor mansion, I had a feeling this was going to be quite the experience. Walking into this immense two-story house was like walking into the pages of *Architectural Digest* meets *Sports Illustrated*. It oozed

220

fine design with contemporary furnishings and reflected success and a distinctive sense of accomplishment. The colors were gray and black, with bold splashes of purple and green. The textiles were top notch. This was a home of a champion, and as we would learn more about him, a long way from where he had started: a low-income neighborhood in Oakland, California and six years in the Dodgers' minor league system before getting his shot in the majors.

To determine where we should set up the cameras, Dave showed us the expansive main floor with a room dedicated to baseball, with his jerseys, baseballs, and World Series memorabilia. We chose the family room adjacent to the kitchen with a large, purple leather sectional sofa.

The most vivid memory I have of that day has to do with time. As we were putting a microphone on him and preparing to sit down on the sofa, he inquired, "How long is this going to take, Jane?" To which I replied, "It all depends on how long you feel like talking." Then, sliding down in the big couch and putting a foot up on the coffee table, he said in his soft, calm voice, "Well, if I can sit back like this, I'll talk to you all day," and he did. After fourteen years, he still holds the record as the longest of my *One on One* interview sessions: three hours on tape, and another thirty minutes with his daughter and the house tour. Every minute was fascinating. He went into great detail about challenging times. Some topics about the business and politics of the game deserved more time and explanation than I could give, and I knew while listening that they would never make it on the air for my program focusing on his story. However, hearing his tales, opinions, and frustrations helped me understand him more.

Asked about his philosophy of pitching, he explained the pitcher's appearance on the mound during a game might be the first time someone has seen a baseball game, so it is the pitcher's job to show the fan that the pitcher is baseball, that day. I was so caught up in his vision and his passion, I joked, "I'll pitch for you, Dave. Sign me up." He just had a way of drawing you into his world. No wonder he was so good.

At the end of our interview session, he said he had never talked that much about himself, even after combining all the times he had been interviewed. Perhaps it was because I had an unusually large number of questions. It just seemed to me as if he wanted to be thorough in answering each question. He did so with great patience and passion, and if he had the time, we had the time.

Our day wasn't over. He obliged us with a complete tour, taking us up the winding metal staircase into the master bedroom and bathroom with a large whirlpool tub and a skylight for stargazing. I recall we did a lot of ooh-ing and ah-ing, which made it difficult to pick and choose the best snippets for the final show so viewers could feel as if they went along for the ride.

That spring we flew up to Oakland to videotape where Dave grew up and went to school. We gathered pictures from his high school, his mother and sister, and interviewed his sister and a friend. It is a very tangible experience to go to someone's childhood home. You can feel their stories come to life by seeing the neighborhood, hearing the horns honking, comparing and contrasting their life then and now. That sense of accomplishment, and physical and emotional gains over the years, are all the more vivid when I can feel, if only for a few hours, a little piece of their past.

The Dave Stewart edition also taught me a valuable lesson to frequently SAVE a working document. I began writing the show one late afternoon at my office. Five and a half hours later, at about nine, something went wrong—my script was gone. I hit UNDO and every other thing I could think to do, and all the words that I had written in the cells of the formatted Word document were gone. I called every person I could find in the Information Technology department after nine o'clock at night. They said if it was not there and not in the computer's trash, it was lost. It had to have been an operator error—mine—but it was still maddening.

In tears, and nearly hyperventilating, I called my mother. At first she said I should take a break, go home, and get some sleep. I said I wouldn't be able to sleep. She then suggested I say a prayer, take a deep breath, and try to write everything I remembered. I don't know how it happened, but in an hour and a half, I rewrote the first part of the script that had originally taken five and a half hours to compose. Our brains are amazing organs; all that thinking, planning, and writing poured through my fingers and onto that screen. I'll never know which version was better, but I was happy with what I did. Since that night, I save, save, save as I go.

Dave Stewart went on to be an assistant general manager and agent. His role in Padres history is important, and it was good to see him as part of the ten-year reunion celebrating the 1998 World Series year and personally, to hear his comments about his *One on One* experience all these years later. His edition is a *One on One Classic*.

Here's the script from the original show debuting June 4, 1998.

• • •

From his humble beginnings to his magnificent dream house, five-time World Series pitcher Dave Stewart is cloaked in mystique and making his mark as the Padres pitching coach.

DAVE: Whatever it takes to make you better. I'll make you better.

Dave Stewart may never have landed in the big leagues if it weren't for a bold move he made. A move based on an amazing level of self-confidence. With a reputation as a tough guy on the mound, you might think he's unapproachable. Not so. His reputation is only part of his story, a story of intrigue, struggle and success. His menacing stare could melt ice.

DAVE: If you can create one inch of fear in anybody, you can win.

His magnetism and conviction could melt hearts.

DAVE: I believe all good things come through God.

His soft voice, but powerful message could make a novice or veteran eager to adopt his pitching philosophy.

DAVE: When I take the mound on my day, I'm baseball. I am the guy that when you see me play, you saw a good performance.

DON SUTTON: When you watch Dave Stewart, you say, "Here's a guy that walked out there, and if you're going to take the ball, you'd better have a forklift and an armed guard, because it's his mound and he was a take charge type guy."

He made an impression during fifteen years in the big leagues to win an astonishing minimum of twenty games, four years in a row.

DAVE: For years I had been telling my best friend that I was the best pitcher. I didn't hesitate. I said, I'm the best pitcher in the game if I get my chance.

He has pitched in the World Series five times, three of those the teams were World Champions. He retired as a player in 1995. Dave Stewart's first appearance with the San Diego Padres in 1997 seemed almost cameo, quietly working as special assistant to General Manager, Kevin Towers, to scout talent to build on the '96 National League Western Division champion team. But after a losing '97 season ...

KEVIN TOWERS: There was some hidden talent there that hadn't come out yet.

After some coaxing, Stewart did something even Hall of Famer Don Sutton admits few marquee names ever do.

DON SUTTON: He stepped down from what could be considered an ivory tower to go on field and to convey that to other people.

DAVE: I'm not going to take it for granted that they respect me. What I'm going to do is try to earn their respect.

KEVIN BROWN: Every time you see him, you think about the way he pitched, and that's how you want to approach the game.

KEN CAMINITI: All those games that we were losing, [he'd say,] "We're gonna win this game, watch. We're gonna win this game."

BRUCE BOCHY: He's been cut, been released, given up on. He knows what it's like to struggle, but he also knows what it's like to make a pitch in a big situation.

KEVIN TOWERS: I think our pitching staff has an identity now. It's known now throughout baseball as one of the better pitching staffs in baseball.

You don't have to be a player to understand why he's been effective. All you have to do is listen to his message that could be applied to many professions.

DAVE: I can't run for them. I can't condition for them. I can't do that. What I can do is condition their minds. If you say, "Today, Roger Clemens is pitching today, and I'm going to pitch until he is out of the ball game, and if he's out of the game, you know you've won," that's what you need to do. And that's training your mind. You're preparing yourself to battle. I want guys to be aggressive. I want them to be unafraid to make mistakes. I want them to go out and do the best they can every day. What I want them to do is be the pitchers that they are, and if they don't know what they are, then it's my job to let them understand that this is what you posses. This is who you are. If you can write down what you're weak at, I'll develop a program for you that will allow you to win, if you trust me.

And building that trust reveals part of the Dave Stewart mystique.

DAVE: I expect them to take this personal. It is a personal insult when you don't succeed. When you don't pitch as well as you're capable of pitching, it's a personal insult. It should be a thing where we pass the baton every day. The next guy, it's your responsibility, okay, it's my day to carry twenty-four guys.

Dave Stewart is raising the chinning bar, requiring more discipline, more focus.

DAVE: I want to win the World Series. I don't want to be just, "Well, we got this far, let's do it again next year." Wrong. I want to win.

While the team had its best start in club history, nothing is easy. You can see how he burns with frustration and yearns for success.

BRUCE BOCHY: Those pitchers are like his babies. He looks after them.

Dave Stewart cheers them, consoles them, balancing high expectations with compassion.

DAVE: I am for them. I'm 100 percent a pitcher.

He can imagine what they're thinking.

CARLOS REYES: He knows how to pick my head. He knows, when I'm doing something wrong, he knows what to say.

TREVOR HOFFMAN: He is riding your highs and lows with you as a pitcher as you're out there performing.

Even the best closer in baseball, Trevor Hoffman, was open to Stewart's advice after some frustrating outings.

TREVOR HOFFMAN: He sat me down in the training room and he goes, "Listen, you need to relax, these are some of the things you're doing right." I go, "Yeah, you're right there," and he goes, "Chill out. I understand where you're coming from. I'm a pretty intense guy myself, take this from it."

Some challenges, like Joey Hamilton's inexplicably rough first innings, aren't as easily fixed, but Stewart approaches the problem the same way.

DAVE: I'm going to try to think what he is thinking at this time, and if I think it's not the right thought—maybe not right at that time, but at some point—I'm going to say, "Joey, this is where I want you to be, and if you can put yourself here you will do this for the rest of this game, for the rest of the season, or the rest of your career." That's what I have to do. I have to be these guys. It will help me to understand what I need to do to get them past whatever it is that's keeping them from being the great pitcher instead of just being an all-right guy.

The most public display of how he works with pitchers when they're struggling is the meeting on the mound.

JOEY HAMILTON: You really don't want to hear what they're saying. But it's a different story with Stew. I try to listen to what he says.

For example, a game in May. Depending on the pitch, Hamilton could allow the other team to break the game wide open.

DAVE: The first thing I always ask, how he's feeling physically?

JOEY HAMILTON: I told him I felt fine.

DAVE: I'm not here to take you out of the game. I'm here to give you a breather.

JOEY HAMILTON: It's really good to have someone come out and have faith in you that you're gonna be able to get the job done or get out of this inning within a couple of pitches, and fortunately, I was able to get out of that inning and it made Stew look really good!

DAVE: It was luck!

Dave Stewart is still adjusting to being a coach.

DAVE: When it's frustrating, it's really frustrating. It's disappointing, because you're always searching for answers. But when it's good, it's good.

And he boils down his goal to its simplest form. You'll know how he's doing by reading the box scores.

DAVE: We are here to play the game in every aspect, so that when it's done, it equals a "W."

Where do Dave Stewart's insight and motivation come from? Up next on *One on One*, how his rise to the top from child prodigy to World Series hero was no easy climb ....

We see Dave Stewart as a tremendous success story, but his success came after years of trials and tribulations. Many would have thrown in the towel after being dubbed a has-been. But that's not his style. On the mound or in the dugout, Dave Stewart, standing 6'2" weighing 230, can seem daunting.

> **DAVEY LOPES:** He's known for that famous stare of his.

Maybe even seem like the song "Bad to the Bone," but in slang, bad can really mean good.

> **KEVIN TOWERS:** Team player, tremendous intensity.
> **GREG BOOKER:** He's real down to earth. He listens to other people.
> **DAVEY LOPES:** Very dedicated, pretty much a perfectionist.

He is all that to the core.

> **TREVOR HOFFMAN:** He's as soft and as caring a human being as they come. He's a class act.

Therein lies the dichotomy of Dave Stewart. He was born February 19, 1957 in East Oakland, California, grew up in a small house, the second to the youngest of eight children with one brother, six sisters.

> **CAROLYN** (sister): He was real boy, harassing his sisters, a know-it-all.

They didn't have much money. His mother worked in a cannery, his father was a longshoreman.

> **DAVE:** My dad taught me to fish, taught me how to fight, taught me how to be what a boy is supposed to be ... rough, tough.

Stewart was just sixteen when his father died unexpectedly.

> **DAVE:** I didn't realize how much I would miss him early on, until later in life, after becoming an athlete. A lot of guys do share that particular part of their lives with their dads.

Part of Stewart's guidance came from church every Sunday, and his mother hoped attending a small Catholic high school, St. Elizabeth, would help keep him on track.

> **CLAIRE** (friend): There was no death stare in high school. There was more like practical jokes and fun loving.

Still, the streets and some friends got rougher.

> **DAVE:** I mean gangsters, they knew that they had a chance to get busted or popped, and they wouldn't let me be involved, because I was an athlete. They took care of me.

Not just an athlete, but a three-sport star in basketball, baseball, and football.

> **DAVE:** Football was my first love. I was aggressive, game day, I was mean.

Sports would be his ticket to a college education. He was offered some thirty football scholarships, but wasn't too thrilled about what most coaches told him.

DAVE: I'd have to put on another thirty pounds in bulk to compete.

He signed with the Dodgers in 1975.

DAVE: I didn't know much about pitching. I didn't really want to pitch.

He told his minor league manager he preferred catching.

DAVE: "If you want to catch, I'll give you a bus ride back to Oakland, California. You can catch there. Otherwise, I don't want to hear any more." And I never complained about catching again.

DAVEY LOPES: When I first met him, he was very shy.

Davey Lopes, already the Dodgers' veteran second baseman, took Stewart under his wing during spring training.

DAVEY LOPES: He was like a sponge soaking up everything. He didn't add much, he just listened a lot.

Listening to Dodgers' instructor Sandy Koufax helped tame his wild pitching.

DAVE: He said, "Use your cap as a way to lower your sight." So that's when I lowered my cap.

His trademark also dramatically improved his pitching.

DON SUTTON: About once a week, there was someone from the minor league system who would remind us there was a kid tearing up the minor leagues that was after one of our jobs.

Stewart had a taste of the majors in '78, but went back to the minors until '81. By then, he figured he'd more than paid his dues, but Manager Tommy Lasorda said he was to stay in Triple-A. Stewart took a risk by speaking his mind.

DAVE: I said, "I'm better than Don Sutton, I'm better than Burt Hooten … I'm better than Don Stanhouse." I said, "No, I refuse to go. I'm not going back to Triple-A. I don't have anything to prove there."

Then he met with the general manager, Al Campanis.

DAVE: "If you don't play in Albuquerque, you'll never play again." And he says, "Do you realize what you're getting into?" And I said, "Yeah I realize what I'm getting into," and I said, "Do you realize what *you're* getting into?"

Stewart recalls Don Stanhouse's prophetic words as he left the building.

DAVE: "Sometimes there is just no justice," and I said, "You're right," and he says, "Good luck kid."

Later, Stewart received a call to return to the stadium.

DAVE: And Stanhouse was coming out and he looked at me and said, "Kid, I told you in this game sometimes there's just no justice." I walked in and I was talking with Al and those guys, and they said, "We just did something that we've never done in this organization's history." I said, "What is that?" and he said, "We ate a big chunk of contract to keep a rookie." And I said, "Really?"

And he said, "We just released Don Stanhouse." And I said, "Wow," and that's how I made the team. That's how I made the team. It was a good year; a good rookie year.

He even pitched in the World Series in which the Dodgers beat the Yankees. But 1983 marked the beginning of a dark time, an unwelcome trade to Texas.

DAVE: Was not good. I don't care how you look at it.

The team was not good. He had a bad relationship with the manager. The silver lining, which he'd see only later, was that Texas is where he learned to throw his vaunted forkball. The trade to Philadelphia wasn't much better. He was released early in the '86 season. He'd been winless for twenty months. A pitcher no one seemed to want; no one seemed to believe in.

DAVE: I was more embarrassed than anything.

A lucrative offer to play in Japan was tempting.

DAVEY LOPES: Don't do this, don't do this, I really believe something is going to click for you.

Sure enough, he accepted an offer to go home to the Oakland A's. At first he was pitching mop-up, but then an incident, which gave him a new level of respect: Cleveland was beating the A's two days in a row.

DAVE: I came into the game after back to back to back home runs. The first guy I faced was Julio Franco. Sandy always told me that if you can create one inch of fear in anybody, you can win. The first pitch I threw was in his ribs. Pat Corrales came out. He was screaming profanities about me to the umpire—things that I really didn't care to hear. I kept looking and he said, "What the *** are you looking at?" And I said, "I'm looking at you and I don't appreciate what you're saying." He says, "Well what are you gonna do about it?" I said, "I'm not gonna do anything. You're the bad one, you come out here." So he started coming out to the pitcher's mound and I popped him pretty good.

On national television.

DAVE: It was the first time that people didn't see a pitcher running away from somebody; they saw the pitcher attacking somebody.

In mid season, the A's new manager, Tony La Russa, called him.

DAVE: "My first game as manager you're going to be my starter." I said, "Yeah right," and hung up. I thought it was somebody playing a joke, so I hung up. He calls back and says …

TONY LA RUSSA: We need a starter for my first game Monday and Duncan and I have talked about it and we'd like it to be you.

DAVE: He said, "You're pitching against Roger Clemens [laughing]." So I said, "Okay." So he says, "Are you ready for that?" And I said, "Hey, I've been waiting for this opportunity for a long time."

DAVE DUNCAN: It more or less showed Stew the confidence that was there and what our opinion of him was.

And something almost magical started happening. He burst from mediocrity to making his mark in the game. Stewart's scheduled starts were an event. With the A's, he won twenty games or more four years in a row. He's the only two-time American League Championship Series Most Valuable Player, and while never awarded a Cy Young, he was named MVP of the 1989 World Series.

DAVE: I pitched with passion, but I also pitched with a great deal of pride.

A trade to Toronto meant another World Championship in '93. But just as he had realized after six years in the minors, he felt again he had nothing left to prove.

DAVE: When I realized I couldn't turn the switch back on, I left the game. I dropped some seeds and some crumbs along the way. There are people that play for other ball clubs and you look at how they wear their cap, or how they walk, or something that they do—that's a little Dave Stewart.

His success has not been without sacrifice or without a celebration of his faith. When *One on One* continues, peeling back yet another layer of Dave Stewart's story and a look inside his spectacular home ....

Dave Stewart remembers his humble beginnings in East Oakland. He realizes just how far he's come every time he looks at his spectacular custom home.

DAVE: This is the house I want to die in.

Every time he glances at the scores of glass block or looks through one of the 282 windows.

DAVE: The feeling of freedom, that's why I put the windows in. I didn't know it was going to be 282 of them.

It even has a fully equipped surround sound home theater.

DAVE: It's my favorite place in the house. When you close that door you can't hear anything in here. When you come from a big family with a bunch of kids, you really appreciate space when you get older.

And he appreciates how he got here.

DAVE: Baseball has allowed me to move my mother from her first house to her first new house. I slept with my brother until I was about twelve or thirteen in the same room. Shoot, my kids, they have separate rooms. That makes me feel good.

A trophy room showcases souvenirs from his career.

DAVE: Just a lot of different things in here that remind me that I played. There are some great players in this game, and they'll never know what it's like to have the party after you've won it all, to go shake the President's hand.

Baseball's brought him celebrity, including appearances on TV shows for kids—*Silver Spoons* and *Square Pegs*. But he recognizes all that came at a price.

DAVE: The road I chose was to sacrifice everything first for baseball. I might still be married had my wife been as important to me as baseball. But she wasn't, and I admit that. If I had to rearrange things and set things so that they work right, I probably would have stayed single until I'm forty years old and then looked to get married now.

He married his high school girlfriend, Vanessa. They have two children, Adrian and Allyse. He was away from them a lot as they grew up.

> **ALLYSE:** When you see most of your friends, their dads are there for performances and stuff; I'd never see my dad there.
>
> **DAVE:** What I can do is be the best father that I can be today.
>
> **ALLYSE:** I respect my dad a lot. I love my dad a lot. He wants me to be open with him and I feel like I can tell my dad almost everything and anything.

If he thought being a pitching coach would be challenging ...

> **DAVE:** Raising girls is tough, it's really tough! She's never worn makeup before and this morning she comes downstairs to go to school. She had makeup on and fingernail polish, and her toes were painted. I'm looking at her like other guys are going to be looking at her and I'm like, oh man!

While he has a good relationship with his children now, Stewart says the lack of time he spent with them inspired him to give to children in each community where he's lived. He's been a long time supporter of the Boys and Girls Clubs of America where he worked in high school. He co-founded KIDSCORPS to support sports and motivational programs for inner city youth. And in San Diego when Classics for Kids needed help, he not only paid for more than six hundred students to attend the concerts, he performed, reading Lincoln's Portrait.

> **DAVE:** Even though you're Mr. Athlete and Mr. Money Bags, you have time, you're not just throwing money on me. To these kids, most of the time that's the most important thing.
>
> [In house foyer] You can see my room if you want, it's kind of different.

It's up the stairs, over the bridge, and up again.

> **DAVE:** It's really a pillow and candle room. I have a telescope because I'm a peeping Tom! The light colors take the edge off of it, but it's definitely a man's house.

His friends like the master bathroom. Who wouldn't? The tub has a retractable roof. But if he revels freely in his luxuries and his novelties, it may be because he is grounded in something else.

> **DAVE:** I believe all good things come through God. There's no doubt about that: I'm a witness. I was a rough-neck kid in a rough-neck area, and I could have easily gone in the other direction. I've been in some real compromising situations that could have ruined my life when I was younger, and I was able to get past that.

Dave Stewart's faith is something he holds close to his heart, yet rarely volunteers.

DAVE: Unless you ask me like you did right now. When people say, "Are you a Jesus freak?" Yeah I am but in my own personal life. I'm not going to overwhelm you with that, throw it all over you, dump a bucket of God on you.

It's very personal, but Stewart shares that it might not be just coincidence that at the same time he started winning games with the A's, he learned the practice of Tae Kwon Do.

DAVE: It teaches you to take that aggressive nature, and instead of being angry, it teaches you to channel it into something positive.

The one constant in Stewart's life seems to have been finding a way to turn hard times into good times.

RICK SUTCLIFFE: It was the adversity he faced in his life and in the early part of his career that would help him more as a pitching coach than all of the success that he had.

CAROLYN: He's a kind-hearted person that wants to make you think he's big, and bad, and mean.

With his look, his hat, even his walk that make an impression on fans, friends, and former teammates.

DUSTY BAKER: There's a guy that called me and asked me why I don't walk to the mound as cool as Stew, and that I need to work on my walk. My walk is my walk. There's only one cool Stew and he's in San Diego.

Dave Stewart thinks someday he'd like to be a major league general manager; that may happen in time. After all, he's living proof of just how far patience, persistence, and hard work can take you.

DAVE: I'm not going to take credit for just being lucky, that's not just luck. My house is a blessing, my beautiful daughter, that's a blessing, my mother,

"My first reaction to anyone coming into my space is, 'I don't know about this,' and then it passes ... This was of a more personal nature that took some getting used to, versus just talking about a victory, or a loss, or a spectacular play. The focus is on me and how I live and that is uncomfortable for me. I don't like to talk about myself. I thought things flowed, that would be the best way to put it. I don't really know if that's because of Jane, or just the circumstance of being in my house doing the interview ... I saw the show for the first time in a long time the other day. It was well done, natural in appearance. It really expressed a lot about me, gave the public I think a different look at me, who I really am ... That would be the best part of *One on One*. It does give you insight into the players that you live with during the season. These guys are supposed to be your family, yet unless you watch the show, you really don't understand fully what your teammate is about, what he's been through to be here today ... I enjoyed the experience with Jane. She's good at what she does."

—Dave Stewart, 2010

helping my family, those are all blessings to me. And if all of this is taken away from me tomorrow I'm not going to sit here and mope and be sad and worry about what's going to happen tomorrow. What's going to happen is I got faith enough that I can do it again.

Dave Stewart was taught if you can create fear in your opponent, you can win. But perhaps the lesson from his story is if you have confidence, faith, and tenacity, it's never too late to become the person you always thought you could be. I'm Jane Mitchell. Hope you'll join me next time for *One on One*.

TREVOR HOFFMAN

"You knew the end result would be well done and you would be happy with it. Jane is genuinely interested in the person's story."

—TREVOR HOFFMAN, 2010

In February 1997, a trip to Texas had two purposes. I was traveling with the Padres' Director of Entertainment, Tim Young, and videographer, Mike Howder. Our first stop was Dallas to meet and interview Trevor Hoffman and his family. *One on One* had not yet been "born" (not until after we returned from that trip and my Ken Caminiti interview), so the assumption going into the Hoffman visit was to do a Padres profile feature story for the pre-game show once the season began. Trevor and Tracy Hoffman had an off-season home in Texas. They knew Tim and Mike, and were welcoming to me. Who would have known how many times in the future I'd be knocking on their door to tell the Hoffmans' amazing story?

Trevor, still early in his closer career, had been key in the Padres' success in 1996 and clinching the West in the final game against the Dodgers. When we talked in their living room, I learned a few things that offered some good insight into his colorful personality and way with words. Rather than just "butterflies" in his stomach as he was waiting to come out of the bullpen, he had "pterodactyls ... big old birds in your stomach." Also, when I asked if he was a "tough guy" saying,

"You really do have the aura about you—steely-eyed, tough guy," Trevor shook his head and said, "Turn that camera off. I don't want anyone else in baseball to know I'm really not." Of course, we didn't turn it off. He was joking, but there's often some truth in a joke. For the sake of competition, he was somewhat protective of his professional image. We didn't want to jeopardize that, but we would learn that our stories showing him off the field had no bearing on how incredibly talented he was on the field. Most of the competition probably wasn't watching Channel 4 at that point, anyhow.

With our visit fairly short and the interview just scratching the surface, I did a five-minute profile as planned that spring. But I knew Trevor's story demanded more exploration.

1997 wasn't a great season for the Padres, but it prepared me for what a season was like: the highs and lows, being on the road compared to the homestands, the routine of the players—what they liked and didn't like, figuring out the logistics for me to do my job as it overlapped with their schedules, and understanding when they had to do theirs.

Looking ahead to 1998 and the second season of *One on One* shows, I had in the line-up centerfielder Steve Finley, broadcaster Jerry Coleman, and new pitching coach, Dave Stewart. I wanted Trevor Hoffman, but I wasn't sure how close he would let me get. I had observed his closer mentality, and remembered his notion he didn't want the competition to know he was really a nice guy, but I didn't buy that a television show would strip him of that armor. I kept him on my radar; he was too intriguing not to. The team was off to a great start in 1998 and Trevor was broaching a National League record for consecutive saves. The Padres had started playing the AC/DC song "Hell's Bells" when he came in to save a game. That energy in the stadium was so intense and indicative of what he and this team were capable of doing that year. I had him on my to-do list, but it was just a matter of finding the right time. Trevor apparently knew what I was doing in terms of my *One on One* show, because this is how it finally happened ...

I was on the road with the team in Arizona, staying at the team hotel. One evening after a game, I was in the hotel lounge with some of the other broadcasters when I saw Trevor. I went up to him, just to be social, and the subject came up of Channel 4 and *One on One*. I boldly asked, "So when do I get to tell your story?" To my surprise, he said, "Well, it's about time. I've been waiting for you to ask." I was stunned, but seized the moment and said, "Okay, let's do it."

It wasn't as easy as that, but we did it. The first weekend back after the All-Star break, the Padres were on the road playing the Dodgers. We coordinated to meet Trevor at his mother's home in the area where we would interview Trevor, his wife Tracy, and his mother

Mikki. Because it was a game day and Trevor had his routine, he gave me one hour to interview him before he had to go. It was just a one-camera shoot. Trevor sat on the couch. I was in a chair. We covered a lot of topics, and for a moment of levity, he lay down on the couch, as if I were a psychologist and he was telling me his problems. Trevor Hoffman, I was learning first hand, could be quite the jokester.

Another question in particular triggered a very telling and serious side of Trevor. I asked what bothered him, and he said, "When things don't go right. Confusion. Confusion adds to more confusion, and I get a little stressed out about that stuff, and there's no doubt about it. And I have a hard time dealing with it."

It wasn't just what he said, but how he said it. It may not translate quite as well in print as it does hearing his voice and seeing his face, but what I observed was a distinct certainty and almost crack in his voice that came from deep inside.

It was the little moments like this that showed me—and because I chose to use it, showed fans—that Trevor, like other strong, bold athletes, had vulnerabilities too. That doesn't mean they can't overcome them or don't deal with them, but those vulnerabilities are there because they are, in fact, human.

That first one-hour interview ended quickly, but we got it all in. I remember thinking, *Wow. He just revealed so much about himself, so much about who he is and why he does what he does.* I was eager to produce this show. The other key element of this edition came a few weeks later. We needed to see him with his family, and he agreed to let us come to their modest home in North County. The house was still a bit bare with a pool table in the dining room and their little boy Brody's crayon markings on the wall. The three of them played in the backyard for about fifteen minutes, just enough to capture some family time, including Tracy, pregnant with their second baby.

In the interview, Trevor shared that the ocean was an escape from chaos and confusion, especially at sunset: "The sun is just starting to go down and it's lighting up the sky. There's nothing like that, that puts me in a good mood, and there's nothing better than watching Mother Nature show her glory." Rather than just talk about it, it was important for us to be able to show him actually doing it. He was hesitant to have someone else be a part of such a personal time, especially someone

with a camera, but I helped him see that it was significant to his story. He acquiesced and invited me to drive with him in his black Porsche® to the beach. Dan followed in the Channel 4 truck and met us at the cliffs of Del Mar.

It is awkward but necessary in television to say, "Just act like we're not here," as a camera is focusing on someone doing what they normally do. Perhaps it was the performer in him, like his parents—the dancer and singer—but he understood my need. He ignored the camera, and for a few minutes, he watched the waves at sunset. And he did it while being himself.

Trevor also agreed to my request to tape his baseball routine. We arrived at the stadium at two o'clock one day when he was running around the field's warning track. Just as we had seen in spring training, he was wearing drawstring shorts and a medical scrubs shirt. When he got hot, he took his shirt off, showing his cut and defined, muscular body—shoulders, abs, and strong legs so important for a pitcher. During a game, we waited under the stands by the bullpen out in left field to see how after the fifth inning, he made his way back to the clubhouse to go through his ritual. While we couldn't go into the clubhouse during the game, Dan went in one day when no one was around to videotape "point of view" shots, showing Trevor's viewpoint during that ritual. This was a way to take the viewer into Trevor's world, using his descriptions, without being there in the moment and interfering with his actual routine. Plus, MLB rules wouldn't allow cameras inside during a game.

There had been a few articles written about Trevor and his closer mentality, including how in the minor leagues he ate bugs to send a message to his competitors that he was a tough guy. But *One on One* was the first in-depth piece on his whole story. I think it was one of the most powerful editions because it allowed me to show how this dominant player on the field was someone who was the sum of his many parts—his childhood, his failures and successes, being a husband, a father, and a leader.

One day, soon after the show debuted, I went to the field for batting practice and pre-game. As I walked out of the elevator toward the clubhouse, before going down the tunnel, Trevor walked toward me, gave me a big hug and said, "Thank you." Neither the team nor the players have editorial control over their pieces, so there's a big trust factor involved. In 1998, I was still establishing my role and my reputation. I was relieved that he liked it, not just for telling his story, but his family's story, too. I even got a hug and thank you note from his brother Glenn, the Dodgers' interim manager at the time.

> "I thought the piece you did on Trevor was great. You really did your home-work and it came out well. I know my family will always remember it. Thanks again. Glenn Hoffman."

After Tony Gwynn retired in 2001, Trevor Hoffman became the face of the active Padres: a team leader, a popular and beloved guy for all he had done in the community, considered another future Hall of Famer. Still, he had preferred to hold off on a *One on One* show update with me, partly because he was working his way back from surgery, although we did videotape him during his rehab to have if and when we did another show. By late in the 2005 season, on the verge of being the All-Time Saves Leader, we revisited Trevor's story. While many may have been familiar with his history, work ethic, and family, I felt it important to reintroduce those elements to bring new viewers or fans up to speed, as well as address new information of what had happened since 1998.

We elaborated on a few facets of his life beyond his pitching prowess. First, we saw him with his three sons reading a favorite book, *Inch and Miles: The Journey to Success*, by the legendary Coach John Wooden. I received several emails and phone calls from people wanting to know about the book, as it inspired them to act on something the Hoffmans were doing. Second, we showed how Tracy had not only been the glue keeping the family organized behind the scenes, but how she had expanded her world by starting a business focusing on children and exercise, with the added dividend of showing their boys their mother had professional qualities and strengths like their father.

The highlight of the shoot at their home, however, was Trevor showing us his amazing collection of memorabilia from his baseball career, starting in the game room with pictures and awards, moving out to a hallway with a custom made wall of shelves, cases, and drawers separating his younger years, college, minor, and major league play. Most fascinating, and what fans still talk about, is how he had kept a ball from every game in which he earned a save. Every game. He had dated each ball, put the team match up, and in later years, started writing another item of significance on the ball to help him remember the moment—whether it was the day something happened with his family, a young player making his debut, or getting his first hit. Standing in the hallway, he looked back, laughed, and said, "They'll have me back in here, I'll have Channel 4 Padres going and all the *One on Ones* up on the TV one day … I'll just be back here just pretending I'm still playing." This truly was a wow experience and worth the wait.

We held off editing the final thirty seconds of the show until that last few days of the season when we would know for certain that the Padres would clinch the

West Division. I was able to weave in a wonderful moment of Trevor after the game, with champagne drenched hair, sitting next to his proud mother in the dugout.

This was a message left on my home voicemail on October 31, 2005:

"Hey Jane, Trevor Hoffman calling. And I just wanted to call and say how much I appreciate the job you did on our *One on One* ... really turned out pretty special. And I know I give you a hard time not wanting to do it ... but it's always a pleasure when it is done and get a chance to see your product at the end. So again, I hope your off-season is going well. I know you guys don't have much of an off-season. You guys just shift gears and go onto something else. I know Hawaii's calling ... pretty sure you get out there every now and again so ... again I appreciate all your efforts and all your crew. Tell them I said thanks and we'll be talking to you. Bye."

Trevor Hoffman was re-signed in November 2005, and by the end of 2006, he indeed became the All-Time Saves Leader, breaking Lee Smith's record, after which we updated his story for the 2007 season. He played for the Padres through 2008, and that November, the Padres announced Trevor would not return the next season. He then signed with the Milwaukee Brewers. I was disappointed the parties did not find a way to keep him in a Padres uniform. His presence was powerful and valuable to the team on so many levels for an unusually long time. Thankfully, after the 2010 season when he decided to retire, the Padres welcomed him back to be part of the team in the front office and around the players. Both in uniform at spring training, and in street clothes at PETCO during batting practice, he told me it feels good to be home and part of an organization he loves.

Opening Day 2011, when he emerged from the bullpen for the pre-game ceremonies to the gong of the bells, there was no question, Trevor was where he was supposed to be.

I hope they someday erect a bronze statue of him in the Park at the Park near Tony Gwynn's, and with or without a television crew, I plan to be in Cooperstown when Trevor Hoffman is inducted.

Here's the script from the all-encompassing edition debuting March, 2007.

• • •

We first revealed what made the mysterious, tough-looking Trevor Hoffman tick in 1998, then again in 2005 as he helped the Padres clinch a division title. At the time, he was chasing history. In 2006, he made it: breaking Lee Smith's long-standing all-time saves record. Just another amazing feat by a man whose story about tenacity and class is timeless.

Trevor Hoffman: marquee player, busy father, relentless workhorse, fierce competitor.

TREVOR: I'm going to go at you strike one and I'm going to give you everything I've got.

Trevor Time.

[music/crowd cheering, etc.]

It started as an idea from the Padres marketing department in 1998: play the AC/DC song "Hells Bells" to inspire the crowd as Trevor Hoffman is called in to try to save the game, the bottom of the 9th. But in 2005, Trevor Time is an ingrained and celebrated part of the San Diego Padres vernacular. Not because it's catchy, but because of Trevor Hoffman's consistency. The closer has delivered nine times out of ten in save opportunities, securing a victory for the team with every save. He has pitched his way into the hearts of Padres fans, the organization, and into the team and Major League Baseball record books. When we sat down with him in 1998, he had just returned from his first All-Star game appearance.

> TREVOR: There's like forty million people in there so the reality of where you're at really finally hit.

At thirty-one, Number 51 was emerging as one of the best in the game. At thirty-eight years old in 2005 …

> TREVOR: I think we could probably use a different word than emerging, maybe evolved. And maybe at the time I was evolving and it's an ongoing process, I think, that I'm constantly learning based off of the parameters changing. Maybe a little less, a little more velocity on any given day, but the parameters of age and where the team's at, all these things kind of are factored in to where I am in my career.
>
> JANE: But to be the second all-time best …
>
> TREVOR: I wouldn't have thought about it back in '92 when I made the transition to pitching. And in '98, I would've said, "Jane, we don't want to talk about things like that." And as we sit today, I just don't think I've allowed myself to look outside the box in a sense.

Rather, he's always just focused on getting the job done. Pitch by pitch, inning by inning, milestone after milestone.

> TREVOR: I've enjoyed the ride so far, but to sit back and pat yourself on the back is the minute you'll get clipped, and the game'll humble you, and you'll be gone.

His wife Tracy and their three boys were there in St. Louis to cheer him on for his 400th save.

> TREVOR: But it was nice to have it done with my family in the stands.
>
> JANE: What do people say to you after something like that?
>
> TREVOR: It was nice to come into the clubhouse on this particular night in St. Louis 'cause to a man, they were standing in front of their lockers and applauding as I came in. It was a very humbling moment, and one that you always look forward to get from your peers that you're doing things the right way.
>
> [Game call Save #425—passing John Franco]

Then, save number 425, passing John Franco was an amazing accomplishment, considering where he was a few seasons ago. In 2002. Another stellar year, marking his 350th save. Even so, he would be tested, because he was playing through pain.

JANE: By the end of that year, what was telling you that something was …
TREVOR: My arm was done.

The last game he threw was against the Dodgers.

TREVOR: And I thought it was a perfect pitch on the inner third of the plate where I, everything mentally and mechanically felt like that's where I was putting the ball, and I missed my spot by a foot and a half. And that's not the way it was supposed to register. And I hit him and I'm going, "I'm in trouble."

A simple arthroscopic surgery on his rotator cuff didn't solve the problem by that December.

TREVOR: And that became frustrating. That became scary. And a part of— out of control that I didn't like 'cause I'm usually always in control of what I want to do.

Spring training 2003, news came of Plan B, a more invasive shoulder surgery with months of rehab.

JANE: Is it hurting?
TREVOR: A little bit, but that's kind of part of the thing you have to go through as well. There are really no guarantees. There's no forecast of where you're going to be at, a little scary. I know through this whole thing it's kind of been an eye opener knowing what guys have gone through in the past. And how determined you have to be and how much you really do care about doing this.

TRACY HOFFMAN (Trevor's wife): He realized he wasn't ready to retire [saying] "I still love this game so much that I am going to do whatever it takes to get back into it." He wasn't cranky. People give you the horror stories about, "Oh, good luck for you, not for him." But he was actually very good.

He stayed home when the team traveled, taking advantage of extra in-season family time …

[With boys at a Little League game]

When the team was home, he stayed connected.

RICK SUTCLIFFE (announcer): Trevor's not only a role model on the field, but off the field. You can't help but improving by being around him.

Still. Hoffman felt a little vulnerable watching Rod Beck having success in the closer role.

TREVOR: And you start going, *Is there going to be a place for me?* You know, *Where do I stand?* I'm contractually, I'm almost at the end here, you know. *Just worry about your own thing, Trev, don't worry about the big picture.*

Taking it one step at a time, he was back in the game that September.

TREVOR: I was most appreciative of the minute I toed the rubber in the bullpen mound that the folks that are always down in the bullpen in Qualcomm started applauding. And then you kind of heard, like a wave, the whole stadium started clapping and appreciating that I was getting ready to go into a ballgame. This was the seventh inning and I don't even know if we were winning. And that was cool. That kind of, *All right, this makes sense.* And not that I'm back, but it made all the hard work worth getting to that moment that, *Okay, now we go to the next level. Let's get back to where I've been before.*

MARK GRANT (announcer): *A perfect seventh inning: one, two, three. Pardon me while I stand up and applaud.* [standing ovation]

Shoeboxes with pictures, a shelf with a few trophies—that might work for some, but considering his career, Trevor Hoffman needs a little bigger set up. We begin inside his home's west wing and the billiard room.

TREVOR: Pretty cool, isn't it? I didn't think I collected very much stuff over the amount of time I've played, but there's been some significant pieces and pieces that kind of painted a picture over time.

Over time …

TREVOR: It's a neat story.

Beating the odds from the beginning, at six weeks old Trevor William Hoffman had a defective kidney removed. Small for his age and always the underdog, he strived to be like his two older brothers—Gregg, who'd become a high school coach and teacher, and Glenn, a major league infielder and coach.

TREVOR: It kind of completes me in a sense that the history of where I've come from even as a little rug rat, the age that my guys are right now, what that kind of means, and how that made me, in a sense. A favorite article about Dad, just kind of talking about the first closer of the family …

Trevor values his parents' influence. His late father Ed, a marine, became a singer *[audio of father singing "Quartet"]* and married his mother Mikki, a British ballerina. They raised their three boys in Anaheim. Ed, a postal worker, sang the national anthem at Little League and Angels games. He wouldn't allow Trevor to pitch after Little League to protect his arm, so Trevor played infield at Savanna High School, Cypress College, and at the University of Arizona.

TREVOR [career collection tour]: These guys are pretty important here just 'cause they're Wildcat Hustle Awards. They give them out to the kid in fall baseball that basically showed a little bit more effort than the others, so that's important to me, and then the Hank Lieber Award. I was the leading batter on my college team.

The Cincinnati Reds drafted him as a shortstop. But when he couldn't make the transition from aluminum to a wood bat, instead of releasing him, they tried him as a pitcher. His ability and mindset, including eating bugs to create a scary mystique, set the stage for big league success. Alongside him since meeting in the minors, his wife Tracy.

TREVOR: Allows me to be me and it's huge. It's, you know, to be able to go to the yard every day with that comfort is priceless. And so, to take all these different areas and factors in, it's a pretty good gig. It's been a lot of fun.

[career collection tour] That's where it all started in Kenosha, Wisconsin. 4/22/91, first save ever, minor league ball. Those are the spikes that I was wearing, the glove I used.

His immense popularity among Padres fans is a far cry from when he first arrived in San Diego in 1993, part of a five-player deal sending fan favorite Gary Sheffield to Florida.

TREVOR: I understood that there was a lot of work to do and not only from the fans accepting me, but I had to earn their respect.

He did, becoming an integral part of the team's march toward the playoffs by '96.

TREVOR: The feeling I got in '96 was that it's a pretty good team, that we got a chance to go a long way on chemistry. The pictures are really the story. I mean, when we clinched '96 and all the pitching staff on the mound. And the '98 ballclub was like, "We're stacked. We got some horses in the stable." The hat there's been a little more weathered than others. This is when we really only wore one hat …

JANE: Uh-huh.

TREVOR: … throughout. So …

JANE: Put one on at spring training, right?

TREVOR: Put one on in spring training and let 'er ride. That one's kind of nasty. It went through a couple of celebrations. It was a good run. We just ran into another ballclub [the New York Yankees] that was equally as talented and got ahead early and made it difficult for us to come back.

Keepsakes aren't just from obvious big moments and milestones. With the joy and diligence of a kid, Trevor Hoffman has been collecting a ball from every game he's saved.

TREVOR: Probably '95 on I've been able to keep the ball from the end of the game. And if it's a guy's first win, he definitely gets the ball, or a milestone for somebody else, I'll get a game ball from that game and just say first ball went to so-and-so. And this is cool, too, 'cause it kind of—it can pull out. [opening cupboard]

JANE: Ohhh …

TREVOR: And you can kind of expose them all.

JANE: Wow.

JANE: Do you remember when you look at these? Do you have that vivid of a memory that …

TREVOR: No, that's why I've kind of started writing on more of them now, like a diary of what's going on, just so that you have an idea. It'll take you back to that moment. It's like … like this one. Date, number of what it was. 9-6 in LA and it was when my nephew was the batboy of the game.

JANE: Wow.

TREVOR: And I remember him in uniform and his—the first ball went to him.

JANE: Ties Rollie, breaks Rollie.

TREVOR: You remember certain things … if you write them down. And, you know, I obviously hadn't done that 'cause I didn't think I would have this many but …

JANE: Yeah.

TREVOR: It would've painted a better picture.

JANE: And how about in these drawers here? These are the—all the …

TREVOR: These are the ones past .300 …

JANE: Wow.

TREVOR: Wilson gave me a glove to commemorate the date and when I got .300. It makes a statement. It's kind of cool where it's a clean display. And you can see it when you walk in, not that I'm looking to honk my horn, but just kind of looks cool.

JANE: Yeah, it's sentimental though.

TREVOR: It's kind of neat it's not spread out throughout the house. Trace lets me have this little area in the big, empty hallway.

JANE: This is the baseball wing.

TREVOR: "And go and—go and relive your glory days, Trev." They'll have me back in here, I'll have Channel 4 Padres going and all the *One on Ones* up on the TV one day.

JANE: There you go, see?

TREVOR: I'll just be back here just pretending I'm still playing.

He hopes that pretending isn't for a few more years. Yet when it's all said and done, might he be what many refer to him as a future Hall of Famer?

TREVOR: I feel very uncomfortable talking about things like that because it's something that is very hard to attain. And you don't want to—that let-down. If it never happens, it never happens. You know, I'm not done putting up numbers in the game. I'm not done trying to win championships in the game. When it's all said and done, if it's enough, you know, Tony Gwynn'll tell you, if it's enough, they'll let me know.

Trevor Hoffman is chasing Lee Smith's 478 saves, and Smith is not in Cooperstown. Only three closers are, including Dennis Eckersley. And during induction weekend 2005, the Oakland A's legend was asked on ESPN radio if more closers belong there.

DENNIS ECKERSLEY: There's going to be more to come whether it's Trevor Hoffman …

TREVOR: Thanks, Eck. You know what? That's fantastic and it kind of gives me chills thinking about a guy like him even thinking about mentioning my name because, not for all that it stands for, but I watched Eck go to work. And I watched how hard he worked at being as good as he could be. And I think he's partly what confirmed the way I wanted to go about my business in the game. He solidified that by the way he would be out there every day running and getting his sprint work in and doing the things that he needed to do to prepare himself for seven hours later. All right, I'm on the right track.

On the right track with a routine that now requires a different focus. That's next on *One on One,* plus a new dimension to the Hoffman family; life beyond baseball....

Trevor Hoffman likes pressure. But Opening Day 2004, back from shoulder surgery, was a lot to handle.

> **TREVOR:** You're aware of the situation. I mean, that throws knots in your stomach. But to not have pitched for a whole year, get that little month in, and then come back on Opening Day in a one-nothing ballgame and a brand new stadium and everybody jacked and to, you know, it couldn't have been any worse. You visualize the best situation and you also are seeing the worst situation, and you're just going, "It's happening."
>
> *MATT VASGERSIAN: And the Giants lead it 2-1.*
>
> **TREVOR:** Nothing you can do about it. Just kind of pick your bootstraps up, tighten them up, and let's go.

He's undaunted by a bad inning, a rare blown save. Teflon® by nature, he's tough due to discipline and plain hard work. Through the years, it's a visual that's distinctly Trevor Hoffman. On the road or at home, he arrives early to stretch, run, and prepare for the game. By the fifth inning he heads to the clubhouse. Watching the game on TV as he shines his shoes, soaks in the whirlpool, works with the trainers. His routine ...

> **TREVOR:** Is much more calculated on how the game's going and where I'm at in the sixth inning.

Because unlike Qualcomm stadium, PETCO Park doesn't have a direct route to the bullpen: he can only get there by crossing the field with players during a half inning.

> **TREVOR:** And at times I get rushed, where before I never had to rush through anything 'cause I knew I could always make it up going the back way 'cause I was going to get there.

He gets there always prepared. Trevor Hoffman sets a great example not only for his peers and fans, but for his three boys, Brody, Quinn, and Wyatt, a fixture with their mother Tracy watching from behind home plate.

> *[kids cheering at a game]*
>
> **JANE:** You guys never lose each other, do you? Because you're always wearing the same outfit.
>
> **BRODY:** Ya. Not all the time though.
>
> **JANE:** How are you lucky?
>
> **QUINN:** Cause our dad plays for the Padres, and he's famous, and he lets us go on the field.
>
> **JANE:** What do you think about your mom?
>
> **BRODY:** Um, she's a really good baseball player.

JANE: What do you like about your brothers?

WYATT: They love me and they play with me.

They have grown up in baseball and in the Padres family. As their boys have grown—as well as Hoffman's big league salary—Trevor and Tracy have gone from a house in Texas to a modest house in North County with crayon on the wall for art, to a spacious custom home with new art by their boys, a wall of family photos, a work-out room, and reflections of their faith.

TREVOR: I'm a very blessed man, you know. I think that God plays a role in our family, and a role in me being healthy, and I am very thankful for the many blessings that I do have.

TRACY: That's what we work for. I mean, that's who we are, you know. It's an important part of our life. Our life would be incomplete without it.

The Hoffmans also look to a book by legendary basketball coach, John Wooden. It's called *Inch and Miles*.

[Trevor, Tracy, and boys sitting on floor reading book]

TREVOR: Here's the gist of the whole book. "You'll meet special friends who are good teachers too. Each one has a message especially for you: to learn how to try one hundred percent. Just ask them for clues. You'll be glad that you went."

JANE: This is a tough game and a lot of marriages don't last.

TREVOR: I'm able to focus on doing my thing that everybody watches on TV and really associates me with and defines me, but she's the rock behind our group.

TREVOR [reading]: "Loyalty. I wag my tail when you're feeling bad. I'll cheer you up if you're kind of sad. I'm honest and fair and my word is true. When others run out, I'll be there for you."

Family and her husband's career have always come first for Tracy.

TREVOR [reading]: "Hard work. I may be small, that's very true, but I succeed, and so can you."

But now she's in business at a Carmel Mountain Ranch shopping center with a boutique …

TRACY: I gear it towards moms, a lot of jeans, and T-shirts, and fun things.

And at the Rock 'n Tumble Gym, she teaches tumbling and values from their favorite book with its pyramid of success inspiring children to do their personal best.

TRACY: Because one may be able to do a round off back hand spring, but the other child may just be doing a summersault, and that's just as important, because that child just accomplished something that they thought they couldn't do.

[Tracy cheering for a child]

Her partner Mary has run gyms before. And Tracy was a realtor and Buffalo Bills cheerleader when she met Trevor. But this venture is about more than making a business work.

> **TRACY:** It's kind of nice that my kids think that Mom's job is pretty cool, too. For so long it was always about Dad's job.
>
> **TREVOR:** She's not just Mrs. Hoffman. She's got it going on. She's got a lot of character and she just is such a loving person and takes care of everybody around her. And it's nice that she's kind of had an opportunity to do something for herself.
>
> **TREVOR** [reading]: "Enthusiasm. The energy and pep you show will rub off on those you know. Don't make excuses, complain or whine, enjoy your work and success you'll find."
>
> **BOYS:** Hootie-toot-toot!
>
> **TREVOR:** That's what we're talking about.
>
> **TRACY:** Yeah.
>
> **TRACY:** We are preparing ourselves for life—not just with baseball, but just life as a family. So San Diego is where we're going to stay. We love it here.

Their community service includes bringing Kidney Kids to the field, saluting the military in honor of their fathers, both veterans ...

> **TREVOR:** Say thanks for all that they do to protect us, and our freedom, and allow me to go play a game for a living.

And putting on a tux for *Cox Presents: A Salute to Teachers* ...

[Enters stage in tuxedo to Hell's Bells music]

> **TREVOR:** That was awesome. I mean, talk about energy, people rootin' and tootin' for their teachers.

For his efforts, Trevor Hoffman has received team awards, and in 2005 national recognition in Seattle with the Hutch Award for honor, courage, and dedication to baseball on and off the field.

> **TREVOR:** It's something that I learned from my mom and dad about being active in your community, and I hope that's something I, in time, can pass to my kids and let them understand that this isn't normal, you know? There are a lot of families out there that aren't as blessed as we are. And they need to understand that through hard work things can happen. And through charitable efforts, you realize how lucky you are.

He's passionate about a lot of things. Take the issue of steroids.

> **TREVOR:** They're bad. They're cheating. They're wrong. I don't think you can get much more poignant than that.

With his matter of fact attitude and experience, he embraces leadership.

> **MARK SWEENEY:** I know he won't say this, but this is his team.
>
> **JAKE PEAVY:** Ever since Tony retired, he's kind of taken over. This guy's Mr. San Diego in the clubhouse.

SCOTT LINEBRINK: I've learned a lot from him, not just the way he goes out there on the field, but just his preparation and everything he does before he even gets out on the mound.

MARK LORETTA: We wouldn't be where we are today, that's for sure.

RAMON HERNANDEZ: He's going to give you good advice. He's one of the greatest players I've ever played for.

KEVIN TOWERS: A lot of people wrote him off a year ago when the arm went bad. Not me. I mean, there's no telling what he'll still accomplish. I think he's got a lot of years left in him.

BRUCE BOCHY: It's remarkable really, over the years how consistent he's been, and that's why he's going to the Hall of Fame.

He has a special relationship with the team and the fans …

TREVOR: It's been unconditional love from everybody here.

FAN: Go get 'em Trevor!

And on September 28, with an eight-run lead over the Giants, he's invited to the mound to close the game.

MATT VASGERSIAN: The Padres are Western Division Champions in 2005.

[Champagne bottles being popped and poured on heads]

TREVOR [with Jane on field postgame]: There were six or seven guys down there that could have had that opportunity. Pitched well enough all year long to have had that honor. I'm truly privileged to have that honor myself and wear this uniform and get that done.

MIKKI HOFFMAN (Trevor's mother): [in dugout] I'm so proud of him. I could bust!

He has a few more baseballs to add to his collection.

ANNOUNCER: And everyone in the ballpark will turn their attention to the center-field gate that will swing open and take a listen.

On his way to helping the Padres clinch the division two years in a row, it happened. September 24th, 2006.

STEVE QUIS (announcer): Shortstop … gotta hurry … Oh, he got 'em! Yes! 479! Trevor Hoffman has become the All-Time Saves Leader in Major League Baseball History and they're all chasing him!

TREVOR: [on field to crowd]: You people deserve to have it. My teammates deserve to be part of this, at home. It's something tremendous for the city of San Diego.

STEVE QUIS: It's a touching moment and it is a big day in the life of that man and his family.

The saying goes, "The only thing constant is change." But Trevor Hoffman's story also underscores how there's a lot to be said for consistency with one's work ethic, passion, and core values—a combination that undoubtedly equates to Trevor Time. I'm Jane Mitchell. Thank you for watching *One on One*.

"The final show is kind of like a keepsake. It had that kind of personal feel. It was great to have input from a lot of different people. It was nice to hear people speak about your career who have had a profound impact on it—coaches, teachers, friends, and family."
—Trevor Hoffman, 2010

JUNIOR SEAU

"You make the interview process easy. You're always well prepared and the questions are thoughtful.... you've obviously done your homework."
—JUNIOR SEAU, 2010

In 1999 it was time for *One on One* to branch out beyond baseball and to our partnership with the San Diego Chargers. The unquestionable first choice of players to profile for the show was Junior Seau. His productivity, popularity, and personality both on and off the field were great ingredients to this local star's success story. The Chargers asked Junior if he would do the interview, and he agreed. I then met him in preparation of the shoot to map out where we would do it and the elements we would need—his family, his home, working out, his restaurant, and his Junior Seau Foundation. This was a savvy athlete, businessman, and philanthropist. He understood why I needed to gather so much and was helpful in pointing me to the right people to interview. This included his parents, who still lived in Oceanside.

On our shoot day that September, we arrived at his home in La Jolla. It was a spectacular house with big windows, a view of the ocean, and a tasteful amount of football memorabilia items and pictures reflecting his life and career.

Junior was a great listener and a good talker. He has a natural gift of speaking passionately and intensely about things and experiences he cares about. Similar to my experience with Tony Gwynn, knowing Junior was the leader on the Chargers, I wanted this experience and the show to go well, as I believed his reaction could set the tone for other Chargers' willingness to be interviewed down the road.

After the interview, we went to Bird Rock Beach where Junior and Gina, his wife at the time, played in the water with their children for us to capture their family in action. After that day, we checked off a number of locations to round out Junior's story: Seau's the Restaurant, a meeting with the Junior Seau Foundation, Oceanside High School, the Oceanside Boys and Girls Club, working out at the Chargers complex (at six o'clock one morning) to see him in his real element, and of course, shooting him on the sidelines during a game. A few days after the show debuted on October 19, I received the most beautiful peach-colored roses and a note, that read, "Great job and thank you for the *One on One*." I still have the large, green glass vase they came in.

In 2003 the Super Bowl was in San Diego. At the time, Junior was among the few Chargers who had played in the annual championship contest. With thousands of visitors coming to San Diego, his story was great programming as we tailored Channel 4 to visitors and locals alike for Super Bowl Week 2003. By the time we shot the updated interview that December, he was living in a new house. He played to the camera as I played his piano while touring the spectacular Tuscany-style home. I did not have to cover his whole life story, because I could use parts of the original show detailing his childhood and early career. In this edition, I acknowledged his divorce and added more content about his passion for the game and the challenge and frustration of being close to the playoffs again, but not in them.

Over the years, even as he was traded, and twice "retired," Junior Seau has shown me the utmost respect and appreciation. We often cross paths at community and charity functions, such as his foundation's "Shop with a Jock" event each year in December. It is nice to know that no matter how big a star he is—and he is a big

star—Junior Seau still remembers the little part I had in telling his story.

This script is from the edition debuting January 17, 2003.

• • •

San Diego's Junior Seau: his enthusiasm, perseverance, work ethic, part of San Diego's Super Bowl legacy.

JUNIOR: If you're consistent with what you believe in and what you do, eventually it'll come your way.

From his humble beginnings to his high profile status in San Diego and the National Football League, Junior Seau has had quite a journey, one that's a reality check on how tough the game of football is and how hard it is to make it to a Super Bowl. We first explored his story in 1999, and while he and the team have seen many changes, the core of what makes Junior Seau a local hero remains the same.

Number 55 Junior Seau lives for competition. He exudes concentration and commitment.

JUNIOR: I just want to get the edge. I have been blessed with a certain amount of talent and I want to make sure that I work to help that talent.

And when Junior Seau feels thrills? He gets chills ...

JUNIOR: The chills of winning down your spine does not change from now, to when I was five years old.

Being a team player seems natural for Junior Seau. He's from a big family with strong parents who taught them to love each other.

TIAINA SEAU: Love inside the family, love for the parents, and take care of them ...

And to love their heritage. Tiaina and Luisa Seau are from American Samoa in the South Pacific, where tuna packing is the main industry, where a grandfather was a respected village chief, and honoring the family name is a sacred value. In 1963 the Seaus' first child, David, needed medical attention, so they came to San Diego, where they had relatives in the military, and settled in Oceanside.

JUNIOR: They found their way through the church.

Their faith helped them through the death of a baby twin and the joy of the birth of their other children, including Tiaina Seau, Jr., January 19, 1969. They lived in a small house, just two bedrooms—one for his parents, one for the two girls. The four boys slept in the garage.

JUNIOR: It was a tight knit group.

Junior's parents spoke only Samoan at home, so learning English when he started school at age seven was a challenge.

JUNIOR: And we had to make the adjustment quick or else we were going to get lost.

LUISA: The most important to me is the education for the kids.

His father worked at a rubber factory.

JUNIOR: And he worked hard.

His mother stayed at home.

JUNIOR: I think that if Mom had her way, we would be playing bingo and having a great time. Dad was always the one that had the structure.

Even with his strictness ...

JUNIOR: My dad was the guiding light for me. At five o'clock every morning, you would hear some mumbling going on upstairs, and it would be Dad reading his Bible, every morning. That is special and I remember that.

And he remembers the evening family prayers …

LUISA: [saying Lord's prayer in Samoan …]

JUNIOR: We always had time to get together and thank God for the time we had together. The best days of my life were sleeping in the garage with my brothers, listening to them communicate about sports and what they were going to do, and how they were going to do it.

And growing up where the Seau boys did, both his family and his focus would serve young Junior well. Oceanside's East Side was a tough area at the time.

JUNIOR: I knew there were gangs there, but they knew that I didn't want any part of it. My gang was football, my gang was basketball, my gang was track, my gang was school. My gang, my purpose, was to get my parents out of Oceanside and help them see another side of life that they deserve. That was my goal. My drug in life was winning, and it is today.

Winning came early, so did developing his work ethic.

JUNIOR: I used to do ten pushups before I went to bed because I knew my brothers weren't doing the pushups, so I felt like I was getting ahead of them.

By the time he was in the eighth grade, all his older brothers and sisters had won the Jefferson Junior High School sports boys and girls of the year honors.

He wanted to win that, too.

JUNIOR: I think that was probably the start of the chills because I knew that was the pressure, that I had to fight, and it was something no one else knew about but me.

And at the awards dinner …

JUNIOR: It felt like I was the best in the world. It was an eighth grade banquet and for me to receive [an] award, where I can take home and show my brother and sister and say, "Listen, I won it too," was a start of something.

DON MONTABLE: He always said that basketball was his love, but football was going to be his career.

Don Montable was Junior's basketball coach at Oceanside High School and remembers him as a leader and a standout on campus. Junior advanced to the varsity level early, as a sophomore, helping to lead the Pirates basketball and football teams to championships. But one day his senior year, 1987, was a defining moment for young Junior. After an outburst of frustration in front of the basketball team, he risked not playing if he didn't apologize.

DON MONTABLE: He says that from that he learned that he wasn't the star at all costs. He believed that he was someone that had to adhere to the rest of the policies and rules.

Still, he was a star and in demand, inundated by offers for college football scholarships. He wanted to play at University of Colorado where he had friends, but at the last minute, his father wanted him to consider USC [University of Southern California].

> **JUNIOR:** He wanted to share my college career with me. It was important to him and I knew that, therefore, I honored it.

[music: USC fight song]

But there would be another painful defining moment before Junior would be a fighting Trojan. The college entrance SAT scores. The minimum to be eligible to play his freshman year: 700. His score: 690.

> **JUNIOR:** Because I was highly touted, an All-American athlete, it hit the head-lines and it hurt my family. Because it hurt my family, it hurt me. You know, suddenly Junior Seau was a dumb jock. Junior Seau won't play his freshman year. That he won't have the crutch of using football. He is going to have to be just a student. A lot of people didn't think that I would be able to do it.

He wanted to prove to himself and others he could do it.

> **JUNIOR:** It was fun fighting back.

He earned above average grades. And after setbacks due to minor injuries, he earned respect on the gridiron his explosive junior year, leading the Trojans to the Rose Bowl. He earned All-American honors and was the Pac 10 Defensive Player of the Year. He chose to leave USC, expecting to be drafted by the Patriots.

> **JUNIOR:** So I go to New England in my shorts and tank top and it is below zero … cold, cold, cold.

But Junior was hot, hot, *hot* and one of the top three athletes in the 1990 draft. The Chargers' General Manager Bobby Beathard wanted him.

> **BOBBY BEATHARD:** His effort on the field, his effort in practice and every-thing fit.

New England and Tampa passed on him.

> **JUNIOR:** And that was the best thing that ever happened to me.

Up next on *One on One*, exploring Junior Seau's discipline, drive, and emotion-al journey which have taken him from rookie to leader, and one of the best in the game ….

> **JUNIOR:** I thought I knew football until I stepped on the field with the San Diego Chargers, and they put me in the middle.

In college, he'd been a defensive end with a straightforward assignment.

> **JUNIOR:** Go find the ball on the opposite side, and that was mainly the quarterback.

The Chargers changed his role to middle linebacker, the guy in what's called the "thinking man's" position.

> **JUNIOR:** They wanted me to do coverages and wanted me to make calls, and it took me a long time to adjust to that. Now, I had to learn football.

But old habits die hard.

> **JUNIOR:** I was running fast. I was hitting my own players, but I was running fast!

It began to click, especially after being selected as an alternate to the Pro Bowl after his rookie year.

> **JUNIOR:** That gave me some hope and I started studying the position itself.

The results showed year by year, as Seau emerged early in his career as the heart and soul of the Chargers' defense. In 1991 he became the team's top defensive playmaker and named to the Pro Bowl, an honor he'd receive twelve years in a row through the 2002 season, tying an NFL record for consecutive trips to the Pro-Bowl. His numbers—impressive. He has been a constant even as the Chargers have had a number of losing seasons, what he calls "the drought" …

> **JUNIOR:** There'll be times when it's hard to get up in the morning to go work out, it's hard to go to practice, it's hard to sit in meetings. It's hard. It's hard to talk to the media to try to be positive, to try to find a positive out of the negative. And whenever you hear people talk about the Chargers, yeah, it hits home. And if it didn't, then you shouldn't be part of it. But what you have to do, you have to believe it's going to turn.

And if and when it does turn, he knows what to expect by just thinking about 1994, a one-stop shopping season playing through pain, and playing in the ultimate game. If making 155 tackles wasn't impressive enough, consider his injury that year. Mid season he hurt a nerve in his left shoulder—getting a shooting pain, then numbness, with every impact.

> **JUNIOR:** During the course of a lot of the games, they knew my left side was the weak side and they were running right at it. And after the first play, I knew I had fifty-nine more plays that are going to come to the same side.

His tenacity was key that season, as the Chargers made a run for the playoffs under Head Coach Bobby Ross.

> **BOBBY ROSS:** It's amazing when you have so many people, a group, and you're fighting for the same goal and it turns your way. You know it's your time. And that was our time.

The most dramatic do or die face-off was the AFC Championship game against the Pittsburgh Steelers in Pittsburgh.

> **JUNIOR:** We didn't have a chance. Well, no one gave us a chance. The only ones that believed in us were, you know, our team on that plane. And as we were up there in Pittsburgh, they were preparing for their Super Bowl shuffle and their dances and then we started to get angry because everyone started to talk bad about us. And we took that to heart and went out there and found ourselves in an opportunity with the last play on the line to win a game. Time just stopped. You know, suddenly the terrible towels were nowhere to be found. It was quiet, and all day it was so loud. The only cheers that came

out in that stadium were from our bench. We didn't know what to do. We just started running everywhere.

JANE: How emotional was it? And how emotional did you get?

JUNIOR: Well, I remember crying. I was overwhelmed with the impossible. There are a lot of great players in the league that don't have that—that never had the opportunity to play in the Super Bowl. And we took care of that.

Just knowing they had that chance would have been reward enough. But on the plane, Ross informed them they were in for a big surprise.

JUNIOR: He says, "They're having a pep rally at the stadium. The city of San Diego is waiting on you." And that just started a roar. And that is definitely my highlight of my career thus far.

JANE: Then, you play the game. What sort of pressure ...

JUNIOR: Ah, I don't want to go into that—cut this! We were definitely over-whelmed with a lot of talent with the San Francisco 49ers and we didn't play well. And it hurts, you know, embarrassment. Just feeling down not only yourself but, you know, obviously for the team and the city.

Getting a chance to get back to a season like that, to get back to the playoffs, back to the Super Bowl, certainly drives number 55, game by game.

JUNIOR: All I want on Sunday night, after the game, is to be able to lay my head on my pillow with peace.

To get that peace he has to know that he's done everything he can to help his team.

JUNIOR: I refuse to be out-worked.

Even on Tuesdays, the team's day off, he's at the training facility.

JUNIOR: I am in there getting treatment, making sure that every part is ready to go for the next week.

Wednesday and Thursday begin before the sun comes up.

JUNIOR: I like to get up at 5:30 and work out, because I know that my op-ponents are sleeping.

Every day is film day.

JUNIOR: I play my opponents five times a week. We win every day.

Alone in a quiet room, Junior plays a copy of the upcoming opponent's most recent game, dissecting every move. Friday is spent being quiet and mellow.

JUNIOR: Saturday I get in my hot tub and sit there. I visualize the game.

Sunday, Game Day, begins at the stadium five hours before kickoff.

JUNIOR: I walk around the field and visualize again what is going to happen today.

He listens to his song of the season, this year, one by Fiji ...

JUNIOR: I go out and joke around with my trainers and have a great time. Then I get quiet. And then I am in my zone.

[Game action]

JUNIOR: I have approximately five to eight seconds to assess it and to position our defensive line and to know where to attack. I look at the formation and I know the weakness and strength of that formation. I have to find that in eight seconds and we go.

On the sidelines, Junior Seau is in constant motion. On the bench, talking to coaches, looking back, looking ahead, the wheels are turning. His energy burning with sweat, and scrapes, and intensity increasing deeper and deeper into the game. Junior Seau doesn't hold back—running on months worth of adrenaline.

JUNIOR: It takes you back to the off season workouts, trying to build yourself to that point that you can perform on Sunday and it's hard to bottle that up. Wherever the chills go, I shake. It just happens that it runs through my spine and my legs. There are a lot of people who are not my fans that would love to critique that. I like to say, that it is not meant to be any harm [to] anyone. It is a person that loves the game. I want my team to win. I want my players to be successful. I am not going to sit back and hang up my helmet and say that I wish I was able to be me.

Junior Seau's focus and energy go well beyond the football field. When *One on One* returns, getting personal—about some of the things that matter to him most….

Football Sunday in San Diego, number 55 is plastered on cars, kids, and on fans of a guy some call Mr. Intensity.

FAN: He is defense.
FAN: Wherever the ball is, Junior is there.
FAN: He is a family guy. We love him in San Diego. Junior!

Loved in San Diego, known nationwide, and often in the limelight, and all the opportunities it has to offer, Junior Seau, in his trademark shorts and flip flops, has a good beat on life and enjoys mixing work with play.

JUNIOR: [Community event] Hey little man, how you doing?

He makes the most of the fact that there are twenty-four hours in a day. He's a man on the move.

JUNIOR: How ya doing?

Tackling photo shoots …

JUNIOR: Hi, I'm Junior Seau.

Including Seau's, the Restaurant, a sports bar, opened in 1996.

JUNIOR: I'm not a guy who's going to lend my name and put it on top of a building and let someone else run it. I need to fall and rise with it.

The restaurant almost fell before it rose. Junior, earning a multi-million dollar salary, was one of the high profile athletes victimized by financier John Gillette, convicted and sent to jail for stealing his clients' money. But Junior bounced back.

JUNIOR: It's my place and I take that to heart.

He also takes to heart the Junior Seau Foundation …

JUNIOR: [Foundation meeting] Let's go to the scholarship in excellence program.

The foundation, established in 1992, has given out more than one million dollars to charities and for college scholarships. Its mission is to educate and empower young people with resources and messages.

KID: Not to get into gangs, not to smoke and drink.

KID: He just encouraged me to play my best at what I do.

Junior's charity work started where he once played, the Oceanside Boys and Girls Club. Club 55 is just for teens.

JUNIOR: To have a place to go rather than hanging out in the street where they can get in trouble.

With academic and mentoring programs.

KID: He gives us a role model to look at.

To help make all that happen, the foundation's biggest fundraiser is the Junior Seau Celebrity Golf Classic, one of the premier events in the region with active and retired players on the guest list. An event with less sizzle, but plenty of emotion, comes during the holidays when more than 200 youngsters who win an essay contest Shop with a Jock ...

JANE: What is that moment like to be with some of these kids?

JUNIOR: What I see is, I see Junior, that's what I see. I see Junior. I see my brothers and my sisters. I mean, I was there. That's what I see. It's a tear jerker, it really is, to see kids that aren't able to have a Christmas tree. To be able to take two hundred and fifty kids shopping with a jock, whether it's a Padre, a San Diego Charger, San Diego State athlete, UCSD athlete, we all come together and every single one of us gets paired with one kid.

With the help of volunteers and corporate sponsors, the foundation gives each child one hundred dollars to buy something for a family member and then something for themselves. He hopes to take the program to the national level to every city with an NFL team.

JANE: It will be part of your legacy, too.

JUNIOR: It's part of our legacy. It's something that San Diego started.

And that's more important to me than anything else.

Family is also important to Junior Seau, and while his marriage of ten years did not work out, his three children, Sydney, Jake, and Hunter, remain a priority. Spending time with them at his new home: one with a view, plenty of space, a piano, and just a few awards and memories on display in his office. While that pinched nerve in 1994 was his worst injury to date, his foot and ankle injuries in 2002 put him on the sidelines for three games, bringing his total of missed games to just eight in thirteen years. Yet at thirty-four years old ...

JANE: How beat up can you get though? How many years can you play, do you think?

JUNIOR: I'm looking to play two to three more years. I am.

JANE: Is that Super Bowl ring still just kind of pulling you? I mean—is that the ultimate for you?

JUNIOR: I have rings in life, you know. I do. Do I want to win a Super Bowl ring? Yeah, I do. I'm hungry for one. That's probably the only thing that I haven't done yet in my career, that I haven't accomplished. But I'm not going to say that's going to fulfill my career, fill my life. I'm living in San Diego. I have great friends. I have a great pastor. I have a foundation here. I've been able to plant seeds in the community to make my home. So there are a lot of rings there that I've been able to gain in thirteen years. I'm proud of those rings. So for me to say that I'm going to give all that up for a Super Bowl? You know what? I'll take my rings of life. So am I after one? Yes. But I already won.

However long he plays, however well the Chargers do, Junior Seau has already made his mark in the game: considered by many to be one of the best linebackers in NFL history. He says he just hopes he'll be remembered as a guy who was fair. Fair to his sport, fair to his community, and fair to his family. I'm Jane Mitchell. Thank you for watching *One on One*.

> "I am totally comfortable with you.... The final shows were good. I remember thinking they were on target ... We have used your *One on One* stories for the Junior Seau Foundation as we honored those you have interviewed—they are informative and fun. Keep up the good work."
>
> —Junior Seau, 2010

TED WILLIAMS

December of 1999, my plate was full. We had had a so-so baseball season with the highlight being Tony Gwynn getting his 3,000th hit. I had just finished my first Chargers programs and was planning to go to New York for a winter vacation. I was preparing to move into a house after New Year's. I had my reservations for my annual trip to Maui just before spring training. Then things changed. I received a call from Ron Phillips, then the Executive Director at the San Diego Hall of Champions Sports Museum. I thought he was just checking-in about what was coming up at the Hall, but it was more than that. He said, "Jane, Ted Williams is going to be in San Diego for the Hall of Champions awards dinner in February. We like your show, so we would like to know if you'd like to do a *One on One* interview with Ted Williams." Wow. What a compliment.

I knew Ted Williams was big enough to have a parkway named after him, and that he had been a big influence on Tony Gwynn, but as much as I appreciated history and valued the older generations, I wondered if this would make a good *One on One* program. Would fans want to hear from and about him? Would that

"Ted was brutally honest and didn't suffer fools easily.
Had you not prepared and asked the right questions, you would
have known immediately."
—STEVE BROWN, TED WILLIAMS' FRIEND AND BIOGRAPHER, 2010

be sexy, sizzling, contemporary, and interesting enough? Again, it took only a few short conversations with Dennis Morgigno and the Padres' Charles Steinberg to realize this was an opportunity not to be missed. I rearranged my Maui vacation travel plans to fly out a day later and began the preproduction process.

I still did not realize just how big a legend or how revered a player and feared a hitter Ted Williams was in baseball. I figured it out fast as I started my research and mentioned to people that I was interviewing him in early February. That is why January turned out to be a month with a nonstop knot in my stomach. The more I learned—especially about his reputation of not having much patience or tolerance for many reporters in his day—the more nervous I felt, and the more I prepared.

"I'm just finishing up the magazine once more for the annual induction ceremonies at the Ted Williams Museum in Florida, and one of the pieces I needed to write was on Ted's .406 season in 1941—this being its 60th anniversary. You know, I gratefully received the video tape of your *One on One* show featuring Ted back when you sent it last year, but I, shamefacedly now, admit I never got around to watching it until tonight. I've been really, really, busy.

I brought it out tonight, found a bit in there which I was able to use, and mainly really, really enjoyed it. It might be the best piece on Ted I've ever seen. I think you did an *excellent* job—confirming the instincts I had when we met and talked later. Thanks for the credit at the closing, too.

Congratulations!

I hope you won some San Diego award for that show.

Hope you are well."
—Bill Nowlin, Author and
Boston Baseball Historian, January 10, 2001

Ted Williams was born and raised in San Diego. The librarian at Hoover High School was very helpful in providing images, background, and a hard-to-find copy of Ted Williams' 1969 autobiography, *My Turn at Bat*. I read that book cover to cover, taking notes and extrapolating important defining moments, stories, and explanations about his life. I talked to people who could offer information and perspective about what was known or thought about Williams over time. Some of it was obvious; some very helpful. I became really excited about it after a conversation with my good friend from Tulsa, John Anderson, who had moved on to anchor at ESPN's *SportsCenter*. I called him at work to ask, "If you were going to interview Ted Williams, what would you ask him? What would you want to hear him talk about?" John replied, "If I had the opportunity, I wouldn't even know what to say, I'd be in such awe." Knowing that I had never cared about sports, he kidded, "This isn't fair. I should be interviewing him. I'm the one who loves baseball!"

On Friday, February 4, 2000, our crew arrived at the San Diego Hall of Champions Sports Museum. It is a unique and beautifully designed museum celebrating San Diego sports established by Bob Breitbard in 1946. We set up downstairs in a room displaying several Ted Williams and other special baseball memorabilia pieces. I wore a conservative long-sleeved blue sweater, pearls, black pumps, and a straight glen plaid skirt—the same skirt from my 1986 job interview that I shortened for the late '90s. The crew was set. I was excited.

I believed the best way to break the ice with the great hitter known as the "Splendid Splinter" was to find some common ground. My father, a retired Navy Commander, was in three wars, liked to hunt, and had taught me how to fish. That day, I brought three photographs: my father in uniform, my father with his hunting pals, and one my mother took of my sister and me in a boat with my father holding fishing poles somewhere in Montana when I was about ten.

Ted Williams arrived downstairs at 11:30 that morning. Mr. Williams, who had suffered two strokes and had heart problems, was in a wheelchair and accompanied by a personal medical assistant. My heart was pounding. Like a college student cramming for a big exam, the knot in my stomach had lasted several weeks, until the moment we said hello. Photographer Dan Roper was rolling tape.

JANE: Mr. Williams, Jane Mitchell, how are you?
WILLIAMS: Hi Jane.
JANE: I actually interviewed you a couple years ago about Jerry Coleman.
WILLIAMS: Oh yes, and what I said was true, wasn't it?
JANE: Absolutely!

He seemed to remember me, or else he was just being polite. A man known for being feisty, he graciously accepted my adrenaline-rushed attempt to connect on a personal level.

WILLIAMS: Your dad was in the military.
JANE: And I brought you a picture. I wanted to show you something. He was born in October 1919, so he would've been just about your age.
WILLIAMS: Was he a pilot?
JANE: No, aviation maintenance in World War II, Korea, and Vietnam. But he raised me fishing, so that's me fishing [laughing].
WILLIAMS: Oh isn't that something. Did you see any bears on that trip?
JANE: Yes we did, and picked giant blueberries.
WILLIAMS: How big?
JANE: This big.
WILLIAMS: Wow! No kidding.

He seemed genuinely interested and inquisitive. I was relieved. We were off to a good start, but then referring to the photograph of us with our fishing poles, he asked, "So, what kind of rod did he use?" After all that strategizing to bond, to try to connect on some common ground, after the anticipation that this would give me an edge—he got me. I didn't know the answer. I laughed and said I would have to get back to him on that. I never did, but for the record, I found the old green rods in our basement and they were made by Heddon.®

What Ted Williams didn't know is I had never worked so hard in advance of an interview in my career. I had tried to enter that day respecting this man's accomplishments and life story by being prepared and ready to listen. I believe he came to realize that as the interview was underway.

This was an unusual situation for a *One on One* shoot—he was an icon and this was not in his home or a familiar environment for him. For the first time, we had a small audience, including my boss, Dan Novak. I had to ignore that and block any potential added pressure. I had been told we had about one hour, or less, depending how Mr. Williams did and how he was feeling. As we started, I felt my body vibrating with a hint of anxiety, and my throat was tight through the first question. After

listening to him, hearing this legend answering *my* question, I shook off the nerves and settled in, but had my work cut out for me.

My first question was a door opener about how it felt to be back home in San Diego. He responded with an all-encompassing answer. As I somewhat anticipated, I quickly realized in that answer I had to be specific and diligent in having him talk about personal topics, such as his childhood, his parents, his struggles, and successes. I wanted to get inside his head, heart, and history, and to understand the reasons behind those elements and his feelings now that he looked back at his life. The statistics and facts could be filled in with narration and other interviews. I had read his book. Most people who would be watching probably had not. I felt a tremendous amount of responsibility to explore aspects of his life that most did not know about, or certainly had not ever heard him talk about.

Sometimes his answers meandered from topic to topic. Due to some health

issues, it was difficult to gauge how he would do, or the degree of his stamina in that situation. With a limited amount of time for the interview, and eighty years to cover, I not only had to listen, but take control; more than with anyone I had interviewed, and more than anyone since. Still, in recounting his journey, Ted Williams had a good grasp of details, such as when he signed with the Pacific Coast League Padres as a senior at Hoover High School for $150 a month, planning to stay in San Diego at his mother's request. He was sharp and expressive. He had eight decades of details in his vault of memories, and some were certainly more top of mind

than others—namely, the topic of hitting.

The Hall of Champions had a bat Ted Williams used in 1941: his .406-season. Mr. Williams held it in his hands as if he were ready to step up to the plate. Being the interviewer, I was not expecting the following exchange with the interviewee:

WILLIAMS: What did I tell you was the most important thing? Well, I told you …

JANE: For hitting? To be relaxed and to anticipate what the pitcher's gonna throw.

WILLIAMS: I made it a lot simpler than that.

JANE: Tell me again.

WILLIAMS: You are always ready for what?

JANE: You're always ready for the fastball!

WILLIAMS: Ah, ah, ah! That's right!

When I replied with the correct answer, he put his hand on his heart, and his three "ahs" punctuated how he was overjoyed I had been listening. Ironically, I believe my final answer did not come from listening that day, because after more than an hour of intense questions and answers, I cannot always remember details immediately; I have the recordings to rely upon later. However, because I had read his book and had that important part of his hitting philosophy in my mental file, I was able to retrieve it. I was pleased he was pleased. After a little more than an hour I asked:

> JANE: What would you like to be remembered for in fifty years when people look back at Ted Williams?
>
> WILLIAMS: That I contributed to this game of baseball at a high level, that they can always say, "What a hitter he was." And I think that might happen. And they can always say when he walks down the street, "There's as good a hitter as ever played this game." I don't say the greatest. I don't think I was the greatest. But I was a pretty good hitter. And that would be good enough for me.
>
> JANE: Well, that's good enough for us. Well, thank you for your time.
>
> WILLIAMS: That's a documentary. You gonna write a book, or what?
>
> JANE: No, it's a documentary, though.
>
> WILLIAMS: *[Laughing]*

I would never have anticipated a decade later, that day's experiences would indeed end up in a book. After wrapping up the formal interview, the crew and I posed for several group photos with Mr. Williams. Then, I made sure—practically insisted—we go to the North Park baseball field where he played as a child and now bears his name.

This once strong, robust man stood tall, but a little hunched over, as he used a walker to balance himself. I walked beside him, and step by step, we made our way onto the dirt around home plate. While his medical assistant seemed nervously protective, Mr. Williams was enjoying the trip back in time, describing where he played and where he hit balls some seventy years earlier. We were there

for only fifteen minutes, but in that time, I saw a glimpse of what is possible, and what is often inevitable—greatness from humble beginnings and eventual physical decline, despite an athlete's mindset. He offered advice to youngsters with great passion and conviction in his voice and his expression. Were it not for his physical limitations that day, we would have meandered and reminisced for much longer.

After I said thank you and goodbye, my work was just getting started. I did take my Maui vacation and went to spring training for the regular baseball stories and other *One on One* shoots, but the Ted Williams edition had a long to-do list to make it what it should be.

Even with the interviews, locally collected pictures and archival film, I felt the one-hour special edition would not be complete without a trip to the Ted Williams Museum in Florida. That is where we would not only gather more historical pictures and elements, but we might be able to interview him at his home. My boss agreed, and photographer Tod Lilburn and I made a three-day trip to Florida. Try as I might to persuade his contact person to let us meet with Mr. Williams, there was no budging, and that part didn't work out. However, I was persuasive enough that his fairly quiet and protective son, John Henry, agreed to sit down for a brief interview to talk about his father and the mission of the museum. We also interviewed several museum visitors, adding a nice dimension to the breadth of Ted Williams' influence and impact. Tod and I then flew to Palm Beach to spend part of a day interviewing the legendary broadcaster Curt Gowdy who called Ted Williams' last game on the radio.

Upon my return to San Diego, I mapped out the show, wrote one section, and Dan began editing. Then I wrote the next section, and he would begin editing that as I moved onto the next. I wrote at home where I could focus and figure out this immense jigsaw puzzle. The challenge of the "writing at home plan" at the time was I had just moved into my house, so I had to move my computer and notes as the painters were painting one room then the next. At an average of one hour of writing for each minute that hits the air, that was nearly sixty hours just to get it to script form.

Dan and my associate producer at the time, Lya Vallat, were digitally piecing the elements together in the edit room. Technical difficulties were maddening because the computer Dan used to edit crashed and we lost a lot of time and work. I panicked fearing we would miss a deadline for the debut date. I couldn't imagine sacrificing quality for a self-imposed deadline, so I shared that concern with Dan Novak. He said there was no reason we could not delay the debut date, and trusted we knew what it would take to make an excellent program. We extended our editing about another week, allowing us the time to do it right. I have no doubt this reasonable thinking in a technical crisis, and the fact we had control of the programming on the channel, made all the difference in how the show turned out.

We shot the original stand-ups at Hoover High School in the gym, and after one month of intense production, the show was finished and ready to debut. Because this was so special, I had a small debut party at my home with about a dozen people from work who had a part in it and some local historians.

Very few people know this story, but in the interest of honesty and a learning milestone, here goes .... Dan Roper and I have always put a high value on accuracy, especially with pictures. One key to Ted Williams' story was his high school baseball coach, Wos Caldwell. There were a few pictures of Caldwell in the school's yearbook and some loose photos. He was clearly identified in the items we had gathered and had been given from the library.

All the other facts were double checked, so we felt confident that everything was correct.

Then, as the group gathered around the television in my living room, in the middle of a segment talking about Ted Williams' high school years, Dan and I heard Bob Breitbard say fairly softly, "That's not Wos Caldwell ..." Commercial Break. "Coffee anyone?" Pit in stomach. Had we made a mistake?

I quietly conferred with Bob about the possible error and the next day, Dan and I looked at the pictures. We were operating off a photograph that clearly identified the man as Wos Caldwell, but the photo itself had apparently been misidentified by whoever had originally marked it. Because the picture was old, small, and black and white, it took some comparing with other pictures that were of Caldwell to see the mistake. We replaced the wrong one for the next showing. It's an awful feeling to think you've made an error, and even worse when you realize you have.

Since then, anytime Dan and I question a picture, asking if that really is the person, we look at each other and say, "That's not Wos Caldwell," and we know we're making sure we have it right.

In 2001 I had the pleasure of meeting Bob Costas, first in Cooperstown during Dave Winfield's induction, then later that October at the ceremony for Tony Gwynn's retirement. During a brief conversation in San Diego with Bob, I offered to send him a copy of the show on Ted Williams because a little part included Bob at the Fishing Hall of Fame event. I sent him the copies of the Ted Williams program along with a few others—if I had his attention, I might as well show him the breadth of my work. January 7, 2002 I was sick and stayed home to work. I checked my office voicemail only to hear one of the best messages I had ever received in my career. It was from Bob Costas. He indicated he was busy getting ready for the Olympics, but wanted to let me know he had watched the Ted Williams show and said it was excellent. I was euphoric. I saved the message and ran searching for an old tape recorder to record it so it would not be erased or lost. Then I had my mother listen to it, and she shared in my jubilation. Other than that, I mostly kept it under my hat—I didn't want people to think I was boasting or showing off. In all humility, it gave me an added boost of confidence and validation I was doing things right.

> "Over the years, Jane Mitchell's work with contemporary and historical sports figures has been consistently thoughtful and well crafted. She blends a fan's passion with a reporter's curiosity and eye for detail."
>
> —BOB COSTAS, BROADCASTER, 2010

July 5, 2002, Ted Williams died. He was eighty-three. Not long after that I received a phone call from Charles Steinberg. In 2010, he reflected on what the edition meant to him.

"Another one of the shows that springs to mind was her *One on One* with Ted Williams. It was so well done that several years later, when we left San Diego to join the Boston Red Sox, and Ted Williams passed away, and we were having a public celebration of his life, it was that *One on One* that we showed during the day at Fenway Park, so that people got as vivid a portrait of their hero as we could provide. So it had legs far beyond San Diego."

—Charles Steinberg, MLB, 2010

I didn't know for the longest time whether Ted Williams had ever seen the show, and with his death, I wasn't sure I ever would. Then Steve Brown called me in 2008. He told me he was Ted Williams' long-time friend and was selected and authorized by Mr. Williams to produce a documentary for children called *Ted Williams: The Greatest Fisherman to Ever Play Baseball*. Mr. Brown, in his seventies, had also been chosen by Bobby Doerr to produce his documentary. Doerr, the Hall of Fame Second Baseman, was also Ted Williams' friend. Production had slowed following Ted Williams' death, but then Mr. Brown contacted me about using part of the *One on One* interview in his project. Out of curiosity, I asked if Ted had ever seen the show. I was stunned when he said yes, and by what he relayed as Mr. Williams' impressions of it. I am grateful for the letter Mr. Brown wrote to help document those impressions.

"It was good getting to talk to you from Bobby's home, and you getting to hear from his own mouth what Ted's best friend thought of your interview, since it was the last one he did before he left us. As Bobby told you and I confirm, we appreciate your work, as you left the world with a wonderful understanding of one of the last true American Heroes …

For the record, when Ted and his son came back from San Diego, Bob Breitbard sent Ted a copy of your Channel 4 interview. We watched it in its entirety, and all agreed it was very well done. Days later we watched it again. This viewing got the response from Ted that you had captured what the fans wanted to know. He compared your interview with some of the greatest sportscasters', Gowdy, Costas, and Firestone.... Ted gave you, Jane, his proof by his response. Ted was brutally honest, and didn't suffer fools easily. Had you not prepared and asked the right questions, you would have known immediately.

He knew you had touched him and presented him, the man, that only those who knew him best could attest, and as he should have been presented to legions of fans—as the last great American hero. Jane, in closing, Bobby Doerr, my film crew, and I concur. The production value, the use of visuals in weaving the story line, and the depth left us with more insight into the life of the Greatest Fisherman to Ever Play Ball."

It's humbling to even be named in the same category as those respected and nationally acclaimed sportscasters, and ironic, considering I knew so little about

Ted Williams when first presented with the opportunity to sit down with him. I am so honored that he had the interest to watch the final show. Had he not liked it, I might have heard that criticism some other way. I'm just glad he did—for him, his family, and his legacy, and I'm still touched when viewers comment on that show.

With a myriad of elements to manage as the writer and producer, the final show would not have been what it was were it not for Dan Roper and Lya Vallat. While others contributed on shoots and production logistics, Dan and Lya were deeply committed and connected to this production as well. Despite the challenges, there were no shortcuts, no excuses, and no complaints. There were, however, many long days and nights, and equally as much pride in ownership.

The edition was nominated for an Emmy for best Biographical/Historical program and for writing. I received one for writing, but we did not receive an Emmy for the program category. While we found that a bit odd, and we don't do it for the awards, it was one show early on we hoped would win. Regardless, its longevity is award, and reward, enough.

The show is among the *One on One Classics*. By all accounts—from his inner circle, including Steve Brown, Williams aficionados, and producers from other entities wanting to view it—my 2000 interview was his final television interview. Of course we could not have known that at the time, but that makes me all the more proud, and humbled, to have been a little part in telling the Splendid Splinter's legacy then and now.

Here is the script from the *One on One* debuting May 16, 2000.

• • •

Baseball's best hitter, Ted Williams. From humble San Diego beginnings to major league icon, war veteran and a great outdoorsman, his passion for life reflected in his passion for hitting.

TED: Boy, boy oh boy, the greatest feeling and greatest sound in the world.

The word *legend* can evoke mythical, bigger-than-life images. But with Ted Williams, because of what he achieved in the game—the last man to hit .400 in a season sixty years ago—time emphasizes that his accomplishment was certainly no myth. And much of his success began here at San Diego's Hoover High School where his picture hangs proudly on the wall of the gym with other Hoover standouts. You don't have to be a baseball fan to appreciate the story about this baseball player, this baseball legend. It's a story about luck, loss, love, and learning, sometimes the hard way.

Ted Williams the player, his presence, his stature, his swing. At 6'4", 198 pounds, he had a look made for the job—the John Wayne of baseball. The Kid, the Splendid Splinter, Teddy Ballgame: nicknames befitting a man whose statistics and style make for a remarkable career, a remarkable story.

TED: I would have to say that I am as lucky as you could be as an individual. Considering everything that has happened to me, a career with a lot of excitement connected to it, and I am still kicking at eighty-something. I know more than anyone else how lucky I've been.

Thirty years ago, Ted Williams told his life story in a book *My Turn at Bat*. He wrote, "If there ever was a man born to be a hitter it was me. As a kid, I wished on every falling star, please, let me be the hitter I want to be."

Fate would have that wish come true for Theodore Samuel Williams born August 30, 1918 in San Diego. He and his younger brother, Danny, grew up in a little house at 4121 Utah Street in North Park, just a block and a half from the playground on which Teddy Williams would begin his amazing journey. And from as early as he can remember, he had a bat in his hand.

TED: I mean it was baseball, baseball.

JANE: Where did you get that drive and that conviction to work at it so hard every day, even as a kid?

TED: The most fun I have ever had in my life was holding a bat and hitting a ball, and then really hitting one on the button and what a feeling. It could just vibrate that through my body. Oh what a feeling. That just kept going for the next thirty-five to forty years.

His drive also was the result of essentially growing up by himself. His father, Sam, was a former Marine in World War I, a quiet man who owned a little photography store on Fifth Avenue downtown and didn't get home until late in the evening. His mother, May, from El Paso and of Mexican heritage, was dedicated to serving the poor.

TED: My mother was with the Salvation Army and her whole life was that. She was going that way, my dad was that way, and I was going some other place.

His brother had leukemia and no interest in baseball, and the two were never close. So Ted Williams filled a void and followed his heart, baseball, which motivated him to be the first to arrive every day at Garfield Elementary School.

TED: It was easy for me to get up early in the morning and be there when that janitor got there, open the clothes closet and get the ball and bat. Then I would come home in the afternoon, same thing. I had other kids or their fathers and they were at the ball field, opportunity galore.

Williams remembers well Rod Luscomb, the playground director at North Park.

TED: He was just a frustrated old ball player, who loved it, wanted to be with it. Loved to tinker around the playground and was just as eager to practice with me as I was with him. I have always given him credit for stimulating my great desire.

He was young Ted's first real hero because he cared and taught him about the intricacies of facing different pitchers. With Williams getting up to 100 at-bats a day, and with his keen eyesight, practice began to make perfect.

TED: I always wanted to, as I started to play, to excel and I had the opportunity. I had some natural talent and all of a sudden I was a good hitter.

For seven years Williams played ball with Luscomb at the playground every day but Saturday. Saturday was for exploring San Diego's great outdoors, a landscape in the early '30s dotted less with traffic and more with natural targets.

TED: I would go down to Mission Valley and start hunting rabbits or find a duck still sitting there in the pond.

After a Saturday of being outside, he and his friends would listen to USC games then Benny Goodman and swing music on the radio.

As a kid with not much of a home life, Williams bonded with Les Cassie, the father of Les Junior, Williams' friend and teammate in school.

LES CASSIE: He just naturally took to Ted from the first time I brought him over to the house, and my mother the same.

TED: Mr. Cassie, one of my most dearest memories in life. He was a fisherman and at an early age I started making my own bamboo—calcutta rods and the fishing was good at some of these beaches, nice Corvinas, nice Croakers …

Les Junior didn't like fishing, so Williams and Mr. Cassie often spent Friday nights on the shores of Coronado.

TED: We would go by that Coronado hotel at eight or nine at night and saw the big chandelier ball room, and we would fish until twelve and then drive back again.

While fishing and hunting were his recreation, the baseball diamond was young Ted's calling. By tenth grade, Williams had a choice of high schools. San Diego High was the area's biggest at the time. Hoover High was smaller and newer.

TED: I was right on the line, I could have [gone] that way or this way and I decided that I had a better chance at making the team at Hoover than San Diego and I wanted to play.

He visited Hoover's batting practice and hit two balls further than anyone off baseball coach Wos Caldwell.

TED: "What's your name kid?" "My name is Ted Williams and I'm signing up, I'll be here on Monday!" And that's how it all started!

So Hoover, it was. That's where he met Bob Breitbard, a football player and class president.

BOB BREITBARD: We had a wonderful teacher, Mrs. Hamilton. Never forget her. She loved him and he had a loud voice. And he'd say, "Hi Teach!"

Hitting was Ted Williams' obsession. Running, an obstacle, so coach Caldwell challenged him with racing around the bases.

TED: He could run, for a coach he could run. Here I am a gangly seventeen years old, who could not run at all, just arms and legs.

But his young beanpole body was conducive to hitting and pitching. He won All Southern California honors as a pitcher his junior year, and as an outfielder his senior year, 1936. On the mound, he pitched his team to playoff spots. His ability and potential caught the attention of scouts from Detroit and Los Angeles, but they didn't like his lean and hungry look. He was 150 pounds, 6'1" and still growing. He turned down offers from Saint Louis and the Yankees.

TED: My mother wanted me to be around San Diego, around her, so I signed with San Diego.

The new Pacific Coast League San Diego Padres, fresh from Hollywood, needed a local draw, and Williams, the best high school player in town and a prospect, fit the bill for $150 a month.

TED: I signed in June because I was going to graduate from high school and they said, "You sign with us and we will pay you for the whole month of June and for the rest of the season."

At seventeen years old and still months away from getting his high school diploma in January 1937, Ted Williams was a professional ballplayer.

The beginning of his professional career would deliver much more than expected. Up next on *One on One,* the brash and brilliance of a rookie with the Boston Red Sox and the story of his still unmatched record setting year 1941....

At seventeen Ted Williams was a wonder boy, not just for his knack with the bat, but for his unbridled enthusiasm for baseball—always swinging an imaginary bat, even while shagging balls. With the Pacific Coast League Padres, he pinch hit, pitched, and played the outfield. He threw right and batted left and it was his classic swing that impressed Red Sox General Manager Eddie Collins. While visiting Boston's affiliate, he saw Williams play and asked for an option on him.

TED: So when I got a little better goin', they would buy me and I would become a Red Soxer.

Ted grew an inch and added ten pounds so by the '37 season, his swing delivered line drives and home runs, finishing the year hitting twenty-three out of the park. The Red Sox were convinced and bought Williams' contract for $25,000 and four ballplayers.

TED: And at the time, I thought it was a terrible break. Here I am going from San Diego to the furthest I could go Northeast, never been to the snow, never did this or that, and I thought, *Oh boy!*

He was greeted at spring training in Sarasota, Florida with fans and ballplayers ribbing him for being from small time baseball and the West Coast. Not afraid to respond he was soon dubbed the Fresh Rookie and California Cookie.

TED: I was not sure whether I had said the right thing or not. I'll tell you, I was scared as anyone else when I was ready to get going, hoping I could do it.

He couldn't quite handle major league pitching, so he was bussed to the Red Sox farm team, the Minneapolis Millers. He vowed he'd be back. But first he had a little growing up to do. The new Miller was described as both a sensational rising star and a spoiled kid who seemed to have it too easy professionally. Tearing up the clubhouse after going hitless in three consecutive games, not hustling to first after a hit he hoped would be a home run wasn't, seeming bored unless he was at the plate. Signs of immaturity magnified in a new world under the scrutiny of the press.

> TED: But they never had anyone like me at that time, and I was brash and sounded cocky.

He really just wanted to excel. So to read a 1938 sports column by Charles Johnson, you see why Ted Williams is special. On the heels of criticism about his antics Johnson wrote, "Instead of crawling into his shell and complaining that everyone is picking on him, Ted has turned over a new leaf. To us, that means he has the qualities of which great stars are made." Williams indeed listened to his manager, Donie Bush, and instead of tearing up the clubhouse again, he tore up pitchers, leading the league batting .366 with forty-two home runs.

Off the field, he showed his softer side with children, visiting hospitals and sending autographed balls to kids he'd met with or without cameras around. One magazine called him "Baseball's Bad Boy, Boston's new batting idol, to delight and despair of the fans." And Ted Williams was favored to be the outstanding Rookie of the Year before the '39 season started.

> TED: I was in some place that I had dreamt that would never be, it looked different, the weather was different. The fans were great. Here I am a young kid, and I was hitting pretty good and they thought that this guy was interesting. I was doing things that no other left-handed hitter had done there.

Eccentric and energetic with a graceful swing and powerful wrist action that virtually guaranteed success at the plate, Ted Williams seemed destined for greatness. The next Babe Ruth, the best hitter since Joe DiMaggio, the headlines predicted his future. He wore the Rookie moniker well. Clean cut, clean living, named The Kid by the clubhouse manager and with his smile and quick wit, he was the story in Boston and in baseball, splashed and celebrated for his sensational start.

> TED: I always did better, no matter what it was in life, if I went into anything I said, "Geez, I hope I can do it." I always had more success that way than if I said, "Just get me up there, no problem." Before I knew it I was 0-for-8. But if I went in there with an attitude, boy I hope I can do it and grind a little bit, I always did better.

The fans loved him. He loved the fans. He wouldn't just tip his cap, he'd wave it. With no official award at the time, he won every unofficial Rookie of the Year honor.

> TED: All of a sudden, they thought I was great.

But 1940 was another story. The Red Sox reconfigured the outfield, hoping Williams might get more long balls to challenge The Babe's home run record. He was moved from right to left field to keep him from staring at the sun. The fans didn't like it. They thought he hadn't earned so-called special treatment, yet. The honeymoon was over.

> TED: Boston was a funny town that year. There was plenty of competition among the writers to get some new angle on something. Sometimes it was good, sometimes it was bad, but they had a story.

To add insult to injury, a columnist blasted Williams for brooding on the bench over a bad performance and criticized him for being extremely selfish, including for not visiting his parents in the winter, disparaging his upbringing. Getting personal, Williams thought, was a low blow.

> TED: I might have said things that I should not have said.

He was baffled, felt betrayed. Williams' response was a vow never to tip his cap again. The love-hate relationship between the kid, the writers, and the fans would follow him his whole career. His relationship with the broadcasters, including Red Sox announcer Curt Gowdy, far different.

> CURT GOWDY: His big thing was the radio/TV people boosted the game and the writers tore it down.

Williams forged ahead and at spring training 1941, he's quoted as telling the sportswriters, "Sure I look forward to this season. How can they stop me?" Prophetic words. Ted Williams, confident, ambitious, and prepared was ready for anything a pitcher wanted to throw at him.

> TED: Fastball pitchers never bothered me, it was those little cuties out there, knuckleballs and screwball, and not wanting to give you anything to hit. That guy that had the almighty fastball. WOW, I could hit that.
>
> JANE: What did it feel like to hit that time after time after time?
>
> TED: The greatest feeling in the world for a ball player or a hitter when he has really mashed one. Bow, boy oh boy the greatest feeling and greatest sound in the world.

And in 1941, it was a symphony of hits, a duet actually with Yankee Joe DiMaggio on pace to break Willie Keeler's all-time 44-game hitting streak. For Ted Williams it was one multi-hit game, then another, and another, and by early June, a 23-game hitting streak during which he hit .488. Williams was now seen as the Red Sox's most dangerous hitter, more so than slugger, friend, and veteran Jimmie Fox. And people began to realize The Kid could become the first major league hitter to hit over .400 for the season since Bill Terry in 1930. Williams and DiMaggio, creating intrigue and excitement in baseball, took center stage as teammates in the 1941 All-Star Game.

> TED: Boom, I come up and hit a magical home run, gave me a real good pump.

DiMaggio snapped his streak just after the break at 56, so the focus shifted to the chase for .400 and the kid they would call "King." Despite a nagging ankle injury, Williams went on a tear. Teams tried to stop Ted by pitching around him, walking him, but he was hot through the summer. In a game of inches and decimal points, just a few strike outs and outs had Williams clinging to .400. And baseball history would come down to the last game of the season, September 28.

The Red Sox were out of the race, and in Philadelphia for a double header. Williams' batting average was .39955, rounded up to .400 for the record books. A few bad at bats would jeopardize his average.

> TED: The manager of the team, Joe Cronin, said that you don't have to play today, you are .400 officially. You don't have to play. I was dumbfounded to think that they were talking that way to me because I never had an ounce of idea that I was not going to play. I said, "I am going to play."

And play he did, both games, going 6-for-8 with a couple monstrous home runs with his batting average at .4057 rounded up to .406.

> TED: It is sixty years since that has happened. Sixty years, as I say it I can hardly believe it, sixty years since that has happened and it has been connected with me all of the way.

The 1941 baseball season was truly a time to celebrate Ted Williams' awesome achievement hitting .400 for the season. But that winter, the course of his life, the course of the world, would change.

[Bombing of Pearl Harbor]

December 7, 1941 the Japanese bombed Pearl Harbor. The United States was at war. Ted Williams heard the news while at home in Princeton, Minnesota. He had registered that November with the local draft board. But soon after the attack, his status changed. He could be called into service anytime. Considering his mother's financial dependency because she was divorced, he filed for deferment but was refused. But he won his second appeal and was not likely to be called to duty right away.

> TED: I was accused of ducking the service and I was this and that, they were all taking a shot at me, someone in those papers.

But applause came from fans at home and around the league. He won the battle of public opinion and kept on swinging, then chose to enlist. By night he studied to qualify for flight school. By day, he pummeled opposing pitchers, right up to the last game of the season.

> TED: All I was concerned with actually, that day I was hitting against Dizzy Trout, a pretty good pitcher. I did hit a home run that day before I left—home run.

Ted Williams finished 1942 winning the Triple Crown. But now it was time to serve his country in the Naval Cadet Corps.

> TED: I never flew a plane in my life. Used to drive a car pretty fast because I had a good car, but I didn't know what to expect and what might happen.

He earned his officer's commission, completed flight school, and was on his way to the Pacific fully prepared to face combat when the war ended, and Ted Williams came home.

>   TED: I was lucky, I didn't even notice it, swish. I was just getting better all of the time.

1946 was a very good year for Ted Williams and the Red Sox. They clinched the pennant on September 13. But while the 13th was lucky, the days after were not. His elbow was hurt and a New York newspaper reported he may be traded. Ownership wouldn't comment. Ted was in the dark. Between that and St. Louis pitching that stymied Sox hitting, Boston lost the series 3-4. Late after the game on the train, he broke down in tears.

>   TED: We got there and we didn't win. And I did poorly and I don't know why, today. I don't know why.

He did win the Most Valuable Player award and another Triple Crown, and would prove forceful again in '48, leading his team to a mid-season comeback. The Red Sox fell short in that bid for the pennant and '49 would be a similar year with one of Williams' worst moments in his career in a pennant-deciding game. Williams juggled a ball in the 8th, allowing a man to reach third, then Yankee Jerry Coleman was at the plate.

>   *[Coleman gets an RBI, Yankees score]*

It was home again without a ring for Ted Williams, but world events were conspiring again to make that disappointment seem minor in comparison. In 1952 he was married with a four-year-old daughter, at the peak of his career, and the U.S. was at war with Korea. As a Marine reserve, he was recalled.

>   TED: I didn't like it because I could not play ball.

But he accepted his assignment as one of four major league ball player pilots, including Jerry Coleman, called to fly again. On April 30, Boston bid him farewell in an emotional pre-game ceremony. The crowd sang "Auld Lang Syne" and the teams lined up like the shape of a wing, dugout to dugout. It seemed this would be the end of Teddy Ballgame's fourteen-year career. He hit a home run to win the game, then Ted Williams went to war.

>   TED: … lo and behold, here I am in Korea.

He was flying [F-9 Panther] Corsairs, making bombing runs, serving with future astronaut, John Glenn. The weather was cold and damp, but he flew anyway. Then, the odds caught up with him. His was hit by enemy fire and he remembers thinking …

>   TED: I said in the cockpit, "If ever there were someone up there to help me this would be it. "
>   JERRY COLEMAN: "MAYDAY, MAYDAY!"

And with a pilot in another plane trying to guide him, Williams made a dramatic landing, skidding more than a mile.

TED: And I got over the field the plane blew up … [demonstrates]. Blew the wheels, doors off, and everything. That is what happened to me and luckily I got down in one hunk.

He was back flying the next day—no time to recover, and after thirty-nine more missions he was deathly ill with pneumonia, and that sickness and the effects of the crash sent him home. Boston kept his locker for him and at thirty-five years old, he played the rest of the season—thirty-seven games—hitting .407. Ted Williams was back. The next few years, 1953 to '57, were unhappy years for him. He got a divorce, was tired, sometimes sick. At thirty-eight years old, he remembers, "Every move I made was a headline." In 1957 at forty, he was the oldest to win a batting championship. He was just five hits shy of duplicating his magical .400 season.

CURT GOUDY: The one thing about him that made him great, that makes any athlete great, is his pride. He had a burning pride to be really good.

While the Red Sox weren't very good, Ted Williams was still captivating the baseball world with his bat. And finally captivating his critics in the press, who began to see that the once-sassy Kid had turned into a baseball treasure with his work ethic, determination, his achievements—even his long time charity work. Still, age and injuries were taking a toll.

JANE: When did you know it was time to retire?

TED: I remember I was at second base, two men out. Tight ball game and I am on second. I looked at shortstop and second baseman, then I looked at home plate and geez, it looked like it was a mile and a half, and I had to go around this way to get there. I took a couple of deep breaths and said, "Boy, I hope I can make it." That is when I realized as much as any time. But I could still hit. I could still hit a little bit.

That's what kept him going and going. He wasn't expected to field or run like a younger player anymore. Ted was about hitting. After a neck injury just before the '59 season, his friend and Red Sox owner, Tom Yawkey, suggested it might be time to retire. Williams gave his answer in the first game of the season with a 500-foot home run. And the next year, another milestone home run number 500, among peers such as Ernie Banks, Yogi Berra, Mickey Mantle, Jackie Robinson, and Willie Mayes. Ted Williams was named Player of the Decade. He did his legacy a favor by choosing to hang 'em up while he still had something left. September 28, 1960, was the last home game of the season, the last day the Red Sox would ever field a guy wearing number 9.

TED: It was a dreary, wet, and windy day …

Announcer Curt Gowdy learned from the clubhouse boy that Williams wouldn't be going on for two games in New York.

CURT GOUDY: "Don't tell anybody." "Don't worry, I won't."

But he couldn't contain the significance in Williams' last at bat.

CURT GOUDY: Jack Fisher's pitching for Baltimore. And threw him a high fastball, and Ted swung, and as the ball started, I knew it was going to be a home run, started out to right and I said …

Game call: Ted Williams has hit a home run at his last time at bat in the major leagues.

TED: I never thought, well it was my last time I am going to hit a home run or anything like that, I was just trying to hit the ball hard, which I always try to do.

Rounding the bases, he thought about tipping his hat to the fans.

TED: I thought about it, but just for a fleeting second. But didn't.
JANE: Why not?
TED: I just could not do it. I didn't want to. I couldn't do it, I hadn't done it, so I didn't.

He doesn't remember celebrating after the game. It was over, he recalls. That's all. With no tempting offers to stay in the game to coach or manage right away, Williams realized it was for the best because now he finally had his long summers free to fish.

Coming up on *One on One,* Ted Williams the outdoorsman and a museum that holds baseball and personal treasures. And later, a classic from the archives, his speech at the Baseball Hall of Fame….

As much as Ted Williams is one with a bat, he's also one with nature. During his off-seasons as a player, he'd cast aside the pressures of the game for the thrill of the catch.

JANE: What's the biggest fish or toughest catch you ever made?
TED: I am glad you asked me that dear, because when I say this they say, "Boy that guy has been around fishing."

In retirement, he took his adventuresome spirit to new heights. Fishing and hunting all over the country, all over the world.

TED: I have fished the Zambebe River in Africa and I caught the tiger fish that has the big mouth and teeth and they go together like that. I had a chance to fish in Peru, and that is where I caught the biggest fish I ever caught, 1,235 pounds, fourteen feet long and bigger around than I can go like that; fourteen feet. Boy was he big.

At the time, it was the eighth largest Marlin ever reeled in, one of his feats that landed him in the International Game Fish Association's Hall of Fame in Fort Lauderdale. He shared his time with those who shared his love for the great outdoors.

CURT GOUDY: So he started asking me questions about Wyoming. "What's the best stream out there, what's the best time of year, what flies do you use?"
TED: He's the best fisherman I ever saw.

Williams was on the SEARS Sports Advisory Staff and urged people to walk softly and carry a big stick, lending his star name to sporting goods and food, such as Wheaties® and Ted's root beer. A bigger challenge: managing the business of his valuable signature and memorabilia.

> **TED:** I enjoyed doing most of it. Some turned out better than others.

Many of the pictures and mementos from his life's journey, from playing, to flying, to even his stint as manager for the Washington Senators, can be found in a special place in Florida, his home-base since training there during the war years. One hundred miles north of Tampa in the small lake town of Hernando is the Ted Williams Museum and Hitters Hall of Fame.

> **WOMAN FAN:** We're from New England, so he was everybody's hero.

Laid out like a baseball diamond …

> **BOY FAN:** There's a first base, second base, third base …

You experience the different dimensions of his life.

> **WOMAN FAN:** That affects me because I've been a fan all my life.
> **BOY FAN:** It's cool because you see all the different old gloves and bats.
> **BOY FAN:** I learned that Ted has his own root beer and it was delicious and creamy.

> *[Opening of Hall of Fame]*

The Hitters Hall of Fame opened in '95 with a star-studded guest list, including former President George [H.W.] Bush. An event each February inducts Ted's top hitters and contributors to the game.

> **BOB COSTAS** [from ceremony]: You either had to have great statistics or know a lot of good fishing spots.
> **JOHN HENRY:** Where he can honor his friends at his own place and they can turn and honor him back. I can only imagine how great that makes him feel deep inside.

John Henry Williams, Ted's only son, is active in helping his father carry out his vision for his legacy, the betterment of baseball—especially youth baseball.

> **JOHN HENRY:** It's kind of lost that home-grown feeling, picking up a few baseballs and playing in the park like Dad used to do, in San Diego.

The Ted Williams League is designed for skill level more than age group. It's based on fifteen years of research and development by Williams and his teaching protégé, Steve Ferroli.

> **STEVE FERROLI:** Having all the right bases to give kids an opportunity to have self-confidence.

It's expected to expand from the Northeast to franchise leagues including Alaska and San Diego, eventually, with championships played on the museum grounds.

> **TED:** It is not competition as much as it is teaching.

Teaching and hitting are synonymous with Ted Williams …

[Ted hitting video—"that's what works for me ..."]

Who has fans coast to coast.

> **FAN:** Many of us in Brooklyn read his book on hitting and talked about that. He had a book that was required reading by the high school coach.

While countless kids and big leaguers swear by that book, *The Science of Hitting*, and want to emulate him, John Henry was not driven to try to follow in his father's footsteps.

> **JOHN HENRY:** I had to make choices every summer. Play baseball or go fishing with Dad. And you have to play baseball if you are going to be a baseball player. So there were constantly choices that took me from being a baseball player.
>
> **JANE:** So you went fishing with Dad?
>
> **JOHN HENRY:** Oh, yeah.

He's learned from his father's life that passion is good, but balance is important.

> **JOHN HENRY:** He did everything so to the Nth degree that a lot of other things fell by the wayside.

Including marriage—three times divorced—and time with his children. A bittersweet thing happened when Ted Williams suffered two strokes in the mid '90s.

> **JOHN HENRY:** It forced our relationship to become very close. And it was probably one of the biggest blessings in disguise. Not only did it force that, but it also probably saved his life, because of attention to his health and making sure that he was doing well.
>
> **TED:** ... That they have a lot of love in their heart for their dad because their dad has so much love for the two kids.

Ted's love for children in general stems from what he didn't have as a child, as much as what he admired in his charitable mother. So he's long been devoted to the Red Sox Jimmy Fund, providing help to kids with cancer.

> Williams is caring and, admittedly, cantankerous at times, but perhaps that's the perfectionist in him, a man with high expectations and a quest for knowledge.
>
> **JANE:** When did you become so curious, so inquisitive, a student, not just of the game, but about nature and the world?
>
> **TED:** When I was a kid I was not interested in school work. Then I was in the Navy and I went through aviation training, learning about combustible engines. What makes the airplane fly? Do you know what makes the airplane fly?
>
> **JANE:** I'll never understand it. *[He laughs]*

And he began applying the laws of physics to his game.

> **TED:** I wanted to know why the ball curved; those are things that applied to what I was thinking about. It kept my interest and I was always learning things.

From his museum, to writing books, to videotapes, CD-ROMs, and websites, Ted Williams is devoted to spreading the word on hitting.

TED: I think I know a lot about it and I can give people I think the best description of how it should feel.

[Demonstrating bat to Jane]

Even while holding a bat from his .406 season. Always the teacher, pop quizzes are to be expected.

TED: What did I tell you is the most important thing?

JANE: For hitting? To be relaxed and to anticipate what the pitcher is going to throw.

TED: I made it simpler than that. What did I tell you was the most important thing? I told you. You're always ready for what?

JANE: You're always ready for the fastball.

TED: Aahhh ... ahh! [Ted points to heart]

Teaching and challenging another hitting great, Tony Gwynn, and Ted Williams' San Diego Connection, that's next on *One on One* ....

Red Sox fans revere Ted Williams, retiring his number for what he meant to Fenway Park. He is one of Boston's favorite sons. In 1991, he and Joe DiMaggio received the Presidential Medal of Freedom, the highest honor bestowed by the president in peacetime. Ted Williams is one of America's favorite sons. But his roots are in San Diego.

TED: It is the regret of my life that I didn't spend more time here earlier, but I had other things that I was thinking about and doing. It has been pretty much a busy fifty years.

Williams has enjoyed making up for lost time, returning for events such as the naming of the Ted Williams Parkway and to re-establish ties.

TED: I have so many wonderful friends here.

The Hall of Champions recognized him in 1996 with the All-Time Star Award. The Padres have embraced the former PCL Padre as one of San Diego's favorite sons ...

[Ted Williams throwing out the first pitch]

... and has dedicated a Little Padres Park in his name.

TED [speaking at the Hall of Champions]: I can't thank you enough and everybody responsible, even if there are a few sportswriters involved.

His alma mater, Hoover High School, is dear to his heart. In the history room of the library are newspaper clippings and pictures documenting his career and visits to the campus. Librarian and baseball fan, Dennis Donnely, is the keeper of the collection, which attracts writers, researchers, even occasional honeymooners from Boston.

DENNIS DONNELY: People want to literally retrace his footsteps. You would like to see what he saw and what he felt.

[Hoover High School baseball game]

And for freshmen who want to make the baseball team? A book report on the 1937 grad is required.

> RON LARDIZABAL (Coach): That's a big honor for our kids to say they play on the same field that is named after Ted Williams. So it is important that they know who he is.

In a rare return to his childhood playground, that ball field in North Park, there's a sense that even while he's not the same little kid who once dreamed …

> TED [at Little League field]: I'm trying to see where I used to hit.

… the details of yesteryear seem as if they were yesterday.

> TED [at Little League field]: There used to be a short fence in centerfield and I hit my first sandlot Sunday game home run over that centerfield fence. And I don't know exactly where it is now but, oh, that was a big hit for me. I thought, *Boy, home run.* Yep, home run.

Wherever Ted Williams goes, the subject of hitting .406 inevitably comes up.

> TED: Still I think that it will be done again. You have a guy here in San Diego that might be the next .400 hitter too you know …

[A 1997 game: Tony Gwynn hitting near .400 mid season]

The parallels between Williams and Gwynn are intriguing. Williams number 19 as a PCL Padre, Gwynn number 19 in the majors; both playing to at least age forty; Williams with six batting titles, Gwynn with eight. But while Williams hit for power, Gwynn hits for contact.

In fact, in '97, Gwynn and Larry Walker were on pace to hit .400, the first to challenge Williams' longstanding record in fifteen years. And Gwynn's success, hitting more home runs in two months than all of the year before, came two years after first meeting Ted Williams.

> TONY GWYNN: He is brutally honest. He might not say what you want to hear and that is what I found out the first time I met him. He did not say what I wanted to hear. But the man knows what he is talking about.
>
> TONY GWYNN [Telling story to a small group with Ted]: He said, "Son let me tell you, major league history is made on the ball inside." [laughing] So last year I finally found out what he was talking about and what he's saying is that when they throw inside and you show them you can hit the ball out of the ballpark, that you can handle the ball inside, when you handle that ball, they go back a way. I got to the All-Star break, I had thirteen home runs, I'm doing pretty well and the second half of the season I hit four home runs [chuckles]. And the reason why is, "Major league history is made on the ball inside." *[laughter]* And I owe Ted Williams a big thank … Thank you!

Gleaning such insight is special for those who spend even a little time with him. Reliever Trevor Hoffman joined a small group of Padres talking baseball.

TREVOR HOFFMAN: That's all he cared about. He was so adamant about talking strategy: why do you throw this and what are you thinking when you throw that?

Hoffman mentioned what it meant to be in Williams' presence at the 1999 All-Star game …

TREVOR HOFFMAN: I got choked up thinking about having the opportunity to be there on the field. I'll remember that the rest of my life.

1999 ALL-STAR GAME ANNOUNCER: Ladies and Gentlemen, please welcome, the greatest hitter who ever played the game, Ted Williams….

Number 9 broke his sixty-year covenant and tipped his cap to the fans.

[applause]

And peers from contemporary All-Stars to All-Century players were in awe …

TED: Sammy, where are you? Hello Kenny. Tony, how's your leg?

This magical moment between Ted Williams, players, fans and millions watching on television was as intimate as it was magnificent.

TED: Thank God for baseball. It's the greatest thing that ever happened …

While Ted Williams has called San Diego, Boston, and Florida home, there's one place he will live as long as there is baseball. Turning back the clock to his memorable induction speech when *One on One* returns ….

Ted Williams. At the plate …

JERRY COLEMAN: Only Ruth and Gehrig matched him for average and power. He had power and average. He out hit both of them.

In person …

CURT GOWDY: Besides being a great hitter, what really made him a star was his charisma. His personal charisma.

To his family …

JOHN HENRY: He is a very caring person, extremely caring person. Ted Williams makes a big impression.

For all he accomplished in his twenty-two years, baseball fans ask what if? What if he maintained his average in the nearly 800 games he missed for military service? His projected rankings would be considerably higher in the top four of ten benchmark categories. But what ifs can work in other ways. What if he hadn't played those last two games in 1941 and instead had an asterisk, indicating he hit .39955, instead of a definitive .406? What if that crash in Korea had taken him out of the game? But Ted Williams isn't about what ifs. He's about hard work and doing the best with what you're given and giving back. He wouldn't have it any other way.

TED [HOF speech]: Two things I am proudest of in my life is that I became a Marine pilot. The other thing of course is that I had a good baseball career. And equally important, equally as satisfying, equally proud of was that I became a member of the Baseball Hall of Fame.

In the summer of '66, he was immortalized in Cooperstown. Despite his battles with writers he believes they voted for him because they felt he rated the honor.

TED *[1966 HOF speech]: Thank You, thank you from the bottom of my heart.*

His acceptance speech then juxtaposed with his thoughts now, underscore his life-long connection with the game.

TED *[1966 HOF speech]: I am thinking of my old playground director in San Diego, California, Rodney Luscomb, my old high school coach, Wos Caldwell, my managers who had such patience with me, and helped me so much. Because ball players are not born great, they are not born pitchers or hitters or managers, and luck isn't the key factor. No one has come up as a substitute for hard work. I've never met a great baseball player who didn't have to work harder at learning to play baseball than anything else he ever did.*

TED: I have some regrets in my baseball life; I have some regrets in my personal life. When I was a young kid, I got to read a book by Bing Crosby and the name of the book was *Just Call Me Lucky*. The longer I live, the more I realize that luck has played a great part in my life.

TED *[1966 HOF speech]: To me it was the greatest fun I ever had, which probably explains why today, I feel both humility and pride, because God let me play the game and learn to be good at it; proud because I spent most of my life in the company of so many wonderful people. There are baseball plaques dedicated to baseball men of all generations. And I'm privileged to join them. Baseball gives every American boy the chance to excel. Not just to be as good as someone else, but to be better than someone else.*

JANE [at Little League field]: What do you tell kids who maybe want to pick up a bat and play this game, maybe have big dreams like you?

TED: They gotta show me that they want to hold the bat, play with the bat then give them the best advice you can, swing the bat, and swing the bat, and swing the bat.

TED *[1966 HOF speech]: And I hope that someday the names of Satchel Paige and Josh Gibson in some way can be added as a symbol of the great Negro players that are not here, only because they were not given a chance.*

JANE: Is there anything you would still like to accomplish?

TED: If I had my one wish it would be that I could be connected with a team, of winning in a World Championship or be in the excitement of being there.

JANE: What do you want to be remembered for?

TED: That I contributed to this game of baseball at a high level.

When he was twenty, he said, "All I want out of life is that when I walk down the street, folks will say, 'There goes the greatest hitter who ever lived.'"

TED: When he walks down the street, you can always say, "There is as good a hitter to ever play this game." I don't say the greatest, I don't think I was the greatest, but I think I was a pretty good hitter. That would be good enough for me.

TED [1966 HOF speech]: *So in closing, I'm grateful and I know how lucky I was to have been born in America and to have a chance to play the game that I loved, the greatest game of them all ... baseball.*

Somehow the kid from San Diego, California who could read a pitcher like no other, swing like no other, who was held to a higher standard like no other balanced the kudos with the criticism and excelled. We can learn from that. That practice, practice, practice makes nearly perfect. Dedication can pay dividends. And all of your choices become part of your legacy. Just ask Ted Williams the legend, and Ted Williams the man. I'm Jane Mitchell. Thank you for watching *One on One.*

DAVE WINFIELD

"... I want to thank both you and the crew of Cox Cable for all your hard work you put in for my HOF Induction/Celebration, and to produce a truly outstanding piece of work ..."

—DAVE WINFIELD, SEPTEMBER 2001

February 20, 2001 Dave Winfield was elected into the National Baseball Hall of Fame on the first ballot. He was drafted by the San Diego Padres and played the first part of his career there, then spent about half his career with the New York Yankees. In retirement, he had reestablished a relationship with the Padres as a member of the Board of Directors and was embraced as a fan favorite. Dave chose to have the Padres' insignia on his cap on the bronze plaque in Cooperstown, so the fact that he would be the first to go in as a Padre was significant for the franchise. It was reason to celebrate, and fortunately for me a reason to document the moment.

The Padres organization was committed to documenting this, too. As for the production contingent, we collaborated to have two cameras, two photographers, two field producers, and me. Going as part of the Padres family, we would have special access to Dave. He welcomed us with open arms. He is not only media-savvy but seems to enjoy and appreciate cameras and what they can capture. Major League Baseball (MLB) Productions had planned to be there for many behind-the-scenes events leading up to Dave's induction. I talked with the MLB producer, and we agreed to work together in Cooperstown and swap or share video for our various productions. For example, some of the moments the MLB crew wanted included Dave selecting his wardrobe and preparing his speech. I would want some of that, but with our being out and about the town, gathering interviews, and shooting in the Hall, it would have been impossible and a duplication of efforts to try to be with him all the time. So the collaboration made sense.

Due to the schedule, we had to do some action items out of order. In advance of the trip, I outlined the one-hour show based on what I anticipated we would be doing and incorporated the content about his life story from the first time he was on *One on One*, along with one of the original Padres, Nate Colbert, in 1999. I wrote the on-camera introductions, tags, and conclusion. After learning from the Hall of Fame staff there were various areas where Dave Winfield would be featured in the museum, such as the 3,000 Hit Club display, I wrote based on what I guessed those displays might look like and how the words would mesh with the visual.

I wanted the show's on-camera stand-ups to be from inside the Hall of Fame's Plaque Gallery, hoping it would be quiet, with no one around, so we could have space for lighting, time for getting it right, and no distractions. The Hall's staff agreed and we planned to do it Wednesday night when the museum was closed and there wouldn't be other activities conflicting with the shoot. Our teleprompter was too big to bring, so I would have to memorize each of my segments—and quickly.

While the crew set up that evening, I put on my makeup in the bathroom then walked out to the grand hall to shoot the show open and close. To get the shot, I had to be at least twenty feet from the camera. Dennis Morgigno had suggested I record the words of my stand-ups in a tape recorder, then listen to that recording in my ear as I said the lines. It's an old broadcasting trick, but I just couldn't make it work for me. I panicked a little and my throat got tight as I wondered how I was I going to get this done. Plus, while we had hoped we wouldn't have distractions, it turned out ESPN was there to do a similar shoot in the same place at the same time. I was already stressed that I had to memorize each segment, but then to have network anchors watch me fumble over and over? They didn't say anything and were professional, but I still was nervous and felt the pressure.

I decided to put myself in a better situation and split the difference between my weakness of memorizing and my utter failure to use the recording in my ear. I removed the earpiece and just talked into the camera. I wrote the words, so I could certainly say them, and I did. I was also nervous from the pressure of standing in this new venue, this gloriously grand place, with the spirit of these legends, wanting it to be so perfect. I knew once the stand-ups were in the show, no one would know how fast my heart was beating. I learned a lot that night about performing under pressure. As we moved around to the other areas, it was much easier—the stand-ups were shorter, we were away from the ESPN crew, and Dan, as usual, helped me stay calm. We laughed in between hauling the camera and lights around three levels, asking the cleaners to stop vacuuming so we wouldn't hear the noise in the final show, and finding the maintenance crew to have them turn the display lights back on so we could actually see the items in the cases.

2001 was my first trip to Cooperstown. I had heard about it and seen it on video, but I had a lot to learn and to prepare. Not only was I there to capture Dave Winfield's experience, I would be meeting, and hopefully, interviewing living legends and members of the Hall of Fame, including Al Kaline, Lou Brock, and Yogi Berra.

I had been in baseball five seasons at this point, which was good timing as it was just long enough to appreciate the game's history and recognize names and faces. After gently persuading the Hall of Fame staff it was important for us to be there when Dave and his family arrived in Cooperstown, they granted us access to be at the hotel Thursday evening. My first magical moment was standing on the hotel's porch waiting for the Winfields. Just after they arrived, so did Kirby Puckett, the other inductee. Sometimes, you get lucky. Our mantra at these venues was "just keep rolling" to capture it all, including when Dave and Kirby greeted each other. We followed Dave into the lobby and there stood Yogi Berra and Tommy Lasorda, both bigger than life. I recognized them immediately—their faces, voices, and demeanor. They greeted Dave and I could not help but throw out a question, asking what advice they had for him. Both said, "Keep it short," meaning his speech.

The traditional Hall of Fame golf tournament is held on Saturday of induction weekend. The general credentialed media has access to the Hall of Famers on the first and sixth holes. Even though we had access at other times, this would be our main opportunity to get most of our Hall of Fame member interviews. It was a challenge—deciphering who was who in a short amount of time, introducing myself, and asking about Dave before they jumped back on the golf cart to the next tee. There were several other members of the media, and most were fairly considerate of everyone doing their jobs. I was able to interview nearly everyone on my list, plus several others. There was a bonus, too. It was 2001, the year Tony Gwynn had announced his retirement. When I identified myself as being with the Padres, several Hall of Famers, unsolicited, talked about Tony. I saved those, expecting I would do another show on Tony Gwynn a few years later.

History came alive for me when I saw a man zipping up to the sixth tee on his golf cart. His face was familiar—weathered with a distinctive nose and thinning hair. Puffing on a cigarette, he was older, old school—but how did I know him? When someone said it was Warren Spahn, I connected the dots. He was the pitcher Ray Boone faced in his only at-bat in the 1948 World Series. I learned that in 2000 when I had interviewed Ray Boone who said of Mr. Spahn:

> "He threw me three fastballs down the middle, and I'm telling you, I was on all three of them, and I just missed those things, and finally struck out."

Ray's interview was part of a *One on One* show featuring the Padres second baseman Bret Boone and the Boone family from San Diego, the first three-generation Major League Baseball family.

I just *had* to talk with Mr. Spahn, so as he sat on the golf cart, I told him how Ray mentioned that at-bat and Mr. Spahn seemed happy to hear about it. That brief conversation underscored how closely knit this game is, how destiny can be determined by one at-bat, one more strike out, or one more hit—whatever the case may be. Later that weekend, Mr. Spahn and his daughter were in the gift shop and I told him how I had worked in Tulsa and had traveled throughout Oklahoma, where he lived. Those two conversations may not have meant much to him, but they did to me—to meet someone who had been just an image in someone else's story. Back in San Diego, I relayed the story to Ray Boone, who seemed to appreciate it as well.

That night in Cooperstown, our crew was invited as part of the Padres' family to attend the Hall of Fame dinner as guests—without our video cameras or microphones. I saw Lou Brock at a table with his family. He had been so cordial and respectful earlier in the day that he was on my list of new favorites. I had rarely taken posed pictures with players unless it was after a big shoot, but this was different. I was a guest—a fan. I asked if I could have my picture taken with him, and he said yes. Yogi Berra also obliged. It was a good night.

After the induction on Sunday, the Winfield party moved to New York City for a private event at Cipriani's. The Winfields had parlayed his induction celebration with a Winfield Foundation event benefiting the Boys and Girls Clubs of America. It was a spectacular, sports star-studded event. With permission to be there, and with a brief setup that this was to tell Dave Winfield's story, anyone and everyone I asked to comment was more than willing to share their thoughts. That A-list group included basketball great Julius "Dr. J." Erving, former major leaguer Dave Parker, the spectacular dancer Gregory Hines, former NFL player and sportscaster Ahmad Rashad, and New York City Mayor Rudy Giuliani. Dave was inducted as a Padre, but his decade in New York ingrained him in Yankee history, so it was a fitting celebration.

In the hotel lobby, I saw Chicago Cubs icon Ernie Banks, of "Let's Play 2" fame. I reintroduced myself after meeting him in Cooperstown, reiterating why we were now there in New York. This dashing Hall of Famer told me, "Everyone in the Hall of Fame should have their story told for television." I agreed it was something I would love to do, but at the time, I could only focus on Dave.

After New York, we drove from San Diego to Los Angeles one more time to talk with Dave and reflect on his induction experience. This visit was straight forward, with no surprises as we had on the first trip to his home in 1999. In '99, Dave opened the box with his World Series trophy for the first time when we were there and rolling. He pulled out the dozen or so beautiful scrapbooks for us to sort through, and we met his lovely wife, Tonya, and their two children. We had a challenge that day in '99, too. There was construction going on next door. It would not have been good to hear bulldozers in the background. We took a chance, and explained we were a television crew from San Diego shooting an interview. We asked if they could please stop any of the noisy work for about an hour. They obliged. No such issues in 2001.

Although I had personal wow moments surrounding Dave Winfield's show production from the Hall of Fame in 2001, my job was to organize all these interviews, experiences, sound, and pictures into a comprehensive one-hour show about Dave Winfield in just a matter of a few weeks. Having already done his life story for that first edition, I had about twelve minutes of content that was complete, because his story from birth to 1999 didn't change. After commercial time, I had about forty-two minutes of new content to produce surrounding his induction.

Dave is one of the most accommodating stars I know. He understands the role of reporters and the logistics of getting things done. As busy as he was coming down from the whirlwind of the Hall of Fame experience, he never made us feel as if we were an imposition. He appreciated the effort, and thankfully, the results. In the wake of September 11, he sent a thank you note. Even a decade later, he compliments me, or shares with others upon an introduction, that the show was outstanding. That is nice to hear, especially considering it is still running as a *One on One Classic* program.

After this edition aired that summer, I sent a copy to each Hall of Fame member and friends of Dave whom I had interviewed. I included two copies of pictures I had either taken with them or had created from a freeze frame from the show. All but a few returned one of the pictures autographed to me; several with a nice note of thanks. They are still sitting in those postage paid envelopes in a safe part of my photo closet. A few are in this book and, someday, they will end up in a frame or a scrapbook. I appreciate that no matter how famous or revered some of these men are, they acknowledged my efforts and gratitude in helping to tell Dave Winfield's story.

This is the script from the one-hour edition debuting August 28, 2001.

• • •

His performance and presence, a powerful combination. Now Dave Winfield is the first player to enter Baseball's Hall of Fame as a San Diego Padre.

> DAVE: *[HOF speech] Had I known that I was going to be up here one day, I sure would've saved all my rookie baseball cards!*

Baseball is America's past time. Its diamond offers riches in the simple game of catch, in the dream realized of playing in the majors and in the most brilliant, rare and revered honor, being enshrined here in Cooperstown. This is the story of Dave Winfield's life on the diamond and his journey, which has come full circle.

> DAVE: You think about it, but it's almost mythical. There's no reason to think you're going to the Hall of Fame or even make it to the major leagues, or even be an all-star or do anything special. It was just, I was playing baseball.
>
> JANE FORBES CLARK [at induction ceremony]: As Chairman of the National Baseball Hall of Fame, it is my honor, Dave, to welcome you into our Hall of Fame family.
>
> DAVE *[HOF speech]: I had my choice to be a tight end for the Minnesota Vikings, a power forward for the Atlanta Hawks or Utah Stars, or play Major League Baseball. And I remember the scout, Donnie Williams, after they drafted me—he was with the Padres. I asked him, I said, "Donnie, what do you want me to do?" He said, "Man we want you to play every day. We want you to hit that ball and run." And so the rest is history. I chose baseball because to me, baseball's the best game of all.*

His passion for the game would take him to the top. His classmates: one-time teammate Minnesota Twin and stocky centerfielder Kirby Puckett, whose playing career was cut short by glaucoma; the Pirate's Bill Mazeroski, arguably the best defensive second baseman ever, who after thirty years was finally voted in by the veteran's committee; and the late Hilton Smith, the right-handed pitcher who played in the shadows of the great Satchel Paige in the Negro Leagues. Getting into the Hall is a long and unlikely road considering the odds. Of the three million youngsters playing Little League, only a small percentage will ever be good enough to play in college or be drafted into the minor leagues.

> **JANE FORBES CLARK:** Of those, five percent will ever play in a single major league game. Those who make it to the major leagues are the best of the best. And only one out of a hundred of those players, one percent of the best of the best, is inducted into the Baseball Hall of Fame here in Cooperstown. *[applause]*

It is also a challenge to get here, considering the logistics. Cooperstown is a four-hour drive northwest of New York City or an hour and a half drive south of Albany's airport, through dairy and farmland, on a two-lane road past thick pine forests and in the summer, lush green trees with leaves that rustle in the warm breeze lining the long Lake Otsego dotted with lily pads and swans. Streets named Pioneer and Pine with nineteenth century homes lead to Main, where, even with modern amenities, time seems to stand still. With the flagpole as the town compass, visitors mark the day's "Extra Innings" at the "Doubleday Café," wander by "Where it All Began," or marvel over memorabilia at "Mickey's Place."

> **BOB HURLEY** (fan): It's just the excitement of meeting the ballplayers and seeing the old timers that used to play when I was a kid.
>
> **CHRIS FALTEISEK** (fan): It's the people that played back then who set the example for today.

Thought to be the site where baseball was first played, the National Baseball Hall of Fame and Museum, circa 1939, protects, preserves, and celebrates the game.

> **DALE PETROSKEY** (HOF president, 2001): It's about baseball from the little leagues to the major leagues and everything in between. We really are the spiritual home of baseball at all levels.

The brick walls and the arched gallery are the setting for baseball's crown jewels, the plaques of those selected into perhaps the most elite fraternity in professional sports.

> **JEFF IDELSON** (HOF): Only 188 players out of 16,000 have a plaque in these hallowed halls.

Add managers, executives, and umpires, and the number's just 253. Of the sixty living Hall of Famers, forty returned for this annual induction weekend, staying at the historic and majestic Otesaga Hotel by the Leatherstocking Golf Course. Gracious, they share wisdom about the Hall, the game, and Dave Winfield's qualities that placed him in the Hall the first year he was eligible.

> **WILLIE MCCOVEY:** I'm just proud of what he's accomplished and I'm just happy I had a little bit to do with it, and happy that he recognized me as one of his mentors.

PHIL NIEKRO: I think everyone realized that if this guy stays healthy and doesn't have any problems through his career, you know, he's gonna wind up in Cooperstown. It was just a matter of when he wanted to quit playing baseball and wait five years and he's in.

ROLLIE FINGERS: I saw him when I went to San Diego in 1977. When I first saw him play, he was one heckuva ballplayer. He had a cannon from right field and he could run down any balls out in the gap and could hit a long home run, too, so he's certainly deserving of coming into the Hall of Fame.

GEORGE BRETT: I was playing third base and there was a situation where there was a runner on third and one out and Dave Winfield came up and he hit a line drive, and to this day, I don't know if I dove out of the way of the ball or if I tried to catch it. That's the fear that he could put in a third baseman.

DON SUTTON: Tremendous athlete and great competitor and one of the things I always appreciated about him was that he took the time, because he learned how to play right, he took the time to make sure young players learned how to play the game right. And I think we need that thread to continue through baseball, so not only a good player, but a good guy.

LOU BROCK: I'm glad to see Dave. He's a Padre by nature, no matter what other uniform he put on, he's still a Padre. And so, he is a guy who's one of those five tool players that came along and could do everything.

ENOS SLAUGHTER: I finally got in in '85 and I'll be here as long as I live. If I can get here, I'll be here, because I think going into the Hall of Fame is one of the greatest things there is for a baseball player.

Induction weekend is the most glorious of the year for Cooperstown, as the village of 2,000 swells ten-fold with baseball fans from around the country declaring their team loyalty.

[Little boys waving, saying, "Go Dave Winfield!"]

They collect autographs and pay homage to living legends that come back each year. Fans also celebrate the new inductees, including Dave Winfield, whom they feared or cheered throughout his twenty-two-year career with six teams.

LARRY REESE (fan): Very aggressive, great arm, great all around player, one of the great all around players of his generation.

ED SULLIVAN (fan): He had tremendous talent as a ballplayer and he's a gentleman, a good guy, too.

KEVIN ROONEY (Chula Vista Police Officer): I remember growing up, going to Shea Stadium, and seeing him hit two home runs off of Jerry Kuzman, I mean, he was young, and he was powerful and he was a stud.

VALERIE BARONE (Yankees fan): Dave was playing for the Yankees and we were fortunate enough to be close enough to the dugout, and as he was coming off the field we did get him to respond and wave to us, and I did get a photo of him, and I have it in my family album, and it's very precious to us, and we're here because of him.

RUDY (Blue Jays fan): Always laughing and always friendly. Even when he played against the Blue Jays for the Yankees I always respected him, the way that he carried himself on the field.

JOHN CRAWFORD (fan): I'm so glad that he came into Cooperstown wearing that Padres cap because it means so much to the team and the city of San Diego.

For every person honored with a bronze plaque here in the Hall of Fame gallery, there is a story of how it all began with details that make the earning of such an honor even sweeter. The details of Dave Winfield's story are next, on *One on One* ....

When considering who is worthy of being elected into the Baseball Hall of Fame, baseball writers consider a player's ability, performance, character, and overall contribution to the game. But turning back the clock nearly fifty years, Dave Winfield didn't set out to achieve the highest honor. He just wanted to play. Dave Winfield, in baseball terms, was a five-tool ballplayer. He could run, hit, hit with power, field, and throw. He was also a controversial player, chastised and celebrated, embattled and embraced during his twenty-two years in the big leagues. He's done it all just about. And he's done it his way.

DAVE: I never had limitations on what I thought I could do.

His confidence stems from his upbringing, born David Mark Winfield in Saint Paul, Minnesota, October 3, 1951. His parents divorced when he was three, and while he later became close to his father, his mother and nearby relatives raised him.

DAVE: Grandmother, aunts, cousins ...

His older brother Steve was his best friend.

DAVE: I think we lived, slept, ate, breathed baseball.

The neighborhood field of dreams, Oxford Playground, was headed up by a Marine turned Little League coach who would make a lasting impression.

DAVE: Discipline was important. Not just do what you want to do.

While Winfield, who was always a pitcher, had athletic ability ...

DAVE: I was thin, gangly ...

He struggled during awkward growth spurts.

DAVE: It seemed like I'd be banging into things, I had long arms and long legs.

He grew into his body and learned to play the game he loved by watching his hometown Minnesota Twins.

DAVE: We didn't get to many games, because we didn't have enough money.

By high school he was a star in basketball and baseball. And when Baltimore drafted him as a pitcher, he had a choice.

DAVE: Getting a scholarship for a major college and get your education to carry you throughout life, OR take $500 and a bus ride to Bluefield, West Virginia. HA! There wasn't much of a choice.

He flourished at the University of Minnesota.

DAVE: I thought I was a good baseball player and there was a little cockiness involved in it too, but not overbearing. You go to an American Legion tournament and you tell somebody, "You heard of Dave Winfield?" "No." I say, "You will when this is over."

He made history by being the first athlete to be drafted in three professional sports. Football with the Minnesota Vikings, though he'd never played the game; basketball with Atlanta and Utah; and baseball. One day he's the MVP pitching in the 1973 College World Series and a week later …

DAVE: I'm playing left field occasionally for the San Diego Padres.

No minor league stop-over, just straight to The Show.

DAVE: All of a sudden you have to learn how to play the outfield. I was bad. I was horrendous. Stumbling, tripping. Guys hit the ball hard and far.

Soon known as Daddy Long Legs, number 31 vividly recalls his first defensive play on a ball certain to be a double.

DAVE: I scooped it up and fired a bullet to second. It was waiting for the guy, he was out. I say, "Yeah, this is not so bad!" But I had a whole lot to learn.

He gravitated towards veterans Nate Colbert, Willie McCovey, and Cito Gaston.

DAVE: We'd travel on the planes. That's who I'd be with. I'd sit in the dugout, that's who I'd talk to.

And he implemented what he calls "industrial espionage."

DAVE: I'd send people to ask other people questions on teams. "How do you get the Winfield guy out, what are you doing to him?" Oh yeah …!

He became an offensive star near the top in almost every category, making his first of twelve all-star teams in 1977 and receiving a standing ovation when he signed a $1.3 million, four-year deal.

DAVE: I'd smile and laugh and I couldn't think of anything more exhilarating, men on base and hit a triple, show your speed, clear the bases, hook slide into third and sit there, like yeah. And the fans on their feet, I get excited about it now!

He was also excited about helping kids.

DAVE: I just knew the athletes could influence a lot of people in a positive way. And I just tried to create the format.

The format, the David Winfield Foundation, the first of its kind in Major League Baseball. Thousands of children benefited from scholarships and were treated to parties and ballgames, sitting in the right field bleachers—the Winfield Pavilion—all based on a simple phrase his mother used: "Give a little when you have a little. Give a lot when you have a lot."

DAVE: It started in my family, that's just the way I was. So I always gave back.

But with the cheers came jeers. The year is 1980. Winfield is negotiating his next Padres contract and asking for a $20 million, ten-year deal or he'd become a free agent.

DAVE: Free agent, they want to kill! My car was marked up, my garbage was thrown in the yard and eggs on the house.

The Padres passed.

[Television archive of former Padre owner, Ray Kroc: We don't have the money.]

DAVE: We've been unable to come to a conclusion which is satisfactory for me. I was the top guy in the market at the time, so I was going for it.

Signing with the Yankees made headlines, and owner George Steinbrenner made Dave Winfield the $23 million man, setting a new standard.

DAVE: People said, "You gotta be careful man, it can get crazy in New York," and I said, "I don't cause any problems, I'm not worried." Ha! For nine years, that was something.

The drama was well documented in the media. Steinbrenner hoped Winfield would fill the shoes of Reggie Jackson, but when Winfield went 1-for-22 against Los Angeles in the 1981 World Series, Steinbrenner soured on him and things got ugly: financial and legal disputes, personal jousting.

DAVE: Okay, you're battling with money, I got some money, too. You got some lawyers, I got some lawyers, too. You got PR people, I got PR people.

The nitty gritty details from Winfield's perspective are laid out in his 1988 book, *A Player's Life*, which Steinbrenner blasted. Nevertheless, Winfield was popular with the fans. He ranks among the Yankees' all-time top twenty in home runs, doubles, and runs batted in, and among his stats, the notorious seagull incident. In Toronto, a seagull was sitting on the field near the ball boy ...

DAVE: I threw it in that direction, it short hopped, bam, splat.

After the game, he was arrested on cruelty to animals charges ...

DAVE: They got exhibit A on the table, feet sticking up in the air ...

And despite some teasing around the league ...

DAVE: Flapping their arms out in centerfield ...

Toronto gave him a commemorative bird and forgave him when he helped the city with a charity event.

DAVE: Sorry about the animal, I didn't do it on purpose!

His good intentions include expanding his foundation. From the clubhouse to the White House he shared his message to kids to stay off drugs. His good looks, good works, and style have been recognized in print and national TV, and *Lifestyles of the Rich and Famous.*

After eight years in the "Bronx Zoo," Winfield sat out 1989 recovering from back surgery. In early 1990, the last year of his contract, he negotiated a trade to a team and owner he felt wanted him, Gene Autry's California Angels. In 1992, he played for his former Padre mentor, Cito Gaston, with the Toronto Blue Jays. And the forty-year-old Winfield got a second chance to make a difference in a World Series. In Game 6 against Atlanta he hit an 11th inning double that gave the Jays the lead and they hung on for it all. In 1993 he went home to the Minnesota Twins and achieved baseball immortality, delivering hit number 3,000. He could have retired after Minnesota in '94, but with a strike and no World Series that year, people were disenchanted with baseball.

> **DAVE:** That's really a way for people to forget about you, so I said, "I'm going to come back for one more."

But after not playing as much as he wanted to with Cleveland in '95, he retired. He wishes he'd known sooner so he could have said good-bye to guys around the league.

> **DAVE:** One of the other regrets, serious one, there …

The transition, not always easy.

> **DAVE:** You're used to the accolades, you're used to people doing things for you.

Dave Winfield the businessman managed his twenty-two-year-old foundation and continues to be involved in charity work. He had a stint as a broadcaster, but realized he preferred to control his schedule, to be home with his family, his wife Tonya and their twins, Ariale and David, Jr.

> **DAVE:** They are beautiful and great, and if we can invest our time in the children and their school and community—Dad might be a Little League coach after a while!

Dave and Tonya met through friends when he was with the Yankees. She wasn't a baseball fan, but she was a top corporate sales executive in Los Angeles.

> **TONYA:** After our first date, I knew. He didn't talk about himself. He was more interested in what I was doing and my career. I thought, *I am not ready for this, but, wow!*

Their bi-coastal relationship evolved to marriage in '88. Life in L.A. includes moving into a new home.

> **DAVE** [Unwrapping the 1992 trophy]: You guys are seeing history. I haven't seen this since …

Since he received it after the '92 World Series. He's achieved great things in the game. More than 3,000 hits, 465 home runs, 7 Gold Gloves, 6 Silver Bats. He's been inducted into San Diego's Breitbard Hall of Fame. And when it was suggested prior to the election that entry into baseball's Hall of Fame was inevitable, he was modest, but thrilled at the possibility.

> DAVE [1999 interview]: If it happens, that'll be great. I can't tell you any other words; it'd be great!

Dave Winfield's numbers and career would indeed be remarkable enough to be recognized here among the greats. That honor also brings new challenges, including the biggest public speaking engagement of his life. That's next when *One on One* returns from Cooperstown ....

One can only imagine the awesome sense of accomplishment, and perhaps humility, knowing your name and numbers will live in baseball eternity. The very real and surreal experience surrounding Dave Winfield's induction spotlighted his confidence, courage, and charisma on a whole new stage.

January 2001, five years after retiring as a player, Dave Winfield is eligible for the Hall of Fame. But there are no guarantees.

> DAVE: You're waiting, you're waiting, you have butterflies.

With a record 515 ballots cast by members of the Baseball Writers' Association of America, he receives a resounding 435, 84 percent; well above the 75 percent required. And at his Los Angeles home, the call finally comes.

> DAVE: I had a speaker phone and was holding my daughter. I pressed it one time and I accidentally pressed it again and hung up. And I know it was Jack O'Connell the sports writer because he called right back. So I got the call from the Hall and hung up on them. Ha! It was the stamp of approval—he had a great career. I was ecstatic.

As an inductee, Winfield's early perks are quite presidential, among the Hall of Famers invited to the White House by President George W. Bush.

> PRESIDENT BUSH: One of the great things about living here is that you don't have to sign up for fantasy baseball to meet your heroes. Turns out they come here!
>
> DAVE: It was a beautiful experience.

In early spring, he must make a decision. Which logo will adorn the cap on his Hall of Fame plaque? With much of his career split between two teams, eight years with the Padres, ten years with the Yankees, he chooses San Diego.

> DAVE [at pre-game ceremony]: You gave me my first chance. I got my first hit, got my start here. You've embraced my family. You'll never know how much I appreciate that ...

While three former Padres, Willie McCovey, Gaylord Perry, and Rollie Fingers are in the Hall, Winfield's April decision would make him the first to enter as a Padre. The news coincides with the retiring of his number 31 before thousands of fans wearing replica jersey T-shirts.

> DAVE: I'm looking forward to going into the Hall of Fame wearing a Padre hat proudly.

In May he had the opportunity to fully explore the Hall of Fame.

> DAVE: Oh man, can I touch this? I mean, this is a hundred years old, or Babe Ruth did this, or look at those gloves. No wonder guys hit for great averages, ya know? You emerge once you visit it with a lot more respect, and in my case, reverence, because I played the game and not just looked at it from afar.

The countdown to Cooperstown requires juggling public appearances, working with a Major League Baseball productions crew documenting many events along the way, and planning his speech.

> DAVE: I wrote my own words, what I wanted to say. I got input from different people as to what would the people want to hear. And I watched video tapes of some people who had given presentations, knew their timing. Some people were like from seven to seventeen minutes.

Intertwine that with anxious family and friends from coast to coast.

> DAVE: And everybody says, "How do I get there? What do I do? I need transportation. What are the logistics?"

Thursday August 2nd …

> DAVE: We got on the plane and John Moores was very gracious. Just said, "You guys, let's get on my plane. Let's go up to Cooperstown." Nice jet. And my family we all had our cameras and videotape. So everything, leading up to it we captured every moment we could 'cause we wanted to savor this.

He's greeted at the hotel's gate by a handful of diehard fans.

> FAN: Congratulations to you. You're a class act.

And with special access for the weekend, our cameras are there for his arrival.

> JANE: So how's your stomach feeling?
> DAVE: No, I'm fine. I'm fine right now. We're just gonna relax a little bit and just get ready for the activity this weekend.
> JANE: Tonya, how are you feeling at this moment?
> TONYA: I'm feeling great. Just to get on the plane and get here and see Cooperstown again. You know, you get the butterflies again, so we're excited about this weekend.

Kirby Puckett arrives at the same time.

> KIRBY PUCKETT: Big Daddy! Long time no see.
> DAVE: That's right, only two days. Good to see you.

Yogi Berra and Tommy Lasorda are quick to manage the rookie.

> *[Yogi and Tommy joking with Dave]*

> TOMMY LASORDA: I'm telling him to be careful because these old time Hall of Famers, they're gonna start on him right now, him and Kirby about no long speeches.
> JANE: Mr. Berra, how about you? What's your advice to Mr. Winfield?
> YOGI BERRA: Same thing. He better make it short. Ha, Ha. [grabs Dave]

JANE: Or what?

YOGI BERRA: The gong. He'll get the gong.

DAVE: When your old manager tells you time is up, time is up.

There's little sleep for the inductee-to-be …

EARLY SHOW: *Later this hour, an interview with Dave Winfield …*

7:30 a.m., lights, makeup, a national TV interview from the hotel porch, and another to send home to San Diego. A spontaneous Winfield family stroll down Main Street attracts a friendly crowd. Friday evening, a sense of celebration emerges with VIPs on the veranda. Saturday morning it's back to the old competitive ways on the links. His foursome includes friend Jimmy Jam, music producer and fellow Minnesotan. He and his colleagues are interviewed by the national media …

KIRBY PUCKETT: I want to be 6'6" like Winnie!

Including some writers who helped elect them to the Hall …

TIM SULLIVAN (Sports Columnist, *Cincinnati Enquirer*): He's a guy you don't even have to think about. I mean, at 3,000 hits, Gold Glove, a tremendous athlete.

JAYSON STARK (Sports Writer, *ESPN.com*): He went to the All-Star Game every year, so you knew that his peers and his fans all thought of him as a great player.

Later, with spotlights and applause, the greats and their guests gather in the Hall of Fame gallery in all its glory. Then in the quiet of his hotel room, he prepares what he'll wear for his big moment.

[Pulling out his suit from closet, "Bam!"]

Sunday August 5, induction day is here. Winfield and the Hall of Famers travel a mile from the Hall to a field accommodating twenty thousand spectators in front of a tented stage.

TONYA: I think we're running on adrenaline right now.

JIMMY JAM: This is the baseball mecca. But what makes it doubly special for me is the fact that Kirby Puckett and Dave Winfield are both going in.

KEVIN TOWERS: It's a tremendous place with a lot of great history and our first Padre, couldn't be happier.

JOE WINFIELD: To see some of us here with the Padres shirts. First time in history!

JOHN MOORES: It's really exciting, a chance to be a very small part of Winfield's induction.

DAVE: A lot of eyes are on you. So it's just getting closer to that time. The countdown, you're sweatin' bullets. Ha Ha. You're sweatin'. 'Cause it's hot. I ain't lyin.'

As it once was for others who have gone before him—Babe Ruth, Ted Williams, and Hank Aaron—it is his turn.

JANE: When you're standing up there, what are you seeing?

DAVE: I see my enclave of people, my family and they're proud. I see some Padres hats and you know I saw some Yankee hats and I saw a couple Angels hats. You know, every team that I played for I saw some representation. And then it keeps going and going you know …

In the pasture among those who have made the pilgrimage for this day is a group of San Diegans wearing those replica jerseys …

FAN: Our whole baseball team came, you know, we're here to support him.

FAN: It's overwhelming, it's awesome. I can't explain it.

DAVE *[HOF speech]: I look back, there are a few people that I have to tell you about.*

His retrospective includes thanking people he never met …

DAVE *[HOF speech]: His legend, and his saga, and his story, is just that. Jackie Robinson. We all have to tip our hat to him because he made the game available to guys like me. [applause]*

And pointing out the importance of having heroes …

DAVE *[HOF speech]: You know heroes are ordinary people that have achieved extraordinary things in life. Guys like Bob Feller and Ted Williams, you know we're talking about real heroes, and there's many guys, not only just from the way they played the game of baseball, but how would you like to go off to war? You're in the middle of your career, go off to war, and come back, get injured, things like that and still come back and love this game and play it well. Those are real heroes.*

He is appreciative of coaches, executives, and owners, including the late owner of the Padres and McDonald's founder, Ray Kroc.

DAVE *[HOF speech]: We talked business many times and his belief in quality and service fit me like a glove. And that's what I brought to baseball and that's how I conducted myself throughout my life. That's what that was about. To George Steinbrenner, I want to thank you for bringing me to the New York Yankees. I'm serious. This is an experience that changed my life forever in a positive way. You know, and I'm glad that time, distance, respect, and clear minds has brought about a respect and friendship that we didn't have early on, and I'm glad we have it today.*

And to the current San Diego Padres owner, John Moores, and President Larry Lucchino …

DAVE *[HOF speech]: I appreciate you guys making it very open and very wonderful for me and my family, letting us know that the tradition, you know, me being in San Diego was very important. I appreciate what you've given. Thank you, John. I have to thank all the people that came from San Diego and hopefully the thousands that are back in Qualcomm Stadium that are watching on the jumbotron this ceremony here. Love goes out to you and thank you for your support.*

He acknowledges his late parents, his friends, and confidantes …

DAVE *[HOF speech]: Randy Grossman for your youth, energy, skill and professionalism …*

And his brother Steve …

> DAVE [*HOF speech*]: *This is my brother, my best friend in life. Baseball playing buddy! And last, but certainly not least, my wife, Tonya, stand up. Stand up, Tonya, the love of my life. And my kids, Shanel, David, Ariel, stand up. You guys are my heart. I love you. I really do. Finally, I could go on, but I certainly am not. I know what you want to say Kirby. [laughing]*

Woven throughout his twenty-three-minute speech, his gratitude is part of his message about attitude.

> DAVE [*HOF speech*]: *You know what the secret of being the best is all about? Just giving all. It's not about numbers, it's not about the money. It's about giving the best you've had. It's an inner affirmation. It's here. It's up here. You know you can't buy it, nobody can give it to you, you gotta find it. Yeah, I've had a complete career. How could I not? I played in America's finest city, San Diego, America's greatest city, New York, perhaps North America's classiest city, Toronto, played at home with the Minnesota Twins, Gene Autry and Anaheim. That's probably why I live in California now and Cleveland. All—everybody, thank you. You've made me feel welcome. You've embraced my family. It's been a wonderful journey of personal discovery and development. I've given to baseball everything I've had and baseball's given its best back to me today. Thank you. I love you all.*

It is an experience his family will remember forever.

> LOUISE TURNER (mother-in-law): It is so gratifying to know that my son-in-law has reached the highest level that you can attain in the baseball world. And the best part about it, he has so many glorious friends to share this moment with him.
>
> ROBERT TURNER (father-in-law): Oh, we're just all excited about it. We've had a great time. We just love every minute of it and we're so happy and proud of him at the same time.
>
> SHANEL: I mean, he's my dad, so I mean, that's why he's special to me really.
>
> STEVE WINFIELD: On behalf of our family, thank you to everyone who's ever been any part of my brother's life.

For a guy who awed so many, Dave Winfield himself is in awe of the legends in the Cooperstown landscape.

> DAVE: Wow. Man, all these guys were really gracious….
>
> TONYA: And David and I talk about it, that this is God touching us. No question about it. And we are enjoying every moment of it.

Dave Winfield's induction is cause for celebration, a moment shared by baseball fans, family, and friends. His celebration and sentimental journey befit a guy known for doing things his way and in a big way. That's next on *One on One* from Cooperstown….

He had played in a few exhibition games at Doubleday Field during his career, but in 2001 Dave Winfield joins his new Hall of Fame colleagues in a post induction day tradition, throwing out the ceremonial first pitch. Then he's in for the ride of his life, whisked away on a helicopter, compliments of Hall of Fame Chairman Jane Forbes Clark. An hour and a half flight takes him over his old stompin' grounds, Yankee Stadium, and into Manhattan by the Empire State Building arriving just in time for the big bash at Cipriani's at 42nd and Lexington. What began as his wife's idea to be just a little family and friends gathering, turns into a family, friends, and superstar guest-list gala. Entertainer Gregory Hines, former NFL player Ahmad Rashad, probable Baseball Hall of Famer and former Padre Ozzie Smith, basketball great Julius Erving, "Dr. J," all among the 400 here who know Winfield from different times and dimensions of his life.

> **JOE MORGAN:** Well, when he first came to the major leagues I was already playing. And I look at this big guy, cause I'm not the biggest guy in the world, I said, "Who is this new big guy in the league, cause he never went to the minor leagues." And then we had a chance to sit down and talk and I said, "Not only is he a big guy, he's also a special guy."
>
> **DAVE PARKER:** We both had above average speed, above average arm, above average power. So they always kinda compared the two. And I really enjoyed competing against him. We'd always try to more or less show our talents when we played against each other, so it made for a good game.
>
> **GREGORY HINES:** You know 'cause Dave was drafted in all three big time sports, but when he said "and I chose baseball," the way he said baseball. There was so much affection in his voice and in his timber. He—you know he loved baseball. He loves it.
>
> **MAURICE LUCAS** (NBA): Most big guys don't have the opportunity to play baseball because it's a small guy's game. And he took it to another level.
>
> **OZZIE SMITH:** He was the one guy when people ask me now who was the best all around player that I had a chance to play with, and his name is certainly the name on the top of the list.
>
> **"DR. J" JULIUS ERVING:** You know the Lord gives some individuals on this planet that type of talent. And then they have to come with the resolve to just blend their will with His will and make it happen. And that's what happened to Dave.
>
> **AHMAD RASHAD:** Never changed. Always been the same. And it's a guy that you always root for. It's kind of nice to see him going into the Hall of Fame 'cause he certainly deserves to be there—not only the Baseball Hall of Fame, but the hall of fame of people.

The party setting: marble columns, hologram images of balls and his championship ring, and a stage set with a replica of his plaque and video highlights from his career. It's elegant, classy with Tonya's touch. Albeit star studded, the gala is also vintage Dave Winfield because the auction, with donated jerseys and memorabilia, benefits a cause the Winfield Foundation has long supported, the Boys and Girls Clubs of America.

PAT SWILLING (NFL linebacker): Dave's been so great with all the charity organizations, all the things he's done here in New York and all the places he's played. He is definitely a role model for all the kids. And if kids are looking for someone that they want to be like, Dave Winfield is the guy.

ROBIN SWILLING: He's a great father and he's a great husband to Tonya. And that means a lot more than the baseball awards and all the recognition for other things.

And while it's his night to shine, he takes time to say thank you to the people who have helped him in his efforts: corporate sponsors, volunteers, and supporters all getting hugs, handshakes, and photos to capture the moment. NBA player Jayson Williams grew up hoping to someday meet the three-sport star Dave Winfield, and finally did five years ago.

JAYSON WILLIAMS: He came to a Knicks game and somebody said Dave Winfield's in there and he's sitting on courtside and I was focused on the game and I'm already a bad free throw shooter and I went up there and shot the first one and it didn't hit nothing and the second one didn't hit nothing. I said well at least you know one thing: I made Dave Winfield laugh. So after the game he came to the locker room and I got a chance to meet him and we went out for dinner and the rest is history. Here I am with a man who's making history today.

New York Mayor Rudy Giuliani couldn't miss sharing kudos about the former Yankee slugger.

JANE: He's going in as a Padre, what's your take on that?

RUDY: That's fine. I'll always remember him as a Yankee 'cause I'm a Yankees fan, but I'm also a baseball fan. A credit to baseball, still is.

The San Diego Padres contingent includes owner John Moores, General Manager Kevin Towers, and President Larry Lucchino.

LARRY LUCCHINO: He is big and strong and fast and articulate, and he gets his role off the field. If the Hall of Fame is looking to do a movie and they want to cast someone, I would consider Dave Winfield for a leading role.

But for this night, Dave Winfield has to wait to take the stage until after a little toasting …

JOHN MOORES: I don't think that Dave thought this was such a big deal. He's overwhelmed. I'm overwhelmed.

And a little roasting …

"DR. J": [Brings out jersey] It resembles what people might put in the category of would, shoulda, coulda! [Dave to stage for Sixers' jersey]

DAVE: Everybody in this room has had an impact on my life in one way or another, and right now I'm living one of the most wonderful times of my professional career, and I thank all of you for sharing that and coming out tonight. Thank you!

Dave Winfield has a big, booming presence meshed with eloquence and style.

> **DION LATTIMORE** (stylist): He's very meticulous about the way he dresses, but he likes to be a little fashionable, but he doesn't want to go over the top.
>
> **GREGORY HINES:** It's Dave! I'm telling you—this weekend exemplifies Dave. Have you noticed what Dave has been wearing? You know, yes. Oh yes. Sartorial splendor is Dave Winfield. Oh yes.

Wrapped up with respect and love of course, his inner circle knows how to deliver a tease or two to bring this bigger-than-life image of a man back down to size.

> **JOE MORGAN:** Well, Big Fella, we're there together now. I don't care if you're six-six. I'm only five-five and we're in the same spot.
>
> **JANE:** He was really gifted in all of those sports …
>
> **MAURICE LUCAS:** No, he really wasn't. You know he was a really awful basketball player!
>
> **AHMAD RASHAD:** That I still look younger than him and I'm older than him.
>
> **JANE:** What if he had chosen football and not baseball?
>
> **PAT SWILLING:** Then I'd have had the opportunity to hit Mr. Winfield and that would've been great.
>
> **OZZIE SMITH:** Congratulations on a job well done.

The past earned Dave Winfield a place in the Hall of Fame, but it's what he could do with that moniker that's creating anticipation in the baseball community and specifically from the city and the team he represents, the San Diego Padres. Up next on *One on One*, Dave Winfield's hopes and plans for the future ….

So, Dave Winfield you were just inducted into Baseball's Hall of Fame, what are you going to do now?

> **DAVE:** I take a vacation in about a week.

Not so fast. There are places to go, people to meet, and television shows to be on. Because those who bear the same Hall of Fame moniker have found it's not just a highly regarded reward …

> **JOE MORGAN:** It gives him a little more power in whatever he's doing. He'll never be the same after today.
>
> **DAVE:** I feel that way already. People respect you. It's like doctor, ambassador, ha ha, they're not focused on what you did everyday. I mean twenty-two years, "Did you get a hit today?" "What'd you do for me lately, brother?" Ha ha. You know things like that. I don't have to worry about a slump or a period of adjustment as I would call it. It's just good stuff.

Good stuff, good will: familiar territory for Dave Winfield. It's part of who he is. And part of the reason why his decision to go in as a Padre is not only bringing a little more national credibility to the young, thirty-year-old franchise, but is also bringing great pride in him and the team.

TONY GWYNN: The one thing our organization lacks is that sense of history. That sense of somebody you can go back to and say he started here, he established himself here, he was a great player for San Diego. And to me, he was the first everyday player we can say that about.

BRUCE BOCHY: It was just amazing how well he could play the game. He was just so much better than most of us.

TIM FLANNERY: It's always been great to say that I had an opportunity to play with him and learn from him.

KEVIN TOWERS: Gives every player that ever puts on a Padre uniform something to shoot for now.

FAN: Every time I see him, he has that big smile on his face, and he just seems so appreciative of what he's been given.

FAN: I think it's a great thing that he thought that highly of San Diego and say, "I want to go in as a Padre."

FAN: He feels like this is home to him and we feel like he's part of the family here in San Diego.

Winfield, on the Padres Board of Directors, will have input on the team's future endeavors.

DAVE: Maybe with the players, the ballpark, anything, I will just make sure that my relationship is good. I know my future is not totally laid out. I heard someone say, "Do you want to run for politics?" I said, "Are you kidding me?" Forget about it. I have been public enough.

The scrutiny he can live without, even hoping to close the book on those who looked sideways at his decision to go in as a Padre rather than a Yankee.

DAVE: I don't have to live and listen to all that stuff. I did for a long time in my career and I wasted a lot of time, a lot of energy, a lot of money, a lot of goodwill listening to that stuff; soap opera stuff everyday about my career. It never was easy during that middle part. I survived. I'm here and I feel good.

On the national level, he's not only on the cover of Wheaties®, the Breakfast of Champions™, but is considered a champion representative.

DALE PETROSKY: One of the greatest ambassadors the Hall of Fame will have and that the game will have.

DAVE: Even going in the Hall now there is so much more media and coverage. I mean some of these guys that have gone and you know their name and never saw them play. But they all know Kirby Puckett and they all know Dave Winfield, and in the next couple of years they are all going to know Ozzie Smith, and Tony Gwynn, and Cal Ripken, Jr., and Eddie Murray, and people like that.

On the historical front, he will likely help the National Baseball Hall of Fame and Museum's mission to preserve history, honor excellence, and connect generations.

DAVE: They are not just like, here we are at Cooperstown, you know the holy grail, you must come to us and you can get to the Fiji Islands easier than you can get to Cooperstown. They want to take the Hall of Fame out and about around the country and they know that we can potentially be good spokespersons and good representatives.

Even athletes in other sports see how Winfield's ways, legitimized by his new title, could be adopted by younger athletes.

JAYSON WILLIAMS: We need to get them to have some class like Dave Winfield. You know, Dave Winfield played twenty-two years and you walk down the street and you can stop him and he'll give you the time of day.

Born the day Bobby Thompson hit the home run to give the New York Giants the National League title in a playoff over the Brooklyn Dodgers in 1951— the shot heard round the world, fifty years later, Dave Winfield establishes his place in the game's history. Fate? Perhaps. But as he looks ahead, he is not taking for granted what he has now, because he knows what it really took to get here.

DAVE [HOF speech]: I was a little skinny kid growing up. I didn't know what my future held. I worked extremely hard, extremely hard. I had the basis of God-given tools and ability, but I worked really hard to get there, and even everything else I do in life. I have never sat back and said that people you should hand it to me, because people never did. You think those pitchers said, "Here's a fast pitch down the middle," and said, "Hit it"? Shoot, I worked very very hard all my life and I do it off the field now. I never could sit back. I mean, golf, tennis, yeah, I will go to a country club, but I mean, I work and I want my kids to have that work ethic. That is what life is all about.

When looking at Dave Winfield's career, he is finishing where he started, re-embracing San Diego, where he began; a San Diego Padre again, a San Diego Padre forever. I'm Jane Mitchell. From Cooperstown New York, thank you for watching *One on One.*

"Dear Jane, Although the events of the world can distract us for a while, on behalf of Tonya and myself, I want to thank both you and the crew of Cox Cable for all your hard work you put in for my HOF Induction/Celebration, and to produce a truly outstanding piece of work, 'Road to Cooperstown.' It obviously took a lot of thought, work, and dedication to capture the essence of that very important time in my life. This is a piece that we will always treasure. Continued success in all you do. I'm sure I'll see you soon in San Diego."

—Dave Winfield,
September 18, 2001

RYAN KLESKO

"You do a great job of showing a lot of the athletes around San Diego and how good their hearts are ..."

—RYAN KLESKO, 2004

Ryan Klesko was part of a trade between the Atlanta Braves and San Diego Padres, and it did not take long for him to adjust upon returning to his Southern California roots for the 2000 season. Ryno, as he was called, was a name, an energy, and a bat with a lot of experience, having played for the Braves, the perennial post-season victors in the 1990s. He also brought a natural, easy-going way with fans, the community, and the media. We knew he had a plethora of interests outside of baseball. He had a lot of the charm, ways, and hobbies often attributed to the south, yet he was from Orange County and a surfer at heart. So combine all that with a presence at first base, some good power at the plate, and an affable personality off the field, and I had the makings of a *One on One* subject. To really do it right, we had to participate in some of his hobbies in the off-season in Georgia.

In the meantime, I took advantage of the opportunity to travel with the team when it made sense for productions. In April of 2000, the Padres played in Atlanta and I killed two production birds with one stone. First, I interviewed outfielder Eric Owens' family and followed them attending a Braves game, and second, I interviewed Ryan's former Braves teammates on the field, knowing I would want their perspective and sound bites when I eventually featured Ryan on a show.

An off-season trip to Georgia took a little creativity and coordination. Ryan was up for it, agreeing to take us hunting, let us shoot (videotape, that is) around his property, do the sit down interview, and everything on my list. We just had to get there. I was going to be in New York City for my annual winter holiday with friends. As a resourceful way to get it done, I offered to cut my trip short and fly to Atlanta. Photographer Dan Roper, the pack mule that he can be, loaded the gear, flew from San Diego, and met me in Atlanta. After getting our rental car and

303

staying in a modest hotel, we awoke to an unusually cold winter day and snow. Thankfully, the snowfall was light enough that it didn't hinder travel or our plans.

We drove more than an hour through the backcountry to his property. Ryan was flying in later that night. We had a lot to do, so we started rolling tape with the okay from his friend and business partner, Richard Spear. We shot most of the exteriors while we had light and good weather. The dusting of snow was beautiful by his enormous log cabin, surrounded by trees and the sounds of a brook and birds. As the sun went down, we moved inside to shoot pictures of the shelves and animal horns on the walls. It was well after nine o'clock that night when Ryan arrived. He was a bundle of energy, even after traveling all day. He welcomed us and made a plan. We would be starting the hunting trip the next day at four-thirty in the morning, so rise and shine by 4:00 a.m. Did we have enough warm clothes? No. So he outfitted us with big, warm, hunters' jumpsuits, shoes, hats, gloves, and whatever we needed. We were not expecting it to be this cold.

The script tells much of the story of what we did. Here are a few stories and impressions of note that didn't make the show. First of all, Ryan's hunting friends welcomed us with open arms, hot coffee, and plenty of jokes and stories about him. Some of that could not go on family TV, and even if it could, there was just not time in a half-hour show. I did give viewers the essence of it by capturing their camaraderie and salty fun and humor. Sometimes, you just have to be there for it to make sense. Buddha, for example, got his nickname from his Buddha-like belly. Richard number two (not his business partner) was smart and equally entertaining. My being the only girl made for a fun, just smile and go-with-it kind of time.

The 4:30 a.m. call time was early, cold, and just the beginning of an adventure. After shooting a little video of the gathering, we piled in the pickup trucks and headed an hour to the ranch to go duck hunting. I sat in the truck with Ryan, chatting most of the way. It was still dark when we arrived at his property with a big metal gate.

The Klesko rule was that if anyone with access to the property used the hidden key to the gate, they must return it to the proper hiding place. At 5:30 in the morning, cars loaded with hunters, guns, and a TV crew, arrived to find there was no key—no key anywhere. The only way to be in place before the sun rose was to get in there right away. So Ryan and the others got out of the car, he grabbed his gun and yelled to me, "Jane, you're driving." With flashlights pointed at the lock on the chained gate, he fired a few times, blowing the lock off. Then he hopped in the car and yelled, "Go! Go!" My heart racing, my foot hit the gas and we headed down that road like there was no tomorrow. Actually, as far as hunting and shooting the hunting, there wasn't a tomorrow. We had to get this on this day and that meant we all had to be in place before the ducks knew we were there. Apparently, Ryan explained, ducks are pretty smart that way. When they see, hear, or feel activity, they avoid the area in order to survive. But we persevered.

Once the caravan quietly approached the opening by a pond, we unloaded and gingerly stepped into a few boats to row out to the duck blind. Dan was in one boat with the camera. I was in the other with Ryan, trying to soak it in and interview him in whispers for fear of spooking the ducks. I think we saw about one duck the whole time. No one got anything, but, as they say, the hunt is often more the point than the catch.

Still, Ryan and the other diehard hunters didn't want to be skunked. We rowed back, loaded into the cars, and began the pursuit of dove. Along the way, he explained how ecological efforts to maintain nature's balance included helping the quail repopulate. We saw plenty of wild turkeys, but they were out of season, so they were safe that day.

One would think that adventure would suffice for our purposes. We had the footage to show this hobby, but that was only the beginning. Whenever I talk with Ryan, as I did for this book, the next part of the day often comes up as one of those moments that did not make the show.

The sun was coming out and that winter cold snap was thawing a bit. We still had our winter gear on, along with the camera, batteries, tapes, and microphones, as we were trudging along to the next excursion: boar hunting. Not pig. Not deer. Boar. Yikes. Boars are not welcome in that part of the country where they root crops, ruining them in the process. Besides, they are big, mean, fast, and strong animals with tusks. They are no "Wilburs." With this kind of game hunting not in the mainstream mindset, and perhaps a little much for a family television show for baseball fans, we agreed it might not be appropriate to include, but we still went along.

We alternated being in the all-terrain vehicles and walking. The ground was wet and muddy from the melted snow. It was especially difficult for Dan, who was carrying a lot of equipment. I had the tripod. This was hardly glamorous. We were moving fast and sweating. Gradually, we stripped down the various layers of cold weather gear. The chasing, the strategizing, the listening for their grunts and growls to find the boar would have been excitement enough. Then something unfortunate happened. Ryan's dog met up with a boar, and the boar won. The boar's horn gouged the dog, who was bleeding profusely. Even in all the chaos, the boar was shot dead. The hunting trip quickly turned into an emergency rescue situation for the dog. We loaded up and drove to the nearest veterinarian. While the dog was being treated (thankfully he survived), we took a picture with the dead boar on the back of a truck. We left the boar-hunting escapade out of the program, but that photo of the hunters (and me) and the dead boar made it into a newsletter/magazine for the sport somewhere.

For this book, Ryan and I reminisced about our trip to Georgia:

"I wanted to give you the full experience. Obviously we kept meeting up with a lot of my redneck friends and making sure you were going to be warm 'cause I knew it was going to be cold that weekend .... And the lake being frozen over that wasn't supposed to be frozen over. Oh, and getting lost. Remember, I made the wrong turn and we were late 'cause we were talking so much. And the hog hunting, running the dogs around the pigs, and one of my dogs getting hurt. I don't know, not speaking for you, but I don't think you've had too many *One on One*s with that type of deal!"

After a long, emotional day, I would have understood if Ryan wanted to put things on hold and pick up the next day. Not the case. After returning to the house, everyone took a break with the plan that we still needed to do the sit down interview and see him work out at his gym. Dan and I set up the camera and lights in his living room with its high ceilings, big couches, and fireplace. There was definitely a hunting lodge feel. At about nine o'clock, Ryan asked if we were ready. We sat down and walked through his life story for about an hour. Then we drove to a huge warehouse converted to a gym, and for another hour, until after midnight, we shot him lifting weights. He never said, "Ah, you don't need this, I'm done." He understood what he agreed to, what we needed, and he more than obliged. We were all tired and unfortunately for poor Dan, we had no production assistants to help, just me.

The next morning, we interviewed Ryan's father and shot a few things around the house. The night before, Ryan had shared about his recent baptism, so my "find visuals to illustrate his words" antennae noticed books about his Christian faith. I also saw a little tin can wrapped in paper with the word "God" on it. I asked about it and he shared that when you're worried about something, or unsure, you can write that worry down on paper and put it in the can. Meaning, "when you can't, God can." People don't make things like that up to put in their house so a television crew might see it. That was part of his world, his belief, and his faith. That visual comes to mind when I have struggled, been worried, or burdened by something. I have yet to make an actual "God can," but the symbolism is inspiring. I later heard a similar suggestion during a church service with my friend Tammy in Oklahoma. I didn't include the "God can" element specifically in the show, but I value learning that from him and being able to pass it along.

Dan wasn't the only one shooting that day. Ryan asked if I had ever fired a gun. My only experience was when I was a daily news reporter covering a story

306

related to a police firing range. I did not enjoy it. I'm not against guns, but I don't like them, and certainly don't like holding or shooting them. Even so, Ryan offered to teach me how to shoot a pistol, and I accepted. My target was a shoebox between two trees. I had no idea how powerful a pistol was. I am not tiny, but my five-foot-six, one hundred thirty-pound frame is not designed for that kind of bang. I fired it a few times. I did not hit the box, but it didn't matter. When it comes to shooting, I'll stick to cameras.

When we drove away that day, I had nothing but respect and appreciation for Ryan Klesko. He was, and is, a class act. He made a plan, and not only followed through with it, but was exceptionally accommodating and considerate of both Dan's and my needs as people, as well as a television crew. Granted, this show would be great for him and the Padres, but he demonstrated genuine kindness and professionalism in challenging circumstances and a tight timeframe. He knew I had to get certain elements for me to do my job right, and he made every effort and then some.

A decade later, for this book, Ryan shared: "You're the only person that's really ever done that with me. I've had some other people out and they maybe spend a day or something, but to come out for a couple days and take an opportunity to see exactly what we did ... that's what obviously being a reporter's all about. . . . Thinking deep and getting the truth and reflecting that person the way they want to be reflected. And not just by them, but by their family and friends. That was interesting. It was a really, really great job, and just a fun time for me."

To contrast his southern living, we went to where it all started for Ryan, southern California's Orange County. A day trip up the coast accomplished meeting his high school coach at the field where he played, interviewing his mother and one of his two sisters at the home where Ryan was raised, and shooting his route down to the Pacific Ocean where he surfed as a teenager. Even now, when I see his mother, Lorene, she gives me a big hug and thanks me for featuring her son. Reflecting about that time, Ryan says he especially wanted his mother to be part of the show, because as a kid, while his father was away working in the oil fields, his mother "was very influential in my baseball career and taught me just about everything I knew about baseball ... I told her [then], I wanted that to come out more than anything about me."

I updated his story in 2004 after he returned from surgery. He showed us around his stunning home in La Jolla, his garage jam-packed with surf and fishing gear, and his high-end condo overlooking the ballpark where his mother often stayed during her visits.   After the 2006 season he signed with the Giants and retired in 2008. His original show is a *One on One Classic.*   Ryan married Kelly, a girl from Georgia, and they are parents to a little boy named Hunter.

Here is the script for the show debuting April 10, 2001.

• • •

San Diego Padre Ryan Klesko, a southern California boy with country charm, on the field, in the spotlight or in nature, lives life to the max …

RYAN: I'm doing something all the time, as you well know. [smiles]

Throughout his career people have formed all kinds of impressions about Ryan Klesko. When he was with the Braves, most Padres fans considered him a big, mean-looking guy with lots of power and not a lot of personality. We were all in for a pleasant surprise.

Ryan Klesko, with his 6'3", 220-pound buffed out body, powering balls out of the park, can be a Mr. Tough Guy.

TONY GWYNN: People who watch him on TV, you have this perception of him and then you talk to him and it's completely different.

See him smile. Hear him interact with sincerity and a sense of humor …

BRUCE BOCHY: He's one that will keep you laughing and just has a lot of fun out there.

And it's clear why he's earned respect and admiration not only for being a standout slugger but for being a free spirit.

TIM FLANNERY: His clothing label describes him just perfect. It's Mindless Reaction.

TREVOR HOFFMAN: It's interesting to watch Ryan work.

He's been a work in progress, born June 12, 1971. Ryan Anthony Klesko grew up in Westminster, California.

LORENE (his mother): It's hard to believe that he was a shy kid, but he really was. Very good little guy.

His mother, Lorene, grew up an Oklahoma tomboy. His father, Howard, put a fishing pole in Ryan's hand at two years old.

HOWARD: I took him to one of those trout pond places where you can catch the fish, and he caught it. He was still in diapers, almost.

The Kleskos' modest incomes and their little house on an Orange County cul-de-sac prompted Ryan and his two older sisters, Pam and Paula, to play the old fashioned way.

> **PAULA:** Make forts and stuff together, and he kinda followed me around and we'd go hunting for pollywogs or whatever.
> **PAM:** He and my sister were closer in age. They used to get into it all the time. He always knew he could run and hide behind me and I'd protect him.

As All-Star softball players, he wanted to do what they did. And their mom grabbed a glove for pitching practice in the backyard.

> **LORENE:** When he came along and he started pitching, Mama caught him.
> **RYAN:** She built my mound by hand in the backyard, build a pitch back, and she worked two jobs to take me to pitching and hitting school which I went to for twelve years, and I think that's why I really developed my skills in baseball.

Ryan's sisters took private pitching lessons and at nine years old, the little leaguer was eager to follow with instructor Richard Hickey.

> **RICHARD HICKEY:** He was always at a high level. He had great coordination.
> **RYAN:** I hit off college guys when I was twelve, thirteen years old.
> **RICHARD HICKEY:** He was a big strong kid. He's left handed.
> **RYAN:** I had the experience, so when I went to play high school, it was like, nothing.
> **RICHARD HICKEY:** He loved to compete.

As Ryan entered Westminster High, his home life changed. A workplace accident had left his father with serious health problems. His parents divorced and he didn't see much of his dad for years. But his mom did do all she could to encourage his baseball goals, and so did Coach Bill Whiteley.

> **BILL:** When I got him in high school, I had other good players ... so he was a little bit taken aback.

But not intimidated, even as a freshman on the varsity team.

> **BILL:** In practice, he was hitting balls out to right field hitting those homes out there.

Losing too many balls ...

> **BILL:** It didn't take him but one practice or two to learn to sit back and hit the ball the other way. And that amazed me for a freshman. I mean, most high school players never learn that skill.

Even with his name in local sports headlines, he was humble and popular, stayed out of trouble, and as he had done since he was nine, he often headed across the Pacific Coast Highway to surf with his pals.

> **RYAN:** We just kept surfing. It was great.

As one of the best pitchers in the region, throwing ninety miles an hour, Klesko pitched a nine-inning shutout in the 1988 Junior Olympic qualifying games. He was picked for the team which traveled the world and brought home the gold.

RYAN: Just a great experience. That was something that opened my eyes to a new, a whole new dimension of baseball.

Arizona State University offered him a full scholarship, then the Atlanta Braves drafted him in the fifth round and, in a telegram, hoped he'd give serious consideration to a career in professional baseball. He had hurt his pitching arm, so at a workout at Dodger stadium, a scout put a wood bat in his hand.

RYAN: I took batting practice for the team, they asked me, "How much do you want?" I said, well you know, uh, oh, I'm in trouble. I didn't think they were going to say that. I ended up signing like two days later.

He would bank and live on the $100,000 signing bonus as he headed straight to Rookie Ball in Bradenton, Florida.

RYAN: Wake up in the morning and it's raining, it's hot, it's muggy. There are mosquitoes everywhere. We got, I think, six beds in one room, no TV. And I just, I was like, "What do we do to get out of here?" And they said, "Hit." I told them I was going to give them their money back, go back home, go to school, they said, "No no, you signed!"

So he hit, even daring to break the rules once when he was going to be walked intentionally.

RYAN: So he threw it out over, about a foot off the plate and I stepped over … I didn't step on the plate, because if you do that, you're out. I hit the ball right over the third baseman's head and the runner came in and scored and we won the game. Everyone was freakin' out and I was a hero and everything and my coach calls me and goes, "Whattya doing? For your punishment, you take all the helmets and carry them in and the bat bag by yourself before you go." And I didn't catch it. And then he said, "Did you hear me right? Before you go." And I said, "Go where?" "You're getting called up, you're going to A ball today. You're done with this league!"

From only a handful of fans in the stands in Florida …

RYAN: I went to Sumter, South Carolina, there was 400 or 500 people there a night, I thought I was in the big leagues!

When he moved up to the Durham Bulls …

RYAN: Bull Durham, you know, the movie and everything, I was in heaven!

In 1990, Klesko forged friendships with two fellow up-and-comers, catcher Javy Lopez …

JAVY LOPEZ: Everyone liked to watch him take batting practice because nine out of ten pitches, he's hitting out of the ballpark.

And the nation's number one draft pick, Chipper Jones.

CHIPPER JONES: The first time I ever saw him, he took three of the God awful-est swings I've ever seen in my life. And on the last one he swung, missed, and completely fell down and I'm like, "Why you swing so hard?" And he goes, "Just in case I hit that son of a gun!"

Trying to get an edge, he played winter ball in Puerto Rico. Then after Double-A Greenville, he was named the best power prospect in the minor leagues and landed in Triple-A, Richmond.

> RYAN: That's the first time that I struggled anywhere my whole life in baseball.

Veteran pitching was the toughest he had ever had to face.

> RYAN: Here starts my mental process of actually getting to the big leagues. I mean, it was freakin' me out.

He didn't know how to deal with it. But former Pittsburgh Pirate and Hall of Famer Willie Stargell had joined the staff of the Braves and *he* knew.

> RYAN: Called me one night and said, "Come on to my room, kid, we're gonna work on baseball." He sat down and talked for three hours with me about the game. How it's supposed to be played, how you're gonna succeed, you know, what you should and shouldn't do.

Klesko appreciated Stargell's ongoing mentoring and by the spring of '92, was considered a Brave phenom, a future star "bound for glory" with Jones and Lopez.

> RYAN: And that's when I knew, that year I was going to the big leagues.

But he was motivated by something more important than money, ego, or pride.

> RYAN: My mom hadn't been feeling well. She had been sick for a few months.

A work-related accident left her with chemical induced pneumonia.

> RYAN: And that was my sole goal. It wasn't for me to get to the big leagues. It was for me to get to the big leagues for her. And when I got called up, that was the first thing I thought of was her. So that was real special to me.
> JANE: Did you hear? Was she the first one you called?
> RYAN: Yeah, for sure.
> JANE: How did she react?
> RYAN: "'Bout time! About time those guys called you up." Oh, it was, you know, that's my mom though. She thought I was ready when I was twelve, I guess … [Laughs]

Up next on *One on One*, Ryan Klesko's Brave New World and making a splash in San Diego ....

Ryan Klesko, a Triple-A All-Star in 1992, was anxious to make a good impression after earning a call up to the big leagues with the Braves that September. But it didn't quite go as anticipated.

> RYAN: So that whole off-season I had to live with all my buddies saying I didn't get my first major league hit.

He'd get his chance to redeem himself when recalled early the next season.

[Footage: April 22, 1993 first hit.]

His power surged back in Richmond as the Triple-A All-Star game's MVP and he did well off the bench with Atlanta as the Braves pushed toward the playoffs. But when he was not selected for the post-season roster, instead of just staying mad, Ryan Klesko got ready.

> **RYAN:** I went to the Arizona League and led the league in home runs there. Let 'em know I was ready to come back to the big leagues.

He'd get his chance that spring. The regular left fielder …

> **LOCAL NEWS CLIP:** *Ron Gant was riding a dirt bike and broke his right shin bone. He will be out at least three months.*
>
> **RYAN:** They said, "You're gonna be playing left field." I never played a day of outfield in my life. I was like, "Okay."

When two players vying for the spot were injured, Klesko made the big league roster. Whether by default or destiny, he never looked back. He was named a Topps' Major League Rookie All-Star, finishing third in National League Rookie of the Year voting. Manager Bobby Cox moved him around to keep him at the plate.

> **BOBBY COX:** When he came up here he could hit and he could play.

Cy Young award-winning pitcher, Greg Maddux …

> **GREG MADDUX:** He was a presence in our lineup. Made it tougher to pitch to the guys before and after him.

Ryan Klesko was an integral part of the Braves' successful plan to develop home-grown talent, on a relatively low payroll, building championship teams.

> **RYAN:** We played as a family. We knew what it took to win and that's what I think we won so many years for.

In 1995 Klesko experienced his first post season, all the way to the World Series.

> **RYAN:** It was awesome …

Even making World Series history in Cleveland …

> **RYAN:** … finally, I got a hit. And then I got another hit. Then I hit a home run, then I hit another home run. And then, I ended up hitting three home runs in three straight days on the road.

But more than his personal feat, helping the Braves become World Champions was especially sweet because he could share it with his mom, whose poor health had stabilized.

> **LORENE:** And I'll never forget he picks me up and swinging me around, tears running and said, "Mama, we did it." That was a special moment between the two of us. [crying]

The next year, Klesko would play every day, hammering thirty-four home runs all the way to the World Series again and contributing in campaigns to the post season in '97 and in the 1998 NLCS against the victorious San Diego Padres. But even as he continued to produce, Klesko wasn't himself at the plate. Painful injured wrist ligaments requiring cortisone shots hampered his swing, and he couldn't work out to maintain his strength.

> **RYAN:** I was just trying to get through it.

Fearing surgery and out of shape, he was once again pro-active in the off-season, hiring a former body builder as his personal trainer.

> **RYAN:** I walked in spring training doors and they go, "What happened to you? What have you been doing?"

In 1999 he was back bigger, stronger than ever, enjoying his third trip to the World Series. But after the Braves were swept by the New York Yankees, trade talks that had only been rumors in the past were the real deal.

> **RYAN:** "But, where am I going?" And he said, "San Diego," and I just got chills all the way up. I said, "Yes! Thank you! I love you!"

He'd be going home to Southern California and to a team planning to capitalize on his revitalized strength. General Manager Kevin Towers traded Wally Joyner, Quilvio Veras, and Reggie Sanders for Braves second baseman Bret Boone and Klesko.

> **KEVIN TOWERS:** To be able to go out and acquire an impact type, in our eyes—left handed power hitting first baseman in the prime of his career—was key to us.

Still, there were questions.

> **TONY GWYNN:** One, could he hit left-handers? Two, would he be a good defensive first baseman? Three, nobody in their right mind ever thought he'd ever steal twenty bases.

2000 would be Ryan Klesko's best all around season, unequivocally answering those questions with his bat and his glove.

> **RYAN:** They let me run last year, and let me play my game, back to my natural position, first base. It was the first time where I didn't feel like I was under a microscope.

He found a new home.

> **TONY GWYNN:** He's turned out to be a really good player, very astute as far as picking up pitches and knowing how to attack 'em and making adjustments.
>
> **TREVOR HOFFMAN:** He always gave 100 percent when he was on the field. And it was never fun to go up against Ryan Klesko. And now it's nice for him to be able to be on our team.
>
> **KEVIN TOWERS:** Klesko we think is somebody that we're going to be able to build around. He's only going to get better with time.

Ryan Klesko's playing time doesn't stop when the season's over. Coming up on *One on One*, the other dimensions of Klesko's life: church, charity, and the wet and wild . . . .

With photographs and home video, Ryan Klesko likes to document the moment.

> **RYAN:** Just to have that memory, when I'm sitting in my chair, hopefully, when I'm seventy-five, eighty years old, to remember it.

And has he had some moments to remember, meeting all sorts of celebrities and country music stars from the Grand Old Opry to Brooks and Dunn and Travis Tritt. His video library archives annual off-season trips with the boys south of the border to Costa Rica and Mexico, exploring the back roads, surfing, and fishing. Long respectful of law enforcement, he's wanted to earn a badge. But his baseball notoriety put some of his SWAT tag-alongs on hold.

> **RYAN:** But, you're bustin' a house, and bust somebody, "Hey Ryan Klesko, what are you doing in my house?"

Klesko, at ease in the great outdoors, was asked by the host of the *North American Fish and Game Magazine* show to be a guest sportsman in 1991. And he's been polishing his performance skills to perhaps even play host within the next few years. And when HBO's show *Arliss,* about a sports agent, called the Padre, Klesko delivered. He's not acting when it comes to business. As a partner in a clothing company his surf and skateboarding attire is reaching into the Asian market. The company, Mindless Reaction, suggests instinct, a Klesko trait. As for real estate, he owns thousands of acres of ranch land for hunting, fishing, reforestation and quail preserves in Georgia, Texas, and Oregon. Richard Spear, his business manager and lifelong friend, appreciates Ryan's work ethic and choices.

> **RICHARD SPEAR:** He knows what he wants to do and he goes out and accomplishes that.

Among Ryan Klesko's moments to remember, his renewed faith …

> **RYAN:** It's been a blessing in my life to have.

He was raised going to church, but as he shared at a Padres Day of Fellowship …

> **RYAN:** I was kind of scared. I was scared to take the next step. I thought I was gonna lose my friends. I thought I was gonna lose all my fun.

On Valentine's Day 2000, he was baptized in Georgia along with his father.

> **RYAN:** I wake up and I'm just, life's so much easier and better. It's just something I guess some people need to experience, some people have. [smiles]

Hunting, fishing, having fun, and working out. With Ryan Klesko's all over the map off-season schedule …

> **RYAN:** A little bit of everything …

If you don't join him, you won't see him. His off-season home base is the dream home he bought two years ago.

> **RYAN:** I was saving up to get something special.

About forty miles outside of Atlanta, the property is 250 acres with trees and a stream that, in the winter, dusted with snow, is quiet and secluded. A log cabin house with high ceilings is spacious, comfortable, and cozy with his traveling bull-dog Missy, and decorated with mementos of friends, faith, fishing, and plenty of outdoorsman trophies. But it's the 4:30 a.m. wakeup call at a mere sixteen degrees with a group of buddies that gets his blood flowing. An hour ride toward Macon through a locked gate …

RYAN: All right, let's roll.

… and in the still of the early morning …

[Ryan in full gear walking: "It's froze up solid, it might not be good."]

Ryan Klesko is in his element.

RYAN [whispering]: Aren't you glad you got up early this morning? We ain't seen but one duck. Look how pretty that hawk is. There is some ice on the pond. We're out here in the hardwood timber and pines. It's more the camaraderie and getting out and just getting away from work and the city and everything.

With no luck with the ducks, it is time to move on with the guys. Hunting for food they will eventually eat, a trek through the timbers leads to an opening for doves. Wild turkeys have no worries; they're out of season.

RYAN: It's called hunting. You gotta go out and scout.

The geese elude the hunters as well. After a ten-hour hunting excursion and a late evening interview, Ryan Klesko has one more thing on his to-do list: work out, even at the stroke of midnight, in his home gym converted from a barn, only to get up at 4:30 the next morning to do it all again. Aside from what he does for himself, he is also an accommodating and considerate person, even setting his father up with a cabin by his Georgia home and taking time to hunt or fish with him like they used to do.

HOWARD: I enjoy that. *I enjoy that.* That's more important to me than anything.

RYAN: They didn't give him that much time to live five years ago, and he's still kicking around, so I'm blessed to have him here.

LORENE: You see him tough on the field, but basically, Ryan is really a loving, caring human being.

He shows that through the sharing of his time and money, giving back to his high school with donated equipment, or a thanks to his coach and spending time with Make-A-Wish kids at baseball games and hospitals, inspired by his sister Pam, who treats little cancer patients.

RYAN: If I can make them happy for ten seconds out of all that pain they've been through, then I've done my job.

Back in Southern California at his Solana Beach condo, he's close to the surf and his family. He's come a long way from his childhood adventures and baseball beginnings.

RYAN: I just look at myself. I'm a normal person. I just play baseball. I'm not anybody special.

Humble, appreciative, and driven, number 30 is turning thirty in 2001 and, as expected, intends to enjoy every minute of being in the prime of his career.

Ryan Klesko is the epitome of the modern ballplayer. He's strong, smart, a fierce competitor with a genuine love of the game. But beyond the numbers he could put up this season, he has something else going for him. In an era when rich athletes are often sheltered and aloof, Klesko is a genuinely nice guy. A first baseman who is first rate. I'm Jane Mitchell. Thank you for watching *One on One*.

"Everybody came up to me, the fans, teammates, coaches. 'Cause people, unless they're your friends and around you, they don't know anything about you.

I always watched the *One on One* interviews, and I always got an idea who that person really was and what they liked to do, and what type of lifestyle they had. That's because you went the extra mile and dug deep, and figured out and tried to relate to the fans and the people that this is what kind of a person this is, this is what they like to enjoy and, for the most part, everybody got an idea of who that person was just by watching that, and we appreciate that."

—Ryan Klesko, 2010

DOUG FLUTIE

By mid-season 2001, the Padres were playing below .500 ball, so there were not a lot of expectations it would be a winning season. As it turns out, they finished fourth in the division. While anything could have happened, one thing was sure—on Thursday, June 28, Tony Gwynn officially announced he would retire and that became a focus of our Padres coverage. Nevertheless, as a producer, I had to simultaneously look ahead to the football season. The Chargers' Director of Public Relations Bill Johnston and I decided the two best people to feature for *One on One* would be Head Coach Mike Riley and newly signed quarterback, Doug

Flutie, then a thirty-nine-year-old underdog finally getting a starting position in the National Football League (NFL).

Doug had been around the game as a Heisman Trophy winner, a star in the Canadian Football League (CFL), and a back-up quarterback in the NFL. He had seen it all, but in San Diego, people only knew part of his story. A *One on One* was our opportunity to introduce fans to the next leader on the field. With the Chargers record of just one win and fifteen losses in 2000, many were looking to Doug Flutie to turn things around and to mentor Drew Brees, who had been drafted in 2001 and touted as the team's quarterback of the future.

I didn't know Doug and did not cover the Chargers on a daily basis, so I needed to meet him in a setting that allowed us to focus on what I do, why I wanted to feature him and his family, and what I needed from him. That year, the Chargers were holding summer training camp on the UCSD campus. Bill Johnston arranged for Doug and me to meet during a lunch break on a picnic table outside the cafeteria. In about fifteen minutes, he gave me the names and numbers of family and key people in his life and career so I could do the work of calling and coordinating. We made a plan of what we would shoot—the interview at home, his family (including his son, Doug, Jr., who is autistic), and Doug playing drums. We agreed to keep it in one location at their rented home, and within a reasonable timeframe of about three hours. We planned for September 26, after he picked up his daughter from school. On another day, we would tag along to see the family during a charity event where they played games, including miniature golf. With those plans in motion, no one could have anticipated what would happen in the meantime—September 11. The tragedy of the assault on America that day touched us all. After assessing it was safe to move forward, we all agreed to follow through with the production schedule.

To look back at the list of elements included in this program, I realize how much bicoastal effort went into it. Not only did I interview his immediate family in San Diego, but we also coordinated interviews with his family in Massachusetts, with his brother, Darren, and coaches with the CFL in Canada. His brother Bill, in the Boston area, helped by taking digital pictures of the Fluties' childhood and current house. Doug was such a celebrity in New England, it affected our gathering process. For example, my associate producer on this show,

Kelly Morris, was told the yearbook with his senior picture had been taken from the high school. He was popular and in demand, so we relied heavily on his family for visuals.

Just being around Doug Flutie, I could feel his star power, but not in the vain superstar way. While he was very articulate and engaged during the interview, he was otherwise quiet, almost shy, cordial with a dry sense of humor, a man of few words with a New England accent. We were strictly professional and respectful of Doug and his wife, but his subtle yet ever present charisma admittedly produced a few sighs from Kelly and me afterwards. It was a good day to have our job.

Beyond his compelling football story, Doug Flutie was an example of keeping one's priorities in order. He and Laurie put family first and used his position as a celebrity to champion the cause of autism in the name of their son, Dougie. I don't believe I had been around an autistic child before the day of our interview. I learned it is common for autistic children to be vocal and physical, but when one is not accustomed to that, it can be uncomfortable at first. Dougie, eleven years old at the time, was tall, thin, and full of emotion—sometimes laughing or yelling, and also content and quiet. We were the outsiders, creating unfamiliar commotion with our lights and cameras. I wasn't sure if our presence was interfering too much or was too intrusive. With their assurance everything was okay, that day taught me a lot about the Fluties and about autism. By watching Doug, Laurie, and their daughter Alexa interact with Dougie, I witnessed gentleness and patience, and could see and feel an incredibly strong and determined family. I saw the power of love in motion. I felt more confident and happy to know this television program would share both Doug's football story and help educate people about autism and the Doug Flutie, Jr. Foundation.

Doug Flutie was with the Chargers through 2004, eventually the backup quarterback, mentoring Drew Brees. While he returned home to the New England Patriots in 2005 to wrap up his playing career, San Diego was fortunate to have him for a while, and I'm glad he's one of our *One on One Classics*. No matter what team you root for, Doug Flutie's multidimensional story is worth knowing.

We weren't the only ones who thought so. The FOX Network's *Beyond the Glory* series, which debuted in 2001, wanted to feature Doug. In the process, their producers learned of *One on One* and asked me for some of the pictures and video. With Doug's permission, we passed along what we had received from the Flutie family. That saved his family the hassle of doing it all again, and we were happy to help.

This is the script from the show debuting November 27, 2001.

• • •

From his Heisman-clinching Hail Mary pass to Chargers quarterback, Doug Flutie defies age and size, while his big heart is helping his autistic son.

DOUG: This is his legacy. This is his way to make an impact.

His play on the field has long inspired a play on words, the "Magic Flutie," the underdog who seems to have the magic touch. It's also created an expectation that his magic right arm could always pull a rabbit out of the hat. Doesn't always work that way. The ups and downs of Flutie's playing time mirror his life, one of fortitude, family, good fortune, and fame.

Number 7 is energizing and impressing his new team …

MARCELLUS WILEY: The funky little quarterback that could. He's everything!

JUNIOR SEAU: The missing piece. It's something we've been looking for. Something we've needed.

MIKE RILEY: Every time he takes the field, everybody believes we have a chance. And that's a big deal.

He has instantly endeared himself to fans.

FAN: Cutie Flutie, because he's the best thing that's happened to San Diego in a long time.

And he's quite certain about his biggest asset.

DOUG: Wanting to be the best at what I do or win. You know, whatever it takes to get to that goal.

Since signing with San Diego in the spring of 2001, the veteran with a winning track record has made his mark. At just under 5'10", 180 pounds, he's not doing it with intimidating height, but with unique might, skilled, swift, smart, with a phenomenal recall for strategy and plays.

DOUG: We were down by two with one second left on the clock. He hits his first foul shot, cuts it to one. He hits the second foul shot and they call me over the line and take the point away and that was our only loss of the season. That was when we were twelve.

Sports, the center of his life, it seems, from day one. Born Douglas Richard Flutie, October 23, 1962 in Baltimore, Maryland.

JOAN (his mother): He never sat still. He was very, very active. He climbed out of his playpen a little over six months old.

DOUG: Going a hundred miles an hour all day long, but very shy.

JOAN: If we took him somewhere where there were strangers around, he was always behind me hanging on to me.

Joan and Dick Flutie raised their four children Denise, Bill, Doug, and Darren with this theory:

DICK: You give that child something that he has that's special and he's best at compared to his peers. He will have an easier time going through life.

DOUG: I was one of those kids that had that bat on my shoulder and was afraid of the ball and hoping for a walk and all that. By the time I was eight, I was one of the kids that was pitching and hitting the home runs and one of the better athletes. So I don't know what the transition was there, from there on, I just remember it was the most important thing in the world for me.

While Flutie's grandparents and mother were athletes, his father, an engineer, photographer, and musician, was a committed coach doing research at the library.

DICK: I was going to make sure my children were ready.

Even during tough times in Florida.

DOUG: Living paycheck to paycheck. And as the kids, I mean, we came first. If we needed a new baseball glove, the money was spent on that.

And non-sports entertainment? Richard Flutie and his orchestra practicing in the house.

DICK: We'd play and the whole neighborhood would come out and just clap after every number. We had a lot of fun and the kids grew up around that.

But Doug's first drum set wouldn't get much use, as he was too busy playing or watching sports on TV and tracking his two favorite players, Orioles pitcher Jim Palmer and flashy Miami Dolphin running back Mercury Morris, both number 22.

DOUG: I'd watch NFL quarterbacks and say, "You know, you really shouldn't have called a time out there. You should have waited until this moment, or they should have called a time out before the two minute and used the two minute as their third time out for when they get the ball back." [smiles]

By all accounts he was more knowledgeable than most of his coaches at the Pop Warner level, applying that and acting on instinct, such as the time an opponent caught the ball on kickoff.

DICK: Doug didn't tackle him. Doug ran up to him and grabbed the ball away from him and ran the other way. The officials went crazy. But finally they ruled his way and we won that ballgame.

JOAN: When he stepped on a football field, his charisma just spread.

At thirteen, his family moved and his charisma would catch on in small town Natick near Boston.

DOUG: I always kind of enjoyed it, keeping my mouth shut, not saying much and being that way and then stepping on the basketball court or the football field or something, and impressing people that way.

Hearing of his junior high exploits, Natick High School Coach Tom Lamb tried him out.

DOUG: He saw things in me that I didn't really see in myself at that age.

He made varsity as a sophomore stepping into his brother Bill's quarterback position.

DOUG: The way we viewed it was this was great 'cause now neither one of us leaves the field.

The first day of school that year, the still shy Doug Flutie would meet his soul mate.

LAURIE: We were in the same homeroom.

DOUG: The girl that caught my attention was Laurie, sitting right next to me.

LAURIE: And I just thought he was the cutest thing in the world.

DOUG: I guess I held the door open for her once during the course of that day. And I talked to her a little more than usual, and I guess she went to lunch with her girlfriends and said …

LAURIE: "I found my guy, I found mine!"

DOUG: I was oblivious. I don't know. [blushing smile]

Laurie, a dancer and cheerleader, was also a sports fan.

LAURIE: On Monday morning he would come in and he would like write out what happened in the game and tell me all about it and I was very interested.

Their friendship led to a first date, a June Red Sox game and the beginning of a lifelong relationship.

LAURIE: Neither one of us really cared to go to any of the big high school parties, and neither one of us ever drank or smoked or anything like that, so we had a lot in common in that way, too.

Flutie was becoming a great player with a prowess and knack for making things happen at an acceptable high school height of about 5'10".

DOUG: So I didn't think twice about it until I started getting recruited by college coaches. I remember a guy from Ohio State saying, "You know, let's face it, you're not going to be a quarterback."

His first taste of being dismissed as too short.

DOUG: They've obviously been around football. They must know what they're talking about. I'm just a kid. I play high school football.

None of the hundred-plus Division I schools makes an offer, so he plans to play at the smaller Harvard …

DOUG: I was sold on the fact that that was the type of kid I was, that I was going to go that way. And then Boston College came back and offered me a scholarship. And it was like.... No decision. I'm going, bang. You know. That's what I want.

The Boston College atmosphere also more his style. He signs, wondering if the players he had watched would be a lot better than he.

DOUG: Until I got to school and then you get on the field with the same group of guys. It's just a bunch of guys and you're playing football.

New Head Coach Jack Bicknell, desperate for a quarterback in 1981, sees something special in Flutie, giving the fifth string freshman his chance against Penn State.

JACK BICKNELL: I learned early in his career just let him go because you trust in his athletic instinct and more often than not, you're going to be happy.

Flutie, with his optimism and unconventional, spontaneous style, becomes the lightning rod helping the Eagles soar, a victory drive for a program that hadn't seen any glory for more than forty years. The Flutie factor fills stadiums, draws national television coverage, and by September 1983 he's on the cover of *Sports Illustrated* as the "Little Big Man ... Boston College's Amazing Quarterback," then the Liberty Bowl's MVP, and a Heisman trophy finalist.

DOUG: It was an outstanding season for us. Something we'll treasure for the rest of our lives. And a win over Alabama was unbelievable.

All signs of things to come and more, on what would be their magic carpet ride of 1984. Up next on *One on One*, a pass that's seared into the memories of college football fans, and Doug Flutie's risky and resilient rise in the pros on both sides of the border ....

In 1984, Doug Flutie shatters all-time college offensive records. He plays with his kid brother Darren and is on track for the Heisman trophy, honoring the year's best college football player.

DOUG: We'll wait [it] out, see what happens and I'll keep playing as hard as I can.

Soft spoken and poised, the Computer Science and Speech Communications major is comfortable with the media documenting his and the Eagles' journey toward the New Year's Day Cotton Bowl. Their final game against the University of Miami is meaningless. Or so it seems.

DOUG: November 23rd, 1984.

The day after Thanksgiving on national TV, a high scoring battle to the end.

DOUG: It's amazing on a single play how many decisions you make.

With just six seconds left on the clock ...

DOUG: Should I roll out or should I step up inside ...

ANNOUNCER: *Flutie, rolls back, looks, takes a peak, scrambles, looks to Phelan, did he get it? He did it! He did it. Flutie did it. He got Phelan in the end zone! Touchdown! Touchdown!*

That was the clincher. Flutie is named the fiftieth Heisman Trophy winner and graduates as the NCAA's all-time passing yardage leader.

DOUG: So many dramatic finishes, the entire career. The way things have gone, the undersized guy making it in a big man's game.

But making it in the big man's game on the pro level would be tough because he simply didn't measure up to conventional wisdom in the NFL, that a quarterback had to stand at least 6'2".

DOUG: It's always been a size thing and it's a big variable, and it scares a lot of people.

Projected to be a late-round draft pick, maybe, Flutie, newly married to Laurie, opts to sign with the USFL's New Jersey Generals.

DOUG: I played one year, I earned three year's worth of money.

He's a late round draft pick by the LA Rams, traded to the Chicago Bears, then to New England where his wins and charisma once again captivate fans. But after the '89 season, the Patriots decide he's not their starter. His attitude after being released?

DOUG: The heck with you guys. You know. That's honestly what it was. I'm gonna enjoy myself and play football.

Flutie heads north to the Canadian Football League's British Columbia Lions where he teams with brother Darren, who had previously played with the Chargers. At the time, Mike Riley was coaching the rival Winnipeg Blue Bombers.

MIKE RILEY: I remember our defensive coordinator saying to me, "This is a match made in heaven: Doug Flutie and the Canadian Football League." And it turned out to be legendary.

Legendary indeed. Flutie's second year he's the league's Most Outstanding Player, repeating that with Calgary while leading the Stampeders to a Grey Cup.

DOUG: Our Grey Cup 60,000-70,000 people. You know, it's packed. It's big time. It's the Super Bowl of Canada.

A genuine star, he realizes just how much he was not on the NFL's radar when a scout asked him who he'd recommend as a potential NFL offensive player …

DOUG: I'm like, well, I just won five MVPs in a row. No, I can't think of anybody.

He'd go on to lead the Toronto Argonauts to two consecutive Grey Cup championships. Then on the verge of signing a million dollar a year deal with Toronto, the Buffalo Bills offer him a lot less, about $200,000, but a chance.

DOUG: I was promised an opportunity to compete for the starting job. And that's what I thought I was getting into.

JANE: It wasn't exactly that …

DOUG: But then I get there.

Two weeks later, the Bills acquire the young Rob Johnson.

DOUG: The fact that they gave him eight million up front and they gave me 25,000 up front. He was the starter. And I knew that. And we get to the first mini-camp and it was, Rob would take eight plays, I would take one. Rob would take eight plays. But I did realize that they wanted me as the number two. And that was a good situation. I thought it was great.

John Butler was the Bills General Manager.

JOHN BUTLER: It's very difficult when you've got two people who want to lead the team and are highly competitive. No one wants to be the second guy. It was a tough situation.

Chargers defensive end Marcellus Wiley was Flutie's teammate then.

MARCELLUS WILEY: He just sat there and worked diligently behind the scenes and just showed his character. It was great to see that somebody who had been counted out of the NFL for so many years finally got their chance and they shined with their opportunity.

Often filling in for an injured Rob Johnson, Flutie becomes the NFL's Comeback Player of the Year, goes to the Pro-Bowl, and sets the team record and leads the NFL with rushing yards. And in 2000, wins four out of his five starts.

DOUG: I played my best football that season.

Still, the Bills choose Johnson over Flutie, just as Butler moves west to resuscitate the Chargers from their quarterback quagmire.

JOHN BUTLER: I wanted someone who was a proven winner. A guy who had won in the National Football League. Doug Flutie became available. The minute he did, I wanted to have him here.

DOUG: For the first time I feel like I'm going to be the guy and have an opportunity to take a team as far as we can go.

Even with a six-year, thirty-million-dollar deal, he doesn't rest on his laurels knowing the young quarterback Drew Brees would be in mini-camp.

DOUG: I knew I had to come in and play well, or I gotta compete, I gotta play, and I've gotta get it done, and I've gotta get it done right away.

He's had his work cut out for him with a new style under Offensive Coordinator Norv Turner.

NORV TURNER: Spends a lot of time in training camp getting the terminology and the nuances of the offense. That is the thing that has been most impressive.

MIKE RILEY (Chargers Head Coach 2001): He's the guy who stays out after practice and is running laps in training camp. For this team, it was really important that work ethic showed in the leadership part of his spot on the team.

Veterans respect him.

> **JUNIOR SEAU:** You don't put a tape to his head to his toe to see how tall he is. He has something that is just special. It's an intangible and it's called being a winner.

Young players have been in awe.

> **TIM DWIGHT:** Ever since I was a kid you see the Miami game growing up and you see this guy make a spectacular throw.

Of the Flutie aura.

> **LADAINIAN TOMLINSON:** You didn't really believe until you see it with your own eyes and the things that I have seen this season are unbelievable and I believe it.

Doug Flutie helped the Chargers quickly erase the stigma of their 1-15 2000 season, giving their fans something to cheer; cheering to the hilt during the showdown with Flutie's immediate past, the Buffalo Bills and quarterback Rob Johnson in San Diego. In a game many projected as "personal," Flutie, the consummate pro, just plays to win. While the quick and agile Doug Flutie is known for avoiding sacks and thereby concussions …

> **DOUG:** You just can't control things like that.

And rarely throws interceptions …

> **DOUG:** Hey, if I have the chance, I'll throw a fifth interception trying to win.

They happen.

> **DOUG:** You just move on. You put it behind you. You move forward.

A leader in victory and defeat.

> **DREW BREES:** Doesn't have to say anything. You just watch him and you see what's made him such a great player for such a long time.

Up next on *One on One*, Doug Flutie off the gridiron, his family, music, and mission helping others because of a personal heartbreak ….

There's a lot to be said for a guy who attracts loyal fans, no matter what jersey he's wearing …

> **BILLS FAN:** He just made us all feel good. And he was just a trooper.
> **JANE:** You're wearing a split jersey.
> **FAN:** Because we're loyal to Flutie. Tell him that when you see him, okay!

Even some willing to drive twenty-four hours from Calgary to see him play.

> **CANADA FAN:** He takes good care of Canada and he talks well about us. That's why we love him so much.

As for making a first impression on San Diego?

> **FAN:** I think he adopted this city, as we adopted him.

Jumping right in to the public scene …

> TONY GWYNN: Mr. Flutie, sir, pleasure to meet you. Welcome to San Diego.
> DOUG: Thank you.

Batting practice with the Padres, and supporting the new San Diego spirit.

> TV ANNOUNCER: *There's Chargers quarterback, Doug Flutie, enjoying a little soccer tonight.*
>
> DOUG [*signing autographs*]: *Thanks a lot. You're welcome. Have a good practice. Appreciate it …*
>
> FAN: He handles himself nicely so that people here are falling in love with him as a person.

Down to earth, a family man. Doug and Laurie's first child, Alexa was born when he was with the Patriots.

> DOUG: The whole first couple of weeks I would get up in the middle of the night for the feedings and I loved it.

Doug, Jr. came along three years later.

> DOUG: I'm thinking, *You know he's my boy. He's my boy.*
>
> [*Home video: Where's your belly?*] [*points to belly*]
>
> LAURIE: He walked at eleven months old, started talking, um, mommy, daddy, then started talking in full sentences.
>
> [*Home video: How old's Dougie? Two, two! Happy birthday to you! Yeah!*]
>
> DOUG: When he was two he was hitting a baseball off a tee. He was shooting his Little Tike's hoop in his room. He wouldn't miss. Every football player that came on TV was Daddy.
> LAURIE: It didn't seem like there was anything wrong with him at all.
> DOUG: And at two and a half, he just. It just slowed down.
> LAURIE: Over a six-month period he got from talking in full sentences and playing to not saying a word, kind of off in his own corner by himself.
> DOUG: He withdrew, went into his own little shell. And that was hard.
> LAURIE: Where did he go? Where did Dougie go? And it was very frustrating.

Seeking answers, Laurie showed doctors home videos of how he had been developing. And while tests ruled out a hearing problem, a brain tumor, or a chemical imbalance …

> LAURIE: There was no answer for why this happened to him.

Diagnosed with a form of autism, a neurological disorder affecting communication and social skills, the cause, unknown.

> JANE: Did you feel like you couldn't control this?
> DOUG: Totally out of, yeah. Out of my hands.

Clockwise: On my hometown beach at two years old; my sister Robyn, and my brothers, Scott and Jerry, before I was born; Mom capturing my voice on a tape recorder; early evidence of my interest in performing; Mom and Dad's wedding day November 2, 1946.

This page, clockwise: Mom in her element–
teaching second grade; at 14 in a body cast
after back surgery, with my sister and father;
with Robyn after she was named 1st runner-up
in the Miss Coronado Pageant; my mom
and me at a parade in 1980; Dad in
his element– fishing in New Zealand.
Facing page: Dad's retirement,
NAS North Island, 1970.

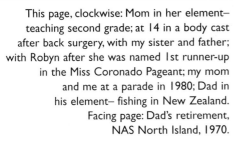

Clockwise: Illustrations from my three school children's books featuring Herman the Hermit Crab, Danny the Dog, and Earl the Pearl & Olly the Oyster; with by brothers' kids Tyler, Elizabeth, and Jeremy; Mom and me on an annual vacation after Dad died; in Europe with a Rock of Gibraltar monkey; with my sister's children Spencer, Ryan and Katharyn.

Clockwise: My favorite picture with Dad taken in grad school; my loving parents during my father's illness; a casual family portrait; the Wally's Walkers team at the annual Walk to Defeat ALS including my youngest nephew, Morgan, in front.

This page, clockwise: with childhood friends Pam Johnson Thomas and Anne Watson Stockdale; visiting my TV "guide" Tammy Payne in Oklahoma; a gathering of creative and talented friends collaborating on the book launch and charity fundraiser, left to right, (back row) Tom Courtney, Elena Haley, Bob Teaff, Kim Beales, Lisa Akoury-Ross, (middle row) Melissa Jacobs, Denise Grimsley, Peggy Halpin, Cathy Brown, Rachel Gershwin, Karen Falstrup, Mom, (me), Mark Mrowka; (front row) Amanda McPhail, Candace Edwards, Angela LaChica, Penny King, James Overstreet. Facing page, clockwise: with Kelly Morris Buh; Claude-Alix Bertrand; Jay DeDapper and his dog Orange; my sister, Mom and me at my "Evening of Eclectic Energy" soirée; with Kathleen Rexrode Durkee. I'm grateful to my "Dream Team" for encouraging me along my journey.

Clockwise: Memorable moments from the evolution of Channel 4 San Diego: 1997 with Dan Novak and Nick Davis in Atlanta; celebrating after the Padres win the West in 1998; our second Channel 4 Super Bowl in 2003 with Dennis Morgigno, John Weisbarth, Jack Gates, Argy Stathopulos and Corrie Vaus; on the road in Boston with announcers Matt Vasgersian and Mark Grant in 2004; Ed Barnes and Bob Scanlan join our team; with Craig Nichols, who gave me the go ahead to use *One on One* archives for my book; after the pre-game show at Qualcomm Stadium with the crew David Robertson, Sheila Simpson and John Bruno, 2002.

Clockwise: We love baseball: Spring Training in Peoria, Arizona with Dan Roper, Jason Bott and Roel Robles; Cooperstown with my *One on One* partner Dan; with my Executive Producer Abbie Smith; enjoying the Padres Division title victory in 2005; a great "Four"some Bill Geppert, Dennis, Dan and Richard Taylor; with colleagues Bernie Wilson, Tim Flannery and Jim Laslavic at batting practice; Opening Day of the new PETCO Park with our late photographer and friend, on left, Tod Lilburn, Michael Saks, Michael Spaulding and Kelly Morris.

This page, clockwise: An unexpected career highlight is when Kermit the Frog joined Dennis Morgigno and me on the TV set of the Holiday Bowl/Big Bay Balloon Parade December 2008; Padres announcers Mark Grant and Mark Neely 2010; a star intern turned Associate Producer Michelle Mattox; and the Channel 4 gang down at the ballpark; and having fun at the office. Facing page, clockwise: My *One on One* experiences with Drew and Brittany Brees, LaTorsha and LaDainian Tomlinson after our second edition in 2005; Trevor Hoffman showing his baseball collection at home; "The Colonel" Jerry Coleman; with hometown favorite Adrian Gonzalez and his wife Betsy.

Clockwise: Just another day at the office interviewing fascinating sports figures including: David Wells; Khalil Greene; broadcasting legend Dick Enberg; and at a STAR/PAL community fundraiser with the Famous San Diego Chicken.

Clockwise: I often have the opportunity to have legends reflect on their colleagues such as Troy Aikman talking about Norv Turner, and Steve Garvey about Tony Gwynn. Also pictured from their *One on One* shoots: rising stars Anthony Gwynn, Jr. and his wife Alyse; and rookie favorite Kevin Kouzmanoff.

Clockwise: An eclectic collection of interviews: Singer-songwriter Steve Poltz; San Diego natives and Chargers standouts, Donnie Edwards; and Junior Seau; and Michelle and me with the 2009 Little League World Series Champions from Park View.

Clockwise: Hall of Famer George Brett in Cooperstown; learning to shoot with Ryan Klesko in Georgia; Hall of Fame Manager Sparky Anderson who commented on Alan Trammell, 2000, and Tony Gwynn, 2007; Hall of Famer Phil Niekro at Dave Winfield's induction 2001; bowling with Antonio Gates his second year in the NFL; and the exceptional day with Ted Williams holding his bat from his .406 season.

From top: The incomparable Tony Gwynn during Induction Weekend in Cooperstown 2007; cruising in a Bentley with the smooth and fun linebacker Shaun Phillips; and a surprise soaking on the field during a live-shot by pitcher Adam Eaton after the 2005 West Division victory.

LAURIE: But then, you get to a point where you have to kinda kick yourself and say, "All right, now. What do we do about it? What do we do to make Dougie the best he can be?"

With love and financial means, they have helped Dougie with special schools and special tools.

LAURIE: But I feel every child deserves to have a bicycle or deserves to have what they need to progress.

Their genuine compassion inspired the Doug Flutie Junior Foundation for Autism in 1998.

DOUG: It's about finding solutions, helping other families, because we know what they're going to have to go through.

Every child, a different story.

DOUG: In general, autistic children don't like to be touched. He loves to be held. He loves to cuddle. He wants to sit with you on the couch.

While their Natick house is still their off-season home base, they're enjoying San Diego …

[Family at an amusement park …]

And don't hesitate to take Dougie anywhere.

LAURIE: Let people know what autism is about, then maybe the parents of an autistic child will feel more relaxed and will be able to do some of those things that you should be able to do with your children.

ALEXA: I see people waiting in line and they're like in wheelchairs and stuff. So I always used to look at them funny, and now I don't look at them like that anymore.

The Fluties, of Catholic faith, believe Alexa will make her mark perhaps on stage, and Dougie's calling in life? The foundation.

LAURIE: And I honestly feel that he is Doug's son because of who Doug is. And through Doug's celebrity status, we are able to do what we can do for the foundation.

Financial aid, education, a future research center …

DOUG: And someday maybe the cure for autism can be in his name.

The foundation, started with half of Flutie's Buffalo signing bonus of just $12,000, has raised three million dollars in three years from his annual Road Race and basketball tournament in the Northeast, with sales of Flutie Flakes, and then teaming up with MCI.

DOUG: Remember that childhood drum set that sat idle?

Practicing on a new one relieves stress and keeps him sharp for Flutie Gang fundraising gigs with current CFL super star, his brother Darren, and an occasional jam in with rockers Lynard Skynard and Bon Jovi. While Doug is in the spotlight, Doug and Laurie beam with pride for their children's achievements.

LAURIE: "Say hi to Nana." And he went, "Hi nananana." I started to cry because that's huge for him.

DOUG: But did I not tell you about my daughter, played on the A travel team and scored goals and they went undefeated three years in a row, you know?

Kind, competitive, a kid at heart, he's well aware of his age. Thirty-nine is past the end of the line for many in his business.

DOUG: I'll play until I drop.

LAURIE: He will.

He's come a long way from that amazing Hail Mary pass …

DOUG: If I didn't play another down of football, there would be something I would be remembered for. That was pretty satisfying at that time. But now, I've got a lot of other memories that are just as important to me.

All of them, no doubt, made sweeter by the memory of those who said he'd never make it.

Doug Flutie wrote a book for kids about his journey. How because of his size, he'd been teased by teammates and mocked by the media. He's not perfect, but he did make it, and is making an impact. The name of his book? *Never Say Never.* I'm Jane Mitchell, thank you for watching *One on One.*

MARK KOTSAY

oward the end of the baseball season, I look ahead to the next season and anticipate who might be good to profile for *One on One.* In March 2001, Mark Kotsay was part of a trade that brought him to San Diego and sent Eric Owens to the Florida Marlins. Eric was a Padres fan cult-favorite for his plays that left him with a dirty uniform and the frequent need for bandages. In 2000, I produced a *One on One* about Eric. With this trade, Mark Kotsay was aware of whom he replaced, and in a sense, felt he had to prove to fans why they should be okay with his being a Padre. Mark did that by just being himself and having enough dazzle and sizzle to keep people's attention, even in between some injuries.

Mark seemed to be unassuming and a "good guy" with Southern California roots, a good fit for the show. Toward the end of his first season with San Diego, he agreed to be featured. He and his wife, Jamie, would be at their new home in Reno, Nevada where Jamie is from, and we were invited to visit them there. After justifying why this would be worth the trip, I received the okay to travel, and Dan Roper and I flew to Reno with our gear for a three-day shoot in January 2002.

We arrived at their large ranch home in the afternoon. It was situated on a big lot with no fences between the houses in a new development. Their view overlooked the valley. It was quiet, cold, and clear. Dan taped some outdoor shots while it was still light. Mark and Jamie welcomed us inside. Jamie, tall, thin, and blonde was stunning, as you might expect of a model, and so down to earth. I was impressed. Their home was contemporary and casual. Their family room displayed a collection of special baseball and sports memorabilia, including a jersey signed by Tony Gwynn.

We did the interview that evening because we had a limited window to get everything done. Dan set up one camera and lights, and Mark and I settled into the sofas. From the very beginning, I sensed he was special and sweet. I just didn't know how he came to be that way until the interview. You will understand, too, as you read his story. What you won't hear while reading the script is how his voice cracked and his eyes welled up when he talked about his childhood, his parents, about feeling like a "gift," and how his father kissed him on the cheek at night. Mark was honest and vulnerable. After being a little choked up, he laughed, saying he didn't expect to get so emotional, but that's just who he is. Later, when I interviewed Mark and Jamie together, it was obvious they had true love for each other.

I was drained, but in a good way, after our more than an hour-long interview. It was emotional and real. By just talking and asking those simple questions of "why," it was like a faucet waiting to be turned on. Mark Kotsay had battled being an underdog his whole career. This was an opportunity to see who he was as a person and how that translated to his profession. I had a good feeling. Fans were going to appreciate this show.

We had more to check off the list. The next day we drove to a snowmobiling spot at Lake Tahoe and had fun shooting us riding through the snow. It's always challenging to be on a moving vehicle with a fifty-pound video camera, but Dan did it. It was a spectacular day with the sun shining on the fresh snow. We went to his mother-in-law's home for a family birthday celebration and to interview her. The next day, we encountered some threatening weather as we drove through the

Donner Pass to his father-in-law's home. He had horses, and because Jamie was also a cowgirl, it was worth the trip to see Mark in her world and on a horse.

Later, from San Diego we drove north to Mark's parents' home in Santa Fe Springs to interview them and see where he grew up in a small, modest home near the freeway. This was the house where he told me he would go to bed wondering if his father, a Los Angeles police officer, would come home each night. The significance of that story came full circle for me as a writer, by being there, meeting his parents, and seeing the house and all his childhood trophies and pictures.

After 2003, Mark Kotsay was traded to Oakland and has since played with the Atlanta Braves, the Boston Red Sox, the Chicago White Sox , and the Milwaukee Brewers. He and Jamie are now parents, and it was nice to hear Jamie express in a recent email, "We had such an awesome experience with you." His show is one of my favorites and replays as a *One on One Classic*.

This is the script from the edition debuting April 23, 2002.

• • •

Mark Kotsay. From motocross to the majors and marriage to a model, he's on the rise with a boost from hitting great Tony Gwynn.

> **MARK:** Hopefully, I can live up to his expectations and I don't think he has expectations. He just has a belief in me.

Trades in baseball are a funny thing. Sometimes they frustrate fans or they fizzle, other times they live up to or exceed expectations. In the case of Mark Kotsay, his second year as a Padre is revealing why many feel his trade was in fact a steal. With no time for an ego, his is a compelling story because of the reason he embraces life and the game. Not for fame, but as a gift.

Mark Kotsay: calm, cool, collected, and very effective. He's the guy who can change the course of a game because of the strength and accuracy of his arm.

> **KEVIN TOWERS:** Kotsay is a bonafide Gold Glove-type defensive center-fielder.

He evokes the ultimate compliment in this game.

> **BRUCE BOCHY:** Solid all around player. He's a ballplayer.
>
> **TIM FLANNERY:** Mark Kotsay, he's a baseball player.
>
> **TREVOR HOFFMAN:** He's always instinctive. He's always one step ahead of his competition.
>
> **PHIL NEVIN:** His baseball skills and his baseball mind are incredible.

Just days before the 2001 season, Kotsay is acquired in a trade sending fan favorite Eric Owens to the Florida Marlins.

> **MARK:** I wanted to show people that hey, you know, this trade is gonna be all right. You know, you lost Eric Owens, but at the same time, you know, I think you might have gained something.
>
> *[Opening Day 2001 Introductions … "Mark Kotsay!"]*

With barely a chance to convince a doubting Thomas, he pulls a quad muscle and is placed on the disabled list.

> MARK: It was frustrating at the time. But fortunately enough for me, being selfish …

Two days later Tony Gwynn, one of the greatest hitters ever, goes on the DL as well.

> MARK: "Hey, Tony, you think you could work with me? You know, break down my swing, now that we have a little time?" We talked pitching, and we talked counts, and we talked situations, and we talked about everything there was and there is to do with a bat. And I think that was really helpful for me.

While Number 14 is sidelined much of his first April as a Padre, and again in September with a hand injury, those months in between …

> MARK: The hits started coming, and the stolen bases and the catches and the throws.

That energy, that potential, that passion evident from the beginning, born Mark Steven Kotsay, December 2, 1975 in Whittier, California.

> MARK: From the age of three when I jumped on a bike and my neighbor took my training wheels off and I rode around the circle by my house. Four years old, out in the front yard playing catch with seven- and eight-year-olds.

And at five, jumped on a bike competing in BMX races, a national champion for his age group at six years old.

> PAM (his mother): He'd come ask me if he could play basketball and I'd say, "Aren't you kind of little?" And he said, "No, come watch me shoot baskets at the park." And I went and he was doing it just like the big guys.

His parents, Pam and Steve, still live in the house next to that park where he grew up with his sister, in a predominantly Hispanic neighborhood in Santa Fe Springs, an industrial area on the edge of East Los Angeles.

> MARK: The gang influence is there. It's not a tough neighborhood, unless you get into the wrong group.

His group played sports.

> MARK: As a kid, it was sports and nothing else.

Kotsay's father, a motorcycle officer with the L.A.P.D., made certain of that.

> STEVE (his father): I saw so much in the streets of how bad kids were, you know, so I wanted him to … I expected a lot out of him and I pushed him a little you know. Maybe I pushed him too hard. I don't know.

> MARK: He just wanted the best for me. And his way of knowing how to do that was pushing me.

And participating as a coach. And his mother, a team mom, worked her at-home beautician's business around Mark's activities. But as much as the young Kotsay lived for sports, he quietly lived with fear wondering if his dad would make it home at night.

> **STEVE:** I lost some partners. I buried some partners you know, different things on the job, accidents, shootings.

So to ease his son's mind …

> **MARK:** He'd swing the door open at 2:30-3:00 in the morning, when he worked nights. Frozen, ice cold, and he'd put his hand on me and you know, to let me know he was home. And I'd hear him and he'd bend down and give me a kiss. And those are good memories of him.

As for childhood memories of his mother?

> **MARK:** She always had a smile, and her face is the warmest face you could imagine.

There is another reason Mark feels especially close to his parents.

> **MARK:** In my mind and in my heart I feel that I'm here because it's a miracle. You know, my parents had a, I would have a brother. They had a baby before me. And he passed away, six days old, of heart complications. My parents—it was the toughest thing for them, and they worked their differences out and here I am, you know. I feel like I'm a gift from God.

So even as a child, he seemed to understand why he should make the most out of life and the most out of his games—football, basketball, baseball—by all accounts with a great attitude, acceptance, yet determination.

> **MARK:** God didn't bless me with the best body. And I don't have the greatest of speed. You know, I'm not the fastest one on the field. I don't have the strongest arm. But I make up for it in little ways. And those ways that I've learned have helped me to be the baseball player that I am.

He sensed his potential. His father did too. But while a solid player, a pitcher and a slugger at Santa Fe High School, no scouts showed any interest in him. Even the coach at a Stanford baseball camp gave a discouraging written assessment.

> **MARK:** And I remember vividly on the bottom of it says, "Not big enough for Division I baseball, might need to go to junior college and play." And I kept that. I used that as a motivational tool too because all the odds were against me. And I thought I was good enough and I never stopped believing that.

After Kotsay's league team went to the Mickey Mantle World Series and the Junior Olympics, his coach had a hunch and recommended Kotsay to a contact at Cal State Fullerton. Brought there to pitch, he made an impression on his coaches.

> **MARK VANDERHOOK** (coach): Mark is a confident person.

Confident he'd make the team as a freshman. Then spring arrived …

> **MARK:** And I didn't really do very well. And I found myself on the bench. And it was the first time in my life I had ever been on the bench. I remember staying after practices and staying at night and hitting and doing extra work. Just trying everything I could to get myself on that field.

Finally, fifteen games into the season Kotsay gets his chance.

> **RICK** (coach): He got a start in right field against UCLA and a guy hit a fly ball down the right field line, and he caught the ball and threw it to third base, and it was like, wow! Where did that come from?
>
> **MARK:** It was kind of a defining moment and the coach ended up putting me in there the next day. I think I hit a home run and had another great game. And from then on my college career started and I just ran with it. And I never stopped working because I knew that there might be another freshman sitting on the bench that comes in one year that could take my job and I didn't want that to happen....

In theory, Mark Kotsay's stature as a freshman—just 6', 180 pounds—shouldn't have allowed him to do what he did, batting a team high .372 and slugging a grand slam as the Titans finished tied for third in his first College World Series. The question at the time was would this freshman sensation last?

In 1995, the sophomore jinx never materialized as Kotsay starred in the College World Series championship game against rival USC.

> **RICK** (coach): It was an amazing—as amazing thing as I've ever seen. He pitched, he hit, he hit home runs. He did everything that was imaginable.

Coming in as the closer the final two innings ...

> **MARK:** I remember standing on the mound and my legs were shaking. You know, I just couldn't control the emotion. Throwing the last pitch, and seeing it hit to the left, I think I had my glove off before it was caught and I was up in the air with my catcher. And the next thing I know, I'm on my back and I can't breathe, because I've got twenty-five, thirty guys on top of me and I was screaming, get 'em off, get 'em off! A dream come true to do something like that.

The series MVP, Kotsay becomes the most productive hitter in College World Series history, honored with the Golden Spikes award, the college baseball equivalent of college football's Heisman Trophy.

> **MARK:** It's an individual award, but it couldn't be done without your teammates and the collective group of guys you have around you.

Launched into the national spotlight, he's ranked 7th on Baseball America's Top 100 College Prospects in the spring of '96. That June, the Florida Marlins draft him high in the first round, the ninth pick overall.

> **MARK:** I didn't say, "When do the Olympics end?" It was like, you know, "When can I go?"

An anxious Kotsay would have to wait a few weeks because as a member of Team USA, he's playing in the Olympic games in Atlanta, first round against Cuba.

> **MARK:** And there's 56,000 people screaming and you couldn't hear. I remember taking my first at bat and trying to take deep breaths, but I just couldn't slow down.

They'd lose the chance to play for the Gold, but beat Nicaragua for the Bronze.

> **MARK:** And standing on the podium and getting that medal put around your neck is pretty special.

From the podium to the pros, Kotsay spends just a few weeks at Kane County, Florida before going to Winter League in Hawaii and then as a non-roster invitee to big league camp spring training 1997.

> **MARK:** Bobby Bonilla was in the locker room. Gary Sheffield was in the locker room. Jeff Conine was in the locker room. Kevin Brown was in the locker room. Robby Nenn was in the locker room. All the guys I grew up watching thinking, *Wow, these are the real deal.*

Kotsay's good showing lands him in Double-A in Portland, Maine, an All-Star his first year. As the fledgling Florida Marlins make their way toward a winning season, on a mid-July day, Kotsay argues with an umpire in a close game that his Sea Dogs lost.

> **MARK:** I argue with the umpire, you know, I figure I'm in trouble.

Instead, his manager asks him if he's okay physically.

> **MARK:** Yeah, I'm fine. He goes, "You think you're ready?" I go, "Ready for what?" He goes, "You're going to the big leagues tomorrow. You're starting centerfield." And uh, I remember my eyes got full of tears and I just was like, "No way, this is incredible." So I sat down in his office and I called my dad and I just started to cry. I mean—I'm *not* gonna cry—but it was a great moment and my mom and dad jumped on a red eye flew all night, showed up. And it was a great day. [Teary eyed]

Getting to Miami for Mark Kotsay, however, is another matter. 5:00 a.m. in Akron, Ohio, he jumps in a cab for the airport …

> **MARK:** Boom. Flat tire. I said, "No way."

No spare tire. Cab number two.

> **MARK:** I'm sweating. I'm like, *Oh, I can't miss my flight. I'm going to the big leagues. I can't miss my flight.*

Gets to the airport, but no ticket is waiting for him.

> **MARK:** I said, "Get whoever you have to get here. I'm going to the big leagues today. Get me there. I've got to get to Miami." They put me on a plane without a ticket. In the back of a little twin propeller, flew me to Pittsburgh. I got to Pittsburgh and they had a ticket for me in Pittsburgh.

The frantic trip finally turns surreal in an empty Marlins clubhouse that afternoon.

> **MARK:** And in walks Leland. He goes, "What are you doing here?" It's 12:30 or 1:00. I said, "I'm ready." He goes, "You're facing Curt Schilling." And I go, "Who?" "Curt Schilling and you're batting third."

Kotsay would spend twenty-one days on the big league roster before returning to the minors, eventually receiving a ring for his part of the Marlins' World Championship season.

With the Marlins' stunning fire sale of high priced veterans that winter, young, cool Kotsay wins the starting job in centerfield in 1998, later shifting to right.

[Game action—defense]

He proves to be one of the premier rookies in the National League and for the next three seasons, even when the Marlins had miserable records, Kotsay turns heads, leads the National League in outfield assists, a statistic that isn't as glamorous as home runs, but is certainly significant.

> MARK: When you throw somebody out from the outfield, not only are you getting an out, you're eliminating a possible run. And if you're throwing someone out at home, you do eliminate a run and you do turn the game around.

Padres third base coach, Tim Flannery, can attest to that.

> TIM FLANNERY: He was, in my opinion, the most feared, anytime I sent a runner, because he was the guy that threw most of them out.

Fellow Cal State Fullerton and Golden Spikes winner Phil Nevin fell victim to Kotsay's accuracy.

> PHIL NEVIN: Oh, I remember! It was a fly ball to right and he threw me out at third base. It was going to take a perfect throw to get me, and usually he makes a perfect throw, and he did.

By spring 2001, the Marlins need pitching and Padres General Manager Kevin Towers wants what he calls a true centerfielder.

> KEVIN TOWERS: We saw how important Steve Finley was to us in '96, '97, '98 and I think Kotsay could become that kind of player.

> PHIL NEVIN: When Kevin asked me about it, I said, "I'll tell you what, you give up whatever you can to get Kots. He's just that kind of a special player that's just going to keep getting better and better."

As part of a five-player deal, outfielder Eric Owens and home grown pitcher Matt Clement go to Florida. Mark Kotsay and his new bride Jamie leave their new home under construction for San Diego on the cusp of the season with high hopes. But in an exhibition game at Lake Elsinore the next day …

> MARK: My first hit was a double into right center. And I took off out of the box and no more than halfway down the line I felt my quad kind of pull a little bit and tighten up.

He'd play through it a few weeks before going on the disabled list—his first time ever—coming back in May, with sizzle and hitting streaks. Wanting to end the year strong in September, a sprained right hand, ironically hurt in Florida, limits his playing time.

> MARK: Now I've got to start all over again.

Considering what the nation was experiencing after September 11, he keeps things in perspective, using his off season to heal and get ready, greeting 2002 with optimism.

MARK: Have a successful season and be out there over 150 games.

Coming up on *One on One*, at home with the Kotsays who blend high fashioned action with old fashioned values . . . .

Mark Kotsay is as rough and ready as they come on the field, but it's his other qualities that his wife Jamie appreciates most.

JAMIE: He's one of the most sensitive and loving individuals. He really is. He's just so sincere. And you look into his eyes and you can just see his soul.

JANE: Tell me about meeting Jamie ...

MARK: Best day of my life.

Jamie Scott was modeling in Miami in the fall of '98 when a mutual friend planned for them to meet at a party. They'd meet again at a Super Bowl party.

JAMIE: It wasn't that I didn't like him, it was just I was dating someone else.

A year later, when she was free, Jamie called Mark.

MARK: I remember vividly. She came in a black dress at a club called "The Bar Room" in Miami. And I was with a friend, Louie, and I told him, I said, "Hey, there she is." And he said, "No way dude." Exact words, "No way dude." And I said, "That's her." And he said, "If she comes over here I'm leaving." I said, "You can't leave," so Jamie walked over and we talked all night.

JAMIE: From that day, you know, it was just the right person. And you feel that, you know. And we knew.

They'd come to know more about each other and their professional worlds, baseball and modeling.

JAMIE: It's actually very compatible 'cause it's someone that understands the traveling, that understands the being on the road and having to pick up and go like that.

Jamie grew up in Carson City, Nevada. Her parents, Jim, a builder, and Sheila, an insurance agent, divorced when Jamie was seven. But both were involved in her life: sports and cheerleading. A natural beauty, modeling didn't even occur to her.

JAMIE: I just wanted to go to school and you know, a normal life.

At sixteen, that changed when her younger sister Jenna pushed her to try out at a model search convention.

JAMIE: I was tall and lanky, just really tall and really skinny and just kind of goofy. And I said, "No, I can't go to this." And she said, "If you don't do it, you'll never know."

Teen Magazine was her first shoot. Then she modeled in Italy, graduated high school, and moved to New York City.

From American to European fashion, provocative, earthy, and romantic styles—even on magazine covers as a bride to be—the camera has captured her versatile look. Her confidence and independent thinking have helped keep her grounded.

JAMIE: Either you can be a model, or modeling is your job. So they are two different things and modeling has always been my job. It's not who I am. And it's emotional and it's very competitive, very competitive.

Mark and Jamie would discover not only what they had in common, but what they could have together. And on a Marlins road trip to Denver in the summer of 2000, on their way back to the hotel …

MARK: … a homeless girl approached us and I put some money in her hand. And I said, "Jamie, isn't it awesome how fortunate and how blessed we are? You know, we have this life and we can do pretty much what we want." And uh, I took a couple more steps and I looked—I turned and looked and I said, "Hey," I said, "We got this trip planned in December or October. We're going to be in Hawaii. Will you marry me in Hawaii? I have no ring. I don't know how to do this in any other way but to ask you, will you marry me?" And she said yes.

So after just ten months of dating, their families gathered in Kauai for a barefoot beachfront wedding deepened by their faith.

MARK: We have God in our lives and we pray together before we go to bed. And they say a family that prays together stays together.

And together they make a good team.

[Working out at gym]

Keeping their bodies in shape is important for both their careers …

MARK: Mentally she's probably one of the strongest people you can be around. 'Cause she'll just do it.

JAMIE: He hates coming here, but once he's here, he's great.

With their workout done, it's time for some real fun …

[Snowmobiling …]

We went along on their first snowmobiling experience. A caravan on the trails above Lake Tahoe …

[Riding, waving, trails]

Mark and Jamie aren't superstars, at least not yet, but their professions could create a bit of competition if their egos allowed that.

MARK: We joke and kid with one another about different things. You know, if she has a shoot with guys there's a guy staring at her like this. And I say, "Are you looking in his eyes?" And she says, "I don't look in his eyes. I don't look in his eyes, I look at his nose." But most of my fans are like fourteen years old that hold up Kotsay signs!

Not to say that Mark hasn't felt a little left out. Case in point, a 2001 national baseball magazine. Inside the front cover …

MARK: Here's my wife running on the beach with two guys side by side, full stride, smile, everything. I flip through and it doesn't even say my name! And I said, "How can you be in a baseball magazine and I'm not? This just ain't right, you know. This ain't right."

Jamie sets her own work schedule to mesh with Mark's and they spend time with their families in Southern California and Reno.

[Birthday Party: Singing happy birthday to you ...]

Her family has embraced Mark for more than his profession.

SHEILA: It's part of his life. And all the other parts are so rich and so full. He's just great.

While they take in some of the bright city night life of Reno in the winter, this city boy ...

JAMIE: He's a cowboy!

... has gone a little bit country at his father-in-law's ranch, learning to rope along with Jamie's little sisters. Bubba the horse was a Christmas present from Jamie's father.

[Roping ...]

Mark Kotsay seems to enjoy exploring new things, new people, and looks forward to the time he and Jamie will start a family of their own.

MARK: And when it comes to us, and when it's given to us, we'll be very grateful and very thankful.

In the meantime, he's involved with Padres community events and is joining Coach Rob Picciolo in the 65 Roses program, giving time and game tickets to kids with cystic fibrosis.

ROB PICCIOLO: He's just a very giving person, a very caring person.

A nice guy who appreciates the history of his game, his sports memorabilia more than just a collection. One jersey reads like this, "Mark—Keep working hard, man. You are just starting out. You're gonna really be good. Best Wishes, Tony Gwynn."

MARK: He didn't have to write something on a jersey that I'll treasure for the rest of my life ...

TONY GWYNN: Is he going to get to the point where he has enough confidence to go out and do the things he can do? I say yes.

TREVOR HOFFMAN: He has had a year to get acclimated to San Diego and knows that his teammates love him and are behind him.

KEVIN TOWERS: Very good defender, good hitter. I think he's going to be a real star.

Whether diving for balls in centerfield or diving into second with a double, Mark Kotsay is cool, confident and effective. A lifelong overachiever who hopes to help lead the Padres back to baseball's promised land. I'm Jane Mitchell. Thank you for watching *One on One*.

OZZIE SMITH

With all the planning involved in producing a program, sometimes I just get lucky. In the early summer of 2002, I learned Ozzie Smith was going to be in San Diego speaking on behalf of the San Diego Chapter of the Society for American Baseball Research, which helps libraries connect with baseball history. Ozzie had been elected to the Baseball Hall of Fame that January for induction that summer. This stop in San Diego was the perfect opportunity to interview him. To do more, namely a *One on One,* I would need at least twenty to thirty minutes with him. I talked with the library and the people managing his schedule while in San Diego and persuaded them to schedule the time I needed. We would be sure to include the main reason he was there, but I knew this was a potential show if it all went well. There were a few moments when that was a big if.

Photographer, Dan Roper, Kelly Morris, my associate producer, and I arrived at the downtown San Diego Public Library in plenty of time to set up. The room farthest away from traffic, and the quietest, was an old study with beautiful wood and basic furniture, but questionable electrical capabilities. We were in place and ready to go when Ozzie came in to sit down. I had met him briefly in New York City for Dave Winfield's induction, but this time the focus was on him. He was a perfect gentleman. Smooth. Courteous. I was a little excited. This was after all "the Wizard of AAAhhhhzzz!" because of his famously amazing feats on the field. I knew my time was limited, so I hit on the main points about his childhood, family, his memories of San Diego, life after baseball, and being elected into the Hall of Fame.

What the viewers did not see in the final show, in between his articulate, eloquent sound bites, and my writing to weave it all together, was how we lost our lights. This old building could not handle the amount of power needed for the lights and camera. Each time, I said, "Hold that thought, let's get those lights back on," Ozzie was cool, unflustered, and understanding, most likely because of his own television experience. We would never have made it had it not been for Kelly.

Kelly Morris and I connected through serendipity. She was graduating from Indiana University, moving to San Diego to be with her then boyfriend, and needed

a place to live and a job. My mother liked to help people during life transitions and would make a spare room available. Kelly visited to see if the room would work for her. After talking with Kelly, my mother called me and said, "I know you hate it when I do this, but this girl is majoring in television, and can you just say hello to her? I really think you'd like her." I obliged and set up an appointment the next day at my office. Kelly met me with a big smile, a solid handshake, an air of enthusiasm, plus a nice résumé. I knew in about five minutes that Kelly was a gem of a person and had great potential as a producer. So with an offer of the going entry-level rate of ten dollars an hour and part-time work, she had a job—if she moved to San Diego. She did by that summer and is on my top ten list of best APs. More than that, even after moving on in her career, she's a best friend.

This is how Kelly remembers my interview with Ozzie Smith:

"We were set up in that old library because he was promoting a reading program. His agent/publicist emphatically said we'd have no more than half an hour with Ozzie, so we were crunched. The interview started and about ten minutes in, the lights went out. It was my job to find the fuse box with the clock ticking. I'm sweating because The Wiz was sitting in the dark and our time is running out. I found the fuse box, flipped the switch, and we were back in business, only for the lights to go out two more times, but Ozzie took it all in stride. He was very gracious and laid back. I think he stuck around for about forty-five minutes."

While Kelly and Dan were sweating that part, I was tap dancing and conversing with Ozzie, who was calm, cordial, and patient. Even with the drama of the electrical situation, I was excited about how much content I had at my fingertips for this compelling man's story. With as much archival videotape as we had of Ozzie as a Padre, the pictures, and videotape he was going to provide us, and working with the Hall of Fame production department to get video of his induction ceremony and speech, I knew we would have plenty for a half hour show. I didn't go to Cooperstown for his induction, but a little ingenuity, resourcefulness, and a gracious guest who let me finish the interview despite the technical difficulties, resulted in a quality show that has since become a *One on One Classic,* just as Ozzie Smith is.

I see Ozzie every few years either in San Diego or in Cooperstown. One time at a Padres game at Qualcomm Stadium in San Diego, I introduced him to my mother, and he shook her hand. Later that night, we saw him walking toward us. He greeted her again, warmly, and gave her a kiss on the cheek. She says, "I guess he felt he knew me well enough by then!" She still talks about that any time I mention his name. Ozzie is a true gentleman of the game, and a man very respectful of others' professions and situations. Some might have really had an attitude about that day in the library and thought we didn't know what we were doing, but he knew it wasn't our fault, and were working within our parameters. He got it and didn't feel put out or make us feel inept. That made me all the more happy to produce a show on another quality athlete.

This is the script from the show debuting August 9, 2002.

• • •

His trademark back flips and dazzling defense combine for a calling card like no other in baseball. Along with giving back, enterprise and entertainment, Ozzie Smith bears the honor of Hall of Famer.

OZZIE: It's been kind of a fairy tale.

It is fitting that Ozzie Smith dons the St. Louis Cardinal cap in Cooperstown. But every story starts somewhere, and for Ozzie Smith his professional career started in San Diego. He is soft spoken, yet proud as he reflects on a life's journey that's led him to the highest honor in the game, being inducted into the National Baseball Hall of Fame.

July 28, 2002: an awesome day for a kid raised in South Central L.A. who was overlooked by scouts and beat the odds of his small size ...

OZZIE [HOF speech]: Getting to the Hall of Fame was not what I started out to accomplish.

A day when that young player who changed the expectation for the shortstop position on the diamond and who represented the game with honor ...

OZZIE [HOF speech]: What I started out to accomplish was to be the very best that Ozzie Smith could be with what God gave him.

... is invited into the exclusive fraternity to be among the best of the best, of the best ...

JANE FORBES CLARK [HOF ceremony]: It's my honor to welcome you, Ozzie, to the Hall of Fame family.

OZZIE [HOF speech]: One of the greatest assets that you can have is the ability to improvise. To me, turning a double play is the greatest improvisational part of what it was that I did, because I never knew exactly what I was going to do.

Smith is known throughout baseball as "The Wizard," for being arguably the best shortstop of all time. But his yellow brick road wasn't paved with gold, and really, not even with childhood expectations.

OZZIE [HOF speech]: Baseball, for me, really didn't become serious until I was a junior in high school. And when I decided to go to Cal Poly at San Luis Obispo, it was at that point that I decided that baseball was what I wanted to pursue. And I wanted to get the opportunity to get the exposure that I needed because I never got drafted out of high school.

Born Osborne Earl Smith, December 26, 1954 in Mobile, Alabama, he's the second of five children. His father Clovis worked at a furniture company, his mother Marvella, at a nursing home. They moved to the tough streets and poor neighborhood of Watts in South Central Los Angeles.

OZZIE: I don't think that that's the story. The story is—it was for me anyway—was not that I lived in those conditions, but what I was able to do with the opportunity when it presented itself.

JANE: How did you do that? What was it that kind of made you believe that you could—and should—do that?

OZZIE: Well, you just had to. You know, I had people around me all the time, starting with my mother that was always preaching the same story. The story was that you get a good education, you work hard, you put your heart into whatever it is you do.

So with a focus on school and belief in his baseball talent, he attends Cal Poly San Luis Obispo. But he wouldn't make varsity as quickly as he'd hoped, and he called his mother ready to throw in the towel.

OZZIE: She called my high school coach who called me and talked to me in no uncertain terms that that was going to be the best place for me and that I was going to stick it out. And I stayed, and about two days later I got a call. The varsity shortstop broke his ankle. And that was the entree for me to start playing with the varsity team and, from that point, I never looked back.

By 1976, Smith would finally get noticed, picked by the Detroit Tigers in the seventh round. But money—a $10,000 minimum—would matter.

OZZIE: But anything less than that, then they weren't very serious. So I asked them for $10,000 and they said they couldn't do it, so I wanted to go back to school and get as close to my degree as I possibly could, which I did my senior year. And being the good businessman that I am, the Padres drafted me in the fourth round and I signed for five thousand dollars and a bus ticket to Walla Walla, Washington!

In the minors, the switch hitter turns heads for batting, runs scored, and stolen bases, but more so for outstanding defense. And by 1978, he's already the Padres' Opening Day shortstop determined to stay in the majors.

OZZIE: I wasn't just doing this for me. I was doing it for my family because, you know, it would make life a little bit better.

His early major league motions are indeed something from the land of *Aaahs,* including one of his most memorable and spectacular of his career. In a game against Atlanta, fielding a shot off of the Braves' Jeff Burroughs …

RANDY JONES: Up the middle, he's diving for it, takes a bad hop, back over the middle of his body, he bare-hands it. That's one thing to catch it, and just stop the baseball and keep it in the infield. He jumps up and *throws him out* by a half a step and that was the unbelievable thing.

JERRY COLEMAN: You can't practice that. You have to have great instincts, great reflexes, and only an Ozzie Smith could do it.

Just one example why he comes in second for National League Rookie of the Year honors. What Smith didn't have in size—just 5'11", 150 pounds—he'd make up for in sizzle.

FAN: The guy had unbelievable range, getting to the ball and when he got there he had an arm like a rocket.

FAN: Not only was he acrobatic, but I loved watching him try to steal bases, and double plays were my favorite. He had a lot of double plays.

FAN: He had a lot of flash when he played. It was with a lot of heart and a lot of flash.

FAN: He's the most exciting player I had ever watched. That was when I wasn't a baseball fan and I used to come to the stadium to watch Ozzie.

Impressing fans *and* teammates …

TIM FLANNERY: As a young player you can get really buried up here. A lot of negative things can happen and he always said, "Focus on the one positive thing that happened during that game and take it with you." So he not only was a great player, he was a great teacher for us young players coming up.

RANDY JONES: Well, being a ground ball pitcher like I was, throwing that sinkerball, I loved Ozzie. I mean, even if somebody might muff one, if I get a ground ball to Ozzie, I get that double play. And that was the important thing to me.

Former Yankee and veteran broadcaster, Jerry Coleman, was the Padres' manager in 1980.

JERRY: And when you're a manager making up your lineup, you put A, B, C, D, and so forth, and then you hope they do well. When you put Ozzie down there, you know exactly what you are going to get every day: a brilliant fielder.

With spectacular defense, earning his first of thirteen consecutive Gold Gloves in 1980, Smith isn't really pressured to develop his offense, something he recalls he wanted to do.

OZZIE: It was always my goal to be the very best player that I could be, both offensively and defensively. I wanted to be well-rounded. You know, there were times when I asked one of the hitting instructors here, I said, "If I want to hit the ball up the middle, where should my hands be?" He says, "Don't worry about that, just aim up the middle." Well, yeah, that helped. That worked.

While Smith improved some—having a batting average of around .220—even being selected to his first of twelve straight All-Star seasons in 1981, the Padres had

343

dropped to the bottom of their division and are looking to do what they can to re-boot the team. So after the '81 season, and after the teams and Smith worked through a no-trade clause …

> OZZIE: I was very impressed when Whitey came out and visited with us three or four weeks ago.

Smith is traded to St. Louis for Garry Templeton. And while it wasn't a popular trade at the time, Templeton would be a catalyst on the 1984 Padres team that finally made it to the World Series. And in St. Louis, Ozzie would become a complete player thanks to the offensive tutelage of Manager Whitey Herzog.

> OZZIE: He said that I was going to be able to get the most out of my ability to run and stuff by keeping the ball on the ground, especially playing on Astroturf®. So we had a deal that any ground ball that I hit, he owed me a dollar; any fly ball I hit, I owed him a dollar.

Turns out, Smith would collect more than he'd pay his manager, and the challenge, along with weight training and a focus on nutrition, would pay great dividends of the World Championship kind. Ozzie Smith's success with St. Louis is next on *One on One* ….

Ozzie Smith will always be part of San Diego sports history, part of the Padres' early years which are well documented here at the Hall of Champions in Balboa Park. For Ozzie Smith, a turning point in his career came after the 1981 season while the Padres and the Cardinals were trying to work out the controversial trade for Garry Templeton. Twenty-one years later, at a news conference just after he's elected into the Hall of Fame, he makes the point of thanking his former manager, Whitey Herzog.

> OZZIE [very emotional …]: Who came to San Diego one day and said to me that if you come to play for the St. Louis Cardinals, we're going to win the World Series.

In fact, Herzog's prediction would come true. In 1982, Smith's first year with St. Louis, he's a key player as the Cardinals ultimately play a seventh game in the World Series against Milwaukee.

> ANNOUNCER: *Sutter from the belt, to the plate, a swing and a miss, and that's a winner! That's a winner, a World Series winner for the Cardinals!*

Fans flocking to the field, a ticker tape parade, the first taste of a Redbird rebirth. The team is in the post season again, just three years later. In the 1985 National League Championship Series with the Los Angeles Dodgers, tied two games apiece, a television graphic says Smith "has not homered batting lefty in 2,967 career at bats." That changes in the bottom of the ninth—a legendary baseball moment— called by the legendary Jack Buck.

> ANNOUNCER: *Smith corks one into right, down the line, it may go! Go crazy folks, go crazy. It's a home run and the Cardinals have won the game by the score of 3-2 on a home run by the Wizard! [cheers …] Go crazy!*

Batting .435 he's the NLCS MVP as the Cardinals go on to the World Series, losing in seven games to the Kansas City Royals. Then in 1987 they're in the dance for the third time that decade, only to be defeated by the Minnesota Twins.

> OZZIE: It was quite a ride there in the eighties for us as a team. And a couple of times there, we just came up a little short.

Smith is not only an integral part of the team's success. He's influencing shortstops on other teams. Alan Trammell, a Detroit Tiger at the time, is half of one of the best one-two punch duos ever, with second baseman Lou Whitaker.

> ALAN TRAMMELL: The old-school way was to stay back on the ball and Ozzie took it with a little more acrobatics, but going to the baseball. I started watching TV, and when I saw film, I said "Hmm, there's another way of going about my business."

But what makes Ozzie Smith's accomplishments and acrobatics perhaps all the more amazing is the fact that during much of his career he had a torn rotator cuff in his throwing shoulder. He first injured it diving back into first base in June of '85. At that time, surgery pretty much meant the end of a playing career.

> OZZIE: And I can remember sitting on the bed and crying, you know, right there by myself, thinking that, *Hey, this could be it if this thing here, if I can't raise this here, you know, how in the world are you going to play?* So I had to do everything that I possibly could to build the strength around it to where I could get myself back to a point or try and maintain that level of excel-lence. I won Gold Gloves from '85 to '93, you know, doing that with a torn rotator cuff.

Even coming in second in 1987 behind the Chicago Cubs' Andre Dawson in the National League Most Valuable Player voting.

> OZZIE: People started looking at me as much more than just a defensive player. You know, it took hitting a home run in the playoffs, and then people started looking at the numbers.

In 1992 he chalks up his two thousandth hit.

> OZZIE: And when I realized that, I said, you know, "What a poignant time in my life and career. Here I am a guy that people have been saying is nothing but a defensive player all his life, I've got two thousand hits. That ain't too bad."

But 1995 is a challenging year. That decade-old rotator cuff injury creeps up on him, he has arthroscopic surgery, and is on the disabled list much of the season. By spring of 1996, however, at forty-one, the major league's oldest shortstop in nearly half a century is fit, feeling good, and determined to keep playing. But with new ownership, a new manager, Tony La Russa, and the young Royce Clayton, Smith is not a lock for the shortstop spot.

> OZZIE [1996 TV interview]: *I'm going to do what I've always done and if that's enough to impress people, then so be it. I don't have anything to prove.*

TONY LA RUSSA [1996 TV interview]: You just give them a bunch of work and let the games decide it later on in the spring.

Indeed, the veteran and youngster would split time on the diamond. Smith was considered the consummate professional.

TONY LA RUSSA [2002]: He had really worked to get himself in great shape and he was in great shape, so he performed an important role and responsibility on that team. We had some very talented young guys and Ozzie was able to give them an idea of what the big leagues were like.

Preferring to play every day, but realizing things didn't come as easily as they used to ...

OZZIE: A ball may go by. You said, "Boy, golly, that ball wasn't that far away."

And knowing he wouldn't be part of the Cardinals' roster plans ...

OZZIE: Could I have gone somewhere else and played? Yeah, I probably could've, but to prove what?

And wanting to end his career in a Cardinal uniform, Ozzie Smith announced that June that he would hang 'em up after the Cardinals' last game that year.

OZZIE [1996 news conference]: I will always cherish the special bond I have made with our fans. And I also want to thank the St. Louis Cardinal organization for giving me the opportunity to succeed as a professional baseball player.... [long pause ... starts to cry ...]

And so Smith is part of the team that makes it to the post season for the first time in nine years, sweeping the San Diego Padres in the Division Series, and then losing the National League Championship series to the defending World Champion Atlanta Braves. He savors every moment of his final playing days.

OZZIE: I was one of the lucky players. Not every player gets the opportunity to take what is termed "the tour." And I was one of those players that every place that I went, there was a ceremony, a special ceremony in every park that I went to.

And at home, the Cardinals give him the ultimate honor a club can give a player. They retire his number 1.

During his playing career, Ozzie Smith was honored with the Branch Rickey Award, given to the major leaguer who personifies "service above self ..." and the Roberto Clemente Award for his work in the community. Clearly, Ozzie's great plays weren't confined to a baseball diamond.

OZZIE [HOF speech]: My glove has given me much, but more importantly, it has given me the ability to give back. That is the ultimate talent in life. That is the greatest trophy on my mantle and I pray that it will so remain.

Among his good works, supporting San Diego's Downtown Library's research center for baseball buffs, part of a national effort to help people build information literacy skills by learning about the game.

OZZIE: We need to reiterate that a lot more with kids. You know, two hours of reading a day becomes very, very important.

And while Smith makes visits to his first baseball home town of San Diego, St. Louis is his main stage for much of his life after baseball.

[Theater Performance video: What is your name sir? Ozzie Smith ... [applause]]

On occasion he's a Show-Me State showman ...

[Ozzie as the Wiz: You want to see new lands, big cities, big mountains, big oceans? Dorothy: It's like you could read what's inside me. Wiz: It's my trade, my calling.]

His life is full of flair and plenty of sizzle as a partner in the upscale St. Louis restaurant, Smith and Slays. For two years, Smith played host of Major League Baseball's show *This Week in Baseball*. That springboards him to an analyst spot with CNN-SI and by August of 2001, his friend Dave Winfield is inducted into the Hall of Fame and at the celebration he is asked can you imagine being next?

OZZIE: You don't know whether or not you're gonna be part of that one percent that makes it.

The day of decision, January 8, 2002, CNN-SI cameras are at his home to capture the moment ...

OZZIE: You never know.

[Phone rings]

The numbers certainly are there. 13 Gold Gloves, 15 All-Star team appearances, a .262 batting average, 2,460 hits, 580 stolen bases, setting six major league records for his position, including most assists, most double plays, and most years with 500 or more assists. The intangibles—factoring in character, contributions to the game—that's up to the voters. The ballots are tallied in New York and then ...

[Voice on phone call]: Ozzie, this is the Baseball Writers' Association. I'm calling to tell you you've been elected into the Baseball Hall of Fame.

OZZIE: And it wasn't till that call, till you get that call, that it's real.

The details of his election are significant. He's named on nearly 92 percent of the ballots, just the thirty-seventh player to be elected his first time around, only the fifth player inducted solo.

JERRY COLEMAN: You know it's about time they got someone in there that could catch the ball and not just hitters. It's a hitter's Hall of Fame and a pitcher's Hall of Fame. This is one of the few great players, brilliant player, who got there with his glove and his bat.

DAVE WINFIELD: So I knew he was going to be good defensively, but offensively, becoming a leader and potent, stealing bases, really made him into the player he became.

TIM FLANNERY: He used his speed, he utilized his strength, and he made himself a Hall of Famer.

TONY LA RUSSA: The first opportunity people have to vote for you, you're in. He's the only guy going in this year. That's the ultimate compliment.

ALAN TRAMMELL: I played this position a long time. He was the best short-stop we have ever seen.

After a spring full of travel and tributes …

OZZIE [San Diego's Ozzie Smith Night]: Thank you very much for being a part of my trip down the yellow brick road. Thank you.

Ozzie Smith goes to Cooperstown for Induction Weekend. The hamlet, home to America's game, is all dressed up for the event welcoming nearly fifty Hall of Famers, including three from Smith's rookie year with the Padres: Gaylord Perry, Rollie Fingers, and Dave Winfield. The private parties and behind the scenes preparation fill an agenda that crescendos Sunday afternoon.

CROWD: Ozzie, Ozzie …

With fans filling the hillside and more watching on ESPN, Ozzie Smith delivers a heartfelt twenty-five-minute speech with thanks all around.

OZZIE [HOF speech]: I would especially like to thank the San Diego Padre organization and the St. Louis Cardinal organization for allowing me to do what I truly love doing. Thank you from the bottom of my heart. This is tough … [pauses]

And while a sign reminds him "there's no crying in baseball" … reaching out to children, he illustrates his experiences twofold, comparing his journey to that of the characters in the *Wizard of Oz*, and by drawing parallels to the layers of a baseball: durability like the cover, strands of love like the string, and a first step like the core.

OZZIE [HOF speech]: All great journeys begin with a dream …

A dream beginning on the steps of his childhood home.

OZZIE [HOF speech]: I would throw the ball up toward the peak of the roof and run around to the other side in hopes of catching it myself. And if any of you are wondering, no I never did, but it never stopped me from trying.

He credits two factors for keeping him focused …

OZZIE [HOF speech]: The first shell is my faith in God. With Him, I have everything. Without Him, I have nothing. [applause] The second, the faith I had in myself which came from my mother who repeatedly told me, "Oz, you can do anything as long as you believe in your dream with all your heart."

[Subtle sound of "Somewhere Over the Rainbow" instrumental]

So like the Scarecrow, Smith had the mind for dreaming, and like the Tin Man, a heart for believing, and like the Lion …

OZZIE [HOF speech]: … the c-c-c-courage he wanted, not just so that he could rule his kingdom. He wanted the c-c-c-courage to face adversity.

While Smith's father has passed away, and his mother's too ill to travel, he shares his glorious day with his brothers, sister, and family in the most personal and emotional moment.

> OZZIE [HOF speech]: *And I want to thank the person who gave me the three most precious gifts of all, my children. Denise, though our journey has taken us down different paths, the good roads far outnumber the rough ones. And the fun that we shared will forever be embedded in my heart. Thank you.*

In the end, unlike the Wizard who hid behind the curtain, Ozzie Smith's story is not about illusion, but about possibility.

> OZZIE [HOF speech]: *Folks, there is no wizard in Oz…. Ozzie Smith was a boy who decided to look within. A boy who discovered that absolutely nothing is good enough if it can be made better. A boy who discovered an old-fashioned formula that would take him beyond the rainbow, beyond even his wildest dreams. A boy who discovered a formula that was, and is still today: a mind to dream, a heart to believe, and the courage to persevere. And the pot of gold at the end of the rainbow is the opportunity to serve others. Thank you, and may God bless you in your journey, and God bless America.*

> [Music ending on instrumental: "Why oh why, can't I?"]

For all the talent Ozzie Smith displayed in his Hall of Fame career, his work ethic is the key to his success. His college coach inspired what would become Ozzie Smith's mantra: "Absolutely nothing is good enough if it can be made better, and better is never good enough if it can be made best." Coming from a Hall of Famer, that's advice worth heeding. I'm Jane Mitchell. Thank you for watching *One on One*.

ANTONIO GATES AND DONNIE EDWARDS

ANTONIO GATES

Several times over the years I've paired two players for a show, and in 2004 the duo for the Chargers reflected some contrasts and common ground. In 2003, a young player to watch on the San Diego Chargers was Antonio Gates, an undrafted tight end. He was quiet in person but a powerhouse on the field. Fans watched Antonio closely his rookie year, and going into his second, it was clear this rising star was a good candidate for a *One on One*. The Chargers' Director of Public Relations Bill Johnston, asked Antonio if he would do an interview with me. Antonio agreed, and we met at the Chargers' facility to work through logistics.

Antonio liked to bowl. Because he was young and single, bowling was an activity we could do together as part of the show. The plan was on a Tuesday, a team off day, we would meet at a bowling alley at about four o'clock in the afternoon, then go to his house for the in-depth interview.

"I think that was the bigger picture for me to be able to sit down with somebody and be able to conversate [sic] where people can see, wow, this is what Antonio Gates is about."

—ANTONIO GATES, 2010

The crew and I arrived early to be ready for him. That day, his plan was to drive to Los Angeles for a meeting, then back for our shoot. He was driving himself in his big SUV—no car service, no friend along with him. He called my mobile phone and was apologetic that he would be late. In reflecting on that day, six years later for this book, he shared this with me:

> "When people think of Antonio Gates, I want them to think of somebody that's trustworthy. That's in sports, that's outside of sports, that's in anything you do. It's just that you can count on him doing the right thing ... I was going to communicate with you because I felt like you took time out of your day to do some things. I owe it to you to say, look, I can't make it, or, I'm going to be fifteen minutes late, because somehow it builds friendships, it builds this way you feel about a person because it's as simple as communicating."

That evening in 2004, I was appreciative and amazed he not only showed up, but was in a great mood. Some could have let getting stuck in traffic ruin the whole day and the plan, but not Antonio Gates. He slipped on some bowling shoes and gave me a bowling lesson I will never forget. His soft voice, smooth style, and huge smile are enough to make anyone aspire to do well, and I did—during the time we

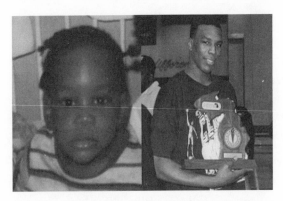

were rolling tape, at least. Those moments, including his gracious support and a high five, made the show.

We then caravanned to his house in the Poway area. The route seemed eerily familiar. As we drove up to the cul de sac, I realized this was where I interviewed Drew and Brittany Brees a few years before. Antonio was renting the townhouse from them. The décor was a bit more bachelor-esque, with sparse furnishings, but the interview was the most important thing to accomplish, and we did that. As you read his story, understand while he is soft-spoken, he has warmth in his voice that comes from his heart.

DONNIE EDWARDS

When I met Donnie Edwards, he was as cordial and accommodating as Antonio, but the veteran seemed ready for prime time—not just on the field, but on TV. He could have been a producer because he was so in tune with all the elements we had to cover for the show. I was excited to feature him, knowing he was a boy who made it out of a difficult neighborhood in San Diego and into the NFL with his hometown team. He was known for his charitable works and quality play on the field.

We met at his home, a gorgeous house with huge rooms and a designer's flair. His wife Kathryn was there. She was beautiful, friendly, and smart. We set up in a grand living room and settled in for the interview. He was articulate, confident, and energetic—a natural in front of the camera. He showed me his collection of military photographs, models, and other items reflecting his appreciation for history. While Dan Roper, the lead photographer that day, was shooting the close ups of the military items in the room, Donnie flipped through his photo library on his computer to narrow down the pictures we would need. He was so open and willing it made producing his segment all the more fun.

After the 2006 season, Donnie became a free agent and returned to play for Kansas City, but his home is San Diego, and he remains a part of San Diego sports history. Antonio Gates became a seven-time Pro Bowler and indeed the superstar fans expected. Through the years, he still greets me with that same smile as when I first met him when his star was on the rise.

This is the script from the show debuting December 8, 2004.

• • •

Antonio Gates and Donnie Edwards.

DONNIE: I'm going to go out there and show you and do it.

Shot for the moon.

ANTONIO: I was just on my way. You know, I had many more blessings to come.

And became stars.

Antonio Gates on offense and Donnie Edwards on defense are two sparks in a surprisingly exciting year for the San Diego Chargers. A team that hasn't had a winning season in nearly a decade is seeing success, and Edwards and Gates are right in the middle of it all.

His second year in the NFL, Number 85 Antonio Gates—jumping, running—is turning heads while making touchdowns: eleven by early December on the brink of the NFL tight end record, which is twelve.

ANTONIO: It was kind of a learning experience for me to have somebody have a vision for you that you just couldn't see as a child.

Antonio Gates was supposed to be a professional basketball player ...

ANTONIO: Everybody growing up wants to pick up that basketball.

... at least according to his childhood plan growing up in the inner city of Detroit, Michigan.

ANTONIO: You see people playing basketball and you see Michael Jordan on the TV and people who you idolize, and so that was the thing to do, is to become a basketball player. Fortunately, things didn't work out for me.

Didn't work out in some ways, but in others? Yes. Partly, because by his senior year in college, he finally accepted that his professional fate would be on the gridiron, not the hardwood. Not as easy as it might seem.

Antonio Dwayne Gates was born June 18, 1980. He's the oldest of five with older step-siblings from his father's first family. Antonio's parents graduated from high school then worked to raise their family in a little house at 15765 Petoskey Street, by all accounts a rough neighborhood.

>**ANTONIO:** In the inner city, you know, obviously there's drugs and gangs and violence going on so, you know, you want to just try to eliminate the temptation as much as possible.

That's where he believes sports saved him, playing year round, traveling with summer leagues. He credits his father with fostering his competitive side—having him play neighborhood pick up basketball games with bigger guys.

>**ANTONIO:** It ain't no rule in the book that said a younger guy couldn't be the best player. It helped me out in life, period, in competition. You know, any time I'm getting involved in anything, I always wanted to be number one.

And he was, playing football and leading Detroit's Central High School basketball team to its first state championship in 1998.

>**ANTONIO:** We was just a group of people who played together and loved one another and would basically leave it on the court for one another, and that alone, it builds something that can never be taken away. So to this day, I still communicate with all those same friends and when I go back home, we go out to eat and the first thing we bring up is that '98 year. And that's just something that I always think in my heart and I'll always remember.

He also remembers how no one thought he could or would get as far as college basketball.

>**ANTONIO:** To hear people say I couldn't become a good college basketball player 'cause I wasn't tall enough or 'cause I didn't have this, or I didn't have the right height, or I didn't have a position or—and it was just a combination of things—and I think that was the drive that got me through college.
>**JANE:** In fact, you had offers to Michigan, but you decided to go to Michigan State …
>**ANTONIO:** Uh-huh.
>**JANE:** … because they said you'd be able to play …
>**ANTONIO:** Both.
>**JANE:** … both sports.
>**ANTONIO:** The football coach had seen a future in me of playing football and he couldn't understand why I wanted to play basketball. I remember his number one thing he would say to me is that, "The NFL is looking for people like you." And I was like, "Yeah, whatever."

Gates had the ingredients of a mismatched player: 250 pounds and 6'4"; big, but fast, with soft hands and good footwork, taller than most receivers, able to jump to catch passes. Still determined to make it as a basketball player, schools said he needed to improve his grades. After getting his associate's degree at a community college, he accepted a basketball scholarship to a small Mid-American Conference school, Kent State.

ANTONIO: What was so crazy is that we had a vision that we were going to go to the Final Four.

The Golden Flashes made it to the Elite Eight, just one game shy of their goal.

ANTONIO: I think that that was a situation for me, throughout the tournament, where I led the team in scoring and I got a chance to show, you know, not just people who didn't believe in me, but to prove to myself that things can be done, you know, with a little hard work.

JANE: At that time, were you thinking, okay, come on, NBA scouts …

ANTONIO: Uh-huh.

JANE: … come find me?

ANTONIO: Yeah.

JANE: Is that what you thought? But that's not what happened.

ANTONIO: Well, it was—it's just such a unique story. No …

JANE: It is unique.

ANTONIO: … after the Elite Eight, it was just tons of football coaches. You know, tons of football agents. Not to say that there wasn't any basketball coaches or scouts coming to the game, but the football scouts were so overwhelming that the basketball scouts are looking at me like, "Well, you gotta go play football."

And then, he finally got it. He finally accepted he didn't have the height for the NBA. but his athleticism, size, and speed were valuable, if he just switched uniforms.

ANTONIO: You know what? I'm going to give it a try.

With plans to soon complete his final few college units, he signed with the Chargers as an undrafted free agent in May 2003.

ANTONIO: And I came to San Diego and, boy, did I think I was going to get cut.

JANE: Really?

ANTONIO: It was the hardest—training camp was the hardest thing I ever went through in my whole entire life. I was just like, man, I thought the NFL was a little bit easier than this, you know.

JANE: What was hard about it?

ANTONIO: I mean, they were so much stronger than I had seen. You know, a basketball player's this—not to take nothing away from a basketball player, you know, 'cause I was one all my life—but it's a different game. You can be a good basketball player with a mentality of, "I don't want to get touched." I mean, to be a good football player, you really have to be physical.

JANE: Did you ever get a little scared?

ANTONIO: No, I don't want to say scared was the word. I don't think I was ever scared. 'Cause I was an inner city kid.

JANE: This is nothing.

ANTONIO: … we play here, this is nothing, you know, so I think it was just the fact that I was more nervous. I was nervous like, wow, okay. You know, but what held up for me was that the fact that I was a competitor. I always wanted to win, and I had no pressure on me. For me not to make the team was no pressure. It was kind of like, "Oh, he ain't making it, he was a basketball player," so it was one of those things though, and I was thinking like, *Well who said I couldn't start? Or Who said I couldn't play?* The real accomplishment was when I made the team.

Coming up on *One on One*, Antonio Gates making adjustments on the field and he does a little coaching with a bowling ball. And later, Donnie Edwards: from National City to the National Spotlight. . . .

Having not played football since high school, the first thing Antonio Gates wanted to do in the NFL is what he did best in basketball, not just play the game, but *know* the game. The transition took a little tweaking and learning technique, especially his rookie year, 2003.

> **ANTONIO:** I was just so robotic. You would tell me to run ten yards and turn, I literally run into somebody and run ten yards and turn. So now it's just so much. It's like the game has slowed down a whole bunch for me. I can see when a guy's trying to jam me on the line, I can see whether I'm getting double-teamed. It's like something you just learn over time.

With the passing game more of an emphasis for the Chargers in 2004, he's become a go-to guy for quarterback Drew Brees. But Gates will never forget his first TD.

> **ANTONIO:** I finally got a chance to receive a touchdown pass from a person that I've watched play since I was a kid—which is Doug Flutie. And that was like something special. And I still have that ball to this day.

Playing football or watching sports keeps him busy, but we asked the potential Pro-Bowler what he'd like to do in his spare time. Shoot hoops? Nope. Go bowling! A game he learned from his step brother growing up.

> **ANTONIO** [at the bowling alley]: Bowling is kind of a competition, but it's settled. It's less energy, it's less physical, it's something you can come do and just enjoy. [coaching Jane bowling]
> There it is! Remember kinda keep your body straight, thumb pointed.
> **JANE:** Thumb pointed at the middle.

You can tell he's a genuine, helpful, and patient guy.

> *[Jane bowls a strike]*
> **GATES:** There you go. Yay, there you go! [high five]
> **JANE:** You have a future in coaching, oh my gosh!

Nice attributes that have no doubt helped him in his journey to overcome adversity. Proud to be the first in his family to go to college, now advising his younger brother.

> **ANTONIO:** That kind of makes me feel good when I'm able to show him the way because I had to learn it the hard way, first hand.

Antonio Gates says he's matured in other ways. The competitor is a pushover as a father of two toddlers in Detroit …

> **ANTONIO:** I'm so soft, man, I tell you, for my little boy it's a little different, but my daughter is kind of, "Okay, baby, you can have this."
> **JANE:** Your mom told me that when you were little, you used to pray before you would do anything.
> **ANTONIO:** Umm-hmm.
> **JANE:** You'd pray before you'd play, you'd pray before you eat.
> **ANTONIO:** Umm-hmm.
> **JANE:** Do you still do that?
> **ANTONIO:** All the time.
> **ANTONIO:** All the adversity kind of changed my life around. You know, it was something, that when you go through tough times and lumps in your life, you learn to appreciate smaller things.

Antonio Gates is young and a rising star; a long way from the hardwood and that house in Detroit on Petoskey Street.

> **ANTONIO:** When you see people cheering and screaming, there's no better feeling in the world than that—to know that one day a little kid wants to grow up and be like you. That's something that you really just need to take heed of and say, "I'm blessed to know that this kid is out here and looking at me as a role model." And I try to continue that process.

It's been a long time since the Chargers have drawn national attention for their tight end, since Charger great Kellen Winslow in the '80s, and fans are ecstatic.

> **FAN:** What a surprise! It's a great pleasure to see somebody who didn't play college ball, but come out of basketball and do so well.
> **FAN:** His size, his leaping ability. No corner can cover him.
> **FAN:** I think he's really been the difference in what people expected from the Chargers this year and what they've really become.
> **FAN:** He shows the other wide receivers what they should do and what they can do. He never quits.
> **ANTONIO:** As long as people can see me as a contributor to the team and something positive to the team—'cause obviously it can easily be the other way around. They can say, well, that tight end, he is really hurting that team. So, it's exciting to know that people look at me in a positive way.

So far, so good. . . .

Number 59, Donnie Edwards, makes being a linebacker sound so simple.

> **DONNIE:** I just happen to be a guy who can just run fast and tackle and hit receivers coming across the middle. That's all I can do. But, you know, I'm a big kid, and I relate well to the kids, and that's how I see myself. I was just like them and if I can help them out, that's all I want to do.

With Edwards, hardly a topic goes by without his passionately linking his present to his past …

DONNIE: It happened for me, it can happen for you.

His profession to his mission …

DONNIE: Now it's my turn to give back. I benefited from it; why not help someone else?

And his NFL opportunities to his humble San Diego beginnings …

[Picture of Donnie Edwards with President Bush.]

DONNIE: Here's a little kid from National City on the USS *Abraham Lincoln* meeting the President of the United States.

Donnie Edwards is a textbook extrovert, an optimist with a fierce work ethic. Take the surreal moment when the defensive star, who wasn't re-signed with Kansas City, returned home to play for San Diego in 2002.

DONNIE: When I was sitting there on my knee looking at my helmet, thinking like, *"Wow, this is pretty amazing. I'm in the NFL. This is my seventh year, and I'm playing for the Chargers when I just grew up down the street?* It was cool. But then [snaps fingers], as the whistle blew, that little moment in time passed and I had to go back on the field.

A field that seemed out of reach as a child. Donald Lewis Edwards was born April 6, 1973 and raised just southeast of the San Diego skyline in National City. His window on the world was limited at first to his inner city apartment complex.

DONNIE: I gotta tell you, it was a little tough. Being in a big family. We had nine kids in our family, my mom and my stepfather. It was very difficult. We were always trying to find next week's meal. Living paycheck to paycheck. At that time, did I know it was difficult? No. I thought everyone else was the same, just like me.

And just like a lot of kids …

DONNIE: My whole room was filled with Charger memorabilia and everything like that.

His jersey numbers reflected those of his heroes, but sports was more than just fun for the young Edwards. At eight years old he traveled with his Pop Warner team to San Jose to play, staying with a host family.

DONNIE: And it was my first time out of the community, out of the apartment, out of my little complex. And to see something different, it was life changing. I mean, I was just looking around like, "Oh, my God, this is amazing." Like, "How did you get this?" And he said, "I went to college." "Okay, well, how do I get to college? And he said, "You can get to college through a scholarship." And I said, "Okay, how do I get a scholarship?" And they said, "You gotta get good grades, do well in school, and stay out of trouble." I said, "Heck, I can do that. That's not too bad, I can do that."

That goal and a lot of athletic talent carried him through Chula Vista High School, part of the 1989 Metro League Champs. Lettering in three sports, he indeed landed a scholarship to play football at UCLA. The Bruin, with dreadlocks, wasn't very big for a defensive player and had to adjust to the competitive academic environment, too.

> **DONNIE:** I worked extra hard, and got tutors, and worked hard in the weight room, and did what I had to do to prove to myself and to everyone that I could do it.
>
> **JANE:** What do you think the difference was between you, who wanted to prove that you could do it, and someone else who maybe believed all that and gave up?
>
> **DONNIE:** For me, it was just like a fear from going back to where I started. I wanted to get away from that so much in my life it just motivated me.

He tried one season of Bruin baseball, but football was his forte, among the best in school history for tackles and sacks, earning All-America honors. NFL scouts came calling after his junior year, but Edwards never lost sight of his goal. The Political Science major graduated in less than four years.

> **DONNIE:** And I was very proud. Trust me, this is like a huge, like monumental, goal that I set for myself, but I wasn't satisfied with that. I wanted more.

Then a serious injury in a game: a compression fracture in his back. He missed most of his senior year, but he healed in time to be the Senior Bowl's Defensive MVP, playing as a graduate student. He was drafted in 1996 in the fourth round by the Kansas City Chiefs.

> **DONNIE:** I met so many great people there. I mean, Kansas City's a really nice community, a really nice city.

It didn't seem to matter that he still wasn't very big for a linebacker. He broke the mold, becoming the first player in team history to record more than a hundred tackles in five straight years. As for playing against his hometown team?

> **DONNIE:** Well, I always got excited when I came home. I mean, coming back to San Diego, all my friends from grade school and high school and junior high are going to be there watching me, and my family. And this is the team that had a chance to draft me. They didn't draft me, so it's payback. I'm gonna get you.

Still, Edwards hoped and expected he'd always be a Chief. But when the struggling team chose to invest in offense, Edwards did not receive an offer for the 2002 season.

> **DONNIE:** And so, hey, when one door closes, another one opens.

He signed on to work again with the man who drafted him, Chargers Head Coach Marty Schottenheimer. Edwards put up Pro-Bowl type numbers and was only selected as an alternate. Then, an opening on the roster punched his ticket to Hawaii with teammate LaDainian Tomlinson.

DONNIE: Finally, I'm here. You know, regardless of the struggle of my life and how I get to places, but I'm here and I'm going to enjoy myself.

As he does every Sunday: a playmaker, a pro.

DONNIE: I've learned from people who showed me the ropes before me. Guys like Derrick Thomas, guys like Junior Seau, Marvcus Patton.

A fan favorite ...

FAN: He's always hustling. He doesn't stop until he hears the whistle. You can't ask for a better linebacker for the Chargers.

FAN: He reminds me a little bit of Seau. His speed, his ability to cover sideline to sideline ...

FAN: Extra hustle and a great guy. Good for the community. An inspiration....

No matter what Donnie Edwards tries, he's polished, personable, open to perks.

DONNIE: I'm really into the reggae music scene and I'm able to meet a lot of really cool artists that I grew up listening to.

He enjoys the extras, but is relentless about giving back, a 2003 finalist for NFL Man of the Year, honoring a player's contributions on and off the field. Someone who knows his generosity, his wife Kathryn ...

KATHRYN: The number one thing that I can say about Donnie is just that he's a good guy. He's a really good guy. He's got a huge heart, and what you see is what you get.

Kathryn, from Milwaukee, was working in advertising when they met through friends in Los Angeles in 1997.

KATHRYN: So he was just a young fellow and I thought, you know, *Nice guy to introduce to one of my younger girlfriends*. But then after I got to know him, he was such a sweetheart and love blossomed.

JANE: Ahh....

DONNIE: I know. Meanwhile, I thought the whole time that she was just my big sis, you know, trying to hook me up with one of her friends. And, lo and behold ...

KATHRYN: I had ulterior motives.

They married in Pebble Beach in 2002.

KATHRYN: I wish I could say I have the passion for life that Donnie does, and his spirit of like, just wanting to go and do everything. He really teaches me a lot with that and it's something that I learn from him every day.

One of the first things he did when he returned to San Diego was select and pay for all new equipment at his high school's weight room.

DONNIE: And the great thing is that the kids take so much pride in it, too.

They are leading a pilot project in San Diego County, Jump for Life, to fight childhood obesity in tandem with Arnold Schwarzenegger's After School All-Stars program.

> KATHRYN: There's such a huge epidemic in our country with overweight children and it's just really a sad situation. And so Donnie's always been a fan of helping kids out and getting them active.

There is also Dad's Day with Donnie, a day at Sea World to give some special children a positive Father's Day experience.

> DONNIE: After an hour or two, they're jumping on your shoulders, on your back.
> JANE: You're a Boy Scout ...
> DONNIE: Umm-hmm.
> JANE: ... in lots of ways.

Still wears a uniform, supports his old troop 32 and is a regional council board member.

> *[Home office tour with photo albums]*
>
> JANE: And this is your grandfather?
> DONNIE: Yeah, this is my grandfather, who just passed, who got me into military history.

His grandfather, a Native American, was in the army, a Pearl Harbor survivor whose photo album intrigued him.

> DONNIE: Without these brave, courageous men like my grandfather, the world would be a much different place.

His curiosity about military history has taken him to France and the site of D-Day ...

> DONNIE: The world got changed right there on that beach. And that was really cool. It was like an eerie calm out there on the beach, and just go to different battle sites on the Normandy Coast. It was pretty amazing.

And then there was the three-day trip at sea ...

> DONNIE: May 1, 2003, I'll never forget it.

On the USS *Abraham Lincoln* with President Bush.

> DONNIE: I was there for the famous "Mission Accomplished" of the [first] war in Iraq. And, forever in history, I was there.
> JANE: Tell me about your army men.
> DONNIE: I spent a long time putting these together. As you see, this is the Japanese.
> JANE: Uh-huh.
> DONNIE: This is the British. You can tell by the helmets.

Even with similarities between football and war—strategy, teamwork, and accountability—he sees the difference.

DONNIE: Well, they're my celebrities and my idols. Every time I meet some-one of military rank, I'm just like, "Wow," you know, "Thank you so much," because they're providing us freedom.

Might his outlook lead him to politics someday?

DONNIE: It definitely excites me when I think about it.

The two-time team Defensive MVP knows how to be ready when opportunity knocks.

DONNIE: It'll never be there if you don't work hard. You gotta work hard at something. That's what luck is—is when opportunity meets hard work, that's lucky. But if you're not working hard, you'll never get there.

There's a saying here at the Chargers: "The will to win means nothing without the will to prepare." Donnie Edwards and Antonio Gates are proving they have the will to prepare and to win, and it's paying dividends with their families, the community, and on the field. I'm Jane Mitchell. Thank you for watching *One on One.*

"It was a long journey.... It wasn't just basketball to football, it was the struggling, basketball, back to struggling, basketball, back to struggling, you know, so it was just the way you presented it and the way people got to understand that I didn't just walk on the football field and became a Pro Bowler.... What really hurt me, and my story the most, was the guy that I would probably prefer was my number one resource [for you to talk to] had actually passed away, which my high school football coach.... That was something that, I wish—if I could've changed anything—is that he would still be alive and have him tell you a little bit more about who I was as a kid growing up.... [Your show] was a way of getting my story on the forefront where people can understand who I was outside of the helmet. You see 85 running around with the helmet, but who is he outside of the helmet? Talk about my kids and my family, how much I love my family, that's something that a lot of people just don't really know 'cause you see me at the game, all my kids are never here. Family Day, my kids aren't here, my mom isn't here. So you just have a assumption that I'm this lonely guy just running around San Diego, probably at every party. You know? So I think it's just good to know a person, outside of the helmet—good to see his face, good to see what he's about, and then you just understand. Obviously I'm a whole other animal when I put the pads on. And sometimes you get stereotyped on who you are on the football field.... I've always wanted people to say, 'Look, I met him and he didn't act like he's been to six straight Pro Bowls. He acted like he was a human being first.'"

—Antonio Gates, 2010

DAVID WELLS

"Jane is very relaxed and not pushy. She kinda lets you, the athlete, carry the interview."

—DAVID WELLS, 2010

I n 2004 David Wells put on the uniform of the team he grew up cheering for: The San Diego Padres. Of those who have made it to the majors out of San Diego, David Wells is one of the most successful and well-known—largely for his tough-guy grit. So with the prospect of featuring him, was I intimidated? No. I was challenged, and his modus operandi gave me more motivation to crack that hard shell and see how he had evolved.

Several factors came into play with this edition of *One on One*. First, I had met David Wells in 1998, but he probably didn't remember me. I wasn't sure I wanted him to either. It was after game two of the World Series at Yankee Stadium. The Padres lost and both teams were heading to San Diego. Mel Proctor, Channel 4's play-by-play announcer, and I were on the road doing post game interviews for the show in San Diego each night. Mel did interviews with the Padres in the visitor's locker room. I got the short straw and headed to the Yankee's clubhouse. I figured I had a shot at interviewing David Wells about being a San Diego native coming home to play, even though he was the opponent. It made perfect sense to me. A quick two-minute interview on tape and we would be done. How hard could that be? Hello, rookie. This is New York. The Yankees. Not a friendly atmosphere, even though they had won the game and were up two games to none in the series. The reporters from the New York media offered me luck when I queried them about getting Wells for an interview. Still, *the naïve, open-minded, nervous, but brave TV reporter girl from San Diego* that I was, got up the gumption.

The clubhouse seemed oddly quiet considering the Yankees had won. That was their norm; they were all business. I hovered around David Wells' locker waiting for him. When he arrived I said, "Hello David. I'm Jane Mitchell with Channel 4 Padres. I was hoping to do a quick interview with you to send back to San Diego for our post game show—just about coming back home and what that means to you." He sat on his chair, packing his things and did not look at me, as he explained, "No, I don't have time." I tried to rationalize, "But it would take about a minute and thirty seconds ... just real quick." He replied, "That's a minute and thirty seconds less time I can spend with my family before I go, so, no."

No? Really? Not even for just a minute and thirty seconds? I was befuddled. In the time I talked and he answered, we could have had it done. I didn't understand, but I was not going to argue. Maybe I should have started interviewing him without asking, that's how others were doing it, but I thought I would be polite and ask first. Different team. Different way of doing things. I stored that little memory and chalked it up to nothing ventured, nothing gained.

This whole experience should not have been a total surprise. The day before, I also had the Yankees clubhouse assignment. One of the Yankees (whose name I will withhold) had done exceptionally well in game one, so he was a logical interview for the postgame coverage. I waited politely at his locker until he finished dressing. I was there with my microphone and explained I would like to do a quick one-on-one for San Diego television when he was ready. He acknowledged that would be okay. As I waited for him, a radio reporter put a microphone close in on his face and started asking questions. I said to the reporter, "Excuse me, but I have been waiting for him to be ready." I assumed the player might actually appreciate manners and my respecting his space while he changed. I was quite surprised when he said to us in effect, *Stop your fighting, or I won't talk to anyone.* Wow, Dorothy, you are not in San Diego, anymore. The next day, a Yankees radio announcer told me that I had made a New York newspaper. Apparently, my naiveté translated to some fun fodder, saying that a San Diego TV reporter had caused a little stir in the clubhouse.

Fast forward to 2004. David Wells, a free agent, signed with the Padres to add power on the mound and sizzle and swagger to a team moving into its new home at PETCO Park. He was an obvious choice for a *One on One,* but how daring was I to ask? In talking with the team's media relations department, we thought it best if the team laid the groundwork. The media relations staff stated my case— that I was part of the Padres family with the Padres TV station—and this would be great for the team and the fans.

He agreed, but didn't want to do it at the house where he was living in Ocean Beach because it was tight quarters. We opted for the ballpark in a new, luxury dining room with wood tones and nice chairs. I would work with him about going back to his childhood haunts in Ocean Beach, but I just wanted to get the interview on tape to start.

Boomer, as he is called, had written a book in 2003 entitled *Perfect I'm Not: Boomer on Beer, Brawls, Backaches and Baseball*. The week before the interview, I read it. Every page. It was chock full of eye opening stories. I felt prepared and excited about the challenge ahead.

The day of the shoot, we had a three-camera setup in that dining room around noon, plenty of time before he had to be at the clubhouse and batting practice. He arrived in a short sleeve green shirt, shorts, and flip-flops. His wife, Nina—tall, slim, with long brown hair—was strikingly beautiful. She and their two boys sat to the side while David and I sat in two chairs for the interview. I had to be on my game, but also warned him in a nice way, just in case, that there were no swear words allowed because this is family TV. He said, "Good luck. You get what you get." With his wife and children there, he said he would be on good behavior. He was and was also very honest and revealing.

We didn't hit only on what people talk about—his reputation for being brash and bold—but several stories he had talked about in his book. These were the stories I wanted to explore as well—his memories of his mother, being poor and embarrassed to be on food stamps, playing through pain, and what he did to avoid it. The way he described his memories, and why he was so driven, revealed sides of David Wells few had seen or heard about. He was a little brash and bold, but also thoughtful and vulnerable. He let down that tough guy façade to share about the people and situations that molded him and sustained him over the years. After more than an hour on tape, we brought in Nina. They had great energy and candor. It was apparent she was a strong, make-it-happen woman who understood his different dimensions, not just what the outside usually sees. I knew this would be a compelling show.

I eventually had the courage to tell him the 1998 story. He figured that to be true and did not seem to think he would have done anything any differently. At least he was honest.

After the interview, I made my move, for the big "ask," presenting how it would be great to see him back where he played basketball as a kid. Thinking this was going to be a difficult sell—because it would require more time and coordinating—surprisingly, he didn't resist, and we agreed to meet on a Saturday morning at the Ocean Beach house where he had been living. He was surprised to see us, however, when we arrived at his home at what I thought was the agreed upon time. Somehow wires had been crossed between the media relations staff, him, and me. I wasn't sure what happened, but this is where experience and diplomacy have to trump fear and intimidation. I explained what we needed to do and how long it would take. He acknowledged the mix-up without pointing fingers and rolled with it. Even better, as I asked questions about the house and area, he seemed even more happy to share things important to him—how the house had been left to him by old friends, the significance of an apple tree, showing me his surfboards, and the motorcycles in the garage. We walked to the Ocean Beach Recreation Center where I arranged to have access, and he reminisced about his days of sneaking in to shoot hoops. He was so relaxed, genuine, engaged, and I think appreciative of the details I was interested in. Maybe he had mellowed a little. After all, this was San Diego. He was not in New York anymore.

To round out his story, I interviewed childhood and high school friends, shot his neighborhood, Little League fields, and Point Loma High School. Point Loma is the alma mater of Don Larsen, also a former Yankee who threw a perfect game. The show received positive reviews around town. I didn't hear from David directly, but I expected it was okay by him, because after he left the Padres and returned a second time in late 2006, I wanted to do an update, and he agreed.

This time, though, we would be at their new home. Construction was still underway in parts of it, so we had to limit what we shot. We arrived at the spectacular mansion filled with beautiful portraits of his family, baseball images, and some rooms with stacks of unpacked boxes.

Nina suggested we use the family room off the kitchen. It had big, oversized furniture, and of course, we had to move things around to make it all fit. While Nina was upstairs getting ready, David came home. He was surprised by all the lights, and how big a setup this appeared to be. Again, experience and diplomacy were on my side. "We're perfectionists, like you are," I explained. I confidently reaffirmed the interview would still be fifteen to thirty minutes as we talked about, but we wanted it to look good. His brusque veneer again melted away as I said we were ready when he was. He sat down for an interview covering the most recent years, and he was a pro. Nina joined us and we broached the subject of whether he was done playing, which was still a question mark at the time.

When we were finished, and everyone was laughing and having a good time, I asked if we could see his pets—dogs and birds—his game room with stuffed game in it from his hunting expeditions, and his backyard. Outside, on tape, he said I could come back and do a follow-up story when it was completed and he was retired. As of this writing, we haven't done that yet.

Their home was threatened by the San Diego wildfires in 2008, and because I keep my contacts in my phone, I reached Nina easily. She and David didn't hesitate when I asked to talk with them about their evacuation. Beyond that, they voluntarily shared they would be giving fire victims extra items from their home, which was untouched by the fire. We talked with them at a downtown hotel where the whole family was camping out in one room with the pets, too. The story was for our nightly sports news show, but it reiterated for me that David is down to earth, even with his rough edges and his fame and fortune. He knew the importance of showing support and acting on it.

On Opening Day for Park View Little League 2010 in Chula Vista, I had the pleasure of being the guest speaker for the ceremony, then introducing David Wells to present the 2009 Little League World Series Champions with their rings. He was thrilled to be there, and my comments to the crowd in part linked the boys to him—a 2-time World Champion and 3-time All-Star who started his baseball career just like they had, across San Diego at the Ocean Beach Little League fields.

While we were on the stage chatting, I reminded him I was writing a book about my experiences and he inquired if I was going to put in there that, "You just can't come into a person's house and move all the furniture around!" I said that's all part of the process, so probably, yes. I enjoyed the friendly sparring. It keeps me sharp. I conclude that by the nice comments about his *One on One* experience, in part, it was worth the little inconvenience. I know it was for our viewers and me.

If tenacity alone would dictate pitching, David Wells could probably do it into his late forties or beyond. In the meantime, he has ventured to the other side of the microphone and camera, as a broadcaster for baseball coverage and is often seen at Padres games just for fun.

His edition is also a *One on One Classic*. This is the original script from the show debuting October 1, 2006 upon his second stint with the Padres.

• • •

Pitcher David Wells: no pain, no gain, no regrets.

DAVID: I've exceeded a lot of things, and I love proving people wrong.

Emotional in the game, sentimental about his family ...

DAVID: So I can watch my kids grow up and have some fun.

David Wells is a big-game pitcher who thrives in the spotlight and under pressure. He seems to be part Teflon®, bouncing back and enduring pain for more than two decades on the mound. Colorful, controversial, candid, in control, and it all started as a kid growing up in San Diego.

David Wells: Big, bold, brash with a booming personality, and an arm that just doesn't quit.

DAVID: I'll go after everybody and if I give it up, you know what, I gave it up with my best stuff.

Nicknamed Boomer, his resilience, presence, and desire to play with a purpose—all compelling reasons Padres General Manager Kevin Towers traded the Red Sox for him in late summer of 2006, just in time to get him on the playoff roster. Boston was out of the race, and the Padres were in the thick of one with the rival Los Angeles Dodgers.

> **KEVIN TOWERS:** I think it showed the ball players that we're getting kind of a real hired gun, somebody who pitches well in September and as well as October. I think it kind of fired up the boys.
>
> **TREVOR HOFFMAN:** Just his presence has been huge, and the ability. With some of the games we know we've got coming up, that's gonna be great that he's gonna be a part of.
>
> **JOSH BARFIELD:** Just the confidence when you go out there to know you have a guy like David Wells on the mound, you feel like you're gonna be in every game.
>
> **CHRIS YOUNG:** He's got that sort of savvy to him that's fun to watch.

At his new Rancho Santa Fe home, the forty-three-year-old Wells settles in to talk baseball and life.

> **DAVID:** I'm not a savior. I'm here to try to help the team as much as I can.

The same attitude we discovered when we explored his story in 2004, his first stint with his hometown team.

The hefty lefty has played in baseball's biggest cities in the most intense spotlight. As a Padre, he has brought all that to the mound with a bonus.

> **DAVID:** I couldn't be happier playing at home where I grew up.

While some people run from their past, David Wells has always gravitated back to it, specifically Ocean Beach, an "earthy" community.

> **DAVID:** Ocean Beach is the job without the J. That's why you got OB!

Yes, he's enjoyed the finer things a Major League Baseball salary, two World Series Rings, and 3-time All-Star success can bring: VIP treatment, a beautiful wife and children, hanging with rock stars, appearances on late night talk shows and *Saturday Night Live*. But he's also dealt with the flip side of fame: media scrutiny, he says, mostly in the East.

> **DAVID:** Terrible, terrible back there. If they don't like you they're going to try to bury you. You know, they're going to put you in there all the time, a lot of negative things ... that's something that they feel that they can make or break you, and especially in New York.

After last wearing a New York Yankees uniform in 2003, he had back surgery and signed with the Padres as a free agent for the 2004 season. Along with his stellar big league stats—winning more than 200 games—he indeed came with a reputation as a guy with an edge who liked post game nightlife and didn't like to work out. Yet moving home at forty, he was nearly twenty pounds lighter, in shape. General Manager Kevin Towers called him a man on a mission.

KEVIN TOWERS: Coming back home a left-hander with a little bit of swagger, we were looking for somebody with a little bit of that edge like Kevin Brown brought to this club in '98. He's been everything that I thought and more.

As for the "partying" part of his unofficial resume?

JANE: So far you've haven't lived up to that. Is it just maturity? Just sort of growing up? Or is it just being back home?

DAVID: My kids are getting older, you know, and it's something that your body can take it for so long. We went out socially and it's not like you try to go out and get hammered every night. That's just not the way to do it. You know, we do have a job to do and you want to be your best that day if you're playing. But, you know, just coming back home, I'm so relaxed.

Sitting in shorts and flip-flops, he certainly seems relaxed considering all he's been through, as described in his autobiography *Perfect I'm Not … Boomer on Beer, Brawls, Backaches and Baseball.* There's a bit of his naked truth, so parental discretion is advised.

DAVID: It's more about baseball and, you know, a little bit about me growing up, a little bit about my mom, my history.…

JANE: I learned a lot about you and about the game as well that I had never really thought about. The cortisone shots, for example. You know you hear about it, but you were quite—you really told it like it was …

DAVID: Well, they can be helpful.

Big, painful cortisone shots: his solution over the years to backaches.

DAVID: You know, I think if I wasn't pitching up to speed, up to my potential, then I don't think I probably would have done it. I would've, you know, just gone under the knife and had things taken care of. But, we do crazy things in life. But, knock on wood, I'm still here. I've gotten through it.

JANE: Let's go back to your foundation, to Ocean Beach. Describe a day for David Wells growing up. What was that like for you?

DAVID: Waking up, cooking some eggs. You know, as a kid, probably about seven, eight years old, my grandma bought me a skillet 'cause I always watched my mom cook, so I always wanted to cook. And I'd get in there and dabble. And so my grandma would—for my birthday—would always give me a twenty-four pack of eggs. We lived a block away from the beach so, you know, put my trunks on and walk right down to the beach and just go down there and spend the whole day.

David and his sister, two of five siblings, lived with their mother in this apartment complex, the party spot on weekends for her and her Hell's Angels friends. David didn't come to know his father until years later.

DAVID: Anybody ever messed with us, or anything of that sort, she was the first one to step up. But, at times, money was hard. We lived on welfare. You know, and the worst thing about it is at Safeway®, when we were there, she'd make me go to the store with the food stamps and I'd be there for hours because I knew everybody in the store and I didn't want nobody to know, so I'd just be going up and down every aisle. "Hey, what's going on? How you doing?" Waiting for everybody I knew to leave and then grab my stuff, what my mom wanted, and boogie out. But, you know, that's how it was. We did a lot, a lot to survive. A survivor. You grow up on the streets, you learn how to grow up quick, and that's what I did.

JANE: How'd she get her name—Attitude Annie?

DAVID: Probably from a lot of the Hell's Angels that she hung out with. She just didn't take any crap from anybody and, you know, if somebody gave her any crap, she'd haul off and nail them. And that was her reputation.

JANE: You too?

DAVID: Oh, me too. My mom and I would have some good knockdown, drag out, wrestling matches. I mean, it never got to the point where it was a slug-fest, but, you know, if I got in trouble, she'd let me have it and let me know who's boss. It was neat as a kid. On Fridays, Saturdays, and Sundays, it was just motorcycles all the way around. And the parties, you know, were going on. It was great. I mean it was fun for the kids. You know, they all treated us all the bikers, Hell's Angels, treated us kids like one of their own. And you know, they're getting a bad wrap.

JANE: And they came to your Little League games sometimes?

DAVID: Oh, yeah. They came …

JANE: You write about that in your book, it's like, wow, that's quite a fan club.

DAVID: They did and the people would look and just like, "Are you kidding me?" They were scared. You know, it was awesome. But, you know, it was kind of cool 'cause I'm out there pitching and I was just like, my chest was out to here. I was like Superman.

An afternoon with him,

DAVID: Nina, "That's little David, right there," … Yep.

His boys, and wife Nina, is a walk down memory lane …

DAVID: This was my sanctuary. We gotta go around, it's locked.

The Ocean Beach Recreation Center …

DAVID: I mean, it was crazy. We'd play stickball here. This is where we learned how to play stickball, pitching mound right here, you know, you'd try to hit it up into the house where I won my first skateboard contest right here, sprung and I jumped over ten of them and landed on the board.

JANE: Ten?

DAVID: Ten cones and landed on the board. That's what won me my Gold Wing® trucks. Terrorized the neighborhood going in and out of everyone's yards, we used to pick the locks and come in here. Every day, especially in high school. I'd ditch. I'd come right here. This is where I'd come. Every day at one o'clock. We'd play 1:00 to 3:30, go down to Robb field 4:00 to 6:30, come back here 7:00 to 9:30. Every day we'd play. It was stupid.

He worked at basketball, his first love, but baseball would be the ticket to his future.

DAVID: I just had the natural ability and the talent. You know, even when I was in Little League and I was pitching.

At Point Loma High School, talent wasn't enough. To stay on the team, he had to work to at least get passing grades, convinced of that by a stern coach.

DAVID: He gave me a reality check, and says, "You got a talent that's unbelievable. Do something with it, 'cause you never know what's going to happen."

He got back on track throwing hard, more than ninety miles an hour, even pitching a perfect game. The Pointers won the CIF Championship in 1982. Wells was courted by colleges and drafted by the Toronto Blue Jays in the second round.

DAVID: I wasn't a school guy and I think they knew it, so I ended up signing, taking the money, and running.

Every stellar career starts somewhere. For David Wells, it was the Toronto Blue Jays' farm team in Medicine Hat, Alberta, Canada. By his third year in the minors he needed elbow surgery and a year to recover. Discouraged, he was ready to call it quits, until a talk with his pitching coach.

DAVID: "Are you going to go home and bang nails? Work in a restaurant for the rest of your life?" He goes, "Just rehabilitate your arm. You got good people to do it." And I took a chance and, you know, the rest is history.

A history with a tough and contentious learning curve.

DAVID: Toronto was bad. They were fining me a hundred dollars a day for every pound I was overweight. Despite the team I didn't really care for, I still went out and did my job.

Part of the 1992 World Champion Blue Jays. Even so, he didn't know his role: starter or reliever?

DAVID: I said, "Just make me one or the other, all right?" Just one, and then they released me. Said, "Hey, take that."
JANE: So what was it like to be in Detroit with [manager] Sparky Anderson?
DAVID: That was unbelievable. Sparky gave me new life. My major league career's probably what it is today because the man believed in me. You know, it was just like I was his own son. And showed me how to be a man on and off the field, how to really accept certain things, and all that even when you're doing bad.

He did it the Wells way, choosing to crank the music of Metallica in the clubhouse.

DAVID: I'm going to pitch like they play.

After a trade to Cincinnati then to Baltimore, David Wells was again in familiar territory—post season.

> **DAVID:** I wanted to be the guy on the mound. Any situation, even now, I mean, during a big game during the season, I want to be the man on the mound 'cause I want to be the one, 'cause I'm not afraid to fail.

He rarely did. As an Oriole, he was known as a Yankee killer, just what the Yankees wanted, so Wells was signed to wear pinstripes, with high hopes. And then troubled times.

> **DAVID:** My mom passed away and so I come back here to bury her and, I think it was the day after I buried her, we were down in OB and with a bunch of friends and we were just saying our goodbyes and ended up getting in an altercation down there and, boom, now the Yankees said, "You know what?"

They had second thoughts.

> **DAVID:** I was like, my dreams of being a Yankee are over because of the fact I broke my hand.

They kept Wells after he was cleared. The fans loved that he was on their team, but he recalls criticism from the press for going out on the town the nights before the day he started. The night before Sunday May 17, 1998, was one of those nights.

> **DAVID:** I went to *Saturday Night Live* that one night. I got home around five or so in the morning and just feeling pretty good, but …
>
> **JANE:** You had a big day that day.
>
> **DAVID:** Big day, huge day.

And became the fourteenth pitcher in major league history to pitch a perfect game.

> **DAVID:** I mean, nobody expects to go out and throw a perfect game, you know, especially in Yankee Stadium. That was a sold-out crowd. Beanie Baby™ Day and, you know, it was pretty bizarre because of the fact that after like the sixth inning you throw a ball a foot outside and the fans are going nuts. They're screaming at the umpire, "That's a strike!" And so it became nerve wracking to me and then trying to talk with somebody in the dugout was just—nobody would talk to me, and then David Cone, there's David Cone, my boy, and he just started talking to me and he just started letting things go and trying to take my mind off it, which I do appreciate it.

In the end, twenty-seven batters up, twenty-seven batters down. David Wells was the second Yankee to pitch a perfect game. The first to do it, Don Larsen, in the '56 World Series, called to congratulate his fellow Point Loma High grad. A magical day, making David Wells a household name and instant celebrity. Later that year, he'd face his hometown Padres in the World Series with some pre-game controversy, thanks to an appearance on Howard Stern's national radio show.

> **DAVID:** And he was trying to get me to predict what we were going to win it in, and I'm like, "Howard, that's not fair to my teammates, my team, or the Padres." And I said, "Howard, if I was to predict, which I'm not, so just to get

you off my back—five." Well, the next day it's printed, pooff, "Boomer predicts five."

JANE: And then coming back to San Diego thinking you're the hometown kid made good.

DAVID: No, I was a hometown villain.

In the end, the Yankees swept the Padres 4-0, and in 1999 the Yankees' ace was axed, traded to the Blue Jays for Roger Clemens. For the next five seasons between Toronto, the White Sox, the Yankees again, he pitched mostly on par—but with pain.

JANE: When you look at that time in your life, why are you thinking you can still come back and still keep pitching?

DAVID: My arm. My arm has always been there for me. Bailed me out of trouble and, you know, just the rest of me started deteriorating.

After surgery he had great comebacks, but by the 2003 World Series ...

DAVID: I felt like I was ninety years old on crutches.

With one last cortisone shot.

DAVID: The shot took effect and that was fine until game five; it just had enough. It just spasmed [sic] so bad where I was, you know, I couldn't even do it. Couldn't even do it, it hurt so bad. And you know, going out that way, you just don't want to go out that way ...

Choosing *how* he'd go out of the game is important to him; all the more reason he seized the opportunity to play in San Diego in 2004 and beyond. That's next on *One on One*. . . .

David Wells has reached a lot of milestones, which have produced a lot of memories from his career, including one from the summer of '04. A Sunday afternoon at Yankee Stadium, David Wells had been here many times before. But this time he's in Padres blue.

DAVID: Oh, my God, it was unbelievable. I expected, you know, some cheers, but a lot of boos, but when that whole stadium stood up, I thought *Wow*. I just had to step off. I was like, *Oh, man, am I going to cry? Am I going to break down and do this?* I'm like, *Nah, I ain't gonna do it. Tip your cap and go get 'em.*

Wells clearly left an impression from his years in New York.

MARIANO RIVERA: David is a warrior. When he's on the mound he wants to give it everything he has.

DEREK JETER: He's a gamer. He enjoyed playing here and pitching in New York, had a lot of success.

Wells has long stayed connected to his hometown and old friends. Where he once borrowed boards at South Coast Surf shop, he now can afford to have them custom made.

SURF SHOP CLERK: He's never forgotten where he came from, never forgotten us.

In '92, the World Champion Blue Jay donated $50,000 for Point Loma High's new gym.

JANE: I bet your mom's proud of you ...

DAVID: She is. I know she's looking down—her and my grandmother, smiling ...

Family means a lot to him. And while he's naturally protective and appreciates privacy, he's also at ease out and about.

DAVID *[on walk with family]: Have a good day!*

DAVID: I'm a happy-go-lucky guy. People perceive me to be this one dude; I'm not that guy. At one point I was, but I'm not that guy anymore. I just want to relax. I'm back home. I want to relax.

NINA: He's really not everything that the press says that he is, like this wild and crazy guy. I mean, he's got his moments, don't get me wrong.

Nina and David met while he was living in her native Florida in 1994 during the baseball strike.

NINA: A girlfriend of mine was trying to set him up with another girlfriend of mine.

He and Nina clicked instead.

NINA: He kept calling her. "Who's that Nina girl?" And all that. And my girlfriend was telling him, "You don't have a shot in the world, don't even try."

They married in 2000.

DAVID: Not bad for a guy who had no chance, huh?

Nina was a successful real estate broker, then the businesswoman behind the David Wells Charitable Foundation for seven years. After having their son, she's back as a runway model for high-end fashion shows. And after the 2004 season when David fired his agent, Nina, his biggest fan, took on that role.

NINA: I think that my own personal feelings got in the way of the negotiations a lot, and it was just a lot of pressure for me 'cause I was scared that I was going to end up doing something that he wouldn't be happy with.

He wanted to stay in San Diego, but ended up taking a Red Sox offer he couldn't refuse. His time in Boston in 2005? Generally positive, but after asking to be traded, his '06 started like this:

DAVID: When I was walking out to warm up, I got booed. And then every hit I gave up, I got booed. Every walk I gave up, booed, especially when I gave up the home runs. I mean, it was terrible.

On top of that? Knee issues.

DAVID: Then I rehabbed it and I got it to where it felt great, and then the line drive. *[hit in a game]* And then right on the knee that I had surgically repaired and, you know, what are the odds of that?

Finally pitching again in late summer was good timing for that trade back to the Padres and home, his two-and-a-half acre estate in progress.

> DAVID: I would've never thought I'd have something like this but, you know, I guess …
> JANE: Why not?
> DAVID: … if you pitch a long time and you're very effective, you can buy things like this. So it's just nice to relax. This is good retirement.
> JANE: Is this it for you?
> DAVID: This is it. I'm looking forward to it, to be honest with you. I still have the will to go out there, sure, I could be effective, but, you know, I've played a long time and I think it's time to come home and hang out with the kids, hang out with my wife.

In an elegant home filled with family pictures of their growing boys, a menagerie of animals …

> DAVID: This is Bruce Bochy [big dog], right here.
> NINA: This is David's baby.
> DAVID: This is my favorite. This is Cabella [little dog].
> JANE/DAVID: Ohh … [bird snipping at Jane]
> DAVID: See? There you go. She don't like women.

And a few deer head from hunting his Buck Falls Ranch in Michigan he owns with Kirk Gibson.

> DAVID: But just the thrill of the hunt is pretty spectacular.
> NINA: I won't say that he will retire. I believe in my heart that he will, but I've been saying that for four years, too, and he just amazes me every single season. So who knows?
> DAVID: I want to feel good after baseball so I can, you know, watch my kids grow up and have some fun.

A big guy, he admits he's put weight and pressure on his knees and knows that what's kept him pitching at times—doctor approved cortisone shots and anti-inflammatories—have taken a toll.

> DAVID: If you keep taking them, I mean, it's not good for you.

On the other hand …

> DAVID: If they keep throwing the money at you, why turn it down? But twenty-five years of professional ball, I think, is, you know, it's good enough. Maybe I can use my knowledge to help guys.

He already has.

> CLAY HENSLEY: There's been some situations here when I've gotten into a little bit of trouble on the mound and he's kind of brought me back and just told me some things to think about while I'm pitching.
> JOSH BARFIELD: He's a gamer. He's a big time pitcher. I think that's something you try and emulate.

CHRIS YOUNG: Personally, I'm just extremely excited to be on the bench with him or even talk with him.

DAVID: And the most important thing I tell all these young guys, and I keep telling them every day is, "Don't be afraid to fail. Because if you're afraid to fail, then that means you're doubting yourself out there on the mound. I mean, be the same person you were when you got here and leave that way as well, and I think you'll earn more respect from the athletes and the people than you can imagine."

David Wells makes a strong first impression with his charisma and candor. But considering all he's accomplished from a poor kid in Ocean Beach to pitching the elusive perfect game, no matter what more he does, he has indeed left a lasting impression on the game. I'm Jane Mitchell. Thank you for watching *One on One*.

> "I was happy to do it because it was for Jane. This interview was more personal; a better setting because it was at my home. I thought the show was edited nicely and gave the viewer a 'real' look at who I am and what I am about. Everybody loved the show and still talk about it every time it is aired. Always, getting a different view into [other athletes'] lives is cool and helps you to appreciate them more."
>
> —David Wells, 2010

JAKE PEAVY AND MARK LORETTA

JAKE PEAVY

Jake Peavy was called up from the minors in 2002 and impressive from the start. Being in the spotlight didn't seem to shake him when he made his major league debut at Yankee Stadium. I would come to know him at spring training and on the field through 2003. He was quiet, respectful, and humble. While young, he was composed on the mound with the confidence of a veteran. However, by 2004, and just twenty-two at the time, a different spotlight, the television show *One on One with Jane Mitchell,* would be a whole new ball game for this boy from Alabama.

"I was nervous about the interview at first, but got comfortable as it went along. I have to give credit to Jane for putting me at ease during the process."

—JAKE PEAVY, 2010

As the San Diego Padres made the transition from Qualcomm Stadium to PETCO Park in 2004, there were high expectations for the team. The pitching staff had great promise with young gun Jake, and many wanted to know more about this wunderkind, so he was on deck for a *One on One* that season. Traveling to Alabama to tell that part of his story was not in the budget, nor did it need to be. That winter, I coordinated with a local television reporter to spend part of a day with Jake and his wife Katie at their home. He went to their house, shot inside their home (including the antler chandelier) and joined Jake driving to a pond where he liked to fish. The reporter used the video for a story there, and we gladly provided him with some video of Jake at spring training. It was a nice partnership—to bring a little bit of the South with Jake in his natural environment to San Diego, his new baseball home.

Once the season began, I arranged to meet Jake and Katie at their nearly empty, rented apartment the morning of a home game. When the two photographers, my associate producer, an intern, and I arrived, I could see the near panic in Jake's face. This was not his comfort zone. "Welcome to the big leagues," I joked. As the crew set up, I talked with Jake and Katie about the process and how we wanted it to be informative and fun, giving my standard advice: "Just ignore the men behind the cameras and talk to me." It was a tight squeeze, and TV lights in such a small space tend to heat the place up a bit. Between that and Jake's nerves, we had to dab the sweat from his brow a few times. I reassured him it was okay, and he did well.

He knew the answers to what I asked, because it was about him. Still, he had never had such an in-depth interview. I was impressed by his thoughtfulness, courtesy, honesty, and depth. When he and Katie sat next to each other to talk about how they met and fell in love, it was sweet and refreshing to see how grounded, wide-eyed, and humbled they were about where they were at such a young age.

Sometimes I'll take no for an answer, but not this go round. Jake was learning the guitar and one of his teachers was Tim Flannery. That same year, 2004, Tim, a former Padre player and coach, had returned to the Padres as a broadcaster doing radio for the team and the pre-game show for Channel 4. Uncertain whether Jake's story would be able to sustain a whole half hour at the time, I decided to do a Tim Flannery update, too. Part of why it made sense to pair the two in a show was the common denominator: they both played guitar, and Tim had been giving young Jake guitar lessons.

I scheduled Tim to come to the apartment with his guitar so he could teach, Jake could learn, and the two could play together. It would be a juxtaposition of music and baseball, veteran and youngster, and a look at Jake's musical sides fans had not seen. Jake seemed nervous and a little leery about doing this on camera because he was still learning the instrument. I justified that process is part of their good story, and Tim encouraged him to relax, play, and sing. It was a perfect little musical vignette.

Soon after his first full year in the majors, Jake Peavy came in to his own. By 2007, he dominated and was named the National League Cy Young Award winner. That was indeed four seasons from our original interview with Jake when he anticipated, "Do I think I'm going to be better four years from now when I'm twenty-six? Of course, I do. You know, I think I'll be bigger, stronger, and better."

I had wanted to do an updated show with Jake and Katie because they had finally bought a home in San Diego, and their family had grown. With an injury, then trade talks, the timing never seemed right. The summer of 2009, he approved a trade to the Chicago White Sox.

Considering he was so young and a bit timid when I first met him, it has been a pleasure to watch him mature on videotape and in person. Few knew anything about him as a rookie, and it is rewarding to know we introduced him in a different way, other than just the highlights. Looking back, I hope the *One on One* experiences did a little something for his confidence and comfort level off the field, knowing he deserved attention for his success and contributions. While we've showcased him, he is the one who has earned his place on the national stage and record books.

MARK LORETTA

"When Jane came to the house, it was as if a friend had come over for a visit."

—MARK LORETTA, 2010

I had a hunch I was going to like Mark Loretta because he went to Northwestern University. What I didn't know is how much I would like him and his wife Hilary for so many other reasons. Fans would love them too. The winter before the 2003 season, Mark, a free agent, signed with the San Diego Padres, back home in Southern California. What made it nice, from a production standpoint, was that he and his wife were already based in Scottsdale, Arizona. After a long hot day at camp, photographer Dan Roper and I (no big crew here) drove to the Loretta home where I first met Hilary and their baby, Frankie. There was something so down to earth and unassuming about them that I was excited to be featuring them. The outside of their house was adobe style, inside was warm and modern. The contemporary, Chicago, city-girl side of Hilary was reflected in her stylish décor.

Once the season began in 2003, I wanted to interview Mark's parents, Dave and Ellen, from Laguna Beach. The Lorettas graciously agreed to meet at Mark and Hilary's rented home in Del Mar. They arrived with bags of fish tacos, enough for everyone, including us. It was a quick shoot on a game day, but the parents' perspective added a lot of texture to Mark's story, especially the part about living in Mexico as a child and growing up a Dodgers fan.

Mark's original story was paired with Adam Eaton in 2003. By 2004, Mark had had stunning success at second base and was named an All-Star, so his story needed an update. I paired that with Terrence Long. When Terrence was traded, Mark's story couldn't be replayed, yet he remained on the team and a fan favorite. I found a way to resurrect Mark's portion with good reason. After the 2004 season, both Jake Peavy and Mark Loretta had received national acclaim. Jake won the National League's ERA (Earned Run Average) title, and Mark Loretta was named a Louisville Slugger Silver Slugger, selected as the best offensive second baseman in the National League. I paired the two for a new show, with the new information, and reintroduced them in 2005.

For the Lorettas' updated interview, we went to their new home in a lovely gated community—a stark contrast in size and décor to their little house in the desert. Even in its grandeur—with high ceilings, big furniture, and a lovely guest-house and big backyard—their home was warm and comfortable with plenty of children's toys for Frankie and his new baby sister due that fall.

There is more to the story about Mark and Hilary that hits close to home for me. When I first met them we had exchanged stories about our timelines, including how I had moved back to San Diego because of my father's poor health and had been involved with the ALS Association. They shared how Hilary's uncle had Parkinson's Disease, one of the diseases that I understood could be greatly helped with a cure for ALS. I explained about the chapter's Walk to Defeat ALS® every October and that if the Padres were not in the post-season, we would love to have them come to the walk. They said they would keep that in mind.

Sometimes people just say something to be polite and don't follow through. Not Mark and Hilary Loretta. On a beautiful October Sunday morning—along with more than one thousand participants—Mark, Hilary, Frankie, and Mark's father came in their walking shoes with Frankie's stroller. They walked our three-mile route, met my family, talked with several of our PALS (persons with ALS), and were touched.

Encouraging or pressuring (in a nice way) a player to do an interview for the good of a show and the fans is one thing. I have no problem with that. However, I am always careful about not using my position to impose or pressure anyone for a cause I care about separate from my Channel 4 duties. I'm not afraid to inform and suggest that the ALS Chapter is open to anything and any kind of help, but I would never want someone to feel obligated or think they have to do something because I asked. When it came to the Lorettas, I didn't even have to ask.

Sometime not long after that walk, Mark said how much they enjoyed the event, and if there was anything they could do to help to let them know. Wow. What an offer. With that, I gratefully asked if he and Hilary would be our honorary chairs for the 2004 walk. They didn't hesitate to say yes. Players have a lot going on during the season, so I promised we would help them with the logistics. Their participation for two years was significant to our cause. To help spread the word, they lent their name and picture, read a script for a public service announcement I produced, did radio appearances, and Mark was on hand to meet and greet several of our PALS and their escorts down on the field. The Padres helped facilitate some of Mark's participation and featured his ALS-related time as a highlight of their community service efforts. Having a true partnership with the team and a player helped the chapter immensely, and we are still grateful to include Mark and Hilary as lovely people key to our chapter's growth.

Their involvement was a legitimate subject during our interview. Not only was a new dimension to their story included, but so was, for about thirty seconds, the story of ALS and the fight against Lou Gehrig's Disease—an example of good synergy all the way around.

In December 2006 the Padres traded Mark Loretta to the Boston Red Sox. He went on to play for the Houston Astros and then the Dodgers, the team he grew up watching. In 2010, he retired and joined the Padres as a special assistant to the general manager. The Lorettas had kept their home base in San Diego, so, as I told Hilary in a congratulatory email, I was glad they had "come a full pretzel-like circle." I count them not only among my favorite show subjects, but also among my friends.

First is the script for the *One on One* featuring Mark Loretta and Jake Peavy debuting March 20, 2005. Following that is an excerpt from the edition in which Jake and Tim Flannery played guitar together in 2004.

• • •

Jake Peavy and Mark Loretta: among the Padres' best, look for another good year.

> **JAKE:** I feel like that I'm kinda molding myself into the kind of pitcher that I want to be.

> **MARK:** Our goal is to win the division. Get in the playoffs and then you never know.

Mark Loretta and Jake Peavy had stellar seasons in 2004, bringing them national and international recognition. That's something San Diego should be proud of, indeed, although it's not surprising to those who have been watching their stories unfold.

You can take the boy out of the country, but you can't take the country out of the boy. And Jake Peavy's quite happy with that. His Alabama roots are as deep as his pitches are strong. He's young, twenty-three in 2004, but mature.

> **JAKE:** I get so tired of people saying, "You're twenty-two years old in the major leagues," you know. I do have some time in and do have a decent idea of what's going on. You know, do I think I'm going to be better at four years from now when I'm twenty-six? Of course, I do. You know, I think I'll be bigger, stronger, and better. But, you know, for the time being, I am what I am. I think I can get the job done now and I think—I don't want people to label me as young and have any kind of excuse to get me out of anything or say I'm not

ready because I feel like I am capable of being a good major league pitcher and helping this ball club win.

He is proving that already. Leading the team with the most strike outs and wins in 2003, he's consistent and growing, going full throttle.

> **JAKE:** I think I was full throttle since the time I stepped on this earth, you know.

He's outgoing and friendly with a warm southern style and beams around his wife Katie, pregnant with baby number two, and their four-year-old son Jacob. Jake and Katie were just fourteen when they were set up at their church's youth group. She ran track and appreciates his competitive side.

> **JANE:** Tell us about Jake. What's he like?
>
> **KATIE:** Oh, he's very, very fun, animated. You know, sometimes he can be hard to keep up with, but it's very exciting. And when I look at my little boy, I see him.

Jacob Edward Peavy was born May 31, 1981, in Mobile, Alabama. He and his little brother Luke were raised by their father, a cabinet maker with the family business, and mother who returned to work at the post office to help put the boys through private school. They lived in the country, their neighbors mostly family.

> **JAKE:** Just the old school way of living, "yes sir," "no ma'am."
>
> **JANE:** How did they teach you to live your life and to approach life?
>
> **JAKE:** Well, I think that all comes from the Christian standpoint, I guess ... the Bible's the ultimate of what to do and what not to do and then we lived by that. And just do unto others as you would have them do unto you.

From the time he was in T-ball, young Jake was hooked on baseball and the dream.

> **JAKE:** I don't think you really realize that it can become a reality till I started getting into high school and scouts started coming to see you play and colleges. And you think there may be a shot, you know, but I really didn't know what I was going to do, to be honest with you. I was very blessed, I guess, with a good arm and, at that I was a six-foot, a buck-sixty, a small kid, but I could throw it about ninety miles an hour in high school, and I guess not many kids back home could do that.

Bound for Auburn University, the San Diego Padres drafted him in the fifteenth round in 1999.

> **JAKE:** We had made it clear that we were going to go to college, you know, for the most part, I didn't feel like I was mature enough. I didn't want to leave the great state of Alabama and head off on this adventure. And we took off on it and agreed as a family. I signed papers and two days later was in Phoenix, Arizona ...
>
> **JANE:** Wow.
>
> **JAKE:** Crying, thinking I had made the wrong decision.
>
> **JANE:** Really?

JAKE: But …

JANE: Tough to leave.

JAKE: It was very tough to leave.

Katie was running track and studying nursing at the University of South Alabama, so there were lots of phone calls to her and his dad.

JAKE: He said, "You know, son, Peavys ain't never quit." And that's—you just have to know my dad to understand where he's coming from. He said, "I've never quit anything I've done in my life, never done anything like this, but we're not quitting," you know.

Peavy's toughness was tested when he went from Rookie League to Single-A, Fort Wayne, Indiana, with a drastic temperature change from heat to snow. His severe headaches and nausea turned out to be viral meningitis.

JAKE: The good Lord was looking after us 'cause my grandparents happened to be in town. I was staying with them and if I wouldn't have been staying with them and they wouldn't have got me to the hospital about three o'clock in the morning, who knows what could've happened. But fortunately, they got me into a hospital that took great care of me. And there for about a couple of weeks, I was down and out, but was able to rebound and then get back on with the season in late April.

By the next year, his homesickness was cured with a big promotion from A-ball at California's Lake Elsinore Storm to the Double-A Mobile Bay Bears in Mobile, Alabama.

JANE: A lot of Peavy fans.

JAKE: It was a …

JANE: Everyone out there showing their support.

JAKE: We had a lot of unknown relatives I met for the first time and friends, guys I went to high school with. But that's all in good fun, I guess.

Marriage and fatherhood added fuel to his professional fire.

JAKE: And I think that was a huge thing for me to be settled down and focused whereas some guys may have been, at twenty or twenty-one years old, having a lot more active nightlife and just having a good time and not really focused on what they were there to do and that's to play baseball. So at that year I really saw that it wasn't that far away being in Double-A for the last part of the season and was really looking forward to 2002.

Starting the season at Double-A, he'd get great news.

JAKE: "You're going to the big leagues and you're starting against the New York Yankees tomorrow." And just started to—I didn't know what to think. Just, you know, I'm not going to lie, I started crying. It was an emotional day for me and to be able, you know, just to realize a lifelong dream was something that was just truly awesome.

When Jake Peavy isn't playing his game, you'll often find him playing his guitar. A talent he has developed just since spring training of 2000.

> JAKE: Never had a lesson, never had any formal teaching by no means, can't read music, but I can play it.

He has organized a notebook with favorite country music songs, throws it in his suitcase when he's on the road.

> JAKE: Sort of sing myself back home sometimes. Up in San Fran, I'm in my hotel room, just—had a bad night or even had a good night, go sit around and play the guitar. It's just peaceful. And it keeps you out of trouble, and you don't get caught up in some of the things a lot of people get caught up in.

He is also in tune with his professional responsibilities, preparing physically and mentally for a game.

> JAKE: And I think you gotta have a certain confidence about yourself—not in any way being cocky. But I'm definitely confident in my ability when I'm on the baseball field.

Confident and composed even in trying times, such as August 2003, when Katie was hospitalized for also having viral meningitis.

> ANNOUNCER: *He wants to say hi to her, thinking about Katie and Jacob watching the game on TV …*
>
> KATIE: And I just knew that he still had a job to do and I didn't want him to just put everything off and stay with me because I knew that I'd be fine. I was going to be taken care of, and I needed him to do what he needed to.
>
> JAKE: And it was a trying time for our family, but those type situations when it's just me and Jacob and we're spending the night at home and he's asking about mommy and we're saying prayers for mommy, those really bind your family.

Jake Peavy's values were instilled in Alabama …

> JAKE: That's just what it's about, going down to see the boys at Ralph's Sporting Goods.

In the off-season, they're at home in the town of Semmes. Their house is decorated with baseball collectibles and artifacts reflecting his interest in Civil War history.

> JAKE [driving in a truck in Alabama]: You just wonder where the USA would be today without the stance that some of those men took back in the day. You don't see many of these dirt roads in San Diego or trucks in front of you that have deer heads on the back of them.

He hunts, but as for those antlers hanging on the chandelier …?

> KATIE: I didn't do that. It wasn't my idea. But it made him happy. It's in his office. It's something that makes him smile when he goes in there. So he can do it.
>
> JANE: You also like to fish.

JAKE: Love to fish. Love to do anything outdoors.

During the baseball season, he'll cast a line with his Padres teammates ...

JAKE [fishing in Alabama]: I enjoy my time in California, love playing baseball, getting to see the big cities I get to see. However long we spend during the season of big cities and big tall buildings you get out here and see little pine trees, and hardwood bottoms, and big lakes. It's a just a beautiful sight to me.

JANE: Tell us about Sundays in Alabama with the Peavys.

JAKE: Well, Sundays are very traditional day back home. Shenandoah sings a song called "Sunday in the South" and talks about a lazy Sunday that your family gets up, I guess, on a Sunday morning and you eat a nice big breakfast. And you get ready in your Sunday best and go down to church, spend some good time talking to the big man upstairs, and then we go over to Ma and Pa's house and have some Sunday dinner. After we eat, the men'll be out in the den or on the front porch watching some—maybe some NASCAR®, some NFL football—and the women'll sit in there and maybe drink coffee and talk ...

JANE: You got the whole men-women thing going.

JAKE: That's just the way it happens, you know. Not to sound—but that's just the ...

JANE: Oh, come on. Don't women like NASCAR® too?

JAKE: I tell you what, some women down south get into it. But it's ...

JANE: Those are special times.

JAKE: Special times.

He takes family, winning, and losing to heart.

JAKE: I want to be respected around the league and around the clubhouse for what I do every fifth day.

Even after missing some time for a strained tendon he came back strong ...

ANNOUNCER: *Jake's done for the year with the third best ERA in franchise history.*

And then some, earning the title for the best earned run average in the majors. No fanfare, but his 2.27 ERA is on a baseball card with some of the greats like Randy Johnson and Roger Clemens.

JAKE: To have your name in front of those guys' names, you can't say that you ever thought or imagined it in all your years, but wow is all you can say I guess.

He joined other Padres for the autumn All-Star series in Japan, and Game 4's MVP then came home to accept the Padres' Pitcher of the Year award.

It was a whirlwind of a year, with Baby Wyatt making this a young family of four. Jake Peavy has a new contract through 2008 and a goal.

JAKE: I don't just want to be a major league pitcher. I want to be a great one. My job is to win ball games for this team and if you go out and do that, you're going to leave your mark. So I just, I know that I'm young, but I feel like I got a good, a lot of good years ahead of me, so hopefully the good Lord willing, we'll play for a long time and leave our mark on San Diego . . . .

"[I remember] first, being surprised that anyone wanted to do an in depth interview, then, being a little apprehensive about what it would be about. At first, I was a little nervous, but eventually I got more comfortable and all went fine. It was different because there were few questions about baseball or any particular game or play. That made it harder because I have plenty of experience with post-game interviews and little experience talking about my personal life . . . .It's probably always a little uncomfortable to see yourself interviewed and have your life described on television, but I thought it was fair and a nice piece. [Hearing others talk about me] is a bit uncomfortable and even embarrassing, but I truly appreciate the great things everyone had to say. The feedback was all positive about the show. . . . I know my teammates pretty well, but it is interesting to see some of the things about their youth and their extended families . . . . Thank you."

—Jake Peavy, 2010

Number 8 Mark Loretta has found a place with San Diego. The former Brewer and Astro came with a good guy reputation. We first met Mark and his wife Hilary in 2003. Their winter home base was in Scottsdale, a modest home with an eclectic style. Then, moving west, they rented a house in Del Mar . . .

> HILARY: 'Cuz we thought, *Hey, we're here for one year in San Diego*, so it was that aspect, away from baseball, was a lot of fun, just enjoying San Diego, getting to know the city a little bit, and we fell in love with it.

Their son Frankie was just walking, now he's walking, talking, and a real jumping-for-joy little boy. And they've expanded their square footage a bit . . .

> HILARY: We had to buy a bigger house because we have guests all the time!
> JANE: You're expecting another baby?
> HILARY: We are, yeah, we are, number two. In November, perfect timing, after the season . . .
> MARK: After the World Series hopefully . . .

Feeling part of a community, they continue a commitment to Padres and other charities.

> MARK: You can learn a lot of life lessons from people who are afflicted with devastating diseases . . .

With an uncle suffering from Parkinson's, they're helping a related neuromuscular disease, ALS, as the honorary chairs for the annual Walk to Defeat ALS, Lou Gehrig's Disease, named after the baseball great.

MARK: It's such a difficult disease because it can take its toll so quickly. So you see somebody in the winter then all of a sudden you see them six months later, there's a drastic difference. It's a very ugly disease that needs some attention.

Their compassion and experiences are woven into a busy and successful two seasons with the Padres.

JANE: What have you learned about yourself? Has anything changed in the last year or so?

MARK: I don't think so, maybe you should ask Hilary more so on that.

HILARY: That's a good question. I don't think so. Mark's the same. He's the same since I met him when he was nineteen.

Born Mark David Loretta on August 14, 1971 in Santa Monica California, at just three months old he moved to Mexico City for his dad's job with Bank of America. Baby Mark was speaking Spanish before English, and home movies show little number 5 enthusiastic about the game.

MARK: My first exposure to baseball being when I was about two or three years old. There was this professor, they called him, in Mexico City, who kind of taught me how to play catch.

But his parents, Dave and Ellen, recall his tendencies far earlier than that.

ELLEN: The first Christmas card we have of him, he's holding an ornament, I mean he's in this position and he's just a little baby.

DAVE: He seemed to have tremendous hand-eye coordination right from the start.

When the family returns to Arcadia near Los Angeles, he's at first too young for Little League. His only option the Boys Christian League.

ELLEN: So I said, "Mark, they want to pick you up on a bus, twice a week and you have to go to the Bible study and you can play on the team. Do you want to do this?" And he said, "Yes." So that's how dedicated he was at five and a half years old.

With a younger brother, Chris, and baby sister, Kelly, among his fans, he plays baseball, basketball, and is student body president at St. Francis, an all-boys college prep high school. A late bloomer physically, Loyola Marymount and UCLA would have kept him on the bench a few years, but Northwestern offers a scholarship with a promise.

MARK: "We'd like you to come in and play right away." And that was really attractive to me, too.

So to the windy city of Chicago he goes …

MARK: And incidentally, I hated Northwestern my first semester.

The weather, the distance, but taking his parents advice, he sticks it out, meets his teammates …

MARK: And just kind of fell in love with the place.

Then fell in love with Hilary Kaplan ...

   MARK: We met at the Fiji DG P-J Party.

A fraternity-sorority mixer their sophomore year.

   HILARY: My girlfriend said, "That guy's name is Mark and he wants to meet you." And I said, "Okay, well, tell me about him." "He's a really nice guy, and he's on the baseball team." And I said, "He's on the baseball team? He doesn't look like he's on the baseball team. He weighs about a buck fifty."

Hilary, from Chicago, went to a small high school in Vermont for ski racing.

   HILARY: I was really into sports and very competitive.

The competitive Loretta doesn't get a big enough offer from a team to leave college early, and not being drafted pays off. His senior year, he's the team captain, the Big-Ten Conference Most Valuable Player, and a Division One All-American—all while maintaining a B average. With Phil Rizzo scouting him, the Milwaukee Brewers pick Loretta in the seventh round.

   MARK: After graduation, I loaded up and went to Helena, Montana into the Pioneer League. And that was fun. I only spent a week there though.

Loretta's age and experience in the summer Cape Cod wood bat league in college gives him an edge over younger guys. He zips through the minors in two years.

   MARK: So, yeah, I mean, that's just a euphoric feeling, getting that first call-up.

His family flies to Minnesota for his debut. He strikes out as a pinch hitter, getting his first hit at a Brewers home game.

   MARK: Got a standing ovation from the crowd in Milwaukee. I remember it was kind of a cold day, so the crowd wasn't huge, but it was still real special.

Loretta's first full year in the majors is 1997, getting extensive playing time as a utility player. Then in '98, he sets a career high batting average of .316, ranking sixth in the National League against lefthanders, and has a combined .991 fielding percentage, making just six errors in nearly 700 chances.

   After that impressive season, a more personal highlight, his wedding. With Mark a Catholic and Hilary Jewish, their ceremony reflects their faiths. On the professional front, he finally feels comfortable in the big leagues and by 2000, he's finally guaranteed the shortstop spot. But then some freakish twists of fate.

   MARK: It was June second. I was actually hitting about .305, off to a great start and fouled a ball off my foot. You know, didn't think too much of it. It was hurting.

The fracture requires ten weeks of recovery ...

   MARK: Obviously derailed the momentum I had going.

Spring 2001, completely healthy ...

   MARK: A foot first slide and just reached out my hand to grab the bag and tore a ligament in my thumb, which required surgery again.

That shifts him back into a utility role in 2002, still cracking his first major league grand slam, dedicating it to his mother-in-law who lost her battle with cancer. And on the last day of the trading deadline, he's dealt to the Houston Astros, bats an amazing .424 in the month of September, finishes the season with a .304 average, and becomes a free agent.

Mark Loretta has become an integral part of the San Diego Padres. His productivity, personality, and pure professionalism also earned him his first selection to an All-Star game chosen by his peers in 2004.

> **MARK:** You play this game a long time, and you really don't allow yourself to think of yourself as an All-Star, even though you feel like you're a good player, that's just kinda reserved for the superstars of the game. And to finally be acknowledged like that was really special. Especially because my peers did it. And I think the greatest part of it, for me, was sharing it with my family, sharing it with my parents, making that phone call to them and having my mom tear up on the phone, and the same way with Hilary. They know what it's taken to get there, and all the bumps in the road, and the endless games, and being away from home and everything, so it was really an emotional time.

It's the kind of success story that just couldn't happen to a nicer guy. A guy who took his own advice and didn't squander his opportunities …

> **MARK:** Well, it was really a dream come true coming back to Southern California.

He signed as a free agent with the Padres going into the 2003 season. Never claiming he'd dazzle with speed or power …

> **MARK:** Well that's right. They talk about five-tool players and I'm probably maybe a one-tool guy. I'm not somebody who is going to steal a lot of bases or hit thirty home runs or whatever, but I think the strengths of my game come out on an everyday basis. If you see me, and if I get a chance to play every day, and that's kinda what's happened so far.

> **HILARY:** It was just so exciting to watch him play every day, and do well, be a part of a team he really felt he could add value to.

The only National Leaguer to have five hitting streaks of more than ten games and lead all NL second basemen with a .990 fielding percentage. The Padres' Mr. July, a good candidate for a trade to a team that needed what he could deliver.

> **MARK:** When you hear your name out there and you're so happy and comfortable in the place that you're in, to think about moving and going to another team is a little unsettling.

Loretta not only got through the deadline, he was rewarded with a two-year contract extension. Then he hit an 0-for-22 slump. On the last day of the season, he was just one away from breaking the franchise record for hits by a second baseman: 184 in 1989 by Roberto Alomar.

MARK: I'd been 0 for 4 that game, and I got two quick strikes on me. And so I said, "You know what, this may not happen." But I hit an 0-2 pitch out for a home run.

His outstanding year earned him the team's Most Valuable Player and the Madres' Favorite New Padre honors.

MARK: To be acknowledged by them is very nice.

In 2004, as one of the best Padres hitters ever, Loretta broke his own franchise record for most hits by a second baseman. The team fell short of the playoffs, but Loretta was again named the Padres' MVP. He received national recognition with a Silver Slugger award, voted as the best overall offensive second baseman in the National League by managers and coaches of all major league teams.

MARK: It's something that'll be real special and it's always kind of been a goal of mine.

He and Hilary were invited for an intimate dinner at the White House with President Bush to talk baseball. And in November came their very special delivery, baby Lucy Ellen. Big brother Frankie is now three, and from birthdays to baseball, Mark Loretta appreciates what he has and what's ahead.

MARK: When people say, "Hey they're playing pretty good baseball there in San Diego," especially last year when nobody expected us to. You know, we felt really good about that, but now, we have got to take it to the next step.

From Mark Loretta's break out year to Jake Peavy's quick start and success, it's clear these are two players who set a standard of excellence on and off the baseball diamond. I'm Jane Mitchell. Thank you for watching *One on One*.

• • •

The following is an excerpt from the 2004 *One on One* in which a young Jake Peavy's story is paired with an update on veteran Tim Flannery. One common denominator: their music.

• • •

At spring training and on the road, Tim Flannery has helped Jake Peavy develop his talent of playing the guitar. So we asked that the two of them get together to share a little of their musical heart and soul, and they were happy to do it.

[Jake and Tim tuning guitars]

TIM: You're singing great ...

JAKE: Baloney.

TIM: This is the hand, it's all perfect chck, chck, chck, timing—just like pitching.

JAKE: But these times right here, you learn a little something and take your game to another level—and it's just awesome.

TIM: You have something lessons will never give you—you can hear it—and you can go figure it out—lessons can't teach you that—that is a gift.

JAKE: I can remember the first time I struggled so hard to hold just a D chord or an A , I just said, "That's it," and the first time I said, "That's it, that's the song I'm trying to play." I can't imagine doing what this guy does and sit up on stage and play in front of people.

TIM: It's no different than walking out with a baseball and a mound in front of 46,000 people and getting big league hitters out—see that is where the parallels and connections are.

And on that note … we thank Jake Peavy and Tim Flannery … two guys at different ends of their career spectrum … who show why the love of the game seems to pass easily through the generations. I'm Jane Mitchell, thank you for watching *One on One*.

"Hilary and I gave Jane a tour and talked about things that didn't remotely concern baseball. In other words, we felt very comfortable with Jane and the situation. In turn, the interview went much deeper than we imagined it would. We discussed the trials and tribulations of the baseball life; in particular, the difficulties that most people don't realize in carrying on a relationship under very unique circumstances…. Because of her personality and her approach, Jane is incredibly skilled at getting her subjects to open up further than they ever expect to…. By contacting, and sometimes interviewing, subjects' parents, grandparents, friends, etc. Jane is able to weave a comprehensive depiction of her subject. In my case, Jane even interviewed my parents. They were overjoyed to be on-camera talking about their son and how he had grown up dreaming of being a big leaguer. The pictures they provided also enhanced the quality of the production and gave it depth. The *One on One* episodes we did with Jane will be treasured family heirlooms for generations to come."

—Mark Loretta, 2010

KHALIL GREENE

In all the years of *One on One*, there are two people I'm asked about most: Ted Williams and Khalil Greene. The two could not be more different. Ted Williams was outgoing, verbal, and bigger than life. Khalil Greene, still a young ballplayer when I interviewed him, was quiet and would be lost in a crowd unless you knew who he was. Yet from my experience, they had common denominators—they were not interested in talking to the media and would be potentially challenging interviews had I not been prepared.

2004 was Khalil Greene's rookie season. His play mesmerized and thrilled fans and teammates. His look and lack of expression were equally puzzling. Fans, reporters, and I were curious about his idiosyncrasies—what made him tick.

Although a virtual highlight reel, he seemed uninterested in or shy about media attention. So I made my case to the Padres' media relations director at the

"Dear Jane, I received the videos and photos the other day and wanted to thank you. We love the interview. You did such a great job. It is one that I know we will watch over and over again. I know you spent a lot of time tracking down the story and Khalil as well, thank you so much. I hope we can meet again sometime when we are more relaxed, usually during the summer!"

—JANET GREENE, MOTHER, 2005.

time, Luis Garcia, that if anyone were to tell his story, it should be me, because I could tell it fairly, comprehensively, and with plenty of time to be complete. I knew Khalil was unusual and it would take a lot of care and thought to pull all the pieces together to do his story justice. I also made my case to my boss that to do this right we had to go to him in the off-season. Khalil was living near and working out at his alma mater, Clemson University, in South Carolina.

After a lot of encouragement and persistence from me, Luis relayed that Khalil agreed to our visiting him at Clemson—as well as a sit down interview. I respected Khalil's choice to coordinate through the Padres, but not having his email or phone number made it more challenging to get things done. His agent, Mike Milchin, was helpful in giving me some insight and contacts. I also coordinated with the head baseball coach at Clemson, Jack Leggett, who was in frequent contact with Khalil and helped me map out the Clemson shoot itinerary. We had a tight window, but Khalil agreed he would be at the school for a typical winter workout the day we planned to be there and would sit down with me for a few minutes at the field. It was still a question mark whether we would be able to interview his parents while in the area. His father had been ill, so we weren't sure what would transpire, but I was willing to take a chance. We agreed to do the long interview in San Diego in February before he drove to Arizona for spring training.

Come January 2005, photographer Dan Roper and I flew to Charlotte, North Carolina. We drove west, capturing scene-setter shots of country landscape and tall feathery plants on the way to Clemson. The next day, we met Coach Leggett. He was friendly, understood our goals for the day, and he helped me understand

Khalil a little better by sharing how he was an old soul, focused, and special. Down on the baseball field, we interviewed some of his former teammates and younger players still on the team. Then Khalil arrived, nodded hello, and went straight to the infield. It was a little surreal. Here was this unassuming young man who could have been the National League Rookie of the Year were it not for a broken finger coming out on a sunny but cold January day where it had all begun. He was removed from the lights of PETCO Park, yet it was a perfect fit for a humble and talented player. I sat in the dugout just watching him take ground balls and, on occasion, talking with the other players. He was serious about every step, every move, every throw.

When he finished, I pulled out the lavaliere mikes and asked to sit in the dugout and talk a few minutes. With my prompting, he reminisced about his time at Clemson, describing what it was like to be there in the moment, and what he thought about as he looked around. That is all in the script, but what's not in the script is how I personally gained a real sense of how Khalil respects people who respect him. I pushed for things I thought were important, but pulled back when I understood why it would not work for him. For example, I encouraged him to let us interview his family, but when he explained it had been a trying winter because of his father's health, I respected his need to not do too much. I was thankful he was coordinating with his mother to gather childhood pictures. Eventually, she and I communicated by email, and between her, his high school, and college we had plenty of elements to include, along with the trip to Clemson.

We spent the balance of that day and the next roaming the college town interviewing people about Khalil and shooting an on-camera stand-up at a big park with the town behind me. Then we traveled home.

We planned to interview Khalil in February in San Diego before going to Arizona. Because of unusually heavy rain, in part, he left early, and had to reschedule our shoot. Plan B: shoot at the complex in Peoria. It wasn't ideal, because we would not have all the equipment and crew we normally used for an in-depth interview; however, we adapted.

I sensed Khalil was not one to chitchat. Some people I can ask, "What were you like as a little kid?" and they talk for five minutes before I ask the second question. I didn't think that would work with Khalil. I felt interviewing him would require more preparation.

I had already done the Clemson connection. I read old newspaper and web articles pointing to other people, coaches, reporters, and friends who had been influential or contributed to Khalil's high school and college careers. I tracked down several of them, and these conversations gave me some facts, perspective, and stories I could then bounce off Khalil in our interview. For example, instead of just asking him, "What did you like to do for fun in college," and expecting him to fill it in, I could tell him that I learned he liked going for milkshakes in college, and ask him to tell me more about that. He might have answered general questions, but having more information than less seemed to be a better fit.

We set up in an empty office of the Padres complex with a couch, a chair, and some plants. It was not warm and cozy, but the interview is what counts. This was not his comfort zone, so I tried to make him feel at ease, saying I wanted this to be fun, but to also learn more about the core of what made him who he is. That is why I broached the subject of his Baha'i faith in the first few minutes of rolling tape. The length of his comments about his beliefs shows how in-depth and thoughtful he was. It seemed to me, it wasn't that Khalil was uncommunicative, but rather, he didn't seem at ease with quick questions and answers such as those that often come before or after a game. From my experience, he was a deep person and when asked something of substance, he gave a substantive answer, especially given that we had time. I intentionally let some of his comments go longer than usual in the show to hear his perspective in his words on topics he was quite comfortable talking about. Some viewers have said that Khalil didn't say much and wondered how I managed what must have been a challenging interview. I always gently remind them of his depth and that he seemed to prefer substance over quippy sound bites. Did I have to work a little harder and prepare more? In some ways, yes, but that was my responsibility to him and the viewer.

Another aspect of the interview process that made it quite enjoyable for me is that Khalil was a very good listener. In some of my questions, I might have assumed or implied something, and he was quick to clarify with a frank grin. For example, when I asked who he played sports with growing up:

JANE: With your sisters?
KHALIL: No …
JANE: Too or?
KHALIL: … not so much the sisters. [smiles]

While Khalil isn't one to smile a lot, he did a few times and those genuine moments offered a peek into his sense of humor and fun side. Players and others who knew him better and saw him with no cameras—as some share in the show—told me they knew that side of him, confirming he was not really a cut-up, crack-up kind of guy, but he did let loose every once in a while. One funny part of our dialogue had to be truncated for the show, but here's the longer version from when I asked him to give me a timeline what he was going to do after the interview:

KHALIL: Probably go home and eat and watch a movie and go to bed.

JANE: And that's it.

KHALIL: Yeah. Floss possibly in the middle there somewhere. Something like that.

JANE: Flossing is good.

KHALIL: Yeah.

JANE: Excellent. I know we've covered a lot and ...

KHALIL: Yeah, we have.

JANE: ... and maybe more than you wanted to cover. But is there anything we didn't talk about? I mean, honestly, just that ...

KHALIL: No, I think you got it all.

JANE: You sure?

KHALIL: You got it. Yeah.

JANE: Didn't miss something?

KHALIL: No.

JANE: What about—Hmm. And I can't think of anything else either.

KHALIL: No, I certainly can't.

When the show aired that spring, I sent copies to his parents, and then that season, I met them at their seats at a Padres game. I told them my mother, as many others did, admired Khalil for his outlook on life and work ethic, and that he was one of her all-time favorite players and *One on Ones*.

One time at batting practice, I did something I rarely do. I asked Khalil if he had seen the show. At the time, he had not. I then told him I wanted to do an update because he had since married. He said he was happy to introduce me to his wife, but wasn't too interested in another interview. I understood. After the 2008 season, the Padres traded Khalil to the St. Louis Cardinals. When he returned to San Diego with the visiting team, I made an effort to catch his eye and say hello, hoping he would know he was not "just a show," but an inspiration.

In 2010, I was happy to hear from his agent that Khalil was agreeable to my using pictures from the *One on One*, and his mother's nice note, and that "he wishes you well on the book." I wish him well, too, and hope to see him again and meet his wife someday.

This is the script from the edition debuting April 9, 2005.

• • •

Khalil Greene, sensational shortstop. From Key West to Clemson to California, the secret's out.

KHALIL: My expectations are probably going to supersede those of anyone else's that's around.

Khalil Greene—from his name, his look, his abilities—is not your typical or text-book baseball player. And he certainly could be considered one of the most intriguing rookies to enter the game. Sizzle aside, spending time with him and exploring his story, we find he is a young man who is as deep and thoughtful as he is talented.

If you didn't know his name or where he works, you might think he's a surfer kid: long light hair, an unassuming gentle presence. Then you see him in action. In 2004, the San Diego Padres' rookie shortstop, Khalil Greene, was a virtual highlight reel, not just in local TV team coverage, but nationally on ESPN. Productive at the plate and in the field.

> **RYAN KLESKO:** Oh, he's like a cat! You know the guys think they have hits and the next thing you know the guy is diving, getting up, and throwing them out by five feet, and guys are just going, "WOW!"

Juxtapose his performance with his solid stance, stoic style with rarely a smile. At just twenty-five years old, a sophomore in the majors, it's just his way. He's simply complex.

> **ADAM EATON:** Gifted in humanity, gifted in sports.
> **TREVOR HOFFMAN:** I think the fact that he knows what he is trying to do is kind of the biggest compliment you can give him.
> **JAKE PEAVY:** He's a team guy, he doesn't want any attention, but when you got that kind of talent, you can't run.
> **MARK LORETTA:** He's soft-spoken, yet when he does speak, he has some great things to say.

So while he has caused quite the commotion among fans, to focus only on the wow of this whiz kid would indeed shortchange the very real and fascinating person at shortstop.

> **JANE:** Were you always this laid back, even as a kid and growing up in high school?
> **KHALIL:** I don't know. Don't know, probably, probably the same way. I don't think too much has changed, honestly, in terms of the way I was growing up and then. I'm not necessarily looking for that much attention. That's something that I kind of don't really want, honestly.
> **JANE:** Umm-hmm. Well, I know. That's the difficult thing being in a very public profession because you're kind of out there and …
> **KHALIL:** Right.
> **JANE:** … people are curious.
> **KHALIL:** Well, I guess you gotta adapt.

And adapt Khalil Greene has, in his own way, on his own time. To understand how he views the game and life, go back to the beginning. His name, Khalil, means "friend of God." He was born October 21, 1979, four days after the Pittsburgh Pirates won the '79 World Series, interesting in that he was raised twenty minutes outside Pittsburgh in Gibsonia, rural western Pennsylvania, where he first picked up a baseball.

KHALIL: I remember my mom and dad were into it, and they were big into sports and nothing really organized, but it was a lot of just backyard type deal.

JANE: With your sisters?

KHALIL: No …

JANE: Too or?

KHALIL: … not so much the sisters.

JANE: No?

KHALIL: My older sister's not really athletic. She wasn't into it that much. But it was me and my mom more than anything 'cause Dad was at work. So we'd go in the backyard and beat the whiffle ball around or something like that.

JANE: Really?

KHALIL: Oh, yeah.

His mother, Janet, stayed home with the three kids, then became a Montessori school teacher. His father, Jim, a Vietnam vet, was a jeweler and picture framer. How they raised their family was influenced by their adopting the Bahai faith.

JANE: Can you describe for us what that is and how that was important to you even as a child?

KHALIL: There's so many aspects of it that I owe my whole developmental years to. And knowing right from wrong and being certain about it, and there was no real gray area. And you knew what you were doing and it was a conscious choice on your part whether or not you wanted to do it, growing up, and we knew that. So I think throughout, you had the basis to—as you grew up, and you knew what you were doing, and there was a certain independence, I think, associated with it.

Part of the mantra: to live in a pure and kindly way with a radiant heart …

KHALIL: It's a oneness of mankind. It's a big element of it, and that's something you're searching for and it can be used in all areas of life, and it's helping to get to know yourself better and your relationship with God, and also keeping in mind everyone around you and trying to, hopefully, reflect some of the attributes that are in what you're trying to live up to, I guess.

At five years old, the Greene family moved to Key West, Florida when his dad got a new job as a jeweler. Khalil played soccer, football, and his favorite, baseball.

KHALIL: I never looked at it as if I wanted to do it for a career move. It was always the enjoyment of the game and was something I wanted to do.

Khalil, a natural athlete, benefited from Brooks Carey, a former minor league teammate of Hall of Famer Cal Ripken, Jr., involved in Key West Little League.

KHALIL: And there were a lot of guys like that, so you were learning fundamentals and you were learning little ins and outs of the games that a lot of people don't have the opportunity to learn about until they're in high school or college.

At Key West High School, number 5 helped his team to the state championship his sophomore year.

> KHALIL: I focused a lot more on hitting than I did defense, and I knew that if I was ever going to go anywhere it had to be with your bat.

With colleges and scouts seeking standout seniors, Khalil did more than the required practice routine.

> KHALIL: I felt like if you wanted to get to the next level, you had to—it had to be on your own and a lot of it had to be individual.

Khalil was a star as they won the Florida State Championship. But some scouts believed he was getting too heavy to be a shortstop. And even after Coach Carey invited Cal Ripken, Jr. to watch Khalil, Ripken's nod didn't sway teams.

> Khalil was not drafted. Not what he expected.

> KHALIL: I was just—kind of questioned the system, so to speak, 'cause at that point I felt like if you did what you needed to do in the certain showcases, and if you ran under this amount of time, and if you showed off this amount of arm strength, and you had a good year, then you would be drafted—from this round to this round. And I felt like I qualified in all those areas and I didn't get drafted at all. I wouldn't say I was disappointed about it. The one thing I could say and I can remember being disappointed about is, you know, I felt that my family was definitely disappointed by it and, for me, that disappointed me more than not getting drafted 'cause I knew that I still could go to college and then I'd just do what I had to do there.

The St. Louis Cardinals had interest, if he'd become a catcher. He told them ...

> KHALIL: No, I didn't want to get to the big leagues and then be a big league catcher basically. So I figured if I can't do it as a shortstop, third baseman, or second baseman, then I guess I'm not good enough to get there.
>
> JANE: That's a pretty bold decision to make as a seventeen- or eighteen-year-old kid. I mean, a lot of kids might've just snatched at the opportunity.
>
> KHALIL: Right, well, I never looked at it in those terms. I figured if I went to school and continued to get better, then I'd have an opportunity to prove myself at another time.

And prove himself he has. When we return on *One on One*, a trip to South Carolina where Khalil Greene took his game to another level ....

> Pristine lakes, wide-open skies, crisp air. It's January in South Carolina. Just off the interstate, towering pines and a rock wall frame the entrance to Clemson University. Established in 1889, it's now ranked as one of the best public schools in America. You know you're in Tiger country from all the tigers and paw prints on roads, in the shops, in the town.
>
> FAN: What is a Tiger fan? Solid orange, my blood runneth orange.
>
> KHALIL: I really wanted to go to a school that had some national prominence and was known throughout the country, and they kind of fit that mold.

What would lie ahead is why he now he drives forty minutes from his family's home near Greenville up to Clemson's baseball stadium three to four days a week for his winter workouts, taking infield during Tiger practice.

> **CLEMSON PLAYER:** It's been a joy to me just to take ground balls with him and talk with him, because it's not every day you get to take ground balls with a big leaguer.

> **CLEMSON PLAYER:** Well it gives everybody hope and he's kind of set a path for some people to take, especially players who have come into this with that kind of ability.

It didn't start out so easy. As a freshman, Khalil was adjusting to the climate and was homesick.

> **KHALIL:** You know it was hard, and I look back on it, and I'm glad I had baseball because I could come down here—'cuz this was the one thing that I always did have here. And when it was a little bit more tough socially, I think, I could always come to the field and it was something I could get at least a few hours enjoyment out of.

Coach Jack Leggett and former teammate Bradley LeCroy recall their first impressions of him.

> **BRADLEY LECROY:** He's just a little different. You know, guys were a little bit hesitant to get to know him because he was shy and did his own thing.

> **JANE:** So what was his own thing? What did he do?

> **BRADLEY LECROY:** You know, he'd take walks at night after study hall.

> **JANE:** They'd find you taking walks at night to get a Jamocha shake at Arby's™.

> **KHALIL:** I did. I did. I just didn't have anything else to do around there really.

> **JACK LEGGETT:** A major transformation took place in the four years that he was here. He was very introverted and quiet, I think, at the beginning, and just did his job and worked at his game.

> **KHALIL:** I don't really cause any waves and you kind of let other people get to know you, and in that way, I think I find out a lot more about other people.

> **JACK LEGGETT:** He opened up more and just started to evolve as this tremendous person to be around and a fun person to be around before it was all over.

As for baseball, after his freshman year, Khalil focused on weight training, wanting more power as a third baseman, demanding more out of himself.

> **KHALIL:** I used to go to the library and read like the body building magazines and stuff just to get a new workout. And they used to always stress how important the diet was. I definitely went at it hardcore from the beginning and I just stopped eating all the stuff that in the magazine they said you weren't supposed to eat, and I just started eating all the things they had, and tuna fish happened to be one of them.

> **JANE:** Oatmeal.

KHALIL: Oatmeal was another one, yep.

JACK LEGGETT: You could smell tuna fish. You'd look and Khalil would be eating his own tuna fish before the game in the locker room.

Khalil's considered a pioneer of healthy eating for players with his tuna and oatmeal routine, and to support Khalil's discipline and nurture his creativity, Coach Leggett gave him latitude.

JACK LEGGETT: Because all great athletes have the ability to express themselves and need to go out and do their own thing a little bit. If you caged them back and hold them back, they're probably not going to be as creative as they need to be or as good as they can be.

Khalil Greene, considered a team player, was on a team that made it to the 2000 College World Series his sophomore year. But once again, Khalil wasn't satisfied, raising the bar for himself.

KHALIL: I wanted to go into my junior year and have really kind of a breakout year for me and put the offense together, and the defense together, and hit for more power. And I kind of didn't, not any of the above. I really didn't do much of anything, I didn't think.

Khalil and shortstop Jeff Baker were flip-flopped, meaning, transition time.

KHALIL: So moving to short was like I had to go back and relearn the position so-to-speak at a different level. But I was excited about it, and I knew it gave me an opportunity to do more things defensively. And I could make more plays and have a chance to do some things at that position, but it was a bit of a learning curve I guess.

With that learning curve came confidence. And his instincts and ability to improvise defensively flourished.

JACK LEGGETT: And then he made a great play here and there and the next thing you would know, he would make another one and then he would start getting more creative, and then he'd realize he could go into another realm on defense.

But come time for the draft his junior year, he was selected by the Chicago Cubs in the fourteenth round. He turned them down to return to Clemson.

KHALIL: I wasn't setting out to prove anybody wrong and say, "You should've drafted me here," or anything along those lines, but ...

JANE: How about to prove to yourself?

KHALIL: Nah ...

JANE: That you could do it?

KHALIL: I always thought I was better than what I'd showed. I just felt like my swing wasn't where it needed to be, and the whole year I was kind of searching for something. So if I found that something I was looking for, I knew that I could put up good numbers.

He found it in 2002. Consistent, coming through in the clutch, a .470 batting average, twenty-seven home runs, and an .877 slugging percentage.

KHALIL: As I was doing it, I was aware that I was having a really good year, but I was just trying to maintain everything I was doing and just try to keep it going.

JACK LEGGETT: I've been coaching for twenty-seven years and I've never seen anybody from start to finish have a season like that, maybe never will. It was just one of those things like, was he ever going to cool off?

[Standing in Clemson town] While Khalil Greene has captivated San Diego Padres fans as an out of the blue surprise, his success is just what Clemson Tiger fans would have expected. Because they know their sports, they know their baseball, and they knew when they were watching a star on the rise.

CLEMSON FAN: Khalil was very laid back while he was here. He never pushed anybody or anything. But he tried to perfect himself.

JACK LEGGETT: On the field he just got better and better. He makes plays that the average baseball player could not make look easy.

And on Sundays, when kids could stand next to their favorite player to sing the national anthem ...

JACK LEGGETT: And he would be embarrassed because everyone wanted to go out and stand next to Khalil. He had this aura about how he played the game.

FAN: You're in class and somebody says, "Hey were you at the game last night? Did you see Khalil hit two home runs?" So he was the person people talked about.

JANE: Were you aware that you were kind of creating that buzz and interest?

KHALIL: No, not really. Not really. It was a—that's one thing about that area that I really like, and even now when I go back is that they are so supportive of athletics, and if you succeed there, you know, they'll let you know that they appreciate what you've done, and they're sports fans. It was a part of me that I'm—a part of my, I guess, life span so far that I'm really happy I had. And looking back on it, the progress I made in the four years from my freshman year to my senior year was something that I don't think I would've predicted and at the time, as you know, coming in as a freshman you kind of think you've got things a little more figured out than you have, but then when you leave you realize how much you really learned, I guess.

JANE: And did you learn about yourself as much as you did about the game?

KHALIL: Oh, yeah. No, I learned a lot. I think that 2001 was a good thing for me. And not having the type of success that I wanted was instrumental in being able to see failure and—and deal with certain instances where things don't go your way and how you adjust and adapt to them.

But 2002, what a year, setting six Clemson career records. In his last home at-bat, he hit a home run. And at the College World Series, the Tigers finished third in the country, the highest Clemson finish ever. Banners at the stadium and a special case in the locker room proudly display the symbols of Khalil's contributions, complete with a can of tuna fish. He was named the 2002 National Player of the Year, winning every national college baseball award including the Golden Spikes.

> **JANE:** What do those awards mean to you? What do they say?
>
> **KHALIL:** It let's me know I had a good year, I guess.

… a very good year, making a big impression on the Padres. Up next on *One on One*, his quick rise to the majors and thoughts on family, the fans, and his future .…

Home Opening Day 2005 …

> **ANNOUNCER:** *Shortstop Khalil Greene!*

It's just what Padres General Manager Kevin Towers and his scouting staff envisioned when they were looking to draft a shortstop in 2002.

> **BILL GAYTON:** A college shortstop who plays hard and gets his uniform dirty.

Bill Gayton heeded regional scouting reports and watched the Clemson senior more closely.

> **BILL GAYTON:** I didn't really scout, I just watched as a fan, and Khalil, you know, continued to make these great plays.
>
> **KEVIN TOWERS:** These guys don't come around that often. Offensive shortstop, a guy who can make the plays he does defensively.

Beyond that …

> **BILL GAYTON:** Here was a kid we were told, and you know, you could see that he takes care of himself and he was going to represent an organization in a favorable way.

Come draft day, San Diego picked him in the first round.

> **KHALIL:** They were the one team in the draft that saw me as a shortstop.

After just one year in the minors, he was called up to the Padres September 20 '03. When asked, back then, about the buzz surrounding his potential …

> **KHALIL [2003]:** I mean, it's flattering, I guess, but I think it's, in the same light you just basically, your performance will dictate whether or not you're going to stick around or what kind of impact you're gonna have.
>
> *[Khalil Greene introduced Opening Day 2004.]*

Impact indeed. After easily winning the starting job in 2004, the reason would be made clear May 14: a throwback game against the Cubs.

> **KHALIL:** I was more fired up about the uniforms, honestly, than anything else.
>
> *[Highlights]*
>
> *MATT VASGERSIAN (announcer): Great play by Khalil Greene … oh the other way! Get him! Get him! Yeah! … The 1,2 from Linebrink, bounced, up the middle. Greene gets it! Gets to Loretta! What more is this guy going to do tonight?!*

KHALIL: It just seemed that the balls were, I guess, maybe a step out of the way where I couldn't get to them [mike noise] standing up so I just had to get down for them.

Khalil Greene became a household name for Padres fans and on a roll for the National League Rookie of the Year through early September. But an injury to his finger likely affected final votes. He placed second, and then graciously accepted the Madres Favorite New Padre award.

KHALIL: It's hard for me to sit back and analyze myself and talk about the things I've done and what I want to do because it's not something that really comes natural.

But others don't mind at all.

JAKE PEAVY: I'll say it for him, he's going to be the next big name shortstop to come into Major League Baseball.

BRUCE BOCHY: Some things that we've never seen around here since Ozzie Smith. He's the talk of the league. When we play other teams, they want to know more about him.

MARK LORETTA: He has the potential to make a spectacular play on any play.

BRIAN LAWRENCE: It breeds confidence in the defense and it goes to the pitching staff and all the way around.

ADAM EATON: Sliding to his right, spinning backwards, and throwing a guy out at first, nobody else does that. He practices that kind of stuff.

TREVOR HOFFMAN: Was a tremendous rookie, just kind of kept his mouth shut and his ears wide open. Old school. Just went about his business and I respect that.

JANE: Your teammates respect not only how you play, but how you live your life.

KHALIL: Well, that's good to know. And, hopefully, I can continue to do that. And that's more important to me than anything else, really, is to be able to have that and, hopefully, be able to connect with other people on a level that just isn't baseball.

Connect on so many levels. From his artistic side—he painted a Pink Floyd mural in high school in order to stay in class—to valuing education, a three-time ACC Academic Honor Roll student in college even after changing majors from art to sociology. Then there's his look: long hair, flat bill, uniform loose. A no-name rookie to fan favorite fast.

JANE: Do you want to be like him?

FAN: Oh, yeah. I even grew my hair out like him last year.

FAN: He's the best player I've seen.

FAN: Like how he dives for those balls and stuff, it's so sweet, he's just like, "Awww."

FAN: It's almost acrobatic.

FAN: Ozzie.

FAN: He brought a lot to San Diego and we are so glad he's with us and he's made our team so great.

FAN: That's who I idolize.

FAN: He's so cute, he's like young and all the girls love him.

[Teenage girls yelling]

KHALIL: You get a chuckle out of it sometimes. So it's interesting to see the progression.

JANE: Umm-hmm. And do you appreciate that?

KHALIL: Oh, of course. Of course, you do. I mean, I'm thankful to everybody that is a fan of mine, I guess, if you want to say that. Or people that like to watch me play.

He's grounded and thankful for his family. And when his father had a stroke August 2004, Khalil quietly flew home to South Carolina and has been dedicated to helping in his father's recovery.

KHALIL: I look back on this off season as one that was as happy as any one just to be able to spend time there and be around them and ...

And again, his faith, very much a part of who he is.

KHALIL: So with my occupation, it's something where you use your work as a form of worship and, hopefully, conduct yourself in a manner that reflects well upon your faith and you could be a productive member of whatever you're doing as a baseball player.

Serious and intellectual, he's also a bit of a closet comedian. Take a question about what he's going to do after the interview ...

KHALIL: Probably go home and eat and watch a movie and go to bed.

JANE: And that's it.

KHALIL: Yeah, floss possibly in the middle there somewhere, something like that.

KEVIN TOWERS: He actually opens up behind closed doors.

JAKE PEAVY: You get him in a hotel room having a good time rappin' and playing the guitar or something, he'll open up.

As for rapping this day?

KHALIL: No. No. I do not care to share it.

JANE: We'll give you a few years.

KHALIL: Yeah. Give me about a decade.

JANE: A decade, okay.

For now, he'll share his talents on the field.

KHALIL: It's been a good year, but baseball's definitely a "what have you done for me lately" type game and you can go from being the hottest player around to being a guy that's on the trading block in a short period of time if you don't perform. I did have a good amount of success last year, but I feel that there's a lot of room for me to do a lot more than that, and I feel that I've got that ability somewhat. So I'm excited about it.

At a time when people are searching for a sense of purity in the game, it's easy to see why everyone from little leaguers to big leaguers find Khalil Greene a breath of fresh air. He's old school and an old soul, with a special spirit, energy, and potential to be one of the greats, and he's only just begun. I'm Jane Mitchell. Thank you for watching *One on One*.

"I got to know Khalil Greene and he's a different guy. Very bright, smart, great baseball player and, he doesn't show very much emotion or didn't open up a whole lot and I think it was awesome for you to do a *One on One* with him because that doesn't seem like him. And for you to make a job fun and—and to make it fun for the players—I think that says a lot if you get somebody like him to go on your show. I watched part of that. That was—that was pretty cool."

—Kevin Kouzmanoff, MLB player, 2010

MARK SWEENEY

"I had a real connection with the fans of San Diego and it was enhanced through my *One on One* interviews."

—MARK SWEENEY, 2010

When I think back to the first time I heard the name Mark Sweeney, it was another first for me in baseball. June 13, 1997, I was on the field with Bob Chandler getting ready to go live for our *Prime Time Padres* pre-game show. We were in Anaheim because it was the first ever interleague game for the Padres, and I had a feature explaining just what interleague play was. Thankfully, one of our field producers, Jason Bott, wrote the story and I voiced it. That was a great help, because I was still very much a newbie and had not fully learned how the divisions were organized within the American and National Leagues. I did know that the best team of each league played each other in the World Series. MLB's new interleague concept, of teams from the two leagues playing each other during the regular season, had thrown a monkey wrench in my learning process.

While I stood next to Bob, getting ready to go on the air a half-hour before game time, he was handed a piece of paper and told something in his earpiece. At the same time, I could see people scurrying about in the dugout—players, reporters, media relations staff. Something was going on. Bob told me there had been a big trade. "A trade? As in right now?" Yes, right now. A six-player deal between the Padres and the St. Louis Cardinals. I got excited. My heart started beating a little faster. *Oh my gosh, a big trade, but then who was gone?* The answer: Fernando Valenzuela, Scott Livingstone, and Phil Plantier. Coming to the Padres were Rich Batchelor, Danny Jackson, and Mark Sweeney. That whole dialogue was like a foreign language. It just did not compute for me at the time. All I knew was that three players I had just met that spring were gone—different uniform, different allegiance. In their place, three new players. My first major league "trade" experience.

I would not meet the new players until the team looped back through Los Angeles to play the Dodgers at the end of a long road trip. I was on the road again in LA for another pre-game show. We did several road pre-game shows in 1997 because we were new and there was talk of an effort for a new Padres ballpark, so we wanted to showcase cities with nice parks—new or well-maintained. I was doing a profile piece on former Dodger star and then Padres First Base Coach, Davey Lopes. Down on the field, I spotted the new players, but it wasn't until the next day at the team hotel that I met Mark Sweeney and Rich Batchelor. The fair-skinned guys transplanted to sunny Southern California stopped by the pool where I was taking a break as well. I introduced myself and remember laughing and joking with them, because they were friendly and unpretentious. While Rich was not with the team for too long, I did get to know Mark well, and that laughter would be part of his infusion with the Padres for the next decade.

In 1998, I was still doing a mix of shorter profile pieces for the pre-game show on players who would not quite "qualify" for a whole half-hour show, but whom I wanted to feature. Mark fit those criteria. At spring training, photographer Dan Roper and I went to his Scottsdale house for the interview. It was a nice tract home that wasn't too big or too small for a young ballplayer. The best part of the shoot was the home tour and on the patio, he suggested I try the hammock. I did, and almost fell out. That made the story. Looking back at that day now, for this book, Mark recalls:

> "I remember wondering why I was asked to be the subject and the reality of showing my first house to you. I was proud and nervous because most players have this elaborate house and I remember putting you in the middle of my house and telling you to just keep turning in a circle to see the whole house. It was very small but that was my starting point and I was proud of it."

His parents, Dan and Peggy, visited him at camp that week, so it was a bonus to interview them in person. His mother sent me pictures, and with photos and personality plus, I knew I could do more than six or seven minutes on him, but at the time, those were the parameters.

In June 1998, I was on the road with the team in Arlington, Texas down in the dugout during batting practice sitting with several players on the bench. I was telling Dave Stewart his show was airing that night in San Diego after the game. While relaying it included the tour of the Jacuzzi® in his master bathroom, Mark Sweeney started comparing situations of Dave's house with his. With grandiose gestures and well-placed humorous drama, Mark described how Dave, a five-time World Series pitcher, had a big house, a big bathtub with a skylight that took all day for us to shoot, and yet, "When Jane did a story on me in spring training, it took about five minutes to show the house, the bedroom, and the prized new vacuum!" He was kidding, of course, but it did underscore the different degrees of their careers and the TV time associated with it so far.

By the time Mark was an established player, a returning fan favorite and with the Padres for a third time in 2005, he more than qualified for a half hour show, and it was a pleasure to do it. This time, his dwelling was a high-end, high-rise rented condo in downtown San Diego with a spectacular view. After the interview, we walked to have lunch at his favorite restaurant, Acqua al 2. The owner, Martin Gonzalez, showed us the plates celebrity guests and players had signed that are displayed on the walls. Mark had one covered with autographs from the 2005 Padres roster. As we sat outside, and the photographers were rolling on us talking and eating, Martin came to me with a plate. I was surprised and touched. I signed it, "Thanks 4 watching and for being part of Mark Sweeney's One on One!" Last I checked, it's still on their wall.

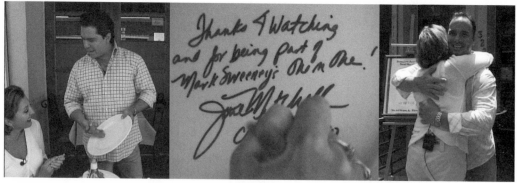

For this half-hour show, I amplified more elements of Mark's life and coordinated new interviews with his parents and a little girl he encouraged when she was sick. He had told me back in 1998, the first time I interviewed him, about how a Boston news anchor friend had asked him to do something while he was with the

Cardinals. She asked if he would visit a girl named Lindsey Dias from Massachusetts who was having a rare double lung transplant at a St. Louis Hospital. He invited her and her family to come to the field after she recovered. In the meantime, Mark was traded to San Diego. True to his word, he saw that she and her family had that visit when he returned to St. Louis as a Padre. As he relayed the story, I wondered if he had stayed in touch with Lindsay but he said it had been a while. I could have stopped at just having him tell the story and showing a picture, but the situation just screamed that I had to find her.

Later, the Cardinals' media relations staff helped me contact her, and I arranged to have her and her parents interviewed. Mark didn't know anything about this until he saw the show. He told me it meant a lot to hear and see her now that she had grown up and was doing well. Likewise, the family said it meant a lot to them to be able to express their gratitude to him. Mark demonstrated such compassion and was so genuine that it made me feel good to know we could showcase and celebrate those quiet moments and acts that truly impact lives. Someone who could attest to that was Dan Rea, a respected TV and Radio anchor in Boston and a Sweeney family friend. I appreciate how Dan helped me navigate the Northeast for contacts and video and has been supportive of my efforts over the years.

Mark's parents visited San Diego that summer, and upon their return home, they emailed me this lovely note:

> "The best part of the trip [to San Diego] was seeing the video. Everyone loved it—all for different reasons. His brothers for the memories; his brother Bryan and myself for the great job you did bringing in the various perspectives on the same subject matter and seamlessly editing it into production; and the grandkids just lovin' him run and hit and be his funny self just as he is with them. Peggy just beamed throughout being proud of her 'boy.' You did a masterful job and with so little time to do it. Jane, thanks so much for all your effort. It was a special job for someone we think is a very special guy."
>
> —Dan Sweeney, August 4, 2005

That summer I had an extreme case of laryngitis, so much so that during a live shot celebrating our 1,000th game, I only squeaked out about one sentence. For the next five days, I didn't talk to save my voice to both track the audio for this show and shoot the on-camera stand-ups. My voice was still a little raspy—the only show like this in fourteen years—but at least it worked.

This is the original script from the show debuting July 22, 2005.

• • •

Mark Sweeney: personality plus, pinch hitter, a Padre again.

MARK: People are special here, they don't forget, it's the '98 thing. They do not forget. And I've come three times and, hopefully, third time's the charm.

If ever there were a player who could light up a room as well as drive a baseball, it's Mark Sweeney. This is his third stint with the San Diego Padres, and while he jokes, "The third time's a charm," he no doubt has made quite a first and lasting impression.

Mark Sweeney, with his ability and magnetic personality, attracts a lot of attention, demands a lot of respect.

TREVOR HOFFMAN: He's always on top of his game. He's prepared. He's everything you could ask for in a teammate and a player.

TONY GWYNN: I knew from the first day I met him that he was gonna turn into a pretty good ballplayer because he asks questions.

BRUCE BOCHY: He keeps grinding it out and doesn't give up, and now he's back to being one of the elite role players in the game.

Even higher praise, because he's spent most of his career as a bench player.

MARK: I always question if I could've been an everyday guy and I really believe I could've; I just wasn't in the right situation. But the way it's evolved is it's kept me in the big leagues for this many years and it's been great.

From being named the Padres Favorite New Padre in 1997 to dousing champagne in the '98 Championship season, with a short return in 2002 and now spearheading the "Show me your pelo" dugout routine in 2005—he's still a favorite.

MARK LORETTA: He brings banter. He brings the gift of gab. He brings the lingo to the team.

TIM FLANNERY: He genuinely cares about others, he cares about the team and he's genuinely funny.

Not really all that different from when he was little. Mark Patrick Sweeney was born October 26, 1969.

PEGGY (his mother): Oh, he was really probably the funniest little boy. From maybe two or three months old, balls started to become very, very important to him. They were in the bed, of course, with him, and he just loved them. And as he got older, maybe a few months older, and could start to sit on the floor, he would even start pushing the balls and crawl to get them.

Mark grew up in a house on a quiet street in Holliston, Massachusetts where his parents still live. Dan works in advertising. Peggy is a college counselor.

MARK: My mom and dad, hands down, have been my biggest influence because they're just hardworking individuals that are based on love and affection.

Mark looked up to, and tried to keep up with, his three older brothers.

MARK: They paved the road for me. I did get into trouble once in a while, but they set me straight. I knew what I had to do.

JANE: So what was it like around the Sweeney dinner table? Were you laughing a lot? It seems like there's a lot of humor in there.

MARK: Food was flying. You know, my mom cooked all the time for us and meals were always eaten together. It wasn't separate. That's what I mean about my mom and dad. They always kept our family together and it was something that's very special.

His hometown is about an hour outside Boston.

MARK: You had all the things that you could do by seeing the Celtics, and the Red Sox, and the Bruins, and all the teams that were there. But you also had that small town living, which I think is special.

With playing sports his focus, he learned a tough lesson about not putting school first his freshman year at Holliston High.

MARK: Yeah, it was a tough thing. I was playing a basketball game that day and I walked down, we got our report cards and I stuffed it in my book bag like no big deal. My mom and dad were going to the game and my grandmother was going to my first basketball game. So all of a sudden I walk down and my athletic director tapped me on the shoulder, he said, "Mark, you can't play today." And I said, "What do you mean?" He said, "You failed off the basketball team." And I didn't think it was possible 'cause I did whatever I could do to get by in school. It didn't come easy. But it just was one of those situations that I didn't—I took it for granted, you know, and I thought sports was my ticket to everywhere and that was wrong. But what I did is I had to make a phone call to my mom and dad, which was very embarrassing, very humbling.

PEGGY: Crying his eyes out, and he said, "I just flunked off the basketball team."

DAN: He had to leave the premises after school. And that was really what bothered him the most. The after-effects of seeing his friends being able to go out and participate either on the field or in the gym or whatever, but he had to board the bus and head home.

PEGGY: He said, "I can't do the school work, Mom. I can't do it. I just can't get everything organized." So I said, "You know what, Mark? I'll come home and I'll meet you here at three o'clock every day. And we will. We'll set up a schedule of how to do this." And we laugh about it now 'cause it did work. And he'll always say, "Thank you, Mom, for that."

By his next report card during baseball season, he was on track. And the star athlete parlayed his new ability to balance work and play with a maturity to bounce back from disappointment quickly. Take his high school Super Bowl game.

DAN: He's a quarterback, three minutes left to go in the game, he throws an interception and a kid runs it back for a touchdown, they go ahead by six points. And, you know, you never bet against him because he always had that ability to, kind of, rise up and he came back, had a nice run back and, sure enough, with less than a minute to go, they scored a touchdown. That's how he was.

Mark landed a scholarship to the University of Maine to play football, his first love. So trying out for baseball was almost an afterthought.

MARK: That was the first time I fell in love with baseball. I knew I was playing every single day. By doing it seven days a week and putting time into it and seeing the progression, I think was very exciting to me at the time.

Baseball became his sport of choice. At 185 and fast, he excelled in centerfield. And while a few scouts had noticed him in high school, more paid attention as he was setting twenty-four University of Maine baseball records—twenty-one still standing ...

> MARK: And every single year I'm saying, "Well, you know, it could happen. If I keep on doing it, it could happen."

His junior year, he passed when the Dodgers drafted him.

> MARK: It was very nice to be drafted thirty-ninth round, and I didn't look at it in a negative way. I just thought that my chances were better if I went back, got my degree, and then went on and hopefully had another chance my senior year.

Not only did he graduate with a Business Marketing degree, he was a finalist for the Golden Spikes award, the most coveted award in collegiate baseball.

> MARK: It was something that just gave me a little more confidence. It gave me that "what if" thought in my head ...

That what if—answered by the Angels who drafted him much higher, in the ninth round, no big signing bonus, but a big opportunity to be in professional baseball.

> MARK: Having the degree behind me and going on to my next phase of my life, I said, "You know what, let's see where it takes me." And it's been pretty special.

... special with adventure and adversity. Coming up on *One on One*, a walk down memory lane, the great year of '98, and a walk downtown with the single guy living in the city ....

> Fresh out of the University of Maine, Mark Sweeney's first stop in the Angels' farm system in 1991 was A-ball in Boise, Idaho. There, out of curiosity, he asked a coach what he thought his chances were in the big leagues. The coach's answer? Prophetic ...

> MARK: He goes, "I really envision you being a fourth outfielder in the big leagues." I was hoping he was going to be wrong in a sense. I wanted to be a third outfielder or second outfielder.

That un-resounding prediction motivated him, his powerful bat moved him through the minors, and by July of 1995, he's traded to the St. Louis Cardinals organization. In Triple-A, the lefty is playing first base for the first time.

> MARK: So I'm like, I'm all for it. And all of a sudden, two and a half weeks into it, I get this phone call saying, "Hey, you're going to the big leagues."
> JANE: What do you remember about that day?
> MARK: I got the call about 5:30, 6:00 in the morning. And the first thing I thought of is I have to call my mom and dad.
> PEGGY: I had just gotten to work and I picked up the phone and he said "Mom, I'm going up!" I said, "What?"

MARK: I said, "Get your tickets to St. Louis, we're playing the Cubs tonight." And, of course, they went berserk.

DAN: You always wish the best for your kids, but you don't necessarily know that they're going to make it until you get that call. It's sort of like a magical call.

MARK: The two things I remember: there was a pitching change. And I was playing first base, like I said, and all of a sudden I looked down and it was the first time I looked at my uniform because everything was just numb. I mean, my legs were numb. Just everything was amazing to me. But I looked down and I said, "Wow, this is the most beautiful uniform I've ever seen in my life." And then I looked up and I realized there were fifty thousand people in the stands and the reality hit. And the second thing that was the most special thing is that night my whole family came down after the game and I got to see them coming up through the stands.

> "You did a masterful job and with so little time to do it. Jane, thanks so much for all your effort."
> —DAN SWEENEY, 2010

Mark Sweeney would find a niche, pinch hitting. He did it unusually well for a young player, even having a seven-game pinch-hitting streak, one shy of the major league rec-ord set almost forty years earlier. All enough to keep him on the Cardinals' big league roster, getting a taste of the playoffs. His optimistic nature helped him grow in that critical role.

MARK: I go through a process of getting ready for every situation, and I feel like I'm going to be successful until that failure happens. And if the failure happens, it's all right now because I've gotten ready. Before, I didn't realize that. I didn't know what it took to get ready, so it was harder to deal with the failures. I think now it's a lot easier. Not that it's easy all the time 'cause some of them hurt worse, but you just always want to succeed.

His ability and positive attitude, a good fit for the San Diego Padres, Sweeney was part of a six-player trade with the Cardinals in June of '97.

MARK GRANT [from game broadcast]: Mark Sweeney is gonna be a guy off the bench, a good over .300 lifetime average. So he's going to be a guy off the bench for the Padres.

He'd lead the majors with twenty-two pinch hits, become a fan favorite fast, setting the tone for even better things to come.

JANE: You mention 1998 in this town and everybody just knows what that was like. So let's walk through that year from your perspective.

MARK: We had a lot of moments. I mean, if you think of that highlight tape that they did. You knew something special was going to happen even in spring training. We were all totally different personalities, but we all came together. I remember Steve Finley's grand slam home run against Arizona to win it 'cause we were down and all of a sudden we got the bases loaded and hit a grand slam. We developed that sense of we were going to win every single day. It was just a special group.

Mark Sweeney's calling card: keeping guys loose and always ready.

MARK: Even if I failed or succeeded, I realized I was going home and we won.

JANE: Well, take us to September twelfth uncorking champagne and pouring it on each other ...

MARK: ... and realizing from day one of spring training all the way through ... the experiences that we've had were great.

They'd win the Division Series against Houston at home.

[on field after division win doused in champagne]

JANE: Mark Sweeney what is this moment like for you right now?

MARK: What is this moment like? This is beautiful!

MARK: I remember the times when we had the rallies when we got home from the games on our trips. There were thousands of people waiting for our buses to come in late, early in the morning, and they're there to give us all the support we needed.

They'd carry that with them on their return to Atlanta after the Braves forced a Game 6 in the National League Championship Series.

MARK: That last out and seeing Carlos Hernandez jump up and run out to Hoffy and just the jumping out of the dugout, and realizing we're going to New York to play in the World Series. It's probably the greatest moment of baseball that I've ever had. This is what it's all about—every player's dream, to go to there and just experience this once is plenty to handle. I'm telling you. I got shivers in my body and it's crazy. And all I remember from my at-bats— and what I did in the World Series is I swung at every pitch. I didn't want to waste any time and it's kind of funny. I got a pinch-hit in the second game off Jeff Nelson. It was the first pitch, and I don't even know what it was. It was just something white coming at me and I swung at it. But it went through the hole and I'm rounding first base and I'm going, "What just happened?" You know, my whole family's there. The whole atmosphere of the World Series and real- izing it's Yankee Stadium ...

Then back home, down two games to none ...

ANNOUNCER: Ladies and Gentleman—welcome to Qualcomm stadium for Game 3 of the 1998 World Series. [fans go crazy!]

MARK: I got to pinch-hit in the third game against [Mariano] Rivera, but I got a hit on the second pitch and I'm saying, "Wow, this is amazing. I'm in front of my home crowd and all of a sudden I'm pinch hitting." But the last at-bat was the most—it was the toughest 'cause I ended the World Series.

On deck, he imagined the scenarios ...

MARK: *Hey, Carlos might hit a single here. I might have first and third. He might hit a double. I might have second,* and all the good things. And as soon as I think of that, he hits the ball to second base and Chuck Knoblauch turns a double play and all of sudden the reality hit that there's two outs, we're down by three—I think, *Four runs and I'm taking the doughnut off my bat saying, I am not striking out and watching the catcher jump into the pitcher's arms.* But ended up hitting a soft liner to Scott Brosius. And that wasn't a great moment, but after the fact, we realized that was the Yankees' year. It was the year that they had. But our World Series was beating Atlanta and going to the World Series. That was our moment.

So many moments that Mark Sweeney will forever be a part of …

MARK *[1998 post season addressing fans]: Obviously we're all disappointed but everyone of us hugged each other, and special memories now, and we're going to look back and say, "You know what, we accomplished a lot." When I was younger and I dreamed about being in the World Series, I couldn't even dream how good it was going to feel. Everyone on this team feels so fortunate to be doing what we're doing. But it's nothing, without you guys….*

After being part of the magical '98 season, Mark Sweeney wasn't sure what to expect next.

MARK: I didn't know I was going to get traded again. I mean, it was something very strange.

A trade to the Cincinnati Reds, the start of challenging times: sent back to Triple-A, off season shoulder surgery and a trade to Milwaukee, with former Padres First Base Coach, Davey Lopes, then the Brewers' manager.

DAVEY LOPES: We took him basically going on what he had done in the past, hoping that he would be able to do some of those things, but because of his injuries, mainly his knee I believe it was at the time, didn't allow him to be the type of hitter that everybody expected him to be and certainly not the hitter that he is today.

With a smile on his face, he'd overcome more adversity, traded, released, signed with the Padres, then released again.

MARK: That's the time that I went home, I watched baseball on TV, and I had—while they were playing, I was at home wondering, *Is this it?* You know, *Am I done?*

After contemplating his future, possibly broadcasting, the Colorado Rockies gave him another chance in 2003.

MARK: We didn't win as much, so that was hard, but the experiences I had there and getting back on track, getting back onto the normal part of how I thought I was as a player, I got to that point.

In '04 he led the majors with twenty-three pinch-hit RBI and five pinch-hit homers. With that comeback he'd be a good fit again for the Padres in 2005.

ROB PICCIOLO: Not only on the bench as a pinch hitter, but he's been a good defensive replacement for us …

And true to form, he bounces back.

TIM FLANNERY: He's eighth on the all-time list ever as a pinch hitter—sometimes, because of how goofy he is, sometimes how funny he is, you forget how good a baseball player he is. He's a pro's pro.

Fans know.

FANS: Pinch hitting. Pi-i-inch hitting.

FANS: That really shows the sign of a true hitter, when they can come up to the plate and get a hit when the team needs it.

FAN: Dedicated player. Always ready to go to bat no matter what the situation is.

FAN: He's got sex appeal! [laughs]

JANE: Whooo!

FAN: And very happy he's wearing number 11, Tim Flannery's old number who I used to love growing up also.

FAN: He's good with kids and everybody else. He's nice to everybody.

Genuinely engaged at community events, one story's special to him: In 1997 a Boston news anchor friend asked if he'd visit a sick Massachusetts girl, Lindsey Dias, having a rare double lung transplant at a St. Louis Hospital.

LINDSEY DIAS: Seeing him, his bright smile, definitely good looks [laughter], coming into my room to, like, surprise me and to greet me, and to, I don't know—it just was a whole sudden happiness all of a sudden.

MARK: But that smile on her face, I'll never forget. And I said to her, I was talking to her, I said, "Listen, I'd like to have—when you get healthy, I'd like to get you to come to the field."

LINDSEY'S MOTHER: I mean, I can remember when he left the room—it was a different child. She was ready to have the surgery. She was ready to get up and she was gonna be at Bush Stadium just like he promised her.

LINDSEY DIAS: The fact that it actually followed through after my transplant was, wow. He's a man of his word, which doesn't really happen often.

Then upon his return to St. Louis, as a Padre …

MARK: The whole family came to the game and it was a special moment. I have pictures still of that day and I need to get back in touch with her because I know she's doing very well.

Mark Sweeney has a big heart, loves his dog, Ali, and hopes to add to the Sweeney portrait with a family of his own someday.

MARK: To my mom and dad's credit, they've made it harder to find somebody because that's the relationship I want. They're best friends, and I'm looking for that, and haven't found that yet. I know someone's out there.

In the meantime …

JANE: You live in Scottsdale in the off-season. You showed us your house the first time.

MARK: It's changed a little bit ...

JANE: 1998.

MARK: ... since. The white walls have changed.

JANE: No white walls? How about the vacuum?

MARK: The vacuum ...

JANE: Is that still there?

MARK: No, I've changed vacuums. I've upgraded a little bit. Yeah ...

JANE: How about the hammock? The hammock?

MARK: The hammock is still there. My mom and dad bought me the hammock. I can't get rid of it. She—when they come down for vacation, they like to sit out there and ...

JANE: I think I almost fell out of that hammock ...

MARK: ... and read books. Yeah.

JANE: ... really.

MARK: Yeah, we'll get the tape on that one. Yeah.

With golf clubs, a laptop, it's sparse, but his rented downtown condo has quite a view.

JANE: Beautiful.

MARK: I like it. I see the field. Yeah, like I said it gives me a reminder that I have to go to work. Then I see this [view of the bay] and I don't want to go to work. It's nice to come out here in the morning and after a game and just relax and see the sights.

JANE: And you like to eat downtown ...

MARK: I do. Actually, I have a friend of mine that has a restaurant down here. It's really good food.

JANE: Well, we're ready, ready for lunch.

MARK: All right, sounds good. I'm hungry.

[At Acqua al 2 restaurant]

MARK: Carlos, good to see you. This is Jane. This is my spot.

Acqua al 2's owner, Martin Gonzalez, describes how special guests sign plates.

MARTIN GONZALEZ: And also I like to do it for celebrities like my friend here. [Smiles and winks]

MARK: I feel like something special's going to happen in 2005, so I thought we'd get the plate first. And he put it up in the front.

After a photo op with the staff, lunch, and an invite to sign ...

GONZALEZ [giving the plate to Jane]: Can I have your autograph? [Jane signs plate—"Thanks 4 watching and being part of Mark Sweeney's *One on One*"]

JANE: What's around your neck?

MARK: I have a cross. I have a cross here that I wear all the time. I don't wear it during the game, but that's my Catholic upbringing.

While he doesn't always have time for church during baseball season ...

MARK: But I'm always doing my little prayers and, you know, praying for my family and praying for my teammates and so forth.

[Jane and Mark hug outside restaurant.]

JANE: Thank you so much.

MARK: See ya!

He's grateful for different experiences in life, including meeting the legendary Jimmie Reese who had spent seventy years in professional baseball and was with the Angels organization by the time Mark met him at spring training in '95.

MARK: He just wanted to be in uniform. He was baseball to me and the way people needed to treat the game.

He writes Jimmie Reese, the names of his parents, and of two late uncles on his hat and glove.

MARK: When you fail, taking my hat off and looking down and understanding, you know, it's all right. You need those things in your life to remember, hey, this is where I came from, these are the people that have been a huge influence on my life, and everything's going to be all right.

His 2005 salary, just less than $600,000, is his highest yet.

MARK: Getting a check every two weeks to play baseball is still funny to me. I mean, it really is.

But at thirty-five, he's happy to take it for the love of the game.

MARK: Until they take the shirt off my back, I'm going to play. I mean, there are certain guys that have done a lot in this game, like Tony Gwynn retiring. I don't have the luxury of saying I'm going to retire. I'm going to say, you know, thanks for the opportunity.

Mark Sweeney learned early on to be ready and resilient. That and a good sense of humor have served him well in a game where a strong bench is often the key to a successful season. I'm Jane Mitchell. Thank you for watching *One on One*.

"Jane makes you feel very comfortable and she also laughs at ALL my jokes, which is nice. ... She wanted to know the reason for my success and my family, especially my parents, are the main reason for all my success and passion that I have had in my career. When you hear other people talk about you [in the show] it is very humbling and amazing in the same sense. I have truly been blessed in my career, and the people I have shared my career with have been amazing! My mom really was gleaming with pride, and if you can do that to your mom that is all that matters in life!"

—Mark Sweeney, 2010

DAVE ROBERTS

"We all felt really good about having Jane be the voice of our family as I returned home for the first time in my professional career. With this approach, she was able to get more candid and honest answers from me. There has not been a *One on One* special that I have seen where I don't feel closer to the athlete and his family."

—DAVE ROBERTS, 2010

I never tire of telling the "coming full circle" story, especially in sports and about someone who gets to play for the team he grew up watching. That's the case of Dave Roberts. The Padres were close to winning the division in 2004, but petered out toward the end of the inaugural season at PETCO Park, so there were high hopes for the next season. Dave Roberts would be part of the 2005 equation. The Boston Red Sox traded him to the San Diego Padres. Dave was an exciting injection considering he was coming home and had been a Red Sox hero in 2004. He's best known for a stolen base in Game 4 of the 2004 ALCS, key to the Red Sox' eventual victory, and known as "The Steal of the Century." The Red Sox went on to be World Champions that year.

Dave Roberts was grateful and accommodating when asked to do *One on One*. It was early in the season. I could do the high school and other elements when the team was gone, but we had get the sit down interview shot while the team was home. We chose the morning after a road trip. His wife, Tricia, was not feeling well, but she understood the nature of our deadline and that we had so many people to coordinate. She put on some makeup and a smile and powered through for a few hours. Thankfully, Dave and Tricia also asked Dave's parents to be there to watch their son and baby girl during the interview, and talk with me, as well.

"I think sometimes there is a disconnect with fans and athletes, but Jane does an incredible job of bridging that gap. The fans in San Diego always support their team and this show allows them to be more invested in the players, which I believe is incredible."

Their family is an ethnic rainbow. Dave's father is black. His mother is Japanese. Tricia is white. They shared freely about their ethnic and cultural mixture, and how they are raising their son Cole (who looks like Dave) and daughter Emmerson (who looks like Tricia) to have open minds and hearts.

Dave's father was a Marine. Being from a military family also, I could appreciate and relate to Dave's experience of traveling and being raised with a sense of authority and respect for protocol. That spawned questions about how it affected his growing up and ability to adapt to change. Hearing Dave's story and admiration for his father reminded viewers of the work service men and women do in uniform and the sacrifices they make in their personal lives—missing weeks and months of their children's lives due to their tour of duty with a modest salary at best. It also underscored the great examples of integrity, honesty, honor, and respect they teach their children who then have the option of carrying that on in their own lives. Dave certainly did.

After the interviews, we went in the backyard to shoot the family playing baseball. Little Cole could make contact with the Wiffle ball and mimic the moves from watching his father and other players. Cole signed a real baseball with a black marker and gave it to me. If he grows up to be a major league player, it might be worth something someday. Either way, it's a special keepsake from a sweet boy.

Dave had so much to say in our interview I could have let his articulate sound bites go longer to fill out the show. But because he was local, it was all the more important to have others describe him, and what he meant to the school and community. While the Padres were on the road, we visited his high school, Rancho Buena Vista, to talk with teachers who knew both Dave and Tricia, his coaches, and students watching Dave in a Padres uniform.

To see Dave in action in the community, we taped him visiting children at a Boys and Girls Club event. Even if they didn't know who Dave was, they enjoyed having a Major League ballplayer spend time with them and teach them a few things. We put a microphone on Dave and followed him around. Microphone or not, Dave was sincere and enthusiastic with youngsters.

One of the bonuses of this process is meeting a player's parents. I never would have known the people sitting a few rows in front and to the side of my season ticket seats were Dave's parents until I interviewed them. Since that day, anytime I see them, there's a warm greeting and appreciation for our time together and the show. That makes me feel good, because *One on One* is not only about the player, but his family's role in his life.

At the Boston Red Sox home opener in 2005, Championship rings were presented to the 2004 team. Dave Roberts, already a Padre, was invited to the ceremony. It showed true sportsmanship and a respect for the game from both the Red Sox and the Padres to allow Dave to travel to be a part of that momentous occasion.

> "I don't think it's a gender thing. I think it's a Jane Mitchell thing. I didn't feel like I was being interviewed, it felt more like a conversation. Her show is honest. The more we talked the more I wanted to open up and that is a credit to her."

Dave Roberts was with San Diego through 2006. As a free agent, he signed with San Francisco for 2007, battled some injuries, and was then released by the Giants during spring training in 2009. Tired and sore, Dave retired and immediately expanded his broadcasting experience. In 2010 the Padres hired him as a special assistant to baseball operations, another loop in his full circle story. That spring, he was diagnosed with cancer—Hodgkin's Lymphoma. Even between treatments, he was at spring training and around the ballpark with a smile on his face. After a year of treatments, he was cleared of cancer and returned to the game as the Padres First Base Coach for 2011. Dave will always be part of San Diego sports history and a hometown favorite. I hope Red Sox fans enjoy learning more of his story beyond his baseball heroics there. Again, in the grand scheme of things, there really is more to the game than one's uniform.

This is the script from the show debuting May 15, 2005.

• • •

The fun and fast paced Dave Roberts: dynamo, dad, ready to deliver.

> **DAVE:** Because I'm a big believer in the one thing you can control is your effort.

In baseball, getting on base is one thing. How you make it home? That often comes down to speed: Dave Roberts' calling card. But his talent isn't only a catalyst for changing a game; it literally changed the course of history. It's all part of the story of a homegrown talent who has a special spark wherever he goes.

Call him a sparkplug, a little bit of lightning, a centerfielder who can get something going, make something happen with his speed.

In 2005, Dave Roberts is a San Diego Padre, on the team he grew up watching. With San Diego roots a plus, his tangible speed and intangible energy largely factored into the trade that brought him from the World Champion Boston Red Sox to San Diego for the '05 season. A good match, considering Roberts had what's been called the "Steal of the Century."

> **DAVE:** Stealing that base, I didn't know what it was going to amount to. I really didn't. I wish I could say I knew that after that point, we were going to go out and win eight straight games and win the World Series, but I had no idea.

It's a dramatic story that would unfold a decade into his career on a journey that began a half a world away in Japan. His father, Waymon Roberts of Houston, was a private in the Marines stationed in Okinawa, where he met Eiko through friends.

> **EIKO:** His best friend was roommate.

Neither spoke the other's language.

> **DAVE:** So my dad had a dictionary and kind of like the English to Japanese translation dictionary. And so I guess he found a way to make an impression on my mom and won her heart over.

They married and David Ray Roberts was born May 31, 1972.

> **WAYMON:** Dave was kind of into everything from day one. He was always very inquisitive.

At three months old, the family was stationed in North Carolina, then Hawaii, Orange County, and eventually San Diego's North Coastal area when Dave was twelve. Vista became their home base, even as his dad was at various duty stations retiring as a Master Gunnery Sergeant.

> **DAVE:** My dad, being in the military, he had that tough-man demeanor. And when I was younger, I was always afraid of him. But I loved him to death and respected the heck out of him, but I was always kind of afraid of him 'cause he's a big guy. But he wasn't that drill sergeant type dad. But I've come to learn he's just a big softie. You know, he was always there to support me and my sister as long as we kept our grades up. And my mom was pretty shy, laid back, but she always kind of just pushed the academic side of things and just wanted me to be my own person. That's her whole thing.
>
> **WAYMON:** I wanted to be the dad to do things for him that my dad wasn't able to do, and didn't do, for me when I was growing up.

And whatever sport Dave was involved in ...

> **DAVE:** Seemed like every game—Wednesday, Friday game or weekend game—they were always there. And a lot of parents don't have that luxury and can't take time off, but my parents found a way to be there.
>
> **JANE:** And how do you think the fact that you come from the military family might've affected you or influenced you in terms of moving around or getting along with kids?

DAVE: Obviously, it forced my sister and me to assimilate with people in different situations a lot. I mean, if we didn't then we were going to be outcasts. It's kind of I've had that background of being able to go out there and be outgoing and meet different people. So it's really helped me out. Actually, it's been a benefit.

JANE: Well, we went back to your high school.

DAVE: Oh, boy.

After his freshman year at Vista High, he was assigned to the new Rancho Buena Vista High School, home of the Longhorns, where he played varsity baseball, football, and basketball.

DAVE: And I called myself a defensive specialist, so I wasn't that good of a basketball player, but I enjoyed it. I enjoyed competing. And football was my first love.

Even though Dave wasn't big, Dan Hancher, an offensive lineman, recalls how Dave, the quarterback, made up for that with speed and smarts.

DAN HANCHER: He'd be fiery. He'd try to motivate us all into block better, carry the ball better, to hang onto the ball and he definitely would carry his own in, too.

DAVE: So my whole life, the way that I could compete with the guys that were bigger or more talented than me was to kind of outwork them or have the energy and go out there and out-compete them.

As for baseball …

DAVE: I took playing baseball for granted. I didn't really see myself playing baseball at any higher level, 'cause I—my love was to play football.

Former head coach, Steve Hargrave, put him in centerfield and as the leadoff hitter.

STEVE HARGRAVE: He changes the complexity of the game. When he's up to bat they are thinking bunt—everybody—the infielders would move in and you could hear the other coach would say, "Hey this guy has wheels."

Jason Schmeiser, a shortstop, was a teammate.

JASON SCHMEISER: He was the only guy I ever saw who hit a chopper off the plate that the pitcher fielded, and I'm talking about a one bounce off the plate and Dave would beat it out without a throw.

He made an impact, beyond his skills.

STEVE HARGRAVE: He came to play and he led by example.

JASON SCHMEISER: You know the stereotype is that the drama people don't get along with the athletes, but you know, Dave was one of those guys who was involved with everybody and just was—just a good guy and someone you wanted to be around.

But his personality and character would be tested after his sophomore year with an injury to his knee during spring football drills.

DAVE: I tore my anterior cruciate ligament, so that was kind of like a wake up call for me, and just realizing that my career, my sports career, let alone just my football career, could be in jeopardy. And so I missed my entire junior season of all three sports and just rehabbing. And the first doctor I went to had said that I would no longer be able to play sports again. I was sixteen years old, actually, and that was just devastating to me and went to the doctor who ended up doing the surgery, Dr. Woody, and he just said, "We'll fix you up and it'll take about nine months, and we'll get you back out there." And sure enough, I came back and played football.

But it was a tough junior year on the sidelines. U.S. History teacher, George Roswell, recalls Dave's focus on his rehab and studies.

GEORGE ROSWELL: He always came to class prepared, did his homework, was up to date on things, and was good to have in class.

And his senior year he returned to the gridiron, leading his Longhorns to the CIF Championship on a foggy winter night in 1989.

DAVE: As a kid growing up in San Diego and going to what was then Jack Murphy Stadium and seeing the Chargers play and wanting to be a Charger someday, and watching the Padres play and wanting to be Tony Gwynn someday, you know, that's a dream of yours. And at that point in time, that is the pinnacle of anything, of all sports, winning CIF and playing in that stadium.
JANE: Before we go on to college, I just have to tell you that—reveal that we have looked at your yearbook.
DAVE: Umm.
JANE: And so we know that not only were you a three-sport guy, but you were also senior class president and, yes, you were the prom king.
DAVE: Oh, I—I … [laughs] That was a big surprise to me, a big shock. We had it at the convention center. That was kind of like the first big event at the downtown convention center that—was our prom. And that was a huge surprise to me, so I got to dance with my then girlfriend, my bride-to-be.
JANE: How did you meet?
DAVE/TRICIA [in unison]: Spanish class.
DAVE: Spanish class, she was a cute little girl with fashion sense, so …
TRICIA: Oh, yeah.
DAVE: I was trying to do everything I could to disrupt the class to get her attention basically.
JANE: Well, it worked.
TRICIA: Yes, it did. It did.

By their senior year, the high school sweethearts would face the first of many decisions together. She was going to U.C. Riverside. He received a full scholarship to play football at the Air Force Academy. But he didn't want to be so far from Tricia. And a game he once took for granted, baseball …

DAVE: Kind of started to become the forefront of my future, but I signed a letter of intent to go to the Air Force Academy, but my heart just really wasn't there to play football anymore.

He was a recruited walk-on at UCLA, with no scholarship.

DAVE: I just figured if I didn't make the team, worst-case scenario, I can get a UCLA degree and I'm one step ahead of the game.

He made the team. And after his freshman year, not only did he get scholarships, his coach, Gary Adams, helped him realize he didn't have to be the typical big slugging centerfielder.

DAVE: He said that, "Every team needs a guy like you who's going to be able to bunt, be a good teammate, play hard, play good defense, steal base, and things like that."

He set career and single season stolen base records at UCLA, two records he still holds. Still, he was only a late-round draft pick both by the Indians and Tigers his junior and senior years.

DAVE: It was pretty frustrating, pretty humbling. It was just a matter of—you feel like you're kind of slighted.

He wasn't going to sign with the Tigers until he talked with a teammate.

DAVE: And he just said, "You know what, you have your choice, but if you don't sign, professional baseball's not going to miss you. It's going to move on and it's going to go on without you, but you could regret it for the rest of your life. But if you feel you can play and you feel that you should—you should. You have an opportunity. You did get drafted. Then show them that you should've been a higher pick."

Inspired by that, Dave Roberts signed with the Tigers and after graduating with a History degree, he was looking forward to what his professional baseball future would bring. That's next on *One on One* ....

Paying dues in the minor leagues is the norm and Dave Roberts is no exception. First stop, 1994 Single-A Jamestown, New York. And by '96, an unusual assignment back west to Visalia, California to play on a co-op team for the Tigers and the Arizona Diamondbacks.

DAVE: To have the organization tell me that it was a lateral move and to go up to Visalia and to be a co-op team was very disheartening. And that was the—kind of the point where I said that I'm—that's it, I'm out.

But Tricia encouraged him to go. Then his manager gave the team a pep talk.

DAVE: He says, "I know you guys are upset that you're here, but you're playing baseball. You're getting a check, and this is an opportunity for you guys to shine."

He did with sixty-five stolen bases, the most in all the minors that year. Through it all he could count on Tricia commuting from her job as an insurance broker in Carlsbad.

DAVE: Looking back, that was some of the best times of our life together.

TRICIA: For sure.

DAVE: Because some of our best friends in all of baseball came from the minor leagues, and it's like, you know, when you're all kind of struggling and fighting that same fight together and all you can all ...

TRICIA: Nobody has any money and ...

DAVE: Yeah, and you can all relate to each other and ...

TRICIA: Yeah.

DAVE: ... things like that. It just makes it a lot more fun.

And nearly a decade of dating ...

DAVE: To have somebody that was there, coming to my baseball games on a Wednesday in high school, you know, knowing exactly what I'm about.

They married in La Jolla, in November of '97. Then another dream came true after a trade to the Cleveland organization in '98, his major league debut in '99 in Tampa Bay. The night Wade Boggs marked his 3,000th hit.

DAVE: I remember when I got my first hit. I think it was with John Flaherty, he said that, "Well, you only got two thousand nine hundred and ninety-nine to go to catch Wade Boggs." So I got a big kick out of that.

Good things would follow. The rookie Roberts was on the Indians' post season roster, then on Team USA qualifying for the US Olympics. He spent off seasons playing in the Mexican and Puerto Rican Winter Leagues. Then after a trade to the Los Angeles Dodgers, he wins the centerfield job in 2002.

DAVE: They let me have the ability to just go out there and run at will and make things happen and be creative.

He found his niche, developing into one of the best lead-off hitters and stolen base threats in the game. But July 31, 2004? A big surprise.

DAVE: At the time, I was devastated, to be honest with you, because spending three years with the Dodgers and, you know, we got ridiculed for underachieving for those years and not winning the division. And at that point in time, we were leading the division and things were looking great.

An eleventh-hour trade to Boston was part of two bold deals by the Sox to catch and beat the rival New York Yankees. Manager Terry Francona would use Dave Roberts to fill in for the injured right fielder or to pinch run.

DAVE: Right when I got there, the guys welcomed me with open arms.

JANE: Describe your teammates. Kind of an interesting bunch ...

DAVE: Well Johnny, Johnny proclaimed us idiots, so that's smart. But no, it was just a group of rock stars. It's amazing how guys with long hair and twenty-five different egos and personalities and, but the amazing thing though is once game time hits, everyone's on the same page.

A Red Sox documentary captures the season of keeping the faith, achieving the impossible with different post season heroes, working toward that goal.

> DAVE: I just watched a lot of videotape: Anaheim pitchers and the Yankee pitchers and potential teams that we were going to play and just waited for that one opportunity to shine and make my contribution.

That opportunity: Game 4 of the AL Championship Series with the Yankees. The Red Sox down three games to none. It's a must-win ball game, bottom of the 9th, 4-3 Yankees.

> DAVE: You look into the stands and everyone had their hands over their faces and their heads between their legs, and just the beginning of the end kind of thing. And another cold winter, losing to the Yankees. And you get the best post season closer of all time on the hill.

A rarity, Mariano Rivera walks Kevin Millar.

> DAVE: And so Terry Francona just kind of gave me a wink and told me to go out there and make something happen.

Pinch running for Millar.

> DAVE: I just had so many nerves and emotions, fear, you know, anxiety, nervousness and excitement, and all these things 'cause at that point I hadn't played in like a week and a half. And so I got out there, and a mentor of mine with the Dodgers was Maury Wills, and he always told me that, you know, "You're going to get one opportunity to make a difference in your career and don't let that opportunity pass. When everyone in the ballpark knows you're going to steal a base, you need to steal this base."
>
> ANNOUNCER: *pitcher trying to pick him off*
>
> DAVE: And then the third time he picked, tried to pick over and tried to get me, then it was like: I had played every day for the last month, like I was just locked in at that point in time. And I said, *Once you go to the plate, here it is.* You know, I gotta do something. And so he held the ball, held the ball, and it seemed like an eternity. But then right when he picked his leg up, I took off.
>
> ANNOUNCER: *The pitch high, the throw, the tag, SAFE! That's exactly why Roberts is in the game, the steal of the century.*
>
> DAVE: And I don't really remember a whole lot, but I knew I had a good jump and he had a good pitch throwing, and Jorge made a great throw and, you know, fortunately Joe West called me safe. But I thought I was in there pretty good, but when I looked back at the videotapes, and it was a bang-bang play, and it was just after that I kind of jumped up and the emotion in Fenway Park was just completely changed, you know, and there was hope.
>
> *[Fans going crazy cheering]*

Hollywood couldn't have scripted it any better. Dave Roberts scored the tying run that night and the next as the Red Sox won eight straight through New York and St. Louis and into the record books as World Champions, the first time since 1918.

After the euphoria of the locker room, champagne showers, and celebratory parade, the business of baseball: the Red Sox didn't have a full-time spot for Dave Roberts, but the Padres wanted an everyday speedy lead-off hitter. So a trade sends him home to San Diego.

After an optimistic spring training, a lingering hamstring injury puts him on the disabled list the first two weeks of the 2005 season. Unable to play, the timing was such that he could return to Fenway to receive his World Series ring.

DAVE: And that's something that I'll always be proud of because that's not an individual accomplishment, it's a team thing. And to have an opportunity to get that ovation and the closure from the Red Sox fans was awesome, was an awesome feeling.

JANE: Well, it was called the steal of the century. I mean, it really turned the tide. They probably will love you forever.

DAVE: Yeah, you know what, they're great fans and I'm just—I'm very happy I had an opportunity to go there and a lot of times they saw me on the top step, giving high-fives and cheering for my teammates, and if that was what my role called for, I was going to do it to the best of my ability. And when I get an opportunity, I'm going to do whatever it takes to win and be a teammate and try and win. And now to have an opportunity to come back home to San Diego and I hope some of that rubs off because this is where I've always wanted to be.

With so many variables in the game of baseball …

DAVE: I'm a big believer in the one thing you can control is your effort. No matter how talented or how not-talented you are, how good you feel or how good you don't feel, you can always go out there and play hard.

Dave Roberts proves that every day he plays.

MARK LORETTA: Well a legitimate lead-off hitter means that you can get on base and you can run. That's what Dave can do.

DAVEY LOPES: And it's great for the guys hitting behind him because you know the pitcher is going to have to pay attention to him, and you might get a mistake out of it.

With his track record, Roberts is always been seen as a threat.

DAVEY LOPES: When a guy of that magnitude, of Dave Roberts, gets on base, the center of attention goes to first base pretty much. So you take away the hundred percent attention of focus that you're supposed to have on the hitter.

BRUCE BOCHY: But the other thing he brings probably as important is that infectious enthusiasm when he plays the game. He plays with a lot of fire. He keeps the bench loose; he keeps 'em fired up. He's always pumping guys up.

Dave Roberts' positive energy isn't limited to the big leagues.

DAVE [At home in Dave's backyard]: I wanna see a home run with that one, dead centerfield. Home run!

TRICIA: *Run around the bases!*

DAVE: *I'll be the third base coach!*

He's just as impassioned at home playing ball with his four-and-a-half-year-old son, Cole, with Tricia and baby Emmy cheering them on.

TRICIA: *This is for the World Series!*

DAVE: *The Padres are going to win the World Series! The crowd's going crazy, everyone at PETCO Park. It's a day game at PETCO Park!*

COLE: *Ramon Hernandez behind the plate!*

DAVE: *This is for the World Series for the Padres! Strike three! Yeah!*

They've been based in San Diego, but now not only did he have the dream of playing with the Padres, now they're able to work and live here.

JANE: … what's that like for you?

TRICIA: Like winning the lottery. I mean, we are two people who love being at home.

JANE: How does faith factor into your lives?

TRICIA: It's the center of our lives. It's the biggest …

DAVE: Yeah. I think with what we do, there's a lot of negativity and a lot of things that bring you down, and separate marriages and things like that, and families. So I think that, you know, our faith is the stronghold of our lives.

They see what they call the "Roberts melting pot" as a positive.

DAVE: And so the diversity that's always around our …

TRICIA: The kids.

DAVE: The kids are …

TRICIA: Great.

DAVE: … great. And I think that, you know, Cole and eventually Emmy, they're going to see no color, and I think that's the great thing about it.

Dave has made several trips to Japan to visit relatives. But his mother regrets Dave didn't learn Japanese, so she's making sure Cole does.

GRANDMA [in Japanese]: Baseball.

COLE: Baseball.

GRANDMA: Can you count? [Cole shakes head.]

Cole is quite confident on the topic of baseball.

COLE: My favorite position is centerfielder, but I really want to play catcher.

JANE: Why is your favorite position centerfield?

COLE: Because it's just a great position and I want to catch fly balls and home runs, and I just want to be in the World Series.

Like father, like son.

DAVE: When I see my son and he's playing baseball and he's talking about going to the World Series, and I lived it. You know, and no matter what, no one can take that away from me. And that's something I'll always be proud of because that's not an individual accomplishment. It's a team thing.

From videos to baseball hats, they have many mementos from his career, but soon they'll be relocated.

[Tour of new home.]

To their new house in North County.

> **JANE:** Well tell us about some of the features.
>
> **DAVE:** It's kind of got the U shaped feel and it's a Tuscan Ranch, is kind of the motif, the theme so ... sixty-inch TV is going to be right there, flat screen right on the wall.
>
> **JANE:** Channel 4 Padres.
>
> **DAVE:** Channel 4 in High Definition, Padres will be there.
>
> **JANE:** [laughs] Love it. How involved were you in the design and the ideas and, you know, your hit list of all the things that you wanted?
>
> **DAVE:** Well to be honest with you, not very ...
>
> **JANE:** Really?
>
> **DAVE:** I leave that stuff up to my wife, she's a lot better at that stuff so ... Every room surround sound and the cool remote features and, I like a lot of toys, so she's kind of given me that luxury.
>
> **JANE:** Well you deserve it.
>
> **DAVE:** Yeah, I treat myself a little bit.
>
> **JANE:** This is looking like a baseball field to me though.
>
> **DAVE:** I know. That's my son. He said you don't see many kids that don't want a pool but he's pretty content with having this as a baseball field.

Having traveled from the simple life in the minors to a late-blooming major leaguer, it was a reverse role in the post season that finally led to Roberts' first million-plus salary. But none of it has changed the way he and his family live their lives.

> **DAVE:** And obviously, we are very fortunate wherever we're at and, you know, every opportunity we do get to contribute and help out. We try to take advantage of it.

Giving back is part of what makes Dave Roberts one of the good guys. He was the Dodgers' club winner of the Roberto Clemente Award and the LA Sports Fans' Choice for Humanitarian of the Year. He's already active with the Padres' community outreach and has long supported his high school. In 2005, he brought former coaches and teammates to a fundraiser and auctioning off his Red Sox post season shoes alone fetched a few thousand dollars.

> **STEVE HARGRAVE** (RBV Coach): Probably the most special time was in 2002, the day of Longhorns' CIF Baseball Championship game, Dave came to the pep rally. His advice: "You guys go out and have fun. You guys are good and you can do it," and that's what they did. And we ended up winning that game.
>
> **STUDENT:** He's been a good influence, a good role model for us to follow, and just kind of model our baseball careers after.

His retired number 10 hangs in the gym, a tribute to his play, contributions and character.

> **STUDENT:** We didn't get the chance to make it, for whatever reason, but you did.
>
> **EIKO:** I'm just proud of my son.
>
> **JANE:** You're proud, too, I'm sure.
>
> **WAYMON:** It's not often a parent sees one of their children chase their dream and actually reach that dream.

Dave Roberts remembers what it was like to have that dream as a kid. All the more reason he takes advantage of the major league stage.

> **DAVE:** I look at it as a responsibility because whether you like it or not, kids are going to try and emulate you. They see you on TV, they come to the ballpark and see you, and you're a role model whether you like it or not. So I really embrace that.
>
> **JANE:** And so what's your message to kids?
>
> **DAVE:** Believe in yourself and work hard, and if you do that, then success is inevitable in whatever you choose.

Dave Roberts' gift of speed has helped him succeed. But perhaps a quote displayed in his home offers an even better explanation for that success. It's from legendary basketball coach John Wooden who said, "Ability may get you to the top, but it takes character to keep you there."

I'm Jane Mitchell. Thank you for watching *One on One*.

"My family is typically a private one, but we knew Jane would be sincere in telling our story. She engages everyone and has a way of making everyone feel included, even my four-year-old at the time. The thing I learned most was how much my wife and I had matured. We have been together since we were fifteen and talking about how much our lives have evolved is amazing. As an athlete, I never spent much time going down memory lane. I was always focused on the future and how I was going to make myself a better ballplayer. So, to see the old pictures, interviews from friends and family, it made me realize the long road I took to get to the big leagues."

—Dave Roberts, 2010

JERRY COLEMAN

"I thought—and I say this very candidly—that you made it look easy for me, and it wasn't. And I thought the way that you handled it was better than the way I handled it, to be honest with you. I think you got to the core of what I was, where I was, and why. And it came over very nicely."

—JERRY COLEMAN 2009

There are some legends that seem bigger than life. They fill a room with their presence, personality, or egos. Then there is the legend and icon, Jerry Coleman. He is an unassuming man with a cordial handshake, who stands tall and proud, not for his baseball career or forty-plus years in broadcasting, but for his service to country. He will tell you emphatically himself that being a Marine was the most important thing he has done in his life.

In 1998, our second season of covering the Padres, I continued the *One on One* mission to include the entire Padres family, not just current players. Jerry Coleman was on my list. When I approached him about the show, he said, "No one cares about me. I'm not a player." I told him he should let me worry about who wants to know his story, but please do the interview. He agreed.

I had come to know Jerry my first year as a rookie sports broadcaster. He was also on our Channel 4 Padres team as the host for *Padres Magazine*—the half-hour show in which we replayed mostly my features that had run in the pre-game show, adding highlights, interviews, and trivia elements. It was a resourceful way of getting a lot of bang for our buck; giving viewers ample opportunity at different times during the week to see some of the work we were producing. By 2002, when we had more reporters, *Padres Magazine* began featuring all our stories. Jerry was still hosting through 2010, fourteen seasons.

Jerry was very welcoming and supportive, and yet could be feisty at times—just his way of adjusting to the new format and a teleprompter. He was a professional with a good heart. Because he was the same age as my mother, born in 1924, I could relate to him quite well. I had heard the stories from her and my father of the Great Depression. My father had served in three wars, and I understood that generation. I felt comfortable listening to Jerry's stories and perspective. The Colonel deserved the utmost respect and to have his story shared for others to appreciate.

He agreed to let us come to his house. He, his wife Maggie, and daughter Chelsea, lived in La Jolla in a lovely ranch style home. We set up in his living room, and, having prepared, felt ready to hopefully peel back some layers. Two parts of that day were the most revealing: first, when I said he was a "hero" and he brushed it off and I came back with the definition of hero; and second, when he walked us around his family room, showing us pictures of his mother and sharing how difficult her life became due to her health. These two moments showed his vulnerability and gave us a glimpse of some very painful times in his life.

Determined to stay healthy, Jerry walked his dog every morning. Dan Roper was willing to drive the equipment home at night then get up early the next day to videotape Jerry doing his morning routine. I didn't need to be there, and I wasn't.

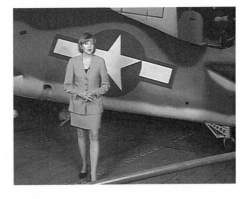

We shot the stand-ups for the 1998 edition at the San Diego Air & Space Museum to incorporate his history beyond the ballpark. The half-hour edition was well received by everyone that year, and as a timeless story, replayed many times. In 2005 Jerry was given the Ford C. Frick Award of the National Baseball Hall of Fame for Broadcasting Excellence. As of 2010, he's one of only four major leaguers to receive the honor.

When I heard he was going to Cooperstown, I immediately approached my station manager, Dennis Morgigno, and said we needed to be there. The Padres would be making a big deal about this and so should we. With nearly thirty minutes from the original show covering his background, we could incorporate all the new video and sound from Cooperstown into a one-hour special edition. Plus, he was going to be inducted into the U.S. Marine Corps Hall of Fame in Washington, D.C., a few days before that, which we could also include. He agreed. We were on.

Having already been to one induction in 2001 for Dave Winfield, I felt confident about what we would need to do and how much time we would need to do it. At the end of July 2005, Dan Roper and I traveled to Cooperstown. It is a long haul, and Dan had to handle most of the gear and luggage. I tried to help, and as the producer, I also managed the car rental, tipping, meals, maps, and coordinating the schedule. I had just recovered from being quite ill with laryngitis. I was feeling okay, but by the time we arrived in Cooperstown, Dan was feeling something coming on and became ill, too.

Through the Hall of Fame, I hired a college student, Philip Zaengle, to be our grip to help carry our equipment. We arrived on a Tuesday night, and on Wednesday, we met Philip and the very helpful Hall of Fame staff including Jeff Idelson, who had been so accommodating in 2001, as well. I had already written everything I needed to say for the on-camera parts we needed to shoot in the Hall of Fame Plaque Gallery and Museum. We would have no teleprompter, so I had to make them short enough so I could memorize them fairly quickly as we moved from backgrounds with plaques to various displays. I did my hair and makeup in the bathroom, and at about seven o'clock, once the museum was closed and the visitors were gone, we shot the opening stand-up in the gallery. I don't know how many takes it took to get it right, but we were up against the clock to shoot nearly ten on-camera elements around the museum in about two hours, so there was little time for nerves or flubbing my lines. This was much less nerve-wracking than the first time in '01.

Dan was so good at times like that, making me laugh and never making me feel bad about my mistakes. I had to keep things moving along and deal with issues such as the vacuum cleaner going when we were in one part of the museum and we needed it quiet. That happened with the Winfield shoot, too. By the time we finished this time, it was after nine o'clock. Dan was sick and near exhaustion, and our week had only just begun.

Thursday was hot and muggy. We were meeting then-president of the Hall of Fame, Dale Petroskey, for an interview by the garden area of the park. We were early and Dan was wiped out. I took a picture of Dan lying on the sidewalk with the camera.

I don't know how he got through that week. I was very cognizant of how ill he  was, so we took breaks when we could. We returned to the house in the town where we were staying so he could rest between shoots. We spent time on the main street interviewing people about Jerry Coleman, surprised, really, to learn how many people from all over the country knew of him. When we identified ourselves as being with Channel 4 San Diego and the Padres, people often said, "You'll have another Padre going in soon, Tony Gwynn." They were right, but this trip we focused on Jerry.

That year the two players inducted were Wade Boggs and Ryne Sandberg, so there were Red Sox and Tampa Bay fans for Boggs and Cubs fans for Sandberg. Because Jerry was not going in as a player, the demands on his time and attention were not as much as for the others. That made it nice to be able to capture his experience. To start, being part of the Padres family, and with my polite but constant reminder of that, the Hall accommodated us so we would have access to Jerry. That access included being at the hotel for his arrival, for several minutes before or during some of the Hall of Fame events, and for an interview downstairs at the hotel on Saturday.

As for documenting Jerry's experience, for example, he was on the main street doing a free autograph session. He signed and talked with people as they came by. With microphones on, we walked with him through the little town over to the Otesaga Hotel, discussing what it was like to be there and how he had prepared for his speech. Saturday, I interviewed him and Maggie, bridging the time gap from the 1998 interview until then, including being inducted into the Marine Corps Hall of Fame that week.

Saturday afternoon, I encouraged Dan to take a rest before we went to dinner. Dinner was often at our favorite restaurant there, Hoffman's Bistro on Hoffman Lane. We naturally loved the name as a sign to us that Trevor Hoffman would be in Cooperstown someday. The food was excellent too, especially the pork chop and sweet potato fries. That afternoon the weather was bad, and everyone hoped it would clear by the next day.

The storm held off for a while. Sunday's induction that early afternoon was warm and wonderful. It was just after that, on the way to the family and friends party congratulating Jerry, the storm hit. The clouds closed in, the sky turned black and ominous, and rain fell fast and hard. Not only did Dan, the camera, and I get wet going from the car into the party, but the sound of the pounding rain was almost as loud as the music. That meant we had a lot of audio issues to deal with, but the goal was to capture the experience and hear from people there, and we did.

After six days of shooting and traveling, I had to write the show. Interns and my associate producers, Brad Williams and David Bataller, logged the many tapes with all the beautiful shots Dan took, and all the interviews we had gathered. The

Marine Corps Hall of Fame provided us with video of their event, so we had a plethora of elements for the production.

With maybe one day off, I sequestered myself at home and wrote for several hours a day for a week so Dan could begin editing. I had to map out how long each segment could be so we would be able to include everything. That is always hard, but in the end, I feel we captured both the essence and the details of Jerry Coleman's life, work, and legacy. I'm very proud of this hour-long program. It turns out Dan had whooping cough. Yet, as sick as he was in Cooperstown, and even while he was editing for the next ten days, he was a master with his visuals. I often asked him to shoot certain things I knew I wanted to relay to viewers and write to, such as the flower-lined streets, and the names on the stores. He always did, and then some.

No matter how long Jerry Coleman is in the broadcast booth, it has been a pleasure and an honor to work with him and share his story for those of his gen-

eration and the younger generation who need to know of his sacrifice, dedication, and integrity. I'm sure there are many men like him, but being in a position in the public eye, he is a reluctant, yet admired icon. I learned in Cooperstown that Jerry Coleman is known and appreciated across baseball and across the country. He is a national treasure, and San Diegans are fortunate he calls San Diego home.

This is the script for the Hall of Fame edition debuting August 19, 2005.

• • •

Jerry Coleman. Yankee, Veteran, Broadcaster ...

JERRY: One of the greatest days of my life is this day here in Cooperstown.

Takes his place at the top of his game.

The National Baseball Hall of Fame here in Cooperstown pays homage to the best of the best in the game. Players, managers, executives, and umpires are inducted with a bronze plaque. There is also a special place for those selected for their major contributions to baseball broadcasting. Jerry Coleman, with his remarkable life, is so honored and is now enshrined in these hallowed halls.

His life spans three stellar professional dimensions, ranked in order of his priority. The military, with service in two wars, a decorated Marine pilot ...

JERRY: Well, you can't discount your country. That has to be number one, I mean, from a standpoint of what it means.

Next, baseball for nine years, a New York Yankee Rookie of the Year and World Series MVP during the Yankees dynasty of the '40s and '50s ...

JERRY: Playing is the best part of baseball. On the field is the best part of baseball. But if you can't be there, broadcasting's just as good because you're there every day.

He's been on television and radio, from New York to San Diego. Jerry Coleman is an integral part of San Diego Padres baseball. But his life, career, and voice transcend a single team.

JANE FORBES CLARK [From HOF ceremony]: What every fan knows is how important radio and television broadcasters are to the game. They paint us a picture, a wonderful picture, letting us feel as if we're in the ballpark. In recognition of this, the National Baseball Hall of Fame has awarded the Ford C. Frick Award for excellence in baseball broadcasting annually since 1978. This year's recipient, the twenty-ninth, is Jerry Coleman.

JERRY: Yes, actually. I'm kind of surprised to be honest with you. I never thought I would get here as a broadcaster or a player, to be quite frank with you. And to get here is really delicious.

But getting to this glorious moment and to Cooperstown is quite the journey, figuratively and literally. From Albany, the state capital in eastern New York, venture west to the country. The drive meanders through rolling hills rich with green trees, golden tones, brilliant wild flowers and thick, hot, humid mid-summer air. Off highway 20, a sign for Cooperstown, fifty more miles and a sense you're heading into history. And indeed nestled in by Otsego Lake a playground for ducks, boaters and golfers, signs of old times, brick buildings, tree-lined streets and hanging baskets full of geraniums celebrate summer. Shop names remind visitors that this village is the cradle of baseball, first thought to be "Where it All Began." A place where anyone in the "On Deck Circle," or at "Home Plate" may thrive on "Rivalries," but from every generation of player in the game, Cooperstown is where "Legends Are Forever."

VINNIE RUSSO: Oh, absolutely.

Vinnie Russo owns Mickey's Place, one of many stores chock full of bats, balls, cards, and memorabilia from every team, every era, where some legends have stopped in or signed autographs over the years.

VINNIE RUSSO: They can remember games that took place thirty and forty years ago as if it were yesterday. So it really is an opportunity to sort of go back in time and relive history.

And you never know who you might meet, by just saying hello.

CHARLES TURREY: Oh nobody takes my cap, nobody. [laughs]

Charles Turrey lives in Cooperstown. He remembers Jerry Coleman from their Triple-A playing days.

CHARLES TURREY: There were things that I probably did on the ball field that might seem stupid today, but he made it a point to let me know. And I never made those mistakes again.

Cooperstown is steeped with nostalgia. With a population of about 2,000, it attracts nearly 100,000 for induction weekend, more than visit the whole winter season. There's a distinct energy here. Team pride is displayed on what people wear, and among families and friends, casual fans and experts.

Everyone's talking baseball. The historic town is wired for the twenty-first century. Still the flagpole at Pioneer and Main is the town's compass. And at the information booth?

> **JANE:** What's the most frequently asked question?
> **INFORMATION LADY:** Where is the Hall of Fame?
> **JANE:** And where is it?
> **INFORMATION LADY:** It's right across the street, about fifty yards up to the left.

Busloads of students and little leaguers are among the tourists who file through to the brick shrine with its gold lettering, the National Baseball Hall of Fame and Museum. The banners announce that the two players inducted in 2005 are Ryne Sandberg of the Chicago Cubs and Wade Boggs of the Boston Red Sox. Inside the Hall of Fame Gallery, with its oak lined walls in all its grandeur, is truly impressive. Sparking conversations and questions, with answers at one's fingertips, amazement at every glance. The tradition of inducting baseball's brightest stars and immortalizing them with a bronze plaque began in 1936, with strict criteria that narrows the field, as the president of the National Baseball Hall of Fame, Dale Petroskey explains.

> **DALE PETROSKEY:** Well to be a Hall of Famer one needs to have played at least ten years and been retired for at least five years. [Jerry Coleman] was a very good major league player, he didn't make it to that ten-year mark and that's the reason he couldn't be considered for the Hall of Fame itself.
> **JANE:** Did you ever think, "Well, I guess I'm never gonna make it?"
> **JERRY:** Absolutely. I'd never get here as a player. I didn't play long enough, and I wasn't good enough. I mean, certainly, I think everybody that's in baseball, going to the Hall of Fame as a player, that's the ultimate honor in baseball, never mind executives or broadcasters or whatever, that's the ultimate. And I think that these players, you know, that I think it's incredible for them. I think it's wonderful, and I'm delighted to be part of it.

A part of it, on the same sacred ground as the Yankee greats he played alongside Yogi Berra, Joe DiMaggio, Whitey Ford, Phil Rizzuto, Mickey Mantle, or those friends he once played against like Boston's Ted Williams. And Jerry Coleman is a part of it, because the Hall of Fame has long recognized other contributions to the game, namely baseball writers and broadcasters.

> **DALE PETROSKEY:** Broadcasters are there for forty years, players come and players go, but the fans' link to the games is through the broadcasters.

The Scribes and Mikemen wing is home to those honorees with photos and a narrative of the annual winners. The Ford C. Frick Award is named after Frick, an inductee devoted to baseball as a journalist, National League president and commissioner. The award carries with it plenty of prestige.

DALE PETROSKEY: So [Jerry's] with Mel Allen, and Red Barber, and Ernie Harwell, and Chuck Thompson, Harry Kalis, the great broadcasters in the history of the game we only select one every year.

As fate would have it, the first two honored are Mel Allen and Red Barber, who Coleman worked with as a rookie broadcaster.

JERRY: Red was a great teacher and he taught me things then that I use to this day of what to eat, what not to eat, who to see, who not to see, and how to do it. He was wonderful. But Mel had a great command of the voice and he, *"How about that?"* You know, and I can still hear him.
JANE: But to go in and to be awarded this honor with these guys who …
JERRY: Yeah, it's kind of neat.
JANE: Yeah?
JERRY: It's kind of neat.

Only three so far (as of 2005) have made the transition from major league player to broadcaster to Ford C. Frick winner. Catchers Joe Garagiola and Bob Uecker, and now Jerry Coleman. While there is a formal description of the award, how it applies to Jerry Coleman is easily found when talking with baseball fans from around the country in Cooperstown.

JANE: What does the name Jerry Coleman mean to you?
FAN: Very colorful announcer for the Padres.
FAN: That means to me growing up I saw him playing second base for the New York Yankees against the Dodgers in all those World Series.
RED SOX FAN: Anybody that's been in baseball for that long has to have the love for the game.
ORIOLES FAN: I remember him doing the CBS games when I was a kid, bringing the game to life, just making it more interesting.
FAN: Whether you're a Yankee fan or a Padre fan you're always gonna remember your beginning as a kid and watching your favorite team and those broadcasters tend to just stick out in your mind forever.
JANE: You resonate with people, not just Padres fans.
JERRY: You know I don't recognize that. It's the game and the microphone, and whether I'm in San Diego or Timbuktu or Kalamazoo, or doing a national game, I really—it never—oh, boy, I'm talking to thirty million people out there. I never thought that. It's just the game, again. You have to divorce yourself from that, from sound, from the thought process. And I'm not being noble, I'm not being shy, I'm not being anything, I just don't think about it.

His humility and talent appreciated also by inductees George Brett and Gary Carter, in town early for Hall of Famer Ozzie Smith's Turn 2 charity event at Doubleday Field.

OZZIE SMITH: Well you know it's what makes all the people that are a part of this Hall of Fame very special. They all have their unique style. And Jerry certainly has his own unique style and hanging stars all over the place and I think it's one of the things that's allowed him to get here.

GEORGE BRETT: I've been an American Leaguer my whole life and he's been in San Diego for how many years, and I know who he is, and I couldn't tell you who the—I know Vin Scully's with the Dodgers, I can't tell you who does the Giant games, I can't tell you who does the Rockies games, I can't tell you who does the Met games, I can't tell you the Cubs on radio who does that. But *you know he does* the San Diego Padre games.

GARY CARTER: I always enjoyed his interviews and just enjoyed his way and his personality. He was always friendly to me whenever we came in to San Diego or even on the road. And he's well deserving of this award and I just, I've always been a Jerry Coleman fan and I'm just very happy for him and he's gonna enjoy this weekend.

It's been a long road to reach this special recognition. Jerry Coleman's story of humble beginnings is next on *One on One* from Cooperstown....

From rounding the bases to radio and now in the broadcaster's gallery in Cooperstown, Jerry Coleman is the boy next door who grew into a man known as a consummate gentleman and professional, with a voice and a smile that's his own special style. His story begins in the city by the bay, San Francisco. He was born Jerald Francis Coleman, September 14, 1924. He lived with his older sister and parents at 424 Broderick Street. His mother was a homemaker, his father worked in the post office. His childhood is not storybook. In the '30s, during the Depression, his parents separated. What made it all the more difficult? His mother was injured and needed a brace to walk.

JERRY: Every time the brace went, she went down. And I used to walk from where we lived up to the UC hospital. It took all day long to get there and back to get that brace fixed. Really sad, she ended up okay, but she had some hard times. The Depression—were hard years.

It still pains him, but it's clear his mother's strength has had a profound influence on him.

JERRY: My mother really raised me. She was my guardian angel.

While his relationship with his father was not strong, Coleman recalls his father playing professional ball in the same company as Ty Cobb.

JERRY: He was a catcher, 5'6", much shorter than I. I don't think he could hit too well, that's what kept him at the Triple-A level or Double-A level in those days. But he gave me my first glove.

With little money and no place to go, summers for Jerry Coleman were spent at Big Rec in San Francisco's Golden Gate Park.

[Jane, Jerry, and Charlie in SF park]

JERRY: We would show up here religiously about what, ten o'clock in the morning and the rest of the guys came and we would make up games. Where was that screen we hit off of?

438

CHARLIE SILVERA: The screen was right here. There was one here and one over there, and there was no diamond, we played on grass.

One of his friends then and now, Charlie Silvera, ultimately became the Yankee's catcher behind Yogi Berra.

CHARLIE SILVERA: Well, ten years old, that's how old we were when we started playing ...

The late '30s early '40s were a time when San Francisco's own Joe DiMaggio, the son of Italian immigrants with a sweet swing, dominated sports headlines ...

JERRY: All we thought about was being Yankees of the future.

Coleman and Silvera were among hundreds of boys hoping a Yankee scout might spot their talent, but it seemed unimaginable.

JERRY: Until one day when I was a sophomore in high school a man came up to me by the name of Joe Levine, he was a scout for the Yankees and he said that he thought I could be a professional baseball player and I go, "Huh, really?"

Coleman was offered a spot on the Yankee's local team for hot prospects—the Kineli Yankees.

JERRY: I said, "I can't do it because I'm playing for the A Romeo Fish Company this year." [laughs]

The next season he joined the Kaneli Yankees, and by his senior year at Lowell High School he had baseball and basketball scholarships to USC. But then came an experience that would change his life's course, the onset of World War II.

JERRY: Anybody who had anything going for them wanted to get in and do their part, whatever it was.

At seventeen, Coleman wasn't old enough to join the service. So he signed with the Yankee's scout and played in the minor leagues in Wellsville, New York, but on the verge of his eighteenth birthday, he returned to San Francisco hoping to join the V-5 Naval Aviation Cadet Program.

JERRY: Gee, that sounds romantic, let's become pilots.

He passed the physical and had letters of recommendation in hand ...

JERRY: Saying that I was a wonderful, sterling character ...

But then the commander saw his mediocre high school transcript.

JERRY: And he said, "I can't sign this." I almost fell off my chair, and I said, "Why sir?" And he said, "Well, it cost $300,000 to train a pilot and you're going to get halfway through somewhere and you're gonna fail and you're gonna cost the government money." Well, I started talking ...

And convinced him to let him in.

JERRY: I was determined to prove to him that I could make it. I held my own, I learned to fly.

And before he was twenty, he was overseas with the Marines in the Solomon Islands, then Guadalcanal, Green Island, and the Philippines under General MacArthur's command.

JERRY: We became the first group of planes to use in-close air support because we were very accurate in what we could do in dropping 1,000-pound bombs and I never had trouble taking an order. I never said, "Why are you doing this?" because I respected the people who were ahead of me.

But even his uniform couldn't shield his emotions about war.

JERRY: It's scary. I don't think anybody that flew a plane and goes on a combat mission is totally immune from a certain amount of fright, there's no question about it, people die.

Life and death in combat: it is an indelible but distant memory.

JERRY: You don't really spend your lifetime thinking about it. It's behind you. And you know we read stories, you know, people write this stuff about whatever you did but there were eleven million people out there helping us you know, there were eleven or twelve million people under arms in World War II.

While he was home on leave the war ended, his duty fulfilled. But for the kid who had to talk his way into serving his country, Coleman more than proved to the recruiter that he would succeed—decorated with two distinguished flying crosses, seven air medals and two naval citations. His first tour of duty changed him. And what he took away from his World War II experiences—more than the fifty-seven missions, more than the medals—is special.

JERRY: The reason it was special to me is because I started out scared to death, very young and didn't think I could compete. What it did to me was it brought me up to the fact that I was able to compete. I was very young, I made it through. It was the single greatest thing I had ever done.

Jerry Coleman's commitment to country would be tested again. How he answered the call and finding his broadcasting voice, that's next on *One on One* from the National Baseball Hall of Fame . . . .

With Jerry Coleman's World War II service finished, that other world he had left behind was beckoning. But he hadn't picked up a baseball for three years. So spring training in Florida in 1946 was like starting all over again.

Jerry Coleman knew he was a good fielder with a great arm, but it took some time to see where he'd fit into the Yankees organization. At the farm team in Kansas City, he played second base for the first time.

JERRY: I made some terrible blunder and the next day I was on my way to Binghamton where I spent the year that was A-ball.

So close, but so far, the last man cut from the big club's roster at spring training two years in a row. Then his minor league manager told him "to make the big leagues he had to do two things ..."

JERRY: "To learn to use your bat and you have to quit smoking." Nobody ever said that to me. Learn to use my bat was one thing, but smoking?

He quit and he was called up to the big club that August.

JERRY: Sat on the bench and shook hoping they wouldn't put me in because it was a pennant race. They never put me in. I just sat there.

And he watched batter after batter. The great Joe DiMaggio, Charlie Keller, Tommy Henrich and realized ...

JERRY: I'm doing this wrong. So I went home that winter and put lead in the end of the bat, swung it every day, half hour in the morning, half an hour at night and got into a choke up situation, and from that point on I got to the big leagues and I made it.

He vividly remembers his first day playing in the majors in 1949, second base.

JERRY: First man up, hit a ball right at me and bam, right through my legs, I was scared to death. Next one hit a one shot right to me. I couldn't think about it, I mean it was a bullet. I caught it like this, made a double play and saved me.

It would come to be known as a storied time in baseball and Jerry Coleman was becoming a part of that story.

CHARLIE SILVERA: Jerry Coleman was a star. He was a star on a club that had stars. He wasn't the greatest star because we had Mantle and DiMaggio and those types of stars and Berra, but Jerry was an everyday player.

Baseball's greatest hitter, Ted Williams, recalls one of his worst career moments came thanks to a hit from Coleman. October 2, 1949, a playoff game, the Yankees versus the Red Sox, bottom of the ninth.

TED WILLIAMS: Jerry was the hitter and he hit a ball that was just a little hump back line drive, and to this day he says it was the hardest, stingiest line drive you ever saw. That ball won the game for them. He has really been a great asset to baseball.

Coleman earned Rookie of the Year honors that season. Then the next year, Most Valuable Player in the World Series.

JERRY: It was a magic time. Baseball dominated sports.

And the Yankees dominated baseball.

JERRY: It was our divine right, you see, to win. We thought that's the way it should be. It was not good for baseball but if you're on that team, you think it's wonderful.

But especially in the days when the teams had total control of a player's fate, the glory and glamour came at a price.

JERRY: It was a desperate struggle every day and every year. The only fun thing about it was when it was over. If you didn't perform you were traded and nobody I knew of wanted to be traded from the Yankees to any place else.

Because nowhere else had players like teammate and friend, Joe DiMaggio.

JERRY: He had an imperial presence that no one else has ever had. I used to kid Joe because I said without us infielders, you're nothing!

Coleman's amused by the fact that the only picture he knows of showing him hitting a home run May 24, 1951 the newspaper caption says the hitter was Joe DiMaggio. But those sorts of things don't really seem to bother Coleman. He loved to play and relished the intimacy of the game.

JERRY: There's nothing that I still remember more than playing at Ebbets Field in the World Series, and there was a woman named Hilda Chester with a cow bell and she was about from here to you clanging that bell at me—"You guys, you bums!" And it was great! I mean there they were right there, you could reach out and touch them. People were right there.

Jerry Coleman, the player, is described as a dancer who played second base with grace and ease.

CHARLIE SILVERA: He was acrobatic. He was quick on his feet.

TED WILLIAMS: Very, very good second baseman, and not a bad hitter. He was a real good cog in that whole outfit.

With another Yankee World Championship barely in the record books, America was at war again. This time, Korea. The Marines, desperate for pilots, asked Coleman to volunteer.

JERRY: I said, "I haven't been in a plane in five years and I have a wife and two children." I said, "I'm not really in the mood to volunteer, if you want to know the truth of it." And he said, "Well, we're going to get you."

Coleman, used to facing fastballs and making double plays, was back in the cockpit dropping bombs. But this time he came face to face with death when his Corsair's® engine quit on takeoff.

JERRY: And I had all these bombs, so I let them go and I think one of he bombs hit my tail and flipped me up. And my propeller was one of those huge propellers and I flipped over and the only thing I remember was my knees were behind my ears and my head was bent over and I was passing out.

Coleman was one of only four baseball players called back to fly in Korea. Ted Williams was among them.

TED WILLIAMS: My closest relationship in my own mind with Jerry Coleman, he was a Marine, a Marine pilot.

Jerry Coleman flew sixty-three missions in Korea and was honored with six more air medals and a Navy citation. He retired as a Lt. Colonel.

JERRY: What I did in the service took more out of what I had to give than anything else I've ever done.

After missing two major league seasons he was welcomed home to a Yankees contract and played four more years. He also roomed and looked after a raw young talent, Mickey Mantle, who received a lot of late-night phone calls.

JERRY: I told the switchboard operator, unless it's the President of the United States, Mickey's wife or my wife, this phone shall not ring.

Jerry Coleman was part of history in the making. While a Yankee, the team played in the World Series eight of nine years, he played in six, missing two because of the war. 1957 was his best year. At the end he hit a home run ...

JERRY: But I had no idea it was my last game.

... his last at-bat in the majors. In the off-season, Yankees management gave him an option to work in the Club's office.

JERRY: Offered me the same salary I was getting as a player and I said, "Well, I have nine and a half years, I'd like to get ten, what if I don't take this offer?" He said, "Well you could be traded." And I said, "I'll take it."

Out of uniform, he tried the front office's personnel department for three years, then was the national sales manager for Van Heusen shirts for a year. But, unlike baseball, he didn't look forward to another season. So he accepted an offer by a friend at CBS television.

JERRY: I said, "Bill, is that job still open?" He said, "Yep." He said, "Come on in." So Pee Wee Reese, Dizzy Dean, and I made a trio for the game of the week for CBS every Saturday and Sunday.

So begins chapter three in Jerry Coleman's career history, as the baseball pre-game show host for CBS.

JERRY: The third game I did, I'm interviewing Cookie Lavagetto on the field in Comiskey Park. He's managing the Senators and they play the national anthem. I don't know what to do. Shall I keep going? Well, I guess I keep going. I found out at that point when the national anthem is played, stop.

By 1963, he returned to the Yankees as their radio broadcaster, in the booth with Mel Allen and Red Barber ...

JERRY: Two of the great broadcasters of all time, Hall of Famers, and Red was a great teacher and he liked me and taught me a lot.

In the early '70s his first wife and family wanted to be in California, so he left the Yankees' broadcasts for the Angels' and did sports at KTLA. For the Padres fourth major league season in 1972, Buzzie Bavasi hired him to be the lead broadcaster. Other than one year when he served as the Padres field manager in 1980, Coleman has been known as the radio voice of the Padres, and for nearly a decade, the host of Channel 4 San Diego's *Padres Magazine*.

A fixture of San Diego baseball, he's been there for the great seasons—including two National League Championship years, and he's been there for the tough seasons.

He's done the honors of emceeing significant events in team history, including retiring numbers, retiring players, saying goodbye to the Padres' first major league home and hello to their new ballpark.

For his contributions at home, he's been gracious in accepting his induction into the Padres Hall of Fame, an eightieth birthday party at a ballpark filled with friends and fans and a painted star by the broadcast booth, a gift befitting the icon who's given so much to San Diego.

Being honored at the Hall of Fame is quite the topper to Jerry Coleman's broadcasting career. But before traveling to Cooperstown for the ceremony, the Colonel received yet another distinction for his service to country. That's next, and later on *One on One*, the pomp and circumstance of induction weekend . . . .

While some major leaguers left the game to do their military duty, Jerry Coleman is the only big leaguer to see active combat in two wars. For that and more, the United States Marine Corps commends him with a national honor. Just outside the nation's capitol at the U.S. Marine Corps Base in Quantico, Virginia, this patriotic, yet modest luncheon setting bestows new dimension to the pride of being the few, the proud, the Marines.

JANE: What did it mean for you to be honored and to be inducted into the Marine Corps Hall of Fame?

JERRY: Well, the commandant was there, General Hagee, and had a chat with him and get to sit with him and talk to him, and that was neat.

Then the four-star general Mike Hagee addresses the audience and honorees.

MIKE HAGEE: *Whether they were wearing the uniform when they were playing, or whether they just had that eagle globe and anchor in their heart, it didn't matter. They were representing the United States Marine Corps.*

And with a video tribute ...

JERRY: The film itself was a highlight, but I think you don't have to explain a lot of things if you see that.

MIKE HAGEE: *Upon graduation, Coleman departed to Guadalcanal and was assigned to the 341 Marine Scout bombing squadron, the Torrid Turtles.*

JANE: Did you get emotional at all? Did you get flashbacks of those times?

JERRY: Yeah, a little bit.

JANE: Yeah?

JERRY: And try to stay away from that because there are some sad moments.

JANE: Yeah. Yeah.

For his valor, he's a decorated pilot, and his country and fellow citizens call him a hero.

JERRY: Well, I don't know about hero. The only heroes I know, they're all dead. To me, I discount that because, you know, there were eleven million people under arms in World War II and there were a half a million people in Korea. And I was just one of the guys, you know, and I think I was lucky to survive, period. I wasn't a hero, but I had to do the best I could do and that was all. And I think people tend to, the farther away you get from that, the more they glamorize it and the more heroic it becomes, and it's not heroic. It's dirty, mud, and sometimes death.

JANE: You've said in the past that being a Marine, though, was the most important thing.

JERRY: Absolutely. Absolutely, no question about it because of what it represented. It was our country. And I've always had a philosophy: My country, right or wrong. And once you're in there, go for it. Don't give up, keep going.

Jerry Coleman's award will be displayed with others including Ted Williams' in the new National Museum of the United States Marine Corps. Coleman's wife Maggie, whose father was a Marine, underscores how this is so poignant and special to her husband of twenty-five years.

MAGGIE: For Jerry, it's family first, country second, and baseball third. And he is a patriot of the first order and so proud of being a Marine. So it was a wonderful day.

From Quantico to Cooperstown, Jerry Coleman's weekend of national accolades continues next, on *One on One....*

TED LEITNER: Here's the Colonel.

JERRY: And we're ready to go.

It is the last week in July and Jerry Coleman is on the job with Ted Leitner ...

JERRY [in booth]: Jerry and I will miss that Thursday game because he has this Hall of Fame thing. [laughs] Yeah, like it's no big deal.

JERRY: And you're going to hold my hand through all of this?

TED LEITNER: I will, absolutely.

JERRY: I'm going to need help.

TED LEITNER [overlaps]: It is a big, big deal.

One of Coleman's trademark calls has roots in his junior high spelling class. A gold star meant perfection, something he never got. So he's selective when giving one away.

JERRY [in booth]: Woody fires ... WHOA, hard shot up the middle ... OH WHAT A STOP BY LORETTA! OOH DOCTOR! YOU CAN HANG A STAR ON THAT BABY! WHOO!

Meanwhile, Cooperstown is ready for the weekend. New Yorker Ken Stevens is hoping to have Jerry sign some long-saved memorabilia.

KEN STEVENS: One is a 1978 family fun center post card and the other is an old advertisement that he had doing some kind of ad here.

Jerry Coleman is still at the Marine Corps induction, as thirty-eight Hall of Famers and guests are on hand at a Friday afternoon ceremony for the re-dedication of The National Baseball Hall of Fame and Museum after a major expansion project, with the Hall also building an endowment. Million dollar donors are recognized with a plaque. One says "San Diego Padres, in honor of Jerry Coleman." Across town, the stately Otesaga Hotel by the lake is secured for Hall of Famers, honorees, and those with special access. After leaving Quantico, Virginia and re-boarding Padres' owner John Moores' plane, the Coleman clan arrives.

> **MAGGIE:** It's so exciting!

Inside, who better to greet him but former teammate, Yogi Berra.

> **JERRY:** It took me fifty years to get here. [hug]
> **JANE:** How was he as a player?
> **YOGI BERRA:** Fine, saved me from a lot of errors!

Then Jerry and his family zip away to a private party for Honorees, Hall of Famers, and guests, including childhood friend Bobby Brown. The two started in New York's farm system together.

> **JERRY:** The four of us got together and had some pictures taken, which I'm going to get copies of. That'll be fun because I'd like to see the pictures in 1949 and '50 and then these in 2005. It was great.

Saturday morning, time for the Hall of Fame and friends golf tournament. Jerry's not on the links but there's no shortage of thoughts about him. Oriole Brooks Robinson once idolized him.

> **BROOKS ROBINSON:** When I was still in high school Jerry was playing with the Yankees I guess and I was a real student of the game. I knew all the players and we knew all the Cardinal players, the Brooklyn players, the Yankee players, of course Jerry was part of that.

Detroit's Al Kaline played against him in 1953.

> **AL KALINE:** He was one of the strengths of the Yankees in those days, Rizzuto-Coleman double play combination, so he was an outstanding ballplayer. I'm very happy to see him go in the hall.

And teammate Whitey Ford.

> **WHITEY FORD:** Jerry really helped me and told me how to behave in the big leagues and he's always been a gentleman. You know between World War II and the Korean War I think Jerry probably missed about five seasons.
> **JANE:** Do you remember talking about it and his making that choice and what that was like?
> **WHITEY FORD:** Jerry was so quiet about it, he never said anything. All of the sudden one day Jerry's gone and we said, "Where did he go?" And they said, "He's back in the service." But Jerry never talked much about it.

When talking became his next profession, Coleman affected more guys, like Braves pitcher Phil Niekro ...

> **PHIL NIEKRO:** I used to get knocked out early in the Padres games. I'd go down and listen to him on the radio. Don't get to see him as much, but looking forward to seeing him up here and I know it's well deserved and it's well overdue, too.

Reds catcher Johnny Bench was a broadcast partner ...

JOHNNY BENCH: He loves being part of the game and it shows. He gets so excited sometimes that emotionally he malapropos, but don't we all? And I think that's what's so lovable about Jerry Coleman is that he is what we as baseball players appreciate because [makes fake radio voice] he doesn't have the announcers' voice, he's got the guy that everyday inflects into his thoughts, what happens on the field, and that's as simple as it gets.

Dodgers' pitcher and Braves broadcaster, Don Sutton …

DON SUTTON: When you listen to Jerry Coleman you're listening to a guy you know is genuinely in love with the game and genuinely in love with the responsibility that goes with bringing that game to people who can't be there.

As for new inductee, Ryne Sandberg …

RYNE SANDBERG: We go back to the year, the '84 year, Cubs-Padres. I know he was around for that, although I don't want to think about it. His style, he was very comfortable for me, being a former player, just talking the game, and just having an appreciation for the players.

Oakland A's closer Dennis Eckersley …

DENNIS ECKERSLEY: I respect what he's done in his life along with his long career. Great personality, and it always comes across. He's just a very friendly, warm guy. It's nice to see in this game.

And of course, two former Padres, Rollie Fingers and Dave Winfield, who played for him and listened to him …

ROLLIE FINGERS: I don't think I ever heard him rip one guy, but I bet in the four years I played in San Diego I heard "Oh doctor" about 7,000 times.

DAVE WINFIELD: More than a niche for himself, he's carved his own piece of history and he deserves credit for it.

JOHNNY BENCH: All the things he loves now say, "We love you, and we appreciate Jerry Coleman," and now he's in the Hall of Fame, wow, that's just a great, great thing for all of us.

By mid-morning, Jerry Coleman is signing autographs in town with his share of proceeds going to charity.

FAN: Good morning, sir!

He's alongside friend Andy Strasberg and one-time broadcast partner, Ralph Kiner.

JERRY: We were brilliant! [laughs]

RALPH KINER: Really good, huh.

Fans are cordial in seeking autographs and sharing stories.

FAN: My grandfather used to work for the Newark Bears, Frank Smith?

JERRY: You're kidding!

FAN: Used to be the head groundskeeper.

FAN: Ah, and I also had a 1951 Yankees team photo signed which, you know, if you can find the players these days catch up with them, it's great to add 'em to your collection.

Stopping by is the author of *Pride of October*, Bill Madden.

> BILL MADDEN: And Jerry was the first interview I did for the book. And when I got done with the interview, I remember going home and telling my wife, "If they're all as good as this guy was, this is going to be some book."
>
> JANE: Show us that bat?
>
> FAN: It's a NY Yankee bat, with seventy autographs on it.
>
> JANE: Where did he sign that one?
>
> FAN: Ah, right there, right. I had him sign two bats, and a book, *Pride of October*. And he played for the Yankees back in the '50s when he beat my Brooklyn Dodgers all the time. So I really hate them, but I still get their autograph, huh.
>
> FAN: Jerry's linked to Yankees of the past and everybody today. He really transcends baseball for all generations.
>
> *[Jerry signing baseballs and walking away after autographs.]*

True to form, Jerry Coleman walks back to the hotel.

> JANE: A compliment, though, to know that they want your—to be a part of that …
>
> JERRY: At this stage, yes, very complimentary because I left the Yankees [thinking] almost fifty years ago and started with them fifty-seven years ago. It's been a long time. And the fact that there are still people who are interested fascinates me.
>
> JANE: So are you getting ready? You have a big night ahead of you now.
>
> JERRY: You never get ready. You know what I mean? It's always a challenge about how you gotta wear a shirt and tie tonight, and a jacket.

He manages and is prompt for a private reception on the grand lawn of the Otesaga, where he says hello to old friends in his new Hall of Fame family. Then after a formal dinner he takes a trolley ride to the Hall of Fame for a dessert reception where baseball meets Hollywood. Fans line the streets, cheering as Hall of Famer after Hall of Famer and honorees arrive to a red carpet. A night to remember, before a day he'll never forget. . . .

In his eight decades Jerry Coleman has experienced the thrills of baseball, the gravity of war, the satisfaction of a life well lived. And on July 31, 2005, this veteran would experience a new wave of emotion as he reached yet another milestone.

> *[Baseball game in Cooperstown]*

A game like this was just the beginning of a dream for Jerry Coleman—a kid from San Francisco who wanted to be a Yankee. A lifetime later, nearly 30,000 fans take their place on a green field to celebrate how dreams come true, and then some.

> HOF ANNOUNCER: *This weekend, the star will get hung for him, The Ford C. Frick Award winner, Jerry Coleman [Jerry enters stage, applause]*

The stage is filled with forty-eight of the sixty living Hall of Famers. Peter Gammons, honored for writing, the two inductees, along with a national ESPN audience, are part of the day when Jerry Coleman takes his place in history.

> JERRY *[HOF speech]: Good afternoon. I am delighted to be here. There's no question about that. One of the greatest days of my life is this day here in Cooperstown. I would like to introduce to you my family: My wife Maggie.*
>
> MAGGIE: Always feels like somebody's more deserving, somebody's worked harder or somebody's done something more important. So it's just nice to be with him, and he is allowing himself to enjoy it.
>
> JERRY *[HOF speech]: My daughter Chelsea.*
>
> CHELSEA: All he has ever wanted to do for me and his entire family is provide. It's good to see him sort of sit back and just relax and realize that for a day it's about him.
>
> JERRY *[HOF speech]: My daughter Diane.*
>
> DIANE: I've adored him forever and I am so proud of him. He's an incredible role model and I just couldn't be more proud of him.
>
> JERRY *[HOF speech]: My granddaughter Courtney and my grandson Christopher, and a pot full of extended family all over the place. Also, I've had a partner in broadcasting for twenty-five years, and I can't go by without introducing Mr. Ted Leitner, one of the best broadcasters you've never heard.*
>
> *The best owner in the history of baseball Mr. John Moores. I'm delighted to be on this platform with a couple of guys, Yogi Berra and Whitey Ford, and I'm sorry that the Scooter, Phil Rizzuto, isn't here who I shared broadcast duties with and double play duties with for sixteen years in New York Yankees. I'm here because my peers put me here. My fellow broadcasters brought me in. Wherever you are, whoever you are, God bless you and thank you so much.*

He didn't want to write a speech, but ultimately follows some notes.

> JERRY *[HOF speech]: In the beginning, the first job I had was to do the interview on the pre-game show on the CBS television network. There were twenty-five to thirty million people watching. I didn't know where the microphone was, anything. I was out there like a, you know what, nothing. And I had a floor manager who counted me down, five minutes, four and a half, and on down, then finally when he pointed to me, my knees turned to mush and I had Red Schoendienst, he's my interview guest over here, I looked to Red and said something very inquisitive like, "How's it going, Red?" And he talked for five minutes and he didn't stop for five minutes, and finally the floor manager said, "Wrap it up, wrap it up." I said, "Now back to Pee Wee Reese and Dizzy Dean." Red, you don't know how close you came to getting kissed right on the spot.*

In a dominant sea of Chicago Cubs blue, a group of forty in Padres gear and Oh Doctor T-shirts travel here with the Padres' radio station.

> FAN: We all came because we wanted to honor him and respect him for all he's done for us in the community and as a veteran.

> **FAN:** Very fruitful life and a very giving life and he's done a lot for San Diego and done a lot for the country.
>
> **FAN:** And it's really nice that other people appreciate him, too. And he's not just San Diego, he is a national figure.

Some Padres family and friends at a reception in Cooperstown share their sentiments.

> **ROBERT HORSMAN:** When I was a kid I had his baseball card, I still have it.
>
> **SANDY ALDERSON:** Jerry was really a true patriot in the best sense of the word.
>
> **ANDY STRASBERG:** He's a San Diego treasure. But he's also a national treasure.
>
> **DICK FREEMAN:** And Jerry always represented class in major leagues.
>
> **JOHN MOORES:** Jerry's the real deal. We're never going to see his like again.
>
> **BECKY MOORES:** I didn't know him as a baseball player or as a Marine but I know him as he is today which is a fine gentleman.

Tim Flannery, who broke into the bigs when Coleman was managing, pays tribute in song.

> **FLANNERY:** *[singing] I can hear that old familiar voice ... radio in Dad's old car ...*

And still others with the team or with especially close ties who couldn't attend watched his short five-minute speech with great affection.

> **TONY GWYNN:** It's the greatest feeling because I've known for a long time he's a Hall of Famer.
>
> **BRUCE BOCHY:** A lot of our players who have not known Jerry very long, they were staring at the TV listening to him. You know it was like a moment of silence in that clubhouse. The TV was on and they were all watching it, and that's how much respect he commands.
>
> **RANDY JONES:** And once again, he goes into the Hall of Fame, you know how proud he had to be, but you know he just did the professional job like he always has.
>
> **TREVOR HOFFMAN:** It just shows the true character of Mr. Coleman. Very respectful and understands what he's done in his life but in no way shape or form is flaunting it by any means.
>
> **TONY GWYNN:** I've learned so much from him and to this day he still won't give himself credit. He taught me a lot about the game through just through conversations.
>
> **JANE:** Can you summarize your philosophy of how you've lived your life?
>
> **JERRY:** Well, you can say, do unto others. Pretty much, I try to do that, treat other people the way that I would like to be treated. I want to thank the fans for putting up with me for thirty-five years in San Diego. What more can I say?

JERRY [HOF speech]: Also, I'd like to tell you this is a lifetime joy of mine. I've been in baseball my entire adult life and I've loved every minute of it, the road, the journey's incredible. I've done clinics in Europe. Stan Musial made that one, he remembers, yes, we were all over the place. I was in Japan broadcasting games, I played exhibition games throughout Japan, Okinawa, in the Philippines, on Guam, in the Hawaiian Islands, and I broadcast games in the Hawaiian Islands. I made a trip to Vietnam for baseball. All of this is for baseball. And I have broadcast and been in every small village and major city in the United States, but today, on this golden day here in Cooperstown, a journey that started sixty-three years ago, I feel that finally, finally, I've come home. Thank you.

Jerry Coleman remembers what it was like in his junior high school spelling class to never receive a gold star, his definition of perfection. But for his service to country, his brilliance in the big leagues and in broadcasting on his entire journey, which places him here in the Hall of Fame, you most certainly can hang a star. I'm Jane Mitchell. Thank you for watching *One on One* from Cooperstown, New York.

> "You make the person that you're interviewing always look good, and they're not always good. There are times when they don't look so good and, occasionally, you just have to, I guess, make a left turn. It happens occasionally. Get the wrong person and they're mad, they're upset and they don't talk well or whatever.... But you always make the person you're interviewing feel good that what he says is okay. Everything isn't okay all the time. And the way you handle those things always fascinates me because it's very difficult. It's the presentation that counts, and it's good, always has been. That's why you're here. Fourteenth year. I haven't missed any of them. I watch the channel all the time."
>
> —Jerry Coleman, 2009

DREW BREES AND LADAINIAN TOMLINSON

Few professional athletes stay with one team their whole career, but that does not negate their sweat, success, and maybe tears in that uniform. Consider that trading cards and Halls of Fame would not have retained their place in our sports value system if we, as a culture, did not value history. So it goes, to some degree, with my *One on One* profiles. Where someone begins is as significant as where they end up. The exciting thing for me is to meet them at different parts of their journey, both looking back and looking ahead.

Drew Brees and LaDainian Tomlinson are now household names for NFL fans. LaDainian has set and broken many NFL records. Drew led the New Orleans Saints to victory in the franchise's first Super Bowl in 2010 and was named the Most Valuable Player. Turn back the clock a decade, though, and these names were among what might be, what could be, and what should be.

"I remember being very excited because *One on One* was a very popular local show and I was still just a young guy trying to make a name for myself."

—LADAINIAN TOMLINSON, 2010

In 2001 the San Diego Chargers drafted LaDainian first, then Drew second, anticipating they would be future cornerstones of the team. But they would have to prove themselves, and everyone was watching. As I was planning what Chargers to feature for the 2002 season, it seemed like the right time to profile these two young players in their sophomore year. This pairing not only made sense because of their positions on the team, but also because their paths had crossed in high school, and they were good friends. I first interviewed them at their individual homes with their wives.

LADAINIAN TOMLINSON

LaDainian and LaTorsha lived in a nice-sized house in Poway. LT, as he's nicknamed, was quiet, so it would take some patience and some listening to get him to open up, which he did. He had a million-dollar smile. His eyes twinkled when he talked, and I was not confusing that with his signature diamond earrings. LaTorsha, or Torsha, was vivacious, outgoing, and expressive. She made sure we had everything we needed to coordinate pictures and video of LT from their collection and his mother's house in Texas.

The evening of our interview, we also videotaped their animal trainer giving them lessons for their teacup-sized dog. A little dog was not LT's first choice, but to see someone who is rough and tough and intense in uniform with a small dog showed the softer side fans had not yet seen.

DREW BREES

At Drew and Brittany's townhouse, they welcomed us and our camera gear with enthusiasm. I interviewed Drew first, then brought in Brittany, his fiancée at the time. Both were articulate and funny. A favorite part was how they described meeting in college. Later during editing, we alternated their interviews back to back to let them tell their story. That day, they openly brought up Drew's unusual birthmark on his right cheek—not embarrassed by it, but rather quite matter-of-factly, anticipating people's curiosity. Everything about them seemed direct, honest, and transparent. They often finished each other's sentences and seemed to be a pair that would last.

Drew gave us a tour of his office with some of his Purdue memorabilia and a poster of his favorite movie, *Caddyshack*. While that made the air, what did not was the banter between my associate producer, Kelly Morris, and Drew Brees. Kelly went to Indiana. Drew went to Purdue. That college rivalry is deep-seated. Kelly's brother also went to Purdue. We took a picture, and later I asked Drew to sign it for Kelly. She was grateful, especially to be able to show it to her brother, who idolized Drew Brees.

Two other elements added to capturing their story the first time. First, Drew's father was visiting during our production schedule, so we were able to interview him. Secondly, Drew and Brittany were planning their wedding, so we went to the Hotel del Coronado to capture them at the beach and taste-testing for their wedding menu. Imagine a royal crown shaped chandelier hanging from a two-story-high ceiling. Now imagine a camera angle that would, unintentionally, place that crown on top of Brittany's head as she sat at the table tasting the items. That made for an unexpected "visual," and why I wrote that Drew had a few "crowning moments" aside from his bride Brittany.

The show mapped out how Drew and LaDainian crossed paths at a high school All-Star game in Texas before coming to San Diego. While this edition profiled them as individuals, I wanted to show them together off the gridiron, too. We found an activity they had done together, one that would be easy to coordinate— playing basketball at the Chargers' facility. We didn't need much time, just ten to fifteen minutes to show their friendly but competitive nature. We didn't want any injuries, so they didn't go full throttle. Capturing that interaction was the perfect visual punctuation to their tandem story line.

As the team continued to do well with Drew and LaDainian at the helm in the 2002 season, I remember my boss, Dan Novak, popping his head into my office after he had seen the show, saying, "Putting those two together in a show made us look like geniuses!" It was a logical coupling, and sometimes we get lucky. It was good for everyone that they had success, and I was glad we could help connect the dynamic duo with the fans and viewers.

ROUND TWO, 2005

Over time, just watching on television or talking to him in person, LaDainian matured and grew in his confidence speaking to the media, either on the spot or in a more relaxed mode. That was particularly evident by fall of 2005 when I wanted to do an update of the *One on One*. This time, though, the main interview would be LT and Drew together, to reflect on their five seasons playing with the Chargers. We would shoot it at LaDainian's house.

Since our first interview, LT and Torsha had moved up. Their previous house could fit in their new house a few times over. The crew and I arrived late in the afternoon and LaTorsha and LT greeted us. Drew and Brittany arrived later. The Tomlinson's new Tuscany style home had high ceilings, big furniture, an enormous fish tank in the entryway, a game room with football memorabilia, a home theater, and a backyard with a pool, waterfall, and palm trees. It was a big step up from his rookie year home, and certainly from his roots in Texas.

To set up the three cameras for the best angles, photographer Dan Roper and the crew had to move some of the furniture around. That is not usually a problem, but Dan decided instead of going around the roadblock of the couch, he would jump over it, and he fell. He didn't damage any of the Tomlinsons' items, but he did hurt himself by hitting his head. He was okay, but had a headache and didn't feel well, yet he kept on going. I was having my own problem as well. I had learned long ago (at Dave Winfield's house in 1999) that I couldn't go too long without food, especially before a shoot. For whatever reason that day, I had not eaten enough. As we were waiting for Drew and Brittany, I felt the low-blood-sugar headache coming on and had no backup cheese in my purse. I asked LaTorsha if she had any cheese or orange juice. She had both, and that got me through.

When Drew and Brittany arrived, we were ready to go. This was a first for *One on One*, with two main subjects seated next to each other for the interview. We covered the five years Drew and LT had played together and what they had learned. How they talked demonstrated the dynamic of their friendship, their shared Christian faith, their sense of humor, respect for each other and for their team and city. At the time of the interview, in November during the season, it was not clear if Drew would be re-signed by the Chargers after the 2005 season. From the time we did the interview until the time it would air, much could happen. To keep it less time-sensitive, I simply asked about what they hoped would happen.

Later, each of their wives sat beside their husbands to touch on what they had experienced in the last few years as well. Both couples seemed as genuine as before, but clearly more mature, wiser, and even stronger. For our activity, they laughed and joked as they played pool in the game room, bejeweled with jerseys and footballs from LT's stellar career to that point.

After the usual writing and producing process, the show debuted about a month after the sit-down interview. We wove in the latest images and information, while still leaving things open as far as Drew's contract. Eighteen days after the debut, in the last game of the 2005 season against the Denver Broncos, Drew injured his throwing shoulder and underwent arthroscopic surgery. There were questions whether he would recover. After negotiations, Drew did not accept the Chargers' offer, became a free agent, and signed with the New Orleans Saints in 2006. Earlier on August 29, 2005, Hurricane Katrina had taken a disastrous toll on the Louisiana area, and Drew said he felt drawn to be part of the rebuilding of the team and the region. As much as I cheer for the Chargers, I am thrilled to see his success with the Saints. I appreciate a friendship with Brittany and Drew, based not just on the show but also on conversations over time. And they have supported my fundraising efforts by donating a signed jersey for ALS fundraising auctions.

Even with their connection to New Orleans, Drew and Brittany didn't forget their first NFL city, maintaining a home in San Diego and the *Brees Dream Foundation*. In 2010, Drew became the new partner in what had been the *Stan Humphries Celebrity Classic* developed by Dave Miller and *Integrated Sports Marketing*. The new chapter of the event included my employer as the title sponsor for the *Cox Celebrity Championship* hosted by Drew Brees. During the cocktail attire dinner, in front of about a thousand people, I was asked to introduce a video about Drew and Brittany's foundation's efforts, and in part, this is what I said:

"While cheering for Drew with a bunch of other people on vacation in Maui, I was happy for him and his Saints. But when I saw Drew and Brittany on

Oprah, I literally flashed back to sitting with them in their living room that first time, and realized how, even with all their challenges and successes, they are the very same real, genuine people we all came to know and love. Tonight, and with this weekend's events, we see how their hearts continue to make a difference in others' lives, and to make dreams come true.... Ladies and gentlemen, please welcome a World Champion on the football field, and a World Champion in life, Drew Brees."

In early 2010, the Chargers released LaDainian and he signed with the New York Jets. That spring, Junior Seau invited him to the Junior Seau Foundation's annual Legends Awards event. The event was honoring John Lynch—another stellar San Diegan—but Junior wanted LT there for a special sendoff from an appreciative crowd. I saw LaDainian, and like many other times over the years, he said hello with a genuine hug and smile. It's nice to know LT and Drew are among the superstars who do not forget those who helped them or celebrated them along the way. I am deeply touched LaDainian offered his thoughts for this book. He's right, he was a young guy trying to make a name for himself, and he certainly has.

Drew and LaDainian matured and made a tremendous impact on Chargers football. Even though that tandem on the field changed with the business of football, their stories, grit, and character are still relevant and respected. I am happy to have been a tiny part of their exposure early in their careers. We even made the updated edition a *One on One Classic*, for the timeless value of this twosome's story.

This is the script from the edition debuting December 13, 2005.

• • •

Drew Brees and LaDainian Tomlinson: unstoppable and inspiring.

> **DREW:** I got the same thing that I got coming out of high school, which was, you're too short, you're too slow, not strong enough arm.
> **LADAINIAN:** Every single year, you have to prove yourself.
> **DREW:** As long as we take it one game at a time—that every time we step on the field, we can beat anybody, anywhere, anytime.

Call them the dynamic duo, an offensive one-two punch, and on a personal level, the best of friends. We first met Chargers quarterback Drew Brees and running back LaDainian Tomlinson *One on One* in 2002, their sophomore year in the pros. They have indeed come into their own, taking the reigns as leaders on one of the most successful and exciting teams in the NFL.

Drew Brees—confident, resilient, optimistic—is carving a place for himself in Chargers quarterback history. LaDainian Tomlinson, with quickness and agility, has been called one of the best to ever play his position in the NFL. They have more than lived up to the expectation placed on them in 2001; the one-two draft picks to be the cornerstone on which the Chargers would build the franchise's future. In the midst of a competitive 2005 season, at LaDainian's new custom home, we sit down with the two friends to reflect on the past few years and a bond that started at a Texas State High School All-Star game.

LADAINIAN: We both put up huge numbers but, you know, none of the big schools came calling. So we felt like we had something to prove.

DREW: I knew I'm going to be watching this guy at TCU because, you know, he's got something, and he made a heck of a catch for me in the All-Star game, too, so I kind of owed him one.

They were finalists for the Heisman Trophy.

JANE: So then when you ended up both coming to San Diego, what was the first thing you said to each other?

DREW: I remember specifically. We just kind of looked at each other and said, "This is our time to turn this organization around."

Brees learned a lot from quarterback Doug Flutie. Tomlinson started every game his rookie year. Both recall how they tried to block out external pressures while focusing on the veterans.

LADAINIAN: We were taught how to, you know, lead a football team because of those guys. So when you first come in, you are looking to Junior and Rodney. You're kind of looking at everything they do, and you just kind of sit back in the background and say, you know, what do you guys want me to do? [laughs]

DREW: Yeah.

LADAINIAN: You know?

JANE: Well, because within just a short amount of time, you then become the leaders.

LADAINIAN: Right, exactly.

In 2002, Drew Brees won the starting quarterback spot from Doug Flutie.

DREW: But I think when you get in that position, you just understand that the team goes as maybe you go, and so you gotta make sure that every day you approach it with that kind of focus and intensity.

Tomlinson held nothing back, turning heads as he tied and set team records for rushing and catches.

DREW: I wanted to be good, and I had a lot of goals for myself, but not only that, I wanted to prove that I belonged in this league and I can play and be great at it.

2003 started off with a twist, with Brees catching a twenty-one-yard touchdown pass from Tomlinson.

LADAINIAN: I guess it kind of brought back that feeling of we're having fun again.

DREW: Right. None of the pressure....

LADAINIAN: That play right there, it was kind of like—it was exciting for the fans and everybody, and it was exciting for us because it was something different. I don't think any one of us expected that, you know.

DREW: No. And you only get that opportunity once every couple of years ....

LADAINIAN: Yeah.

DREW: ... and maybe once in a career ....

LADAINIAN: Yeah.

By mid season 2003, Drew Brees wasn't playing well, wasn't effective, benched for five games.

DREW: It was extremely tough. Definitely one of the hardest things, if not the hardest thing, I've ever had to deal with in my professional career. I mean, in all of my athletic careers, 'cause I've always been the guy—the starting quarterback, the guy that everybody looks to come through in the clutch and win games and all that. And I felt like I learned a lot by kind of being removed from the field and being on the sideline and watching. I realized how complicated I was trying to make it, and how simple the game can be if you just go out there and play it and have fun doing it.

LADAINIAN: He proved it to me that Kansas City game our rookie year when he brought us back. I mean, you go in and perform like that as a rookie? You just showed everybody what you can do.

Meanwhile, Tomlinson was the first player in NFL history to rush for a thousand yards and catch a hundred passes in a season.

DREW: That's what made it fun to come to work, is to watch this guy run around and make the plays that he was making. There were times, obviously, during that season, tough times, where he would come up to me and say, "Drew, I believe in you." Just kind of, "Weather this thing and everything's going to work out." And I probably never told him how much I appreciated it, but I did.

That mutual belief in each other helped in what could have been a deflating experience when the Chargers drafted Philip Rivers, another highly touted young quarterback. Lucky for Brees, Rivers held out of training camp just long enough for Brees to prove that he still deserved to lead the team.

JANE: Did you ever think my time as the Chargers quarterback was over? Or short lived? Or did you just ...

DREW: No, honestly I never did. I always believed that I was the starting quarterback of this team, and I never visualized myself as anything else.

Their work ethic, vision, and execution helped turn the team around in 2004....

LADAINIAN: But for us, it was never a doubt. We were going to be good.

DREW: All we needed was just a little bit of success, just to continue to get that confidence. The winning breeds confidence.

They made it to the playoffs for the first time since 1995, but the AFC West Champions lost a hard-fought playoff game against the Jets in overtime.

DREW: I think it was disappointing just because we felt like we had the ability to go all the way, but I walked away from that game feeling very good about our team, just because we had fought so hard. We had fought so hard all season long, and we had defied all kinds of odds.

JANE: Everyone nationally was recognizing how you had come back. And what was that like to get that kind of recognition?

DREW: Well …

JANE: Did you feel like you had come back?

DREW: … in my mind, I had never gone anywhere. [laughs]

LADAINIAN: Yeah, exactly.

DREW: But it's a tremendous honor because, you know, obviously people recognized that you've had some struggles and that you fought through it.

2004 was Brees' first and Tomlinson's second pro bowl year. Number 21 led the NFL with seventeen rushing touchdowns among a lot of impressive statistics, and it continues in 2005.

LADAINIAN: I'm like on a one-track highway. I don't look to the side. I don't look behind me. I kind of have tunnel vision, and I'm going straight ahead, and I don't want to look back. When I'm done playing and I hang up the cleats, I'll look back and I'll reminisce on the kind of career I've had. But right now, we got some Super Bowls to win. [both laugh]

To appreciate LaDainian Tomlinson and Drew Brees' success, we revisit their stories first told in 2002.

Drew Christopher Brees was born January 15, 1979 in Dallas, Texas. Even in diapers, he seemed adept at handling a football.

DREW: Whether it was football, baseball, wiffle ball, I was swinging it, throwing it, doing something.

Athleticism runs in the family. His father, Chip, an attorney, played basketball at Texas A & M; Uncle Marty Akins quarterbacked at the University of Texas; and Grandfather Akins is the second winningest high school coach in Texas. Young Drew rarely missed his grandfather's pre-season practices.

DREW: I remember going out there and sitting out there in the heat and humidity. But thinking, *Gosh, I want to be like these guys someday.* And that was the high school level.

His father doesn't think Drew's dreams and eventual success were ever a given.

CHIP BREES: For Drew, every time a door opened for him, giving him an opportunity to play at the next level, he was able to succeed, in large part because of being just a hard worker.

Drew's work ethic and independence are partly a result of his parents' divorce when he was seven, the same year the family moved to Austin.

DREW: That almost made me grow up faster in a way 'cause it was my brother and I, and we would spend two days at one house and then two days at the other house.

Hearts heal, parents remarry, and Drew becomes consumed with school, sports, and a mantra instilled by his parents.

DREW: They said if you're going to do something, you're going to give it everything you've got.

After only having played flag football at his middle school, he's the fourth string JV quarterback at West Lake High School.

DREW: We went 8-and-2. Those are the only two losses I ever had in high school, which we never should've lost! I can tell you who we lost to and why! From that moment on, I kind of had where I wanted to be.

He wants to be the leader, and number 15 wins the varsity quarterback spot his junior year. As a senior, he's a high school hero, crowned homecoming king while leading his team to an undefeated 16-0 season.

DREW: Which, in the state of Texas, is pretty incredible. You have to play six games just to get to the state finals.

It seems Drew Brees should be getting calls from college recruiters ...

DREW: No calls came in.

He wonders if his smaller size, just 6', or his post-junior-year knee surgery, are counting against him. So as a three-sport star, lettering in baseball and basketball, he figures he'll likely get a baseball scholarship instead, then winds up leading the charge to a state championship.

DREW: Then all of a sudden, I get a call from Purdue and Kentucky. I know University of Kentucky is in Kentucky obviously, but where the heck is Purdue?

Neither program had recent winning records, but he's drawn to the Indiana school's tradition, picks Purdue, and wins the starting spot his sophomore year.

DREW: Of all places to have your first college start, at USC, in the Pigskin Classic, the first game of the year.

And despite losing to the Trojans ...

DREW: I thought, *You know what? I can do this.*

So begins the Brees era under then new head coach, Joe Tiller.

JOE TILLER: Drew's always been a confident guy, a great quality to have in the sense that if he does throw an interception, or he does make a mistake out there, he's on to the next play mentally.

ANNOUNCER: *One of the biggest touchdown passes in college history. They'll be replaying this for years!*

The Big Ten underdogs are not only winning, they're winning big games....

ANNOUNCER: *Scans the field, knows he has it, and doesn't miss it. What a play.*

DREW: I felt like at Purdue, whenever we stepped on the field with a team like Michigan, Ohio State, Michigan State, Penn State, Wisconsin, whoever it would be in the Big Ten, we were outmatched. But somehow we'd always get in the game. We just wanted it and we wanted it bad.

Early success means prophetic questions about his skills and style.

> DREW [college interview]: *People like to compare me to Doug Flutie. I don't know— just because he's short and I'm short.*

As a junior, Brees is a candidate for college football's most coveted award, the Heisman Trophy. He is also eligible for the NFL draft. But instead of following the hype—quitting school to go pro—he follows his heart. Because, despite being part of setting a school record for three straight bowl games ...

> DREW: Our ultimate goal was obviously to win a Big Ten Championship, go to the Rose Bowl, and we hadn't done that, and I just felt a little empty.

His senior year at Purdue is all about finishing what he's started.

> DREW: All four years just kind of wrapped into one moment.

The Boilermakers had gone from worst to first in four years, earning a trip to the Rose Bowl, the school's first appearance in more than thirty years. Despite losing to the Washington Huskies, Brees is again a finalist for the Heisman and for the Maxwell Award for the College Player of the Year....

> MAXWELL AWARD ANNOUNCEMENT: *The best of the best is Drew Brees of Purdue University.*

He leaves Purdue as the Big Ten's and the school's all-time leader in several categories, including passing yards, nearly 12,000, and touchdown passes—ninety. He does all that while making academics a priority. Graduating with a degree in Industrial Management and a 3.4 GPA, he's the first recipient of the Socrates Award for the nation's finest athlete in terms of academics, athletics, and community service.

> [PSA for the American Lung Association: *Enjoy the breeze. Don't smoke.*]

He lends his name to causes and helps kids with reading and math, underscoring how school should be first.

> DREW [school PSA]: *That's the way it's gonna be until I actually get out of college and hopefully make football my job for a couple years.*

Even he isn't sure he'll get a chance to prove himself at the next level.

> DREW: I got the same thing that I got coming out of high school, which was, you're too short, you're too slow, not a strong enough arm.

Come draft day 2001, teams he thinks might pick him take a pass until round two, and the call from Chargers General Manager John Butler.

> DREW: "You healthy? You feel good? You ready to work?" "Yes sir, yes sir, yes sir." "All right, let's go." Click. And that's it.

LaDainian Tomlinson's story is next on *One on One*....

LaDainian Tomlinson is already a household name for football fans across the country, but that recognition comes because of a lifetime of work and focus, as we first learned meeting him his second year in the NFL. While some kids only dream about playing professional football, LaDainian Tomlinson visualized it.

> **LADAINIAN:** I was always a goal-oriented person. You know, and I always looked at the bigger picture.

His bigger picture started June 23, 1979, born LaDainian Tyshane Tomlinson. Among his earliest memories: watching the Dallas Cowboys on TV.

> **LADAINIAN:** The Cowboys played every Sunday in our house. I used to be able to tell my father whatever was going on in the game at a very young age.

His eyes focus on legendary running backs Tony Dorsett, then Emmitt Smith.

> **LADAINIAN:** You're looking at the guy who has the ball.

His father wouldn't see him play much as a child past Pop Warner. After his parents divorced, Tomlinson, his brother, and sister grew up with aunts and cousins in working middle class neighborhoods in Marlin and Waco, Texas. He's raised mostly by his mother Loreane, a nurse's assistant, with guiding words.

> **LADAINIAN:** Along with faith, it was kind of the idea that whatever you want in life, you have to go out and get it.

His quest to succeed in sports continues at Waco's University High School his sophomore year. He runs track, plays basketball, baseball, and football under Head Coach Leroy Coleman.

> **LEROY COLEMAN:** He had great quickness and speed, had the size and the heart and the character to be a great athlete.

For two years, Tomlinson is a fullback, a blocker, but not the one with the glory or whom scouts might notice. So with his sights set on college, he works hard in the classroom and at his game.

> **LADAINIAN:** I wanted to get a scholarship. That was one of my goals.

Finally, his senior year, he is the guy who gets the ball.

> **LADAINIAN:** 300-yard, 200-yard performances, six touchdowns, five touchdowns.

He's a Texas State All-Star and even the prom king....

> **LADAINIAN:** Yeah, yeah, yeah. Oh, man. [laughs]

Despite accounting for an amazing 2,500 yards and thirty-nine touchdowns his senior season, he's not highly recruited. A few schools want him to red-shirt then to grow in their programs.

> **LADAINIAN:** And I was like, "No, man, I want to play as a freshman."

Texas Christian University in Ft. Worth agrees he should play, and LaDainian Tomlinson becomes a Horned Frog with TCU, in the Western Athletic Conference. He's the back up to junior Basil Mitchell, who'd later become a Green Bay Packer.

LADAINIAN: Who had been through the fire, and he kind of taught me the ropes.

And so Number 5's climb into college record books begins, and fast.

LADAINIAN: My numbers always improved every year.

On his way to helping his team win the Sun Bowl, then a WAC Championship, he sets a major college rushing record of an incredible 406 yards, becoming the nation's leading rusher. Going into his senior year, he's a projected Heisman Trophy candidate.

LADAINIAN: It was just like one of the names thrown out there and you have to prove yourself throughout whole year.

No pressure. There's only a little school campaign saying, "LT for 2000. He loves his Momma. He loves his Big Uglies [that's his offensive line)], and he loves to run, too."

LADAINIAN: I didn't think they would give it to a guy like me from TCU, which is a smaller school.

So the quiet but strong 5'11", 217 pound Tomlinson, who bench presses 450 pounds, just plays with his mother's picture tattooed on his arm as his inspiration. He counts the Senior Bowl in Mobile, Alabama as a pivotal moment.

LADAINIAN: And that was when I really proved to people that I can run the football in a pro-style offense, and I can catch the football, and I was fast. So it kind of changed their views.

Tomlinson leads the nation in rushing again. Carrying a 2.4 GPA, majoring in Radio-TV, he wins the Doak Walker Award for the best running back who also epitomizes sportsmanship, leadership, community service, and academic and athletic integrity. And he is indeed a Heisman finalist, attending the big event in New York and talking with Drew Brees.

LADAINIAN: We just played in a high school All-Star game four years ago, and what if we end up on the same NFL team?

What if? The Chargers had the first pick of the draft, but the day before trade it to Atlanta. Part of the deal, pass on the right to draft Michael Vick. Tomlinson becomes the Chargers' number one priority, number 1 pick, and lands in San Diego with Drew Brees.

In 2005, Brees and LT are consummate pros—Pro-Bowlers, worthy of their own real action figures.

LADAINIAN: An action figure? I mean, that's super hero cartoon stuff. You know....

JANE: Well, a lot of people think you are super heroes.

LADAINIAN: That's the way it makes me feel, you know.

DREW: Yeah, they gotta put a cape on LT.

LT—even that nickname wasn't okay a few years ago.

LADAINIAN: My friends started calling me that at a very young age so I'm their LT.

JANE: Right.

DREW: The new school LT, yeah, all those old school guys, they know Lawrence Taylor's LT. We know LaDainian Tomlinson is LT.

Even though the two and their team are often the talk of the town …

DREW: I'll talk on the radio and I'll talk on TV, but I never watch it. Never listen to it.

JANE: Really?

LADAINIAN: Yeah.

DREW: Whether it's bad or good. What people are saying, it's not going to help you win the next game.

They are committed to the community for the Chargers or with the Tomlinson Touching Lives Foundation, his 21 Club for kids, and the LT School Is Cool Scholarship Fund.

LADAINIAN: That's just the way God made me, you know, to have a kind heart, to be able to try to help people.

DREW: We were both kids once, and we both went to those camps and got to meet those athletes.

The Brees Dream Foundation helps find a cure for and helps those living with cancer, and there's his Gridiron Classic for youth sports and a spring golf tournament: his turn to give back.

The Chargers and Tomlinson showed mutual loyalty with an eight-year contract worth almost sixty million dollars through 2011. The team also placed its franchise tag on Brees with an eight million dollar contract for 2005.

DREW: But I believe that God has a plan for all of us, and if it's not here and it's elsewhere, then it's happening for a reason, and I'm going to make the most of it. But if I had it my way, I'd be here playing with this guy for a long time.

JANE: It seems from what I know of you guys, that faith plays a big role in your lives.

LADAINIAN: Yeah …

DREW: Absolutely.

LADAINIAN: … I mean, absolutely. There is no other way to live than to know that God plays a huge part in my life and my faith, knowing that He has a plan for my life and it's way bigger than football. It is way bigger than football. You know, football is kind of just an avenue of what God wants for my life and my family.

Family now means their college sweethearts. The two couples are friends and competitive when playing in the Tomlinson's game and trophy room. Since 2002, LaDainian and LaTorsha have married, have their dream homes, and completed their college degrees.

"Although I had been doing interviews since college, it took some time before I gained enough experience to be comfortable doing interviews on a professional level such as the *One on One* interview. The first time I didn't really know what to expect, but by the second time I was pretty much a veteran.

The *One on One* interview was more personal and in-depth. It wasn't a typical stats oriented interview. Jane had a way of making me feel comfortable with opening up. Unlike some interviews, she wasn't trying to create controversy. Jane was very sincere in asking her questions and wanting to hear the answers.

It really felt good to hear so many people say such positive things about me. I believe it was their comments that made the interview so personal, honest and different than others. My friends and family, especially my mom, were very impressed. The show definitely helped connect me with fans and the community because it gave the insight into my life other than what they see on Sundays. It helped them to get to know the real LT. I enjoyed getting to see a different side of some of my teammates through *One on One*—a side that most of us wouldn't just openly show to one another. The show allowed us to do that."

—LaDainian Tomlinson, 2010

LATORSHA: I wanted kids to see that education is also important to him. And not only did he already achieve his dream of coming to the league, he went back and finished school. How many people do that?

JANE: Big contract, lots of money. What do you do with that? And how does it change your life?

LATORSHA: And he definitely has grown in that aspect of knowing I have all this money, who do I help? How do I put this money to use? I want to help people, but how do I help? And over the years, he's learned to listen to his heart and just go with what his heart says.

In addition to celebrating their marriage at the Hotel Del Coronado, Drew and Brittany have had an eventful few years with football.

BRITTANY: Went through a lot of different things, a lot of different struggles, a lot of great times, and I think it really helped us kind of learn a lot and mature a lot, and value the things that we have more, and appreciate things more, and kind of take a better outlook on life.

Dedicated to their charity work and traveling the world, from Australia to South Africa.

BRITTANY: Now we can really kind of help people in different situations that maybe we wouldn't have been able to do before. So …

DREW: Yeah.

BRITTANY: … we're very blessed.

With a solid support system, the dynamic duo is on a roll.

LADAINIAN: We were faced with a challenge and we looked it dead in the face, and we answered it, and we became champions.

DREW: I think that just goes to show that if you believe it can happen, I mean, you can will it to happen, then it will.

Drew Brees and LaDainian Tomlinson have matured and made a tremendous impact on Chargers football. When faced with challenges, their true grit and character shine through as they're determined to take the team to new a level. I'm Jane Mitchell. Thank you for watching *One on One*.

GEOFF BLUM

"Jane did a great job of shining a light on things I had not thought about for years. She did a lot of research and did a wonderful job of showing my path through life to the big leagues."

—GEOFF BLUM, 2010

There are some movies or television episodes that, no matter how many times you see them, they always make you laugh or cry. That's how it is with Geoff Blum's story and his *One on One* show of 2006. I just didn't realize it until the day I interviewed him, and part of the reason for that, even, was very personal.

On Wednesday October 27, 2005, I was in bed watching the Chicago White Sox and Houston Astros play game four of the World Series in Houston. I didn't have ties to either team, although I was fond of Chicago from my grad school year there and had vivid memories of celebrating in the streets when the Bears won the Super Bowl. I was happy for the White Sox, mostly because they hadn't won a World Championship since 1917, and it seemed time for Chicago baseball fans to come out on top. Otherwise, there was no emotional connection in it for me. Then my phone rang.

On the other end was someone I had just been introduced to the week before, a blind date to be, and we had only talked on the phone once, the Friday before. He had told me then that he was flying home to Chicago to be around the excitement of the White Sox being in the World Series. The night the White Sox won, he was obviously happy for the victory, and I was flattered he would call me from a bar in Chicago in the middle of all the pandemonium. He was deliberate in telling me he called his father first, then me. *Nice*, I thought, *to be number two on his list behind his dad.*

He asked if I had seen the Geoff Blum home run the night before. I had not, but had seen his picture on the front page of the sports section that day. As we talked, I walked in to my kitchen, pulled it from the recycle pile, and set it aside. He reiterated he had called his father, which I figured a natural thing for a family of Chicago baseball fans. Then, it started to hit me. In a vulnerable, and somewhat tentative tone, he shared how that call was a big deal, because the White Sox' success in the post season had given him and his father something to talk about, a conduit, of sorts, bringing them close again, after they had drifted apart. "Ahhh," I said, "common ground. That's nice."

He elaborated on how the night before, when Geoff hit that home run in the fourteenth inning, giving the Sox the lead, Geoff became an instant hero for far more reasons than he would, or could, ever know. That home run meant the White Sox finally had a chance to win the World Series; it meant he and his father—despite their differences—could celebrate and share in a moment they had talked about and waited for their whole lives. I already understood the great feeling of my team clinching a title and going to the World Series from my experience with the Padres in 1998, but this was different. The sound of joy and relief in my new friend's voice told me not only about how the win affected a personal relationship, but enlightened me about the depth of emotion and connection people from Chicago have for their teams, and how that connection—especially in victory—can transcend the communication gap or years of disconnect. I would soon learn stories like his were multiplied thousands of times over.

Three weeks later, the blind date to be and I finally had an official date. We met at a restaurant near my office, and I came bearing gifts: A T-shirt from the Walk to Defeat ALS® in October and that newspaper I had pulled from the trash with Geoff Blum on the front page. It was the start of a beautiful friendship. Beyond that, the insight was the main

"I didn't realize what a production it was having it at home with all the lights, cameras, and people. It was better and harder than the typical pre and post game interviews. Better because we were in a comfortable environment at our home; it made it easier to open up and give real, unplanned answers. Harder because I couldn't give cliché, generic answers."

reason I put Geoff Blum on my *One on One* list the very next week, when he re-signed with the Padres as a free agent.

At spring training in Peoria, Arizona, 2006, I introduced myself to Geoff, congratulated him on his success, and shared I had heard how much that World Championship had impacted people's lives. I said I wanted to do an interview for my *One on One* show, and he seemed excited and grateful for the invitation to feature him and his family. We made a plan to shoot early in the season.

I did my homework and mapped out the timeline of his story, specifically 2005 and the trade to the White Sox midseason, after his triplets were born. I could anticipate some things, but not what unfolded within the first half hour of our time together at his house that spring.

After the crew set up the three cameras and lights in the main family room, we decided to do the house tour before sitting down. We walked upstairs to a room that had a number of jerseys and pieces of personal baseball memorabilia. He pointed them out very matter-of-factly, like a timeline getting from point A to point B. He mentioned that the picture of him the night of the home run was in the bedroom. So we followed him down the hallway, and he beamed as we passed pictures of his daughters. As we walked over to a wall at the foot of the bed, he pointed out the picture and started describing it: "This is what I took away from the World Series. That's me, my daughter, my brother Greg in the middle, my mom, Connie, and my wife, Kory. They were all there for the home run and, you know, obviously they were sitting in the stands when I threw that kiss up there after the home run."

Between the time I looked at the picture then back at him, his eyes had welled up, his voice cracked, and he joked: "Good grief. Do you do this to everybody?" I really didn't do anything, other than allow him to share with us a special moment. You can't fake stuff like that. Geoff Blum is a sentimental guy. Once we sat down, he moved along in the interview with energy, humor, and humility, as we talked about his childhood. He had a great grasp of his defining moments and realistic expectations of being just a guy who loved to play the game.

Earlier that spring, I had gone to Anaheim when the White Sox were playing the Angels to interview his former teammates, Manager Ozzie Guillen, and Sox fans. Those fans, some transplants living in Southern California, had similar stories of how they appreciated Geoff Blum's role in making their collective dream come true. When we talked about 2005, I relayed my friend's story about his father and others' experiences. Geoff was genuinely touched by the outpouring of love and thanks from Sox fans. Throughout, he was honest and transparent, with seemingly no walls and no machismo, especially when I asked him to describe what went through his mind when he hit that ball to go out of the park for a home run.

This was not a play-by-play of where the ball went, and how fast he ran around the bases. From the first words of his answer, I could feel how this home run was truly like no other. He went back in time to illustrate his real life movie, frame by frame describing those defining moments of highs and lows, of pain and passion, of an opportunity of a lifetime, and how all those moments passed before his eyes and through him every step he took. I didn't interrupt. I didn't need to. I just listened and even had to subtly wipe a tear from my cheek as he took me right along with him in this eloquent, genuine description of the hit, the run, the memories from his mind's eye. He fought back the tears and pushed through the lump in his throat, saying, "It's a part of me, and it's something that I get to take with me forever. You know, it's something that, hopefully, you know, my girls'll be proud of, and it'll be good."

In that moment, before we even brought Kory in for their interview together, I knew his description would be at the end of the show, as the culmination for the viewer to really understand, like he did, the bigger meaning of that home run. With Dan Roper's editing, inserting powerful and perfectly placed music, along with a blend of slow-motion and visuals from Geoff's journey, you can imagine why it's an episode—a story—that makes me laugh and cry every time.

When Kory sat beside him and they described their odyssey with their triplets, the dimension of their agony and ecstasy became clearer to me. I even exhaled after hearing about their emotional roller coaster. Sometimes people forget that just because someone is a professional athlete, they are still people first, and for Geoff and Kory, they were a young couple facing a medical and moral question about her pregnancy.

The results, as you'll read, were all good, and they had quite the handful to prove that. So in addition to the serious subjects, the shoot was fun. As a couple, their humor worked in their favor, as triplets in high chairs and a fourth daughter, too, all wanted food and attention as we were shooting video and asking for pictures and other elements for the show. It was good that we scheduled the shoot on a non-game day. That allowed us to take the time we needed, with no sense of a deadline to finish so he could get to the field. I count it as one of my favorite interviews and one of my favorite days at work.

Driving up to their house between San Diego and Orange Country, I was going into the interview with an open mind. I did not promise this would be a half-hour show, especially because he was a bench player on the Padres' roster and not necessarily considered a star or marquee player at the time. As photographer Michael Spaulding and I were driving back to the station, Michael said he hoped it was going to be a half hour, because he was so moved by Geoff's story. "Oh yeah, for sure a half hour," I concurred. "That was amazing."

As I say in this edition's introduction, sometimes the regular guys don't get the attention they deserve; sometimes it takes being a hero to get noticed. For me, Geoff Blum's journey would have been special even without the home run. His story of working hard, living his dream, balancing the tug of the heartstrings from his family and the pull of the pressure of the game all combined for a real life drama we can all learn from and appreciate. Still that home run was a moment seared in the hearts and minds of White Sox fans, and it served as an additional vestibule to tell his story fully.

After the 2007 season, Geoff Blum was a free agent and signed with the Houston Astros. In 2008, the White Sox erected a monument celebrating the 2005 championship. As one of the key players, Geoff's tie-breaking home run in game three of the World Series is replicated in bronze, and I look forward to seeing it sometime in Chicago.

As for that blind date? We eventually went our separate ways, but as friends, he tells me he still has that newspaper featuring his hero and will always have the good memories of the 2005 season to share with his dad.

This edition was awarded an Emmy. Here is the script from the show debuting May 13, 2006.

• • •

Geoff Blum, a South Side of Chicago Hero, returns home to Southern California, his hands full with an all-girl infield of his own.

GEOFF: The timing of everything that has happened in the last couple years is what blows my mind.

In a game where super stars often get all the limelight, it's encouraging to find great stories in those "regular" guys, like Geoff Blum. In one season, he went from being happy just playing off the bench to being an unlikely World Series hero. But his journey is laden with happiness and tears: faced with tough choices about his triplets, and realizing how one swing of the bat changed his life and the lives of countless baseball fans.

> ANNOUNCER: *And another welcome back to number 27—infielder, Geoff Blum!*

In 2006, Geoff Blum is in a San Diego Padres uniform for the second time. His first time, 2005, he was a free agent, grateful to make the team knowing he and his wife Kory were going to be parents again. Number 27 didn't disappoint: a key contributor to the first half of what would turn out to be a Western Division Championship season. But his proven versatility catches the attention of the Chicago White Sox, and he's crushed, at the time, to be traded to the AL Central Division leaders.

> GEOFF: This is memory lane right here.

At their home in San Clemente …

> GEOFF: As you can see, I was blessed with a linebacker number: 50. But, you know, I would've worn anything at that time, anything to be in the big leagues.

A collection of jerseys and balls …

> GEOFF: The 500th hit and the fiftieth home run …

Chronicles his professional baseball years …

> GEOFF: I think that's actually the jersey I wore when I hit home runs from both sides of the plate …

Especially proud to be part of two Division Championship teams in 2005.

> GEOFF: At least one TV in the clubhouse would be on the San Diego game. I definitely left my heart there when I left and got traded.

He, of course, has the bat and ball from his World Series Game 3 go ahead game-winning home run. Geoff Blum is sincere, yet matter of fact, in describing his mementos and newspapers capturing the rock-star like hoopla with his Chicago White Sox teammates.

> GEOFF: That's Aaron Rowan, myself, and Joe Crede on top of a double-decker bus and going down the streets of Chicago in front of about a million and a half people, you know, just screaming for us. And, you know, a good thing the hair was good that day. [laughs]

But it's a little photo collage in the master bedroom that triggers what that day in October really means to him.

> GEOFF: This is what I took away from the World Series. That's me, my daughter, my brother Greg in the middle, my mom, Connie, and my wife, Kory. They were all there for the home run and, you know, obviously they were sitting in the stands when I threw that kiss up there after the home run. Geez, [gets choked up] just a kiss of relief after the whole thing was over. Good grief. Do you do this to everybody?
>
> JANE: Ahh….

To truly appreciate the depth of his emotion …

GEOFF: Wasn't ready for that …

Go back to the beginning. Born April 26, 1973, Geoffrey Edward Blum was a smiley, blonde, rambunctious boy in Redwood City, moving with his parents to Ontario and the Los Angeles area at four.

> **GEOFF:** I was just the typical Southern California kid. Constantly outside, wiffle ball, you know, riding bikes, playing soccer, trying to do as much as I could, just wearing myself out until the streetlamps came on and Mom said to come in.

His mother was a school office manager. His father worked several jobs, including as a sporting goods distributor.

> **GEOFF:** Just basically did enough to sustain the family with my mom.
>
> **JANE:** And when your brother finally came along, how were you as a big brother?
>
> **GEOFF:** I was awesome. I was the best. Why wouldn't I be?

Five years apart, Greg, who'd have a stint as a minor league catcher, developed a close relationship with Geoff, despite some childhood hi-jinx.

> **GEOFF:** My memories are of putting him in the doorway with the Johnny Jumper that hangs there, and just sling-shotting him across the room.

Geoff hit a growth spurt as a freshman.

> **GEOFF:** I think I was 5'9" in eighth grade and went straight to 6'3" in about a summer and a half.

Good at basketball and varsity baseball at Chino High School, but as a fan, his favorite moment? Watching a hobbled Kirk Gibson hit the game winning home run off Dennis Eckersley in Game 1 of the 1988 World Series.

> **GEOFF:** I fantasized about it, you know, and I said wouldn't it be awesome? If I could do anything in the world, I'd be a ballplayer.

Fantasy approached reality when recruiters showed interest. With college tuition a strain on his parents, he took advantage of baseball, accepting a scholarship to the University of California, Berkeley, as the starting shortstop his freshman year. His Cal team made it to the College World Series in 1992. By his junior year, he told scouts if he flopped, school tuition had to be part of a deal. The Montreal Expos agreed. The seventh round draft pick was off to a good start his first year in Vermont.

> **GEOFF:** The first year was really good to me. I hit about .344 and had a good season. So immediately it planted that seed of maybe I am good enough to play this game. And then in 1998 I went back to Triple-A, and two weeks into the season blew out my right elbow and had elbow surgery. It was minor surgery, it was nothing great. It was just arthroscopic surgery to take out some bone chips I had in my right elbow, but it was a huge setback. That year, I thought about actually going back to school.
>
> **JANE:** So why'd you stay?

GEOFF: Did some soul searching. And January 16th of 1999, I met Kory.

Kory Sweaney: an LA area native pursuing an acting career. She thought he might be in the military because of his haircut.

KORY: I finally asked him—I said, "What do you do for a living?" And he said, "I play baseball." "No, what do you do? Like, for a living? Cool, you play baseball in a league or—that's fun and all. What do you do?" "No, I play baseball, Kory." "Okay."

Two weeks later, the Expos invite him to his first big league camp.

GEOFF: All of a sudden I'm close to the big leagues where I'm getting a taste. They send me a letter. I'm going to big league camp. I've got a beautiful new girlfriend who is totally behind me and supporting everything I do …

KORY: He would call and I'd ask him how his day was, and I knew nothing. I went 0-for-4 and this and that and I was like, "Oh well, that's good." That's not good. That's not good at all. Then when he would go 2-for-4 I would go, "Ok." Then I started learning more.

And Geoff started doing better.

GEOFF: Made the All Star team in Triple-A and was just living it up …

And on August 8th …

GEOFF: Kory and I were in Ottawa watching *The Thomas Crown Affair.*

And that night, an injury on the Expos created an opening, and he got his call to the majors, debuting against the Padres, the start of a sixty-day stint.

GEOFF: If that was my only sixty days, and the way those sixty days went and who I played with for the two-month period, and having my family enjoy it as much as they did, I would've been perfectly content going back to school and, you know, maybe getting a teaching degree and coaching high school kids or something. I would've been perfectly happy with that.

Coming up on *One on One*, from joining the Killer B's to babies in threes, Geoff Blum's winding road to the World Series ….

January 2001, between seasons with the Expos, Geoff Blum and Kory exchanged wedding vows. As for developing into a valuable, versatile, switch-hitting guy? A little Blum luck.

GEOFF: And somebody, out of the blue, said, "Hey, can you play left field?" Pffft, you kidding me? Yeah, for a big league paycheck, I'll pretty much run anywhere on the field you want me to, except catcher. Not yet.

Next stop—a 2002 trade to Houston and the "Killer B's."

GEOFF: Lance Berkman, Jeff Bagwell, Craig Biggio. Geoff Blum normally does not follow in that line of names. Everything I know, everything I've learned is from those guys: how to be a professional on and off the field, how to handle myself as a professional ballplayer. I mean, that's the first time I ever got to play every day. I was playing every day, third base, for them.

And also getting noticed for his unconventional hair. His positive experience in Houston by December '03 is topped off by the birth of their first child, Mia ...

GEOFF: I've got the owner of the Astros calling and congratulating me....

And then during the new father euphoria, the GM called. He'd been traded to the Tampa Bay Devil Rays.

GEOFF: I mean, you went from the peak of the mountain to the bottom of the lowest lake, you know. It was awful. You know, and then two hours later you get a phone call from Lou Piniella saying, "Oh, you're going to be our starting third baseman." Get into spring training, sit on the bench the first four games of spring training, get no shot. My daughter contracted bacterial meningitis. Watching her getting spinal taps and having an IV, a PIC line in her scalp, and right from there, you know, we should've called it in. We should've said, you know what, this might not be the year for us.

With his batting average below .200 at one point, a well-publicized turbulent relationship with manager Lou Piniella became obvious from the fallout when he was quoted in an article about Blum ...

GEOFF: Saying, "Oh, he was worthless, I don't know why we traded for him, we lost out, he's unproductive, I don't know why we have him on the team. I don't know how much longer we can keep him on the team." You know, we were toe to toe for about ten minutes in the visiting dugout, and from there on out, it was miserable.

JANE: And hence the [Tampa Bay] jersey in the bathroom.

GEOFF: Yes, yes. And that is why the jersey didn't make it into the hall of memories. It made it into a, you know, a little less fortunate area.

As he'd hoped, Tampa Bay released him that winter, and on the verge of signing with another team for a little more money, he made a last ditch call to Padres General Manager Kevin Towers.

GEOFF: And ten minutes later he called back with the offer we were looking for, and December 9th I signed with the San Diego Padres, and that changed everything.

By now, in San Clemente, their daughter Mia was only eleven months old, and Kory and Geoff were expecting twins.

KORY: We're going to do another ultrasound because a lot of times there's a disappearing twin very early when you find out that early. And I went in and it wasn't a disappearing twin, it was an appearing twin.

GEOFF: An appearing triplet, yeah.

KORY: Yeah, an appearing triplet. Well, which was one of the twins. It was just—I mean, both of us were floored, totally floored. She was like, "Well, I think they're monoamniotic and it's very high risk and da-da-da-da-da," and all these things are coming out of her mouth that were just like—you just told us we're having triplets. And what is all this other stuff?

The rare monoamniotic pregnancy presented high risks.

> **GEOFF:** In their professional opinion, and the statistics, and their experience, and everything involved in the whole situation …
>
> **KORY:** And our best interest …
>
> **GEOFF:** And our best interest for …
>
> **KORY:** For—for the twin …
>
> **GEOFF:** For the third.
>
> **KORY:** For Kayla …
>
> **GEOFF:** Kayla.
>
> **KORY:** … was to eliminate the two, the twins. And it's like, what do you do? Do you—do you save the one baby and not have the other two? Or … ? So it was tough. It was tough.
>
> **GEOFF:** Well, and we eventually got to the point we didn't choose to have triplets, they were given to us, so … why should we choose whose life …
>
> **KORY:** Yeah. I didn't—I did not want to take that.
>
> **GEOFF:** … to …
>
> **KORY:** … into my hands. God gave us these babies and it was…
>
> **GEOFF:** If He wanted us to have them all the way through, He would give them to us. Which He obviously—I mean, He did.
>
> **KORY:** Yeah. And we just had faith it was going to be fine.

With the delicate pregnancy on his heart and mind, Geoff Blum still managed to play well. Then a collision put him on the disabled list May 2.

> **GEOFF:** Nobody ever says that going on the DL is a good thing, but at the time I went on the DL, you couldn't have planned it any better. You know, the girls were born on May 3, and I got to be there for every single minute of it.

Healed, on track, and the triplets fine and out of the hospital, things couldn't be better for Blum. Until the July 31st trade deadline.

> **GEOFF:** Next thing you know I get a tap on the shoulder and it just went through me like ice. I was just like, oh.

Recalling a somber mood in manager Bruce Bochy's office …

> **GEOFF:** "It's not something we wanted to do, but we had to do." And, you know, in between, I shed a tear. I broke down. I couldn't help it. It wasn't about getting traded, it was about leaving, you know, leaving home.

As for breaking the news to Kory …

> **GEOFF:** And I come out there, I'm just sobbing. I'm like, "Baby, baby, I got bad news." And she goes, "What?" "I've been traded." She's like, "Oh, that's okay. What team?" Yeah, there were two things you said: catch up on your sleep.
>
> **KORY:** Right.
>
> **GEOFF:** She said, "The kids aren't coming, and come back with a ring." And …

KORY: And he did.

GEOFF: And we did both.

KORY: He did both.

Geoff Blum's magical moment is next, on *One on One* . . . .

Even as Geoff Blum is once again coming off the bench as a San Diego Padre, one night getting the go-ahead run on base in the 14th inning, no less, his 14th inning feat from game three of the World Series follows him. His home run made history. He's only the second player to hit a go-ahead or game winning home run in their only at-bat of a World Series. The first? His hero, Kirk Gibson. But what Blum did, coming in after not having an at-bat in nearly three weeks, is vivid and appreciated by fans and by his former team and manager, Ozzie Guillen.

OZZIE GUILLEN: The last thing that went through our mind, that Geoff would hit a home run. Not because he can't—he can—but it's the time, the playing time, so much time on the bench. I think I was more happy for him than for the ball club, because a lot of people love him on this ball club.

AJ PIERZYNSKI: I'd been giving him ribbing the whole time, because he played in Houston and I said, "C'mon Geoff, do something to break all your fans' hearts."

JOE CREDE: Words couldn't describe how happy we were and how happy I was for him.

PAUL KONERKO: Such a good guy—not just last year—but word gets around the league; he's well respected.

CHRIS WIDGER: And that's kind of the exclamation point showing that it was a team victory. It took everybody, and he'll be part of White Sox history forever.

FAN: Geoff Blum, thank you so much. White Sox fans all around the world love you.

GEOFF: It's probably the last thing you think about, too, when you're out there playing.

FAN: Perfect timing, right place, right time, and I know it made everyone's day when he hit that home run.

GEOFF: I've gotten so many letters. I mean, I can't even express enough gratitude towards the city of Chicago and Chicago White Sox fans for what they've given back to me after the World Series.

FAN: Geoff Blum, he means a lot. He means a lot to the city of Chicago because we waited eighty-eight years for a moment like this.

GEOFF: But the craziest part is getting the letters from the people who say, oh, my dad, you know, he can finally rest in peace, you know.

FAN: I can remember going to games with my grandpa and he's eighty-two years old and never saw them win a championship—a World Series—and we finally did it, and it was worth it.

GEOFF: And to know that, you know, you'll be remembered for something like that is pretty special.

Geoff Blum is a family guy who's never made the "big" big league bucks—averaging less than $700,000 a year, only wanting something simple from his career.

> **GEOFF:** If I can be a consistent good person and a consistently good Major League Baseball player, I think I'll be pretty happy with that.

Humble, sure. But he'll still take the ring! He's certainly grateful to be back in San Diego, signing just the second day of free agency. With Kory, juggling their bundles of joy, Mia and the triplets—Ava, Audrey, and Kayla—lunch time at the Blum house is a three-high-chair process. The triplets are a year old, a lot stronger than when, at barely three months old, he had to kiss them and his wife goodbye to meet up with his new team, the Chicago White Sox.

> **GEOFF:** Well, you almost feel like you're crashing the party.

Brought in as insurance, playing off the bench as needed, Blum and the White Sox clinch their division, sweep the Red Sox in the Division Series, beat the Angels for the American League Championship, then sweep the Houston Astros in the World Series. More than a million line the streets of Chicago as the South Siders celebrate a remarkable happy ending eighty-eight years in the waiting. But Geoff Blum might not have been such a memorable part of that story, were it not for the circumstances of World Series Game 3 in Houston against his former team. Recounting the details almost in slow motion, as if it happened just yesterday ...

> **GEOFF:** I took BP with a different attitude because we're in a National League park, and the pitcher's hitting and, you know, you gotta use your bench, and you gotta use double switches, and you don't know how these things are going to play out.

Eventually tied at five, the game goes into extra innings.

> **GEOFF:** I was down at that end of the dugout constantly because I wasn't bugging Ozzie in the sense that I was going, "Hey, Ozzie, Ozzie, put me in, put me, you know, put me in, I want to play, I want to play." But I wanted to let him know that—be fully aware that—I was more than prepared to come into the game whenever he needed it.

During the top of the 13th inning ...

> **GEOFF:** Ozzie comes to us and says, "Pablo, if Iguchi makes the last out, you're going to go to second base on a double switch. We're going to bring in Damaso Marte. Geoff, if we have to hit in this inning, if the pitcher comes up, you'll be the pinch hitter."

But with Iguchi's out, Blum assumes he's missed his shot.

> **GEOFF:** Ozzie comes down the tunnel. And, you know, in all of his craziness, stares at Pablo, stares at me, and goes, "Blum, go to second base."
>
> **JANE:** Wow.
>
> **GEOFF:** And I'm going, *Man, did I bring that glove out?*

Top of the 14th, his thinking while on deck: get the bunt down to get the guys on base in scoring position. That changes with a double play. The count goes to 2-and-0.

"It was an eye opener. As a ballplayer we get interviewed around the game all the time, this was my first experience doing an at home interview. I didn't realize what a production it was having it at home with all the lights, cameras, and people. It was better and harder than the typical pre and post game interviews. Better because we were in a comfortable environment at our home; it made it easier to open up and give real, unplanned answers. Harder because I couldn't give cliché, generic answers. I don't know if I learned anything [from the interview] or just learned to appreciate everything I have a little bit more. It's always nice to hear people say nice things and hear how incredible our story is, but having our experiences documented for all time is something I will always appreciate. My family is growing so fast now that it is nice to sit back and watch our episode to show our family where we were at that time. It's like our own little time capsule. Thank you for the opportunity to be on your show. You did an amazing job."

—Geoff Blum, 2010

GEOFF: I convinced myself that this was my count. It was a great hitter's count. He was going to throw me a fastball, I guessed right. It took every childhood experience and every like fantasy I ever had. And it took me remembering what Kirk Gibson did, 'cause I about jumped through the ceiling when Kirk Gibson hit his home run. And it just slammed everything into that contact point when that ball hit the bat. And you hit it and you're like, oh, God, I really got a hold of that ball. And your second thought is, oh, God, run the bases. And I didn't hit it—I do not remember watching the ball go out of the park. You look down and you see Tim Raines is three feet off the ground with his arms in the air and I'm like, holy crap, it happened, you know?

To silence 45,000 people in an instant is probably one of the most unbelievable things ever. And then you think about 2004. You know, you think about the triplets. You think about not seeing your wife for two months until you get to the playoffs. You think about your mom, who played taxi cab for, you know, thirty-two years to get you to this point. I mean, you think about everything that led up to that point and, you know, it's not that you have everybody on your shoulder, but you want to do so much to, you know, repay them. I mean, not so much *repay* them, but let them know that you appreciate them.

It might as well just have been a huge eraser I swung 'cause instantly it erased the horrors of 2004 and, you know, the doubt of ever playing again, and it erased every illness that our kids had, and, shoot, I didn't play this game wanting to be a footnote in anything. I just wanted to play because it was a good living, my family was getting something out of it, and it makes a good story around the keg when you're with your buddies having a barbecue. And now it's like, you know, if I go back to Chicago, you know, it's—people remember those kinds of things. Yeah, it's just amazing. I mean, there's so many stories that came out of this thing, and I don't know why it happened or, who cares, you know? It doesn't matter now. It's a part of me, and it's something that I get to take with me forever. You know, it's something that, hopefully, you know, my girls'll be proud of, and it'll be good.

Regardless of what team Geoff Blum plays for from this point on, his story transcends a uniform. It reminds us that when you're ready for good things to happen, sometimes, they actually do. I'm Jane Mitchell. Thank you for watching *One on One.*

LUIS CASTILLO

"Sometimes people drill you instead of asking you questions and letting you share your answers. And it's not to say she didn't dig and do her job as a journalist, but she allowed me to tell my story in a way that I felt comfortable."

—LUIS CASTILLO, 2010

No one is without their secrets, their regrets, or even a defining moment that could come back to bite them. No one. Few are willing to share it and risk embarrassment or their career. Some would rather that part of their story just go away and move on. For Luis Castillo, the subject was using an NFL-banned substance before he was drafted, and admitting to it in advance. When it came to featuring Luis on *One on One,* I was not going to act as if a defining moment in his life did not happen. I also was not going to exploit something and fall in to the trap of the sensational. So while I would never promise not to talk about a key part of his life—already in the public realm—I could commit to exploring the subject, understanding it, and treating it with proper proportion and perspective. I knew how I felt about it; I didn't know if that was agreeable or enough.

In gathering players' reflections for this book in 2010, I learned part of the back back-story about why Luis agreed to doing *One on One* by his second year. In an interview with my colleague, Kelly Morris, Luis rewound the clock:

"San Diego had just picked me up, and there was a little bit of controversy with them bringing me in, coming out of college. And I remember at the time our PR staff at San Diego was being careful to not throw me to the wolves— to really allow me to tell my story to the right type of people. And I remember them saying to me—pretty much right when I got here, bringing Jane's name up, and obviously I didn't know anything about her. I had just gotten to town. . . . They said it's somebody who we trust who will do a great job with the story, be fair with it, be candid, and really help you tell your story in the best way. So she came highly recommended."

So by the summer of 2006, Chargers Public Relations Director Bill Johnston and I talked about how Luis would be good to feature. He had personality plus, was a key part of the Chargers' defense, active in the community, was a Northwestern graduate, and had Latin roots. I knew about the controversy, and told Bill I would treat him fairly. Luis agreed to the interview, and we were able to schedule it on a day his mother, Maria, would be visiting from New Jersey. While Maria spoke English well enough to get by, she felt she would be able to express her thoughts and feelings better with a translator. So I asked a bilingual colleague, Sandra Torres, to join us for the interview.

Luis was ready for us when we arrived. While his new house was still in the decorating mode, his pool table in the living room was covered with pictures, newspaper articles, and DVDs with snippets of television appearances, charity events, and early football years. I had asked him to gather things that would help visualize his story, and I was so impressed he had followed through.

Luis' large family room had big sofas and a large flat screen TV. We had to ask his roommate to move in order to set up the three cameras and lights. His roommate was Charger Shaun Phillips, whom I didn't know at the time. (By the next year though, I would know him well, as we did a *One on One* featuring him.) Photographer Dan Roper was on this shoot and lit decorative candles, adding warmth and comfort to the brown, amber, and orange palette. Luis, wearing a T-shirt, jeans, and barefoot, plopped down and was ready to go.

I told Luis—as I tell all people who have had a fair amount of media coverage—to assume people watching this show do not know anything, or very little, about him. So if there were some things he might think people know, it didn't matter, I wanted to hear it from him so I could paint the portrait with lots of information and options. He understood, and we began.

We walked through his childhood, his mother's journey to raise her son in America, his education, and then his college career. Next in the chronology: his

injury, his rehab, and a critical moment in his life—his choice to take something that would help him in the recovery. It is never easy to broach a difficult subject. Years of experience had taught me a few things when on the precipice of such a subject in an interview. He had to know it was coming. I knew it was coming. It was part of his timeline. I didn't know how he would respond, but with a decade of *One on One* experience buoying my confidence, I was prepared if he didn't want to talk about it.

Regardless of his willingness to elaborate on the pre-draft steroid use, I would have been sure to explore the incident in the script so it was fair to him, fair to me, fair to the story. He actually made it much easier for me than I expected. He did not try to downplay it, skim over it, or make me feel like I was being invasive or inappropriate by giving me a "big leaguer" attitude. He did not try to avoid it; rather, he faced it again for me, and eventually for the fans. I was so impressed by his honesty as a Northwestern senior and his honesty in our interview.

He understood my need for him to retell it and answer my questions. What I told him then, and even later, was that his honesty, humility, and candor showed his true character, set an even better example for kids, and sent a positive message to his peers and fans. Everyone makes mistakes, but when you're in the public eye, taking an opportunity to explain a mistake can score points in the integrity department.

In the twenty-four minutes of the final show, about seven and a half minutes was spent on that topic. While he might have been a little concerned how it might turn out (no one gets to approve the script), I asked him to trust me. He did, and his feedback, as well as the feedback from a number of people in the Chargers organization, the community, and fans, was positive.

I don't know what the show would have been like had someone else done that interview and written his profile. I can only speak to my style and my approach. Some things are not a matter of public knowledge, nor do they need to be.

This part of his story, however difficult, was known by NFL teams and reported in various media featuring him surrounding the draft. I feel that one of my strengths is how I assess various facts and aspects of someone's life and decide what stays, what goes, what I hint at, and what I elaborate on. As a journalist and a storyteller, aware of my audience, I'm satisfied with how I approached this particular aspect of Luis' life.

What you won't hear when you read his story is the music when he was dancing in the Dominican Republic. You won't see his enormous smile and true adoration and admiration for his mother, but I hope the words and descriptions will jump off the page as big and as boldly as Luis's zest for life.

Apparently, Emmy judges agreed, and this edition was awarded an Emmy in the category of Best Sports Program. It was part of a sweep in the category along with shows featuring Igor Olshansky and Geoff Blum.

This is the script for the edition debuting October 29, 2006.

• • •

Luis Castillo: the Chargers' future with a challenging past.

LUIS: They could've easily made me an outcast, but they didn't. They gave me the benefit of the doubt.

Determined to make his team and his mother proud.

It's something you just don't hear about in professional sports. Someone who used a substance banned in the NFL then takes the initiative to admit it, knowing he's put his career at risk. But that's what Luis Castillo did as a college senior. It's just part of his story. One that transcends the gridiron and goes to the heart of the old expression: honesty is the best policy.

Number 93, Luis Castillo.

LUIS: I'm not one of the strongest players in terms of three-hundred-pound defensive linemen, but I'm one of the quickest. And in terms of being mentally prepared, in terms of understanding what an offense is going to do, in terms of understanding how to play certain techniques, when somebody's trying to do something to me, that's where I gain my edge.

The defensive end's agility and moves were influenced by high school track and wrestling.

LUIS: One-on-one, learning to use your leverage against another man.

And perhaps by his Latin roots …

LUIS: Dominicans can dance now, so a little Merengue, and Salsa, and Reggaeton.

While we're just getting to know the young Luis Castillo …

LUIS: Nobody knows d-linemen in this league!

In the Dominican Republic?

JANE: You're a real superstar.

LUIS: It was like walking around in LT's shoes out there!

Also impressive about this charming, clean-cut, cordial, Northwestern University grad—his humility and honesty. He knows that being the Chargers' first-round draft pick in 2005—signing a five-year contract worth up to some seven million dollars—could have just as easily not have happened because of a mistake he says came with a one-time use of steroids in college.

LUIS: It was more of, you know, I knew I was doing something wrong than knowing exactly what I was doing wrong. But I knew I was. I mean, I knew I was doing something I shouldn't have done

The details of his personal drama later, but first, a look back....

LUIS: One of the things that's made me the proudest in the last few months is having the opportunity to bring my mom here and see my mom laying by the pool and just sitting in the backyard just enjoying the view and enjoying the fact that she knows that it's her son's house, her son who graduated from a great university with an economics degree, who's now a professional at twenty-three years old, and has his own house. When I see that pride in her eyes, man, that makes it all worth it, and it's just such a special feeling.

His mother, Maria Castillo, understands English, but feels she can express herself better with an interpreter.

MARIA CASTILLO [through her interpreter]: We were very poor. My parents worked in the fields, and we worked very hard in our family.

She is from the Dominican Republic, a family of eight, raised in a house with no running water, no electricity. Seeking more, she started a business, and would travel to New York City to buy clothes to stock her Dominican boutique. On one such trip, she had a love affair, became pregnant, and chose to be a single mother at thirty-nine years old.

MARIA CASTILLO: My mom really wanted me to have kids because she would always tell me that I worked very hard and that I needed to have kids. Luis came into my life and he was a great surprise, and the best thing that happened to me.

Luis was born August 4, 1983 in New York, where they lived briefly with a relative in the projects. Then they returned to the Dominican Republic, so her family could help care for him, but she wanted more for Luis than her country could offer.

MARIA CASTILLO: I wanted him to be in the United States. I wanted him to grow up to be someone very important.

So it was back to New York with Luis to pursue the American dream by building her Dominican hair products import business. They lived simply on the top floor of a five-story building in the low-income area of Washington Heights.

LUIS: My only memories are spending time with the babysitter while my mom was working, going to school, and going straight back to the apartment and being there locked up without being able to have a backyard, without being able to go out and kind of hang around town with my friends, just 'cause it was a dangerous place to grow up, and a dangerous place to be walking around the streets as a young kid with all these bad influences.

But even the walls of an apartment couldn't contain little Luis' energy.

> **MARIA CASTILLO:** He would always be playing with his cars, crashing them into something, crashing them into the wall. He just couldn't sit still.
>
> **JANE:** He was a real boy.
>
> **MARIA CASTILLO:** Si. Yeah, yeah. Every night, no matter how much I worked, I would come home and sit in bed with him, and always tell him a lot of great things, that he was born to do something great, that he had a big future ahead of him.

His aunts and uncles gave him the same encouragement.

> **LUIS:** And when you're a little kid and you hear this over and over and over again, it puts a sense of responsibility on you, but it also—I mean, it just—there's just no way you could let them down.
>
> **MARIA CASTILLO:** He had a special charisma, and because of that, I always instilled that. He would look in the mirror and make sure that he knew that he had to be that person.

To help him get there? A move when he was eight, a half hour away to a working class community, Garfield, New Jersey.

> **LUIS:** When I got the chance to live in a place where I had a backyard, I had a basement I could play in, and I could go out on the street and ride my bike and play catch in the backyard, well, I mean, it was just a whole different world.

He struggled in school until the sixth grade when he became fluent in English. Signing up to play football at eleven came with an unexpected benefit for a kid growing up without a father.

> **LUIS:** My mom did everything she needed to do to give me a great life, but she wasn't that male figure in the house. And I think it made a big impact in me when I got the chance to play a sport where I had all these male figures that now changed my personality a little bit and helped mold me into the person I am today.

Namely, Garfield High School Football Coach Steve Mucha.

> **LUIS:** From just going out there every day and just playing a sport, to really devoting myself to it, and dedicating myself to taking that next step, and to putting in the work that it took to gain that college scholarship. He showed me that *that* was a possibility, that *that* was something I could achieve.

Starting with talent and skill, a big kid at 6'1", 200 pounds, Coach Mucha brought him in to play varsity the last game of his freshman year.

LUIS: It was like the third quarter, and I'd been hiding all game, trying to stay away from Coach so he wouldn't put me in, 'cause I was this scared little freshman.

It's his first play of the game ...

STEVE MUCHA: And Luis hits a swim move, a pass-rush move, and sacks the quarterback, and it was like ... wow ...

Luis was well rounded, popular, a leader—as a math and Spanish honor society student, involved in school activities as well as track, wrestling, and football, developing confidence on the gridiron and making local headlines by his junior year.

LUIS: Regardless of your physical abilities, regardless of the times you have, when you have that confidence, it opens up a world of possibilities.

He proved himself two years in a row in the state playoffs against Ramapo. Luis Castillo was voted an All-State player, and colleges showed interest.

LUIS: It was just such an amazing experience to feel that you'd taken that step and accomplished something, knowing that you were going to save your mom all that money, and she wasn't going to have to pay for you to go to school, and to know that you were making your family proud.

Up next, a decision that tests Luis Castillo's character. And later on *One on One*—grit, gratitude, and giving back ....

When Luis Castillo had interest from more than thirty colleges, he accepted a full scholarship from Northwestern University in Chicago. He chose it for its academics and football program. The Wildcats were Big Ten co-Champions in 2000, and he wanted to play under Head Coach Randy Walker.

LUIS: He pushed us, and he pushed us hard 'cause he knew what we could accomplish if we really dedicated ourselves and put our entire mind, body, and heart into achieving what he wanted for us.

And what Luis Castillo wanted for himself.

LUIS: And I remember being in college listening to the media talk about the defensive tackles at USC, or Texas, or Florida, or Ohio State, and Michigan, and I'm sitting there thinking, *Wow, those guys are so good. I'd love to be like those guys.*

As a junior, he realized he *was* like those guys, those NFL prospects, because of his success against them on the field. Coach Eric Washington remembers.

ERIC WASHINGTON: The first game watching him chase the ball, watching him compete, watching him neutralize his opponent. I think that it was really clear to me that he had a chance to play at the next level.

It all came down to his life-changing senior year.

LUIS: 'Cause you know that NFL teams have you on their radar. You know they're giving you the possibility of becoming a first day draft pick. And all of a sudden, the second play of my first game, I tore my ulnar collateral ligament in my elbow. They kind of taped it up and wrapped it up and I was able to finish the game kind of just with my arm at my side.

He had two choices: play, hoping he'd do well enough to be drafted; or have surgery and return for a fifth year. Prepared to have surgery, he recalls a conversation with his coaches about the team and his future.

LUIS: "We feel like we could do some pretty amazing things and we need you, and we have nobody else. So we feel like you could be a good enough player for us, one arm and all, and without being able to practice." And I made the decision to stay. I couldn't let them down.

Contributing, but not to his standards. Post-season surgery would mean six months of rehab. With the clock ticking just two months away from the Combine—where NFL teams assess what young players can do—he decides …

LUIS: … to not have the surgery and try to just push through it.

The pain subsided, but he was behind in his strength and weight training. So he says—not to gain a competitive advantage, but just to cope and catch up—he accepted a tempting offer.

JANE: Who offered you what? And did you know what they were offering?

LUIS: It was something—it was just somebody that was around the program and had been around for a few years, and had seen us play, and when he saw me in that situation, it came up. But it was honestly something where I just couldn't allow myself to go into the Combine and to go in and let myself be presented to thirty-two NFL teams and to hundreds of scouts in all this training and not be the type of player I was, and not be prepared like I wanted to be.

JANE: Did you know you were taking steroids when he gave them to you?

LUIS: It was something where, honestly, I put—it was more of, you know, I knew I was doing something wrong, than knowing exactly what I was doing wrong. But I knew I was. I mean, I knew I was doing something I shouldn't have done, and I made the decision that, you know, I've worked so hard to get to here, I gotta do whatever it takes. I gotta do whatever it takes to make sure I'm where I need to be. And I made the decision I did.

JANE: Did you tell anybody else about it?

LUIS: No, no.

Turns out he took Androstenedione or "Andro:" A supplement the body converts to testosterone, said to improve strength and muscle development. It's banned in the NFL.

JANE: How did that affect your ability to perform?

LUIS: It was something, honestly, where there was so much involved in that whole process of recovering—I was doing rehab on my elbow five days a week, we were training six days a week, lifting twice a day, and doing all we needed to do to be able to get back. So, honestly, I mean, I don't know if it made that big of an impact or not.

JANE: So how did you perform at the Combine?

LUIS: Performed well.

But that decision to take Andro, even as a college student, would come back to haunt him two weeks before the 2005 NFL Draft.

LUIS: It's the ugliest situation I've ever been in [sic] my life, and it was so tough to deal with, because for the first time in my life, I'd really let people down.

Flying back from meeting with the New England Patriots, he landed in Chicago. He returned a call from his mother, who was worried because a letter had arrived from the NFL saying he had tested positive for steroid use.

LUIS: I just went to my car and cried and just, you know, couldn't believe the fact that I'd worked so hard to put myself in a position to take that next step and become an NFL player, and all of a sudden, to me, it was all gone. I mean, they—it wasn't a possibility anymore. I thought as soon as I heard, I just—I thought it was all gone. I thought there was no way that somebody was going to give me the chance to prove myself.

He called his agent, Mike McCartney.

LUIS: And kind of what I talked to him was, you know, I've already made this mistake and I don't want to go out there and lie and try to make excuses for it, because in the end nobody really believes the excuses anyway. A lot of agents would've pushed me to say a lie and to try to make up some kind of excuse, to make up some kind of, you know, I didn't know what it was, or, I didn't know what was going on, it was something in my orange juice or something. And I'm real thankful that he encouraged me and helped me make the decision I did.

The decision to write a letter to every team in the National Football League....

LUIS: I just remember sitting down and trying to type this letter in which you admit to the biggest mistake you've ever made in your life

The letter was part of a package showing his track record, and that the 3.5 Academic All American had never failed a drug test in college. It was sent to all thirty-two NFL teams, including the San Diego Chargers' Head Coach Marty Schottenheimer.

MARTY SCHOTTENHEIMER: He recognized that an error was made and he fully accepted responsibility for that, and assured us that it would never happen again, and assured everybody that it would never happen again. And when you put all the pieces together, and you do your due diligence, it became very apparent to the San Diego Chargers that this is a young man that would fit in nicely here, not only as a player, but importantly, as a person.

JANE: So take us to draft day.

LUIS: Wow. Wow. You know, when you talk about the NFL draft, it's the biggest unknown there is. When you talk about the NFL draft and the situation I was in, I had no idea. I mean, I had no idea if I was going to be a first round pick or if I was going to be a free agent.

He'd finally know with a call from Schottenheimer. San Diego had two picks in the first round. The Chargers took Shawne Merriman and Luis Castillo.

> **LUIS:** "Thank you for the opportunity, thank you for believing in me, thank you for giving me this opportunity to go out there and prove myself. Thank you, 'cause that's all I ever wanted, was the opportunity. Thank you, thank you, thank you." And that's how the entire conversation went.

Meanwhile, some players commentating on ESPN's television coverage of the draft criticized Castillo …

> **JANE:** … saying, hey, you know, here's a guy who cheated the system.
> **LUIS:** I wasn't going to get mad at somebody for voicing an opinion or for stating what they felt, 'cause I realized I had no right to try to get in anybody's face or to try to be mad at somebody for stating something that was pretty real.

Humbled but proud, Luis Castillo joined the Chargers at training camp.

> **LUIS:** I'm so thankful to my teammates because they really treated it the right way, and they could've easily gone against me. They could've easily made me an outcast, but they didn't. You know, they gave me the benefit of the doubt.
> **SHAUN PHILLIPS:** To come out, and be up front about it, that says a lot about his character. It shows that he's a man, and it's hard to find that in some guys.
> **DONNIE EDWARDS:** That's one chapter in your life. You put it behind you and move on to the next chapter.
> **LUIS:** We're going to give you the chance to come out here and be one of our teammates and help this team win.

Luis Castillo is chalking up a lot of firsts: his first sack of 2006 against rival Oakland …

> **LUIS:** You talk about the Raiders. You talk about the first week of the season. You talk about *Monday Night Football.* It just couldn't have been any better.

His first interception *ever* … and the first to be drafted by and play in the NFL representing the Dominican Republic—the Caribbean nation where baseball dominates. So while he often visited his mother's homeland growing up, returning as a Charger, it seems the whole country celebrates his success.

> **LUIS:** From government officials to people on the street, to see the love and the support they'd give me in a sport which they really don't understand and a game where they really had never watched before, and all of a sudden, to have one of their own in that game and they're going to support him, and they're going to give him a lot of love, and they did. And it was just such a fun experience, and such a great experience, and such an honor to be out there, knowing that I represent that country in this game.

Not a bit shy, singing in Spanish, his natural stage presence parallels his confidence and moves on the football field, even with the pressure as a rookie in 2005.

LUIS: You come in as a first round pick and there are so many expectations, especially for me with everything that had happened.

A sprained foot early on didn't help, but then with other player injuries, Castillo became a starter, fast.

LUIS: I can honestly say, you know, the first six, seven games, even though I was the starter, I wasn't playing anywhere near the level that I should've been at because it—there was just so much I still needed to learn.

By mid season …

LUIS: It was the Kansas City Chiefs, the eighth game of the year, I had my first sack. I think I had a sack and a half that game. And everything started taking off from there.

The defensive lineman is appreciated by his team for both his talent and personality.

SHAUN PHILLIPS: He's funny. He hugs everybody's mom. He kisses everybody's mom. He calls everybody's mom, "Mom."

DONNIE EDWARDS: I mean Luis Castillo's one of those guys that always has a smile on his face, that's so energetic, and always ready to play.

PHILIP RIVERS: Only his second year, he's really playing great for us. Certainly a big key to our defensive success and stopping the run.

MARTY SCHOTTENHEIMER: The sky's the limit for him, because A, he has the physical skills that are necessary, and B, he understands football and knows how to go about the preparation part, which is so critical. And he's got a great, great competitiveness about him. And when you put those pieces together, you come up with a pretty solid player.

As for ever considering using steroids or the like again?

LUIS: For the rest of my career, I never have to worry about that. You know, I made a promise to this team. I made a promise to my family, and not only in terms of my character, but in terms of money, too. I promised to give it all back if I ever made that kind of mistake.

Lesson learned. Lesson shared. He embraces being a role model at his former schools and part of the Chargers' efforts in the community with autograph signings, talking with kids, and going south of the border to Mexico.

LUIS: I got a chance to go down there and visit and really spend some time and show them what an NFL player is like. You know, you don't have to be a stuck-up, cocky guy. You can be a humble person and do the things you do and have fun with it.

Luis Castillo works hard, works out—a natural athlete who is all about preparation.

LUIS: I devote my week to getting in the best shape possible to know that I'm going to be fresh when somebody else is tired in the fourth quarter.

In football lingo it's called having "a motor." When Castillo isn't working, he's usually at home.

> **LUIS:** Growing up in a big old project building in New York to all of a sudden having this great backyard and this great view where I can just hang out and relax. And I'm a firm believer, if you work hard, you rest hard, and that's what I do. I enjoy just laying around doing nothing.

On game weekends his mother, who lives out east, is here, too. Inside, his bachelor pad's in the decorating phase, with a pool table serving as a temporary display for photos, awards, and media coverage—in English and Spanish. A sentimental guy collecting his experiences, such as guest hosting a Latino American TV show—a long way from his mother's starting point.

> **LUIS:** It all goes back to seeing the things she was able to do in her life because of her dedication, because of her hard work. To know that she had that sense of responsibility, that when somebody was trusting her to accomplish something, she couldn't let them down. That's kind of the way I am, and that's the reason why I was able to be successful in school and in football. Because—and it was the same way whether it be on the football field or taking a test—I couldn't go into something unprepared.

Maria says Luis and her company, now a multi-million-dollar business, grew up together.

> **MARIA CASTILLO:** I'd always heard people talking about the American dream and I know that I've done it and really thank God and my son. I want to take this opportunity to thank the San Diego Chargers for believing in my son. And I'm a big San Diego Charger fan—look at my nails. I dress up in the colors. I'm always there. It's just something really great.
>
> **LUIS:** I would love to sit with my mom at a football game that I'm playing in. For a little woman from the Dominican Republic who had never seen football before, to seeing the love and the understanding she has for the game now; it's truly amazing.
>
> **JANE:** Do you want to meet your dad?
>
> **LUIS:** I do. And I actually, you know, I was lucky enough; through the NFL, I was able to find him.

Planning a trip to Europe to meet him, with his mother …

> **LUIS:** She never ever said that he was a bad man, that he didn't care about me, she just said, you know, he was younger and he really wasn't ready, and he made a bad decision. And people make mistakes, and sometimes you gotta forgive them. So I'd love the opportunity to go out there and get a chance to meet him.

Forgiveness and understanding: subjects he knows something about.

> **LUIS:** I'm thankful to the organization for giving me this opportunity and giving me this chance, and I feel like I owe them a lot. Every day, my goal is to go out there and do everything I can to make them look good.

JANE: So your mom was right, you were destined for something great.

LUIS: I guess the family had it pegged right, man, and I'm just thankful I was able to live up to all their expectations, because they definitely had high, high expectations.

Luis Castillo's plan going in to college was to graduate, then take over his mother's business so she could retire. As he puts it, football got in the way. Not a bad detour for someone who, although not perfect, seems determined to make the most out of an NFL opportunity of a lifetime. I'm Jane Mitchell, thank you for watching *One on One.*

"The idea of sitting down with somebody—especially for me—coming from something a little controversial, and having to sit down and find the right format to be able to share your story and allowing somebody to pull that out of you in the best way, isn't that easy. But Jane had the ability to sit down in a happy kind of easy-going way; allowing me to tell the story while enjoying myself.... and I love the fact that she was able to take my life, put my story together in a seamless way like she did, and tell a very heartwarming story like she did, and incorporate my mother and my family, and all the steps that brought me to this point in my life—I thought she did a wonderful job with it. And it's something I know my family's enjoyed, my friends have enjoyed. And it's something that's still around that I still get comments about ... The neatest thing for me was hearing somebody like Marty Schottenheimer—the head coach at the time. Because you're a rookie, you don't really know the head coach very well. You don't necessarily have that great of a relationship with him yet. And it's kind of awkward to sit down and watch something where that person is talking about you. That was pretty neat for me to hear what he had to say, the positive remarks and the comments he had for the show."

—Luis Castillo, 2010

ADRIAN AND EDGAR GONZALEZ

January 6, 2006, Padres General Manager Kevin Towers made a significant deal with the Texas Rangers. The Rangers traded Adrian Gonzalez, Termmel Sledge, and Chris Young to the San Diego Padres for Billy Killian and pitchers Adam Eaton and Akinori Otsuka. Adrian was a hometown boy, but he was young, and Ryan Klesko was still the starting first baseman, so I don't recall having Adrian on my action items list to talk with at camp. Rather, he was just "one to watch." Later that spring in San Diego, a photographer and I were on the field shooting Dave Roberts meeting baseball players from Eastlake High School. The team was the beneficiary of Dave's equipment program that I was featuring as part of a "Padres in the Community" show. Adrian was at the field at the same time, and several of the Eastlake players wanted to meet Adrian. He obliged, quietly saying hello and

"The first thing I remember when asked about doing the *One on One* show with Jane was, 'Cool, I get to be on the show I enjoyed watching while in high school before I was drafted and left home.' The second thing I remember is my mom will get her wish and have her son on the show she loved."

—ADRIAN GONZALEZ, 2010

signing hats and balls. He was either shocked anyone cared about him, or was just so cool, he didn't let his excitement or sense of being flattered show. Either way, I remember thinking we'd better save that tape to have down the road.

By the end of 2006, things had changed sooner than expected for Adrian Gonzalez. He was playing for Ryan Klesko, who was injured. Adrian performed well. By that off-season, Ryan was a free agent and signed with the San Francisco Giants. Adrian would likely move in to that spot as the starting first baseman in 2007, so he became the perfect candidate for a *One on One*.

Adrian and his wife, Betsy, lived in Surprise, Arizona near several major league baseball spring training facilities. In the off-season, we planned to shoot part of their story while we were at camp. One afternoon, photographer Dan Roper and I went to their home. We would do the in-depth interview back in San Diego at his parents' home, so this day was about seeing Adrian and Betsy at home, with their dogs, walking through his library with his awards and pictures, and cooking. Betsy and Adrian were very sweet and helpful. They had seen the show, so they knew the types of things I liked to incorporate. We made a list of what other elements would be good to have, including interviews with his parents, his brothers, and going to Tijuana to see his father's business, and where he and his brothers played baseball.

By April, with the team at home in San Diego, I did the interviews at his parents' home. While I am always glad to have pictures in boxes or photo albums, never have I seen such a collection and display as the one Adrian's mother had of her boys. It was fantastic—almost a mini-museum. There were two full rooms

and a hallway with pictures and trophies from her husband's playing career and the playing years of all three of the Gonzalez brothers. Huge frames were filled with their Little League, All-Star, and high school teams. Adrian and his mother gave me the tour that day, and many of those pictures were in the program.

Spanish is the first language of his Mexican-born parents. I interviewed them in English, and while a little difficult to understand at times, their short sentences were valuable and from the heart. I wanted to include both his brothers, David and Edgar. David, a businessman, met us in Tijuana and showed us the relevant places—their old neighborhood where the boys grew up, the fields where they played ball, and their father's manufacturing company and office. Edgar was in the St. Louis Cardinals' minor league system at the time. The Cardinals assisted me by doing a short interview with Edgar using my questions.

In 2007, the show featuring just Adrian debuted. It was comprehensive and touched on how he hoped that someday his brother Edgar would make it to the majors. By that winter, Edgar signed a minor league contract with the San Diego Padres and was invited to camp to compete for a spot on the 2008 roster. What a wonderfully natural follow-up for Adrian, and, should Edgar make the team, it would be thrilling for them and would make a great story.

At spring training in 2008, Dan and I captured video of Adrian and Edgar at camp together for the first time. We arranged for an interview session at Edgar and Cristina's home. Seeing the four of them together, it was clear how close they are and the strength of their friendship and faith. As for the baseball side of things, there was no way to know what would transpire—if Edgar would make the team—but at least we knew they were in camp together, one step closer to their dream.

At the end of camp, Edgar did not make the Major League roster and was sent to Triple-A in Portland, but the show would still go on in April. With my father's words always inspiring me, "Don't wait. Anticipate," I wrote and produced the show two ways. The first set of on-camera stand-ups referenced that the brothers were "almost" together in the Major Leagues. The second set (I do not believe in jinxes) said their "dream came true." I was ready for it, so if and when Edgar made the majors, we would be able to replace parts of the show with the new information. I just had a feelin, and sincerely hoped for them that it would happen.

I continued to work on other shows, as well as a full-time after-hours effort to help my mother. On May 6, she had major hip replacement surgery. It was a very difficult recovery process for her, and I was exhausted from work and being up all night with her in the hospital. On Sunday, May 11, Mother's Day, I took about an hour break to go to Home Depot® when my phone rang. It was Cristina Gonzalez. "I have news, but you can't tell anyone!" I knew immediately—Edgar's time had finally come. She enthusiastically said, "He got called up, and he's going to Chicago to meet the team tomorrow!" I was so happy for them all, and I had to keep myself from jumping up and down in the store. I knew my updated version plan was ready to be put in to action.

"Jane is super down to earth, and a great person. She made our Rookie TV appearance comfortable for the both of us!"

—Cristina Gonzalez, 2010

The team was on the road that week, so we scheduled an interview with Adrian and Edgar at the ballpark their first day home, May 19. Adrian and Edgar sat side by side as I asked them about getting the news of Edgar's call-up and his major league debut in Chicago. They were happy and grateful it had finally happened. That homestand, another photographer, Jay Conner, and I met up with their family in the stands to document their fresh reaction of this very special time for the Gonzalez family.

Adrian and Edgar's dream played out for the balance of 2008 and 2009. Adrian was elected to his first All-Star team in 2009, and earned his second Gold Glove. With no guarantees to start every day with a team, Edgar opted to play in Japan in 2010.

two boys in the Major Leagues...

After the 2010 season, Adrian was traded to the Boston Red Sox and signed a seven-year, $154 million contract. While this is a remarkable amount of money, Adrian is not boastful, attributing the deal to the baseball marketplace. I have no doubt he will work hard, remain true to his values, and continue to do good things with the significant financial means.

Every time I see the Gonzalez brothers, their wives, and their parents, I am greeted with such warmth and appreciation. I have helped Adrian and Betsy by covering or emceeing their charitable events. It is a good feeling to know I can be a professional, do my job, and develop bonds. They have graciously supported my endeavors as well and friendships with genuine and well-meaning people such as the Gonzalez family.

This is the script from the May 30, 2008 edition.

• • •

The stars have aligned as Adrian and Edgar Gonzalez achieve a lofty goal.

ADRIAN: It happened while we were both with the Padres in San Diego.

EDGAR: We're having the time of our lives now.

For Adrian Gonzalez, his fairly quick rise to the majors and establishing himself as the Padres slugging first baseman make for a rewarding ride, no doubt, especially in his hometown. But personally, he's wanted something more: to see his older brother make it to the majors, too. Five years apart, they've traveled different roads hoping to both be in the big leagues, and they finally made it. On Monday May 12, 2008 at Wrigley Field, one of the most storied ballparks in America, the Gonzalez brothers' story begins a new chapter.

EDGAR: Now it's worth it. No matter what happens. It's worth it because I at least achieved my dream. That was the main thing—achieve my dream.

Just the day before Mother's Day, Edgar was an infielder at the Padres Triple-A Portland team when he receives word from his agent he's going to the show, the big leagues. At thirty years old, it's the first time in his career.

EDGAR: I started getting tears down my eyes, and I started getting pretty excited, and I called my wife, first thing she did when she heard it, she just started crying.

JANE: What did your parents say when you talked to your dad?

EDGAR: He couldn't believe it. He told me he was shaking and he couldn't believe it. 'Cause, everybody knew Adrian was going to go up eventually. Nobody really knew if I was going to go up.

After Adrian's game in San Diego, that afternoon his wife, Betsy, who already knew, urges him to call Edgar.

> "The show was really tastefully done. I feel that we all got to say what we needed to say, and I really enjoyed watching it. I still have the copy at home and plan to show it to my children one day."
>
> —EDGAR GONZALEZ, 2010

ADRIAN: For a second I was like, he might get called up, but then for a second I was like, he might have been traded.

EDGAR: I'm not a guy to really show emotion, but inside I feel it. And I just really felt it.

Edgar flies to Chicago to join the team.

EDGAR: And I remember the first time I walked out to Wrigley Field, and I was like whoa, but I'm like it looks bigger on TV. And then that's what I told Adrian, the Ivy, and you got to go and touch the Ivy in the outfield and then, when I put on the Padres uniform, I mean, I've been a Padre fan, and now playing for the Padres—pretty exciting.

Edgar finally has his moment, put in at third, then faces Carlos Zambrano: one of the best pitchers in baseball.

EDGAR: I think my legs were a little wobbly, but I wasn't too nervous. I was focused, and I just wanted to put a good swing on the ball.

MATT VASGERSIAN (announcer): And Edgar has a base hit in his first major league appearance.

ADRIAN: The only thing that kept me from jumping up and down was the fact that we were losing by seven runs after he drove in the run, so it's kinda hard to jump around in the dugout when you're losing.

This magical Monday, the first of many firsts, and a long time coming for two brothers growing up in South Bay and Tijuana as ballplayers and little Padres fans. Edgar had been on the St. Louis Cardinals' Triple-A team, but after the 2007 season, and a free agent, he signed a minor league contract with the Padres, which included being a non-roster invitee to big league camp to compete for a bench job.

EDGAR: I couldn't refuse it, and being with my brother, too. I mean, I couldn't beat that chance.

Their bond, strong and significant, as we learned when we first told Adrian's story in 2007; one that explains a lot about the whole Gonzalez family, with Adrian's drive to win and play in his blood.

[From 2007 edition] His grandmother, a San Diego native, was a lefty softball player in Sonora, Mexico. His uncle, an athlete and U.S. soldier, had to pass up an invitation to try out for the 1969 Padres. Adrian's father, David Gonzalez Senior, was a player-manager with the national amateur team for Mexico.

DAVID GONZALEZ, SR.: I like too much baseball. I play every Sunday.

Adrian's parents, David and Alba, met in their home state Sonora, married in 1973, and opened an air conditioning company in Tijuana to be closer to his ailing mother. When it was time to start their family, they moved north to San Ysidro with relatives and had David, Jr., Edgar, and Adrian—born May 8, 1982. The walls of his parents' Eastlake home showcase a love for their boys, baseball, and documenting the moment.

ADRIAN: As much as we tell my mom that it's too much, we always end up kind of looking through everything every time we come in here, and looking at the pictures. And it's good because it brings back memories.

Many surrounding his father.

> **ADRIAN:** Those are all pictures and clippings of everything he did when he was playing in Tijuana or across Mexico. Just every day was just baseball. We went home and we would play baseball with my brothers. And it's funny 'cause my competitiveness is always something they'll talk about.

One time, when Adrian was five, playing T-ball ...

> **ADRIAN:** They put me at pitcher 'cause it was T-Ball and I missed the ball.
> **DAVID:** And he was real mad because he can't see—he can't catch the ball.
> **ADRIAN:** And I went home that day, and I stayed up 'til—from like six at night 'til ten at night, throwing a ball against the wall so I wouldn't miss it.
> **DAVID:** And he'd do that maybe for two months. After two months, he catches the ball like a pro, you know—*incredible.*

[Home tour with wall of framed photos.]

> **JANE:** Oh, my gosh. This is amazing. Look at these. Is that you up there?
> **ADRIAN:** That is me ...
> **ALBA:** Yes.
> **ADRIAN:** ... up there, holding a bat. Probably three, two, three years old.

When still a baby, the family moved back to Tijuana. Of the few homes they lived in, it's the one near the racetrack that Adrian identifies with most when recalling a typical day as a kid.

> **ADRIAN:** A bunch of the guys from school would stay out and play either in the school backyard or in the parks until seven, eight, nine at night. And then we would come in, have dinner, do our homework, and go to sleep.

The Little League field next to his father's company now bears Adrian's name, honoring him for what he's become. But as a kid, all that mattered was that it was a place to play ball.

> **ADRIAN:** It's called "Municipal" and they're all dirt fields. But you know, it's definitely a competitive league.

His big league aspirations fueled by seeing his team, the Padres, in person.

> **ADRIAN:** Tony Gwynn was definitely the person that I always admired and always wanted to go watch.

At six years old, Adrian started wearing Tony Gwynn's number 19, and met him at the stadium.

> **ADRIAN:** It was one of those days where they'd fill up the fences along the outfield line, and we actually got some pictures of us jumping on the wall pretending we're robbing a home run. So it was a lot of fun to be able to meet the players.

By the fifth grade, Adrian's parents moved the family back to the U.S. to a modest Bonita neighborhood.

ADRIAN: They just wanted us to have that opportunity to be able to choose either Mexico or the States as far as college and for our future.

With the move, a new challenge.

ADRIAN: I didn't speak a word of English when I came to elementary school over here.

He learned, becoming a good student while still consumed by baseball, playing year round on both sides of the border and at Eastlake High School. Even at home, Adrian and his brothers put their imagination and skills to work. The setting? The batting cage their dad built in their backyard. Their game? Emulating players picked from a whole set of baseball cards.

ADRIAN: And you pick nine guys to be your lineup, and they had to be position-by-position, and not just nine guys.

One time, he picked "to be" Chipper Jones of the Atlanta Braves ...

ADRIAN: I used to just kind of like put my foot down and swing, and then I started doing that kind of t-tap back, and that was one of the big reasons that helped me start driving the ball better, because I was able to get low instead of just a straightforward swing. So actually, playing those games helped me a lot.

Eastlake's Baseball Coach Dave Gonzalez, no relation, coached Adrian's brother Edgar first, and had no reservations about putting Adrian on the varsity team as a freshmen.

DAVE GONZALEZ: The swing he has relatively stayed the same. It was incredible from the very first time I saw it.

Tall at 6'2", but lanky, scouts first liked Adrian as a rare commodity: a left-handed pitcher they could develop. But that changed as he developed at the plate.

ADRIAN: And once I started really building some strength and starting to drive the ball, I would play in some summer tournaments and scouts started taking notice. And then after my junior year, I went to the Area Code Games, and I think that's where scouts really got a chance to watch me.

His senior year, 2000, Adrian began as the number twenty-six high school prospect in the country, moving up fast, hitting .645 with thirteen home runs, named the CIF Player of the Year, considered by Baseball America as the "best pure hitter" in the nation. Still he hadn't been projected as a high draft pick. So to be smart, he signed with San Diego State to play baseball and study engineering.

ADRIAN: But you know, the draft came about and they threw an opportunity I couldn't refuse at the time.

Coming up on *One on One*, Adrian's road to the majors and his brother's twists and turns in the minors. And later, at home for a little poker with the guys and their wives ....

Adrian Gonzalez was the number one overall draft pick in the nation in 2000, receiving a hefty signing bonus from the Florida Marlins of three million dollars. Along with that? He felt pressure from the Marlin's organization, media, and mostly, he says, his teammates.

> ADRIAN: I started off real slow. And so the minute I was hitting like a buck fifty for my first two weeks, everybody's like, uh, he's not that good. And they're expecting me to be this, you know, I guess there you will find, once in a while, like a phenom guy that just stands out, and I never really stood out. You know, they just liked my defense, they liked my swing, they liked the fact that when I got bigger and stronger, I was going to be able to drive the ball. And so I was more like a pick for a couple years later, not for the immediate impact. And so that was a lot of pressure. I was trying to hit home runs and when you try to hit home runs, you don't do well. And so there's definitely a lot of jealousy and things like that that go on and …
>
> JANE: So how did you work through that?
>
> ADRIAN: Just kept playing. I mean, I just kept working hard and always just my competitive nature. But once you start having success, people are starting to be like, okay, okay, you know, he's okay.

In Single-A, he's named the MVP of the league and selected to the 2001 All-Star Futures team. But then, 2002, the Marlins owner bought the Red Sox, taking the coaching staff and scouts to Boston.

> ADRIAN: And all of a sudden you have a whole new set of guys. They changed my stance. Everything they could change, they changed. And so that was very tough for me that whole year.

Then, being hit by a pitch on his wrist meant surgery and rehab into the next season. With a loss of power, he could have used steroids or other substances illegal in baseball.

> ADRIAN: I'm not going to lie to you. There was definitely a thought in my head of doing something like that. But I think my faith in God and doing what's right played a big role in why I didn't do it. You know, there was a lot of pressure at the time. Everybody was doing it.

Still, with it taking a while for his wrist to mend …

> ADRIAN: They thought that my power wasn't going to come back, or it was never really going to evolve.

So in '03, the Marlins trade him to the Texas Rangers. His new start really kicked in as his wrist fully healed, playing in Triple-A with the Oklahoma RedHawks.

> ADRIAN: And so Oklahoma's a ballpark that was suited for the way I was hitting at the time 'cause it's got a really short fence in left field. And so I didn't have to pull the ball and still hit home runs there.

Encouraged, but not hitting all that well, he got his major league call up when the Rangers' first baseman, Mark Teixeira, got hurt. Adrian's debut: April 18, 2004 in Seattle.

ADRIAN: It was definitely a lot of nerves, a lot of excitement, adrenaline. And I didn't get a hit that game, but just being able to get that game over with was a lot of—just kind of like what I needed.

His two-week taste was enough to propel him to work especially hard going into big league camp in 2005.

ADRIAN: They put me in every situation they can think of and if—I guess in a way, hoping for me to fail so I can get sent down, and I just took advantage of everything they threw at me.

He made the Opening Day roster, but after a few weeks, it was back to Triple-A, and by January 2006, he's traded to San Diego.

ADRIAN: At the time it was like, "Awesome, I'm going to play with the Padres," but at the same time, Klesko was the first baseman.

Turns out, Ryan Klesko needed surgery and was out for most of the season, and Adrian Gonzalez would finally get his chance to play every day.

ADRIAN: Just being able to step on the field, look to the outfield fence, and see number 19 out there, and see number 6, and, you know, all those numbers, 35 from Randy Jones [retired numbers display].

Gaining confidence with every game, every at bat, as the Padres clinched the West Division again, and earning him MVP honors.

ADRIAN [from Awards Ceremony]: I thought they'd take this award and split it in twenty-five, and put it into the middle of the clubhouse, and say, "Hey guys, everyone deserves a part of this." You know, it was definitely a team effort.

At just twenty-five, he's earned respect from his team.

JAKE PEAVY: And those batters can pull the bat back and swing the bat, but he's fearless over there, and I hope he gets recognized for what he does over there defensively at first base.

BUD BLACK: He makes plays. For a first baseman, you can't say that a lot of times.

KHALIL GREENE: When you throw a ball in the dirt, I think, that's not where I want to throw it. But at the same time to have a guy over there who has the ability to pick it—that's definitely nice to have.

Already showing flashes of Gold Glove Award-winning potential …

JOSH BARD: With Gonzo, you see him do something awesome and you go, "Wow, that was a really unique play," and I don't think I've seen another guy do that.

Take that 3-6-4 play in May.

BUD BLACK: He's a defensive weapon. I think everyone on the bench went, "Wow! Did you see that?"

As for his offense, he's drawing comparisons to hitters Mark Grace, Tony Gwynn, Rafael Palmeiro….

ADRIAN: I'm always thinking of a way, or trying to analyze a way, for me to get better and that way I can help the team more.

That maturity and approach recognized by two Padres he grew up admiring, pitcher Trevor Hoffman …

TREVOR HOFFMAN: Adrian is just a quality guy, salt of the earth. What you see is what you get, and he's willing to help out any way he can.

… and of course, Tony Gwynn.

TONY GWYNN: From a skinny kid in high school who was all glove, they thought wouldn't hit with power, he's evolved to the guy who was as good with the glove as everybody said, but is much better with the bat than most people thought.

ADRIAN: If I just have half the career they had, I'll be a happy guy.

Adrian has wanted to share the spotlight with Edgar, the middle of the three Gonzalez brothers, born June 14, 1978. A little guy, Edgar discovered he wasn't a standout athlete starting in Little League.

EDGAR: I actually wanted to stop playing baseball for a little bit because I wasn't very good and my coach would just tell me to stand there and take pitches and walk. Get a walk 'cause I was not very good, and he wanted to win, instead of just trying to make a kid learn. And one day, I hit my first home run. After that, I started loving baseball because I started to become successful at it.

Taking it one level at a time, especially because he was a skinny kid at Eastlake High School.

EDGAR: Then at college, I started getting stronger with all the weightlifting I did here at San Diego State and stuff. And I started gaining weight. And that's when I started thinking, oh, maybe I could play baseball. Then, I got signed the same year as Adrian, way later in the round. I didn't care. I just wanted to go try it, and then if I couldn't, I could just finish. I'm two classes away from graduating San Diego State.

Edgar was a 30th round draft pick by the Tampa Bay Devil Rays, receiving a $2,000 signing bonus—pennies compared to Adrian's 1st round three-million-dollar deal. While some might expect sibling rivalry, jealousy, or envy—that's not in their vocabulary.

EDGAR: I always understood he was the first pick overall, and I always understood he was gonna go fast, and actually, I think I get more happy for him than I do for myself, just because he's my younger brother.

Through 2007, and before signing with the Padres, Edgar had been in the minors with Tampa Bay, Texas, Washington, Florida, and St. Louis. They were productive years playing at literally each level, even an MVP. He's really shined in winter ball, Mexico's equivalent to the majors, where he and Adrian have been standouts, and

Edgar won a Gold Glove for his defense at second base in 2007. Still, no taste of the majors had been a source of frustration for Adrian.

ADRIAN: And just because a lot of times there's politics involved in base-ball.

On the other hand …

ADRIAN: Baseball comes down to being in the right spot at the right time, you know, for me, I just happened to be blessed with being in the spot where Ryan Klesko got hurt. Imagine if he wouldn't have gotten hurt; where would I be?

EDGAR: I think what's happened with me, I think it helped me that I've gone through the minor leagues slower. At times in the minor leagues I was ready to quit too, because I wouldn't see any progress, I wouldn't be playing, even though I was doing better than the other guys, I still wouldn't be playing, and they wouldn't put me in the lineup, and I think it was just my faith in God that He had a plan for me, and just saying, "Yeah, I'm not gonna quit."

Adrian started the year in San Diego; Edgar, in Triple-A. The timing wasn't there to play together, but Edgar's tenacity? No question.

EDGAR: I started out pretty hot and so they started playing me a little bit more, little bit more later.

And finally, it was his turn. Their San Diego homecoming when *One on One* returns. . . .

While Adrian and Edgar Gonzalez are all about teamwork on the field—around the dining room table with their wives playing Texas Hold 'Em—it's every man and woman for themselves. The competition is all in good fun for two pair who have aced their hands at love. First, Adrian and Betsy . . . .

BETSY: I was born in Guadalajara, Jalisco, Mexico.

Betsy Perez moved to Chula Vista at seven with her parents and two brothers. While her mother preferred she dance, Betsy joined the boys in the streets.

ADRIAN: I would be playing with the guys—sports—in my skirts, but I would be playing, you know, football, baseball, and everything. But she didn't let me actually play the sports though.

Adrian and Betsy attended the same middle school.

ADRIAN: So I liked her. She didn't know about me.

Until he asked her to dance at the Sweethearts' dance.

ADRIAN: And that was kind of like the first time we spoke.

BETSY: Umm-hmm.

ADRIAN: And so it was love ever since.

[Two couples at card game.]

It's a similar story with Edgar and Cristina. She's from Bonita, and at sixteen, lost her mother to cancer. Her father wanted her to see the world, so after graduating from Bonita High, Cristina traveled for two years and met Edgar, back from rookie ball, upon her return.

> **CRISTINA:** I said I would never date him, because he went out on like, three dates with my friend, but....

Until their two groups of friends bumped in to each other during a weekend trip to Vegas.

> **EDGAR:** What ended up happening was I told her, "Ok, if we win money … if we go to the craps table and we win money, it's meant to be." We won a thousand dollars.

> **CRISTINA:** We had so much chemistry that we just couldn't fight it, and we got along, and we're best friends, and we've been best friends ever since that day in Vegas. It's just undeniable.

They married in 2003, together traversing the minor leagues.

> **CRISTINA:** I didn't know anything about baseball before I got married, and now I'm just his biggest fan. I love baseball. He's just a fighter!

That fight, fire, and faith shared by Edgar and Adrian savored all the more when they returned home to San Diego to play in front of their hometown crowd a week after Edgar's call-up. Two rows of Edgar's friends turned out to cheer him on, but no fans in the stands more proud than their family. Their parents Alba and David....

> **JANE:** Look at you! You're so happy [laughs]! Did you cry [nods]? Did you cry when he called you?

> **DAVID, SR.:** The hard fight to be here. That everything he did, he did to show the people that he could play in the majors. And it was a long way, but difficult a lot of times, very nice most of the time.

> **ALBA:** We cry a lot, and I tell all my friends. There is not a lot of mothers that have two boys in the major leagues and in the same team [laughs].

Their wives....

> **CRISTINA:** I'm so fortunate to have him accomplish his dream. Of course without God, you can't do anything. I'm just so blessed.

> **BETSY:** When I found out that, I was like, oh! It was almost like when they had called up Adrian because, you know, we're so close and I'm going to get to be with her. We're like sisters. And I'm so excited, excited for the family. He works so hard and she works so hard with him. It paid all off; it paid off definitely.

> **CRISTINA:** We're enjoying it. Yeah.

And their big brother David....

> **DAVID:** He's put up the numbers in the minor leagues, and we were just waiting for the time, the right moment where he was going to have the opportunity to come down and be able to show his talent and show what he can do.

> **JANE:** And you're proud of him?

DAVID: Oh yeah. Definitely. Most definitely.

MATT VASGERSIAN (announcer): We're doing a Gonzalez pop around here. We saw Dave, we saw Edgar for a moment ago. Boy, that Gonzalez tree shook out the same three dudes, didn't it?

When they're both in the game, they're true to form …

ADRIAN: He kept telling me about how much Shawn Estes' ball was moving, and you know, he's got more of a view from second base and …

JANE: So you're really talking baseball out there?

ADRIAN: Yeah. Yeah, we're always talking baseball …

EDGAR: Talking about the game.

They are among some 350 sets of brothers to have made it to the major leagues, and among the even luckier few to play on the same team at the same time.

EDGAR: I remember we would tell my mom we were going to play for the Padres in the big leagues, both of us when we were little. My mom would say, "No, no, no. You guys are going to school and study. That's what you guys are going to do, get a degree, because nobody makes it," and, we're like, "No, we're gonna make it," and all of sudden, we both got there.

Adrian's power and presence continue to impress and make an impact.

ADRIAN: God has a time and place for all of us, and whether it's the major leagues or whatever it is, He's got a plan for us, and we just have to stay with it.

Edgar is seizing his first big league opportunity.

EDGAR: And of course I want to stay here for a long time and be able to produce and have a great career, but, uh, at least I'll be happy knowing that I got here.

"Jane is very detailed in the preparation, she asked for everything you can give prior to the interview, so it almost seems like she knows you better than some of your family members by the time the interview starts, which is good, because I personally hate the 'tell me more about yourself' question. Jane also made me feel relaxed and allowed me to say what was on my mind, and the direction of the story wasn't what she wanted it to be, it was the real you…. To hear these people close to me say those words was very touching. Usually, your close friends, coaches, and teammates don't ever tell you nice compliments and those nice words to your face…. I've heard all great things, everyone really enjoyed it, and best of all for me, people got to know what I was really about…. I personally do not think it makes a difference that Jane is a woman. But I do think that her kind heart does come from being a woman, and that allows you to feel more relaxed and comfortable."

—Adrian Gonzalez, 2010

For all the games they played in the backyard pretending to be big leaguers, and for all the Padres games they watched growing up, hoping it would be them someday—the work, the timing, the patience paid off for both Adrian and Edgar Gonzalez, whose different journeys finally intersected where dreams and the majors merge. I'm Jane Mitchell. Thank you for watching *One on One.*

"We were really excited to hear that Adrian was to be featured on the show. We really couldn't wait to see it. Edgar remembers the show coming up to Memphis to interview him about his brother, never considering that in the near future, they would play in the same organization. Then, when Edgar signed with the Padres, it was an exciting time for them both.... It was really neat how Jane was there every step of the way. Jane was one of the first people I called when Edgar heard the news that he made it to the big leagues. She is really special to us both!"

—Cristina Gonzalez, 2010

MIKE CAMERON AND KEVIN KOUZMANOFF

"I've always been a thinking man, more so, and I was able to let people in on that because a lot of people don't get a chance to see that side of me; the joy that I tend to have."

—MIKE CAMERON, 2010

Sometimes the most powerful stories come from the quietest of people. For different reasons, Mike Cameron and Kevin Kouzmanoff are in that category. At different places in their careers they both faced adversity, were tested, and prevailed in a game that isn't always forgiving, a game that doesn't always allow for a second chance.

MIKE CAMERON

In November of 2005, Mike Cameron was traded to the Padres after a dramatic on-the-field injury that season as a Met. I first met him at spring training 2006 and did a short interview about joining the Padres. He was quiet and thoughtful, his words heartfelt, and his voice almost mesmerizing. I had a feeling he would be a good *One on One*. With his family still in Alabama and not certain I would do a whole thirty-minute show on him, I knew we could get the interview done and take it from there. Early in the season, he was staying at the Hotel Solamar near the ballpark. The hotel graciously agreed to let us use a room near the lobby. The exquisitely designed space was modern with orange and brown color splashes. Dan and the crew created a nice arrangement so it felt like a living room and was certainly comfortable for us to sit and talk.

Mike came down from his room and was approachable. He spoke so softly I wasn't sure how he would do, but I was pleasantly surprised. He seemed grateful to be sitting there and telling his story, and with his incredible eyes, smile and that voice, one would hardly guess this handsome man and rock-solid ballplayer had been through a traumatic ordeal.

We walked through his life chronologically, arriving at August 12, 2005—the day of his on-field collision and when the course of his life would change forever. Mike explained what happened that day. He was with the New York Mets, playing right field in a game in San Diego, when he collided head first with another player, sending Mike flat on his back. He described in detail what he saw, what he did not see, what he felt, and what he feared. I asked some questions I wanted to know, and I'm sure others would—how different does he look and how could he come back and try again after knowing what is possible? He didn't hesitate in telling me how his experience affected him deeply, about his healing, and how his gratitude runs deep.

In the course of the conversation, he mentioned how writing poetry had helped him heal from the injury and from other sadness in his life. I asked if he

would share some, and he agreed. In June, he had moved into a condo, so we met him at his place a few hours before he had to go to the field. His wife and children were still in Alabama, so he enjoyed going to the beach sometimes to relax. He was a little shy about sharing his poetry at first, but I asked if he would bring it with him.

We all drove about five minutes to a quiet beach in La Jolla. At first, we taped him walking along the shore in one of those "scene setter" artsy shots that make for great visuals in the show. Some beach-goers asked who he was (he wasn't too recognizable to fans yet) and they were excited to see a Padre. I asked Mike to sit down with me and share what he liked about the beach and to read us one of his poems. As you are reading the script, envision us on a sunny day, barefooted, seagulls flying over, waves softly crashing, and Mike Cameron opening his heart as he reads his words. Not everyone would do that, but Mike is an old soul and wants to connect with people. I'm glad we were able to provide a venue to peel back the layers and let people see and learn about him.

By the middle of 2007, he had demonstrated a remarkable comeback and I wanted to celebrate his strength and success. I asked Mike for an interview down at the field to update his segment. He suggested we do it right out in centerfield; not by it, but *in* it. Great idea. One hot August afternoon, I wore shorts, a white T-shirt, and flip-flops. Mike was in his workout shorts, top, and tennis shoes. That grass felt good on my feet. With photographer Steve Sanders following us on the ground, we recorded with the rooftop camera from our new building just behind centerfield. It was a great visual for fans to see his point of view, and from up top, how far and wide Mike roamed when he was working.

What I didn't realize until talking with him for this book was why he suggested the centerfield location:

> "I think that I tried to take you on a ride with me back in time to where I was. . . . That's why I took you out to centerfield ... to take the people there, where I started at, where it ended at, and where there was a new beginning."

Mike and the Padres did not agree to terms after 2007 and as a free agent, he moved on to the Brewers. His story still moves me. He could have seen the potential for another injury as his nemesis, but instead, he embraced his recovery and second chance.

In talking with him in 2010 about his *One on One* experience, I was reminded of his depth. Consider our conversation about how some players can be derailed by the limelight:

"And those are some of the things that we forget as young men and as professional athletes. We have to grow so fast and sometimes life is not designed for you to grow that fast. It's designed for you to evolve into what kind of person you're going to become. And I think what happens is in the game, sometimes young men have the stage that the people have put them on and they think that that's what has made them, and you lose the sense of everyday life and that's how you evolve into a man. . . . It's not just hitting the ball out of the ballpark twenty-five or thirty-five times a year, or being a really good defensive player, or a good baseball player, or winning a championship. That doesn't make you a man. You know, that makes you a good team player. What makes you a man is what you go through every single day outside of the ballpark, inside of the ballpark, and the types of experiences you have to go through and deal with as you evolve as a young man."

Another reason many consider him a leader. On a personal note, Mike is genuine and appreciative about my part in supporting him. I tell him, it was his story, I just told it. Mike is an inspiration, not just for his children, or for other ball players, but for anyone who has faced physical and emotional trauma. We can all learn from his faith, fortitude, and attitude.

This script is from the September 27, 2007 edition updating Mike's story.

• • •

Baseball isn't usually considered a contact sport. But in those rare and often dramatic moments when passion and speed meet a wall or another person, the results can be devastating. Mike Cameron knows that all too well.

MATT VASGERSIAN [home run call]: Cameron. Deep! Bullpen bound!

We watch him in action from a distance or on TV.

MATT VASGERSIAN [defensive play]: In front of Cameron, dive and grab!

But take a walk out on his home turf ... [Jane and Mike walking into centerfield]

JANE: What's it like for you once you get out here, centerfield, inside the white lines?

MIKE: I would think predominantly, a lot of focus.

... for a different perspective and appreciation for Mike Cameron's typical day at the office.

MIKE: A joy of freedom.

JANE: It feels so much bigger when you're down here.

MIKE: There's a lot of space, a lot of territory to cover and everything. I still can't watch people get close. But most of the time, I'm like full speed so these guys can see me. And it's hard. It's hard for me, as it is, enough, especially coming back from what I came back, and everyone's saying, is he okay from his injury and everything else. But that's why we're here today.

Here today, after an amazing comeback we learned about in depth when we first sat down with him *One on One* in 2006.

MIKE: A lot of guys have surgeries and injuries that just don't allow them to come back.

Coming back seemed unlikely, if not unimaginable, after one fateful day the summer of 2005 playing against the San Diego Padres in PETCO Park. Cameron was the right fielder for the New York Mets. Not his natural position. He'd been moved to right because the Mets had brought in Carlos Beltran to play center. Cameron had steadily been making the adjustment by August 11. Then in the bottom of the seventh ...

MIKE: David Ross blooped a ball over in right center and thought I had the ball. And the next thing you know, it's like I got hit by a freight train.

ANNOUNCER: *Oh, terrible collision!*

MIKE: My mind is puzzled. And, you know, I'm dazed. I have no idea, but I do know that—the only thing I know is that I'm alive, but I can't move. My body won't move. I didn't know the extent of the damage or anything else like that. I just knew that, you know, why didn't I catch the ball? And so they kept me pinned down on my back for the longest, and I'm trying to move my legs to let them know that I need to get on my side so I can breathe 'cause I can't, I'm choking on blood. And finally, I think once the trainer, Ray Ramirez came out there, he turned me on my side a little bit so now I'm able to talk. They found out, you know, my neck is not broken or whatever. Everything's in place and I want to get up. I want to get up. I want to get up and look around at my body. I want to see myself and make sure everything is okay, but they won't let me get up. I'm split, got both of my lips split. My jaw is like unhinged a little bit. My face is burning extensively. I had a headache out of this world. But I was calm though, I don't know why. I don't know why. Until I got in the ambulance and they started cutting my clothes off of me. I knew I was—they only do that when there's something serious. I was really seriously in distress inside because I knew that, you know, when they took me off of that field that may have been my last time going back on the baseball field.

How he would eventually deal with his injuries is rooted in his history, a guy able to adapt and bounce back even as a quiet, yet adventurous kid.

MIKE: Jumping off the back of the house, jumping bicycles, I mean, trying everything.

Born Michael Terrance Cameron January 8, 1973, his hometown is La Grange, Georgia where he first played baseball in the neighborhood at six.

MIKE: I was kind of like a little guy in the middle of the whole thing, but I could run. I could do everything.

Even though his parents were in his life, he and his brothers and sisters spent a lot of time at Grandma Fannie Mae's house. After his grandfather died, she adopted young Mike.

JANE: What did you learn from her?

MIKE: Hard work. I mean, just dedication. You know, she was like the most sound person in our family.

Toughened up from playing football, he preferred baseball, which might have been his ticket to college. But he couldn't pass up the Chicago White Sox, who drafted him out of high school in the eighteenth round.

MIKE: I didn't know if I was ready to do it, but that's what I wanted to do.

And just four years later, he made his major league debut. Exciting for him and his family.

MIKE: I was living out some of the parts of their dream, and I'm finally made to be the player that they thought I could be, but I really didn't know yet.

As a top prospect, he started the next season in Triple-A, but once called up, he stepped up finishing 6th in the American League Rookie of the Year balloting. After struggling his sophomore year, the White Sox traded him in '99 to the Cincinnati Reds for Paul Konerko. After establishing career highs in every offensive category, he's traded to Seattle in 2000.

JANE: That was a pretty high profile deal with Ken Griffey, Jr. as part of that mix.

MIKE: Not only am I going to Seattle, I mean, I'm going for the guy who's been, psshhh, probably the best player, you know, in the league for the longest.

The team's advice?

MIKE: Be yourself. Do what you are capable of doing.

As part of the sensational Mariners season, Mike Cameron proved himself, earning the first of two Gold Gloves, picked as an All-Star, and in 2002 against his former White Sox, hit four consecutive home runs—the first time it had been done in the American League since 1959.

MIKE: I felt like I had something to prove to them all the time because I just didn't know the reason why I was traded from there.

As a free agent, and Seattle not an option, Cameron signed with the New York Mets.

MIKE: I thought I was ready for it.

JANE: You weren't?

MIKE: Well, you aren't quite prepared for everything that's going to happen there.

With his first serious injury, a torn tendon in his hand, and with several players already on the disabled list …

MIKE: I just couldn't allow myself to go on the DL. I struggled with the game of baseball and I was getting plastered. I was getting booed at home. It was everything. I never got booed at home before, but it was a good experience for me. It was a character-building situation for myself as a man.

Even under the microscope, he broke the Mets' home run record for centerfielders and became the eleventh player in Mets history to hit thirty home runs.

MIKE: I thought I had crossed a bridge, you know, in New York City and everything, but there was more to come. I mean, there was more to come.

Which brings us back to August 2005, the collision, and a six and a half hour surgery.

MIKE: The lower half of my face, they had to like reconnect it to my—put my sockets and stuff back together. And I was really fearing the fact that I wasn't going to be able to see.

JANE: Do you feel like you look different?

MIKE: Yeah, a little bit. I would say a little bit. Throughout here it's all like plates [gesturing to face]. I guess it took a long time for this stuff to settle in, you know, these things here to settle in and everything. My eyes are kind of— got maybe one of them is not quite as—like the other one. I got a couple of cuts and scars, and I got … screws in here. Just, they cut me in the top of my lip, cut it all the way across, and it's like *Face Off.*

JANE: Wow.

MIKE: It was a pretty gyrating experience, I guess. And I didn't know if I could go back and play right field again. I didn't know if I could do it.

With the Mets' centerfield spot taken, San Diego took a chance in a trade for Xavier Nady. And at spring training in Arizona …

MIKE: I felt like I was free again.

He missed the first two weeks of the 2006 season with a strained oblique muscle, returning April 23rd, ironically against the Mets. It didn't take long for Mike Cameron to get his baseball groove back.

MATT VASGERSIAN (announcer): [Cameron stealing base] Cameron's running. Estrada's throw is too late. How about Mike Cameron? Lighting things up tonight!

[Mike walking on beach] He appreciates San Diego's beaches.

MIKE: It's refreshing. It's good for your mind. It's peaceful. It's all of the above. The only thing is that I'm a long ways from my family.

Here he often reflects on his recovery and his sister's unexpected death from a pulmonary condition.

MIKE: The reason why you should never take each day for granted.

He misses his wife, JaBreka, and their three children who will visit from Georgia for the summer.

[Jane and Mike sitting at the beach.]

JANE: Tell me about your writing. Why do you do that?

MIKE: It started out being a secret, but it's no longer a secret! Just having some positive thoughts in my mind that I want to put on paper.

MIKE: [reading poem]: My swing, so graceful as a willow tree, but so quick as a cobra strike …

MIKE: There's a lot of different obstacles in life that we go through as human beings and if you're able to live through it, then it's only going to make you stronger.

JANE: Knowing what's possible now with that type of injury, why did you want to come back?

MIKE: That's a good question. I think I needed to come back just for the sake I've always come back, you know, through everything. And I don't think there was a particular reason why I couldn't.

MIKE [reading poem]: … smooth like the ocean on a peaceful night, yet so powerful and thunderous as a wave crashed on the land site.

MIKE: Not only that, just for my little ones, to show a little bit about—they saw me go through everything, too, and they saw all of those different days that I had to go through and couldn't see, couldn't eat, losing a lot of weight to get my strength back, to get back to what I always do. I think it was a good opportunity for me to show them that you go through certain things in life.

MIKE [reading poem]: … my swing, my swing. Can you feel it? My swing …

Since that day at the beach in '06, he's earned a third Gold Glove, is considered a clubhouse leader, and even with a late season finger injury, he's a big part of the team.

MIKE: The first year, I was like, man, you know, everybody's got on Jake Peavy T-shirts and Trevor Hoffman T-shirts, I want to get a T-shirt. And so it's good to see people in the stands having on your shirt. That means that, you know, there's a very great amount of support for the individual. And there's a lot of respect for what type of player you are, regardless of the situation. You know, people have seen enough of you now to know that, "Man, this guy is pretty good."

[Jane and Mike standing in centerfield]

JANE: What can you hear down here in centerfield?

MIKE: You can hear everything.

JANE: Really?

MIKE: If you want to hear it, you can hear everything.

His confidence is balanced by a gentle spirit and sense of humor even about the challenge of the sun in his eyes.

> **MIKE:** You can hear everything. You can't do anything about it. I mean, it's—the sun is there, it's been there forever.
>
> **JANE:** Yeah.
>
> **MIKE:** Not even going to try to guesstimate how long it's been there, but it's been there for a long time and it still heats up the world so you can imagine what it does to your eyes. I mean people, they're so accustomed to seeing you make all these plays look very easy, so when they think that that's a ball that you should've got that you couldn't get, but they just don't really know …
>
> **JANE:** Yeah.
>
> **MIKE:** I always tell them, I say, I will just point my glove up there. "If you want to try it out, you're welcome to come down here. I think I got more experience than you do." You know? The best thing you can do is just keep rooting for me, that's the best thing you can do.

While he wants to stay in San Diego, regardless of what happens next in his career, he values what General Manager Kevin Towers and the organization have done for him.

> **MIKE:** For him to give me the opportunity to come out here and play, and be able to sprinkle some of my game out here in San Diego has been pretty fun, pretty special.

Mike Cameron and Kevin K are at different stages in their careers, but both have experienced success and struggles all right out there for everyone to see. They're good examples of why stats are only part of the story. Another important part? Overcoming adversity with class, determination, and resilience. I'm Jane Mitchell.

Thank you for watching *One on One*.

"Wholesome. If there was one word to describe the whole thing, it would be that because Jane, you put it at a comfort level where you kind of let your guard down because you're telling the people about yourself and you just want to be real. So that's what the people get, not something portrayed. . . . It was good because you even got a chance to add the pieces of my family in there and that was probably the biggest thing because everybody was saying 'Wow, this is cool right here.' That being said, with me being hurt we had to find some sense of unity amongst everyone. The one thing that's not going to fail me, although everything around may fail me, but my family won't fail me. That was big, too, because it gave them a view of having that unity and that's the type of bond that I try to create everywhere I've been in the community. I get so engaged in the place that I'm at that, it's almost heartbreaking sometimes when you leave."

—Mike Cameron, 2010

KEVIN KOUZMANOFF

"This big smile came walking through my door. And it was actually
a very fun time.... I think you did a good job of taking a personal
interest in me and I think that kind of helped me open up because
I consider myself a very private person. But I think with you it was
different just because how you approached it."

—KEVIN KOUZMANOFF, 2010

I remember, vividly, sitting in my seats at a Padres game when Kevin Kouzmanoff
came up to bat early in 2007. He was new, young, and one of many in the revolving
door at third base, so his name had not sunk in with me yet. When I heard what
sounded like "BOOOOO" emerge from the crowd, I was shocked our Padres fans
could be so rude to the rookie. It took me a minute or so to realize those were
not BOOOs, but fans saying "KOOOOOZZZ." They were already fond of him
and wanted him to know it.

It's not often I will do a *One on One* on a newbie. Usually, we like to give them
a little time, see if they stick, test the pulse of the public and insiders to see if they
are worth the investment of a show, or in this case, half a show. It took very little
time to determine this was someone we all wanted to know better. I paired his
story with an update on Mike Cameron and his stellar comeback.

I asked the Padres media relations staff to lay the groundwork with Kevin
because I had only met him briefly, and the team was on the road when I was trying to figure out my final show of the season. When the team returned, I went up
to Kevin during batting practice and re-introduced myself. He has a deadpan way
of looking at you, as if he is going to give you trouble. I said I was glad he was a
go for the interview and that all we needed to figure out was when and where.
In that deadpan, low-key way he said, "I don't know, Jane, why do you want to
interview me? No one wants to know about me." Again I wouldn't let anyone's

joking or insecurities influence me, and I assured him, "Yes they do, and you just let me worry about that part. I just need to set up the shoot." With his cute half smile and a twinkle in his eye, he said okay. He kept trying to put restrictions on my ideas, such as videotaping him riding his bike to the ballpark and his four-block commute. I did not agree or disagree with his veto, and just said we would figure it out that day.

So address and phone number? Check. Date of shoot? Check. His mother's number for pictures? Check. In preparing for the interview, I talked with his mother for some good tidbits and stories I could bounce off Kevin. With the team going

to Colorado where his parents lived, we coordinated getting them to the field so the game producer, Nick Davis, could interview them for me.

On the day of the interview with Kevin in San Diego, we arrived at his downtown luxury condo building. He was renting a semi-furnished place and had not added much other than a television. I pointed out some of the bachelor indicators in the interview, such as the single, easy-care bonsai plant. He was quiet, even a little nervous, but I was not concerned. I'd done this many times. I suggested he just relax and have fun. He was thoughtful and sincere when he needed to be, and funny when he could be.

Reflecting on his *One on One* experience for this book, Kevin, told me: "I don't share a lot of my feelings. I kind of feel like I'm an onion, I used to kind of have to peel the layers back to get in there. But I think when you and I were sitting there in that living room talking on the couch, you asked a lot of great questions to get me to tell my emotions and how I was feeling, what I was going through in San Diego and all that stuff."

After the interview in 2007, we went on the balcony to show his view, and he took the camera from photographer, Gary Seideman, to see what it was like. Yikes. We made sure he realized it was a sixty-thousand-dollar gizmo. We still needed an activity, and because he refused to play his guitar, I said we had to shoot him riding his bike. He resisted, saying. "No. Not going to do it." I rallied with, "C'mon, just ride back and forth a few times, pretty much like you do when you're riding to the ballpark, and we'll be done. Let's go. Here we go. You can do it. Okay." Of course, he did it, and we even took some fun pictures afterward. Fans loved the show, loved Kouz, and wanted him to succeed.

By 2009, with Mike Cameron gone and Kevin's half of a show in the archives, it was time to update and give him an entire half-hour. He had had two great years and deserved the recognition in his third season with the Padres. Getting him to agree to an updated interview was about the same scenario as the first time, but with a little less resistance and knowing him better as a friend, I just told him there was no saying no, and he agreed with that classic Kouzmanoff grin.

In addition to the original growing up part of his story, there was much to talk about: He had zoomed to the top as one of the best defensive third basemen in the league; he had gone flying with the Blue Angels; he continued to do community work; and he was still an absolute fan favorite. In the script, I point out my observations that he had matured and gained more confidence in his three years. In person, that is even more evident. I see his sincere love and respect for his parents, family, peers, fans, and the game. He exudes a quiet confidence, and yet pure joy about life and his work. He is the real deal. As I titled a blog entry when the show debuted, *Gold Glove? Gold Heart.*

In the winter of 2009, Kevin Kouzmanoff was traded to the Oakland A's. He is missed, but I'm glad we were able to show fans who is at the core of this kid they call Kouz.

This script is from the edition featuring just Kevin, debuting August 28, 2009.

• • •

Kevin Kouzmanoff showing his true colors in a Padres uniform ...

KEVIN: If I prepare myself daily, you know, I'll be ready to go.

And sky high, with the Navy's elite.

[Inside cockpit.]

We've watched Kevin Kouzmanoff progress from a rookie with struggles to a confident, productive player with a track record. He's worked hard to keep his spot in the majors, and along the way, earned respect and affection from fans and peers. Add in humility and good humor, and Kevin Kouzmanoff is just one of those guys you love to cheer for.

In 2009, there's no shortage of highlights crystallizing who Kevin Kouzmanoff is at third and at the plate: solid in routine and in clutch situations. He's twenty-eight, his third season in the bigs, and number five is cool, confident, and not afraid to crack a smile. But if you think "Kouz" is just cruising, think again.

KEVIN: It's a long season mentally and physically; it can be pretty tough. So I figure if I prepare myself daily, you know, I'll be ready to go.

And going from twenty-two errors in 2007 to a fraction of that his third season? He's come a long way, fast.

KEVIN: It's all about how you finish, right? Not how you start.

Before we review that progress, re-visit the first time we explored his story *One on One....*

A classic rock music kinda guy, Kevin Kouzmanoff is in the hot corner at third base. Twenty-six years old in 2007, his rookie season in the majors, he's experienced the good … [home run] the bad … [strikes out] … and the [strikes out again] …

KEVIN: Absolutely terrible.

[Fans: Koooooooooz!]

JANE: So you're out there playing and you start hearing, as you come up to the plate, "Koooooz!" I mean, I think the first time I heard that, I'm thinking, why are they booing this guy? And then I realized …

KEVIN: I thought the same thing.

JANE: You did?

KEVIN: Yeah. Yeah. I mean, why would they be yelling my name when I'm batting a hundred, you know? And it just goes to show, you know, that the fans were very supportive and had my back, you know, and that made me feel very good.

As for the attention he's getting?

KEVIN: It's kind of surprising to me that people know who I am. Maybe the bald head gives it away or something. But, you know, sometimes I go around town wearing a hat if I want my privacy that day. But it's cool that people know who I am.

But being on such a stage? About the last place you'd expect him to be. When you turn back the clock to a little Kevin Kouzmanoff, born July 25, 1981, often the smallest one in a group …

KEVIN: Kind of looking over everyone's shoulders, just quiet and shy. I was more of a listener than a talker.

And usually smiling …

KIM KOUZMANOFF (mother): He's always been a very tenderhearted, kind, considerate kid.

JANE: Your mom tells a story that when you were in kindergarten there was a school production and you were supposed to sing and dance.

KIM: And he would just stand there with both of his hands in his pockets, just looking around and watching everybody perform, and not really getting involved or doing anything, you know, and I said, "Kevin, what is it going to take for you to get really into this performance?"

KEVIN: Gum.

KIM: I said, "You got it." I'll tell you, at that performance he had his hat off and he was dancing and real animated, so it worked for a pack of gum.

KEVIN: And my mom would always say, "Hey, if you make a diving play, I'll buy you another pack of gum," you know, or, "If you get a hit, I'll buy you a pack of gum." So I always wanted to do well so I can get that gum.

JANE: Tell us about your mom and dad. What are they like?

KEVIN: Great people, very happy, very positive, very supportive. Both from Chicago, and just the best parents that sons can have.

Kim, a high school cheerleader, and Marc, a football player, went to the same high school. After college and marrying, real estate and health spa ventures took them to Newport Beach, California where Kevin was born, then to San Diego, when he was two. He's the middle of three boys.

KEVIN: We're a very tight family and we were best friends growing up. We did everything together.

Brant, two years older, lives in Chicago. Ky, two years younger, is in Newport.

KY: He's real just chill, you know, he doesn't boast, brag. He doesn't brag about anything he's ever done in the past, he's just always there and just does what he's supposed to, you know?

His parents live in Colorado now, on hand when the Padres play the Rockies.

KIM: Never in a million years did we think that he would be where he is to-day, and it's only by his tremendous focus.

MARC: Our real goal was just to maximize whatever his potential was.

Sports were a family affair, spearheaded by his dad, a Wildlife Biology major and football player at the University of Montana, who also took a stab at a dream.

MARC: To play middle linebacker for the Chicago Bears was the one goal that I would have loved to have done, and so I had a short stint tryout with the Chicago Bears with four games, and after that, I got cut.

Still the Kouzmanoff family roots run deep in Chicago, and their football team of choice …

KEVIN: The Bears.

As a kid in San Diego, Kevin watched a few Padres games.

KEVIN: I remember I got Benito Santiago's autograph.

But his favorite baseball player growing up?

KEVIN: Edgar Martinez, with Seattle. He was my guy to watch. I loved his swing. I just loved to watch him; great hitter.

By seventh grade, the Kouzmanoffs move to the small town of Evergreen, Colorado, near Denver.

KEVIN: We enjoy the outdoors, and the wilderness, and wildlife.

Elk, ravens, a pet ferret, and their dog Tanner. Sports-wise at an altitude of 7,500 feet …

KEVIN: It's definitely a big change. It's not a whole lot of fun to play baseball in freezing conditions with the wind blowing or in a blizzard.

He plays baseball all four years at Evergreen High and tries a variety of sports. Wrestling …

KEVIN: That wasn't a whole lot of fun because I had to starve myself to make weight for the meets, and so I couldn't eat. And since I love food, you know, that wasn't going to go over well.

Golf ...

> **KEVIN:** I just wanted to go up there and see how far I can hit the ball. I didn't really care about getting the ball in the hole.

And football ...

> **KEVIN:** I thought it was more about yelling, and making guys do pushups, and punishing players, rather than playing the game. You know, so I said, "Go yell at somebody else. I'm outta here." [laughs]

While he was okay about not following in his father's football footsteps ...

> **KEVIN:** I didn't want to let him down. I always wanted to be a good son. And I think my parents always wanted us to be doing something.

Even the swim team: he and his friend agreed to join as divers to help the team get points at meets. Their baseball coach said they had to choose: diving or baseball.

> **KEVIN:** So Justin and I talked about it and we're like, "Fine, we're going to dive, we're going to have fun the last year of school, senior year." And that's what we were going to do, and our coach said, "Okay, wait, hold on. Hold on a second, we can work this out."

After graduating, during summer ball he's recruited by just one coach, who he'd play for at a junior college.

> **KEVIN:** So that's probably the time that I realized that I wanted to take it beyond high school.

After a stint at the University of Arkansas, he walks on to be a star at the University of Nevada Reno, named the WAC Player of the Year.

> **KEVIN:** Got all my work done in class and then I was a baseball player. And all I could think about—all I want to do is just get drafted. That was my main goal.

The Cleveland Indians pick him in the sixth round in 2003. Signing for just $30,000, he's off to the minors.

> **KEVIN:** My goals shift. Now I want to just make it to the majors.

He makes it, with a September 2006 call up. First game in Arlington, Texas. His parents are in the stands with their video camera and the bases are loaded for his first at-bat ...

> *[Parents screaming, "Go Kevin!" on home video]*

The third guy in major league history to hit a grand slam in his first at-bat, the *first* to do it on the first pitch ...

> **KEVIN:** I was just happy that my parents were there to see it.

And there would be a lot more to see. Up next on *One on One*, coming to San Diego, and later, Kevin Kouzmanoff goes where only two other Padres have gone before: on the ride of his life....

Kevin Kouzmanoff might be a Bears fan, but some of his motivational mantras come from the legendary coach of the Green Bay Packers.

KEVIN: "The harder you practice, the harder it is to surrender." My dad always said this one: "Physical strength will weaken the enemy, but mental toughness will break them." He was a big Vince Lombardi guy.

That was a good foundation for his next endeavor, traded to San Diego in fall of '06 for the highly touted second baseman, Josh Barfield. Kevin felt a little pressure.

KEVIN: I can't control any of that stuff. You know, I can just control what I'm in control of, and that's my work ethic, and how I go about things, and just playing the game that I know how to play. As soon as I heard that news, that I got traded [for Josh Barfield], from that day on, my goal was to be the starting third baseman.

Once again, he achieved his next goal, but with a shaky start, batting a low .108 by May 7. He welcomed veteran support.

MIKE CAMERON: There's a reason why you're here and it's because you're good and you—somehow, deep down inside, you gotta dig that out and make yourself believe that.

BUDDY BLACK: I had talked to enough people in the Cleveland organization that also said, "Hey, stay with this guy. This guy's going to hit."

GEOFF BLUM: He stuck to his game plan. He knew what he did that made him successful in order to get here and I think he's gotten back to it here of late, and I think that's what's helped him out the most.

Sizzling through September at the plate …

[Kouzmanoff home run]

ANNOUNCER CALL: *And that ball is gone!*

And at third base …

ANNOUNCER CALL: *Up the line, a good play by Kouzmanoff; an impressive play by the Padres rookie.*

FAN: You just got to keep rooting for the guy 'cause the guy was the underdog.

FAN: He just kept trying so hard and he never gave up, and that's what I like. I'm a teacher and I tell my kids never give up.

FAN: We got the shirts, we got the hats. We're out here supporting Kouz 'cause he's the man. And we hope he does great. We know he will.

He's a good sport—being part of the Padres promotions. *[outtakes]* Feeling comfortable is also a result of being back home …

JANE: You've got the couch. You've got the bonsai, lamp, TV …

KEVIN: It's just—this is it, this is me.

JANE: And a guitar.

KEVIN: I basically just have it just to make myself look cool, so when somebody walks in, like, "Oh, you play guitar?" Yeah, you know.

Yep, he's a bachelor.

KEVIN: I just choose to be single right now.

In his rented downtown apartment ...

KEVIN: I got my binoculars and my spotting scope so I can check out the ships that come in.

He often rides his bike for fun. Sometimes commuting—five blocks—to PETCO Park.

KEVIN: A good ride for me is about ten blocks before I start dripping sweat and have to sit down.

While Kevin Kouzmanoff is hard core about his music ...

KEVIN: I like the grunge bands, you know, like Alice in Chains, and Smashing Pumpkins, and Nirvana, and Metallica.

He has a soft side for his family and charity.

KEVIN: As a child, I was star struck when I saw a Major League Baseball player, so I know that kids love it, and just show them that I'm supporting them and that I want to give back.

And he's a guy with faith.

KEVIN: I was born with what God gave me, and I tried to make the most of it.

After experiencing his first full year in the majors, he has a new goal ...

KEVIN: Now I want to stay here. I want to stick.

ANNOUNCER: *That's another base hit for Kouzmanoff!*

KEVIN: Fifty thousand people to come out and watch you play baseball, you know, is pretty neat.

JANE: And for more than a pack of gum.

KEVIN: Well, my mom still sends me gum. [smiles]

[2009] The signs are there, Kevin Kouzmanoff is still a bachelor ...

JANE: Last time we had a bonsai, now we have an elephant.

KEVIN: The bonsai didn't make it. Man, it said soak that thing in water for five minutes, you know, once a week. And that I did, and it just—the leaves just kept falling off it.

JANE: Last time you said you had a guitar just to impress people. Do you have that guitar still?

KEVIN: I don't have a guitar just to impress people.

JANE: Do you play the guitar?

KEVIN: Nope.

JANE: I'm thinking that's not so. I'm thinking you really do play the guitar.

KEVIN: Do you see a guitar in here?

JANE: I'm thinking you put it in the closet.

Then there's his fridge ...

KEVIN: I have a bad sweet tooth. I just gotta have candy.

JANE: Do you have a favorite?

KEVIN: Kit-Kat® or Mr. Goodbar®. Yeah.

JANE: Kit-Kat® or Mr. Goodbar®. Okay.

All part of the rented condos he likes; this one with a different view.

KEVIN: I can get away from everything right here because I'm not looking at the city or into the ballpark. I'm looking over the water.

A perfect place for perspective on his first three seasons with the Padres.

After a rough start, he ended up ranking among the National League rookie leaders in several offensive categories, including doubles, RBI, multi-hit games, and home runs.

KEVIN: I expect myself to be at the top because of the amount of work I put in.

The Padres' long time booster group, the Madres …

SUSIE BUTCHER: Just admired him so much for pushing himself, and trying, and never giving up.

KRIS HARDESTY: He just won our hearts. The Madres'—everybody's.

Naming him the Madres 2007 Favorite New Padre, on the road to that recognition …

JANE: Not to bring up something negative, but you had twenty-two errors in 2007.

KEVIN: Wow.

JANE: I know, sounds like a lot but …

KEVIN: It is a lot.

JANE: At the end of that year then, how do you tell yourself I'm going to change that?

KEVIN: Well, gosh I didn't realize I had twenty-two errors. There's always room for improvement, and I think I can always get better. I'm never satisfied.

So he tapped into the expertise of third base and defense coach, Glenn Hoffman.

GLENN HOFFMAN: Worked on his footwork at spring training and just made him believe in himself, that he was a good fielder, and he just ran with it. He wanted to do ground balls early, so we'd go over to the half field and I'd challenge him, and I'd do a couple drills with him, and then we worked on specific things.

He cut his errors in half in '08 to eleven, and to a fraction of that in 2009.

ANNOUNCER: And another diving catch for Kouzmanoff! Add that to the highlight reel!

KEVIN: The more reps you get and the more experience you have, I think the easier things become.

Another confidence booster: when the Padres had Chase Headley—their second round draft pick third baseman—try the outfield, keeping Kouzmanoff at third.

> **KEVIN:** You know, hearing that, I'm like, okay, so basically it's my position to lose.

Allowing him to solidify his spot in tandem with the every day first baseman, Adrian Gonzalez.

> **ADRIAN GONZALEZ:** I've gotten to really get adjusted to his defense, his throws; got to know where he's going to be, especially on bunts or certain plays where I like to throw to third.
>
> **KEVIN:** I kind of know his tendencies. If there's a guy on second base and Adrian gets a hard-hit ground ball, I know that Adrian's going to come to me at third base if he has a chance.
>
> **ADRIAN GONZALEZ:** Just different communications where we can now have signals that don't mean anything to the average person, but we know what they mean.
>
> **KEVIN:** He's an All-Star first baseman. He can pick it over there at first.

His fielding percentage is the third best among third baseman in '08, and he's been the leader in '09.

> *ANNOUNCER CALL: He can make that play in his sleep!*
>
> **ADRIAN GONZALEZ:** I really believe he should get the Gold Glove, just for the way he's played this year.
>
> **KEVIN:** I'm just out there doing my job.

A job that risks injury: take a play the last week of the '08 season against the Dodgers ...

> **KEVIN:** Just jammed my shoulder up into the socket and then just jammed the whole thing together.

After six weeks of rehab—surgery. And depending what was found, he could have been out of commission for six months.

> **KEVIN:** I woke up, they're like, "Great news, only a couple months of rehab and you're good to go."

So far, so good. A work horse, he starts his work day where cameras rarely go, inside the batting cages.

> **KEVIN:** To be a good hitter, you gotta hit a lot. And I'm trying to hit a lot. And why not practice what we're going to see out there on the field?

Taking live pitching and front toss to work on his unusual swing, which he describes as "quiet."

> **KEVIN:** Not a lot going on. I was never one to have my hands here and then get loaded up and go. I felt like I always had to start loaded up, which looks awkward because most people aren't like that.

Despite a revolving door of Padres hitting coaches, he's just been fine-tuning his swing. Hitting around .260, he's admittedly streaky at times.

> **KEVIN:** Baseball's a strange game. One day we can go out and beat a team 10-0. And the next day they can come out and beat us 10-0. Why is that? Or one day you get a fast ball right down the middle and you can hit that ball, and the next day it's like, you swing right through it. It's like, why is that? But I don't know. If you have anything for me, I'm all ears.
>
> **JANE:** No, I don't. [chuckling]

But when he's hot, he's hot.

> **ANNOUNCER CALL:** *That's Kouz's third hit of the game.*

Away from the field, he's enjoying big league opportunities, such as the Padres' exhibition trip to China.

> **KEVIN:** I'd probably never go there, but because I play ball, I was able to go. We ate a silkworm, I think. We ate some snake. Might as well have eaten a rubber band.

In San Diego, he's among the first to say yes for community appearances for the military …

> **KEVIN:** I like giving back to the community because they're there for us at PETCO Park.

Kids …

> *[Reading Cat in the Hat]*

And fundraisers, such as the Kevin Kouzmanoff Look Alike Contest, benefiting Children's Hospital.

> **KEVIN:** For the children who don't have insurance, and so when they go in there and don't have any money, this money is going to help them out.

But ask about a favorite once in a lifetime experience? It came thanks to Captain Jack Ensch, a former POW who heads up the Padres Military Relations, who fulfilled a Kevin Kouzmanoff request to fly in a fighter jet. And not just any jet …

> **KEVIN:** He's like, "You want to go on a Blue Angel?" I'm like, "Of course."

So he put on a flight suit at Marine Corps Air Station Miramar. Flight staff briefed him on what to expect from the Navy's F/A-18.

> **BLUE ANGEL TRAINER:** Keep that head back in the seat just like this. When he goes through that transition to high performance climb, your head's going to be pushing back in the seat.

Lt. Frank Weisser in the front seat, Kevin squeezing into the back.

> **KEVIN:** I knew right from the takeoff that it was going to be an interesting flight because we were just hovered along the runway right there, and then we went straight up, I mean, it was pretty cool. And then within a couple seconds, we're fifteen thousand feet in the air—and just the power, the *power*, and the turning capabilities, I mean, it's pretty unbelievable how strong that machine is.

"It was nice to open up and let you and let the fans know where I was coming from with the trade because I know at first it was kind of difficult on the fans because they weren't happy with the trade because of the other player I was being traded for [Josh Barfield]. . . . And it was nice to just lay everything out on the table in your interview because the fans, I don't think, really knew who I was as a person or as a player at that point. I was still new. . . . You made it fun and I think that's what was nice about you, Jane, about having you around, is you actually seem like you enjoy your job and you have fun doing it and you like to associate yourself with others. . . . I remember at first I didn't want to do the interview but, when all was said and done, I was very happy and very pleased the way things turned out. As time went on [for 2009 interview] I had a lot more to say. As the fans started to embrace me and support me ... that made me feel good. I really enjoyed myself there."

—Kevin Kouzmanoff, 2010

JANE: And you have to be in excellent shape. I mean, Ken Caminiti and Trevor Hoffman are two other Padres that we know have gone flying, and now Kevin Kouzmanoff.

KEVIN: I didn't have a G-suit on. We did up to seven G's and ...

JANE: You didn't have a G-suit on?

KEVIN: No.

JANE: Wow.

KEVIN: No, so I mean it was pretty intense. It was pretty taxing on the body. I was sweating. When we were going, doing those loops, and the twists, and turns, the pilot was sitting there coaching me on how to breathe the whole time. I mean, that just goes to show what kind of shape he's in to be flying one of those things. But it was pretty intense. A lot of fun.

While that was a solo experience, he relished his family being part of the Padres tribute on Father's Day 2009.

KEVIN: I know my dad had a great time throwing out the first pitch. And when they yelled, "Kouz," my dad had a great time.

[Ends game on a Home Run!]

Whatever more comes with Kevin Kouzmanoff's major league journey—a pay raise above the league minimum, more highlights, more recognition—he says his family, friends, and young fans keep him grounded as evidenced by a baseball given to him by his friend's little brother on the Oceanside American ten-year-old All-Star team.

KEVIN: Just kind of makes me think back when I was their age and what I was going through, what I was feeling, and how cool it'd be to be a Major League Baseball player. So that's why I keep that right there.

JANE: Do you still like hearing the fans' reaction when you come to the plate?

KEVIN: Yes. Yes, it's flattering. I know that they're in our corner, in my corner, you know, rooting me on.

Kevin Kouzmanoff has evolved from a quiet kid with some kinks to work out to a Gold Glove contender. In person, and on video tape, we've also seen him step out of his shell with equally as important fourteen-karat qualities: an inviting charisma, confidence, and compassion. I'm Jane Mitchell. Thank you for watching *One on One.*

SHAUN PHILLIPS

"I thought the show was amazing. It showed who I was, and that's where it did a good job of depicting where I was from, where I started, who motivated me to get where I am today, and what inspired me in the path that I took, and the ups and downs."

—SHAUN PHILLIPS

I n 2006, a player sitting on Luis Castillo's couch watching TV kindly moved to another room so we could set up for our interview with Luis. What I didn't know then was that a year later I would be coming to that player's house, featuring him on *One on One,* and going into his closet.

What a difference a football season can make. That person was outside linebacker Shaun Phillips. He was a rookie with the Chargers in 2006, proving himself on the field, but not that many people knew about him because he was somewhat in the shadow of Shawne Merriman. When a coach from another team mentioned how they had to beware of "the other guy," meaning the other Shaun, a weapon in the Chargers' defensive arsenal, people started attaching Shaun Phillips' actions with his name and the number 95.

Shawne Merriman was on my list of Chargers to profile in 2007, but when it turned out he wasn't an option, Shaun Phillips was among the candidates the Chargers suggested I feature. When I met him in person at the Chargers facility, he was very enthusiastic and excited to be on *One on One*. He had seen a number of the shows and was ready to go.

We scheduled our shoot and activity on a Tuesday, the Chargers' usual day off during the season. That was also when *Dub Magazine* scheduled a photo shoot with Shaun at his house with his luxury cars, including two Bentleys. Perfect. I suggested we shoot their session, for some fun and colorful video, and then do the interview. That day, when

"I didn't know much about [the show] at all. But after Luis, that's when I started being interested and I started seeing that this is a common trend. If Jane's doing something on [you], it must be pretty good. 'Cause you do your work. You do your due diligence, which is good."

the magazine shoot was finished, I asked Shaun to show us his cars and take us for a little drive. Two photographers, Dan Roper and Jorge Corrales, sat in the back seat of the Bentley convertible, while I stepped into the passenger side. I interviewed Shaun as we drove around the neighborhood. It would have been nice to go out by the ocean, but time didn't allow for that and just looking at the details of the car in those few minutes provided an opportunity to also ask about his first car and show fans what a contrast this was to the life he knew growing up.

Shaun was a talker. He had so much to say and was zealous about each subject. I asked what we could see in his house, and the entertainment continued. From his movie screening room, down the hall with lots of "Phillips" jerseys from

various athletes named Phillips, to the pièce de résistance: his closet. He is a clotheshorse, and being a clotheshorse, myself, I had "closet envy." From his color-coordinated organization to his "bling" belts, his closet reflected his enjoyment of being a person now with means. He was reaping the benefit of his talent, but said his mother and his son helped keep him grounded and his ego in check.

While I could not travel to New Jersey where he is from, a local station worked with me to interview his mother and shoot the various areas where Shaun grew up. That, and his mother's limited photographs, helped tell his road to riches story. Had Shawne Merriman been available, we might not have profiled Shaun Phillips for another year. I take things as they come and appreciate how Shaun opened his doors and his heart to share about his long, challenging journey.

He was happy and eager to share his thoughts with me in 2010, about my telling his life story back in 2007: "It really helped me reflect, and I really felt like I was reliving all those experiences again. . . . I wouldn't say that I hadn't thought about [my life experiences] but we definitely dug deeper into appreciating it more and I appreciated the fact that I was blessed and it was a blessing more than anything, and that's what's most important."

He also reminded me how he felt when I asked him to relocate from the living room couch for our Luis Castillo shoot in 2006. I recall asking politely. In his charming, playful way, he describes the moment like this: "'Get out of the way.' Like, geez, I already feel bad. You saw how I moved out the way, like I'm chopped liver here. Like give me a little love."

I felt bad. I think I made up for it, because any time I see Shaun, he lets me know how much he appreciated the show with a hug or comment. Or if he sees me talking to a *One on One* prospect, he offers, thankfully, a ringing endorsement.

This is the script from the edition debuting November 23, 2007.

• • •

Charger Shaun Phillips, from Philly's inner city to a Bentley in San Diego …

SHAUN: As much as I take care of myself, I take care of my family.

Take a ride through the life and times of number 95. Shaun Phillips has become a key component of the San Diego Chargers' stellar defense. For a while, you might say he'd been one of the best linebackers you've never heard of. But just as this Purdue graduate has worked hard to get here, he's still working hard and making a name for himself with an interesting and likeable mix of humility, flash, and confidence.

Number 95, Chargers linebacker Shaun Phillips, knows exactly what his job is on game day.

SHAUN: Destroy all quarterbacks. Anybody that really touches the ball, just try to hit them as hard as you can.

And in 2007, he's doing just that, either directly or in assists. In his fourth NFL season, we're hearing his name more and more.

ANNOUNCER CALL: Shaun Phillips charging through!

But go back to 2006. A coach with the Tennessee Titans, Norm Chow, referred to Shaun Phillips as "the other guy," meaning the guy other than the dominating Shawne Merriman, a proven defensive threat to a quarterback. Shaun Phillips took that "other guy" comment as a compliment, capitalizing on the positive PR potential.

SHAUN: A friend of mine actually made some shirts up that said "the other guy" on it. And it was kind of funny. It got a little extra media exposure. It got me a couple extra fans. You know, people, "Oh, the other guy, SP, the other guy."

While that moniker may stick or fade away, his actions are getting him noticed, including by network broadcasters.

ANNOUNCER: *Shaun Phillips and Shawne Merriman the "sackmasters" for San Diego…. Shaun Phillips has got that cobra-like quickness.*

SHAUN: I want everyone to know Shaun Phillips, or the other guy, however they want to put it. It's great, and I love it, but I want them to know it because I was a great player with my team. My *team*—I play for a great team.

Born May 13, 1981 in Philadelphia, Pennsylvania, being the best on a big stage is something he's long prepared for.

SHAUN: If you asked my mom from when I was growing up, I always wanted to play with the bigger and better kids so I could be better, you know. When I had to play with kids my age, it was like taking candy from a baby. I was destroying them.

His drive and determination, largely inspired by two women in his life. First, his mother Sherri, whose mother raised her and her five siblings alone. Just sixteen when she had Shaun, Sherri lived at home, finished high school, and had an idea of what to teach her son …

SHERRI (mother): How to be responsible, grown up. Do what you have to do to get where you want to go, and be respectful.

JANE: And did you know your father?

SHAUN: Oh, yes, I knew my father. He was around. I mean, he wasn't a bad guy, so there's nothing I can say bad about him. He wasn't a bad person, but he just wasn't there for me, to teach me how to be a man. My mom taught me how to be a man. But he was there for me, you know, a little bit financially, and I could call him and talk to him if I wanted to, and he supported me with my sports and different things like that. But, yeah, like I said, I pretty much, with my mom there, she did everything for me.

The other important female influence? Sherri's mother, he called Nana.

SHAUN: I helped her bake cakes or I helped her cook. And every time I came over, she always made something that was a favorite for me, like strawberry cake or something like that.

Nana was a professional league bowler who competed with her U.S. Post Office team.

SHAUN: That's where I get my bowling skills from, I assume, 'cause I can not play—I can not bowl for three months and go to the bowling alley and bowl a 170, a 180. And it's kind of funny. That's just genetic; it's in my genes.

Their North Philadelphia neighborhood was entrenched for a while with gangs and drugs. While the area improved somewhat by the mid '80s, young Shaun still faced challenges.

> SHAUN: It was like a typical city neighborhood, I would say. You know, you still had the drugs and things like that in the city, but my mom did a great job of keeping me away from that.

Mostly by encouraging him to play sports.

> SHAUN: I was out playing basketball, or playing tennis, or playing baseball or something. I always had something going on where I couldn't miss it. If I was to miss it, then obviously I'm doing something wrong if I'm missing it.
>
> SHERRI: Even though we went through a lot of trials and tribulations as we grew, he was my best friend because it was just us, me and him for a time, until I met my husband.

And by seventh grade, the new family moved about a half hour away to a suburb, Willingboro, New Jersey.

> SHAUN: People were a lot smarter, a lot stronger, a lot wiser about making decisions about who they hung with and the things that they were getting into.

Shaun, an only child until he was ten, soon had a baby brother, a sister, and a stepfather.

> MARK (stepdad): He didn't understand why I had to push, but he had a gift, so I had to push.
>
> SHAUN: We had a long talk, and come to find out, you know, he was looking for my best interest. He was just trying to do the little things that my dad didn't do.
>
> JANE: What was it like, suddenly being a big brother?
>
> SHAUN: It was different. You know, I was the only child. I got my way all the time and I wasn't used to sharing attention again.

He got used to it. As for his pro-sports aspirations? Shaun was convinced he was destined for the NBA because he was better than the older kids he played hoops with in Philly. Ironically, when he moved to Jersey his nickname was "Turtle."

> SHAUN: My freshman basketball coach gave me that. He said the way I run, it looked like I run like the turtle and the hare. And I don't know ...
>
> JANE: Slow?
>
> SHAUN: No—not really slow. Just like the way I run, I really don't.... He never really elaborated on it, but he said it one time and then from then on, everybody on my team took it and ran with it, and the whole school, the whole neighborhood, everybody still back in my neighborhood call me Turtle or T, either one.

While basketball was his favorite and forte ...

> SHAUN: All my friends went to go try out for the football team, and I was like, "Well, I guess I'll give it a try. All my friends are doing it."

He'd always been slender and tall for his age; 6'4" by his freshman year. He ran track, but with football new to him, he learned on the field named for alumni and Olympic track great, Carl Lewis. Coach Tyrone Belford remembers first watching Shaun as a freshman …

> **COACH BELFORD:** If he continues to grow like he was, long lanky kid, and continues with his good attitude, he might be able to play on Sundays.

Guiding him with this advice …

> **SHAUN:** "Just play basketball on grass now." So I thought about it like that, you know, whether I was running a passing route, I'd just go like I was playing basketball, whether I was like wiggling somebody or just running past somebody, however I had to do it.
>
> **COACH BELFORD:** He was a tremendously hard working athlete, and then he became a better student, as time grew closer to go to college, he buckled down to get to school …

Phillips was selected to the Governor's Bowl, the New Jersey-New York All-Star Game, and received recruitment letters from colleges who'd been watching.

> **SHAUN:** And my coach told me one day, he was like, "You're a Division One AA basketball player, you're a Division One A football player." So right then, immediately, I was like, I want to be a star, so I want to play Division One football.

He accepted a scholarship to play football at Purdue University. That and achieving his NFL dream are next on *One on One*. And later, his million dollar garage, inside his fabulous closet, and how Shaun Phillips shares his wealth….

When Shaun Phillips chose Purdue University, the Indiana campus was far different from what he was used to. But the culture shock had its unexpected rewards.

> **SHAUN:** Whether they were white, Greek, Mexican, black … I met a lot of great guys that I keep in contact with, and they pretty much showed me that there is more out there. You know, I'd go home with my friends for their holidays and stuff like that, and hang out with their parents, hang out with their family. And they let me know that there's more out there. There's more out there to life, and you develop friendships, and you develop trust, and people that you respect—grow to, learn to, grow and respect. And it was great. Like, Purdue was probably the best experience I had. It was probably one of the better decisions that I made in life.

On the football front—he generated quite the buzz.

> **SHAUN:** We had guys in the NFL already and they're telling me I'm the best defensive end that ever played there, or I could potentially be the best defensive end. I had all the tangibles. So my freshman year went great. I think I had like seven sacks or something like that my freshman year. After that year was when I told myself, *Okay, I'm going to do whatever I gotta do to get to the NFL.*

And do whatever necessary to graduate, a semester early, at that.

SHAUN: I stayed every summer. Every single summer I was at Purdue taking classes, taking classes, working out, working out, 'cause, like I said, I wanted to do everything I could do and give myself the best possible opportunity to get to the NFL as I could. I put all my eggs in one basket.

His Plan B was his degree in Hotel-Restaurant Management, but it carries a deeper significance, as he's the first in his family to graduate from a four-year university.

SHAUN: When I was coming up, I really never thought about college. I didn't know what to think, what came after high school. I don't remember, like, maybe you just get a job after high school, you know, 'cause that's what everyone did. You got a job after high school. But now my brother and sister know that they can go to college and that they can make a difference. The sky's the limit for them. If I made it, then they know they can make it also.

As for his NFL dream? That basket of eggs worked out. He was drafted in the fourth round by the San Diego Chargers, learning early that he'd spend a lot of time in the gym.

SHAUN: In college I didn't really work out that much. When I got to the NFL, I learned that you should work out all the time, so now I'm working out once or twice a day. Whether you go do just a little bit of something, whether you just go do some abs, or you just go do like fifteen minutes of cardio, you still outworked the next person, and that's just the mindset to have if you're going to be a professional athlete, I think.

In an era with a strict NFL policy banning steroids or performance enhancement drugs, Shaun Phillips is open about the subject.

JANE: You've never done them? Not going to do them?

SHAUN: It just doesn't appeal to me. I don't have to because I know my work ethic, you know what I mean? The only thing I take now is I drink protein shakes, I take a multi-vitamin, and I take glucosamine, and those are things already in your body.

Realizing the importance of taking care of his body and his workout routine his rookie year, he was also motivated to do well by being a fourth round draft pick, rather than going higher.

SHAUN: So everyone that didn't pick me, I was determined to prove them wrong, and that was my mindset going in and out every day. That was all I was thinking about was getting on the field and being able to make plays. And I was able to make a few plays as a rookie.

JANE: You had the second most sacks among rookie linebackers.

SHAUN: Yeah. It wasn't good enough 'cause I want to be first all the time. I always want to be first at what I do.

In 2005, veteran linebacker Steve Foley was hurt, so Shaun Phillips filled in a lot.

SHAUN: I was actually a lot better my second year than my first year, as far as knowing what I'm doing, and knowing pass coverage, and understanding offense, and understanding defense.

In '06 Foley was due to return. Then, in an unfortunate, well-publicized incident, Foley was shot by an off-duty police officer in an early morning chase a week before the regular season. With Foley injured and out for the year, suddenly Phillips became the everyday guy.

SHAUN: As much as I felt bad, and I was like hurting inside because Foley's a good person, I was excited, though, 'cause I'm like, all right, cool, I get to start. Like, watch this.

While Shaun Phillips was learning and contributing, the Shawne most people talked about and knew about was the established linebacker, Shawne Merriman.

JANE: Tell us what that was like for you.

SHAUN: It was somewhat tough, but the reason it wasn't as tough, because Shawne's a friend of mine. Like if Shawne wasn't a friend, then there could be some jealousy involved, or something like that, but …

SHAWNE MERRIMAN: We both want each other to succeed, and I just want him to be the best player he can be.

SHAUN: He goes out and gets seventeen sacks, or he goes out and, you know, gets two or three sacks in the game, goes to the Pro Bowl, different things like that. I see how he works, so I'm going to do the same thing he does.

SHAWNE MERRIMAN: How far he can go, who knows? The potential is there. He was waiting for his time to get his thing out on the field. He's done that. He's done that so far.

NORV TURNER (Chargers Head Coach): When you see him make the plays, he makes you say, "Yes, he can continue to grow and be a dominant player in this league."

JOHN PAGANO (Chargers Outside Linebackers Coach): Being out there rushing the passer, dropping into coverage—you see the different plays that he can make, and it makes him a very versatile linebacker.

LUIS CASTILLO: He's a cocky guy, and he's the type of guy who—every time he steps on that field he thinks he's the best football player to ever play the game, and you know, you can respect a guy who has that type of attitude and backs it up.

IGOR OLSHANSKY: He just never stops working—whether it's on the field or whether it's talking—he just keeps going and going.

MATT WILHELM: Coming in here, earning playing time, getting the big contracts, so everything's really coming with hard work, and he knows and understands that.

LUIS CASTILLO: That star has been waiting to shine, and he's been looking forward to it, and he's doing a great job of it.

But despite an incredible 14-2 season and getting to the playoffs in 2006 …

SHAUN: It was great, but it wasn't great enough, because we didn't win the Super Bowl, and that's what we play this game for. I don't care about nothing individual at all—we play to get this ring.

JANE: Do you feel like you're a different guy when you're out there?

SHAUN: Completely. Like, all right, my normal life, I'm just a nice guy and I like to have fun and joke around, but I get on the field, it's like a switch like flicks on. It just like goes to like crazy mode, and you just want to just hurt everybody and try to beat up everybody you can.

Phillips is indeed carving out his own identity beyond his performance. Take his victory routine: part team move, part tribute to Nana.

SHAUN: I went over to Steven Cooper's house one day and he was like, "Hey, I got the dance you need to do." And I was like, "What?" And so he did it, the bowling thing. And immediately that hit at home.

JANE: What is just, like, a great day for you?

SHAUN: Honestly, football Sunday. Being able to go out and play … nothing like game day to me. I don't care what's wrong. I can have the worst week in the world; once Sunday comes and we got our helmets on, we're running out on the field. Every time I run through the tunnel, I think of that, like, I just love football. I love football Sundays. Ain't nothing like it.

It's a Tuesday afternoon and Shaun Phillips is the focus of a photo shoot for a national high-end car magazine *Dub*. It's featuring Phillips and the contents of his garage: two Bentleys and a Lamborghini. With the last shot snapped, he takes us for a ride.

SHAUN: We got the black Bentley Azure convertible. They just pretty much came on market so, I mean, I love it. It's a great toy.

JANE: Wow. A toy, I would say.

Bentleys are essentially handmade.

SHAUN: From the stitching in the leather, to the wood grain on the doors, to the chrome package inside, to the rims to, you know, everything.… At the end of the day, it's still just a car. You know.

JANE: Easy for you to say. Oh, wow.

This one, with a V-12 engine, is customized to Phillips' liking.

JANE: So what kind of car did you have when you were a kid?

SHAUN: Uh, my first car was a Neon.

He's come a long way to now be able to buy this kind of car.

SHAUN: As much as I take care of myself, I take care of my family.

And he can after signing a six-year contract extension with a guaranteed thirteen million dollars the first two years.

SHAUN: The first thing I did was bought my mom a house. I bought her a nice house back east, and it actually got built from the ground up, and got to get all the bells and whistles that she wanted in it. And so that was the first thing for me. I know—take care of home first.

Home and family includes his son, Jayden, six years old who lives in Texas. They see each other about every two weeks.

SHAUN: And we talk on the phone almost every night.

JANE: Having been raised by a single mom with your dad around but, you know, not a lot in the picture—how do you want to be different?

SHAUN: I basically want to teach my son how it is to be a man, to teach him how to, you know, the right and wrongs in life. And I want to make sure I'm there for him. Unfortunately, I can't see him all the time but, when I am with him, we gotta make the most of that time that we are together.

When Shaun Phillips is home in Poway, his house is a pretty nice place to be. Starting with his home theater ...

SHAUN: I got the super big movie screen projector, four of my favorite movies. I got *Gladiator* and *300*—street tough guy movies—*GoodFellas*, another tough guy movie. And, you know, all time favorite of mine is *Menace II Society*—just a another tough guy movie.

JANE: Not the romantic comedy kind of guy?

SHAUN: Nah. I mean, I'll watch them if they're on the TV, but as far as going down as my favorites, I can't really have *Love and Basketball* as one of my favorite movies. It's just not really ...

JANE: Right.

SHAUN: ... a macho thing to do.

A walk down his hallway shows an artful display of jerseys of pro athletes named Phillips in different sports.

SHAUN: Here's Jason Phillips, he plays for Toronto. I got him to autograph it. And this is when I threw the opening pitch at the Padres game, they made me my own jersey, Phillips 95, obviously. I gotta have my own jersey. Gotta have it.

JANE: Of course.

SHAUN: This guy plays hockey out in Montreal. I really like this jersey. They do a good job of like stitching these jerseys together. This is Shaun Wright Phillips. He plays soccer. He's one of the top five players in the country.

JANE: Well, I'm dying to see your closet.

SHAUN: One of my hobbies, dressing a little bit.

All a bit reminiscent of growing up around his grandmother, who liked to sew ...

SHAUN: She was really good at it. I think that's what got me hands-on towards, like, clothes, and liking clothes, and liking fashion, and things like that.

JANE: Oh my gosh. [Surprised walking in to 15 X 15 closet]

SHAUN: I try to organize everything: got all my coats over there, shorts and T-shirts here, dress shirts here, suits here, T-shirts here, Polos....

JANE: Look at the shoes.

SHAUN: Button-ups. I got a lot of different types of shoes.

JANE: I love how you're so color coordinated. Look at this, you've got the whole, you know, rainbow ...

SHAUN: 'Cause you gotta mix it up a little bit.

JANE: ... colors and ...

SHAUN: You gotta mix it up a little bit. You got solid colors, you got bright colors, you got dull colors, you got light suits, dark suits. There's so many different occasions ...

JANE: Is this the one you wore on the *The Bachelor?*

SHAUN: Yeah, I wore this suit right here on *The Bachelor,* yeah.

JANE: Your grandmother would be proud.

SHAUN: If she was still alive, she'd probably be living out here ...

JANE: Yeah.

SHAUN: ... 'cause that's how much she loves California and loved me.

JANE: Ohh, that's nice. Are you pretty particular with what you wear?

SHAUN: Yeah, this just downplays it. I kind of like either really rock star type look, or more like, really like button-up with a nice sweater over it, or a suit. So I do a little bit of everything. It just depends on the mood.

JANE: What's your most rock star thing you have in your closet right now?

SHAUN: I got some buckles. Like this belt buckle right here is a pretty rock star belt.

JANE: Wow.

SHAUN: Like, a lot of people love this. This is a pretty cool toy.

JANE: This is Highway 95.

SHAUN: Yep, the Phillips 95 T-shirt.

JANE: Okay, well, thanks for letting us in.

SHAUN: My pleasure. My pleasure.

The closet, the cars, the contract ...

SHAUN: Sometimes I gotta pinch myself to see if it's true.

It is allowing him to achieve another goal he set day one in the NFL.

SHAUN: I want to be a star, but not only be a star, you know, on the field, I want to be a star off the field.

He's doing so, with the Chargers' community efforts and on his own. He and teammate Quentin Jammer have a private Christmas dinner for a dozen youngsters from the San Pasqual Academy, a home for abused and neglected kids.

SHAUN: We get them, I'm talking about like, PlayStations®, X-Boxes®, bicycles, computers, laptops, shopping spree, whatever, you know. We take these kids and we just spoil them to death. We don't have any media involved.

He's partnered with the After School All-Stars. For every sack Phillips makes, he contributes $1,000, which is matched by three other sponsors, to make it $4,000 a sack.

SHAUN: Which I think'll go a long way, you know, to give these underprivileged kids something to do after school.

In 2007, he and other Willingboro alums in the NFL returned to their high school for a football camp offering guidance, the same tips he shares with any kid who will listen ...

SHAUN: Set your goals, and write your goals down so you can measure the success of your goals.

Taking his own advice, he attended a four-day course for entrepreneurs, a program set up by the NFL with top business schools, including Northwestern.

SHAUN: I believe entrepreneurs pretty much make the world go around.

He's having fun, traveling with his buddies, launching a website featuring his different interests, including modeling and social activities. And while he can, clearly, taking advantage of opportunities that often come with being in the NFL …

[Throwing out first pitch at Padres game]

ANNOUNCER: Shaun Phillips with our ceremonial first pitch!

JANE: What's that world like for you to know that you can go to the ESPYs or go to Wimbledon, or, you know … ?

SHAUN: It's fun. You know, 'cause you get to mingle and rub shoulders with a lot of other celebrities. I don't even look at myself like a celebrity. I mean, I look at myself as an everyday person, you know. It's kind of funny, like, I get star struck seeing other stars, whether it's a John Elway, or a Dan Marino, or a Quentin Tarantino.

JANE: How do you stay grounded?

SHAUN: You stay grounded by your everyday life and knowing the fact that I have a family at home that I mean a lot to, and that I can't let my head blow up, and I'll go to the sky, and forget about them. I am thankful for everything I have, and I know that it came from a higher power. Through God anything is possible.

Humility and confidence, a combination that, since he was a kid, has served him well in life and on the field

SHAUN: I always was the one that wanted to play with the better kids and I always had the mindset that I want to be better than everybody. And, you know, that's the mentality I believe you got to have as an athlete, whether you are the best or not. As long as you internally feel you're the best and play as if you're the best, then you are the best, because when you say you want to be the best—that's inside yourself. You know, long as, you know, you're working harder than the next person, you should be content with it within yourself.

Like a lot of kids, Shaun Phillips imagined he'd be a professional athlete. What separates him from many is that he not only followed his heart, but he followed sound advice from those he admired and trusted: his single mother, grandmother, his coaches. Knowing that he's beaten the odds and still has so much more to accomplish, makes *him* a guy to watch on his favorite day, NFL Sunday. I'm Jane Mitchell. Thank you for watching *One on One*.

"As soon as the piece aired, a lot of people hit me and said, oh, like, "Oh, I didn't know that about you. I didn't know you graduated from school. I didn't know you were so into fashion. I didn't know how much a role your grandmother had and how much of an influence your mom had." No one knew those things, you know. They just see Shaun Phillips the football player, but I do so many more things off the field that it really should out [shine] my football, but it doesn't. . . . Personally, I would like to have another piece done, because I've grown so much since the last time we did our piece that I would say my core values are sort of the same, but my overall outlook on things has changed a lot, and seeing everything for what it's worth and understanding who to trust, who not to trust, how important it is to stay in focus and building your brand. . . . Bad news always sells and it's kind of annoying that we can't have a positive piece like yours be more publicized and more glorified . . . .The world should be the other way around. We should want to hear positive stories all the time and see a positive message on things and see a positive outlook because it's infectious."

—Shaun Phillips, 2010

MARK MERILA

When you think about teams such as the Padres and Chargers, it is easy to imagine some of the players it would be natural to profile for *One on One*. I am proud of every show, but of all the super stars, the up and comers, the veterans, and Hall of Famers whom I've featured, there is one person who stands out for the beacon of hope, strength, and love that he is. Not because he led the team to the playoffs, or won a national award, or has his name on jerseys all over town. None of those things applies to him.

Mark Merila stands out because he has led a different battle with good humor, kindness, and respect, never wanting or expecting anything because of that battle. I'm not alone in feeling this way about Mark, and that is why everyone I asked to contribute to his story did so without hesitation.

I met Mark in 1997 at the onset of Channel 4 San Diego. One of our producers, Jason Bott, produced a feature about Mark, and I voiced it for the pre-game show. At that time, Mark had overcome a health setback with a brain tumor and was thrilled to be in remission and the one catching Trevor Hoffman in the bullpen. I had seen Mark at spring training, down on the field, on the road when I traveled with the team, and met his wife and children. I didn't know him well, just that he

"I have difficulty answering questions now due to the complications of my brain tumor. Jane was so patient and helpful through the entire interview. I think I learned a lot about how much people are really pulling for me out there, and how my association with the Padres has helped build awareness towards brain cancer and its effects on a person. I was really proud of the work she did, and was happy to have this memory forever, no matter how things go."

—Mark Merila, 2010

was easygoing and always there for Trevor. By summer of 2005, I heard something had happened regarding his brain tumor, but he was still with the team for the playoffs, so it didn't occur to me how serious it might be. At spring training 2006, he did not look like himself.

We have all experienced this: Sometimes you see someone who looks different or has been sick, and you want to act as if nothing is different and everything is okay, to not make the person feel bad. I think in part because of what I learned from my father's illness—being in denial that things weren't "normal"—I make an effort *not* to do this, especially when it's someone I know who has been through something. So one morning at camp, while pitchers and catchers were doing their drills, I sat next to Mark in the dugout. He had difficulty talking and grasped for some words. Maybe it also was my experience with my father who often didn't have the strength to speak because of his ALS, or the times in high school I sat with my Great Aunt Sade after she had a stroke, but somehow, I could figure out what he was trying to say. With tact and compassion (I hope), I broached the subject about what he was going through. I felt for him and his family, but I did not factor Mark's odyssey into my work and production plans. Not yet.

Another year went by and it was spring training 2007. Mark was there for part of the time, more swollen than before. We talked again, and again, we muddled through some words as he described how the chemo had affected him so much. Spring training 2008, I saw Mark, and this time, he was more mobile and able to get in and out of his scooter. Most of the swelling had gone down. His speech

was much improved. We sat for a few minutes, and he was just so humble and grateful to be in a better state. I asked if he would be okay to interview him there at camp, thinking I would do a little profile piece for the pre-game show. He agreed, and when we talked outside on that green hill above the fields, I was amazed at his perspective, his attitude, and his aura.

I had to do more than just a little story. I called his wife Wendy, and we put a plan in motion. She started gathering the pictures and video; I would check back in a few months, and we would come to the house. With other shows in the cue, we finally did the interview that summer.

This show would require a lot of dimensions. From a production standpoint, this was our shooting checklist: At-home interview with Mark and Wendy; doctor's

interview at the hospital with brain scans; physical therapy session; family time playing baseball at a park; Mark speaking to a church group about his faith and testimony; and interviews with key Padres, including former manager, Bruce Bochy, who I talked with when the Giants were in town.

I wanted to visualize Mark's ride on the subway in New York when he had his second seizure. Not wanting it to be hokey, I thought home video or digital pictures could "take the viewer there" as his teammates and Mark told about the sequence of events. I emailed my dear friend Jay DeDapper (from grad school and a political reporter with WNBC at the time) with my request: "Could you ride the subway out to Shea Stadium and take pictures along the way? Here's the story line … what do you think?" He agreed, and delivered, and the masterful editor Dan Roper was able to use the digital pictures just as I had imagined.

What struck me about Mark Merila is how matter of fact he was in sharing his story. He had such faith, gratitude, and strength, that his voice didn't crack once; he did not shed a tear. That is not the case of some of his friends I interviewed, or even me, when I was writing the script. Wendy said they had their bad days, and no one would expect anything less than some tears and emotion for such a traumatic and uncertain situation. Wherever they get their strength—from their faith, from needing to be solid for their young children, or from being grateful for the blessings—it is remarkable, inspiring, and beautiful.

It was lovely to hear from Mark and Wendy about how they felt about being on the show. Mark wrote:

> "You do not always get the chance to tell these people how much they mean to you, and this gave me a chance to hear others' thoughts. Since the show aired, I have heard nothing but positive remarks for our family, and praise for Jane for doing such a piece on me. I just appreciated an opportunity for my wife and me to get the opportunity to thank those who had been pulling for me."

Many people deal with matters like this, but most do not have a television show telling about it, and that's where the power of television can be used for positive purposes. Mark has since become the ambassador for the San Diego Brain Tumor Foundation. His story, and maybe with people reading about it here, should give encouragement, strength, or inspiration to someone else with a brain tumor or any kind of life-threatening and life-changing disease.

A beacon such as Mark Merila is hope for someone, and being able to tell his story is why television can be used for good. While I never do my work for the hardware, we won an Emmy® for Outstanding Sports Program for this edition. Mark was thrilled to learn the news.

This is the script from the edition debuting September 5, 2008.

• • •

Mark Merila: He's not a household name like some on the roster. But after you hear his story, he will be.

MARK: I just wanted to be the guy they can trust every time.

Mark Merila is a remarkable Padre, not for his batting average or fielding percentage—he's never played in a regular season major league game. But hearing his journey, you'll understand how seizing one unexpected opportunity early on eventually led to his being in the right place at a very bad time. A place where his extended family has given him a chance to fight for his life, and a chance to live an unusual version of his major league dream.

For more than a decade, he's worn a Padres uniform, shared in some of the team's biggest moments, and he cares how his team, and relievers especially, are preparing for battle.

He's crouched behind the plate in the bullpen, warming up pitchers before and throughout the game. Most consistently and faithfully for the All-Time Saves

Leader, Trevor Hoffman, who shared the spotlight with Merila at a ceremony in June 2007, celebrating Hoffman's certain Hall of Fame-worthy accomplishments. Mark looked different than the last times he'd been at the ballpark. Just out of the hospital, his body was swollen from chemo therapy, medication, and steroids; all ammunition to control, even reduce, a brain tumor.

> MARK: But I'm glad at least I got to be there. But at the same stuff, it's like, man, you look terrible.

With a sense of humor, in 2008, he is winning the battle. Right beside him is his wife Wendy.

> WENDY: Every day he gets a little bit stronger.

He has some damage, sometimes needing to spell words he knows but can't say.

> *[Jane and Wendy guess Stanford as he spells with fingers]*

Still, his vivid memory, passion and love of baseball, family, and faith are evident.

Mark Merila is a northern boy born November 9, 1971 and raised in Plymouth, Minnesota, fifteen minutes from Minneapolis.

> MARK: When you're in Minnesota, you've got to be—find a way to get out of—when it's cold. So hockey was a big part of my life. Fishing was a big thing with my dad and I.

His father worked construction. His mother stayed home raising Mark and his older sister Tracy.

> MARK: She was always going to my games, whether it was baseball or hockey. She was always a great, great sister.

A Minnesota Twins fan, he admired future Hall of Famers Rod Carew and Kirby Puckett.

> MARK: And so it was nice to see a shorter guy like me, see a guy fly around everyway.

Out of high school, Mark had several hockey scholarships, but accepted one from the University of Minnesota—the only school that wanted him to play baseball, too. Wendy Sue Smith, two years older, was a country girl from Minnesota and a cheerleader for the U of M's Gophers' hockey team.

> MARK: That's when I saw her the first time. And I've been big into hockey all my life, and then blondes have been a big thing for me. [Wendy and Mark laugh.]

While a lot of his new friends knew he was a two-sport guy, Wendy didn't, making for a mischievous moment, and love at first "skate."

> WENDY: There was a challenge between one of the baseball players and another one of the girls, you know, who could skate faster or whatever.
> MARK: So as we started, I let her take way off, and she's way ahead of me. And I'm trying to just catch up to her. And then she got to the other side, and she was coming back the other way, and then finally had to skate like normal and get by her. Then I blew by her and she's like—"What ..."

WENDY: ... he had blown by me, then turned around and skated backwards faster than I could skate forwards! Yeah. So then I was like, "You know what, I like that guy." You know?

MARK: So, definitely, that was the ...

WENDY: The challenge was there.

Wendy graduated with a Sports Marketing degree and worked for a local TV station, on hand for his baseball games. Mark chose to pursue baseball, mostly because of his height. At 5'8", he'd have to be much faster on the ice to progress through the professional hockey ranks. In baseball, his shorter stature wasn't an issue.

MARK: Hopefully that'll be a better, easier way to try to make it.

With the skills to prove it at second base, one of the best freshman baseball players in the country, then an All-American. After his junior year, the hometown favorite was drafted by the Twins in the tenth round. But negotiations didn't pan out. So he moved forward, was picked to play for Team USA, and his senior year 1994, got off to a hot start, hitting .488 in the first month of the season until April 9.

MARK: I was sitting and all of a sudden my right eye and stuff kind of starting flashing out of my eye. And I was like, that's kind of weird. And then next thing you know, you got stars or whatever. And then next thing you know, I started getting feels like if she was pulling my shirt—pulling me down. And the next thing you know, I came to and I was—just as I was going in the ...

WENDY: Ambulance.

MARK: Yeah, and I had no idea. And I said, "Did I already play? Aren't we playing today?" And I had—didn't—had no idea what had happened.

He had a grand mal seizure.

WENDY: They did a biopsy of it and actually went in and they found a astrocytoma.

A slow growing brain tumor—golf-ball sized and inoperable. So the game plan?

WENDY: Let's do these MRIs every three months; let's see where we go.

Nine days after that seizure ...

MARK: They said I can play again, so that was basically in my head then, I want to get back and, hopefully, have the year that I want, thought I was going to have.

An All-American again, the Padres picked him in the 33rd round of the June '94 draft. General Manager Kevin Towers ...

KEVIN TOWERS: A guy that we felt had the ability and the tools to maybe someday get to the big leagues. And we were excited to draft him.

Aware of his health history ...

KEVIN TOWERS: We felt that it was certainly worth the risk, and there was a chance that, you know, it could go into remission and be able to have a good playing career.

In early 1995, Mark took his doctor's advice to try to stop the tumor in its tracks.

> **WENDY:** The best course of action at that time would be to do radiation right before he left for spring training.

The radiation zapped his energy and enthusiasm some, but he managed to go through the motions, performing well in the minors.

> **MARK:** I'm starting to feel better. All of a sudden, okay, I want to play again.

But the Padres had their concerns about his tumor.

> **KEVIN TOWERS:** When he continued to have his problems with it we felt hey, you know, this would be a great guy to give an opportunity to get into the big leagues, put on a big league uniform. If it's not going to happen as a player, this would be—you know he's got great hands, we'll put him in the bullpen.
>
> **MARK:** I've never caught before. And so it's like, well, half of me's like, "Well, this is great, they think of me to have a chance to do this stuff and go in the big leagues." And the second of me's like, "Well, I can never try as a player." I'm like, "Okay, what should I do?"

He agreed to the fairly new idea of being a full-time bullpen catcher, boosted by an invitation by Manager Bruce Bochy to play in an exhibition game just before the season.

> **BRUCE BOCHY:** There was no fear there and he seemed very, very excited about it, and the guy—every time I put him in there, he goes out there and gets hits, and hits line drives all over.
>
> **MARK:** And all of a sudden these guys are like, "Oh, maybe this new guy that we got, maybe he is a baseball type of guy; that it's good that we have this new thing and, hopefully, this'll work out for everybody." And next thing you know, I'm done with the game, and next thing you know, Tony comes over. "Nice job, kid." And I'm like, "Wow, this is great that he knows that I had two hits and wanted to make sure that he said good job."

Then the real work began, learning to be a bullpen catcher.

> **MARK:** I just want to be the guy they can trust every time. If they are going to be ready, I am going to be ready for them, whatever they want to do.

Since 1996, Mark Merila embraced his new world with a positive attitude, apparent in person and in pregame show features over the years.

> **MARK:** I became a bullpen catcher. I guess you gotta be at the right place at the right time.
>
> **BRUCE BOCHY:** The pitchers were very comfortable being around him. And he became part of the bullpen.
>
> **MARK:** The littlest things I was doing the guys would make me feel that I was a big part of it.

Even accepting their nickname for him, "Stump."

> **TREVOR HOFFMAN:** He's short and squatty. He's a stump, you know, he's a tree. He's a short tree.

544

Competitive to the core ...

> **MARK:** My little way to play every day, I always wanted our guy ready so he has a great day.
>
> **TREVOR HOFFMAN:** We had guys that had great years and you know, you wanna think a lot of that had to do with the preparation getting ready to go into a ballgame.

Mark solidified his role through the spectacular season of '98, as the Padres won the National League Championship. After that season, Mark was offered a coaching position at the University of Minnesota.

> **MARK:** And Hoffy's like, "What are you talking about?"
>
> **TREVOR HOFFMAN:** We needed him, you know? I, selfishly, basically said that this is where you need to be.

Feeling flattered and valued, he chose to stay. Mark and Wendy married in 1997 and used the unexpected bonus money from the '98 playoffs to buy their first home, a condo.

> **WENDY:** Every time we looked, the pieces would fall into place for us, including, every other year having a child.

Their daughter Brooke, then sons Boston and Brody. In between seasons they'd return to Minnesota for doctors to monitor Mark's brain tumor, considered dormant.

> **WENDY:** We were so busy with all that, and the baseball schedule, and me working, that I think we really thought about it every year, for like four or five days, and then we just were kind of thankful.

In November 2004 they celebrated ten years with no tumor growth. All seemed to be going well until a hot summer day, July 19, 2005.

The Padres were on the road to play the New York Mets. As usual, Mark joined his good friend and bullpen coach, Darrel Akerfelds, and trainers Jim Daniels and Todd Hutcheson to catch the 7 train to the stadium.

> **TODD HUTCHESON:** Right after we came out of the sunlight I was sitting right next to Mark and he goes, "You know what, I'm not feeling very good." "Well do you want to get off at the next stop?" And he goes, "Nah, I think I'll be all right." I kind of glance over and he's slumped over and his head is now on my shoulder, and he starts to convulse, and I just grab a hold of him. I'm like, "Hey, I need help over here," and I grabbed a hold of him and laid him across my lap, and then gradually we worked him to the floor.
>
> **DARREL AKERFELDS:** I saw him on the ground and I saw Hutch and J.D. take care of him,
>
> **TODD HUTCHESON:** I just held on to him and made sure that, you know, he didn't injure himself any further.
>
> **DARREL AKERFELDS:** The people on the subway, they were awesome, as far as getting the train stopped.

TODD HUTCHESON: Paramedics finally got there and we gave them as much information as we could, and they stabilized him and took him to the hospital.

With the immediate concern of the seizure over, doctors cleared him to return to the game, travel with the team to Philadelphia, then back to San Diego.

DR. KOSTY: This is an MRI of Mark's brain …

Dr. Michael Kosty is Mark's current oncologist.

DR. KOSTY: This large white, irregular area is the tumor. Tumors send out tentacles. And so there's always that fear that at some point it will recur, and much of the time it does, and that's where Mark found himself.

Mark's teammates were told he might not make it. And Mark had a visit from the team's chaplain.

MARK: I had a good place at peace if everything had changed. So …
JANE: Your faith carried you.
WENDY: Yeah.
MARK: Exactly.

As did their determination to fight.

WENDY: It's just me and him against, you know, against time, trying to figure out what this was.

To find answers, their best ally, Padres owner John Moores.

WENDY: John wanted to make sure that we had the best care and knew that—I mean, with three kids and our resources, it was great that family stepped in along with the Padres' doctors, just saying, "We're going to hold your hand, we're going to get those scans out."

It took until that September to determine UCLA was his best chance. While enduring radiation and some oral chemo, baseball was part of Mark's therapy, returning to the bullpen on the weekends, even there the night the Padres clinched the division.

For the next year they commuted to UCLA for treatment, which included a new drug called Avastin. It was working, and so was Mark until the end of the 2006 season. That's when the brain tumor began affecting his right side. Number 71 faced the toughest year of his life. His "treatment central" moved to San Diego's Scripps Clinic with Dr. Kosty.

DR. KOSTY: It was relentless. It wasn't that it was growing more quickly, but it kept growing, and growing, and growing, and the therapies that he had been on had minimal or no effect.

So they added more conventional intravenous chemotherapy and steroids to control the swelling on the brain, a catch-22.

DR. KOSTY: Started having the effects that you see in somebody that's on chronic steroids—swelling of the face, muscle weakness, fluid retention.

Apparent by spring training 2007.

> **DARREL AKERFELDS:** It just seemed like he needed to take a little step back so he could just regroup, and even though we were missing him, he was doing the things where he knew he could get back here pretty much on a full-time basis.

Mark attended only about ten games in '07, but rarely missed watching his teammates on TV.

> **TREVOR HOFFMAN:** I missed his presence. But I think that I didn't miss his support, because I knew that he was watching from whatever venue he could get it from.
>
> **MARK:** I always called him and say, "Hoffy, you know, congratulations—good job."
>
> **TREVOR HOFFMAN:** "Good job for you—you know, I know you're tired, I know you want to go to sleep. I know you're not feeling very good, but you should be proud of yourself to sit through a ballgame and be excited that the Pads won."

Up next on *One on One*, Mark Merila's recovery game plan, and lessons learned from his valiant fight....

> *[Merila kids singing: Take me out to the ballgame ...]*

With the joyous voices of their children, Mark and Wendy Merila are grateful to be living an unusual major league dream, and grateful Mark is *living*.

> **WENDY:** In 2007, it was more bad days than good days. In 2008, it's been all more good days than bad days.

With the tumor essentially stagnant, so is the chemo. He's on lower doses of medicine, off steroids that caused swelling; moving, looking, and sounding more like his old self. He's restricted from flying to avoid blood clots. So team road trips mean more quality family time.

> **MARK:** Now I can do the dad stuff again.
>
> *[Merila pitches to his son at local baseball field]*
>
> **JANE:** So what's the prognosis looking ahead?
>
> **DR. KOSTY:** This is a tumor that's not curable. It's one that can be controlled for hopefully an extended period of time. If and when the time comes that we need to get Mark back on therapy, we have the therapy that worked before as a possible option, or we have things that are in the pipeline and almost ready for primetime.

In the meantime, with the discipline of an athlete, he has regular physical therapy.

> **JANET TROCHE:** What's everything feeling like today? Better than usual, same as usual?

Janet Troche is a physical therapist with Sharp Rees-Stealy, specializing in neurology patients.

JANET TROCHE: It's not so much that I'm treating one body part, but everything, because the brain is the control center of everything. Some exercises mirror baseball moves, being able to throw a ball hard again. That's just—that's bonus, that's great. But yeah, the important thing is just activities of daily living right now. It's hard to know if he'll crouch down as a catcher again.... He's gone against the odds already.

Already back contributing as part of the Padres staff.

DARREL AKERFELDS: Oh absolutely, all through spring he sat down by the catchers when all the guys were throwing, and talking to some of the new catchers about guys' certain pitches, and, "Hey that was a good one," and, "Hey, that one wasn't so good, you better get ready for a good one."

About a half hour before home game time, look for Mark Merila coming out of the dugout by first base.

DARREL AKERFELDS: Hey that's one of the best parts of our day, you know. It's game time, and walking across the field, and having him go out there, and getting ready for the first pitch.

Observing, instructing—a welcomed presence, the whole game.

TREVOR HOFFMAN: Dedication, discipline, perseverance. Just because you're seeing progress doesn't mean he doesn't have a daily fight, and it's exciting to see him push through.

Mark Merila wasn't supposed to make it through that second surge of his brain tumor. They are confident he did in large part due to the financial and logistical support from the Padres, and in particular, owner John Moores, who gave them a chance to fight.

MARK: John obviously doesn't want me probably to talk right now about that type of stuff, but definitely for everything his family has done for our family, obviously every day, I just can't thank them enough.

WENDY: Like Mark said, we're just the bullpen catcher and I'm his wife, you know. They have made us feel like we are, you know, that I've won the Golden Glove Award, I'm MVP. From Tony Gwynn doing things, to Ken Caminiti, I mean, there's always been one of these guys that has continuously done something, or a memory that's come back into his head now that has got him to the next step.

TREVOR HOFFMAN: It has nothing to do with the game of baseball anymore. It's, you know, give yourself the amount of time you need. We want you to see your kids grow up.

JANE: What are some of the things that you do to help your dad?

BROOKE: When he asks for something I get it.

BOSTON: Like if he's trying to say a word, and he can't say it, I'll help him.

BRODY: My dad plays puzzles, and baseball, and Padres.

Also key to his recovery? Friendships. From seeing how former Padre Scott Linebrink wears Mark's number 71, to an on-line CaringBridge support system from Minnesota to San Diego.

> **DARREL AKERFELDS:** I'm not sad for him, I'm just so proud of him. [emotional]
>
> **BRUCE BOCHY:** For him to endure what he's had to go through and never has complained of his situation. I've never heard him once.
>
> **JANE:** What have you learned from him?
>
> **TODD HUTCHESON:** No matter what you've been hit with, there's always hope. And you know, you can always strive to make things better for everyone.
>
> **KEVIN TOWERS:** Every time I see him walking to the clubhouse, it always brings a smile to my face, and always makes me feel how lucky we are, you know, to have our health, and to be able to be a part of this great game.
>
> **DARREL AKERFELDS:** We might be in the midst of losing some games on the road, and you get here and he's positive, and, "Let's go get them today boys," and, "It's a new day."

Mark Merila's outlook on life comes from deep within. At the Green Valley Church with Padres Josh Bard and Adrian Gonzalez along side, Mark talked about how church was just a must-do growing up.

> **MARK:** For us, we always went at eight o'clock. So I'm like, "Oh that's a little rough. You sure we can't go at 8:00, 9:30, 11:00?" [*audience laughter*]

But since being surrounded by Christian teammates, his priorities have changed.

> **MARK:** Last year was another rough one for me, but obviously God wants me to be here, and I think that's part of my life now, definitely. [gesturing levels of priorities] Being with God is here, and then my wife and my family, and also baseball is third, if not fourth, you know.
>
> [*Applause*]
>
> **JANE:** He says he wants to stick around as long as you're here, at least.
>
> **TREVOR HOFFMAN:** He'll be around even after I'm gone. Trust me. He loves the Padres, he loves baseball. You know, it's part of his makeup.
>
> **KEVIN TOWERS:** I don't think Mark will ever wear another uniform other than a Padre one, so as long as he wants to be a Padre employee, he'll be one.
>
> [*Kids singing: For it's 1,2,3 strikes you're out at the old ball game! Yey!*]
>
> **MARK:** Good job Brooke and Boston!

I asked Mark Merila if he looks at the box score any differently now, if the team's wins or losses aren't as big a deal as they used to be. He laughs saying that's how it should be, but the *competitor* in him always wants to win. Another indicator that in *so many ways*, Mark Merila has the heart of a champion.

I'm Jane Mitchell. Thank you for watching *One on One*.

"When you asked Mark and our family to be featured, we were honored and flattered.... Jane, you have an amazing talent to reach into the core of the person you are interviewing with your heartfelt interviewing techniques.... You made us feel so comfortable like we are talking to a long lost friend that we may not see all the time, but we can pick up where we left off. You are respected by all for your heart, honesty, and friendship. I appreciate your support of Mark and our entire family."

—Wendy Merila, 2010

TINA MICKELSON

"I remember being very flattered that Jane would think of me, because the show generally focuses on male athletes....
Jane was one of the most professional reporters I have ever worked with for many reasons...."

—TINA MICKELSON, 2009

Channel 4 San Diego launched a new half-hour 10:00 p.m. sports news show in 2007 called *Postgame*, an extension of the post-game show during the baseball season. It would need content, and one idea for the winter months was for me to expand my *One on One* franchise and niche to shorter *One on One* segments featuring athletes from non-traditional sports, or at least from sports other than baseball and football. That opened the door for college, extreme sports, and golf. One person who fit the bill was golfer Tina Mickelson, younger sister to golf super star Phil Mickelson. We had met at parties and charity events over the years and hit it off as friends. I tried to coordinate a shoot that winter, but between travel, some rainy weather, and her grandmother's death, that January flew by, and then it was baseball season. By the summer of 2008, I teed up the plan again.

We went to Tina's and her husband Eric's home. I expected a thirty-minute interview, enough to touch on her life story, her golf endeavors, and gather several pictures and videos from her career. We would do a little golf outing another day, and combined, I would have enough for about a five-minute segment. My idea changed that day, because her interview was so open, intelligent, and inspiring. When I learned her parents lived in San Diego in the same house where Tina and her brothers grew up, I wanted to interview her parents, which I did a week later. Seeing where the Mickelson kids learned to golf in their backyard, and borrowing home movies transferred to DVDs—capturing their wedding, Phil, Sr. on a Navy aircraft carrier, and the Mickelson children growing up on film—I felt this had to be a half-hour show. This was a story that had never thoroughly been told about a wonderful San Diego family.

For the show to be a half hour, however, and to do the Mickelson family story justice, I needed to include the whole family; especially considering Tina's brothers lived in San Diego and Phil was one of the most famous golfers of our time.

I called Tina to ask if she could help recruit her brothers for an interview. She said she would ask, but made no promises. Tim was the golf coach at the University of San Diego. Phil did not do many television interviews away from tournaments, especially local. With their schedules and my schedule, there was one day that could work: the day Tim was returning from a golf trip; a few days before Phil was going to China, and just before I took a vacation. Just asking on my end paid off. She confirmed they would be there at four in the afternoon on October 28th to play a hole and sit down with me for an interview.

Before that, I wanted to showcase Tina's teaching abilities, so I was a willing student. At the Santaluz Golf Course in Del Mar, where Tina was teaching, she was patient and helpful in giving me some tips about my stance, holding the club, and just handing the club back to her, then letting it go. I hit a ball about seventy yards by my third or fourth whack. Tina gave me a high-five, and I figured I would quit while I was ahead. We included some of that, along with her teaching some serious students. This *One on One* was about Tina, so reporter participation was at a minimum.

The day of the Mickelson sibling convergence, the crew and I arrived at Santaluz to set up in the library. Tina arrived early and said she had been reminding her brothers with text messages. At 3:55 p.m., Tim and Phil, in golf attire, walked toward the front driveway, friendly and pleased to be there. Phil's first questions to me: "So what's this about? What's this for?" I said it was for my show featuring Tina, and that they—her brothers—were part of her story. "Great," he said, "let's do it."

For as many famous baseball and football players I have met, Phil rates as a pretty big deal, considering his international stature. After only seeing him on television playing with the likes of Tiger Woods, I was calm on the outside, but admittedly, my adrenaline was pumping.

Tina, Phil, and Tim walked the course. My associate producer, Michelle Mattox, intern Casey Nakamura, and I drove the carts, while photographers Dan Roper, Michael Spaulding, and Paul Gugliotti followed them to capture their conversations and get various shots. Phil hit his ball a ridiculously long distance, some three hundred yards or so. When he came over to my cart to get a club, the conversation, recorded on tape, went like this:

JANE: Tina taught me and I hit it about 70 yards. She thought I was pretty good.
TINA: She is a good student.
PHIL: She was just being nice! [Laughs]
TINA: Welcome to my world! [To Phil] No, really, she has an athletic swing. [We all chuckled]

At the end of the hole I wanted to take a picture of them and noticed how "teeny-tiny" Tina was next to her brothers. Phil, again, was witty and teased,

"Oh, you gotta pull out the fat jokes, huh?" I noted how interesting it was that three siblings can look so different—short, tall, broad, small—yet all swing a mean club. Wow.

We spent a total of an hour and twenty minutes with them, between the course and a thirty-minute interview, the first time the three of them had been interviewed together. I stayed true to the mission at hand, exploring their family dynamic over the years. They were funny, cordial, sincere, reflective, and professional. Tina said Phil had never sat that long for an interview, and she was very appreciative of that. So was I.

Not to overlook the love-interest in Tina Mickelson's life, we spent part of a morning with her husband, Eric Topacio, a firefighter at Chula Vista Fire Station #4. He had been a runway and magazine model over the years, so I expected he would be ready for the cameras, but Eric was excited and a little nervous to have us there shooting him and his fellow firefighters around the fire truck. It was a quick visit because a real call for a fire came in as I was interviewing them and they had to leave.

When I was writing and producing this show, I realized this to be a rare situation with having the three Mickelson siblings together for the first time, and having Phil do a sit-down, personal interview, different from a news conference. I did not want to hype or exploit that. In fact, I didn't alter the proportions of the show segments just because I "got Phil." It was all in the context of telling the story of Tina and a wonderful San Diego family with military, golf, and a famous name as components. The feedback I received seemed to reflect that I stayed on course, and I am proud of that.

Beyond what was shared in the program, I appreciate Tina's character and insight, navigating love, life, family, and work. This edition truly came with the friendship dividend.

This is the script for the show debuting November 18, 2008.

• • •

Tina Mickelson on the links, in the community, married to a model and firefighter, sister to Phil and Tim.

PHIL: Golf has been very good to our family.

A home-grown success story that runs in the family.

Golf is part of the San Diego scene, a refined and sometimes frustrating game that can be played and enjoyed by hackers and pros alike. While only a tiny percentage who hit the sticks make it big, Tina Mickelson has found her niche. As have her brothers. We'll have a first-ever conversation with the three Mickelson kids later, but first, Tina's story.

She approaches the course with calm and confidence, inspired to teach, often on national TV on the Golf Channel and on the sidelines for her famous younger brother, Phil Mickelson. Phil has made his mark—an international name, winning the first of his two Masters titles in 2004, finally ridding himself of the title "best player never to win a major ..."

> TINA: Very, very proud of him.

But Tina is succeeding in, loving, and sharing the game in her own way. And a library of Mickelson home movies helps visualize her story. Father Phil was a Navy pilot and flight instructor. Mother Mary was a San Diego native. They met at a Navy dance and married. He became a commercial pilot while she was a nurse. Both were athletic and adventurous, and their children would be, too. Tina Marie was born January 12, 1969 in San Mateo. Then the family settled in San Diego the next year.

> PHIL, SR.: She was just very, very special.

Blonde and bouncy, she was the first grandchild in the family ...

> MARY: So everyone—aunts, uncles, and grandparents—I mean, Tina was the thing in our lives. And then along came Philip.
>
> TINA: I remember the first Christmas my brother Phil was about six months old, and we were taking this Christmas picture, and he kept crying, and we had to keep taking the picture over and over, and I remember thinking, *Who is this? It would be so much easier if it was just me, and we didn't have to deal with this.*
>
> MARY: As a little girl, she was very patient, she was happy, very athletic, would try anything, excited about everything; a mother, mothering Philip. She wanted Philip to do, you know, certain things, and they played well together.

Their dad put a club in their hand once they could walk, and a precious snippet of home movies captures their early enthusiasm.

> TINA: Instead of trying to give us advice or trying to form a golf swing for us, he just put a club in our hand and just let us hit the ball, and as you can see, we were just so excited just to hit the ball.

Evolving to swinging sticks on a camping trip and playing Pee-Wee and Junior Golf ...

> JANE: Did you two compete? Were you competitive?
>
> TINA: In everything but golf—we were not. I don't know why, maybe because I just knew he was better, and I didn't even bother. But we played video games, and we had record books where we would log in every score. I mean everything we could be competitive at, we were.

After baby brother Tim made three, golf was a whole family affair, led by their dad.

> TINA: So his love for the game, he passed that on to us, but at the same time, he didn't force it on us, so whenever he wanted to go to the golf course, he always would say "I'm going to the golf course, does anyone want to come with me?" If we wanted to, great, if we didn't, that was ok, too.

At ten, Tina set golf aside for gymnastics.

MARY: I think it's been harder on Tina because everyone, even as a youngster, compared her to Phil, which wasn't fair. And that was one of the reasons why we encouraged her gymnastics, because we knew it was something that he could not do. And she was very good at it, so that gave—that really built her self-esteem.

TINA: What I loved about gymnastics was you were always in control of yourself. In golf, once you hit that ball, it's out of your control; the wind, the grain, the grass has control over that.

With gymnastics somewhat limited, her career aspirations returned to the course.

TINA: I did not want to compete in golf. There were so many other things in golf, there were so many other things in life that I was interested in, and teaching was a big part of that.

After Patrick Henry High School she attended the University of San Diego, graduating in '91 with a major in Communications and a minor in Business. While working at Steele Canyon Golf Course she learned that to become a golf professional, she had the option of qualifying for a PGA membership or an LPGA, Ladies Professional Golf Association, membership.

TINA: I personally felt that getting a PGA membership would make me a little more equal with those that I work with. The playing ability test was a lot more difficult. I personally felt it was more well rounded for the whole golf industry, and I did not want to be gender exclusive.

She was among the few women opting for a PGA membership.

TINA: There were about 350 people at one of the business schools that I went to, and there were six women, so it was just, it was just something I felt I had to do in order to establish myself as an equal.

With her PGA stamp of approval and teaching as her goal …

TINA: There were a lot of myths about the golf swing and about golf in general that I wanted to dispel, and I thought the more—the larger the audience, the better.

After convincing a syndicate company to carry a column about her golf tips in newspapers across the country …

TINA: Somebody at the Golf Channel saw one of these tips and asked me to come work for them.

[Golf Channel lessons]

Moving to Orlando might have given her a bigger role on the Golf Channel …

TINA: But it's not as important as my family and the time spent with my grandparents and my parents now.

Her parents live in the same house where they raised Tina, Phil, and Tim.

Tina's grandparents, on her mother's side, lived into their late '90s.

TINA: Just this no nonsense guy who had a heart of gold, and my grandmother was just this little angel who was always smiling, and always up for anything …

She values their example of the qualities to look for in a partner. In her mid-thirties, Tina had just resigned to being single. When she went to a birthday party in 2005 for her and her friend, Charger Junior Seau, a mutual friend said …

TINA: "You know, you really need to meet my friend Eric," and, "You would really like him." I said, "You know, I don't know, I'm—my life is going good right now, I don't wanna deal with that."

The friend suggested Eric come by the party anyway.

TINA: And he came in and I saw him, and I was hoping that would be the guy he was talking about. And it was.

Eric Tapacio grew up on a chicken farm in Jamul, graduated from Valhalla High School, then Cal Poly San Luis Obispo, and became a Chula Vista firefighter. Along the way—flexing his good looks as a print and runway model.

TINA: I was so excited that he asked me for my number and that was it.

While dating, Tina discovered his attitude about being a firefighter reflected his approach to life.

ERIC: I'm actually paid to help somebody and I'm, you know, anyone of us would probably do it, and so I'm more fortunate to do it.

They married September 17, 2006, her grandparents' wedding anniversary. Tina and Eric have remodeled their first home in San Diego near her parents …

JANE: The fact that you have three TVs, I think a lot of people are going to be very envious.

TINA: I know, it's really for football season, and that's why we did it.

ERIC: Well, we may have three TVs, but we just don't have any furniture to go. [laughing]

JANE: Sports fans and soul mates, so you know where our priorities lie.

JANE: Do you ever get called Mr. Mickelson?

ERIC: Um, no, but—well, actually, yeah I have. But I have been called the favorite son because I'm the only person, or son in the family that Phil, Sr. can actually beat. So I mean, I don't know if that's good or bad, but …

While Tina's nieces think Eric's the rock star with his uniform and fire truck, Eric's had to adjust to being with someone in the public eye.

ERIC: When we would go out to dinner, or we'd go out and people would come up and talk, and I wasn't use to that, so that took a little bit of an adjustment, and I don't think about it anymore.

JANE: But you do get to play some nice golf courses …

ERIC: Yeah.

JANE: There are some perks.

ERIC: Yeah. I don't ask, but we get to. I only *hope!* [laughing]

Now they're hoping to start their family.

> TINA: We'll probably do what my parents did, and that is just stick a golf club in the hand, let them do what they want. As long as they're not hitting anything breakable, just swing the club and kind of develop their own path.

It's a beautiful day in San Diego and Tina Mickelson is in her element, not just being out on a golf course, but teaching how to get in the swing of the game she's loved her whole life. Her student? [Jane] A perennial novice who hasn't picked up a club in more than five years. Her classroom? The luxurious grounds of Santaluz Golf Resort in Northeast San Diego. She is patient, observant, and positive. Her qualities are much appreciated by me and by women serious about golf: students seeking her tutelage at Santaluz.

> TINA: Women approach the game differently then men. And so they've brought me onboard to be their ambassador for women's golf, to really help their women members. What are they looking for? What would make the game more enjoyable to them? So I'm happy to do that work. Now Calloway Golf is also taking that approach, so they've brought me on board to do the same work for them. And I really like the fact that they have this foresight to understand that women are a large part of this game, but sometimes they approach the game a little differently.
>
> JANE: How so?
>
> TINA: Women sometimes are a little more serious about the game, and there are ways that you can be competitive, but still also enjoy the game and help make others feel comfortable as well. It's great to be competitive, but it's not so much about that. It's about the experience you have out on the golf course. There are a lot of aspects about golf that are very difficult. I'm not gonna lie and say it's easy. It can be easier. It doesn't have to be quite so difficult.

As a teacher, Tina tests her own teaching skills.

> TINA: I love going out and playing with friends and giving them a tip here or there, because they will be the first to say, "That doesn't work, that's ridiculous." Somebody else who's actually, you know, students, not that they would ever say, "Oh this doesn't work," but they're very honest. So when you have the honesty of your friends, "Ok, I see what you're trying to get me to do, but that doesn't make sense, explain it another way." That has helped me a lot as well.

Her golf career spans teaching, television, and a series of golf tips. But her connection to the game has taken on a spiritual dimension. Deepak Chopra, an author on mind-body medicine, was writing a book linking his ideas to the game of golf …

> TINA: I thought, *He needs someone to edit that book, because if he's not a golfer, if he's new, there would be the verbiage that might kinda set the tone for that.* So one day, I went to his office and I just said, "I think you need me to do this," and he looked at me and said, "I think maybe I do."

The book, *Golf for Enlightenment*, meshes with Tina's open mind.

> TINA: I was brought up Catholic and I do still have my Catholic beliefs, but I believe there's a lot more to life than maybe what we just have defined through certain religions.

Tina embraces the celebrity that comes with her profession.

> TINA: It's been fun for me because a lot of the same celebrities or athletes go to a lot of the same charity events, and it's nice because you build relationships with them.

Supporting each other's causes, helping community groups and fans, and three specific projects: Dinner with the Pros, teaming up with former Charger John Carney and former Padre Phil Nevin, to raise funds to benefit organizations helping teens in crisis. Then there's Fresh Start, giving children medical treatments to fix birth defects, and third, the Burn Institute.

> TINA: To support everything they do, the Burn Institute is amazing in the things they do for not only the victims, but their families; it's pretty remarkable.

Tina and Eric value their time together and apart with their careers. While he still models on occasion, Eric's home away from home is Chula Vista Fire Station Number 1. He landed the coveted job well before they met. Part of his job is ensuring the equipment is ready to roll. Taking a few minutes, literally, to share about life at the fire house and with Tina in the mix, is golf a hot topic? [With a group of firefighters]

> ERIC: We talk about everything else but golf.
> JANE: What do you talk about?
> ERIC: Sports. We're all Chargers fans. Kurt's a Dodger fan, so we make him sleep in another room. *[alarm goes off]* We actually have a call.
> JANE: Oh my gosh.

TV time's over when Eric and company respond to what turns out to be a routine call.

> ERIC: I have a lot of passion for my job and she has a lot of passion for her job. She goes into her office, she—she works on her tips, she comes up with ideas, and it actually helps me, because I come home from the golf course and I say, "Look at my swing." She always has time to come look at my swing and she says, "You've been hitting the ball left all day." Which is right, and she shows me kind of a little tip, and she always has a good tip that makes sense. And so, I mean it's hard not to like that.
> JANE: She does know what she's talking about. *[laughing from Tina]*

Up next on *One on One*, golfing and talking with the three Mickelson siblings....

Phil Mickelson is a world-renowned golf pro who rarely does one-on-one interviews, but when I asked Tina Mickelson if we could figure out a way for me to sit down with her two brothers, Phil and Tim, to talk about her and her family's story—

they all said yes. With a four o'clock TV time, they even surprised Tina, arriving five minutes early on an autumn afternoon at Tina's golf course of choice, Santaluz.

JANE [greeting Phil and Tim]: Nice to meet you ...

Phil Mickelson was in between trips, back from South America, headed to China. Tim, the head coach at the University of San Diego, flew in that day from a golf get-away in Oregon. The three converged for an exclusive and special conversation.

JANE: Is this the first time the three of you have been interviewed all together at one time?

TINA: Yeah, Tim and I try to avoid that.

JANE: How does it feel?

PHIL: Yeah, you know, we—we have fun. We—we have—we grew up with a great family, and we have fun. We give each other a hard time, but we laugh about it. It's all in good fun. It's never mean spirited.

TINA: It's the way I think we show each other affection, at least I hope so, 'cuz there's a lot of it that goes on, and then, so it just—it's just our way of—of showing each other.

TIM: So when you dressed me up as a girl when I was four—how—how was that showing affection?

TINA: You were three.

TIM: Oh, three.

TINA: And I really wanted a sister.

In 2008 Tina is thirty-nine, the big sister, confident, cool, petite at 5'4". Phil, thirty-eight, is the middle child, a lefty from mirroring his father's golf swing as a kid. He gets his height, 6'3", and broad shoulders from their grandfather. And Tim, thirty-one, the baby they call the surprise, is strong and fit at 6'1".

JANE: Who was the loudest of the three of you?

TINA: Oh, him [pointing to Phil]. Yeah, Phil definitely.

JANE: Who was the funniest?

PHIL: Come on Jane.

TINA: Probably Philip.

Their dynamics play out playing the first hole, a par-five.

[Begin sequence of the siblings golfing over interview]

JANE: We've seen the video of when your dad first gave you guys a golf club when you were out there swinging away, and we watched the home movies over time with the three of you. What do you remember about those early days playing golf?

TIM: I just remember being, obviously a lot younger and—and losing a lot of money on the golf course to this one especially 'cuz I wouldn't say he would cheat, but he would fabricate scores against me, and he would tell me how I was going to miss.

PHIL: I felt I was doing him a favor.

TIM: Doing him a favor, of course, you say it all the time.

JANE: How were you doing him a favor?

PHIL: Well it was my job to—to toughen him up, and now he's a golf coach. He does the same stuff to his own players so …

TIM: Oh, you can't say that. They're gonna see this, you can't do that. It's true though; it's true.

JANE: And how did Tina fit into the equation?

TINA: Good or bad, they would follow me.

PHIL: I remember when I was a little kid and I wanted to eat some candy, so I asked my dad if I could have a little piece of candy, and he said no, I had to wait till after dinner. So Tina said, "Come here." So I followed her up and she takes me into her closet, and she brought her candy there, and she said, "Here, you eat this now and he'll never know." Well, my dad walked up and opened the closet door and said, "What are you guys doing?" I said, "Well, we're eating candy of course." So he grabs it and he threw all the candy in the fireplace. But you know who was most upset about that was Mom.

TINA: She cried.

JANE: When we were at your parents' backyard, your parents were showing us how you played the games.

[Mickelson family home]

MARY: That area there is where Philip would get behind a tree and create his own shot, saying he had to get up above the tree, and land it on the green, or he would get over different areas and say, "Okay, this is my third shot, I've got to get it through the branches over the other tree. So that's why you see him a lot on TV when there's an opening between trees, that he'll do that, and same thing with Tina.

PHIL: Yeah, I don't recall these two either breaking any windows. Did you ever break any, our next door neighbor windows?

TINA: I never did.

PHIL: Yeah, I broke two or three of them, I remember where I had to pay those back, so they didn't try all the risky stuff that I did uh …

[resume golfing]

They've had different levels of public exposure: Tina as a correspondent. Tim, a college star, coached USD to its first West Coast Conference Championship, and is on the Mid-Amateur circuit. But none as much as Phil, who knew at eight he wanted to be a pro, who was an outstanding high school and college player, evolving into one of the most exciting and best golfers of his generation.

PHIL: The greatest thing about Tina and Tim is that they are both supportive of what I've done, and they're both genuinely happy for my success, where a lot of times there's a sibling rivalry where people are jealous of others' success and don't want them to succeed. That's been the greatest thing, and why we have such a great relationship, because we are all supportive of each other's careers and we are all genuinely happy for each other when they are successful.

Tina with her husband Eric, Phil with his wife Amy and three children, Tim, who's not married: a trio of San Diego siblings who call San Diego home.

MARY: They're good, honest people. So when others notice that and come up to you to mention that, I think that's the proudest thing for us: what they're like as people.

PHIL: Don't you think parents have to say that?

TINA: Yeah, kinda!

TIM: I think we probably feel the same way about them, too.

TINA: You have families where they love each other, but they don't really like each other. Our family, we love each other, but we really like each other.

[Golfing]

A day of conversation and convergence to remember for the Mickelson family and the San Diego sports scrapbook ...

[Golf, finishing hole, taking picture]

JANE: Let's see, we have one, two, three ... Can we have age and beauty go first?

PHIL: Thank you.

JANE: Look how tiny Tina is next to her brother.

PHIL: Oh, you got to pull out the fat jokes, huh?

[Jane takes picture]

Finding her place in the game of golf may seem like par for the course for Tina Mickelson. But she attributes her short game and much of her success to something her parents witnessed time and again: Tina and her brothers embracing the idea of "practice makes perfect," and finding their professions in their passions, starting in their own backyard. I'm Jane Mitchell. Thank you for watching *One on One*.

"Jane worked tirelessly to maintain the consistency of who I really am without trying to stuff it into a preconceived idea. Her open mindedness contributed to the show in a big way. I also loved the fact that she included my relationship with my grandparents.... It was very interesting because my brothers and I have never ever been interviewed all together before. It was so much fun! I know it meant a lot to my parents, too. Hearing my brothers' answers to some of the questions was hilarious because it reminded me yet again how similar all three of us are ... Because I don't talk about my work a lot, most of the comments from family and friends started with, 'I never knew you did that,' or, 'Why didn't you ever tell me,' Jane did so much research and was so thorough, but the process was very enjoyable. I just really appreciated her professionalism. I trusted her completely to accurately portray who I am and who my family is; and that really says a lot!"

—Tina Mickelson, 2009

DAVID ECKSTEIN

"During the interview, I realized that this special was more about who I am as a person. I really liked how the fans got the opportunity to learn about my life off the field. I love playing video games, and I had never talked about that side of me in an interview before."

—DAVID ECKSTEIN, 2010

I n case you don't know, Eckstein is pronounced *Eck-STINE* as in Albert Einstein, not *Eck-STEEN*. David Eckstein might not be a physicist, but he is a smart, warm, and personable man. When I heard the San Diego Padres signed him in January 2009, I put him on the list for a *One on One* show. At first, it was just because I had heard his name, remembered his play, and learned he was the 2006 World Series MVP. He seemed feisty and fun. Then I learned his wife, Ashley, was an actress. It just kept getting better.

The Padres' media relations staff checked with the Ecksteins' agent right away for me and relayed they were a go. At spring training I introduced myself to David, and he was cordial and even excited about it. He gave me Ashley's contact information to coordinate details. She gathered pictures and videos, and we set a date for the interview. He preferred to do it when the team had a day off, so the first one that would work was Monday, May 18, my mother's eighty-fifth birthday.

The crew and I arrived at their rented condo near the beach a little before ten that morning. They were both in their sweats, which was fine, because it takes an hour or so to set up. David had co-authored a book *Have Heart* after he and the St. Louis Cardinals won the World Series. It was geared toward younger readers, but provided both an outline for me about his life and perspective and also a mechanism to weave throughout the show.

I interviewed David first, then Ashley and him together. They were open, expressive, and thoroughly engaged. Afterward, they made sure we had what we needed at the condo and for the production. We needed to see them together, other than sitting on a couch. I suggested a walk on the beach, but Ashley said that was not something they would normally do, so she suggested seeing David in his video game glory, playing Nintendo®. It is so old school, which fit him.

The other dimension of his story was his family's history of kidney disease. Three people in his immediate family had transplants. That impacted both his life and his *perspective* on life. This show allowed him to express that and allowed us to provide information on his cause, an important one—the need for organ donation.

A few weeks after the show debuted and the team was back in town, I saw David at batting practice. He intentionally walked over to me, thanked me for the envelope with a copy of the show and pictures, and said thank you for the show itself. In a very humble, sweet, almost embarrassed way, he told me he probably would not watch the show until after the season because, "That's just how I am about baseball and these kinds of things," but he said many people had told him nothing but good things about it.

Beyond that, he shared how something surprising happened. In the show, I had described how before every home game, David goes by the stands on the first base line for five minutes to sign autographs, and that he liked Nintendo®. So to his surprise, the first homestand back after the show debuted, he said when he came out by the first base line to sign autographs, several kids were there and told him, "You always sign for us, so we thought we'd do something nice for you." They gave him a few old Nintendo games. David was touched by that, and so was I. I asked him if I could share that story and with his okay, I first wrote about it in my *Channel 4 San Diego One on One* blog, including my applause to those boys: "Good going guys. Keep it up."

I was so impressed that those boys not only watched the show but also paid attention to the details and wanted to then do something for David. Some say what we do is "just TV," but that little moment—a microcosm of life, good will, and good people—is one reason I love my profession. It is not "just TV." In big and small ways, television has the potential for bridging gaps and bringing people together.

This is the script from the edition debuting June 26, 2009.

• • •

David Eckstein, a World Series MVP, is a spark plug for the San Diego Padres.

> **DAVID:** I love being in the situation when the game's on the line.

Off the field—a love story of how his Hollywood stars aligned.

> When you meet David Eckstein or even just watch him play, you immediately feel his positive aura and energy, his enthusiasm for life. Learn his background, and you understand why he beat the odds to become a big leaguer, how his family's health crises have made him a man on a mission—and then there's the Cinderella story of how he met his actress wife. But we begin with chapter one, David Eckstein, the underdog.
>
> Right off the bat, let's get the pronunciation of his name correct.

> **ECKSTEIN:** Definitely, it is Eckstein. It's a German lineage.

That's Eck*stine*—like Ein-stein. Of course, physicist Albert Einstein is famous for his theory of relativity, and specifically $E=MC^2$. Look it up and the formula implies that any small amount of matter contains a very large amount of energy. A patent description of David Eckstein …

> *[Game call: Diving stop—Eckstein!]*

Small, but mighty in the field …

> **ANNOUNCER:** *He just does everything right, everything.*

… and at the plate …

> **ANNOUNCER:** *And it is gone! Eck has tied it up!*

After being named the MVP of the 2006 World Champion St. Louis Cardinals, he co-wrote a book called *Have Heart*. Its tone is more for youngsters, its message, in his own words, good for any age.

> **DAVID** [reading from his book]: Ever since I picked up a bat, I've been the shortest player on the field. I stand just five feet seven inches. Some Little Leaguers are taller than me. Some baseball people said I'll never play in the major leagues. It's true that I don't hit many home runs. I'm not the fastest on the field, and my arm is just strong enough. However, I always had the desire to be the best baseball player I could be since I was old enough to hold a bat. I never gave up, and I never lost heart.

David Mark Eckstein was born January 20, 1975, in Sanford, Florida, a fighter from the beginning. As a baby, he didn't gain weight because of a blockage in his stomach. Emergency surgery saved his life, and as he writes, the scar is a "constant reminder of the miracle of life and how blessed I am to be alive."

> **DAVID:** I was very fortunate. I had two great parents.

His parents, Whitey and Pat, University of Florida grads, were school teachers who raised their five children in the Catholic church.

> **DAVID:** My oldest brother is Kenny, the next one in line is Christine, then goes Susan, then goes Ricky, then it's me. So …
>
> **JANE:** You're the baby.
>
> **DAVID:** I'm the baby.

David recalls how, because his father came from a broken home, he wanted a big family.

> **DAVID:** And he wanted us to be close together. And so whatever we did, we did as a family.
>
> **JANE:** And you loved baseball from the beginning.
>
> **DAVID:** Yes, that's what I've been told. I mean, it's something that I've always loved to watch, and I can remember like, around three, I was like, "Okay, name the starting lineup for the Pittsburgh Pirates."

His favorite player growing up? Dale Murphy. His first family vacation? A Braves game in Atlanta, and at five, a trip to the Baseball Hall of Fame in Cooperstown. They lived thirty-five miles from Disney World, a place for special occasions, but his favorite amusement park? His backyard, playing with his brother Rick who had a great arm.

> **DAVID:** So he would go back and just fire it in, and we had a game like, you know, I mean, he'd get as close as possible and throw it as hard as he can, and I had to hit him.

David played T-ball early, and while he felt he was ready for Little League early …

> **DAVID:** They said, "You're too young, you're not allowed to." And my mom wouldn't let me go back to the lower leagues, like, "You'll learn more here being the bat boy as opposed to playing T-ball again."
>
> **JANE:** Now were you always kind of the little kid, the smaller guy?
>
> **DAVID:** I always was the small guy.

He values his little league coach's philosophy. No bats at practice, just gloves.

> **DAVID:** You hit on the field when you played the game, but you learned how to play defense and be in the right spot at the right time, and that's how you win games. And we won championships every year.

His father rarely attended games.

> **DAVID:** My dad's very intense, very intense. And we're not allowed to fail. We have got to be the best, and so it was one of those things. He did not want to become one of those parents that, you know, you see screaming at the umpires, because if he was there, he probably would've been that guy. But it was something that we had to come home every night after the game and sit on—we had a little fireplace—sit on the fireplace and we had to go through detail for detail of what happened during the game.

565

JANE: How did you handle that kind of pressure though? 'Cause that's, you know, that's kind of a lot.

DAVID: It's a lot. Loved it. Loved it. Oh, gosh, I think that's, if you look at my abilities, if you look at who I am, without that, you wouldn't push yourself to be better every single day and expect to be the best.

While not in the stands before high school, when David was in ninth grade, something changed. His father had a stroke.

DAVID: And when he came back from the stroke, he is like, "I think I should go watch my sons play."

A conclusion perhaps also due to a compounding of health crises in the family. David's father was diagnosed as a teenager with kidney disease. But when David was in seventh grade, they learned it ran in the family when his sister Susan had complete kidney failure.

DAVID: And all of a sudden she's in an ambulance being rushed up to go—to get her stabilized and to get her onto dialysis as quick as possible. And then all of a sudden we all were getting shipped up to Gainesville to be tested to see if we had the same disease. My mom ends up donating to Susan, her kidney, and actually the day Susan was coming home from the hospital with my mom, they pulled into the driveway, they walk into the door, the phone was ringing. My mom picks up the phone and finds out that Christine and Kenny both were six months away from losing their kidneys. They would have to go on dialysis, and the whole process would happen again. And so that was something, at such a young age, it was very difficult to understand.

He and Rick were cleared of kidney disease, and David embraced the opportunity to make the most out of his life, writing that he "didn't smoke, drink alcohol, or go to parties." At Seminole High School, the honor student and infielder was a two-time All-State selection, a key part of their state championship team his junior year, and as a senior, he expected to be recruited by a Division One school, undeterred by what one junior college told him.

DAVID: I felt like in order for me to reach my goal, I had to play at the highest level, once again, going back to when I was younger. Because if, in my opinion, if the size I am, if I play at a lesser school, in people's minds, that there would be question. "Oh, the competition wasn't as good."

But no Division One offers came. So with good grades and a friend in the admissions office, he could enroll at his parents' alma mater, the University of Florida. But he'd have to earn a spot on the baseball team.

DAVID: I still had to walk on.

He hit in the cages, and when a second baseman transferred out, the coach told him …

DAVID: "You might not be that good, but at least you showed dedication enough to the team that you want to be a part of the team, because you're the only person that has showed up every single day." On the final day they go, "There's no guarantee, but here's a hat." Because I was wearing my own uniform. They were all in their University of Florida stuff, and I was wearing my own stuff the whole time.

He made the team, and by his sophomore year he earned the starting second base-man spot and scholarships for the rest of his education. He set five school records for offense and defense, often in the spotlight on college and local TV.

ANNOUNCER: *Eckstein driving in a team-leading thirty runs on the year.*

His favorite memory: making it to the College World Series where they placed third and playing with his brother, who had transferred to his school.

DAVID: Then the following year, having him coach me, 'cause he was a volun-teer coach, I mean, it was almost a dream come true at that stage of my life.

The next stage, a risk to make it to the majors. That's next on *One on One*, and later, meeting actress Ashley Drane, who's taken a starring role in his life....

At the end of his senior year at the University of Florida in 1997, David Eckstein took a calculated risk to make an impression on major league clubs. He chose to turn down an invitation to play with an independent league.

DAVID: If I go there, it shows these clubs that I'm willing, and think that's what type of player I am. And if I can't make it on a major league club, then I need to go to law school.

Just a few credits shy of his Political Science degree, his strategy paid off. He was drafted by the Boston Red Sox in the nineteenth round.

DAVID: And I just couldn't believe it happened so fast.

With some 500 players selected before him, he was hardly a high dollar pick.

DAVID: My signing bonus was a $1,000 and my father wanted a hat. So they gave my dad a hat. And so that was my—it was even like an adjustable one. It wasn't even like a fitted one! [laughing]

He moved through the minors as both a shortstop and rated as the best defensive second baseman in the eastern league by Baseball America in 1999, making only nine errors in 600 chances. That's a .985 percentage. As for hitting ...

DAVID: I was never a guy that people coached, if that makes sense, because I was never a priority. From the first day when I was in Little League, I hit.

As he writes in his book....

DAVID [Reading]: My toughest experience in the minor leagues happened when I was on the Triple-A Red Sox team in Pawtucket, Rhode Island ...

DAVID: I've hit .300 my whole career, every level, and about two weeks into it, I get a hitting coach that tells me I have to change the way I hit because I can't hit that way in the big leagues. And being from the disciplined family, from my father, in the sense that you always listen to your elders and the people that are above you, I said, "Yes, sir, how do you want me to hit?" And so I went through this process where I finally had to actually think about what I was doing at the plate, and it was the worst thing ever for me.

He went 2-for-97, dropping to a .160 batting average, and his brother Rick visited him.

DAVID: He watched me and said, "What are you doing? That is not you."

Despite his coach, he resumed his swing at practice.

ECKSTEIN: He looked at me and he said, "What are you doing?" And I looked at him, and this is probably one of the more defining moments of my life, when I said, I stood up to him. I said, "I apologize. I can't hit the way you want me to hit." And he looked at me and he goes, "I've never told you how to hit." And that was very crushing to me, knowing that I know he's going back into the meetings not taking the credit for what he had done. If I would've done great, he'd have been, "Yeah, I told him!" And that was like—that was a wake-up call to me to find out who I was and to be who I am.

That summer, the Red Sox put him on waivers, and the Angels claimed him and sent him to Triple-A.

DAVID: And it was complete and utter freedom when I was able to go over there, because they knew me from what I was in Double-A. And I got called into the office as soon as I got there and Garry Templeton was our manager, and he goes, "I just want you to be who you are."

Invited to big league camp in 2001, he proved himself. With Adam Kennedy hurt, Eckstein not only made the team, he got bigger news at an exhibition game from Manager Mike Sciosca about his major league debut.

DAVID: So I'm waiting right by the dugout to hit and Sciosca goes, "I just want you to know that you're gonna be starting." Opening Day, too.

Even with Kennedy's return, the Angels did something rare: They kept the energetic Eckstein to be short stop, a position he had only played in twenty-three games in the minors. Padres Manager Bud Black was the Angels pitching coach at the time.

BUD BLACK: Taking on that challenge—to change positions at the highest level possible, the big leagues—in a way that he didn't—he didn't skip a beat as a player. He got better as a player.

Eckstein set a rookie record, hit at the plate twenty-one times. In '02, the X-Factor became the first player in major league history whose first two grand slams came in consecutive games.

DAVID: It was a magical season. You know, we were never out of any game. We played as hard as any other club and we never gave up. And I think that was the testament to the final goal, which was winning the World Series.

After nagging injuries in 2003, he was part of the 2004 West Division Champion Angels, who did not tender him a contract after the season. So as a free agent ...

DAVID: Not knowing what was going to happen and basically two days later was able to sign a three-year deal with St. Louis.

He was popular, put up numbers, voted in '05 to the first of two All-Star teams. Late in '06, Eckstein, with a torn oblique and strained hamstring, was out until the playoffs, battling injuries from San Diego through to Detroit.

DAVID: Believing in one another. Finding a new hero every night …

Against the Tigers, he started off hitting 0-for-11. Then got eight key hits, named the World Series MVP.

DAVID: So it's one of those things that maybe later on in life, it'll mean a lot more to me than it does right now, because the most important thing was winning the World Series.

After another season in St. Louis, the shortstop signed with the Toronto Blue Jays in '08, traded in late August to the Diamondbacks, and that winter, the Padres called …

DAVID: They said, "We want you. We've got no money." You know …

Used to making three or four million a year, he signed for $850,000 to go back to his natural position.

DAVID: This is where I wanted to come. I wanted to come here, and I wanted to play second base, and they were giving me that opportunity.

[Spring training hitting and fielding]

DAVID: I just try to do stuff to find a way to make the pitcher throw a lot of pitches and find a way to get on base.

Number 3 David Eckstein is the epitome of taking one for the team.

BUD BLACK: This guy can hit, he can turn a double play, he fields grounders, he plays baseball the way it should be played, and he plays it with talent.

He chokes up on his bat to have control.

DAVID: I've always choked up, never choke up in batting practice. So I just pick up the bat and wherever it feels nice, that's where I keep it.

BUD BLACK: All the intangibles he does bring are great for the team, great for the guys in the dugout, in the clubhouse.

Intangibles, including leadership …

DAVID: I believe in the ability to show up every day ready to play with what you're supposed to do on hand to execute that. You don't go out there just to play and say, "Okay, we go home tonight, we're going to end our season, you know, September 30th." No, you play this game to win championships, and you want to be able to be a key contributor to a club to win a championship.

Even in his ninth major league season …

DAVID: I call my father after every game and he's like, "Not good, come on, you gotta get better. I waited up for sixteen innings to only see you get one hit?"

JANE: Does he tell you that he's proud of you, too?

DAVID: Oh, yeah. Oh, yeah, he always does. He always tells me that. I mean, every conversation ends with, "I'm proud of you and I love you."

Good words, especially considering 2003. His father had to go back on dialysis, turning down David and his brother Rick's offer to donate a kidney …

DAVID: Not only because of the careers that we were leading, but also the fact that there's definitely a possibility when we have kids that we could pass on the trait to our kids, and just having the ability to donate to our kids.

Injuries shut him down by the end of the season, but as he writes …

DAVID [reading]: "Something wonderful did happen in September of 2003."

Her name is Ashley Drane. She grew up just south of Orlando. Her father worked at Disney World.

ASHLEY: He was in the Food and Beverage Department. He bought all those, like, giant turkey legs that people walk around with and eat.

Athletic, but by twelve, she fell in love with acting. After a brief stint at the Cincinnati Conservatory of Music, she followed her dream to Hollywood.

ASHLEY: And at the time I was nineteen, but I looked thirteen. With my connections, they said, "You know, you'll never have this opportunity again where you'll be older than eighteen but look so young."

She landed roles on the Disney Channel, on Nickelodeon, and starred on *Blue Collar TV*.

So how did actress Ashley meet the X-Factor? It's like a Disney ride, so hold on. Her friends knew they were from the same area and had a six-degrees-of-separation type connection with someone who had played college ball with David.

ASHLEY: He sounded great, but I just brushed it off 'cause it's like, well, how am I supposed to meet a Major League Baseball player? You know, that doesn't seem so easy.

Then she heard him interviewed after the Angels won the World Series.

ASHLEY: He was talking about his morals and values, and I remember watching it and thinking, *Yeah, my friends are right, I think I would get along with him. He seems like a cool guy.* But again, they'd just won the World Series, so I'm like, oh yeah, right. Like now there's no way I can meet this guy. So I just brushed it off. About a year and a half later, I ended up going to an Angels game and this is the part of the story that sometimes he doesn't like me telling because …
DAVID: Now you want to hear it.
JANE: Of course.

Her friend bought her an Eckstein shirt to wear in their front row seats.

ASHLEY: And so whenever he made a great play or he got a hit, it was just like, "Oh, hey, that's your boy," you know. And about halfway through the game, one of the Angels had scored. And I was just looking over at the commotion and David happened to look over and we made eye contact. And we locked eyes for about five seconds. That's the part he doesn't want me to tell ...

JANE: Aww....

ASHLEY: ... 'cause it sounds like he broke focus.

DAVID: It was something that I was very disappointed in myself that it made an impression on me. So ...

ASHLEY: Yeah, and it wasn't like it was, like, this romantic thing.

DAVID: No.

Six weeks later she needed a date to the premiere of an independent movie. And in true Hollywood fashion, her publicist contacted the Angels' media relations director, who suggested that David call her.

DAVID: Because in the email they described her as angelic.

But he wouldn't go to the premiere on Thursday without meeting her first.

DAVID: I go, there's no way. I wasn't really the Hollywood type.

The one day they could meet—that Monday. This is where it gets magical, based on her fourth grade teacher's comment.

ASHLEY: I've been waiting ever since I was ten for my golden birthday because he told me something special would happen. And it turns out that Monday was September 22nd, my twenty-second birthday, and he was number 22.

A month into their dating, she revealed they had seen each other earlier that summer.

ASHLEY: He goes, "Understand this, the only reason I remember it is because that's the first time I've ever looked into the stands, and I was so mad at myself."

Regardless ...

ASHLEY: We're two peas in a pod ...

DAVID: Definitely.

ASHLEY: ... I guess you could say.

DAVID: Yeah.

Ashley adores *Alice in Wonderland*, so David proposed to her by putting a ring inside a Cheshire cat purse, and their wedding at Epcot Center was truly a fairytale, captured even in celebrity and wedding magazines. Their happily ever after is also based on their common Catholic faith.

DAVID: Definitely, there's a higher power watching over us, and that we try to live our life the right way and in respect of Him.

Faith has helped during his family's medical challenges. Over time, his father, sister, and brother have all received kidney donations.

DAVID: Our family has been stricken with the kidney disease, but there's a lot more organs that are in your body that can help someone else out.

Teamed up with Donate Life, he urges people to check that donor box on their driver's license. His compassion is evident, part of the Padres community outreach and at home games, like clockwork, he puts down his glove and signs autographs for five minutes before his final warm up. An example of what Ashley calls his self-lessness.

ASHLEY: It's about is his mom taken care of? Am I taken care of? You know, or his sisters, or nieces, nephews—do they have everything they need? And that's what matters.

And as much as he appreciates the beautiful view of the Pacific from their rented condo, he is thrilled to have one little toy …

DAVID: I love playing the old school Nintendo®, and my favorite game is Baseball Stars.

He lost his childhood Nintendo® sets in a move, so Ashley surprised him by tracking some down on eBay.

DAVID: I have the original Opening Day starting lineup for the Padres, and I go out and play other teams.

They lead busy lives, with David playing and Ashley's career, now the voice of a character in *Star Wars: The Clone Wars* on the Cartoon Network.

ASHLEY: I will fly in to do my job, and then I'm on the next flight out to go be with him. I think we want to be together.

And with children in their enchanted equation someday, you can imagine there will be lots of bed-time stories, including his own.

DAVID [reading]: Reflecting on my life and the struggles my family has endured, I am reminded to cherish every moment, and to persevere no matter what. That is why I play so hard. It is what having heart is all about. It means that no matter what happens, no matter what curveball life may throw you, you never lose faith, you never lose respect for yourself or others, and you

"You never know how you are going to be received when you go to a new team. There is always that nervous feeling like you would have on the first day of school or at a new job. … We were surprised that [Jane] would pick us, being as though we were brand new to the team. It gave us a very welcoming feeling from the beginning. Jane has a vision for what she wants the special to be before the day of taping. She comes extremely prepared, and knows exactly the right questions to ask to create a truly great product. Being new to San Diego, I had no idea how many people watched and looked forward to Jane's *One on One* specials. People still come up to me today and tell me how much they enjoyed the show."

—David Eckstein, 2010

never lose the belief that every second of your life is worth giving the best effort you can. It's all about having heart.

David Eckstein, bold and fearless, has found his place in the majors. Even so, to him, the game, as in life, is about the bigger picture; saying if you make it about you, you'll always be searching for happiness, because it's hard to celebrate alone. I'm Jane Mitchell. Thank you for watching *One on One.*

ANTHONY GWYNN, JR.

"One on One gave us fans a perspective of the other side of the players and who they are off the field. Waiting for the game to air during a rain delay, we could always count on the *One on One* show. I felt like the person she was interviewing was sitting in my living room with me, and the next time I saw that person at the ballpark, I felt like I was even closer to them because of *One on One."*

—TONY GWYNN, JR., 2010

May 21, 2009, I was at my Channel 4 desk. An email popped up from the Padres announcing that Anthony Gwynn, Jr. had been traded from the Milwaukee Brewers to the San Diego Padres. While it had been more than a year since I talked with him, I sent him a congratulatory text and received an immediate response of thanks. The next day I went to batting practice to see him, and there he was with number 18 on his jersey. He gave me a big hug as I congratulated him again. "I think I feel a *One on One* coming, and this time on you," I said. He agreed. I took pictures to document the significant day.

As the season progressed and I featured other players I had already planned on, I looked forward to coordinating with Anthony. I will probably always call him

Anthony, because that's what his father calls him, and that's how I was first introduced to him at his home in 1997, the day I met his father, Tony Gwynn, for the first time.

A dozen years later, I took a mental inventory of the pictures, video, and interviews we had in our archives that would help tell his story: Anthony shooting baskets at their backyard in 1997; the times he was on hand for his father's events, interviewing him at San Diego State as a student

on his father's team, and in Cooperstown, when his father was inducted into the National Baseball Hall of Fame. I was already anticipating how hard it would be to capture all this in a half hour show, considering his famous father was such a big part of Anthony's journey.

In July, at the field, Anthony and I coordinated a date when the team was home for the sit-down interview with him and his wife, Alyse. Then I went upstairs to the broadcaster's booth where Tony, Sr. was preparing to announce the game that night. I told Tony that Anthony had graciously and enthusiastically accepted the invitation to do a *One on One*, so now I needed to interview him and Anthony's mother, Alicia. Tony replied in his classic voice, trying to halfway sarcastically squirm out of the interview, "Do we have to do another one of these?" I said, "This is about your son, not you, so, yes, you do!" "Okay, you're right. Okay, let's do it." Of course he was going to do it. He was so proud of his son, plus, he knew I would not take no for an answer.

The day of our shoot at Anthony and Alyse's home, we arrived before ten in the morning. (It was fitting photographer Dan Roper was on this shoot, considering he shot our first Gwynn show in 1997.) Their home was a three-story, two-bedroom townhouse in the middle of a beach town. It was a tight squeeze for our cameras with their big couches, big-screen TV, and piles of baby toys. Its coziness was evidence of how he was still climbing the major league ladder and living prudently, within his means.

As expected, Anthony shared about the good times growing up around baseball and his father, and eloquently elaborated about details of his childhood. His voice and mannerisms were so similar to his father. I could not help but have déjà vu, but we got past that and kept talking. Also like his father, he was forthright about challenging moments in his life. One revealing topic was how he could have jeopardized his potential career had he not taken his parents' advice regarding school. I had never heard this, nor had he shared it before, but he was intent that I realized—and fans, especially kids, realized—how his decision to improve his grades was significant to his path. His admission and humility were admirable.

His beautiful, athletic, and down to earth wife, Alyse, was not accustomed to the limelight and a little hesitant when we talked in advance of the day. I had promised I would make it easy and comfortable for her, and she agreed because it was important to her husband. She did well, and seeing them together, I could sense their strength of character and compatibility. Another morning, we videotaped the family walking to the park. Their two girls were wearing matching brown and pink outfits with rhinestones decorating their father's jersey number, 18, on their tops. Asked just to play as they usually do, Anthony—a tall, healthy, ballplayer—sat down inside a little pink playhouse with his oldest daughter to have a pretend tea party. The visual was precious and genuine, and a perfect juxtaposition of him *as* a father and him *with* his father, in pictures from years before.

When we later went to his childhood home in Poway, Anthony's mother had boxes and albums of pictures waiting for me to peruse, and Tony and Alicia were beaming with pride. The challenge in producing this edition was two-fold. First, Tony, Alicia, and Anthony are wonderful storytellers, and it was fun to listen to them. Choosing which stories to include at length was difficult with so many options. I had to edit for time, deciphering which were the most significant to Anthony's journey. Second, I had to keep in mind this was *Anthony's* story, and put more emphasis on that, while keeping the perspective that he was from a well-known family with a superstar father. I felt a responsibility to the Gwynn family and the fans who had watched him grow up. It was rewarding to see how the Gwynns appreciate how the fans have embraced the younger Gwynn, too, as he is proud and respectful of where he's come from, while making a name for himself.

This is the script from the edition debuting October 2, 2009.

• • •

Anthony Gwynn, the son of Padre great, is grateful making a name for himself.

> **TONY, JR.:** I've got nothing but love since I've been out here, and it's a blessing, it truly is.

And has his hands full with his girls.

> Anthony Gwynn's trade to the San Diego Padres in May of 2009 makes for one of those feel-good, full circle, hometown stories. But if you think being the son of Hall of Famer Tony Gwynn gets you an automatic ticket to the top, listen to Anthony's journey and how he could have jeopardized his chance at a baseball career had he not heeded some sage advice.

> Anthony Gwynn, Jr. grew up in baseball watching and learning from his father, Tony Gwynn. And at the ceremonies the night number 19 retired in 2001? Seeing Anthony running into centerfield as his father had twenty years before was both symbolic and prophetic. Over the years, the younger Gwynn's been by his father's side on television, in magazines, even *One on One* as we've documented moments in Mr. Padre's stellar life and career.

> *TONY GWYNN, SR. [at home answering phone]: Hello?*

> *CALLER: Tony I'm calling to tell you that the baseball writers have elected you into the Hall of Fame. Congratulations.*

> *TONY: Wow.*

> *[Applause]*

Now, it's Anthony's turn. Anthony Keith Gwynn, Jr. was born October 4, 1982, the day after his father's major league debut season. He was big at eight pounds, fifteen ounces.

> *[Tony and Alicia's home]*
> **ALICIA:** And I remember the big, broad shoulders that he had. But he was actually a really delightful baby, very busy …
> **TONY, SR.:** He never sat still, you know, just like his dad. He was, you know, always inquisitive, looking, you know, take stuff off the table.

Beginning that next spring training, Tony's wife Alicia went to games with baby in tow.

> **ALICIA:** He'd look at Da-Da, Daddy, you know, and so he—I took him every day. We never missed a game his first three years, never missed the game.

And acquiring a few nicknames …

> **TONY, JR.:** The first one, really, that everybody called me was a nickname that my dad had given me, and that was "Pooh-Pooh."
>
> **TONY, SR.:** Pooh-Pooh? [laughs]
>
> **JANE:** Where did that come from?
>
> **TONY, SR.:** It wasn't 'cause he did it in his diapers, it was just, you know, when he was born and we brought him home that first night, I really didn't know what to call him. Eventually he said, "Dad, you know, you just can't call me Pooh-Pooh no more, you know."
>
> **TONY, JR.:** Little T, Little Tony, Anthony, Antny …

With the arrival of his sister Anisha two and a half years later …

> **TONY, JR.:** This little girl in my life? I remember all the attention left me. I remember that part.

As pioneers of using video to study Tony's swing back in 1983, little Tony learned to press the play button early.

> **TONY, JR.:** I'd see him on the film and I would get up and try to replicate what he was doing. And I do nothing left-handed. I have no coordination in my left hand at all. But that, I think that's the reason why I became a left-handed hitter.
>
> **ALICIA:** And then he would go outside and he would want you to play baseball with him, but he always wanted to hit a home run. I said, "Baby, you can't hit a home run all the time." "Yes, I can." You know, and he was like, "Deep to right field, way back, way back, gone!" All the time.
>
> **TONY, SR.:** "Oh, doctor!"
>
> **ALICIA:** "Oh, doctor!" Yeah, you know.
>
> **TONY, SR.:** Yeah.
>
> **ALICIA:** He knew exactly.
>
> **TONY, SR.:** He was—he was the player. He was the announcers, and he was the crowd. 'Cause he'd say, "Oh, doctor! Hhhhhh …" [crowd noise]

Among Anthony's first memories, going to the player's clubhouse …

> **TONY, SR.:** You come in the clubhouse, you know, you got rules to follow. You follow the rules.
>
> **TONY, JR.:** Be quiet and don't bug anybody. You know, he was really big on that. The second one was stay out of everybody's way.

Anthony had a rule, too.

> **TONY, JR.:** Once my dad came to the plate, I mean, it was—I needed complete silence, so if there was people around me talking, and whether they were my family members or just fans, they got a stare from me if they were talking during his at-bat, like, I needed to have absolute quiet, and I needed them to understand that.

In 1993, when Anthony was eleven, his grandfather died of a heart attack. Tony was forever changed, knowing their last conversation the night before had been an argument with no chance for resolution.

TONY, JR.: So I think from that point on, though, my dad really made that effort to have a different kind of relationship than he had with his father. You know, that's when we began to start traveling together, just me and him. That's when we began to just talk more about life in general, you know, growing up.

Anisha also joined some of their road trips.

TONY, SR.: When my dad passed, I kind of realized, you know, life is short. I really want them to be a part of, you know, of my life and what I do. And we had the time of our lives. I mean, these kids—those two loved room service. They loved jumping on the bed. They loved pillow fights. I mean, we did all of that.

TONY, JR.: I'd say probably right around the time I was in like fifth grade, it kind of dawned on me that, you know, my dad was a little different than everybody else's father. You know, because my dad was the subject at school.

Attending the private Francis Parker through eighth grade ...

TONY, JR.: I'm getting to go to all these different places and watching him play, and I go back to school on Monday and people are asking me questions about it. So it was always cool, but it never really—I don't know if it never really sunk in, but I just always looked at him as my dad, you know.

But his mother acknowledged the magnitude of what their All-Star, Gold Glove, batting titled-dad was doing.

ALICIA: And I told Little Tony, "No matter what you do, you are always going to be Tony Gwynn's son." And I said, "And that's okay. You use it to your advantage, but you create a name for yourself."

With fame, at times compliments and criticisms about his father or the team ...

TONY, SR.: He didn't let it bother him. He just was going to go ahead and do what he wanted to do.

ALICIA: Yeah, he pretty much made the most of it, but as long as he kept that humility. And I always taught my kids, you know, you are blessed to be here, so don't take it for granted.

JANE: Just describe for us what it was like as a kid, sitting there in the stands, 20, 30, 50,000 people, and your dad comes up to the plate.

TONY, JR.: It gives me chills really, thinking about it. You know, it was—my dad has gotten so much love from the people of San Diego that, you know, when those moments came up and the crowd started, you know, screaming and yelling, I'd always get chills, even as a little boy.

After years of Little League, Anthony made the transition to a big league field as a teenager ...

TONY, JR.: After I kind of proved that I can catch a fly ball in the outfield without hurting myself …

Allowed to shag balls during batting practice, even so, baseball wasn't his first love.

TONY, JR.: I'm a huge Laker fan, so I grew up watching Magic Johnson and those guys play, and I really developed a love for the game of basketball because I was always playing it.

Basketball became his focus when switching to the public Poway High School, closer to home, with kids he knew and a good basketball program.

TONY, JR.: After my eighth grade season the varsity coach came up to me and was like, "We want to put you in our program," and, you know, from there it kind of just took off.

By his sophomore year, the point guard helped his team become Palomar League Champions. A standout on the hardwood, but not in baseball, early on, by his junior year …

TONY, JR.: I was on the cusp of just quitting and not playing anymore before the season started. And kind of went to my dad and he was like, you know, "Why not just play? You've got something—it gives you something else to do." You know, "You never know what could happen."

Or what could *not* happen. Up next on *One on One*, Anthony Gywnn's ah-ha moment that changed the course of his career. And a Gwynn hit some fans would rather forget....

By the time Anthony Gwynn was at Poway High School, he'd seen his Uncle Chris help the Padres clinch the West in 1996 and the team become National League Champions.

JERRY COLEMAN *(announcer): And the Padres drape the National League flag around their shoulders for 1998. Oh doctor!*

Facing the New York Yankees in the World Series in '98 …

JANE: So how much did you talk about baseball with him?

TONY, SR.: Other than my—what I was doing, what the Padres were doing, and what I was trying to do—not much.

TONY, JR.: And I think that's also why I was able to establish a love for the game kind of by myself without, you know, him telling me different things, or him pushing me in a certain direction, to kind of allow me to realize why I liked the game.

JANE: And why did you realize that?

TONY, JR.: I just liked the competition.

Whether through osmosis, talent, or just timing the baseball, the late bloomer bloomed in the Palomar League, one of the nation's toughest.

TONY, JR.: I hit .400 my junior year and got invited to the Area Code Games. And at this point, you know, I'm still pretty much all about basketball.

That Area Code Games Showcase August of '99, scheduled just as his father broached a milestone: his 3,000th hit. Anthony joined his family in St. Louis ...

>   TONY, JR.: Hoping he would get the hits there. It didn't work out.
>
>   *ANNOUNCER CALL: Number 2,999!*

Next stop, Montreal ...

>   *ANNOUNCER CALL: Line drive centerfield. There it is! Number 3,000 for Tony Gwynn!*
>
>   TONY, JR.: And it's funny how things work. You know, I have to leave to go to showcase, I miss my dad's 3,000th hit. But I'm pretty positive: if I don't go to that showcase, I'm not sitting here with you, talking right now.

Within days after what he calls a "decent showing" at the showcase, college coaches were on the phone.

>   TONY, JR.: From Miami, from Arizona State, but there's one problem. At this point, I'm not taking my school very seriously. And I think that is when it dawned on me that I needed to kick it in gear 'cause I was in pretty tough shape academically.

With a GPA just below 2.0 ...

>   ALICIA: Little Tony was lazy, and I will never forget. I finally got him—I said, "You know what, if you can't do your work, then you can't play any sports; that's the bottom line."
>
>   TONY, JR.: And the best decision my mom ever made was hiring my tutor. Her name was Maureen Roadman, and she played a huge factor.

Most colleges stopped showing interest, uncertain if he'd turn around part of a difficult time, not because of the external expectations ...

>   TONY, JR.: It was more so the disappointment that I felt like my mom and my dad had, and I didn't want to be the kid—I didn't want to mess up anything.

His grades improved even with a rigorous senior year.

>   TONY, JR.: Six classes at school and then I had three more classes in night school that I had to go to. And this is all during basketball season.

At first, Anthony didn't want to be compared to his father, the legend at San Diego State. So he committed to Cal State Fullerton.

>   TONY, JR.: That's when my dad started putting a little birdie in my ear about maybe wanting to coach. You know, Coach Dietz was real adamant about when my dad retired, he wanted him to be the one to take over the job.

Anthony was persuaded by the Aztec coaches and wanted the chance to maybe play for his dad. He and Tony both say it was Anthony's choice.

>   TONY, JR.: I graduate, end up changing my mind from Cal State Fullerton to San Diego State. And ...
>
>   JANE: Thinking that he might end up there.
>
>   TONY, JR.: With that in the back of my head.

Out of high school, Anthony could have been an Atlanta Brave. But despite being offered a substantial $400,000, he didn't like being drafted in the thirty-third round, the 1,000th pick.

> TONY, JR.: I thought I was going to be drafted a little bit earlier, but it didn't work out that way. But let's just say I had a huge chip on my shoulder from that point on. And as I went into college, I carried it with me.

With pride and determination ...

> TONY, JR.: I was going to improve that draft number regardless of what happened.
> JANE: So how'd you do that?
> TONY, JR.: I got to work. I got to work.

Receiving academic All-Conference honors and invited to, then cut from, team USA.

> TONY, JR.: Okay, that's just another log I can throw on the fire.

The summer of 2001, Tony Gwynn announced he was retiring, so Anthony joined him on the road as teams said thanks and farewell.

> TONY, JR. [television interview in dugout]: It's been a great experience so far. I don't know how emotional it's going to be for me, but I know it's going to be pretty emotional for him.

And at home ...

> *[On field ceremony]*
>
> *BOB COSTAS [announcing]: Just like that night in 1982, there's a Gwynn starting in centerfield tonight. Along with Tony's original Padres teammates, in center tonight, that's young Anthony Gwynn.*
>
> TONY, JR.: It was awesome to be a part of.
>
> TONY, SR. [addressing crowd]: Thank you. Thank you. Thank you.

The next day they were both at San Diego State, Anthony a sophomore. Tony the volunteer hitting coach, later named head coach in 2003.

> TONY, SR.: For me it's a blessing to watch him do what he does every day.
> JANE: You treat him the same?
> TONY, SR.: Absolutely.
>
> *[From San Diego State interview]*
>
> JANE: What are your aspirations?
>
> TONY, JR.: Oh I definitely want to play in the big leagues some day. I'm a long ways away right now. I need to work on a few things. Hopefully my body will mature a little more.

He had improved his batting average every year up to .360. What helped? A trip, in '02, to the premier collegiate summer baseball program, the Cape Cod Baseball League ...

TONY, JR.: I think everybody knew I could play defense, but nobody really knew how I could handle the bat.

Come draft day 2003 he was on San Diego's radar with potential pressure to follow in his father's footsteps right away.

TONY, JR.: So I'm a little skeptical about that, but second pick comes around and the Milwaukee Brewers take me. And I'm excited. I've reached my goal, you know, I wanted to better than a 1000th pick, and I did.

It's a mid September morning and Anthony Gwynn and his wife, Alyse, have loaded up their stroller with their dog Coast, and daughters Makela and Jordan. This outing is a long way from when he was first drafted by the Brewers in 2003.

JANE: You're starting the minor leagues and probably people are saying here's a guy who's just going to …

TONY, JR.: Cruise right through, started off great. Started off good, you know.

But in his next full season, 2004, he struggled …

TONY, JR.: I think the first three months was probably the most difficult, not necessarily on the field, just being lonely.

While he worked on his game, he also dealt with a matter of his heart: Alyse Malek. They met when he was in college and she was visiting a friend on campus.

TONY, JR.: We talked for the entire night, pretty much, you know, in the dorm rooms, just about life, what she did, what her interests were.

Discovering that she was adopted by a single mother with a son …

ALYSE: She just kind of explained it as a, you know, a thing that she was—it was almost more special for her because she was able to pick me, and she was a single mom, and the love that she gave me was just incredible.

She loved soccer, and after Rancho Bernardo High School, she played with the San Diego Surf soccer league. When they met, baseball was not on her sports fan radar …

ALYSE: Basketball was what I watched on TV, so I had no clue of how huge his dad was.

TONY, JR.: You've always got to have your guard up for who's being genuine and who's not. And the fact that she didn't really know who my father was made it a lot easier.

But it took him until 2004 to commit.

TONY, JR.: I realized I didn't want to be by myself all the time.

He says that stability improved his game, having Double-A and Triple-A back to back All-Star years, and by July of 2006 was called up to the majors.

TONY, SR.: I know I was almost in tears when he said, "Hey, Dad, I made it! I made the big." I—and I was like—I was screaming in here.

His parents and sister made it to Arizona for his debut.

[Interview of Tony in stands at Anthony's big league debut: Man, I flew across the desert, and here we are.]

TONY, JR.: The first thing that I really remember is walking in and seeing my name on the back of my jersey with my number, my own number. It's my own thing right now. This isn't my Pops' last name or his number, this is me.

His first major league hit coming a few days later in San Francisco ... then twenty-four years to the day of his father's first major league hit against the Giants ...

JANE: Which was a double.

TONY, JR.: Which was a double. Which was off of the announcer for the Giants at the time, so there's all kinds of eerie things going on at this point.

That season was topped off by their wedding. As for baseball, frustration, sent back to the minors by mid-summer.

TONY, JR.: What else do I gotta do? I'm hitting .300 at this point, I'm scoring some runs, I'm doing everything you guys are asking me to do; what do I gotta do to stay?

The silver lining? Being in Cooperstown to support his father at his induction into the Baseball Hall of Fame. Anthony Gwynn understands baseball's pivotal moments. He was part of one, ironically, the spoiler on the Padres' push to clinch a playoff spot ...

[Anthony Gwynn singles to right for the Brewers]

And while the Padres went to Colorado to be defeated in a tiebreaker, Anthony returned to San Diego.

TONY, JR.: I wake up the next morning and answer the door and it's the UPS® guy. And the first words out of his mouth were, "Why'd you have to do that to the Padres?" You know?

His hopes to prove himself in 2008 were stifled with a pulled hamstring on day three. He eventually healed in time to make the Brewers' playoff roster.

TONY, JR.: I'm just enjoying the fact that I'm in this clubhouse in September, getting to be around this atmosphere.

In 2009, he missed half of camp due to shoulder pain. The Brewers put him on waivers. When no team claimed him, he went to the Triple-A club in Nashville thinking ...

TONY, JR.: It was going to be a chance for me to show the other teams out there that I could play.

And on May 21, the usual manager-player protocol went out the window. Padres owner John Moores called Anthony's mother.

ALICIA: He said, "We picked up Little Tony, Tony, Jr.," and, I mean, all I could do was cry ...

Tony was in Texas with the Aztecs for the Mountain West Conference baseball tournament.

TONY, SR.: She said, "Your son is coming home." And I said, "What?" "Your son just got traded." And I said, "To who?" And she said, "The Padres." And I said—I can't even repeat what I said. [laughing]

Then he dialed Anthony on the road in Portland.

TONY, JR.: He's like, "You sitting down?" I'm like, "Yeah, I just told you, I'm eating breakfast. I'm sitting down." And he goes, "All right, well, um ..."

TONY, SR.: I said, "Has anybody talked to you today?" He said, "No, why?" And I said, "'Cause you just got traded."

TONY, JR.: And so the next question was, "Well, where to?"

TONY, SR.: So I said, "The Padres!!" [arms in air] I'm screaming. [laughing]

TONY, JR.: And I'm like stunned. And I felt like God blessed me with another opportunity to not only get to play in the big leagues, but to have a chance to play in my home town, you know, with my family.

Not only his parents, now doting grandparents, his sister, and cousins he grew up with, but also the fans who have watched him grow up, as he recalls getting in the game that night in the 9th inning ...

TONY, JR.: I get a standing ovation, which was chills. Sent chills down my arms and my back.

ANNOUNCER: *Left field! Base hit! Padres win it!*

TONY, JR.: And end up scoring the game-winning run. And like, from that point, I just felt so comfortable, like, I think most people assumed when I came over here that it would be added pressure that I was playing in the same city my dad played. In reality, I just felt more relaxed.

TONY, SR.: I'm not a good fan, to be honest, 'cause I am pulling so hard for him. I like to scream at the TV.

While he often videotaped number 15's basketball games, now he's making up for the youth baseball games his schedule rarely allowed him to attend.

TONY, SR.: It's been great having him home. I can tell you that.

Whether in a pink clubhouse with his children or in the Padres' clubhouse with his father, a lot of love runs in the Gwynn family. Anthony opted to be number 18 rather than take the Padres' offer to wear his father's number 19 ...

TONY, JR.: I felt like that was out of respect to my dad that that number stay retired.

TONY, SR.: Well, that's my son. You know, he's a very thoughtful—thinks about other people before he thinks of himself.

Regardless of their similarities or differences on the field, Anthony has long realized ...

TONY, JR.: I want to be, I need to be, exactly like him. I mean, as a professional athlete, I think that is the way to go. You know, never heard anything bad about my dad getting in trouble, never heard him going out and doing anything other than playing baseball and being a good family man. And that's what it's all about.

Like father, like son.

> **ALYSE:** He's a good, good person. And he's just so kind to everybody, and treats everybody as equals, and with tons of respect, and I just admire that about him.

But he is still carrying that chip to prove to those who passed on him, his potential as a major league player.

> **TONY, JR.:** I still want to show people that's just what I can be.
>
> **JANE:** Maybe you were just meant to be here.
>
> **TONY, JR.:** I think you're—I think you're absolutely right. It just—I mean, the pieces just have fallen into place when it didn't seem like there was no way they could fall into place sometimes, and I'm just really grateful in being here.

He may have grown up with a lot of nicknames, but now he'll answer to most anything—Anthony, Tony, Junior—as long as there's a first name paired with Gwynn. He's proud of that name, not for its cachet, but because of what it's taught him, especially when he struggled in school. Something his grandfather told his father, and his father told him, "If you work hard, good things will happen."

> I'm Jane Mitchell. Thank you for watching *One on One*.

"From my childhood to becoming an adult, I remember Jane Mitchell being the same then as she is today. I remember as a child saying to my sister, Anisha, 'NeNe, there's that lady that's on TV!' I was always excited because I thought she was a star then, and I still think she's a star now. She is the consummate professional, and really made a difference for the San Diego Padres with her *One on One* show. It gave us fans a perspective of the other side of the players and who they are off the field. . . . All the *One on Ones* in my dad's archive are fond memories of growing up in baseball and watching Dad evolve into a Hall of Famer. When I became a Padre and Jane interviewed me, she made me feel comfortable, as if she had known me all of my life. It was cool to see the end result—getting to see my children playing, getting to see my family and how everyone else views me; whereas when you're going through the process you're not necessarily getting to hear those things from different people, so it was nice. It was a good experience. I was a Jane Mitchell fan then, as a kid, and I'm still one."
—Tony Gwynn Jr., 2010

PARK VIEW: 2009 LITTLE LEAGUE WORLD SERIES CHAMPIONS

"I would like to thank you for the extraordinary job you did capturing my experience in the Little League World Series. The show has put my memories in words and pictures and is now something I can relive or share with grandchildren, God willing. As with all your shows, you captured the emotional side of the story that showed how special this group of kids and families really was. I am honored and fortunate to have had you be a part of this great experience that will live in my mind and in your *One on One* show forever. Thank you."

—COACH RIC RAMIREZ, 2010

After I produced the Anthony Gwynn show at the end of 2009, I felt his would be the final back-story and script for my book. It was the perfect bookend to the anthology covering the first thirteen seasons of *One on One*. How fitting, I thought, to have the son of one of my most significant subjects from the first year, and many subsequent years after, be the last one in this amazing journey. Then I met twelve more stellar boys, and my new conclusion was how perfectly fitting to end with rising stars in their own right, regardless if they ever wear a major league uniform. That Anthony and others were a part of this show made it all the more imperative I include their inspiring story.

On a beautiful summer day in 2009, I was working out at my local gym. The doors were wide open, letting the ocean breeze flow in. It was a welcome respite from the workweek, in a summer in which the Padres had been struggling on the field. Beyond the team's standings, I was excited to be focusing on the Anthony Gwynn show that would debut toward the end of the season. A man at the gym who knew I covered sports said, "How about those PV kids? Aren't they amazing?" *PV kids? What was he referring to?* "The Little League team from Chula Vista—they're doing great, right?" *Oh, right.*

Usually, I ask when I don't feel dialed in to something, but this time I didn't feel it was that significant. It was Little League, after all. I didn't feel bad that I wasn't up on everything happening in the non-Padres baseball world, I just thought, *Good for them.*

Fast-forward a few weeks. It was Saturday, August 29, and I was having a barbeque at my house for some friends. I thought it odd so many people were running late to my party. When Cathy Brown, my first guest, arrived, she said she had driven quickly between commercial breaks so she wouldn't miss any of the game. Then I remembered the Little Leaguers from Park View were playing. We turned on the TV and watched the last innings with joy. When they won and were headed to the World Series Championship game, we cheered, and within a half hour, the rest of my guests arrived. Several of them had been home, glued to the television set, watching the Blue Bombers in Williamsport. Clearly, I had been out of the loop.

I watched with enthusiasm that next day as they won the title. A week later, I received a call from a friend, Ceanne Guerra, who works in the Community and Government Relations Department at Cox. She wondered if I might consider doing a *One on One* on the new champions. *Hmmm,* I thought, *a show on twelve twelve-year-old boys and Little League? Would our viewers be interested?* It only took a few minutes of discussing how rare this feat was and what good kids she heard they were, and to learn that there had been another championship team in 1961, for me to conclude this could be a great show. First, though, I wanted to meet the boys.

On September 12, the Padres planned a special night for the boys to go to the

field early to meet the players, then be honored during the pre-game ceremonies, including throwing out the ceremonial first pitch. That Saturday I spent the afternoon observing them at the field, introducing myself to the coach and some of the boys, and just watching this wonderful interaction between them and the major leaguers. I followed the group up to a suite where they were eating hot dogs and nachos. I wasn't sure if they wondered what I was doing there, but then a few of the boys, including Luke Ramirez, said hello and recognized me. I said I was thinking about doing a *One on One* segment on them. Kiko Garcia chimed in, "It wouldn't be a *One on One*, it would be a *One on Twelve.*" He was right, and that sealed the deal and my creative wheels started turning.

I envisioned a show centering on the boys' story but having a broader scope of history and the romance and reality of the pursuit of the major league dream. I learned about the 1961 Little League World Series Champions from San Diego. I knew I could interview Padres players about being twelve-year-old kids and ask them to offer advice about how they achieved their goals. As I exuded excitement in telling my executive producer, Abbie Smith, about my vision, she said, "Don't make it a half hour with all those elements. Make it an hour." The green light to do an hour special? This was going to be fun. (We also did a half-hour version, so it could

"I'm very grateful to be allowed to share our story on Jane Mitchell's show. I really appreciate everything she's done for us! I'm so glad I met her!"

—MARKUS MELIN, 2010

replay more often, but the priority was *sixty-minutes.*)

I had Padres baseball and Chargers football ahead of me, but this was not the kind of project that could wait until the last minute. With twelve boys, twelve families, many school schedules to consider, plus our production calendar, I started coordinating and planning in October. I could not have made it all happen without Rod Roberto. Rod was the president of the Park View Little League and the point person to give me the back-story and coordinate the shoots—the interview, the day at PETCO Park, and a few others to feature the story behind the championship season.

I first thought we should interview the boys outside at their field, where it all began. Weather was a concern, and setting up outside is always risky. One morning as I was having coffee with my friend, Andrew, who is not an avid baseball fan, I told him what I was trying to envision. He said, "Janie, you know what you're doing, just bring them down to the ballpark and have them sit in the seats with the field behind them. That's where they want to play someday, anyhow, right?" Right. While I opted to do the interview inside at our studio (protected from weather, and a more controlled environment), what that conversation triggered was the other visual that became part of the show and the experience.

I wanted to see the boys in their uniforms out on the field where they might play someday. It would provide a creative vehicle to introduce them, as if in an Opening Day lineup, show their baby pictures and learn about their personalities, and to "just imagine" what their futures might bring—a juxtaposition of now and someday.

With the help of Padres Media Relations Director Warren Miller, we set the shoots for January and February, after the holidays, between vacations, and before spring training. Everything on the to-do list had to go just right—a massive production effort to set up lights, cameras, and microphones for a dozen boys, two coaches, and me. Everyone had to show up, including the parents, whom my associate producer Michelle Mattox interviewed with our combined questions that day. On the day of the PETCO shoot in February, everyone had to show up, be in uniform, and the weather had to cooperate (the winter rain stopped three days before). So far, so good.

Chico Leonard, a member of the 1961 Little League Championship team, was my valuable point person in rallying several players for the segment on them. "You name the day and time, and we'll be there." Northrop Elementary School coordinated mowing schedules so we could shoot on the field where they once played. On a warm January day, we set up bleachers for the players and coach in the middle of the outfield and rewound the clock nearly fifty years to talk about the championship and its impact, then asked them their advice for the twelve boys. When they grabbed their gloves and threw the ball around the diamond, and a few had some at-bats, everyone was laughing and joyful about a game that had meant so much to them for so long.

"The *One on One* experience was a lot of fun. I really liked it when we got to go out on the field at PETCO Park. My dream is to play professional baseball and this gave me a little glimpse of what playing on a pro player's field like this would be like. Thank you for making this all happen."
—NICK CONLIN #8, 2010

After I spent hours producing and writing that portion of the script for the show, colleague Jay Conner edited the piece. He added a digital texture to some of the pictures and images to take us back in time. Together we blended the emotion of then and now and melded the relevance of their story with the Park View team's story. After that nine-minute segment was completed, I sat in the editing room and watched it. My eyes welled up at the point when I asked them how this game had impacted them. This is what life is about. It's not just in the moment. It's learning from experiences, valuing them, and sharing them. Seeing their life in pictures and movies (the actual game they played was on film) and now in their sixties, reminded me, too, that that is all of us. It might not be on television, but we all have a story.

Every time I saw the twelve boys for shoots or at events, they hugged me hello and goodbye. They were so sweet, funny, well-behaved, and appreciative. They were good boys. Not only did they

"It was a lot of fun doing the 'One on Twelve' show with you. Thank you for documenting our Little League World Series run so well."
—SETH GODFREY #13, 2010

have good role models in their lives, they chose to follow those good examples. They seemed genuinely happy to be part of the *One on One* process, and never complained for a moment about anything I asked them to do. Their parents were the same—each agreeable and timely in gathering pictures and following up with phone calls or emails, especially when we were down to the wire.

At spring training, I interviewed five Padres for the juxtaposition of major league dreams and reality: Chris Young, Heath Bell, Adrian Gonzalez, David Eckstein, and Anthony Gwynn, Jr. Each was willing to share their thoughts and perspective, knowing it was for a show celebrating these young champions.

This edition was more complicated than any I had produced because it wasn't just one person's life, but twelve little lives; not just a life's journey, but also an epic that many people had been watching, in part, on television. People who made this production a success on both the technical and creative dimensions include Abbie Smith, who encouraged me to think big, let me follow my heart, and help rally the troops and resources to make it a quality production; Gary Seideman, John Spriet, and Rick Gord, who navigated uncharted waters for that big in-studio shoot; Jay Conner, Erica Simpson, and Shannon Hull, who captured the beautiful images of the 1961 team and the boys at the ballpark against blue skies; Michelle Mattox, whom I am so proud of, for elevating her producing skills by helping manage the many details and interviewing the parents; Candace Edwards, our intern extraordinaire, who helped quiet the lawn mowers during interviews and scanned pictures endlessly; and of course, Dan Roper, who edited all but the 1961 segment, and not only

interpreted my "roadmap jigsaw puzzle," but made it sing. Special thanks to ballpark announcer Frank Anthony whose voice introduces the boys as if it were Opening Day, adding to the ambiance of where reality meets imagination.

After the show debuted, the texts, emails and Facebook® messages were plentiful. I was touched that they were touched. I, like many, look forward to watching the boys grow and mature over the years. With a lot of help—from colleagues, family, and the Padres—I'm glad I had a part in telling their story.

This is the script from the one-hour edition debuting April 8, 2010.

• • •

With big bats ...

    [Hits and action]

... and big smiles, the boys of the Park View Little League All Stars became the Boys of August. The Blue Bombers. The 2009 Little League World Series champions. Follow their glorious journey from little boys to young men to champions.

Lots of little boys dream of being part of a big league clubhouse, and for the Blue Bombers, we just might see their names on major league uniforms some day. But what they have already accomplished is something few can claim and we all can celebrate. Park View's story is centered around baseball, but is so much more, as the team from Chula Vista not only captured a title, but captured our hearts.

[Orchestra music builds]

With every pitch, snag, throw, and hit, the team of tiny and not so tiny giants blazes their victory trail. From hot summer, less than glamorous games to the spotlight on national television and ESPN, through adversity, they find triumph. Through it all, they've grown up.

The Park View All-Stars have their Little League World Championship, and baseball has sustained its place in our culture because of moments like this, moments not only of achievement, but of such meaning, momentum, and magnitude that their victory is *our* victory. Their year is part of our collective memory. Their dreams are part of our imagination…

ANNOUNCER: *Ladies and gentleman, here is the Blue Bombers starting lineup. Number six, Andy Rios …*

ANDY: I'm thirteen years old. My position is shortstop. My favorite baseball player is Dustin Pedroia because he's on my favorite baseball team.

ANDY RIOS, SR.: Thirteen months old, and he would hear the garage open up, and he'd be running out the garage with a bat, a ball, and two gloves. And he was barely talking, and all he would say was, "Ball, ball, Poppy, ball, Poppy."

And it is in learning more about them and hearing from their parents that we appreciate more their journey and what might be ahead.

ANNOUNCER: *Number 19, Kiko Garcia …*

KIKO: I'm centerfielder and pitcher. I'm thirteen. And my favorite player is Tony Gwynn because he's Mr. Padre.

SHARON GARCIA: He started playing when he was two with the YMCA, two or three years old. He has always been really high energy. Whatever he does, he does fully—100 percent.

ANNOUNCER: *27, Luke Ramirez …*

LUKE: I'm thirteen. I play first base and pitcher, and my favorite player's Adrian Gonzalez because he grew up around the San Diego area.

RIC RAMIREZ: He was a really good kid.

CASEY RAMIREZ: A good baby.

RIC RAMIREZ: He had this one little bat that he played with all the time, and there was this little plastic ball that he would hit when he started crawling.

ANNOUNCER: *Welcome number 20, Bulla Graft …*

BULLA: I'm twelve years old. My position is second base. My favorite baseball player is Derek Jeter 'cause he's an all-around great player.

PUA GRAFT: Bulla is a very big-hearted child. He is—he thinks of everybody else but himself. He's a very humble kid. He's just a loving kid. He has an older brother, so his older brother's a senior this year, and so Bulla got to grow up around the baseball field in Pampers®.

ANNOUNCER: *Here is number 16, Bradley Roberto …*

BRADLEY: I'm thirteen. I play right field and my favorite player is Adrian Gonzalez because he plays first base, he's a left-hand—he's a great role model.

CHRISTINE SANTOS (Bradley's mother): He's always happy. Nothing ever gets him down. If you can ask him to do anything—you can ask him to do all the chores for all six kids and he'll just, okay, you know, he'll be really happy, and he'll just do it. So he's always been my easiest kid.

ANNOUNCER: *Number 24, Oscar Castro …*

OSCAR: I'm thirteen. I play third base. My favorite player is Jake Peavy because he's an all-around great pitcher.

LORENA VARGAS (Oscar's mother): When he started playing Little League when he was very little, he came home after practice and he said, "I want to do this forever, Mom." I said, "Okay," you know, "You can do whatever you want to do as long as you're willing, and you put, you know, a big effort into it." So baseball is a big deal for him.

ANNOUNCER: *Number 7, Daniel Porras, Jr. …*

DANIEL: I'm thirteen years old. I play catcher and my favorite player is Joe Mauer because he's a great catcher and he won MVP.

SYLVIA PORRAS: We have video of him, like, a one-year-old, like, hitting the ball really hard. He's extremely shy around adults and people that he's not comfortable with, but he is hilarious around his friends. He's like the class clown and the group clown in the baseball team.

ANNOUNCER: *Now from the dugout, number 23, Isaiah Armenta …*

ISAIAH: I'm thirteen and my position is pitcher. My favorite player is Heath Bell because he doesn't crack under pressure.

MARTHA ARMENTA: We had a Suburban® because we had five children and we had to sit him in the back seat, and we had to make sure there was nothing around, next to him, close to him, near him, behind him, nowhere, because he would literally grab it and throw it at us. And he wouldn't throw like a baby throw, he would throw really hard. And we'd joke around, "Oh, Isaiah's going to be a pitcher."

ANNOUNCER: *Number 13, Seth Godfrey …*

SETH: I'm thirteen years old. I play third base. And my favorite player is Josh Hamilton because he has the home run record with the Home Run Derby.

DIANA GODFREY: Seth is a very quiet, humble, responsible, caring, thoughtful young man. He was this little statistician that knew all the MLB players from across the country, and was following all the games and the aspiring new rookies and all.

ANNOUNCER: *Number 12, Markus Melin …*

MARKUS: I'm thirteen. I play centerfield, and my favorite player is Manny Ramirez because he used to be on my favorite team.

ANNA MELIN: He's funny, silly. He's a good kid. He cares about people.

CURTIS MELIN: Yeah, I just taught him, you know, a lot about responsibility, you know, and basically, once you start something, you stick to it, no matter what.

ANNOUNCER: *Wearing number 15, Jensen Peterson …*

JENSEN: I'm thirteen. I play catcher and my favorite player's Honus Wagner because he's a great baseball player.

KIM PETERSON: Like a teddy bear. He looks kind of big and gruff on the outside, but he's got a really soft heart and is very—pretty sensitive. So he's very caring towards other people

JEFF PETERSON: Outspoken, and he will do just about anything. He's a little bit—a lot of antics, a little crazy. [laughs]

ANNOUNCER: *And finally, number 8, Nick Conlin …*

NICK: I'm thirteen. I play outfield, and my favorite player is Tony Gwynn, Jr. because he plays outfield, too.

LISA CONLIN: His first word in life was ball. When he's doing an activity or something that he really likes, he just goes for it, and it's pretty hardcore.

JIM: He puts himself into everything. Kind of makes him who he is. But he loves to win. It's all about winning.

And winners they are. Twelve boys, twelve backgrounds, twelve personalities, with the leadership of coaches and parents, they became one.

ANNOUNCER: *Ladies and Gentleman, your 2009 Little League World Series Champions …*

Up next, the story of how it all began, then reliving the nationally televised moments with the dazzling dozen in our studio. And later on this special one-hour edition of *One on One*, generation to generation, world champions from nearly fifty years ago remember their glory days....

For the Park View Little League All-Stars, becoming 2009 Little League World Champions began with a love of the game, talent, and a vision of what might be. Not the boys' vision, at first, but the vision of a father who had an epiphany and another dad who stepped out of the classroom to coach. Rod Roberto makes his living crunching numbers, thinking strategically as a financial planner. But his shiny professional awards on display don't compare to his wall of priceless pictures …

ROD ROBERTO: This is when we finally beat Rancho Santa Margarita here at Clairmont in San Diego, at Clairmont Mesa …

Reminders of his son Bradley's special summer of 2009 …

ROD: When we finally get to Williamsport, the first game is Kentucky. Luke hit two home runs that game; Kiko threw a one-hitter; and Bradley hit a triple and a home run.

Rod, from a Navy family, grew up in San Diego's South Bay, played Lucky Waller Little League, then graduated from Bonita Vista High School and UCSD. When he became a father to three boys, he made sure his job had flexibility to be at their T-ball and Little League practices. Bradley's mother, Christine Santos ...

> **CHRISTINE:** He's been out on the field since he was two and three. So as soon as he could, you know, hit a ball off a tee, he was just out there.
>
> **BRADLEY:** I just loved hitting and got fielding, just throwing the ball and catching the ball.
>
> *[In the back yard swinging]*
>
> **ROD:** Everybody thinks I helped him with his swing and the way he played, but he was just very natural at it.... I remember going to the first practice. He goes, "Dad, where's my team?" It was—me and him, we're the team.

Finally at Little League age, Rod coached Bradley and Park View teammates Daniel Porras and Seth Godfrey when they were seven, five years away from the twelve-year-old category to compete to be the best in all of Little League. Then came Bulla Graft and Andy Rios and a conversation with their parents.

> **ROD:** All of a sudden, we had five kids and we said, "Wow, this is pretty good. Wait till these kids turn twelve." And then we found Markus.

When San Diego's North County's Rancho Buena Vista team went to the Little League World Series in Williamsport in 2005 ...

> **ROD:** We said we can probably do the same thing. And so that's what we did.
>
> **JANE:** So is this you trying to relive your childhood dream?
>
> **ROD:** I think it was more for—we wanted to get the kids better.
>
> **JANE:** And what are the kids thinking from your perspective at this time?
>
> **ROD:** They're not thinking anything. They're just kids. They don't know what's going on, you know.

In 2006, the boys turned nine. Rod Roberto was a team manager and on Park View's Board. He and parents of the core group created a travel team to play in the off-season.

> **ROD:** Park View Little League, at the time, was a league that everybody beat in All-Stars. It wasn't well known. And so I just wanted Park View to be the league that everybody came to, that you played baseball, and you did it the right way. But unfortunately, you gotta win, and so we figured that we have to get these kids more repetition.
>
> **ROD:** In travel teams they take kids from other leagues and put them to-gether. I didn't want to do that. I only wanted Park View kids. And so that's when I met Ric Ramirez and Luke.

Ric Ramirez is a fifth grade teacher ...

> *[In classroom with kids sitting at tables]*

... at Finney Elementary school in Chula Vista. This day the tables are turned. Instead of his students sharing for an assignment, he takes us to a favorite moment from his summer of 2009.

RIC: Hey guys, let's go! [in classroom with kids]

[Talks about the end of the game and the dog piling, etc...]

RIC: I couldn't even feel my body, I was just jumping up and down, Yes! Yes! Yes! And then watching all the kids pile...

Like Rod Roberto, Ric Ramirez also grew up with baseball, playing at Park View Little League, Chula Vista High, Southwestern College, Upper Iowa University, then first base at UC San Diego, and in the Division 3 World Series.

RIC RAMIREZ: All along I wanted to be a teacher. Baseball was the thing that kept me motivated in school as well, 'cause I knew I needed to have an education to play baseball.

He and Casey Klazer, a basketball player at Hilltop High School and teacher, married in 1995 and had Luke, May 15, 1996.

CASEY: He was eight pounds eleven ounces, not as big as people expect. They expect me to, you know, say ten pounds, but he wasn't.

RIC: Before he could walk, he would hit this plastic ball, and the ball would go shooting across the room, crawl over to the ball again and then hit it.

The family went to Padres games. Ric started coaching their younger son's Little League team, but at eight, Luke was not a standout player, only mildly interested in baseball. Although his brother Ben, a shortstop, looked up to him.

BEN: Luke always helped me out when I needed help in baseball. And it was cool.

Luke struggled with being bigger than other kids in an awkward way.

RIC: He was clumsy and just not very coordinated, and so we looked at our—we looked at each other and just kind of said, "Well, you know, maybe he's not going to be a baseball player." And ...

CASEY: Basketball.

But as Luke adjusted to his growing body, something clicked when he was nine.

LUKE: I hit my first home run and I guess that kind of sparked it, and I just had that drive to get better, and I just wanted to hit more home runs and stuff, so I think that was probably it.

Rod Roberto noticed as he was following his epiphany to develop the future All-Star team ...

ROD: I remember him sitting on the lawn. I go, "Hey, does your son pitch?"

RIC: He knew what players he needed to make a good team.

ROD: And he goes, "Yeah, he pitches." And I said, "Well, I'm thinking about drafting him first." And he said, "That'd be great."

RIC: And little did I know that that team he was thinking about was the All-Star team.

ROD: Every team that goes, if you watch the Little League World Series, always has a kid bigger than his age. And we got that kid. We got Luke!

A journey they'd take together for the next three years ...

[Classroom]

In addition to their real jobs, Ric, wearing both coach and manager hats ...

RIC: There's a huge transition from being a teacher and going into something different with a whole bunch of kids. I really liked it. Baseball's my passion so, little by little, I started to learn how to manage the kids and do things with them—how to make them listen and things like that.

Throughout, backyard batting cage practice would become a regular routine. Finding balance between new roles for the fathers and sons ...

LUKE: He kind of looked at me to, you know, perform a little better and be kind of like a role model, and that was kind of hard at first. Then I started getting used to it and I actually liked being a role model, and having him as my coach, too.

JANE: Did he treat you differently than the other boys?

LUKE: No, he—I don't remember him ever doing that.

[Rod and Bradley batting]

BRADLEY: He was trying to get me better. And then he was always just helping me and being there for me.

And while the idea of growing an All-Star team might seem black and white on paper, even for a numbers guy, retracing the journey and all it would bring reveals how emotion and heart were part of the equation.

JANE: As a father of Bradley, at this point, though, how are you feeling watching him and seeing what he's doing and, you know, your involvement for all these kids but, you know, for him in particular ...

ROD: 'Cause you know the kids, you know, it isn't just Bradley ... [tearing up]

JANE: Yeah.

ROD: ... it's all of them.

The work, the challenges, and validation that they were doing it right. Up next on *One on One*, the boys re-live the Championship season, and later, their Padres heroes go back to the future....

Winning the Little League World Series Championship is impressive. Just consider the scope of the competition. There are about 7,000 teams from around the world and more than 16,000 games are played to get the field to the final sixteen teams to go to Williamsport for the International World Series Tournament for the Little League Division. Chula Vista's Park View was there in 2009 representing the West, and we invited the champions to our studio to reminisce about becoming a dream team.

While taking pictures and putting on microphones, they have the energy of twelve- and thirteen-year-old boys, and they're well mannered.

JANE: Welcome to our Channel 4 studios and to *One on One*. And as Kiko told me the first time I met him, it's not really one on one, it's one on twelve. Right? And with your two coaches, one on fourteen.

We start with their love of the game ...

BULLA: When we were a little kid, playing baseball wasn't like for something, it was just to have fun and, yeah, I had fun a lot.

Unaware of the adults' strategy to get them to the World Series, the boys on the travel ball club are first selected as the ten-year-old All-Star team. Park View wins District, then Sectional for the first time. Then lose in the sub-divisional round.

JANE: There was one team that you guys could not beat.

BOYS: *[groans]*

Rancho Santa Margarita, a team ninety miles northeast of home.

OSCAR: We were ten and eleven, and every time we always went to the losers' bracket because of them, then we faced them in the championship. We'd always lose. So then this year, we were just hoping, this year, to break the streak this year since it counts.

And breaking that streak meant keeping the team together. While Little League rules allow outstanding eleven-year-olds to move up to twelve-year-old All-Star teams, Park View President Rod Roberto convinced parents and the board to keep this team intact. So come time to pick the 2009 All-Stars to wear the green, black, and white PV uniforms, the ninety-six players from eight Park View teams vote for seven of the boys.

MARKUS: To have the players around us believe in us to go this far was cool.

The coaches pick the final five. With Ric Ramirez, now coach, and Oscar, Sr., the team manager, their primary goal still isn't Williamsport, but to continue to do whatever's necessary to beat their nemesis, Rancho Santa Margarita, at their own game.

OSCAR, SR.: They just seemed like better athletes overall. So we just felt that in order to beat a team like that, we needed to become better athletes, so we just, you know, we had a friend bring one—you know, an instructor out and basically have the kids running all over the place and doing all sorts of speed and agility and, you know, we found that it was helping.

JANE: And to lose a little of their baby fat, I read.

OSCAR, SR.: Yeah, a little bit. That was a bonus.

SETH: We needed to get more in shape and be athletic to beat the tough teams that we were going to face.

It pays off. At the end of July 2009, Park View beats their arch rival, Rancho Santa Margarita. Then after beating Torrance in the best of three series, Park View advances to represent Southern California in the Western Region tournament in San Bernardino, California. It's August, and hot, and they're living in dorms. For ten days, no parents, except coaches Ric and Oscar, are allowed in the complex, just in the stands.

KIKO: It was kind of funny. We were the only team doing homework.

The coaches give them an option …

OSCAR: "Do you want to have fun, or you guys just want to go out, actually try to win this thing?" I—of course, I want to win this 'cause I want to go to Williamsport. And we had the team that could do that.

KIKO: We were so close already.

JANE: So close. So everybody was agreed?

BOYS: *[Assent—yes.]*

BRADLEY: We knew if we won that the fun would come in winning, so, yeah.

They beat Utah, Hawaii, Arizona, and Nevada by a combined score of 72-to-9. After defeating Nevada again, the final game against Northern California is televised nationally on ESPN.

JANE: Okay, well, going into the fifth inning, bases are loaded, right? Game is tied, 3-3, right?

MARKUS: Right.

JANE: Bradley, you're at the plate.

ANNOUNCER: *Here's 3-2. Walks in a run. Great at-bat by Bradley Roberto.*

That run puts them ahead as they eventually win …

[Victory call to Williamsport]

Home of the Little League World Series since 1947, arriving late the next night …

LUKE: We pulled up in the bus. I guess they left the lights on for us to get there. And it was just amazing. I've never seen anything more beautiful in my life than to—I mean, it was just like the number one dream of any Little Leaguer is to just see that field. And for us to be able to play on it was just incredible.

JANE: I heard that when you were there, and this is a pretty cool place to be, that somebody was asking girls for extra hugs.

BOYS: Jensen.

JANE: How'd that work out for you, Jensen? I'm sorry. *[laughter]* Bulla, what did you think when you first saw those baby blue uniforms that you got that said …

BOYS: Ohh …

BULLA: They're so pretty. God, they're cute.

JANE: Nick, what did you think of when you first put on that uniform?

NICK: We made it.

Unbeknownst to the boys, Little League volunteer Tony Garcia had asked some Padres to record a message, which Ric and Oscar played for them right before their first game.

ADRIAN GONZALEZ: I want to wish Park View Little League a lot of success, a lot of fun. Good luck at Williamsport and bring back a title to Chula Vista. You're making us proud, and keep doing a good job guys.

DAVID ECKSTEIN: I just want to wish you all the best at the Little League World Series. Go bring it home for San Diego. Make us proud. I know you will. Just go out there and play hard.

KEVIN KOUZMANOFF: Just wishing you well and wishing you good luck at Williamsport. Hope you guys bring it back to San Diego with a Championship. Good Luck. Have fun.

ANTHONY GWYNN, JR.: Just want to wish you guys the best of luck. Keep up the good work and bring it home to San Diego.

ISAIAH: Oh, I thought it was great just seeing our heroes, all of our heroes from the Padres just showing that they support us and that they want us to win and bring it back to San Diego.

They're one of eight teams from the United States playing for four spots in the elimination round, while another eight teams compete in the international grouping.

Park View starts off hot beating Great Lakes 15-to-0 and New England 14-to-0.

JANE: Did it seem easy?

BOYS: No.

JANE: Not easy. Andy, what do you think?

ANDY: Teams showed up like they wanted to play, but we came out with our A game, so that showed us that we can—we can hit, pitch, and field.

JANE: ESPN featured what you guys were doing and they called you, you know, the Blue Bombers …

[Off-screen ESPN compilation tape being played]

JANE: Good stuff, huh? [reactions, some nods]

Then they face their toughest test—Texas. With that one loss, they must win the next game or they're done. Determined on their day off, they practice by playing Whiffle ball.

OSCAR, SR.: We just kept working. You know, we knew that although we were hitting the ball well, we still weren't, at least where I felt that's where we needed to be.

JANE: The next day you come back, and I just think that Georgia game had a little bit of everything in it.

[Off-screen ESPN highlight tape. Markus' catch, throw—great double play]

MARKUS: I love diving, so I just ended up going down on the ground and catching it. Then getting the guy out was—getting the double play was cool.

Then, an admitted defensive collapse …

[Off-screen ESPN highlight clip, Ric motivating the team]

JANE: Jensen, what were you thinking during the middle of that game?

JENSEN: That we still had a chance to beat them and all that—and that we were the better team.

JANE: ... And then finally in that game—there was some awesome base running that happened in the bottom of the sixth in that final inning that proved to be key.

NICK: I knew the guy had the ball and Coach was sending me, but the catcher had the ball, so I just went back to the bag 'cause I didn't want to get out. [boys react]

JANE: Good call. Good call.

They move on after winning a rematch with Texas.

[Aug. 29, ESPN, Victory—US Champions. Move on to the championship game]

JANE: Did you have butterflies in your stomach?

BOYS: [nodding] Yeah.

ISAIAH: I remember when we went out for our run to centerfield, and Luke said, "This is what we've been working for for our whole lives, our dreams, guys. Let's do this."

Facing Chinese Tai Pai ...

[Off-screen ESPN highlights and win]

BRADLEY: To see that moment over and over again and to actually know that we're the best team in the world. It was just an amazing feeling.

An amazing feeling the whole San Diego community was celebrating. Next on *One on One*, the homecoming and hoopla surrounding their victory, and later, what do they want to be when they grow up? Their plans might surprise you....

In the moment their long journey ends, euphoria begins with emotion from both sides of the fence as Oscar's mother remembers.

LORENA VARGAS: And I was walking away, and he started screaming, "Mom, Mom!" And I came back and I got on my knees, and I dropped my bag, I dropped everything. I got on my knees and he said, "I did it, Mom, I did it." And we—it was just—after that, it was just one emotional day after another, after another, after another.

OSCAR, SR.: It's something that we lived through together, you know. And the special part for me, you know, and I'm sure it is for Ric as well, is you spent it with your son, too.

JANE: Did you look up at the stands?

LUKE: I did, saw Mom crying. I was going to give her a hug, but ...

For parents, it was worth having their boys in those dorms in San Bernardino with no access to them for ten days for the tournament.

MARTHA ARMENTA: I understood and I respected it. And I even agreed with them. But I think that my heart was just not ready to let him go that fast.

It was worth juggling their families' lives, and finances, or accepting community donations to be able to be there.

> **PUA GRAFT:** So I know the boys are very thankful to have their parents and their families to be able to go and watch them play, 'cause we didn't plan this. We didn't plan on going to Williamsport. So we hadn't, you know, not all of us had the money to get there, and then let alone take the whole family. So we were very blessed to be a part of San Diego and Chula Vista.
>
> **ANDY, SR.:** It was a great joy as a father to see him and the rest of the team mature.
>
> **DIANA GODFREY:** Each player would take a turn being the hero of the game or star of the game.

Crowned champions, their celebrity ignites and the whirlwind begins. After flying back west, a bus ride brings them home to a spontaneous welcome at Southwestern College.

> **PUA GRAFT:** The coaches really grounded them that way, and so they didn't see newspapers, they didn't get to see any media, so they didn't know how huge all of this was.
>
> **SETH:** We knew in Williamsport, we knew that like, San Diego was behind us. We wanted to try to like, show and like, prove ourselves, but as soon as we got home, it was just like, wow. All these people are supporting us. It was just like, an amazing feeling.
>
> **LUKE:** We thought it was just going to be our families and just like, a couple of people from around the area but, I mean, it was just amazing how many people were there.

Even more so at a planned victory rally that Friday. Their various schools offer accolades at assemblies. VIP treatment includes a trip to Los Angeles for an appearance on NBC's *Tonight Show* with fun in the Green Room before Conan O'Brien tries to keep their ring. The Key to the City from Chula Vista and a private dinner at Donovan's Steak House hosted by Padre Adrian Gonzalez …

> **JANE:** And what did you have? Steak?
>
> **BOYS:** Steaks.
>
> **KIKO:** Heath Bell cobbler.
>
> **UNIDENTIFIED:** Ketchup.
>
> **JANE:** Somebody ordered ketch—asked for ketchup?
>
> **BOYS:** Bulla. [Bulla raises his hand]

On September 12 they're guests of the San Diego Padres in the clubhouse … Batting practice … A surprise, a giant banner for all to see at the ballpark, and throwing out the ceremonial first pitch. The San Diego Chargers welcome them with high fives and autographs.

> *MARKUS ON TV NBC: It's awesome because the Chargers are my favorite football team and it's nice coming out here to see them.*

And they're featured in the Holiday Bowl's Big Bay Balloon Parade and on a float in the Rose Parade in Pasadena. February 2010 they're honored at the Hall of Champions' Annual Salute to Champions dinner. With tickets compliments of Southwest Airlines, they venture to the nation's capital, where even in the midst of a snowstorm, the Champions and their families meet President Barack Obama at the White House.

LUKE [in DC]: *He's really cool, to invite us here, we're very thankful.*

They come full circle in March for Park View's Opening Day ...

JANE: Have any of you gotten big heads because of this?

BOYS: No.

JANE: You know what? That's what I—that's what I sense, and that's what I hear. So what do you think kind of keeps you grounded?

JENSEN: Coaches.

LUKE: Mom. Mom.

ISAIAH: The moms.

UNIDENTIFIED: School.

Upper Deck made trading cards for the boys and their families, and proceeds from a book about their journey will benefit Park View. So while there are rewards, there's thought behind what they do as a group with a big focus on community and charity.

ROD: We didn't want to do events that kind of just promoted a business, just to kind of exploit the kids, in a sense. I wanted them to learn that—to give back.

ROD: We did things for foster kids, for abused children, you know, for the Kidney Foundation ...

Along with their home digital photo albums, many have captured the moments of their odyssey, including local newspaper and television stations ...

ANNA MELIN: So I'm glad people recorded, and we can go back and we can look at video footage, and read newspaper clippings of things that happened here in San Diego, because I just felt everything moved so quickly, and being there, you couldn't really experience what I'm hearing that happened here in San Diego.

KIM PETERSON: Like, they want to say where they were at when they were watching it, and what they did, and all the details, and they're excited to share that, and that's just a neat experience that, I mean, we didn't have before that.

BRADLEY: We had the best fans. To know that we're—they're supporting us. Even though we're all the way across the country, they were at home watching us and cheering us on. And then to when we get back and to celebrate our victory was just amazing how—how awesome our fans were.

JIM: We just thank everybody for their support and their backing, and the— believing in the kids, and the way they treat the kids.

JEFF PETERSON: ... I can't describe it. Every once in a while I still think about it, and think, I can't believe they're World Champions, I can't believe it went this far.

JANE: When people think of you, what do you want them to think of? Luke?

LUKE: Probably just how hard we worked and that, you know, even thirteen-year-old—a bunch of thirteen-year-old kids can go mess around on a big baseball field in front of some cameras and do a lot for a—a city and—and the whole—and the whole entire city, and that's just what I want to be remembered by.

CHRISTINE SANTOS (Bradley's mom): They became, you know, a band of brothers, and they're just—they're going to be brothers forever.

A band of brothers no longer Little Leaguers, but still enthusiastic about their Park View chant.

UNIDENTIFIED: Call it out, Luke.

LUKE: Ready, one, two, three ...

BOYS: Ali, alo, ali mom-ba, Park View, Park View rah, rah, rah.

JANE: That's awesome. Awesome.

When we return on this special edition of *One on One*, we go back in time to vivid memories from San Diego's first World Championship....

When Park View became the Little League World Series Champions it had been forty-eight years since a San Diego area team had earned that title, and for those on that first championship squad, the summer of '09 takes them back to another place and time. The year is 1961.

PRESIDENT KENNEDY 1961: *Ask not what your country can do for you, but what you can do for your country.*

John F. Kennedy is inaugurated as the thirty-fifth President of the United States. The average price of a new house, about $12,000. A gallon of gas costs just twenty-seven cents, and the number one single? Ben E. King's "Stand By Me." On the Major League Baseball front, Yankee Roger Maris hears cheers and jeers as he chases and breaks Babe Ruth's record of sixty single season home runs. In San Diego, a big league baseball franchise is still eight years away, but fans celebrate America's pastime watching the Pacific Coast League Padres at Westgate Park. Fourteen miles east in La Mesa at Northmont Elementary School, a baseball field is the center of summer activity for fourteen boys: the El Cajon-La Mesa Northern All-Stars.

CHICO LEONARD: Really, it brings back a lot of memories being on this field. We played so many games, so many practices right here. I'm Chico Leonard. I played second base, and I'm now a project manager for a foundation repair company.

MICKEY ALESANTRO: It was hot here, dusty 'cause of the wind. 'Cause there was no grass, and the wind would always be blowing. I'm Mickey Alesantro. I played outfield and first base, and pitched the last inning of the World Series, and I'm a ceramic tile contractor.

GENE OKRESH: I'm Gene Okresh. I played third base, and I'm working at Bob Baker Chevrolet in El Cajon—mechanic.

JIM DOLAN: My name's Jim Dolan. I played shortstop, retired, San Diego Gas & Electric. It feels amazing. I mean, like it never—was only a couple days ago that we were here playing here.

Their All-Star team led by two coaches, Jim's late father, Don Dolan, and Jim Pursely.

TODD LIEBER: I'm Todd Lieber. I played first base, pitcher, and retired.

Todd Lieber has some residual affects from a stroke, but he and the seven other players who could came from across San Diego and even Nevada City, at our request, for a reunion in 2010 on the same field where their boyhood quest began.

BRIAN SIPE: I'm Brian Sipe. I played catcher. I'm a football coach at San Diego State. The experience of going to Williamsport was something that all boys knew about when they were growing up. There weren't other sports and other championships to dream about at that age.

MIKE SALVATORE: I'm Mike Salvatore. I pitched, played second base, shortstop sometimes, outfield, and I'm a real estate appraiser.

STEVE JUPIN: Steve Jupin. I was like fourth string catcher, fourth string second, fourth string outfield. But it was really fun. And right now, I'm district sales manager for Webb Service Company.

Thanks mostly to scrapbooks compiled by Chico's and Gene's mothers, their magical moments are preserved.

[The 1961 team looking at scrapbooks and keepsakes]

On this day, some are seeing those yellowed pages, headlines, and boxscores for the first time in nearly a half-century. Turning back the pages to 1961 and the All-Star team made up of boys from the various La Mesa-El Cajon Little League teams, now called Fletcher Hills Little League.

BRIAN SIPE: These were the best guys in the league. You know, and I was still in awe of them. I was the young guy on the team. I was an eleven-year-old. And watching these guys flip it around the infield was pretty impressive.

JANE: Jim, do you remember anything in particular about what the coaches told you in terms of how far you guys might be able to go?

JIM DOLAN: Yeah, they told us we'll never go to Williamsport and win the World Series on home runs. That's exactly what they told us.

JANE: … win on home runs.

BRIAN SIPE: And we proved them wrong.

JIM PERSLEY: These guys were just phenomenal. You know, they just wouldn't be beat. We had five one-to-nothing ballgames, and all of them was home runs, see.

At the tournaments in San Bernardino, the All-Stars had to win every game to qualify for the World Series. Single elimination in those days; lose one and they're done.

JIM PERSLEY: And we won the State, and then we won the Regional …

JANE: Okay.

JIM PERSLEY: … and that's when we loaded the plane.

MIKE SALVATORE: When we arrived there, we were just grateful for being there. And some of the teams we watched, like Mexico, were intimidating. So we might be going, "Wow, I hope we don't have to face them."

A black and white film of the ceremony sets the tone of the series. Game one was against the defending World Champions from Levittown, Pennsylvania.

MICKEY ALESANTRO: I don't even remember it. All I know is, we won. That's what counted.

CHICO LEONARD: You were oh for four, that's why you didn't remember that game. Sal pitched seven innings, shutout, and then Todd thought he better come up in the bottom of the 7th and hit one out …

TODD LIEBER: I did.

CHICO LEONARD: … and that's how we beat the defending World Champions.

JANE: Game two.

CHICO LEONARD: Game two. Hawaii—Hilo, Hawaii.

In extra innings and behind …

CHICO LEONARD: Sal thought he better hit one out and did, and that's how we won that game.

JANE: Wow.

MIKE SALVATORE: I don't remember hitting that one. No. I do remember hitting the one in the final game.

Against El Campo Texas …

MIKE SALVATORE: It was the last inning. It was two outs. It was—I was holding back tears and some of the players on the team were teary-eyed. I mean, it was like it was over. And no expectations. Only, I'm not going to make the last out.

[From the VHS of the game: Call of Home Run]

Three games, winning each with a walk off home run, and the World Championship, their lives instantly changed. When they landed at Gillespie field in San Diego, they were welcomed by five thousand people and a fire truck for a parade.

JIM DOLAN: La Mesa, El Cajon, you know, San Diego, Chula Vista. They all kind of came together for us.

Bonded by their common experience, their journeys, all different. Brian Sipe became the only pro athlete of the group … playing football at San Diego State, then in the NFL, mostly with the Cleveland Browns.

BRIAN SIPE: You mentioned my having aspirations back then, I really didn't. Just like the rest of these guys, I was just in the moment.

JIM DOLAN: My dad was a pilot for PSA. I wanted to be the same thing for as long as I can remember. I was flying since I was probably fourteen years old.

And that's what I wanted to be. And then some things came into play and kept me out of it, so …

JANE: Yeah.

JIM DOLAN: … a little trip to Vietnam …

Gene Okresh returned home from his duty in Vietnam to work on his passion—cars.

GENE: And I think the beginning in this Little League, and working together, and coaching, is what helped develop that train of thought, and what you need to do to be successful.

JANE: Did you know you made that kind of impact on them now?

JIM PERSLEY: No, you never know, you know, but—but I'm glad, you know. If it helped them, I'm happy.

MIKE SALVATORE: We got so much praise; that carries you through life. That gave me the confidence to do other things in life where maybe I wouldn't have.

All have had families, love, and loss. High points and lessons in humility …

CHICO LEONARD: The impact has lasted a lifetime. I don't know a year's gone by that someone hasn't said something about the Little League team or has talked about the Little League team.

MIKE SALVATORE: Well, I—I feel older. Shoulder's stiffer and things like that. But it's funny to watch.

August 30, 2009, the 1961 team watched the Blue Bombers play their way to a championship title.

MICKEY ALESANTRO: I think they handled themselves just like we did. It looked like they had a good time. Their team is—they got to know each other and they, you know, everything they did was like a team effort, which was the same with us.

BRIAN SIPE: That's something different, was media attention. We didn't have it. In fact, my biggest compliment to them and their coaching staff is that they were able to stay focused given all the distractions.

JANE: What would you want to share with them in terms of how they refer to or value this experience?

CHICO LEONARD: Well, it's something that's going to be with them forever. But it doesn't make anything that's coming any easier. They still have to work for that, too.

BRIAN: They will be ambassadors for that sport, for the city of San Diego, for Chula Vista, for their families, and I would just encourage them to wear that responsibility well.

STEVE JUPIN: We used to joke about hitting it into where the jungle gyms are, and now a couple of guys can actually hit it that far, you know?

CHICO LEONARD: Man, there'll come a time in your life where you're not going to keep playing. And doesn't mean you're a bad person, doesn't mean you're a failure, it just means that you moved on to something else. And that's what life is all about, 'cause life's all about change. And there's going to be tons of changes, but nobody can take away what you got.

Up next, what do the boys want to be when they grow up? Major leaguers offer advice on how to get there. Plus, the Blue Bombers take on a *One on One* assignment....

They have already dared to dream. Now they dare again with an invitation to step onto the field where they could play some day. Most of the Blue Bombers want to be Major League Baseball players. Bulla and Jensen prefer pursuing football. Having such lofty goals wasn't all that long ago for several San Diego Padres who never were Little League World Champions, but remember being twelve. San Diegan and son of a Hall of Famer making a name for himself, Tony Gwynn, Jr....

> **ANTHONY GWYNN, JR.:** I was probably a lot more into basketball at that point but baseball was still a passion of mine.

First round draft pick out of Eastlake High, All-Star Gold Glover Adrian Gonzalez.

> **ADRIAN GONZALEZ:** You have twenty-five different dreams and one of them was always being a baseball player. The game of baseball was something that I always loved, and I always really enjoyed playing.

An infielder who at just 5'7" beat the baseball odds, World Series MVP David Eckstein ...

> **DAVID ECKSTEIN:** I wanted to play baseball. That was my dream.

An undrafted pitcher relentless in becoming a major leaguer, closer Heath Bell ...

> **HEATH BELL:** And I knew it was going to be hard to get there. But I just knew in my heart that I was going to be one, one day.

A tall Texan who became a two sport star at Princeton, six-foot-ten pitcher Chris Young ...

> **CHRIS YOUNG:** Even when I was twelve years old I always wanted to be a Major League Baseball player. I just always believed I would have that opportunity if I continued to work hard and continued to set goals for myself.

The accomplished big leaguers applaud Chula Vista's boys of summer.

> **CHRIS YOUNG:** Being some of their idols, they've looked up to us, yet we appreciated what they were able to accomplish and what they have been through.
>
> **ANTHONY GWYNN, JR.:** And they represented San Diego in the best way they could, and bringing that championship home. So I think as, San Diego—we're all proud of them.

Do the boys feel pressure to continue to excel in baseball?

> **OSCAR:** It's not that it's more pressure, it's just like, it's more expected from you. Like ...
>
> **ANDY:** People look up to you.

OSCAR: Yeah.

MARKUS: Yeah.

ANDY: Someone can look up to you and know what you have done and learn from us.

They plan to play sports through at least high school, but what do they want to be if being a pro athlete doesn't work out? For Isaiah, a lawyer. Kiko, a sports agent.

KIKO: Yeah. I love arguing.

Luke, a sportscaster.

LUKE: I want to take up journalism and kind of, actually, do what you're doing right now.

Oscar, Bulla, and Nick connect with the military …

OSCAR: Join the Air Force, become a fighter pilot.

NICK: Because I'd just give back to my country and stuff.

Jensen and Seth foresee coaching. Junior, a CIA agent. And Markus and Andy, like his father, could be police officers. So far, no "Plan B" for Bradley.

BRADLEY: I just want to keep working on baseball.

With hindsight on their side, big leaguers offer advice for the boys and anyone with a dream and a desire to reach their full potential.

ADRIAN GONZALEZ: Whether you're a doctor—or whatever your career goal is, you have to work hard. There's always going to be obstacles, but you just have to kinda fight through them.

HEATH BELL: Have fun. Keep working hard and never be satisfied.

DAVID ECKSTEIN: Understand your strengths and your weaknesses, and work on them, and try to find something that you can add to a club to help that club win.

CHRIS YOUNG: There's going to be enough people out there to tell you, "You can't do this, you can't do that." You got to continually believe in yourself. Never get down, and stay focused.

Especially on school …

ANTHONY GWYNN, JR.: You can have academics without sports, but you can't have sports without academics.

CHRIS YOUNG: I think education is what provides the opportunity to achieve your dreams, whatever they may be.

ANTHONY GWYNN, JR.: Whether you're a boy or a girl, make the right decisions. You know right from wrong. And just follow your heart. That usually leads you in the right direction.

The boys, wise beyond their years, also have their own life lessons to draw from.

ISAIAH: I think that learning everything and bringing all this experience together has taught not only me, but all of us, that if we work hard and put our mind to something, we could accomplish it.

While we "just imagine ..." that they could someday be in uniform for their hometown's major league team, on this day, they are still happy, free-spirited boys, and it's their idea to recreate an indelible moment—the last out that crowned them World Champions.

[The Blue Bombers jumping into the dog pile]

Before they came to our studio, I gave the boys an assignment: to write answers to essay questions about their journey. They then read a few of the thoughts they penned ...

BRADLEY: The lessons from my coaches, family, and friends have all taught me many different things in life, and how to achieve my goals, and to be successful as an adult when I take on many obstacles in the world.

KIKO: The most important thing I learned from this entire journey is that in order to succeed, you only share determination and persistence.

NICK: The coolest thing that I have done in this whole journey was when we went to Donovan's Restaurant to have dinner with Adrian and Edgar Gonzalez. It was really fun because we got to hang out with some of the players, and the food was really good.

JENSEN: The coolest part of the journey for me was to go to the Chargers game. Even though they lost, it was a lot of fun. And I got to hug a Charger cheerleader.

JUNIOR: I think the coolest thing on this journey is when we got to be on Conan O'Brien and be on national television in front of all the people.

ANDY: The coolest thing so far is when we went to PETCO Park to meet the Padre players. We got our jersey with our names, signatures, go take batting practice, play catch, and go to our positions with the Padres players during the National Anthem.

MARKUS: After winning every big game everyone yells, "Party at Andy's." We would all meet at his house, for pizza, swimming, playing football and pulling an all-nighter.

BULLA: Thank you San Diego City. I was thankful for them to support us, and also for flying our parents out to Williamsport.

SETH: For me, mine is to all the people in San Diego who helped fundraise, because without them, I don't think my family would've made it out to Williamsport. So thank you for that, and for my family to be out there and supporting us.

ISAIAH: The most important thing I've learned since winning the World Series is that true friends will always be there for you. We are a family, and we will never give up, even when it gets hard.

OSCAR: The most important thing that I've learned is probably stay humble, because not every kid can say, "I won a Little League World Series," and most kids don't get to do what we have done since the series.

JANE: Does anyone else have anything they want to say before we wrap it up?

JENSEN: Thanks for letting us be on the show.

JANE: You're welcome. Thanks for being here.

Park View's story underscores the value of celebrating an achievement, not only in the moment, but over time, and not just for the twelve boys and their families, but for the greater community, a part of this positive experience. I'm Jane Mitchell, thank you for watching this special edition of *One on One* about the boys who not only captured a title, but also our hearts.

"Wow!! Just finished watching the *One on Twelve,* and I wanted to express how deeply the show touched my heart!! We were all so excited to watch and knew it would be good, but you blew us away! It made me cry, and was so heartwarming on so many levels! Thank you so much for doing the show, such a special keepsake we will cherish for years, and years to come!! I want to thank you for spotlighting all the boys and showing them in such a respectful and honorable manner."
—Kim Peterson, 2010

"When we watched it for the first time, it brought back all those feelings I had experienced through the journey and reminded me of what my son and these boys worked so hard for and I hope their story will encourage others, to never give up. . . . Thank you again Jane, this show was a perfect closure to an exciting and emotional year for Markus and our family."
—Anna Melin, 2010

"The best part of the show was the 1961 Little League team coming back to share their stories with all of us. That's when I finally lost it and all the tears out. I thought, 'How great is that?

Those men will always share something special together no matter what and no one will take that away from them.' That's what Bulla and his friends will be able to say. Bulla will have this group of boys to call friends forever and that's what I love. Again thank you Jane for all your time that you put into our community and San Diego."
—Pua Graft, 2010

"I truly was, and am, impressed with the One on One combined segment about the Park View LL story and the 1961 LL old and new story.... It was awesome to meet the Park View Champions and their coaches and it was great to see and reminisce old times with the 1961's and reflect on some interesting angles that you provided. We share many wonderful memories (although fuzzy for some). I am honestly honored to have been part of your endeavor and above that, to have met you."
—Chico Leonard, 2010

"It could be because of the shared experience we had together, but getting together with the team will always be enjoyable because of the friendship we have. And for that I thank you for a day of remembering, with friends."
—Jim Dolan, 2010

Afterword

For a *One on One* show, I wrap it up with a verbal bow, leaving viewers with something to contemplate about the guest, what we can learn from them or what they might inspire in us. Following suit, here are a few bows.

Back in '97, I was surprised by players' salaries—even the rookies. It certainly wasn't in my financial ballpark. I once heard a player's wife talk about a cheap sixty-dollar white t-shirt when I was still buying a three-pack of men's T's for ten dollars. Some things didn't compute, but that wasn't my world, that was theirs. Still, the topic of salaries opened a door to exploring what they did with their various paychecks. I saw how many did good things, such as caring for their extended family or sending underprivileged kids to school. I could relate to philanthropy and included that as part of their journeys. While there is skepticism about the state of professional sports, I embrace and try to "perpetuate the positive" in what I call the "good sports story." Along the way, I've learned some of the biggest impressions come in small packages.

In June '98, after shooting my stand-ups for the Dave Stewart edition, I stopped by my mom's house. My two-year-old nephew, Spencer, was in a diaper watching the Padres game on TV. Wearing heels, I told him we were going to learn to hit like Tony Gwynn and Steve Finley. Using a fly swatter as our bat, we planted our feet, tapped the floor, wiggled our backsides, and swung when the pitcher threw the ball. Spencer eventually played T-ball but found his voice in song. Still I treasure that moment of sharing my new love of the game.

In 2007, I interviewed Charger Igor Olshansky from the Ukraine, asking what he liked about America. He said, "The reason America is so beautiful is it has everything for everybody. It makes everyone happy in their own way. Like when you go to the grocery store, you could buy a tomato for this price or you could buy a tomato for three other prices and there are three other tomatoes. And everyone has the ability to go home and have a tomato and enjoy it, and I think that's why it's great." Going beyond the topic of football, I was reminded to appreciate the simple things and hopefully others who heard his comment were, too.

Then there was the Facebook® message on April 14, 2010: "Hi Jane, You probably don't remember me, but back in 1997 you did an interview about Tony Gwynn and at the end you got fans' comments about Tony Gwynn, and there was this kid at the end of

the interview with a San Diego Fire shirt that said 'He's a hard working man.' Well, that kid was me. I wanted to let you know I've been watching you the last few years and you have inspired me to become a journalist. I am currently working as a member of the Padres media. I wanted to thank you for the work you have done throughout the years. See you around the Press Box. Eric Fowler." Of course I

remembered him and cued up that sound bite about Tony: "He's a working man, helps people, good guy." You never know what five seconds of fame might ignite, and I'm touched Eric not only liked Tony Gwynn, but is pursuing his own dream.

My years in television have opened doors to interviewing people of all walks of life, including elite athletes, enterprising artists, pioneers, and even Kermit the Frog. Kermit joined Dennis and me on the set of the Holiday Bowl/Big Bay Balloon parade for forty-five-minutes in 2008. Talking with Kermit was everything I hoped for and more. I was excited and told viewers we were going to have a "ribbiting good time!" I'm lucky. I do get to have fun meeting rising and established stars.

The access and "celebrity" aspects of my career present both exciting and meaningful experiences. With the support of the Padres and Cox, I began offering special behind the scenes tours to watch batting practice and visit the announcers' booth. In thirteen years, those little tours have raised more than $150,000 for charity. I share this because I've learned when you have the chance to do something to help others and make somebody's day—especially if it's just a matter of time and effort—then do it. And do it for your own friends and family. I've begun a tradition of an "Evening of Eclectic Energy" bringing people together and creating new connections.

For the television show, pouring through pictures, interviews, and piecing it all together is not just a process or a routine. I feel like I'm inside their family's life, not as a voyeur, but a translator. This book has required me to do the same for myself. Many have wondered how I can remember my timeline so well. I know people who recite the lineup of World Series games or a player's stats. I can't do that. I think my personal time tracking ability stems from my family marking our calendars by our long summer trips, but this book process has even surprised me. No matter your profession, I encourage you to take stock of your journey; it's amazing the memories it will trigger, the dreams it can re-ignite, and the portals it can open to an unexplored part of your life.

Just as I began this afterword, my mom showed me a letter from the Commanding Officer in Guam, recommending a promotion for my father. It said, in part, "CDR Mitchell... possesses a high degree of initiative, has a progressive viewpoint and displays sound judgment.... He is a neat, gentlemanly officer, courteous, pleasant, and cooperative. Forceful, with an alert, imaginative mind, he works methodically and carefully, and produces accurate, timely results.... He has repeatedly proved he possesses a high degree of leadership."

2. CDR MITCHELL consistently performs his duties in an outstanding manner. He is a neat, gentlemanly officer, courteous, pleasant and cooperative. Forceful, with an alert, imaginative mind, he works methodically and carefully and produces accurate, timely results. CDR MITCHELL welcomes responsibility and continually seeks to broaden his field of knowledge and increase his value to the Navy. He possesses a high degree of initia-

That was written in 1968. I was five years old. Reading it forty-two years later for the first time confirmed what I have always thought about my dad: that he was special. Now with a new perspective, I'm even more proud he was valued outside our family as a good man and an upstanding patriot.

This is why I love my job. Story exploring and story telling allows people to connect with their past and places value on their journeys beyond the box score or whatever their playing field in life. One nice surprise in this book process has been hearing players say the *One on One* experience was more than just a TV show; it mattered to them, to their families, and to their fans.

Television is a strange medium, especially when you're on it and your life, in effect, is in living color. From haircuts to hemlines, it's been a study in "aging" and "freezing time" in TV still frames, seeing how I've changed from my first job in Wichita Falls, Texas (my mom's favorite picture) to twenty-four years later in the Padres clubhouse. More importantly, I'm happy I've also grown professionally and as a person.

I have few regrets from the path I have chosen or unexpectedly found. I try to live faithfully and honestly, love, laugh, learn, be grateful, and hopefully leave a little something along the way. I'm glad I poured more than $2,000 hours of my "spare time" into this book—it's challenged my multi-tasking, stick-to-itiveness, and patience, and it's been worth it. I've examined my road, assessing what's at my core and how I became my own person. Even though I grew up in a nice zip code, I appreciate my upbringing with my parents' thriftiness, roughing it, and cutting my bangs (crooked) before school pictures. I am thankful they gave me the tools to be independent and resourceful. Even so, I admit, I can equally enjoy either my three-pack of ten-dollar Ts or a Nordstrom spree, regular appointments with my hair guy, and finally be okay with selling my fifteen-year-old Honda for a new car. It's not really about the material things as much as knowing I've earned my way while following my passion. Ironically, putting some of my personal story out there, I now have a better appreciation for the risk players take when they allow me in to share their story.

Looking ahead, I hope to contribute to my profession, my family, and my community, experience motherhood and hopefully marriage. Like a lot of girls raised in the seventies, I'm independent, self-sufficient and have been open to and in love. Still, I'm told such independence and my profession can be intimidating to men, and might be why marriage has yet to be part of my journey. Regardless, I'm okay that my timeline isn't what I imagined thirty years ago when I told the Miss Coronado judges I thought I could "have it all" like my mother. I still believe I can; it's just adjusting to, and embracing, my "all" and God's timing. As for that eighth grade epiphany about my career? I visualized what it might be like, but so far, I'm grateful it's been *better* than the dream.

Acknowledgments

None of us goes through life alone. None of us has success alone. In that spirit, while I can't list everyone—with pictures and stories throughout this book and on these pages—I want to acknowledge and thank many who have touched my life, my work, and this book adventure.

Thank you to the Padres and Chargers organizations and the National Baseball Hall of Fame for your trust, support, and help over the years, and for being an integral part of my effort and success.

I thank the players, coaches, and their families, friends, and teachers who opened their scrapbooks, homes, and hearts to me and to those who would see and hear the stories *One on One*.

To the sports fans and viewers: Thank you for watching and sharing how much you appreciate the shows, the details, and the connection. I am forever touched. And to the marvelous Madres for embracing me and for your devotion, emotion, and dedication to your boys.

To Dick Enberg and Tony Gwynn: When I first set out to write this book, I visualized what my cover might look like with your names there, and I am honored you both enthusiastically agreed to contribute by writing the Foreword.

To my supervisors at Channel 4 San Diego: I'm deeply grateful to Dennis Morgigno, who believed in me from the beginning; Dan Novak for listening to Dennis, then hiring me and allowing me to "put my fingerprints all over this channel." Thank you to Bill Geppert, a genuine cheerleader, for having faith in Dan, Dennis, and me, and for giving us a canvas and letting us paint. And to Craig Nichols and Abbie Smith, who arrived on the Channel 4 scene a decade into it and continue to appreciate my work and role with the station and community. Special thanks to Craig, Bill, and Cox for granting me the rights to use my notes, images and Cox copyrighted scripts from the television show.

To my partner in creativity, Dan Roper: From show number one, you have been able to feel my writing, interpret my script's emotion, amplifying it with just the perfect music, pictures, and effects to make it all come together. The shows would not have been the same without your incomparable work ethic and commitment to quality. Thank you for all that and for those late nights you gave up with your family to get it done in the edit bay.

To my associate producers: Especially to Megan Mallgrave, Erin Krueger, Lya Vallat, Kelly Morris, Argy Stathopulos, Brad Williams, Michael Saks, David Bataller, and Michelle Witek Mattox for being willing to start at the bottom and do what might have seemed trivial at the time. Every detail and every element helped put the puzzle together.

To the Channel 4 San Diego staff and contributing freelance photographers: I appreciate your talents to shoot, light, and capture every moment.

To the production truck: Tom Ceterski, Nick Davis, Ed Barnes, Jason Bott, and the crew who have always answered the call for "extra shots," and for capturing the highlights and lowlights that come with a player, a team, and a season.

To my Channel 4 Padres game announcers: Mark Grant, Mel Proctor, Rick Sutcliffe, Matt Vasgersian, Steve Quis, Mark Neely, Tony Gwynn, and Dick Enberg for, at different times, in different ways, teaching me about the game, and for keeping the "non stats girl" part of the live game action.

To the Channel 4 San Diego and Cox colleagues: Whether brainstorming around a table or passing in the halls, I value the enviable family-like environment that has contributed to our team making an imprint on the community and on each other.

To sportscasters Jim Laslavic and Jim Stone, my friends and former colleagues at KNSD, and others in TV and radio sports departments: Thank you for helping me when I did not know something, saying "nice job" when I was still just the new kid on the sports block, or having me on your shows to talk about *One on One* or the annual *Walk to Defeat ALS.*

To the small but mighty board, staff, volunteers, PALS (Persons with ALS) and their families with the Greater San Diego Chapter of the ALS Association: While my main job has been telling athletes' stories, time with the chapter has brought me great joy, fulfillment, inspiration, and some tears. Someday we will celebrate striking out ALS.

To Pam, Anne, and Kathleen for our adventures and dreaming what might be, celebrating when things came to be, and consolation when something didn't quite work out.

To Tammy for being my reliable and stunning friend and spiritual compass, and for always being just a phone call away.

To Kelly, my gem from Indiana turned little sister, dear friend, and valuable assistant editor for this book, even while becoming a mother to sweet Baby Boy Buh.

To Jay for your tremendous energy and confidence that has buoyed me from our first meeting in an elevator at Northwestern to our life-changing conversations over fish tacos.

To Claude-Alix for seeing into my heart and core when I sometimes feel lost and for always wrapping me in a hug from wherever you are around the world.

To John for introducing me to sports on television, even when I wanted to change the channel, and for supporting my vision of something more than the box score.

To Mike for your amazing aura and friendship that kept me inspired during some trying times, and for being around to toast the victory of taking the high road.

To Rachel for being ready on cue to "sing and celebrate," and for the book that gave me clarity and strength about my purpose when I needed it.

To Darren, whose spirit was not quashed by unexpected fate, but rather radiates with humor, artistry, and adventure. While still waiting for an original painting, my best Maui memories include my visits with you.

To Charles for celebrating the more than 98 subtle and unexpected surprises as we "just imagined" through an exciting baseball time and special friendship.

To Mark and Joan for being friends and supporters ever since you first saw me catch a football on television during Super Bowl week in 1998, then "bought me" at a charity auction for a behind the scenes tour.

To Michelle, my sweet "sponge" of an intern turned AP, whose energy gives me great confidence that good, hardworking people still want to make good TV and enjoy life.

To Cathy for a brilliant balance of focus and fun, in big and small endeavors beyond the beach.

To Karen, my seventh grade preposition project partner, and, decades later, a "dazzling participle" as a single mom and my go-to gal for fun and philosophical coffee talks.

To Peggy, whose zest for life and love is a daily ray of sunshine amid the island's Orange Blossoms. The desert's loss has been my gain.

To Andrew, who didn't know what I did for a living and thought I paid people to say hello to me when they wanted to talk sports. Thank you for reminding me how laughter is good for the soul, and how we should all be happy "when the kicker hits a home run to score a basket."

To Kim, for ideas, organization, and creative strategy from day one; Amanda for exquisite expert party planning; Candace for your stick-to-itiveness and positively saying "check" after a tedious task; Mark for creative collaboration and brilliantly designing our cover and look; Melissa for capturing our "sparkle" moments; and Lisa for your unstoppable and vibrant dedication throughout this new publishing venture.

To the rest of My Dream Team: Davia, Anthony, Denise, Penny, Rudy, Will, Sheila, Ria, Kari, Barbara and Elena, for friendships, heart to heart talks, and talent that helps keep me on top of my game inside and out.

To the Hall of Champions family, including the legendary Bob Breitbard, Al Kidd, and Angela LaChica for opening doors for a fantastic celebration of the good sports story.

To Bob Teaff, my attorney and sounding board, for a decade of wisdom and guidance while reminding me, with paternal kindness, what my father would say or do.

Finally, to my family: sisters-in-law Jan and Marie and brother-in-law Steve; nieces and nephews, Tyler and Michael Morgan, Jeremy and Elizabeth, Ryan, Katharyn, and Spencer. Watching your contributions to society and seeing your many talents develop warms my heart. I love you all and appreciate your excitement about my success. I can't wait to see what you do next.

To my father for believing in your "Janie Doll," telling me I was a "winner," and setting a high standard for what a husband and father should be.

To my mother for encouraging and nurturing my gifts even when I resisted; for teaching me about capturing the moment through word, picture, and love; and for setting a good example by writing your own stories, *Mama Was a Gypsy: My Wild Irish Mother and Yearnings*. I appreciate the editing and input during this long and winding process. We will publish our children's books someday, too.

To my big brother Jer for your devotion to our family, caring for me as a baby, and cheering me on every step of the way.

To my other brother Scott for your unbridled enthusiasm about my sports gig and for keeping us chuckling with your sense of humor.

And to my sister Robyn ... for being my rock.

I am so blessed.

Frequently Asked Questions

Who was your favorite interview?

Every interview is unique and fun in the moment and the show production, but certainly some rank among my favorites. Ken Caminiti, because he was my first. Tony Gwynn, for his candor and openness. Larry Lucchino, for proving to myself I could hold my own with an experienced litigator. Trevor Hoffman, for surrendering just enough to see both his strength and vulnerability. Ted Williams, because I could not have fathomed how unique that day and its impact would be. And Ryan Klesko, for his down to earth hospitality.

Who was your most difficult interview?

If by "difficult" you mean challenging to actually interview, because they didn't talk much or open up, then really, no one. Even the quieter guys opened up as we went along. If you mean difficult in terms of preparation, anticipating it might be more challenging because of their strong or unique personas, then that list is: Larry Lucchino, Ted Williams, Kahlil Greene, and David Wells. I love a challenge.

How do you choose your subjects?

Some are obvious—the stars and legends fans want to know about. In addition to my own curiosity and observation, I get input from my bosses, the Padres and Chargers organizations, and fans. We factor in if the person is a key part of the team's equation, if they're making or expected to make an impact, or if they just have interesting personalities and stories. That doesn't mean those I haven't featured don't have great qualities, but we have our production limits and can always try for next year.

How do you know what questions to ask?

I understand things better when I know the chronology, so I start there. I research what's already known about the person. Sometimes I ask others who might know about the subject to offer nuggets of insight. Once we're in the interview, I ask what I want to know, and what I think others might want to know. My questions can serve to verify their chronology, but are more of a launching pad to have them elaborate on the topic. Listening is the best way to know what to ask. I've found that simply asking, "why," or saying, "tell me more about that" or "describe that for me" or "anything I've missed?" can open portals to topics, emotions, and great insight into who they are.

Is there any subject you would not touch, or is everything fair game?

In general, everything is fair game, but it's also a matter of judgment, appropriateness, and purpose. I may ask about the challenges of marriage in the fast-paced world of professional sports, or how they deal with those challenges—but I'm not likely to ask straight out if they've cheated. Relevant topics such as steroid use? Nowadays, yes. On the other hand, sometimes people tell me things they want to get off their chest (specific negotiations, agent-team politics, etc.). For the final show, I might touch on that topic to show a difficult time but I need to be responsible about not disparaging someone else involved, if I'm not going to get their side of the story. This generally is not the forum for that. Frankly, the details are often more interesting to the parties involved than to fans or viewers. Again, it's a matter of judgment and storytelling.

Do you get nervous before an interview?

Not nervous as in "scared," but on occasion, the anticipation leading up to the interview has caused a few wracked nerves and knots in the stomach. For example, my first time with Tony Gwynn, Larry Lucchino, Ted Williams, David Wells—all well-known, big personalities. And surprisingly, the Park View Little Leaguers—only because we were doing it in a studio with twelve boys and everyone watching, and I knew we had to get it all done in about an hour or so. For those, once I sit down and get through the first question, I'm fine. There is an adrenaline rush leading up to most interviews. When it is fun, enlightening, or emotional, I am moved, energized, and at the end, sometimes exhausted. They can be emotionally and cerebrally draining.

Are you surprised when the athletes trust you with the details of their life?

Yes, I am. Going back fourteen years, I had no idea what would come of asking personal questions. I didn't know if they would respond, if they would let their guard down. Over time, subjects knew what the show was about and what to expect in theory, but until we're sitting there with cameras rolling and starting with one's life story, I never really know what they will trust me with and reveal.

After you learn those details, do you respect them more or less?

I respect them more because I understand them better. I might not always be able to relate to what they've been through, but their honesty, self-realization, willingness to admit to wrongs, humbly celebrating turning their life around, or even some of their cockiness due to the fight they've had to fight—whatever the case may be—underscores their humanness and their journey, and I respect that.

Has anyone ever been rude or a jerk?

Rarely surrounding a *One on One* interview. On occasion, people are tired and maybe not in a good mood—especially if we're there in the morning and if the team lost the day before. Even so, they understand our mission that day is bigger than the day-to-day events. In fourteen years, there have been only a few players—in the home or visitors' jersey—who have been a little arrogant and not very nice, professional, or respectful. But they are in the minority, and the good guys far outweigh the bad.

Do guests or team officials see the show before it airs?

No. Neither the players nor the Padres or Chargers see a show before it airs or have editorial input or control. I have an executive producer watch it when Dan Roper and I say it's finished, just to make sure we're not missing something and to be sure it makes sense, but that's it.

Has a guest you've interviewed NOT liked their show?

If they didn't, they've never told me, and I've never heard that they didn't. Usually, I hear they did like it either from them or a family member.

Do you go in the locker room or clubhouse?

While they are open to women, I have chosen to mostly stay out of the locker room or clubhouse to do my job. It's not as big a deal now as even ten years ago, but I prefer to give them their space and not see them in their underwear.

You're always around good-looking professional athletes. How do you keep your focus, and have there been any romances?

Yes, I work around a concentration of compelling and cute athletes, but the operative word is work. I'm around them for a purpose, to get to know them and pass that along to fans. Some become friends, of course, and while rules of engagement are not always black and white, there have been no player romances. Maybe if they were out of the game or with another team, but in fourteen years that has yet to happen. I once had a top executive ask me, "How many of these guys have hit on you?" When I said, at the time, just one, he found that hard to believe. I suppose I didn't put that vibe out there, and I'm glad I didn't have to deal with inappropriate advances, especially when I was starting out. Plus the players are mostly either married or too young. I would rather think of them as colleagues, friends, or brothers.

Has anyone refused to be interviewed or turned you down?

Yes, a handful, but I won't say who.

Did they change their mind later?

Not that I know of, and if they did, they didn't tell me about it.

Has there been someone you wanted to feature but it didn't work out?

After his booming 50-home-run year of 1998, I wanted to feature Greg Vaughn for 1999. His off-season home was in Sacramento, and even though he was a little media-shy, he agreed to let us come to his house after visiting where he grew up and his college campus. We planned to do the sit-down interview in San Diego, due to time. After that trip, I went to Florida for Sterling Hitchcock and Jim Leyritz shoots. Upon our return to the office, I heard Producer Jason Bott say out loud, "Okay, who's gonna tell Jane?" Tell me what? Did Hitch or Jim get traded? Nope. "Greg Vaughn was traded to Cincinnati." Bummer. Those tapes sat on my shelf for years, in case he returned. There have been a few other Padres, and as for Chargers, the ones on the list are still with the team, so we shall see.

What has surprised you the most about getting up close and personal with the athletes and their families?

I've been most surprised by how sensitive and vulnerable the players are, despite their some-times strong, confident, or jaded exteriors. They, and those with the less abrasive auras, can be shy and get embarrassed, too. They sometimes are a little leery about showing the non tough-guy side through old pictures. For example, in Houston, Texas for the Woody Williams shoot, I was sorting through shoeboxes of pictures with his mother and wife. When he saw the pile he said, "No way, you aren't using that one of me in high school in a cowboy hat!" I told him, "Oh, you gotta have that, that's classic! C'mon Woody!" He conceded, it made the show, and he was fine with it. If there are pictures someone really doesn't like—including the ones with for-mer girlfriends—I'm okay with their having a little veto power at that stage. I'm also glad to discover many are really quite funny, smart, and have dimensions to them well beyond their sport of choice. While they are tactful, I'm glad when wives share information that might surprise fans. It's nice to see when the player—touched or embarrassed by her comments—sits there and listens, laughs, cries, or challenges her, showing their dynamic.

What are some of the quirky or awkward interview moments?

I wish I had a long list of quirky, odd, or awk-ward moments. I do not. I have pointed out when someone had something in their teeth or their hair was having issues—saying I don't want them to be embarrassed later or be mad at me for not telling them. We've needed to powder some because they were sweating or get them a tissue when they were tearing up. Sometimes, when I have information from their mother or friend they don't know I have, they're taken by surprise, but usually those are funny and make it into the show.

What is your most memorable moment for you personally from the interviews you've conducted?

When Ken Caminiti told me about his faith; when Ted Williams asked me what kind of fishing pole my dad used; when Jerry Coleman said being a Marine was the most important thing he's done in his life; when Tony Gwynn shared about the last conversation with his father; when Darren Sproles felt comfortable talking about overcom-ing stuttering, and as far as his shorter stature, what matters is the size of one's heart. But if I had to pick just one, it was in 1998 when I saw Trevor Hoffman's intensity when I asked about what bothers him, and he said "confusion." It was a moment of honesty, vulnerability, inten-sity, and raw reality. It was just a moment, but stays with me because it shows how, when you ask and when you listen, you can learn, relate, and better understand.

What advice do you have for someone, women especially, who wants to go into journalism and, namely, sports?

I have heard some television veterans discour-age high school and college students from ven-turing into the television news/feature industry due to the lack of jobs and stations trying to do more with less. But here's how I see it: Storytell-ing has been around from the beginning of time. If you are a journalist and a storyteller, if your heart and passion are pulling you in that direc-tion, then go for it. You might have to do more, be more creative and resourceful about learn-ing more ways of telling and showing stories, but don't cast aside your dream. If you want to cover sports—the teams, the scores, the stats—you'd better know your stuff. The sports part of my career was not my passion or my forte, but I adjusted and learned when I was given this opportunity. For others—men and women—who love sports and want to be around them, be fundamentally sound first in your skills, then ready, willing, and capable of not only filling a spot, but creating a niche. Develop your writing. Don't think you know it all at twenty-one or twenty-four years old. You don't. Seek advice and guidance from experienced peers you re-spect and trust to tell you the truth and who will guide you. Do the work. I encourage you to define your values and your work ethic, evolve, adjust to step it up as needed, and strive to fulfill your potential. If you do that, and stay true to yourself, you'll find your bliss.

A Collection of Comments

In the beginning, I just wanted to save the comments that crossed my desk, computer screen or phone, either directly, or ones my supervisors had passed along. Some made me smile. Others, with their unexpected insight, took me aback. I've sorted through my files, finding old emails and folded papers with faded ink. Not all were addressed to me or about me alone. Several were kudos to our Channel 4 team. The comments also remind me how, especially in the early years when we were establishing ourselves, the notes were a barometer of how we were doing and how people felt connected to us—sometimes even sharing personal experiences along with a thank you. Even now, whether in an article, from a fellow reporter, a stranger, or a friend, I appreciate their thoughts and their taking the time to express them. I humbly share a few here.

From Peers, Fans and Players' Families ...

"She asks questions that I would have never have thought of—I don't think that way," Johnson said. "She's asking about the kids, the family and the important things in life that, quite frankly, guys just don't talk about."

—*Don Johnson, Padres VP of Marketing,*
from "Courting the Women,"
San Diego Union-Tribune, 1997

"Hi Jane, I want to tell you that I finally saw your profile of Jerry Coleman. It was, in a word (ok, two words) absolutely wonderful! You captured the essence of what Jerry's all about. I consider him to be the nicest man I've ever known; truly a gentleman. And you fully conveyed that or more ... Cheers!"

—*John Freeman, Sports Columnist, 1998*

"Hi, it's me, the Madre Newsletter Editor again. I just wanted to pass on what I think is a very special compliment to you. I had brunch in the stadium club before the game on Sunday and at two tables near me the people were talking about Jerry Coleman. All based on having seen your *One on One*. They were discussing all the interesting things they had learned about him. Keep up the great work!"

—*Marcia, 1998*

"For a reporter, the interview is the golf swing of journalism. Relaxed precision is the ticket. To spring the interview to life, the other requirements are a limitless curiosity and an innate fascination with the human dilemma. Jane Mitchell holds these qualities, and they have brought her a Golden Mike award, an Emmy, and numerous Emmy nominations. And, along with the honors, it is evident that viewers like her."

—*Don Freeman,*
The San Diego Union-Tribune, 1998

"Just as Einstein's famous formula is more about different perspectives of space and time than the measurement of energy, Jane Mitchell's biographical television essays have more to do with the human essence at the core of baseball than with a player's batting average with runners in scoring position ... Few individuals are gifted with the empathic sense to recognize and relate so acutely to others... Jane Mitchell gave up her career to come home and tend to the man who cared for her. Yet out of the depths of her compassion, she has elevated her art form to another dimension."

—*Susan Reynolds, Living Better, 2000*

"I just wanted to take a few seconds of your time to let you know how much I've enjoyed the pieces I've seen you do on Padres players and coaches that have graced the airwaves of 4SD. Despite the fact that San Diego is seemingly a city of transplanted folks like myself (I've been here a "mere" ten years now!), your *One on One* segments come across in such a "this is my hometown and this your hometown" fashion, that I can't help but feel nostalgic, warm, and fuzzy about both the team and the city ... very well done."

—*Dave Dial, 2000*

"Dear Jane, Last night prior to the San Francisco game, I watched your summation of the Padres' '97 season. The tears started to fill in my eyes because I knew our season was ending, but I was happy because you started with Archi, and he was featured in some plays. I have taped every feature you have done on Archi, and loved every one of them; especially the antics he pulled where he appeared on other peoples' interviews. You did a marvelous job of keeping Archi in the limelight even though he didn't or couldn't play. As you can tell my dear Jayne that Archi is one of my favorite players ... You know Jayne, as a woman who just turned 70 on Sept 10th & who is the main caregiver to my Alzheimer husband who is 74, I look for precious moments to savor. You have filled a void in my life with your enormous talent and the very favorable way you have presented Archi. You also did a superb job on Cammy, Finley, Lucchino, etc. God Bless You."

—*Theresa M., September 1997*

"Dear Jane, Barbara and I were pleased to meet you in person tonight. We congratulate you and Channel 4 for the great *One on One* series. We hope to meet you more and more over the years and to support your work. Your series goes a long way in really making the Padres a family. Thanks!"

—*Frank and Barbara, Padre Fans of Chula Vista, November 1997*

"Dear Ms. Mitchell: Where did you come from? You are like a breath of fresh air on the Padre pre-game show. I never cared much for pre-game stuff, but now, along with my wife, we try to see it as often as we can. Your special features and interviews with players are always very interesting—you have a positive attitude, a winning smile—a combination that is hard to get. By the way, do you know that there are some 1,500 seniors (55 & up) playing softball in S.D.? A lot of us compete in the Sr. Slow Pitch World Championship. Thanks again for your engaging personality and your ability to bring the best of baseball great, past and present, to us. Best Wishes ..."

—*Andy, 1998*

"I admire your ability to put your featured guests so much at ease. It is refreshing and entertaining to be able to see the Padres players, their families, and others you interview talk candidly about themselves in casual settings. Thanks for making it seem as if we are sitting right there beside you, listening in on a conversation with an old friend."

—*Terrie, Hanover, PA, 1998*

"You give San Diego fans a unique and personal look at all the people in the Padres organization—showing a human side that I have rarely seen in the 29 years I've been a baseball fan. Your work and Channel 4's coverage are a major reason Padres fans look at the entire organization as family. The result: a heartfelt showing of affection for the players after the World Series, and a moment I'll always cherish. It actually made me cry."

—*Vinnie, Spring Valley, 1998*

"[Email to Bill] I regard the local Cox Communications service the best I have seen—anywhere. I *completely* enjoy your local programming. The Super Bowl and Padres coverage was among the best and most enjoyable I have ever seen. In Dennis Morgigno, you have the best news guy in San Diego or any other city I've been in. He's broadcast journalism at its most very honest and very best. What a *great* talent. Also enjoy Mark Grant ... great personality, and he knows what he's talking about. I forget the name of the young woman who does so many interviews, but she does a great job. All in all, Cox Communications is so good, I don't even mind paying the bill each month!!! You're worth every penny of it!!!"

—*Gerry, 1998*

"You have such a wonderful way of interviewing the Padres. You bring out the very interesting parts of their lives—told in such an easy way, great personal stories ... Even the tougher questions are answered, and the interviewee doesn't seem to mind answering."

—*Janet, 1999*

"Just wanted to let you all know how much I enjoy the Channel 4 coverage of the Padres. The games, *Padres Magazine*, *One on One*, *PrimeTime Padres* ... it's all a joy to watch (yes, even when the Pads lose.) :-) I'm to the point that when I know I am going to be away from home, I tape the games and everything around them so I don't miss any coverage. Through Channel 4, I've come to know this team better, and am consequently much more involved with baseball than I've been since the last baseball strike. Keep up the great work!"

—*Sandra, 1999*

"Dear Jane Mitchell, My name is Anna ... I wanted to tell you that you have done a wonderful job with your *One on One* features. My son Aaron is 5, and he just loves Sterling Hitchcock, and he loves the *One on One* you did with Sterling.

Because of that video, he feels like he knows his hero just a little more. I'll tell you, he knows that interview by heart :). Anyway, thanks again and keep smiling!"

—*Anna, 1999*

"Congratulations to Jane Mitchell and the staff at Channel 4 for the *awesome* feature on Junior Seau. I've always been a big fan of his, but now I have even more love and respect for this great team player and family fan. Thanks Channel 4 for such a well done story."

—*Trish, 1999*

"Hi Jane: I really enjoy your interviews with the Padres and the Chargers. You ask the questions we all want to know. I look forward to next year's interviews. Speaking of the Padres, do you know if Ben Davis, Damian Jackson, or Ruben Rivera have girlfriends? Thank you for your time!!!"

—*Noel, 1999*

"Your work is so refreshing ... I love the topics you choose. The research you put into the presentation, the production quality, and content you bring with your reporting. Three pieces you have done have moved me. Two have brought tears to my eyes. You do beautiful work! Without standing, the piece on Ted Williams and Jerry Coleman were pieces of history."

—*G2, 2000*

"Jane, it was *awesome*! Wow–what a great job you did! My two best girlfriends and I went to YOGI's to watch it in Cardiff because they set aside the patio for us so we could crank it up as loud as we wanted, and we all sat out there and cried the entire time! You really did capture Eric, and it was truly a tribute to his trials and tribulations thus far.... We always celebrate people's lives and lament about them after they are gone, but it is so sweet to stop and smell the roses along the way and celebrate life as it is happening, and that is what that tape does for Eric. He absolutely *loved* it. It is very thought provoking and really makes him feel the emotions from the past and present. Every time we watch it, we pick up something new. I don't think he can believe that things are going so well for him and that anyone would care enough to spend the time you have talking about his journey to San Diego. It means more to him than you know."

—*Cindy Owens, 2000*

"Just wanted to let you know how much I enjoyed your *One on One* tribute to Jerry Coleman's induction into the Baseball Hall of Fame. It was definitely a home run. And thank you for having it closed captioned. It made it all the more enjoyable. Great job. Keep up the good work. Thanks so much."

—*Walt, 2005*

"I thought the show featuring Antonio Gates and Donnie Edwards of the San Diego Chargers was excellent. They are both truly fine gentlemen. I am going to show it to underprivileged boys that I mentor from Compton. Both Antonio and Donnie are perfect role models for these underprivileged boys, and it is unfortunate that most professional athletes do not provide this type of leadership and guidance. Once again, thank you very much for your efforts and professionalism, and I look forward to viewing future *One on One* programs."

—*Bill, Laguna Beach, CA, 2005*

"The best part of the trip [to San Diego] was seeing the video [on Mark]. Everyone loved it—all for different reasons. His brothers for the memories; his brother Bryan and myself for the great job you did bringing in the various perspectives on the same subject matter, and seamlessly editing it into production, and the grandkids just lovin' him run and hit and be his funny self, just as he is with them. Peggy just beamed throughout being proud of her 'boy.' You did a masterful job and with so little time to do it. Jane, thanks so much for all your effort. It was a special job for someone we think is a very special guy."

—*Dan Sweeney, Mark's father, 2005*

"Dear Jane, I am so excited that you wrote me back! My son has always excelled in baseball, but both of us have had a little trouble believing that this is going to happen .... That is why your piece on the Gonzalez brothers was so special and encouraging to me, so much so that I wanted to share it with him. The story of Adrian Gonzalez is more about the success that some of my son's friends are experiencing now with being drafted right out of high school. The story that I want him to see is Edgar Gonzalez'; someone who had the dream of being in the major leagues, but instead of instant success, was tested, struggled, and his journey may have taken longer, but he ended up in the same place as his brother. Because my son and I are also devout Christians, the Gonzalez brothers' belief in God was also important. So, thank you so much for touching my life with your show, and I know that he will be touched as well. I believe the Lord led me to flip channels last night, just so I'd see it. I'm looking forward to watching it with my son, and also will make sure that I check out some of your other shows as well."

—*Marcia, Orange County, 2008*

"As time has gone on, it has been more and more difficult for the fan to identify with the individual players. A lot of that has to do with the economic structure and the off the field issues of a number of today's athletes. The show, *One on One,* has the ability to dispel a lot of that by getting in depth with the athletes, their families, and personalities away from the field. It creates a person out of what the fan often sees as an icon. Of course the motor that makes the show run so well is the 'One' in the *One on One.* In 2007, at a charity event for the American Cancer Society, I had the unique opportunity to meet Jane Mitchell … It became apparent what makes her so successful with the show … Jane creates an environment that gets individuals to be open and expressive about their personal lives, and paints their humanistic side wonderfully … that gives the show an easy feel that is very captivating and fun to watch."

—*Jim Leisten, 2009*

"I've been meaning to tell you how much I love *One on One.* The other day I came across your interview with a young Padre and was fascinated with the warmth and genuine atmosphere you created for him and his family. What makes your interviews so compelling is that they allow the interviewee to leave his celebrity behind and just be the person that he really is. This is a great gift, not only to your viewers, but to the athlete as well. I'm not even a sports fan, and I enjoy every interview because the human aspect is so authentic. Best of luck on future projects." —*Ann Marie, 2010*

"Jane: Thanks for the memories. Nice to go back occasionally to good times. Other *One on Ones* were helpful to me in getting to know my players, coaches & friends in more depth. Great work and good luck!"

—*Bruce Bochy, SF Giants Manager, 2010*

"*One on One* was the show I looked forward to each time there was a different person featured. Watching *One on One* sometimes brought laughter, tears of joy, and tears of sorrow, watching those that persevered through, or sometimes those who succumbed to, those demons that haunted them because of the pressures. It made me realize that we don't always know what it took for each one to get to where they are, including the ones who succumbed to those demons. I saw heart, determination, competitiveness, perseverance, love for the game, joy, bitterness, and so much more on the show. It was amazing to see the lives come full circle because of the game of baseball. From the bottom of my heart, I just don't believe that anyone else can ever do the *One on One* show like Jane Mitchell. When she calls it quits, *One on One* should go off the air."

—*Alicia Gwynn, Tony Gwynn's wife, 2010*

"Looking back, I would have to laugh about the blonde highlights in my hair! The other (that I remember) is the honor of Trevor Hoffman speaking such kind words about me. What an amazing guy."

—*Kevin Walker, Former Padres pitcher, 2010*

"You were like a rookie coming to your first Little League practice in jeans and tennis shoes and you wore your glove on the wrong hand, but you were a sponge. I think [you really established yourself] probably after the lean years. It's like a rookie coming up in the big leagues and winning the world championship. It's like you expect it every year, and when you [the team] hit the skids, it's how you react…. Not everybody's in a good mood, not everything's rosy, and that's when you really have to work hard and still get the message across. Even though the Padres were in last place, we'd say, 'Hey, Jane Mitchell's *One on One* is on, it's pretty cool to find out about so and so.' We love giving you a hard time you know why? Because we like you. That's what sports is like. If you walk in the clubhouse and someone gives you a hard time, that means they like you."

—*Mark Grant, Channel 4 San Diego Announcer, 2010*

"I didn't necessarily feel there was more pressure [after being featured]. I never ever thought of it that way, but I thought it was almost an honor to be picked, where you would actually spend the time to fill in our past and find the paths that we chose, whether there were difficult times or not. You kind of develop a story line and so I felt like that was kinda neat that you actually pick us to do that."

—*Xavier Nady, MLB Outfielder, 2010*

"People always want to tell me about Jane. They want to let me know about their favorite interview, or suggest someone for her next *One on One* episode. They'll tell me something about their favorite athlete that they learned from watching the show. They tell me when the show touched them on a personal level. It's easy to see the many ways in which Jane has formed a bond with the San Diego community and with the team at Channel 4 San Diego."

—*Craig Nichols*
VP/GM Channel 4 San Diego, 2010

From My Family ...

"What you create is what it is. Your style is like a flavor or art type ... you handle it naturally and use your experience to build on over time. The more episodes you do, the more you can leverage the learning to the next episode ... so it's always building. Until you do the last show of your life, you will always be capable of doing more; and different is good. It mirrors life. This is a great way to go about it. Keep up the good work. Your passion to create is very clear."

—*Mitch Mitchell, Brother, 2010*

"I was eight when Janie was born. In my own version of "sibling rivalry" I rubbed her head, gently, thinking that might keep her from becoming smarter than me. That apparently didn't work. We joke now how I can take a little credit for her brilliance! I was happy when she won Miss Coronado and impressed when she moved home to take care of Dad. Even though I grew up rooting for our San Diego teams more than she did, it's now common ground. Her TV job has never gone to her head and it's been nice she's included our family in the perks of her job,

and now with this book. We all learned a lot from our parents, and our dad would be proud of her."

—*Scott Mitchell, Brother #2, 2010*

"I am a family physician. Janie is a journalist. Growing up I was on the sidelines and an observer, while Janie was always involved and a participant. We both interview, document and retell a story; mine, confidentially, with my patients and hers with interviewees. I marvel at her ability to gather, research and reveal the story with insight, candor, and accuracy, and then produce it for the public. When I was in High School I took AP biology, later she followed me in that course. I think she was sorry that she did. I loved it; she did not. She has become involved in medicine through her dedication to the ALS Association's San Diego Chapter. She has invested her gifts and talents with opportunity, industry, humor and direction, applying them in her profession and in volunteering. We have a lot in common, and I celebrate our differences. She is my sister and she is *no plain Jane*."

—*Robyn Mitchell-Stong, MD and Sister, 2010*

"Every year about January eighth, the anniversary of when my husband died in 1994, Janie and I have a bonfire on the beach to remember him. Sometimes we write little notes, sending the embers to Heaven. We take sticks, wood cut from our trees, and paper to start the fire. One time, in about 1999, we forgot the matches. Janie took a stick and walked to a neighboring group and asked if she could borrow some fire to light our fire. Immediately, the teenager saw her face in the light of his fire and said, 'Of course, you are the Padre Girl. I watch you all the time.' She had no make-up on and was in jeans, but he recognized her voice as well as her face. I am proud of my daughter for her influence on young people, showing that the ball players are good people who are mainly good role models with values that enhance their lives rather than destroy their lives. You can't win them all, but there is the chance to reach many to make a difference."

—*Ann Mitchell, Fan and Mother, 2010*

Special Thanks

My thanks and gratitude to the following partners for not only believing in me, but for contributing their energy, time, and resources. Their creativity and can do attitude have made the book and book launch charity fundraiser a meaningful and exciting endeavor.

Marketing & Publicity
Marketing Division of
Saint Somewhere Holdings, LLC
www.SaintSomewhereMarketing.com

Publisher
Sweet Dreams Publishing
of Massachusetts
www.PublishatSweetDreams.com

Art Direction/Design
M R O W K A Design
www.mrowkadesign.com

Photography
Creative Keepsakes Photography
www.sandiegophoto.com

Event Planning
Creative Affairs by Amanda
www.creativeaffairsbyamanda.com

Make-up Artist
James Overstreet
www.alteredhues.com

Corporate Sales: Cathy Brown

Legal Advisor: Robert Teaff

Cox Communications/
Channel 4 San Diego
www.4sd.signonsandiego.com

Bridgepoint Education
www.bridgepointeducation.com

Charity Partners
The Greater San Diego Chapter of the ALS Association
www.alsasd.org

The Make-A-Wish Foundation®
www.wish.org

The Padres Foundation for Children
www.padres.com

San Diego Hall of Champions
www.sdhoc.com

The Cox Kids Foundation
ww2.cox.com/myconnection/

San Diego Madres
www.sdmadres.org

Taste of San Diego
Charity Event Partners

Acqua al 2
www.acquaal2.com

Bistro D' Asia, Coronado
www.bistrodasia.signonsandiego.com

Chocolat
www.chocolatsandiego.com

Continental Catering
www.continentalcateringsd.com

Hotcha Salsa
www.HotchaSalsa.com

Oceanaire Seafood Room
www.theoceanaire.com

Randy Jones All-American Sports Grill
www.aagrill.com

Ryan Bros. Coffee
www.ryanbroscoffee.com

Stone Brewing Co.
www.stonebrew.com

TOAST Enoteca & Cucina
www.toastenoteca.com

With Bob Breitbard, friend and founder of the San Diego Hall of Champions, 2007.

Bridgepoint ®
E D U C A T I O N

First and foremost, Bridgepoint Education is a San Diego company. We were founded in San Diego and we remain headquartered here. We are proud to be a part of the San Diego community and we want to do whatever we can to maintain our hometown's reputation as America's Finest City. That means we are an active participant in the community and we give back to the community whenever we can.

Our commitment to giving back focuses on three key areas: education, youth, and the military. We realize that communities thrive when the youngest members of those communities are nurtured and given opportunities to learn and grow. Accordingly, we champion numerous charities that serve underprivileged schools and bring hope to disadvantaged youth.

We also recognize the special role the U.S. Armed Forces play in a military town like San Diego. The sacrifice and dedication displayed by active-duty service members and veterans is admirable and truly inspirational. Bridgepoint Education supports the members of the military who have done so much to serve our country.

As an education company, we understand the power of education to transform lives. Through our two institutions of higher learning, Ashford University and University of the Rockies, we strive to offer a quality education that is accessible and affordable for all students who are academically qualified. Learning is a lifelong pursuit, and Bridgepoint Education stands behind all efforts to expand knowledge.

That is why Bridgepoint Education chose to be a part of *One on One: My Journey with Hall of Famers, Fan Favorites and Rising Stars.* The stories contained in this book offer unique lessons on success and achievement. Everyone can learn something from the way sports legends profiled in these pages have overcome obstacles and climbed to the pinnacle of their professions. We are pleased we could help Jane Mitchell bring these stories—and a rich slice of our community's cultural history—to you.

Andrew Clark

Chief Executive Officer
Bridgepoint Education

The Complete List of *One on One* Shows

The following is a list of all the One on One *shows April 1997–November 2010.*

The editions without descriptions are featured earlier in the book.

1. **Ken Caminiti** *April 1997*
2. **John and Becky Moores** *May 1997*
3. **Tony and Alicia Gwynn** *June 1997*
4. **Tim Flannery** *July 1997*
5. **Bruce Bochy and Kevin Towers** *August 1997*

In 1997, Manager Bruce Bochy and General Manager Kevin Towers called themselves Batman and Robin, but wouldn't say who was who. I relied on them for guidance about the plan for the team. We introduced fans to who they were as people—as husbands, with families and pets—and why they were a successful baseball duo on the rise.

6. **Larry Lucchino** *September 1997*
7. **Retrospective** *October 1997*

While 1997 was a landmark year for Channel 4 Padres and me, a sports rookie, the Padres did not fare well. Rather than casting a losing season aside, I wanted to hear how the players and their wives processed a less than stellar year. Who better to look back and look ahead than Tony Gwynn and Ken Caminiti.

8. **Steve Finley** *April 1998*
9. **Jerry Coleman** *May 1998*
10. **Dave Stewart** *June 1998*
11. **Trevor Hoffman** *August 1998*
12. **Randy Jones and Rollie Fingers** *September 1998*

Two former Padres stars known around the game were Randy Jones, a Cy Young Award winner, and Rollie Fingers, in the Hall of Fame. I had met the friendly, iconic Randy around the ballpark, then Rollie for the first time at his home. While I told their stories seeing their scrapbooks took me back to my childhood and the few times I went to Padres games.

13. **Jim Leyritz** *April 1999*

When former Yankee Jim Leyritz came to San Diego, his energy ignited an already dynamic Padres team. I envisioned a show featuring the Padres own Mr. October. A trip to his winter home in Florida, meeting his country music idol Garth Brooks at spring training, and hearing his story through his interesting raspy voice, made for a fun and invigorating show.

14. **Sterling Hitchcock** *May 1999*

With a trip to Florida to interview Jim Leyritz, we added a stop in Tampa to interview Sterling Hitchcock. The NLCS MVP was quiet but surprised me by sharing how a baseball field became his escape from a lonely childhood. Based on his depth and dimension, what I thought might be a short feature became a half-hour show including Sterling's wife, family, and faith.

15. **Nate Colbert and Dave Winfield** *June 1999*

From current stars to stars of the past, *One on One* was a visual vehicle to share the team's history and perspective with fans. Nate Colbert was the Padres' first big star in 1969. We didn't have a lot of highlight reels to choose from, but an inquiry to an Atlanta TV station, WSB, led to the discovery of rare footage of him playing. Dave Winfield, a Padres star for a decade, became the first bonafide million-dollar man in baseball when he signed with the Yankees.

16. **Matt Clement, Ben Davis and Gary Mathews Junior** *August 1999*

Featuring three young stars in one show was three times the process between pictures, interviewing them and their parents: Matt and Ben in San Diego, Gary in Las Vegas at Triple A. Matt was quiet yet mature as a young starting pitcher; Ben, tall, and a young female fan favorite, was outgoing, confident, and very polite. Gary enjoyed the irony of being with the Padres organization, after his father's team, the Cubs, lost the division to San Diego in 1984.

17. **Junior Seau** *October 1999*
18. **Alan Trammell** *April 2000*

Alan Trammell represented the first "coming home" show. He became a Detroit Tigers and World Series hero facing the Padres, and a Hall of Fame prospect. We interviewed Hall of Fame Manager Sparky Anderson about coaching Alan and walked Alan's high school field and where he snuck in the stadium to watch Padres games during his childhood.

19. **Ted Williams** *May 2000*
20. **Eric Owens** *June 2000*

Eric Owens wasn't a superstar, but became a fan favorite for exuding effort and having a dirty uniform as a result. His interview peeled back layers of this modern day "Pig Pen" as he shared how his father's death inspired him to get on the right path. I gained a real sense of the close family—who grew up packed in a VW bug—when I went to Atlanta to interview the family who had driven from Virginia to watch their little brother live his and his father's dream.

21. The Boone Family *August 2000*

Major League Baseball's first three-generation family is from San Diego, and with the signing of Bret Boone we had the makings of a three-generation show. The Boone group included Ray and Patsy, Bob and Sue, and Bret and Susie. Their respect for the game and tradition was reaffirmed by family and baseball friends at Ray's memorial service; sharing stories about a quality man and patriarch of the Boone family.

22. Mike Riley *October 2000*

The San Diego Chargers switched gears in 2000 with new head coach Mike Riley. His childhood and coaching career were rooted at Oregon State University in Corvallis, Oregon, so Dan and I went to see how his background translated to the gridiron.

23. WUSA: The Spirit Stars, *March 2001*

They captured the world's attention and America's hearts, so we focused on three stars of the U.S. Women's Soccer team, playing for the first-ever major league women's professional soccer league in the world. Julie Foudy, Joy Fawcett, and Shannon MacMillan ventured home to one of the league's eight teams, the San Diego Spirit, to live and share their dream. Julie was a vivacious leader, Joy, a quiet but busy mother, and Shannon a young woman with determination to succeed.

24. Ryan Klesko *April 2001*

25. Woody Williams *May 2001*

Pitcher Woody Williams, one of the good guys in the game, had a new perspective after an aneurysm during the 2000 baseball season threatened his playing career and almost his life. We traveled to Houston in the winter to spend time with him Texas-style. It was a pleasure to tell the story of a soft-spoken guy with a strong faith and family ties, as well as a love of the game.

26. Kevin Walker and Adam Eaton *June 2001*

Kevin Walker and Adam Eaton were ones to watch, two pitchers rising quickly to the majors due to injuries on the big club. With Adam

from Washington state, and Kevin from Texas, coordinating photographers in those states helped us illustrate their story. I was only nauseous for twenty-four hours after I played video games with Kevin for our activity, the price of reporter-participation!

27. Dave Winfield Hall of Fame *August 2001*

28. Doug Flutie *November 2001*

29. Mark Kotsay *April 2002*

30. Kevin Jarvis and Bobby Jones *June 2002*

Kevin Jarvis passed up medical school to pursue baseball. His long road led to San Diego where he found stability. The southerner was a down-home guy who loved computers and being a father. Bobby Jones, from Fresno, showed off his cooking skills. 2001 was challenging, but his professionalism during his worst record ever earned him the respect of his teammates and deserved the spotlight.

31. Ozzie Smith *August 2002*

32. Dave Magadan and Kevin Walker *September 2002*

Dave Magadan's reputation as a teacher when he played launched him into the new world of minor league coaching upon retirement. One of the best pinch-hitters of his time, home movies and photos illustrated his growing up with the inspiration of his godfather and cousin Lou Piniella. We paired the segment with an update about Kevin's progress after surgery.

33. LaDainian Tomlinson and Drew Brees *November 2002*

34. Junior Seau: Super Bowl *January 2003*

35. Tony Gwynn: Chapter 2 *April 2003*

36. Mark Loretta and Adam Eaton (update) *May 2003*

37. Ramon Vazquez *July 2003*

Ramon Vazquez was quick on his feet and praised as one of the most consistent players on the team. His story begins with being a poor kid from a small island who started out as a professional volleyball player. We coordinated bilingual interviews with his family and former coaches in Puerto Rico to help tell this inspiring story.

38. Ted Williams: The Interview *August 2003*

A year after Ted Williams passed away it seemed time to hear more extended parts of his comments from 2000—his last TV interview. This concept provided me a first—including some behind the scenes moments and a more personal narrative about my experience. This book has now allowed that in detail.

39. Sean Burroughs and Xavier Nady *September 2003*

Sean Burroughs and Xavier Nady were two young guns making an impact in the Padres organization. Also roommates, we toured this "Odd Couple's" bare bones bachelor pad, and told their individual stories. Sean, the son of a major leaguer and a Little League World Series victor, had success early in his big league career, but also faced pressures from high expectations. Xavier, from Salinas, the lettuce capital of the world, had an impressive three years at Cal-Berkeley before being drafted by the Padres. A visit to his home and a tour of his parents' family room revealed a lot about his early success and determination to pursue his dream.

40. Marcellus Wiley and Tim Dwight *December 2003*

Even when the early 2000s saw tough years for the Chargers, two outstanding individuals on the Bolts' roster were Marcellus Wiley and Tim Dwight. Their personalities alone inspired fans for what they brought to the game and the cities they care about. I spent some time with the boys with their toys—Marcellus' game room and then kayaking with Tim, an extreme sports enthusiast. Both reminded us that the journey is just as important as the destination.

41. John and Becky Moores: Ballpark Opening *April 2004*

42. Jake Peavy and Tim Flannery *May 2004*

43. Ramon Hernandez and Ryan Klesko *June 2004*

In 2004 the Padres traded for the Oakland A's All-Star catcher. Like the salsa music he loved, Ramon was vibrant and passionate. He grew up on some tough streets in Venezuala and his story underscored how few who dream the dream really make it. Seeing him with his family, he seemed appreciative. And with his loveable Latin sense of humor, didn't mind being called Carlos, mistaken sometimes for 1998 fan favorite Carlos Hernandez. Ryan, the team's MVP and willing to switch positions, was returning from shoulder surgery in 2004, when we updated his story, saw his La Jolla home, and his San Diego condo that cost more than his 250 acres in Georgia with three houses on it.

44. Terrence Long and Rod Beck *August 2004*

When most teams considered Rod Beck done, he stepped into the Padres closer role in 2003 with stunning success and contributed in 2004 as a set-up guy. Time with his family revealed the softer side of the tough guy voted the Players Choice 2003 Comeback Player of the Year. Terrence Long, an Alabama native, was the essence of the major league "long shot" preferring basketball to baseball. He gave in to my request to show us his special, never-before-seen closet full of jerseys.

45. Mark Loretta and Terrence Long *August 2004*

46. David Wells *September 2004*

47. Antonio Gates and Donnie Edwards *December 2004*

48. Mark Loretta and Jake Peavy *March 2005*

49. Khalil Greene *April 2006*

50. Dave Roberts *May 2005*

51. Aki Otsuka and Scott Linebrink *June 2005*

Scott and Aki were one-two punch relief pitchers. Interviewing Aki was a bilingual adventure. Through a translator, he spoke of his love of the game and America. Cooking at home with his family showed how they had a taste of Japan every day. Scott, from Austin, Texas was surprised how he ended up in the majors considering he wasn't a very good ball player as a child. A significant coach in his life died of Lou Gehrig's Disease and he and his wife Kelly helped with my ALS awareness effort.

52. Mark Sweeney *July 2005*

53. Jerry Coleman at the Hall of Fame *August 2005*

54. Trevor Hoffman *September 2005*

55. Darren Sproles and Keenan McCardell *November 2005*

This show featured two men at different ends of the career spectrum: Darren, the exciting Chargers rookie whose quickness makes up for size; and Keenan, the durable veteran who was also a Mr. Mom. Both grew up being told they were too short or too small or too "something" to fulfill their NFL dream. I played tour guide with Darren at the San Diego Zoo. Keenan, a two-time Pro Bowler with two Super Bowl rings, also had his hands full with four children, including twins.

56. LaDainian Tomlinson and Drew Brees *December 2005*

57. Sandy Alderson *April 2006*

Sandy Alderson took the helm of the San Diego Padres as the Chief Executive Officer with a stellar resume as a Marine in Vietnam, an attorney, success with the Oakland Athletics in the '90s, and an MLB executive. I prepared for this interview, posing some tough questions Padres fans were wondering about, including trades and building a team on a small payroll. It was fascinating and fun to push my cerebral limits amid a beautiful home filled with unusual baseball art.

58. Geoff Blum *May 2006*

59. Eric Young and Mike Cameron *June 2006*

Eric Young and Mike Cameron—two former All-Stars with post-season experience—were adding speed and sizzle to the San Diego Padres outfield and lineup. Eric Young grew up in New Jersey and credits his parents with teaching him about hard work and goal setting. Becoming a father at just eighteen years old also spurred him on to succeed both in college at Rutgers University and in baseball. Mike Cameron was a comeback kid story which is detailed in this book.

60. Padres in the Community: Peavy, Roberts and Hoffman *July 2006*

With big egos and bigger salaries, some professional athletes often disappoint their fans. But for more than a decade, the San Diego Padres ownership and team had put their money where their mouth is—devoting time, tickets, and money to more than 2500 organizations every year. We profiled three players (Trevor Hoffman, Dave Roberts, and Jake Peavy) at the forefront of both team efforts and causes close to their hearts.

61. Chris Young *August 2006*

To say Chris Young had reached unusual heights was not just a play on words. He has a degree from Princeton, could have been playing in the NBA, and for a baseball player is very tall. At 6'10", he's among the tallest pitchers in Major League Baseball history. Young, from Dallas, Texas, met and married fellow Princeton grad and Georgetown Law School student Liz Patrick. Her family tree includes founders of the National Hockey League. We walked down by the bay to see them exploring their new community.

62. David Wells Returns *October 2006*

63. Luis Castillo *October 2006*

64. Igor Olshansky *December 2006*

Igor was the first person from the former Soviet Union to play in the NFL. At 6'6" and 295 pounds, this giant of a man takes his work, family, and faith to heart. We told the Olshansky family odyssey by going to San Francisco and meeting his parents who immigrated to America because of the persecution they felt in their homeland for being Jewish. Igor married his high school sweetheart, Liya, also an immigrant, and both shared their appreciation for being in football and giving back to the San Diego and Jewish communities.

65. Trevor Hoffman *March 2006*

66. Tony Gwynn: Road to Cooperstown *April 2007*

67. Buddy Black *May 2007*

Buddy Black, a 15-season big league pitcher and San Diego State star in the '70s, made his managerial debut in 2007. He and his wife Nan, a nurse, have two daughters who battled a rare and yet unnamed blood disease. While Buddy was a little reserved and diplomatic in general, Nan was matter of fact about how she hated baseball when they first met. It became clear Buddy's leadership skills would help the Padres through some growing years. (We updated his story, show #95, after he was named National League Manager of the Year 2010.)

68. Adrian Gonzalez *June 2007*

69. Tony Gwynn: The Conversation *July 2007*

With so many great stories and subjects, I couldn't let what I couldn't fit into shows go to waste, so we put most of his interview into a one-hour show which ran leading up to Tony's induction at the Hall of Fame.

70. Tony Gwynn: Hall of Fame *August 2007*

71. Mike Cameron and Kevin Kouzmanoff *September 2007*

72. Shaun Phillips *November 2007*

73. Adrian and Edgar Gonzalez *April and May 2008*

74. Tony Clark *June 2008*

A high school basketball star in San Diego, Tony Clark didn't envision being a baseball player. He had come to realize his vision isn't as important as he once thought and had learned to embrace obstacles as opportunities. Sitting on a couch in a rented condo—his family still in Arizona—a tearful Tony shared about his challenging childhood, the injuries that changed his career, and his religious epiphany that impacted how he plays and contributes to the community.

75. Heath Bell *July 2008*

Heath Bell, with his deadpan expressions and dry sense of humor, has a big booming personality and an even bigger heart. I learned he was a dichotomy: a tough-guy pitcher and nice-guy father who couldn't wait to show me the latest pictures of his children, including his daughter with Down syndrome. Heath's journey had been a fight every step of the way, and in San Diego, with Trevor Hoffman still the closer, Heath was the set-up guy, proving he was the real deal.

76. Mark Merila *September 2008*

77. Tina Mickelson *November 2008*

78. Eric Weddle and Jacques Cesaire *December 2008*

Eric, a smaller sized player, had an attitude of mind over matter. We saw that in action as he studied film, taking copious notes. At home with his wife Chanel and their new baby, we learned how he was very much a family man and grateful guy. Jacques, a self-proclaimed high school band geek, was big and essentially required by a coach to play football. His willingness to adjust was influenced by his parents who fled Haiti to America in 1976 and raised Jacques and his siblings with humble beginnings and strong values. As he was perfecting his piano playing, he and his wife Jill were expecting their first child.

79. Matt Wilhelm *December 2008*

There's an expression that's part of the American vernacular of late, when someone has a desirable job, a great family or opportunities galore … they say they're Living the Dream. Matt was Living the Dream when we met him and his wife Vanessa and their new baby. The Ohio State Buckeye fan became a Buckeye star on the 2003 Championship team. When I asked about his DUI as a Charger rookie, he was up front about how it was irresponsible, almost cost him everything, and underscored his commitment to the community and his family.

80. Will Venable, Nick Hundley, and Josh Geer *April 2009*

Will, Nick, and Josh were three young guys to watch. We met Will at his parents' home in the bay area, and he played catch with his father, Max, a former major leaguer, as they reminisced about growing up in the game. Will, a Princeton grad, was also artistic, bashfully

expressing himself and demonstrating how he likes to sketch.

Nick grew up roaming the country following his father, a college football coach. Exposure to hard work to get to championship games influenced Nick's choice for and approach to his profession. His mother told how Nick "shook her off" at four years old when he was pitching to her. He was humble, funny, and a little nervous the day I interviewed him and his fiancé Amy. He cooked wasabi salmon cakes for our viewing audience.

Josh Geer, a tall, slow-talking Texan, promised me he would stay humble as he progressed in the game. We captured his winter off-season workouts and heard from his proud parents who revealed Josh was often in trouble for throwing and breaking things as a kid. That harnessed energy turned into a promising career.

81. Scott Hairston *May 2009*

Family trees are important in many professions, but in baseball, there's something intriguing when those roots set a record. Scott is among the five Hairstons who have played in the majors. The Hairstons are the largest Major League family in history to date. A soft-spoken Scott talked about how his grandfather struggled during the time of segregation before being signed by the Chicago White Sox, and how his father Jerry grew up in the south in the '60s before his fourteen-year major league career. The family name also meant having a lot to live up to, and Scott was candid about how he had much to prove in school and in the game. Time at home with the Hairstons showed his other dimensions including marrying his college sweetheart Jill and raising their boys who could be fourth- generation ballplayers.

82. David Eckstein *June 2009*

83. Chase Headley *July 2009*

Chase Headley was about brain and brawn: a high school valedictorian, an Academic All-American, and a student of the game. Understated and clean cut, this Colorado boy had adopted a Tennessee accent, having gone to college there. He was thoughtful in his answers about his faith and how learning to temper his emotions on the field as a kid, helped him develop into a major leaguer. We joined Chase and his wife Casey, an outdoorsy couple, as he practiced shooting his bow and arrow, and she shot pictures with her new camera.

84. Kevin Kouzmanoff *August 2009*

85. Anthony Gwynn *October 2009*

86.   Quentin Jammer *November 2009*

San Diego Charger Quentin Jammer had become one of best cornerbacks in the National Football League, but he had also faced fan criticism about his high number of penalties early on. I asked about that criticism. In his soft-spoken manner, he described how he took that to heart and worked hard to improve his game. By 2009, fans told us they were happy to see how his hard work paid off. His story included hard times, hype, and humility, including being the first person in his family to go to college, and a University of Texas star, at that. He credits UT coach Mack Brown for altering his course. We showed how Quentin and his wife Alicia now quietly give back to help improve the course of foster kids who need a role model and encouragement.

87.   Kevin Burnett *December 2009*

San Diego Chargers Linebacker Kevin Burnett's journey had both tragedy and triumph intertwined. The former Dallas Cowboy signed as a free agent in March 2009 and was unabashed about his role on the team. When I mentioned he was not a household name yet, he said in no uncertain terms that he would be by the end of the season. A confident guy, he lost his father at five and was raised by his mother in Los Angeles' inner city and Compton, and earned two degrees from the University of Tennessee. A big kid, too, he generously let me take control of his expensive radio controlled cars on his back yard track.

88/89.   Park View LL World Champions *April 2010*

90.   Scott and Jerry Hairston *2010*

When the 2009 World Series Champion Jerry Hairston Junior signed with the Padres, we revisited the Hairston family story. This time, we added the brotherly love and competition dimension, considering this was the first time the Hairston brothers had played on a team together other than on team Mexico for the World Baseball Classic.

91.   Heath Bell *Update 2010*

Since being featured in 2008, Heath had been named the Padres closer and an All-Star. He had also experienced a personal roller coaster of events. Along with his success, he shared how he almost lost his marriage to his wife, Nicole, but that his newfound faith brought them together. They added another baby boy to their family, plus his father was battling cancer. This was an emotional interview.

92.   Kyle Blanks *June 2010*

Kyle Blanks was a powerhouse universally known by Padres fans for his inside-the-park home run in 2009. At 6'6", projected to be a big piece of the team, we began shooting his show during spring training, driving up to where he played, Yavapai College. At his rented apartment in San Diego, this gentle giant told how he was raised in a paycheck-by-paycheck household in rural Albuquerque and that his future was a blank piece of paper until baseball offered him a chance. He also demonstrated his favorite hobby—making barbeque chicken pizza. By June, he had elbow trouble, and I asked him about the prospect of Tommy John surgery. He said he welcomed it, expecting this delay would be a small part of what he hoped would be a long career.

93.   Dick Enberg *October 2010*

Having interviewed Dick Enberg in 2004, then having him agree to write my Foreword in 2009, I did not expect I'd do a *One on One* on him. But when he became the Padres announcer for 2010, it seemed not only natural but an honor. I enjoyed elaborating on his return to the game he loved and seeing that at seventy-five, and held in high esteem, he still worked hard for his living as a brilliant storyteller.

94.   Norv Turner *October 2010*

I had heard Norv Turner described as misunderstood because of his low-key attitude and look, not fitting the NFL head coach image. Not one for pithy soundbites, an in-depth interview allowed us to listen to his heart and explore the brilliant mind his players and colleagues admire. We went to the projects where he grew up in Martinez, CA, learned how his late mother, who had MS, inspired him, and that he gets emotional upon hearing that Troy Aikman (whom I interviewed) says he is like the big brother he never had. Norv is a family man, funny and smart. Despite warnings he wouldn't, he allowed us to mic him during practice. I think he trusted I would be responsible in what we used, and that I knew what I was doing to show his many dimensions. Misunderstood? Hopefully, not anymore.

The Crew Behind the Scenes of *One on One* 1997–2010

Senior Editor/ Photographer
Dan Roper

Special Segment Editors
Jay Conner
Maya Trabulsi
Steve Sanders
Tod Lilburn
Tom Catlin

Photographers
Aaron Brown
Alan H. Rose
Ann Zevely
Bob Brock
Bob Cross
Chase Peckham
Chris Brown
Chris Hanks
Chris Hardy
Chris Saflar
Cord Cameron
Darren Leary
Ed Baier
Erica Simpson
Erik Meyer
Gabe Rivera
Gary Seideman
Jason Bott
Jason Dutcher
Jay Conner
Jennifer Hughes
John Kabasakalis
Jon Stinebaugh
Jorge Corrales
Justin Renoud
Kerry Strom
Matt Griffin
Matt Hall
Michael Osment
Michael Peak
Michael Spaulding
Mike Howder
Nick Davis
Paul Gugliotti
Rob Amato
Rob Hotz
Roel Robles
Sandy Gonzalez
Sean Popke
Shane Fortin
Shannon Hull
Steve Sanders

Tod Lilburn
Tom Catlin
Tony Gross

Associate Producers
Argy Stathopulos
Brad Williams
Carla Hockley
David Bataller
Erin Krueger
Katie Moeser
Kelly Morris
Lya Vallat
Marc Prescott
Megan Mallgrave
Michael Saks
Michelle Witek Mattox
Ned Radovic

Production Assistants/ Interns
Arbie Clark
Alicia Quintanar
Allison Muehlenbeck
Andrew Tomsky
Brian Jordan
Brian Kim
Briana Sanella-Willis
Brooke Ellison
Buell Brown, III
Candace Edwards
Carlos Pelavo
Casey Nakamura
Cassie Coulter
Charlie Kenneweg
Chris Frost
Christy Eckert
Danielle Hilbert
David Holtzman
David Kim
Ed Barnes
Ekaterina Villa
Elizabeth Christensen
Faye Donalson
Frank Petroskey
Gina Nardoni
Ginger Lange
Grant Wenkert
Holly Fantaskey
Ivan Burgueno
Jared Carr
Jennifer Riley
John Spriet
John Walsh
John Zappola

Katie Eichhorst
Kerry Strom
Kim Ha
Kristen Castro
Kyle Keller
Laura Given
Laura Vogltanz
Lauren LeBeau
Lauren Mickler
Laurie Fisher
Le My Nguyen
Lesley Pate
Lydia Bautista
Mari Katherine Raftopoulos
Maryam Biganeh
Michelle Bergeson
Mike Covey
Mike Flynn
Nassim Bakhitari
Nichole Shanks
Philip Zaengle
Rael Enteen
Randy Borgwardt
Rich Hevier
Ryan Creighton
Ryan Mickler
Sandra Torres
Scott Richison
Sean Condon
Sebastian Turner
Shannon Janko
Shannon Taylor
Sharon Heilbrunn
Sheri McQueen
Spencer Hollison
Tami Wong
Ted Mendenhall
Tom Connole
Tonya Alleyne
Tory Chainel
Willie Williams

Graphic Designers
Brian Jouan
The Dakota Group
Tom McCarthy
Tonya Mantooth

Make-Up Artists
Davia Matson
James Overstreet
Stewart Cramer

Executive Producers
Abbie Smith
Dennis Morgigno

Awards

National Academy of Television Arts & Sciences: Pacific Southwest Chapter

"Outstanding Achievement for ..."

1996 *A Salute to Teachers*—Special Events Coverage

1997 Padres Profiles: Ken Caminiti/Tim Flannery/Archi Cianfrocco—Sports Reporting Feature

1998 "A Season of Heroes"—Documentary

1999 *A Salute to Teachers*—Special Events Coverage

One on One featuring Junior Seau—Historical/Biographical

2001 *One on One* featuring WUSA—Historical/Biographical

One on One featuring Dave Winfield—Writing Other than News

2002 *A Salute to Teachers*—Special Events Coverage

2003 *A Salute to Teachers*—Special Events Coverage

One on One featuring Xavier Nady & Sean Burroughs—Historical/Biographical

One on One featuring Ted Williams: The Interview—Historical/Biographical

One on One featuring Tony Gwynn: Chapter 2—Historical/Biographical

2004 *A Salute to Teachers*—Special Events Coverage

"Tribute to Dr. Seuss"—Writing Other than News

2005 *One on One* featuring Jerry Coleman—Writing Program

"Tony Muser"—Sports Single Story

2006 *One on One* featuring Luis Castillo—Sports Program

One on One featuring Geoff Blum—Writing Program

One on One featuring Geoff Blum—Sports Program

One on One featuring Igor Olshansky—Sports Program

2007 *One on One* featuring the Road to Cooperstown—Sports Program

Forefront featuring Kadir Nelson—Interview Discussion Program

2008 *One on One* featuring Mark Merila—Writing Program

One on One featuring Mark Merila—Sports Program

2009 *One on One* featuring Scott Hairston—Historical/Cultural

One on One featuring David Eckstein—Sports Program

Golden Mike Awards

1993 "Major Dad's Triplets"—Best Light Feature Reporting

1999 *One on One* featuring Jim Leyritz—Best Sports Feature

2001 *One on One* featuring Dave Winfield—Best Sports Feature

2005 "Tony Muser"—Best TV Serious Feature

San Diego Press Club

2003 First Place Sports Feature

2004 First Place Television-Sports Program

2005 First Place Television-Sports Program

2006 *One on One* featuring Jerry Coleman Hall of Fame—Best of Show Television Entry

American Women in Radio and Television:

National Gracie Allen Honorable Mention

1996 "The Cox Convention Connexion"

National CableACE

1997 *One on One* featuring Tony Gwynn

International New York Festivals – Finalist

1997 *One on One* featuring Tony Gwynn

1998 *One on One* featuring Jerry Coleman/ Dave Stewart

2000 **Women Who Mean Business:** Television, *San Diego Business Journal*

2002 **"40 Under 40"**, Metropolitan Magazine

Glossary of Television Terms

Associate Producer (AP): The producer's go-to person for various responsibilities, including research, logging and organizing tapes, photographs, and other elements for a production.

Back-Story: The "story behind the story." Also, background information about a real person or thing that helps the viewer to better understand them or explain things and/or events that led up to a moment.

Beat Reporter: A reporter who specializes on a topic such as education, crime, health, entertainment, or sports. In a newsroom, it's often the beat reporter's responsibility to stay current on the topic, competing with other reporters in the market or venue.

Director: For a live newscast, sportscast, or sporting event, the director leads the team in the production control room or truck and literally calls the shots—the camera shots—which you see on TV.

Editor: The digital artist at the computer screen who weaves the video and audio together with, or sometimes without, the guidance of a script, creating the final product that the viewers see on TV.

Executive Producer (EP): The executive producer oversees production of a particular show or group of shows and/or producers. He or she guides when there are technical, personnel, or production issues, and is the sounding board for ideas and special requests. The executive producer often gains experience as a reporter or producer before moving into a role with more overall responsibility, but often has hands-on involvement in the production details.

Host/Anchor: The on-air talent and main person or persons presenting and guiding viewers through a television or radio program for news, sports, or entertainment topics.

Live Broadcast/Telecast: The local evening news, network, or show broadcast first on the East Coast, or a pre- and post-game show surrounding a live sporting event that is happening as you're watching it. Some things take place on the West Coast, but are aired live on the East Coast and tape delayed per the time zones.

Logging: The tedious but important process of transcribing interviews and/or elements appearing on videotapes. The elements are listed with the tape's digitally "burned in" time code so an editor or producer can find each shot quickly. Logging a tape from spring training, for example, would include the scenes of the green grass, the natural sound of the players playing catch, the names of the various pitchers, a close up, then a wider shot of the ball and glove on the ground, and an interview with a player.

Natural Sound (NAT Sound): The sounds that are recorded and incorporated into a production, such as the crack of the bat, the roar of the crowd, the popping of champagne bottles, chirping birds, people meeting and saying hello, something cooking on the stove…. This can also include music.

On-Air Talent: While people not on the air are talented, too, this term is used in the broadcast/TV industry designating those who are on the air and the face of a station.

Package: The final scripted or unscripted story on tape that is part of a newscast or magazine program. It can be a serious news story or a fun or serious feature story. The package is an all-inclusive combination of interviews, narration, and video.

Play-by-Play Announcer and Color Analyst: The play-by-play announcer calls the main action of the game: the balls and strikes, penalties, and touchdowns. The color analyst, often a former player, adds explanation, stories, and information to give added depth to what's happening on the field, or what a player or coach could be thinking or doing.

Producer: A person responsible for the production of a television story (package) or program, including supervising and/or participating in the advance research, interviews, logistics, writing, and final overall product or project. A producer can be on the air and/or behind the scenes.

Production Assistant (PA): The production assistant helps behind the scenes of a production, from carrying equipment, to pulling cables, to setting up lights and taking them down, and putting it all away. A PA is critical in getting the technical and logistical aspects of a production, especially if it's complex or in a tight timeframe. A production assistant can help anyone involved in a production, from an AP to a producer, photographer, director, or host, depending on the project and need.

Reporter: The person who produces news or feature stories, including writing, voicing, and/or presenting them on the air.

Script: The road map of narration, interviews, and natural sound for an individual story or show. A reporter, producer, or writer writes the narration, weaving the content of sounds on tape, natural sound, and words into an organized final script.

Sound Bite or Sound on Tape (SOT): A part of an interview captured on video tape that's usually about ten to thirty seconds long.

Station Manager: The station manager oversees the overall staff, budget, operations, and production of a television station or production company and is often key in hiring on-air personalities and others in management who report to him or her.

Taped Program: *One on One* and other pre-produced shows that are shot in stages and put together as a final taped program. A magazine program with non-time sensitive news and/or feature stories, can be daily, weekly, or a special and can be highly produced with lots of elements or a simple studio production.

Television/Media Market: An area where all of the people receive the same television stations and other media, such as radio and newspapers. The market can be a major metropolitan area and surrounding areas or a large or small rural area. The market size generally determines advertising dollars, station budgets, and what can be spent on equipment, staff, and salaries. New York, Los Angeles, and Chicago are the top three markets. Wichita Falls, Texas ranks 149th, and Glendive, Montana is the smallest at 210.

Track or Voice Over (VO): A track, or voice over, is the narrator's voice on a live or taped television segment.

Videographer/Photographer: The person with the camera chasing the action or steadily shooting video from a tripod. The "photog" can work closely with a producer/reporter and/or independently.

The Greater San Diego Chapter of the ALS Association

After 9/11 I was moved to give back beyond attending charity events as part of my job. It had been eight years since my father died, and I felt ALS was something I could help with because I knew about its impact all too well. The timing was divine. The San Diego Chapter of the ALS Association had just been formed. At my second meeting, the fledgling board voted me on and the work has been enriching ever since. Even with tight resources, it is rewarding to see how our small but mighty staff, board, and volunteers have hope and heart to help those with ALS and their families. We want to do more.

The Padres have been exceptional partners, thanks largely to the Community Relations team: Sue Botos, Nhu Tran, and Michele Anderson. The Padres commitment and my station allowing me to do stories about ALS and the baseball connection combined for a synergy to help raise funds for the chapter and raise awareness about ALS. I hope this book will too. Part of the proceeds from this book will go to the chapter.

My special thanks to Mark Loretta (pictured at top with Bob Dennis), Scott Linebrink (pictured with Bobby Carter, left, and Gus Fleming, below), Randy Wolf, Scott Hairston, and Nick Hundley; players who have graciously met PALS down on the field, made ticket or financial donations, or helped promote the annual Walk to Defeat ALS. Their interest is sincere; their compassion leaves a lasting impression.

"The Channel 4 story that you did about Gus and ALS was one of the first things Gus showed someone when they visited him. He was so proud that it showed him and the kids in everyday life, and that you provided an opportunity for each child to express how they were dealing with the unrelenting effects of ALS on their dad. I was both surprised and honored that you took time out of your busy schedule to attend Gus' memorial service a couple years later. Thank you for your fight against, and work in educating and raising awareness about, this most devastating disease."

—Letitia Fleming, Gus' mother,
September 2010

You don't have to be a baseball hero like Lou Gehrig to get ALS, but whoever has it is someone's hero. My father was my hero. My work is part of his legacy. I have been blessed to know so many fighting valiantly and leaving their legacy through their attitude and their inspiration. Case in point, Mike Ramirez, who, with his friend Greg Sacks, checked working the infield off their Bucket

List with the help of Padres head groundskeeper, Luke Yoder. We hope one day to be out of business, and to celebrate a world without ALS. In the meantime, we have much work to do.

"Jane, Saying thank you doesn't even come close to telling you how much I appreciate the story you and Channel 4 did last night on Greg and me. I'm humbled and honored to be featured in such a professional and moving production. Feedback has been very positive and supportive. I feel strongly that God wants me to use my resources to raise the awareness of ALS and raise money to help find a cure. I know He has been working through you as well. Last night's segment and part two to follow will go a long way to fulfilling that mission. It has been a year since I was diagnosed and I have had the opportunity to focus and recognize the many blessings in my life, like family and friends. I consider meeting you—and that you feel my story is worth telling—is one of those many blessings. Good luck with your book and please let me know how I can help. Peace, your friend, Michael"

—Michael Ramirez, September 2010

I wanted my book release to be about more than my book and me. I envisioned an event celebrating what I call "The Good Sports Story," open to everyone, to benefit charity. Indeed, on November 10, 2010, some 275 people dressed up for the Veterans Day evening—a date selected to honor service personnel like my father. The event raised $25,000 divided among five charities players or I have been involved with over time: The ALS Association, The Cox Kids Foundation, the San Diego Hall of Champions, Make-A-Wish Foundation of San Diego, and The Padres Foundation.

I'm grateful to so many, including restaurants for our Taste of San Diego, businesses for auction items, media that spread the word, and the Hall of Champions staff at the spectacular San Diego sports setting. I spent many hours alone writing, but the book and launch happened because of an amazing group of friends, colleagues, and family I call my "Dream Team." A special thanks also to Mark Grant, the funny and masterful emcee, Jack Berkman, the ever-energetic auctioneer, and Tony Amat and Johnakin Randolph for documenting the moment in pictures.

Several people in the book attended, including Dick Enberg and his wife Barbara, Park View Little League team members, and players with their wives: Mark Loretta, Mark Sweeney, Geoff Blum, Adrian Gonzalez, Edgar Gonzalez, Mark Merila, Heath Bell, and Randy Jones. Mark Loretta, Mark Sweeney, and Heath Bell took the stage to turn the tables on me asking playful questions: "So do you plan to make someone cry?" (No!) "When you leaned in to ask a question, did you want to kiss me?" (Ah, with cameras and a crew on hand?) "Your mother wants to know, how's your love life?" (Maybe that will be my life's next chapter!)

I produced two videos showing my "haircuts to hemlines" and the evolution of the *One on One* program. I felt as if I received a giant hug from the turnout and the love in the room. It reaffirmed my new mantra for sports and life which I hope others will embrace: "Be Part of the Good Sports Story... Perpetuate the Positive."